DORLING KINDERSLEY

ROME

DORLING KINDERSLEY

LONDON • NEW YORK • SYDNEY • MOSCOW • DELHI

www.dk.com

A DORLING KINDERSLEY BOOK

www.dk.com

PROJECT EDITOR Fiona Wild

ART EDITOR Annette Jacobs

EDITORS Ferdie McDonald, Mark Ronan, Anna Streiffert

DESIGNER Lisa Kosky

DESIGN ASSISTANT Marisa Renzullo

PICTURE RESEARCH Catherine O'Rourke

RESEARCH IN ROME Sam Cole

DTP EDITOR Siri Lowe

MAIN CONTRIBUTORS
Olivia Ercoli, Ros Belford, Roberta Mitchell

PHOTOGRAPHERS
John Heseltine, Mike Dunning, Kim Sayer

ILLUSTRATORS
Studio Illibill, Kevin Jones Associates,
Martin Woodward, Robbie Polley

This book was produced with the assistance of
Websters International Publishers.

Reproduced by Colourscan, Singapore
Printed and bound by Dai Nippon Printing Co., (Hong Kong) Ltd

First published in Great Britain in 1993
by Dorling Kindersley Limited
9 Henrietta Street, London WC2E 8PS
Reprinted with revisions 2000

**The information in every
Dorling Kindersley Travel Guide is checked annually**.
Every effort has been made to ensure that this book is as up-to-
date as possible at the time of going to press. Some details,
however, such as telephone numbers, opening hours, prices,
gallery hanging arrangements and travel information are liable to
change. The publishers cannot accept responsibility for any
consequences arising from the use of this book. We value the
views and suggestions of our readers very highly. Please write to:
Editorial Director, Dorling Kindersley Travel Guides,
Dorling Kindersley, 9 Henrietta Street, London WC2E 8PS.

CONTENTS

Colosseum

INTRODUCING ROME

Moses by Michelangelo in
San Pietro in Vincoli

Fresco in Villa Farnesina

ROME
AREA BY AREA

The Tempietto

Arch of Titus

TRAVELLERS'
NEEDS

The basilica of St Peter's
in the Vatican City

Mosaic in Santa Prassede

SURVIVAL GUIDE

Roman antipasto

HOW TO USE THIS GUIDE

THIS EYEWITNESS TRAVEL GUIDE helps you get the most from your stay in Rome with the minimum of practical difficulty. The opening section, *Introducing Rome*, locates the city geographically, sets modern Rome in its historical context and explains how Roman life changes through the year. *Rome at a Glance* is an overview of the city's attractions. The main sightseeing section, *Rome Area by Area*, starts on page 62. It describes all the important sights with maps, photographs and detailed illustrations. In addition, six planned walks take you to parts of Rome you might otherwise miss.

Carefully researched tips for hotels, shops and markets, restaurants and cafés, sports and entertainment are found in *Travellers' Needs*, and the *Survival Guide* has advice on everything from posting a letter to catching the Metro.

ROME AREA BY AREA

The chapters covering the 16 central sightseeing areas are indicated by colour-coded bars. Each chapter opens with a portrait of the area and a list of the sights to be covered. These are located by numbers on an *Area Map*. This is followed by a large-scale *Street-by-Street Map* focusing on the most interesting part of the area. The main body of the chapter consists of detailed descriptions of all the sights. Finding your way about the chapter is made simple by a consistent numbering system used throughout for the sights. This refers to the order in which they are described in the chapter.

Sights at a Glance lists the sights in the area by category: Churches and Temples, Museums and Galleries, Historic Streets and Piazzas, Historic Buildings, Arches and Gates, Columns, Obelisks and Statues, Fountains, Ancient Sites and Parks and Gardens.

The area covered in greater detail on the *Street-by-Street Map* is shaded red.

Numbered circles pinpoint all the listed sights on the *Area Map*. Palazzo Doria Pamphilj, for example, is **❻**.

1 Area Map

For easy reference, the sights in each area are numbered and located on a map of the area. To help the visitor, the map also shows Metro stations and parking areas.

Photographs of distinctive details of buildings help you to identify the sights.

Colour-coding on each page makes the area easy to find in the book.

2 Street-by-Street Map

This gives a bird's eye view of the heart of each sightseeing area. To help you locate and identify important sights as you walk around, these are picked out in stronger colour.

A locator map shows you exactly where you are in relation to surrounding areas. The area shown in the *Street-by-Street Map* is marked in red.

Palazzo Doria Pamphilj ❻ is shown on this map as well.

A suggested route for a walk takes in the most interesting and attractive streets in the area.

Red stars indicate the sights that no visitor should miss.

Travel tips help you to reach the area quickly.

7

ROME AT A GLANCE

Each map in this section covers a specific theme: *Churches and Temples, Museums and Galleries, Fountains and Obelisks, Celebrated Visitors and Residents.* The top sights are shown on the map; other sights are described on the following two pages.

Each sightseeing area is colour-coded.

The theme is explored in greater detail on the two pages following the map.

3 Detailed information on each sight

All the important sights in each area are described individually. They are listed in order, following the numbering on the Area Map. Practical information is also provided.

PRACTICAL INFORMATION

Each entry provides all the information needed to visit the sight. A key to the symbols used is inside the back cover.

Map reference to *Street Finder* at back of book — Sight number

Address — Telephone number

Palazzo Doria Pamphilj ⑥

Piazza del Collegio Romano 1A. **Map** 5 A4 & 12 E3. **(** 679 43 65. **☷** 56, 60, 62, 70, 85, 95, 160, 492. **Open** 10am–1pm Tue, Fri, Sat & Sun. **Closed** public hols. **⛌** compulsory for private apartments; notify attendant if you want tour. **☐**

Opening hours

Useful bus routes — Services and facilities available

4 Rome's major sights

These are given two or more full pages in the sightseeing area in which they are found. Historic buildings are dissected to reveal their interiors; and museums and galleries have colour-coded floorplans to help you find important exhibits.

The Visitors' Checklist provides the practical information you will need to plan your visit.

The facade of each major sight is shown to help you spot it quickly.

Red stars indicate the most interesting architectural details of the building, and the most important works of art or exhibits on view inside.

A timeline charts the key events in the history of the building.

Introducing Rome

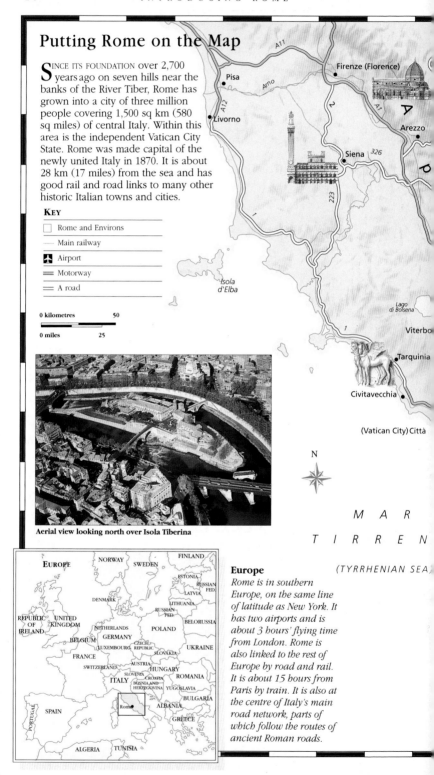

Putting Rome on the Map

Since its foundation over 2,700 years ago on seven hills near the banks of the River Tiber, Rome has grown into a city of three million people covering 1,500 sq km (580 sq miles) of central Italy. Within this area is the independent Vatican City State. Rome was made capital of the newly united Italy in 1870. It is about 28 km (17 miles) from the sea and has good rail and road links to many other historic Italian towns and cities.

KEY

☐ Rome and Environs

— Main railway

✈ Airport

═ Motorway

═ A road

0 kilometres   50

0 miles   25

Pisa

Arno

Livorno

Firenze (Florence)

Arezzo

Siena   326

Isola d'Elba

Lago di Bolsena

Viterbo

Tarquinia

Civitavecchia

(Vatican City) Città

N

M A R
T I R R E N
(TYRRHENIAN SEA)

Aerial view looking north over Isola Tiberina

Europe

EUROPE   NORWAY   SWEDEN   FINLAND

ESTONIA

RUSSIAN FED.

LATVIA

DENMARK   LITHUANIA

RUSSIAN FED.

REPUBLIC OF IRELAND   UNITED KINGDOM   NETHERLANDS   BELORUSSIA

BELGIUM   GERMANY   POLAND

LUXEMBOURG   CZECH REPUBLIC   SLOVAKIA   UKRAINE

FRANCE   AUSTRIA   HUNGARY

SWITZERLAND   SLOVENIA   CROATIA   ROMANIA

ITALY   BOSNIA AND HERZEGOVINA   YUGOSLAVIA

Rome   BULGARIA

SPAIN   ALBANIA

GREECE

PORTUGAL

ALGERIA   TUNISIA

Rome is in southern Europe, on the same line of latitude as New York. It has two airports and is about 3 hours' flying time from London. Rome is also linked to the rest of Europe by road and rail. It is about 15 hours from Paris by train. It is also at the centre of Italy's main road network, parts of which follow the routes of ancient Roman roads.

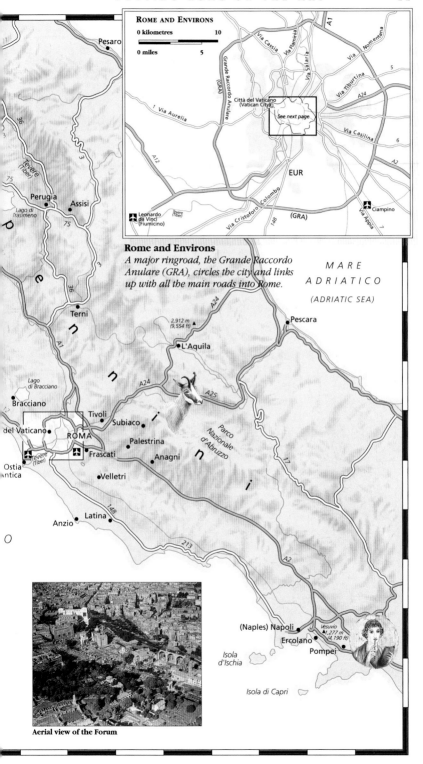

Rome and Environs
A major ringroad, the Grande Raccordo Anulare (GRA), circles the city and links up with all the main roads into Rome.

ROME AND ENVIRONS

0 kilometres   10

0 miles   5

Grande Raccordo Anulare (GRA)

Via Cassia

Via Flaminia

A1

Via Salaria

Via Nomentana

Via Aurelia

Città del Vaticano
(Vatican City)

See next page

Via Tiburtina

A24

5

Via Casilina

6

A12

EUR

A2

Leonardo
da Vinci
(Fiumicino)

Tevere
(Tiber)

Via Cristoforo Colombo

148

(GRA)

Via Appia

7

Ciampino

Pesaro

Tevere
(Tiber)

75

Perugia

Assisi

Lago di
Trasimeno

75

36

Terni

A1

Lago
di Bracciano

Bracciano

12

del Vaticano

ROMA

Tevere
(Tiber)

Ostia
Antica

O

Tivoli

Subiaco

Palestrina

Frascati

Anagni

Velletri

Latina

148

Anzio

213

A24

2,912 m
(9,554 ft)

L'Aquila

A24

A25

Parco
Nazionale
d'Abruzzo

17

A2

*MARE
ADRIATICO*
(ADRIATIC SEA)

Pescara

(Naples) Napoli

Ercolano

Vesuvio
1,277 m
(4,190 ft)

Pompei

*Isola
d'Ischia*

Isola di Capri

Aerial view of the Forum

Central Rome

MOST OF THE SIGHTS described in this book lie within the old city wall in 16 areas shown on the map below. Each of the areas has its own chapter. If you are on a short visit, you may have to restrict yourself to just a few of the central areas: the Forum to see ancient Rome; the Capitol, Piazza della Rotonda and Piazza Navona for the historic centre of the city; Campo de' Fiori for its grand Renaissance palazzi; Piazza di Spagna for its reminders of the 18th-century Grand Tour and its smart modern shops; and the Vatican to see St Peter's and the centre of Roman Catholicism.

PAGES 128–41
Street Finder maps
4, 5

0 metres   500
0 yards   500

Vatican

PAGES 222–49
Street Finder maps
3, 4

PAGES 116–27
Street Finder maps
4, 11, 12

PAGES 142–53
Street Finder maps
4, 8, 11, 12

Piazza di Spagna

Piazza della Rotonda

Piazza Navona

Campo de' Fiori

Janiculum

Trastevere

PAGES 214–21
Street Finder maps
3, 4, 7, 11

PAGES 206–13
Street Finder maps
4, 7, 8, 11

PAGES 102–15
Street Finder maps
4, 5, 12

PAGES 198–205
Street Finder maps
7, 8, 12

PAGES 154–65
Street Finder maps
5, 6, 12

PAGES 250–55
Street Finder maps
5, 6

PAGES 64–75
Street Finder maps
5, 12

PAGES 166–75
Street Finder maps
5, 6

Via Veneto

PAGES 76–95
Street Finder maps
5, 8, 9, 12

Quirinal

Esquiline

Capitol

Forum

Palatine

Lateran

PAGES 96–101
Street Finder map 8

Aventine

Caracalla

PAGES 188–97
Street Finder maps
8, 9

PAGES 176–87
Street Finder maps
6, 9, 10

THE HISTORY OF ROME

ONE OF THE most ancient cities in Europe, Rome was founded over 2,700 years ago. Since then it has been continuously inhabited, and, as the headquarters first of the Roman Empire and then of the Catholic Church, it has had an immense impact on the world. Many European languages are based on Latin; many political and legal systems follow the ancient Roman model; and buildings all round the world utilize styles and techniques perfected in ancient Rome. The city itself retains layers of buildings spanning over two millennia. Not surprisingly, all this history can seem a little overwhelming.

Roman eagle (2nd century AD)

Rome began as an Iron Age hut village, founded in the mid-8th century BC. In 616, the Romans' sophisticated Etruscan neighbours seized power, but were ousted in 509, when Rome became a Republic. It conquered most of the rest of Italy, then turned its attentions overseas, and by the 1st century BC, ruled Spain, North Africa and Greece. The expansion of the Empire provided opportunities for power-hungry individuals, and the clashing of egos led to the collapse of democracy. Julius Caesar ruled for a time as dictator, and his nephew Octavian became Rome's first emperor, assuming the title Augustus. During the reign of Augustus, Christ was born, and though Christians were persecuted until the 4th century, the new religion took hold and Rome became its main centre.

Even though it was the seat of the papacy, during the Middle Ages Rome went into decline. The city recovered spectacularly in the mid-15th century, and for over 200 years was embellished by the greatest artists of the Renaissance and the Baroque. Finally, in 1870, Rome became the capital of the newly unified Italy.

15th-century map of Rome from the north

Detail from 2nd-century AD Roman mosaic from the Temple of Fortune in Palestrina

Rome's Early Development

ACCORDING TO THE HISTORIAN Livy, Romulus founded
Rome in 753 BC. Sometime later, realizing his tribe
was short of females, he invited the neighbouring
Sabines to a festival, and orchestrated the mass
abduction of their women. Although Livy's account is
pure legend, there is evidence that Rome was founded
around the middle of the 8th century BC, and that the
Romans and Sabines united shortly afterwards.
Historical evidence also gives some support to Livy's
claim that after Romulus's death Rome was ruled by a
series of kings, and that in the 7th century BC it was
conquered by the Etruscans and ruled by the Tarquin
family. Last of the dynasty was Tarquinius Superbus
(Tarquin the Proud). His despotic rule led to the
Etruscans being expelled and the founding of a
Republic run by two annually elected consuls.
The uprising was led by Lucius Junius Brutus, the
model of the stern, patriotic Roman Republican.

EXTENT OF THE CITY
☐ *750 BC*   ☐ *Today*

Ceremonial trumpets

Capitoline   Quirinal   **Viminal**

Palatine

Aventine   **Celian**   **Esquiline**

The Seven Hills of Rome
*By the 8th century BC, shepherds and
farmers lived on four of Rome's seven hills.
As the population grew, huts were built in the
marshy valley later occupied by the Forum.*

Iron Age Hut
*Early settlers lived
in wattle and
daub huts.
Traces of their
foundations
have been
found on the
Palatine.*

**Augur, digging
foundation**

TEMPLE OF JUPITER
*This Renaissance painting by Perin del
Vaga shows Tarquinius Superbus
founding the Temple of Jupiter on the
Capitol, the sacred citadel of Rome.*

TIMELINE

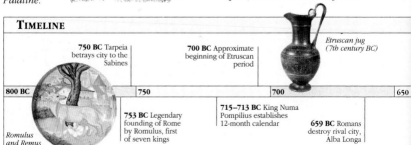

750 BC Tarpeia
betrays city to the
Sabines

700 BC Approximate
beginning of Etruscan
period

*Etruscan jug
(7th century BC)*

800 BC   750   700   650

*Romulus
and Remus*

753 BC Legendary
founding of Rome
by Romulus, first
of seven kings

715–713 BC King Numa
Pompilius establishes
12-month calendar

659 BC Romans
destroy rival city,
Alba Longa

☐ **Rome's Early Development**

The Legend of the She-Wolf
The evil King of Alba threw his baby nephews, Romulus and Remus, into the Tiber but they were washed ashore, and suckled by a she-wolf.

Raven, guardian of the citadel

Apollo of Veio
Etruscan culture and religion were influenced by the Greeks. This 5th- or 6th-century statue of the Greek god Apollo comes from Veio, a powerful, wealthy Etruscan city.

King Tarquin, holding stone worshipped as a thunderbolt

WHERE TO SEE ETRUSCAN ROME
The Cloaca Maxima sewer still functions, but there are few other traces of Etruscan Rome. Most finds come from Etruscan sites outside Rome like Tarquinia, with its tomb paintings of sumptuous banquets *(see p271)*, but there are good collections in the Villa Giulia *(pp262–3)* and Vatican Museums *(p238)*. The most famous object, however, is a bronze statue of the legendary she-wolf in the Capitoline Museums *(p73)*. The Antiquarium Forense *(p87)* displays objects from the necropolis which once occupied the site of the Roman Forum.

Funeral urns shaped like huts were used for cremation from the mid-8th century BC.

Etruscan jewellery, like this 7th-century BC gold filigree brooch, was lavish. Treasures of this kind have given the Etruscans a reputation for luxurious living.

The Legend of Aeneas
Some Roman legends make the Trojan hero Aeneas the grandfather of Romulus and Remus.

600 BC Possible date of construction of Cloaca Maxima sewer

578 BC Servius Tullius Etruscan King

565 BC Traditional date of the Servian Wall around Rome's seven hills

Statue of Jupiter

510 BC Temple of Jupiter consecrated on Capitoline

600

550

500

616 BC Tarquinius Priscus, first Etruscan king. Forum and Circus Maximus established

534 BC King Servius murdered

L J Brutus

509 BC L J Brutus expels Etruscans from Rome and founds the Republic

507 BC War against Etruscans. Horatius defends wooden bridge across Tiber

Kings, Consuls and Emperors

70–63 BC Pompey

ROME HAD OVER 250 RULERS in the 1,200 years between its foundation by Romulus and AD 476, when the last emperor was deposed by the German warrior, Odoacer. Romulus was the first of seven kings, overthrown in 509 BC when Rome became a Republic. Authority was held by two annually elected consuls, but provision was made for the appointment of a dictator in times of crisis. In 494 BC, the office of Tribune was set up to protect the plebeians from injustice at the hands of their patrician rulers. Roman democracy, however, was always cosmetic. It was discarded completely in 27 BC, when absolute power was placed in the hands of the emperor.

Romulus, his twin Remus and the she-wolf who suckled them

107–87 BC
Marius is consul seven times

205 BC Scipio Africanus

218 BC Quintus Fabius Maximus

456 BC Lucius Quintus Cincinnatus

c753–715 BC Romulus

800 BC	700	600	500	400	300	200	100
SEVEN KINGS			REPUBLIC				
800 BC	700	600	500	400	300	200	100

c715–673 BC Numa Pompilius

396 BC Marcus Furius Camillus

c509 BC Lucius Junius Brutus and Horatius Pulvillus

133 BC Tiberius Gracchus

c673–641 BC Tullus Hostilius

122–121 BC Gaius Gracchus

c534–509 BC Tarquinius Superbus

82–80 BC Sulla

c641–616 BC Ancus Marcius

c579–534 BC Servius Tullius

63 BC Cicero

616–579 BC Tarquinius Priscus

60–50 BC Triumvirate of Julius Caesar, Pompey and Crassus

45–44 BC Julius Caesar is sole ruler

Tarquinius Priscus consulting an augur

Julius Caesar, whose rise to power marked the end of the Roman Republic

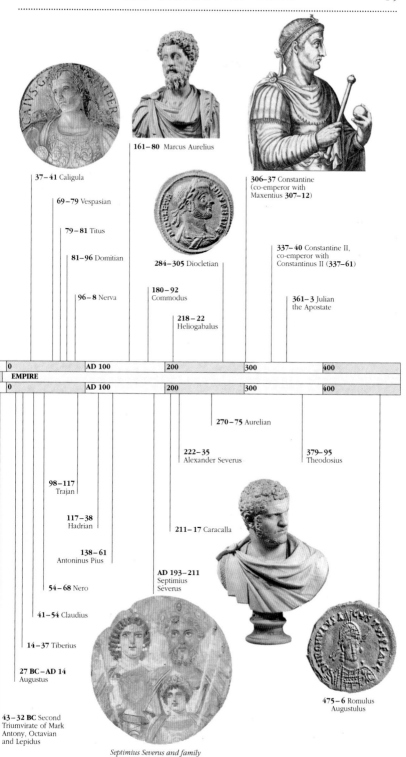

161–80 Marcus Aurelius

37–41 Caligula

69–79 Vespasian

79–81 Titus

81–96 Domitian

284–305 Diocletian

96–8 Nerva

180–92
Commodus

218–22
Heliogabalus

306–37 Constantine
(co-emperor with
Maxentius **307–12**)

337–40 Constantine II,
co-emperor with
Constantinus II (**337–61**)

361–3 Julian
the Apostate

0	AD 100	200	300	400

EMPIRE

0	AD 100	200	300	400

270–75 Aurelian

222–35
Alexander Severus

379–95
Theodosius

98–117
Trajan

117–38
Hadrian

211–17 Caracalla

138–61
Antoninus Pius

AD 193–211
Septimius
Severus

54–68 Nero

41–54 Claudius

14–37 Tiberius

27 BC–AD 14
Augustus

475–6 Romulus
Augustulus

43–32 BC Second
Triumvirate of Mark
Antony, Octavian
and Lepidus

Septimius Severus and family

The Roman Republic

Bronze coin, showing Temple of Vesta (c57 BC)

By THE MID-2ND CENTURY BC, Rome controlled the west Mediterranean, policing and defending it with massive armies. The troops had more loyalty to the generals than to distant politicians, giving men like Marius, Sulla, Pompey and Caesar the muscle to seize political power. Meanwhile, peasants, whose land had been destroyed during the invasion of Hannibal in 219 BC, had flooded into Rome. They were followed by slaves and freedmen from conquered lands such as Greece, swelling the population to half a million. There was plenty of work for immigrants, constructing roads, aqueducts, markets and temples, financed by taxes on Rome's expanding trade.

EXTENT OF THE CITY

400 BC	Today

Arch spanning road

The gradient of an aqueduct was about 1 in 1,000.

Cut stone blocks

Covered water channels

How an Aqueduct Worked
Water from a spring in the hills was collected in a reservoir to build up pressure and ensure a steady supply to the city.

High ground

Cleaning vent

Reservoir

Underground water channel

Arches carrying water across low ground

Cicero Denounces Catiline
In 62 BC Catiline planned a coup. Cicero discovered the plot and persuaded the Senate to condemn the conspirators to death.

TIMELINE

499 BC Battle against Latin tribes; Temple of Castor and Pollux built to commemorate the victory	*Via Appia*		**312 BC** Construction of Via Appia and Rome's first aqueduct, the Aqua Appia
	380 BC Servian Wall rebuilt		
	396 BC Definitive victory over rival Etruscan city, Veio		

500 BC	450 BC	400 BC	350 BC	300 BC

Relief of Capitoline geese

390 BC Rome invaded by Celtic Gauls: quacking geese on Capitoline hill warn of impending attack

264–241 BC First Punic War (against Carthage)

☐ **Roman Republic**

Roman Street
In the 1st century BC, most buildings in Rome were made from brick and concrete. Only a few public buildings used marble.

AQUEDUCT (2ND CENTURY BC)

Rome owed much of her prosperity to her skilled civil engineers. When the city's wells were no longer sufficient, aqueducts were built to bring water from surrounding hills. Some were over 80 km (50 miles) long.

Arches for maintaining a constant gradient over low-lying land

Temple of Juno

The ruins of this 197 BC temple are embedded in the church of San Nicola in Carcere (see p152). Romans consulted their gods before all important ventures.

Scipio Africanus
In 202 BC the Roman general Scipio defeated Hannibal. Rome replaced Carthage as master of the Mediterranean.

WHERE TO SEE REPUBLICAN ROME

This fresco depicting a gang of slaves building a wall can be seen at the Museo Nazionale Romano (see p163).

The Temple of Saturn, first built in 497 BC, now consists of eight majestic columns overlooking the Forum at the end of the Via Sacra (see p83).

Rome's loveliest Republican buildings are the two Temples of the Forum Boarium (see p203). Four more temples can be seen in the Area Sacra of Largo Argentina (p150). Most monuments from this period, however, lie underground. Only a few, like the Tomb of the Scipios (p195), have been excavated. One of the bridges leading to Tiber Island (p152), the Ponte Fabricio, dates from the 1st century BC and is still used by pedestrians.

220 BC Via Flaminia built, linking Rome to the Adriatic coast

168 BC Victory in Macedonian War completes Roman conquest of Greece

133–120 BC Gracchi brothers killed for trying to introduce land reforms

Ponte Fabricio, built in 62 BC

51 BC Caesar conquers Gaul

250 BC	200 BC	150 BC	100 BC

218–202 BC Second Punic War; Scipio Africanus defeats Carthaginians

Hannibal

149–146 BC Third Punic War; Carthage destroyed

71 BC Spartacus's slave revolt crushed by Crassus and Pompey

60 BC Rome has three joint rulers: Pompey, Crassus and Caesar

Imperial Rome

Statue of Bacchus, god of wine

IN 44 BC Caesar became dictator for life, only to be assassinated a month later. The result was 17 years of civil war, which ended only in 27 BC when Augustus became Rome's first emperor. The Empire expanded in fits and starts, but by the late 3rd century was so huge that Diocletian decided to share it between four emperors. Thanks to trade and taxes from its vast domains, Rome was the most magnificent city in the world, studded with the lavish buildings of emperors keen to advertise their civic munificence and military triumphs.

EXTENT OF THE CITY

☐ AD 250   ☐ Today

Cross-vaulted ceiling with mosaic decoration

Apotheosis of Augustus
The first and perhaps the greatest Roman emperor, Augustus ruled for 27 years and was deified by the Senate after his death.

Natatio (swimming pool)

ROMA CAPVT MVNDI

The baths could hold up to 3,000 people. They met to gossip in the central *frigidarium* (cold room).

Area for exercise and gymnastics

The Roman Empire under Trajan
By the 2nd century AD, the Roman Empire stretched from Britain to Syria, and Rome was known as the Caput Mundi, *the head of the world.*

TIMELINE

49 BC Caesar crosses the Rubicon and takes Rome	**27** Augustus becomes first emperor

Emperor Nero

64 Fire during Nero's rule destroys much of city

65 First persecution of Christians under Nero

72 Colosseum begun

50 BC ——————— 0 ——————— **AD 50** ——————— **100**

44 Caesar becomes dictator for life, and is murdered by Brutus and Cassius

AD 42 St Peter the Apostle comes to Rome

13 Ara Pacis is erected to celebrate the peace Augustus has secured in the Empire

67 St Peter is crucified and St Paul executed in Rome

Statue of St Peter in San Paolo fuori le Mura

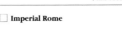

☐ **Imperial Rome**

Roman Revelry
Banquets could last for ten hours, with numerous courses. In order to continue eating, guests would retire to a small room to vomit between courses.

WHERE TO SEE IMPERIAL ROME

There are relics of Imperial Rome throughout the city centre, some hidden below churches and palazzi, others like the Forum *(see pp76–87)*, the Palatine *(pp97–101)* and the Imperial Fora *(pp88–91)*, fully excavated. The magnificence of the era, however, is best conveyed by the Pantheon *(pp110–11)* and the Colosseum *(pp92–5)*.

BATHS OF DIOCLETIAN (AD 298)

Rome's public baths were not just places to keep clean. They also had bars, libraries, barbers' shops, brothels and sports facilities.

The Arch of Titus *(p87)*, erected in the Forum in AD 81, commemorates Emperor Titus's Sack of Jerusalem in AD 70.

Tepidarium (warm room)

Virgil (70–19 BC)

Virgil was Rome's greatest epic poet. His most famous work is the Aeneid, the story of the Trojan hero, Aeneas's journey to the future site of Rome.

A relief of Mithras, a popular Persian god (3rd century AD), can be seen beneath the church of San Clemente *(pp186–7)*.

164–180 Plague rages in Roman Empire

212 Citizenship granted to virtually all inhabitants of the Empire

270 Aurelian Wall begun

Section of Aurelian Wall

150	200	250

125 Hadrian redesigns the Pantheon

Mosaic from the Baths of Caracalla

216 Baths of Caracalla completed

247 Rome's Millennium is celebrated

284 Empire divided into West and East

Early Christian Rome

Crucifixion in Santa Maria Antiqua

IN THE 1ST CENTURY AD, during the reign of Tiberius, a rebellious pacifist was crucified in a distant corner of the Empire. This was nothing unusual, but within a few years Jesus Christ and his teachings became notorious in Rome, his followers were perceived as a threat to public order, and many were executed. This was no deterrent, and the new religion spread through all levels of Roman society. When the Apostles Peter and Paul arrived in Rome there was already a small Christian community, and in spite of continued persecution by the state, Christianity flourished. In AD 313 the Emperor Constantine issued an edict granting freedom of worship to Christians, and soon after founded a shrine on the site of St Peter's tomb. This secured Rome's position as a centre of Christianity, but in the 5th century the political importance of Rome declined and the city fell to Goths and other invaders.

EXTENT OF THE CITY

▢ AD 395   ▢ Today

St Paul

Youthful, beardless representation of Christ

Classical-style border decorated with fruit

4TH-CENTURY MOSAIC, SANTA COSTANZA
Beautiful mosaics, often with palm trees and other oriental motifs suggesting Jerusalem, helped spread the message of early Christianity.

Santo Stefano Rotondo
This 17th-century engraving shows how a Roman temple (top) *might have been transformed* (above) *into the 5th-century round church of Santo Stefano.*

The Good Shepherd
The pagan image of a shepherd sacrificing a lamb became a Christian symbol.

TIMELINE

300	350	400	450
c320 Building of first St Peter's	**356** Legendary founding of Santa Maria Maggiore	**410** Rome sacked by Alaric's Goths	**455** Rome sacked again by Vandals
	Gold solidus of Theodosius		
312 Control of Empire won by Constantine after battle at Milvian Bridge	**380** Emperor Theodosius makes Christianity the official religion of the Roman Empire	**395** Division of the Empire between Ravenna and Constantinople	**422** Founding of Santa Sabina
	Battle of the Milvian Bridge		

▢ **Early Christian Rome**

Epigraph of Peter and Paul
This is one of hundreds of early Christian graffiti housed in the Lapidary Gallery of the Vatican (see p237).

Crucifixion, Santa Sabina
This 5th-century panel on the door of Santa Sabina (see p204) is one of the earliest known representations of the Crucifixion. Interestingly, Christ's cross is not actually shown.

St Peter receiving peace from the Saviour

Lambs symbolizing the Christian flock

Constantine's Cross
Constantine's vision of the True Cross during the Battle of the Milvian Bridge made him convert to Christianity.

WHERE TO SEE EARLY CHRISTIAN ROME
There are traces of early Christianity all over Rome. Many ancient churches were built over early Christian meeting places and sites of martyrdoms: among them San Clemente (see pp186–7), Santa Pudenziana (p171) and Santa Cecilia (p211). Outside the walls of the old city are miles of underground catacombs (pp265–6), many decorated with Christian frescoes, while the Vatican's Pio-Christian Museum (p240) has the best collection of early Christian art.

This statuette, carved out of bone, is embedded in the rock of the Catacombs of San Panfilo, just off the Via Salaria (**map** 2 F4).

The Cross of Justin, in the Treasury of St Peter's (p232), was given to Rome by the Emperor Justin in AD 578.

475 Fall of Western Roman Empire; Byzantium becomes seat of Empire

A Byzantine image of St Paul

609 Pantheon is consecrated as a Christian church

500   550   600

496 Anastasius II is first pope to assume title *Pontifex Maximus*

590–604 Pope Gregory the Great strengthens the papacy

630 Sant'Agnese fuori le Mura is built in Roman Byzantine style

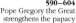

The Papacy

THE POPE is considered Christ's representative on earth, claiming his authority from St Peter, the first Bishop of Rome. Though some popes have been great thinkers and reformers, the role has rarely been purely spiritual. In the Middle Ages, many popes were involved in power struggles with the Holy Roman Emperor. Renaissance popes like Julius II and Leo X, the patrons of Raphael and Michelangelo, lived as luxuriously as any secular prince. The popes listed here include all those who exercised significant political or religious influence, up as far as the end of the Counter Reformation, when the power of the papacy began to wane.

*St Ludovic
Kneels before
Boniface VIII by
Simone Martini*

314–35
St Sylvester I

590–604
St Gregory the Great

*Gregory the Great
leading a procession
to end the plague*

955–64 John XII

222–30 St Urban I

1227–41 Gregory IX

496–8
Anastasius II

931–5 John XI

1216–27
Honorius III
Savelli

217–22
St Callixtus I

891–6 Formosus

0	200	400	600	800	1000	1200

PAPACY BASED IN ROME

0	200	400	600	800	1000	1200

336 Mark

579–90
Pelagius II

**1032–44,
1047–8**
Benedict IX

352–66 Liberius

608–15 St Boniface IV

1073–85 St
Gregory VII

88–97 St Clement

731–41 St Gregory III

42–67 St Peter

1099–1118
Paschal II

772–95 Adrian I

1130–43 Innocent II

1154–9 Adrian IV

847–55 St Leo IV

817–24 St Paschal I

1198–1216 Innocent III

*St Peter, from
a mosaic in
Santa Prassede
(see p171)*

795–816 St Leo III

*Innocent III's Vision
of the Church, from
a fresco by Giotto*

Portrait of Gregory XIII by Lavinia Fontana

1560–65 Pius IV Medici

1555–9 Paul IV

1523–34 Clement VII Medici

1513–21 Leo X Medici

1492–1503 Alexander VI Borgia

1572–84 Gregory XIII Boncompagni

1294–1303 Boniface VIII

1670–76 Clement X Altieri

1484–92 Innocent VIII Cybo

1667–9 Clement IX

1471–84 Sixtus IV della Rovere

1655–67 Alexander VII Chigi

1464–71 Paul II Barbo

1605 Leo XI Medici

1700–21 Clement XI

1458–64 Pius II Piccolomini

1300	1400	1500	1600	1700
AVIGNON	**PAPACY AGAIN BASED IN ROME**			
1300	1400	1500	1600	1700

1417–31 Martin V Colonna

1644–55 Innocent X Pamphilj

1447–55 Nicholas V

1584–7 Sixtus V

1623–44 Urban VIII Barberini

Nicholas V Receiving a Book, illustration from a contemporary manuscript

1592–1605 Clement VIII Aldobrandini

Urban VIII Approving a Building Project in the Vatican's Gallery of Tapestries (see p241)

1503–13 Julius II della Rovere

1605–21 Paul V Borghese

Raphael's portrait of Julius II

1534–49 Paul III Farnese

Paul III Gives his Approval to the Capuchin Order by Sebastiano Ricci

Medieval Rome

Mosaic, San Clemente

SUPPLANTED BY CONSTANTINOPLE as capital of the Empire in the 4th century, Rome was reduced to a few thousand inhabitants by the early Middle Ages; its power just a memory. In the 8th and 9th centuries, the growing importance of the papacy revived the city and made it once more a centre of power. But continual conflicts between the pope and the Holy Roman Emperor soon weakened the papacy. The 10th, 11th and 12th centuries were among the bleakest in Roman history: violent invaders left Rome poverty-stricken and the constantly warring local barons tore apart what remained of the city. Despite this, the first Holy Year was declared in 1300 and thousands of pilgrims arrived in Rome. But by 1309 the papacy was forced to move to Avignon, leaving Rome to slide into further squalor and strife.

EXTENT OF THE CITY

◻ *1300*   ◻ *Today*

San Giovanni in Laterano

Aurelian Wall

Charlemagne Crowned in St Peter's
On Christmas Day in 800, Charlemagne was made emperor of the Holy Roman Empire, a new Christian dominion to replace that of ancient Rome.

Column of Trajan

Column of Marcus Aurelius

Madonna and Child Mosaic
The Chapel of St Zeno (817–24) in the church of Santa Prassede (see p171) has some of the best examples of Byzantine mosaics in Rome.

MEDIEVAL PLAN OF ROME
Maps like this one, illustrating the principal features of the city, were produced for pilgrims, the tourists of the Middle Ages.

TIMELINE

700	800	900	1000

725 King Ine of Wessex founds the first hostel for pilgrims in the Borgo

778 Charlemagne, King of the Franks, conquers Italy

852 The Vatican is fortified with walls following a raid by Saracens

800 Charlemagne crowned emperor in St Peter's

Emperor Otto I

880–932 Rome is ruled by two women, Theodora and then her daughter, Marozia

961 King Otto the Great becomes first German Holy Roman Emperor

◻ **Medieval Rome**

Stefaneschi Triptych *(1315)*
Giotto and his pupils painted this triptych for Cardinal Stefaneschi as an altarpiece for St Peter's. It is now in the Vatican Museums (see p240).

WHERE TO SEE MEDIEVAL ROME

Among the most interesting churches of the period are San Clemente, with a fine apse mosaic and Cosmati floor *(see pp186–7)*, Santa Maria in Trastevere *(pp212–13)* and Santa Maria sopra Minerva, Rome's only Gothic church *(p108)*. Santa Cecilia in Trastevere *(p211)* has a Cavallini fresco, and there is fine Cosmati work in Santa Maria in Cosmedin *(p202)*.

Colosseum

Capitol

Pyramid of Caius Cestius

Charlemagne's Dalmatic in the Treasury of St Peter's *(p232)* was supposedly worn by the Holy Roman Emperor at his coronation. In fact the richly embroidered vestment probably dates from the 14th century.

Old St Peter's

Castel Sant'Angelo

Pantheon

Cosmati Tabernacle
Marblework by the Cosmati family, like this tabernacle in Santa Sabina (see p204), decorates many of Rome's medieval churches.

Santa Sabina *(p204)* on the Aventine Hill has a medieval bell-tower.

1084 Rome is attacked by Normans

1108 San Clemente is rebuilt

1200 Rome an independent commune under Arnaldo di Brescia

1309 Pope Clement V moves the papacy to Avignon

1300 First Holy Year proclaimed by Pope Boniface VIII

1348 Black Death strikes Rome

1100

1200

1300

Mosaic facade, Santa Maria in Trastevere (pp212–13)

1232 Cloister of San Giovanni in Laterano completed

1140 Santa Maria in Trastevere is restored

Cola di Rienzo

1347 Cola di Rienzo – an Italian patriot – tries to restore the Roman Republic

Renaissance Rome

POPE NICHOLAS V came to the throne in 1447 determined to make Rome a city fit for the papacy. Among his successors, men like Julius II and Leo X eagerly followed his lead, and the city's appearance was transformed. The Classical ideals of the Renaissance inspired artists, architects and craftsmen, such as Michelangelo, Bramante, Raphael and Cellini, to build and decorate the churches and palaces of a newly confident Rome.

Detail of Botticelli's *Youth of Moses* (1480s)

EXTENT OF THE CITY

☐ *1500*   ☐ *Today*

Hemispherical dome

Balustrade of small columns

Classical colonnade of 16 Doric columns

School of Athens by Raphael
In this fresco (see p243) Raphael complimented many of his peers by representing them as ancient Greek philosophers. The building shown is based on a design by Bramante.

THE TEMPIETTO
The Tempietto (1502) at San Pietro in Montorio (see p219) was one of Bramante's first works in Rome. A simple, perfectly proportioned miniature Classical temple, it is a model of High Renaissance architecture.

Cosmati-style mosaic floor

Palazzo Caprini
Bramante's design had a strong influence on later Renaissance palazzi. Parts of the building survive in Palazzo dei Convertendi (see p227).

TIMELINE

1377 Papacy returns to Rome from Avignon under Pope Gregory XI

1409–15 Papacy moves to Pisa

1452 Demolition of old St Peter's basilica begins

1444 Birth of Bramante

1350	1400	1450

1378–1417 The Great Schism, a division in the papacy in Avignon

1417 Pope Martin V ends the Great Schism in the papacy

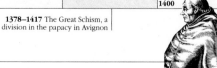

Pope Martin V, reigned 1417–31

☐ **Renaissance Rome**

Sack of Rome
In 1527, the unruly troops of Charles V of Spain pillaged the city, destroying countless works of art. Pope Clement VII took refuge in Castel Sant'Angelo.

WHERE TO SEE RENAISSANCE ROME

The Campo de' Fiori area *(see pp142–53)* is full of grand Renaissance palazzi, especially along Via Giulia *(pp276–7)*. Across the river stands the delightful Villa Farnesina *(pp220–21)*. The most typical church of the period is Santa Maria del Popolo *(pp138–9)*, and the best collection of Renaissance art is in the Vatican Museums *(pp234–47)*. These include the Sistine Chapel *(pp244–7)* and the Raphael Rooms *(pp242–3)*.

The Madonna di Foligno by Raphael (1511–12) is one of the fine Renaissance paintings in the Vatican Pinacoteca *(p241)*.

Pope Nicholas V
Nicholas ordered the demolition of the old St Peter's.

The Pietà, commissioned for St Peter's in 1501, was one of Michelangelo's first sculptures executed in Rome *(p233)*.

Statue of St Peter, believed to have been crucified on this site

Underground chapel

1475 Birth of Michelangelo

1483 Birth of Raphael

1486 Building of Palazzo della Cancelleria

1506 Pope Julius II orders start of work on new St Peter's

1508 Michelangelo begins painting the Sistine Chapel ceiling

Cumaean Sibyl, Sistine Chapel

1519 Frescoes completed in Villa Farnesina

1527 Troops of Emperor Charles V sack Rome

1500

1550

Emperor Charles

1547 Pope Paul III appoints Michelangelo architect of St Peter's

Baroque Rome

Baroque putto

BY THE 16TH CENTURY, the Catholic Church had become immensely rich – one of the chief criticisms of the Protestant reformers. The display of grandeur and extravagance by the papal court contrasted sharply with the poverty of the people, and wealthy Roman society was characterized by sumptuous luxury and a ceaseless round of entertainment. To make the Catholic faith more appealing than Protestantism, scores of churches were built and monuments and fountains were erected to glorify the Holy See. The finest architects in the ornate, dramatic style of the Baroque were Bernini and Borromini.

EXTENT OF THE CITY

☐ 1645	☐ Today

Ceiling portraying heavenly scenes

Monument to Pope Alexander VII
This Bernini tomb in St Peter's (pp230–33) includes a skeleton brandishing an hour glass.

Gian Lorenzo Bernini *(1598–1680)*
The favourite artist of the papacy, Bernini transformed Rome with his churches, palaces, statues and fountains.

Holy Family fresco

Tapestry of Pope Urban VIII
Bernini's most devoted patron, Pope Urban VIII Barberini (1623–44), is shown here receiving the homage of the nations.

A marble rose marks the best place to stand to appreciate the illusion of space created by the artist.

TIMELINE

1568 The Jesuits build the Gesù, prototypical church of the early Baroque

Altar carving from the Gesù

1595 Annibale Carracci begins to fresco Palazzo Farnese

1624 Bernini's sculpture of *Apollo and Daphne*

1626 Work on St Peter's is completed

1550	1575	1600	1625

1571 Birth of Caravaggio

1585 Pope Sixtus V plans new streets

1600 Philosopher Giordano Bruno is burnt at the stake for heresy

Galileo

1633 Galileo condemned to death in Rome for heresy

☐ **Baroque Rome**

Illusionistic beams in ceiling

Chapel painted on flat slanting wall

Figures painted to be viewed from an angle

Queen Christina of Sweden
In a coup for Catholicism, Christina renounced Protestantism and abdicated her throne. In 1655 she moved to Rome, where she became the centre of a lively literary and scientific circle.

St Ignatius, founder of the Jesuits

San Carlo alle Quattro Fontane
One of Borromini's most influential designs was this tiny oval church (see p161) on the Quirinal hill.

Francesco Borromini
(1599–1667)
In the many churches he built in Rome, Borromini made use of revolutionary geometric forms.

POZZO CORRIDOR
The use of perspective to create an illusion of depth and space was a favourite Baroque device. Andrea Pozzo painted this illusionistic corridor in the 1680s in the Rooms of St Ignatius near the Gesù (see pp114–15).

1651 Bernini redesigns much of Piazza Navona

Bernini's Fontana dei Fiumi in Piazza Navona

1694 Palazzo di Montecitorio is completed

1735 Spanish Steps are designed

1732 Works start on Trevi Fountain

1650	1675	1700	1725

1657 Borromini completes Sant'Agnese in Agone

Bonnie Prince Charlie, pretender to the throne of England

1721 Bonnie Prince Charlie is born in Rome

1734 Clement XII makes Palazzo Nuovo world's first public museum

1656 Work starts on Bernini's colonnade for St Peter's square

Understanding Rome's Architecture

Arch of Titus

THE ARCHITECTURE of Imperial Rome kept alive the Classical styles of ancient Greece, at the same time developing new, uniquely Roman forms based on the arch, the vault and the dome. The next important period was the 12th century, when many Romanesque churches were built. The Renaissance saw a return to Classical ideals, inspired by the example of Florence, but in the 17th century Rome found a style of its own again in the flamboyance of the Baroque.

The entablature above these columns has both straight and arched sections (Hadrian's Villa).

CLASSICAL ROME

Most Roman buildings were of concrete faced with brick, but from the 1st century BC, the Romans started to imitate earlier Greek models, using marble to decorate temples and other public buildings.

Plain frieze · Corinthian capital · Triangular pediment · Cornice (projecting section along facade) · Architrave (horizontal section resting on columns) · Fluted column shaft · Podium · Cella (inner sanctuary) · Colonnade enclosing portico

Caryatids were sculpted columns, usually in the form of a female figure. Roman caryatids, like this one in the Forum of Augustus, were often copied in detail from earlier Greek examples.

Roman temples were usually built on a raised dais or podium, to make them prominent. Many were fronted by a portico, a roofed porch with columns.

The orders of Classical architecture were building styles, each based on a different column design. The three major orders were borrowed by the Romans from the Greeks.

Doric order   **Ionic order**   **Corinthian order**

Aedicules were small shrines, framed by two pillars, usually containing a statue of a god.

Coffers were decorative sunken panels that reduced the weight of domed and vaulted ceilings.

EARLY CHRISTIAN AND MEDIEVAL ROME

The first Christian churches in Rome were based on the basilica: oblong, with three naves, each usually ending in an apse. From the 10th to the 13th century, most churches were built in the Romanesque style, which used the rounded arches of ancient Rome.

Basilicas in Rome have, in most cases, kept their original rectangular shape. The nave of San Giovanni in Laterano retains its 4th-century floorplan.

The triumphal arch divides the nave of a church from the apse. Here, in San Paolo fuori le Mura, it is decorated with mosaics.

A tabernacle is used to house the Sacrament for the mass. This 13th-century Gothic wall tabernacle is in San Clemente.

RENAISSANCE AND BAROQUE ROME

Renaissance architecture (15th–16th centuries) drew its inspiration directly from Classical models. It revived the use of strict geometric proportions. The Baroque age (late 16th–17th centuries) broke many established rules, favouring grandiose decoration over pure Classical forms.

A baldacchino is a canopy, supported on columns, rising over the main altar. This Baroque example is in St Peter's.

Putti were a popular decorative feature in the Baroque. A putto is a painting or a sculpture of a child like a Cupid or cherub.

A loggia is an open-sided gallery or arcade. It may be a separate structure or part of a building, as here at San Saba.

Rusticated masonry decorates the exterior of many Renaissance palazzi. It consists of massive blocks divided by deep joints.

COSMATESQUE SCULPTURE AND MOSAICS

The Cosmati family, active in Rome during the 12th and 13th centuries, have given their name to a particularly Roman style of decoration. They worked in marble, producing all kinds of fittings for churches, including cloisters, episcopal thrones, tombs, pulpits, fonts and candlesticks. These were often decorated with

Cosmatesque floor, Santa Maria in Cosmedin

bands of colourful mosaic. They also left many fine floor mosaics, usually of white marble with an inlay of red and green porphyry. Ancient Roman columns were cut up to provide the materials. Several other families of stonemasons used a similar style, and their work is also described as Cosmatesque.

Rome during Unification

U NDER NAPOLEON, Italy had a brief taste of unity, but by 1815 it was once more divided into many small states and papal rule was restored in Rome. Over the next 50 years, patriots, led by Mazzini, Garibaldi and others, struggled to create an independent, unified Italy. In 1848 Rome was briefly declared a Republic, but Garibaldi's forces were driven out by French troops. The French continued to protect the pope, while the rest of Italy was united as a kingdom under Vittorio Emanuele of Savoy. In 1870, troops stormed the city, and Rome became capital of Italy.

Garibaldi in his distinctive red shirt

EXTENT OF THE CITY

⬜ *1870*   ⬜ *Today*

Porta Pia

Tricoloured flag of the new Italian kingdom

Plumed hat of the Bersaglieri, crack troops from Savoy

Allegory of Italy's Liberty
This patriotic poster from 1890 shows the king, his chief minister Cavour, Garibaldi and Mazzini. The woman in red represents Italy.

Vittorio Emanuele II
Vittorio Emanuele, King of Piedmont, became the first King of Italy in 1861.

ROYALISTS STORM PORTA PIA
On 20 September 1870, troops of the kingdom of Italy put an end to the papal domination of Rome. They breached the city walls near Porta Pia; the pope retreated and Rome was made the Italian capital.

TIMELINE

1750		1775		1800
1751 Piranesi's *Views of Rome* revive interest in Classical ruins	**1762** Trevi Fountain is completed	*Napoleon Bonaparte*	**1797** Napoleon captures Rome	**1799** Napoleon expelled from Italy by Austrians and Russians
Piranesi etching of Trajan's Forum		**1792** Canova creates the Tomb of Pope Clement XIII, St Peter's	**1800–1** Napoleon takes Italy again	**1807** Birth of Garibaldi

Garibaldi and Rome

The charismatic leader Giuseppe Garibaldi had taken much of Italy from foreign rule by 1860. Rome still remained a crucial problem. Here he declares "O Roma o morte" (Rome or Death).

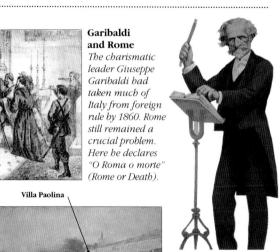

Villa Paolina

Giuseppe Verdi (1813–1901)

Verdi, the opera composer, supported unification and in 1861 became a member of Italy's first national parliament.

Breach in Aurelian Wall

A Freed City

This marble plaque was set up at Porta Pia to commemorate the liberation of Rome.

S · P · Q · R ·
VRBE · ITALIAE · VINDICATA
INCOLIS · FELICITER · AVCTIS
GEMINOS · FORNICES · CONDIDIT

Victor Emmanuel Monument

A vast monument to Italy's first king (see p74) stands in Piazza Venezia.

1816 Work begins on Piazza del Popolo

Fountain in Piazza del Popolo

1848 Nationalist uprising in Rome. Pope flees and a Republic is formed

1860 Garibaldi and his 1,000 followers take Sicily and Naples

1870 Royalist troops take Rome, completing the unification of Italy

1825

1850

1820 Revolts throughout Italy

1821 Keats dies in Piazza di Spagna

1849 Pope is restored to power, protected by a French garrison

Pope Pius IX

1861 Kingdom of Italy founded with capital in Turin

Twentieth-Century Rome

World Cup mania

THE FASCIST DICTATOR, Mussolini, dreamed of recreating the immensity, order and power of the old Roman Empire: "Rome", he said, "must appear wonderful to the whole world." He began to build a grandiose new complex, EUR, in the suburbs, and razed 15 churches and many medieval houses to create space for wide new roads. Fortunately most of the old centre has survived, leaving the city with one of Europe's most picturesque historic cores. To mark the Holy Year and the new Millennium, crumbling churches and monuments have been given a thorough facelift.

EXTENT OF THE CITY

▨ *1960s*   ☐ *Today*

Mussolini's Plans for Rome
This propaganda poster reflects Mussolini's grandiose projects such as Via dei Fori Imperiali in the Forum area (see p76), *and EUR* (p267).

Placido Domingo   José Carreras   Luciano Pavarotti

THREE TENORS CONCERT (1990)
Combining Italy's love for music and football, this opera recital at the Baths of Caracalla was broadcast live during the World Cup.

Pope John Paul II
John Paul II is the first non-Italian pope since the 1520s. A traditionalist, he exerts a tremendous influence on the lives of the world's Catholics.

TIMELINE

1915 Italy enters World War I

1929 Lateran Treaty creates a separate Vatican state

1926 Opposition parties banned

1944 Allies liberate Rome from Germans

1946 National referendum establishes Italy as a Republic; King Umberto II exiled

1900	1915	1930	1945

1911 Victor Emmanuel Monument is completed

1922 Fascists march on Rome. Mussolini becomes Prime Minister

1940 Italy enters World War II; work begins on EUR zone

Poster for EUR

Religion Today

Rome has attracted pilgrims for centuries, and they continue to come, especially at Easter, for beatifications and for the Holy Year of 2000. The city also hosts a large, cosmopolitan religious community.

Conductor Zubin Mehta

Poster for La Dolce Vita

In the 1950s and '60s Rome was Europe's Hollywood. Ben Hur, Quo Vadis? *and* Cleopatra *were made at the Cinecittà studios, as well as Italian films like Fellini's* La Dolce Vita.

Valentino Model

While not as important as Milan for fashion, Rome is still home to some of the industry's leading designers.

City-Centre Traffic

Rome's streets are congested, and many buildings have been damaged by pollution. There are plans to close the historic centre to traffic.

1960 Olympic Games are held in Rome

1962 Second Vatican Council brings about Church reforms

1957 Treaty of Rome initiates European Common Market

1978 Premier Aldo Moro kidnapped, then killed by Red Brigades; Karol Wojtyla is elected Pope John Paul II

1981 Assassination attempt on Pope John Paul II in St Peter's Square

1990 Rome hosts several World Cup games.

1993 Francesco Rutelli of the Green Party is elected mayor

2000 Rome enters the 21st century with millions of pilgrims celebrating the Holy Year, known as the Jubilee

1960	1975	1990	2000	2010

ROME AT A GLANCE

FROM ITS EARLY DAYS as a settlement of shepherds on the Palatine hill, Rome grew to rule a vast empire stretching from northern England to North Africa. Later, after the empire had collapsed, Rome became the centre of the Christian world and artists and architects flocked to work for the popes. The legacy of this history can be seen all over the city. The following pages are a time-saving summary of some of the best Rome has to offer. There are sections on churches, museums and galleries, fountains and obelisks, and celebrated visitors and residents in Rome. Below are the top attractions that no visitor should miss.

ROME'S TOP TOURIST ATTRACTIONS

Capitoline Museums
See pp70–73.

Colosseum
See pp92–5.

Sistine Chapel
See pp244–7.

Spanish Steps
See p134.

Raphael Rooms
See pp242–3.

Trevi Fountain
See p159.

Castel Sant'Angelo
See pp248–9.

Pantheon
See pp110–11.

St Peter's
See pp230–33.

Roman Forum
See pp78–87.

Piazza Navona
See p120.

Interior of the Pantheon, by Giovanni Paolo Pannini (1691–1765)

Rome's Best: Churches and Temples

As the centre of Christianity, Rome has a vast wealth of beautiful and interesting churches. These range from magnificent great basilicas built to assert the importance of the medieval and Renaissance Catholic church, to smaller, humbler buildings where the first Christians gathered, often in secret. Among the most fascinating early churches are those converted from ancient Roman temples. Additions to these over the years have resulted in some intriguing, many-layered buildings. A more detailed historical overview of Rome's churches is on pages 44–5.

Pantheon
This monumental 2,000-year-old building is one of the largest surviving temples of ancient Rome.

St Peter's
At 136 m (450 ft) high, Michelangelo's dome is the tallest in the world. Sadly, the artist died before seeing his work completed.

Santa Maria in Trastevere
Built over a very early Christian foundation, this church is famous for its ornate mosaics.

Piazza di Spagna

Vatican

Piazza della Rotonda

Piazza Navona

Janiculum

Campo de' Fiori

Capito

Trastevere

Santa Cecilia in Trastevere
This statue of Cecilia, showing her as she lay when her tomb was uncovered, was sculpted in 1599 by Stefano Maderno.

Santa Maria in Cosmedin
The decorations in this 6th-century church are 12th-century and earlier. A restored painting in the apse shows the Virgin, Child and saints.

Sant'Andrea al Quirinale
Bernini made maximum use of strong, dynamic curves in this oval interior (1658–70), creating a small masterpiece of the Roman Baroque.

Santa Maria Maggiore
Rich mosaics and relics contrast with the sober interior form of Santa Maria Maggiore. Among its treasures are vestments bearing the Borghese coat of arms.

Santa Prassede
Magnificent Byzantine mosaics cover the walls and ceilings of this 9th-century church. This Christ with angels is in the Chapel of St Zeno.

Santa Croce in Gerusalemme
Saints adorn the facade of Santa Croce. Inside are relics of the Cross, brought from Jerusalem by St Helena.

Via Veneto

Quirinal

Forum

Esquiline

Palatine

Lateran

ventine Caracalla

0 metres 500

0 yards 500

San Clemente
Many archaeological layers lie beneath the 12th-century church. This sarcophagus dates from the 4th century.

San Giovanni in Laterano
The original church was built by Constantine, the first Christian emperor. The Chapel of St Venantius mosaics include the figure of St Venantius himself.

Exploring Churches and Temples

THERE ARE MORE CHURCHES in Rome than there are days of the year, so you'll have to be selective. Catholic pilgrims have always been drawn to the seven major basilicas: **St Peter's**, the heart of the Roman Catholic church, **San Giovanni in Laterano**, **San Paolo fuori le Mura**, **Santa Maria Maggiore**, **Santa Croce in Gerusalemme**, **San Lorenzo fuori le Mura** and **San Sebastiano**. These have a wealth of relics, tombs and magnificent works of art from many different periods. Smaller churches can be equally fascinating, especially those that have preserved their original character.

13th-century fresco by Pietro Cavallini in Santa Cecilia

ANCIENT TEMPLES

ONE PAGAN TEMPLE survives virtually unaltered since it was erected in the 2nd century AD. The **Pantheon**, "Temple of all the Gods", has a domed interior quite different in structure from any other church in Rome. It was reconsecrated as a Christian church in the 7th century.

Other Roman temples have been incorporated into Christian churches at various times. Two of these are in the Forum; **Santi Cosma e Damiano** was established in the Temple of Romulus in 526, while San Lorenzo in Miranda was built on to the ruins of the **Temple of Antoninus and Faustina** in the 11th century. The Baroque façade, built in 1602, looms behind the columns of the temple.

Another church that clearly shows its ancient Roman origins is **Santa Costanza**, built as a mausoleum for Constantine's daughter. It is a round church with some splendid 4th-century mosaics.

EARLY CHRISTIAN AND MEDIEVAL CHURCHES

SOME EARLY BASILICAS, the 5th-century **Santa Maria Maggiore** and **Santa Sabina** for example, retain much of their original structure. Other, even earlier churches such as the 4th-century **San Paolo fuori le Mura** and **San Giovanni in Laterano** still preserve their original basilica shape. San Paolo was rebuilt after a fire in 1823 destroyed the original building, and the San Giovanni of today dates from a 1646 reconstruction by Borromini. Both these churches still have their medieval cloisters.

The impressive domed interior of the Pantheon, which became a church in 609

Santa Maria in Trastevere and **Santa Cecilia in Trastevere** were built over houses where the earliest Christian communities met and worshipped in secret, to avoid persecution. One church where the different layers of earlier structures can clearly be seen is **San Clemente**. At its lowest level, it has a Mithraic temple of the 3rd century AD. Other early churches include **Santa Maria in Cosmedin,** with its impressive Romanesque bell tower, and the fortified convent of **Santissimi Quattro Coronati**. Many Roman churches, most notably **Santa Prassede**, contain fine early Christian and medieval mosaics.

Cloister of San Giovanni in Laterano

UNUSUAL FLOORPLANS

The design of Rome's first churches was based on the ancient basilica, a rectangular building divided into three naves. Since then there have been many bold departures from the this plan, including round churches, square churches based on the shape of the Greek cross, as in Bramante's plan for St Peter's, and, in the Baroque period, even oval and hexagonal ones.

Pantheon (2nd century)   **Santa Costanza (4th century)**

RENAISSANCE

The greatest undertaking of the Renaissance popes was the rebuilding of **St Peter's**. Disagreements on the form it should take meant that, although work started in 1506, it was not completed until well into the 17th century. Fortunately, this did not prevent the building of Michelangelo's great dome. As well as working on St Peter's, Michelangelo also provided the **Sistine Chapel** with its magnificent frescoes.

On a completely different scale, another key work of Renaissance architecture is Bramante's tiny **Tempietto** (1499) on the Janiculum. **Santa Maria della Pace** has a Bramante cloister, some frescoes by Raphael and a charming portico by Pietro da Cortona. Also of interest is Michelangelo's imaginative use of the great vaults of the Roman Baths of Diocletian in the church of **Santa Maria degli Angeli**.

There are other churches worth visiting for the sake of

Michelangelo's dramatic dome crowning the interior of St Peter's

their outstanding paintings and sculptures. **Santa Maria del Popolo**, for example, has two great paintings by Caravaggio, the Chigi Chapel designed by Raphael, and a series of 15th-century frescoes by Pinturicchio. **San Pietro in Vincoli**, besides having the chains with which St Peter was bound in prison, also has Michelangelo's awe-inspiring statue of Moses, while **San Luigi dei Francesi** has three Caravaggios depicting St Matthew and frescoes by Domenichino.

BAROQUE

Interior of Rosati's dome in San Carlo ai Catinari (1620)

THE COUNTER REFORMATION inspired the exuberant, lavish style of churches such as the **Gesù** and **Sant' Ignazio di Loyola**. The best-loved examples of Roman Baroque are the later works associated with Bernini, such as the great colonnade and baldacchino he built for **St Peter's**. Of the smaller churches he designed, perhaps the finest is **Sant' Andrea al Quirinale**, while **Santa Maria della Vittoria** houses his truly astonishing Cornaro Chapel with its sculpture of the *Ecstasy of St Teresa*. The late Baroque was not all Bernini, however. You should also look out for churches such as **San Carlo**

ai Catinari with its beautiful dome by Rosato Rosati and the many churches by Bernini's rival, Borromini. **Sant'Agnese in Agone** and **San Carlo alle Quattro Fontane** are famed for the dramatic concave surfaces of their facades, while the complex structure of **Sant'Ivo alla Sapienza** makes it one of the miniature masterpieces of the Baroque.

Bramante's St Peter's (1503)

Sant'Andrea al Quirinale (1658)

Sant'Ivo alla Sapienza (1642)

Rome's Best: Museums and Galleries

THE MUSEUMS OF ROME are among the richest in the world; the Vatican alone contains incomparable collections of Egyptian, Etruscan, Greek, Roman and Early Christian artefacts, as well as frescoes by Michelangelo and Raphael, priceless manuscripts and jewels. Excavations in the 19th century added treasures from ancient Rome which are now on show in museums throughout the city. The finest Etruscan collections in the world can be enjoyed in the Villa Giulia. More details of Rome's museums and galleries are given on pages 48–9.

Vatican Museums
The galleries and long corridors hold priceless artefacts such as this 9th-century mosaic showing scenes from the life of Christ.

Villa Giulia
Etruscan treasures from Rome's early history are displayed in this beautiful Renaissance villa.

0 metres 500

0 yards 500

Piazza d Spagna

Vatican

Piazza Navona

Piazza della Rotonda

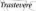

Campo de' Fiori

Janiculum

Trastevere

Galleria Spada
This collection's strength lies in its 17th- and 18th-century paintings. Earlier works include a Visitation *by Andrea del Sarto (1486–1530).*

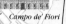

Palazzo Corsini
Included here are works by Caravaggio, Rubens and Van Dyck, as well as a painting of the Baroque sculptor Bernini – a rare portrait by Il Baciccia (1639–1709).

Galleria Doria Pamphilj
Most of the great names of the Renaissance are represented on this gallery's crowded walls. Titian (1485–1576) painted Salomé *early in his career.*

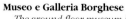

Museo e Galleria Borghese
The ground floor museum houses ancient Greek and Roman sculpture as well as early Bernini masterpieces such as his David *(1619). Upstairs are paintings by Titian, Rubens and other masters.*

Museo Nazionale Romano
This fresco, from Livia's Villa (1st century AD) outside Rome, is one of a huge collection of finds from archaeological sites throughout the city.

Palazzo Barberini
The works of art here date mainly from the 13th to the 16th centuries. This figure of Providence comes from Pietro da Cortona's The Triumph of Divine Providence *(1633–9).*

Palazzo Venezia
The highlights of Rome's most important museum of decorative arts are its Byzantine and medieval collections, including this Byzantine enamel of Christ dating from the 13th century.

Via Veneto

Quirinal

Esquiline

pitol

Forum

Palatine

Caracalla

Lateran

entine

Capitoline Museums: Palazzo dei Conservatori
Pietro da Cortona's Rape of the Sabine Women *(1629) is one of many Baroque paintings in the picture gallery.*

Capitoline Museums: Palazzo Nuovo
Among the sculptures is this head of Giulia Domna (wife of Septimius Severus) from the 2nd century AD.

Exploring Museums and Galleries

ROME'S MUSEUMS and galleries have two major strengths: Greek and Roman archaeological treasures, and paintings and sculptures of the Renaissance and the Baroque. The Vatican Museums have superb collections of both, as do, on a smaller scale, the Capitoline Museums. Fine paintings can also be found scattered throughout Rome in museums, galleries and churches (see pp44–5).

Etruscan clay head, Villa Giulia

ETRUSCAN ARTEFACTS

5th-century BC Etruscan gold plate with inscription, Villa Giulia

THE ETRUSCANS inhabited an area stretching from Florence to Rome from the 8th century BC, and ruled Rome from the late 7th century BC (see pp16–17). It was the Etruscan custom to bury the dead along with their possessions, and as a result Etruscan artefacts have been excavated from tombs all over central Italy. Three main collections can be seen in Rome. The **Villa Giulia** has been the home of the Museo Nazionale Etrusco since 1889. The villa, designed by Vignola for Pope Julius III for summer outings, is one of Rome's prettiest Renaissance buildings. Its gardens contain a reconstructed Etruscan temple. Not

all objects are Etruscan; some of the pottery, statuettes and other artefacts are relics of the Faliscans, Latins and other tribes who inhabited central Italy before the Romans.

The Gregorian Etruscan Museum in the **Vatican Museums** was opened in 1837 to house Etruscan finds from tombs on church-owned land. The Museo Barracco in the **Piccola Farnesina** has statues from the much older civilizations of ancient Egypt and Assyria.

ANCIENT ROMAN ART

THE ARCHAEOLOGICAL zone in Rome forms a huge open-air museum of evidence of ancient Roman life, while the porticoes and cloisters of the city's churches are filled with ancient sarcophagi and fragments of statuary. The largest important collection can be seen in the **Museo Nazionale Romano** at the Baths of Diocletian and its new branch Palazzo Massimo. The museum's many ancient artefacts include, most notably, a sarcophagus from Livia's Villa at Prima Porta just north of Rome. Also on display is some wonderfully well-preserved mosaics. The museum's great collection of Roman statues is now housed in the recently restored **Palazzo Altemps**.

The most important statues are in the **Vatican Museums**, which also have the best of the great Greek works, such as the *Laocoön*, brought to Rome around

the 1st century AD. It had tremendous influence on the subsequent development of Roman art. Splendid copies of Greek originals can be seen in the **Capitoline Museums**.

In the Forum, occupying two floors of the church of Santa Francesca Romana, is the **Antiquarium Forense** with restored finds from the excavations. For those who enjoy history, the large scale model at the **Museo della Civiltà Romana** in EUR gives an excellent idea of what ancient Rome looked like in the 4th century AD.

Centurion's breast-plate, Museo della Civiltà Romana

Victory banner, Museo della Civiltà Romana

ART GALLERIES

Muses in Raphael's *Parnassus* (1508–11), Vatican Museums

IN THE PAST, many of Rome's great aristocratic families owned magnificent private collections of paintings and sculpture. Some of these are still housed in ancestral palazzi, which are open to the public. One is the **Galleria Doria Pamphilj**, which has the greatest concentration of paintings of any palazzo in Rome. It's well worth searching through the dimly lit rooms to find the pearls of the collection, which include works by Raphael,

Filippo Lippi, Caravaggio, Titian and Claude Lorrain, and a portrait of Pope Innocent X Pamphilj by the Spanish artist Velázquez. The **Galleria Spada** collection, begun by Bernardino Spada in 1632, is still housed in the fine original gallery built for it. The paintings demonstrate 17th-century Roman taste and include works by Rubens, Guido Reni, Guercino and Jan Brueghel the Elder. The **Galleria Colonna** contains a collection of art dating from the same period.

Hellenistic faun, Museo Borghese

Other old family residences are now showcases for state art collections. The Galleria Nazionale d'Arte Antica is divided between **Palazzo Barberini** and **Palazzo Corsini**. Palazzo Barberini, built between 1625 and 1633 by Bernini and others for the Barberini family, houses paintings from the 13th to the 16th centuries. It also has *objets d'art* acquired by the state from various private collections. At some future date, the 17th- and 18th-century paintings exhibited in the Palazzo Corsini, on the south side of the Tiber, will

be transferred to join the Palazzo Barberini collection. Another wonderful private collection was that of the Borghese family, also now managed by the state. The **Museo e Galleria Borghese** contains a sculpture collection, including the technically amazing *Apollo and Daphne* by the youthful genius Bernini and the famous statue of Pauline Borghese by Canova. On the first floor is the picture collection with paintings by Titian, Correggio and others.

The **Capitoline Museums** hold collections that were gifts of the popes to the people of Rome. The Pinacoteca (art gallery) in the **Palazzo dei Conservatori** contains works by Titian, Guercino and Van Dyck. There is an art gallery at the **Vatican Museums**, but lovers of Renaissance art will head straight for the Sistine Chapel and the Raphael Rooms. Rome's main modern art collection is in the **Galleria Nazionale d'Arte Moderna**.

SMALLER MUSEUMS

T HE MOST IMPORTANT of the smaller collections is the beautifully laid-out medieval museum in **Palazzo Venezia**, which has exhibits ranging from ceramics to sculpture. Rome has a wealth of small, specialist museums including a **Museum of Musical Instruments**, a **Museo del Folklore**, with tableaux showing life in Rome during the last century, and the **Burcardo Theatre Museum**.

For those with an interest in the English Romantic poets who lived in Rome in the 19th century, there is the **Keats-Shelley Memorial House**, a museum in the house where John Keats died. Focusing on the French Empire, the **Museo Napoleonico** has relics and paintings

Laocoön (1st century AD) in the Vatican's Pio-Clementine Museum

of Napoleon and members of his family, many of whom came to live in Rome.

Portrait of Pauline Borghese painted by Kinson (c1805), now in the Museo Napoleonico

The Deposition (1604) by Caravaggio, the Vatican

Rome's Best: Fountains and Obelisks

R OME HAS SOME of the loveliest fountains in the world. Many of them are the work of the greatest sculptors of the Renaissance and Baroque. Some fountains are flamboyant displays, others restful trickles of water. Many are simply drinking fountains, while a few cascade from the sides of buildings. Obelisks date from far earlier in the city's history. Although some of them were commissioned by Roman emperors, many are even older and were brought to Rome by triumphant, conquering armies. A more detailed overview of Rome's fountains and obelisks is on pages 52–3.

Piazza San Pietro
Twin fountains give life to the splendid monumental piazza of St Peter's. Maderno designed the one on the Vatican side in 1614; the other was later built to match.

Piazza del Popolo
Nineteenth-century marble lions and fountains surround an ancient obelisk in the centre of the piazza.

Vatican

Piazza della Rotonda

Piazza Navona

Campo de' Fiori

Janiculum

Trastevere

Fontana dei Quattro Fiumi
The fountain of the four rivers is the work of Bernini. The four figures represent the Ganges, the Plate, the Danube and the Nile.

Obelisk of Santa Maria sopra Minerva
The Egyptian obelisk, held up by Bernini's marble elephant, dates from the 6th century BC.

Fontana delle Tartarughe
One of Rome's more secret fountains, this jewel of Renaissance sculpture shows youths helping tortoises into a basin.

Fontana della Barcaccia
This elegant fountain of 1627 is probably the work of Pietro Bernini, father of the more famous Gian Lorenzo.

Trevi Fountain
The Trevi, inspired by Roman triumphal arches, was designed by Nicola Salvi in 1732. Tradition has it that a coin thrown into the water guarantees a visitor's return to Rome.

N

0 metres   500
0 yards   500

*iazza
Spagna*   Via Veneto

Quirinal

Capitol

Forum

Palatine

Esquiline

Lateran

Caracalla

Aventine

Fontana delle Naiadi
When this fountain was unveiled in 1901, the realistically sensual bronze nymphs caused a storm of protest.

Obelisk of Piazza San Giovanni in Laterano
The oldest obelisk in Rome dates from the 15th century BC. It came to Rome in AD 357, brought here on the orders of Constantine II.

Piazza della Bocca della Verità Fountain
In this 18th-century fountain, built by Carlo Bizzaccheri for Pope Clement XI, water spills over a craggy rock formation where two Tritons hold aloft a large shell.

Exploring Fountains and Obelisks

Fountain of the Amphorae (1920s)

THE POPES who restored the ancient Roman aqueducts used to build fountains to commemorate their deeds of munificence. As a result, fountains of all sizes and shapes punctuate the city, drawing grateful crowds on hot summer evenings. Ancient obelisks provide powerful reminders of the debt Roman civilization owed to the Egyptians. Architects have learnt to incorporate them into Roman piazzas in fascinating ways.

The Pantheon Fountain

FOUNTAINS

THE TREVI FOUNTAIN is one of the most famous of all. It is a *mostra*, a monumental fountain built to mark the end of an aqueduct – in this case the Acqua Vergine, built by Marcus Agrippa in 19 BC, although the Trevi itself was not erected until 1762. Other *mostre* are the **Fontana dell'Acqua Paola,** built for Pope Paul V in 1612 on the Janiculum, and the **Moses Fountain**, commemorating the opening of the Acqua Felice by Pope Sixtus V in 1587.

Almost all Rome's famous piazzas have fountains. In **Piazza San Pietro** there is a matching pair of powerful fountains. Piazza Navona has Bernini's wonderful Baroque **Fontana dei Quattro Fiumi** (fountain of the four rivers) as its main attraction. The fountain's four figures each represent one of the four principal rivers then known. To the south of this is the smaller **Fontana del Moro** (the Moor), also by Bernini, showing an Ethiopian struggling with a dolphin. At the north end, Neptune

wrestles with an octopus on a 19th-century fountain. In Piazza Barberini is the magnificent Bernini creation of 1642–3: the **Fontana del Tritone** with its sea god blowing through a shell.

More recently, large piazzas have been redesigned around fountains. Valadier's great design for **Piazza del Popolo** (1816–20) has marble lions and fountains surrounding the

Fountain of the Four Tiaras located behind St Peter's

central obelisk plus two more fountains on the east and west sides of the square. The turn of the century saw the opening of the **Fontana delle Naiadi** (nymphs), in Piazza della Repubblica; its earthy figures caused great scandal at the time. The highly original **Fountain of the Amphorae** (map 8 D2) was erected in Piazza dell'Emporio during the 1920s. The same designer, Pietro Lombardi, also created the **Fountain of the Four Tiaras** (map 3 C3) behind the colonnade of St Peter's.

The city also has a number of smaller, and often very charming, fountains. At the foot of the Spanish Steps is the **Fontana della Barcaccia** (the leaking boat) of 1627; the **Fontana delle Tartarughe**

THE TREVI FOUNTAIN

Appropriately for a fountain resembling a stage set, the theatrical Trevi has been the star of many films set in Rome, including romantic films like *Three Coins in a Fountain* and *Roman Holiday*, but also *La Dolce Vita*, Fellini's satirical portrait of Rome in the 1950s. Whatever liberties Anita Ekberg took then, paddling in the fountains of Rome is now forbidden, however tempting it could be in the summer heat.

Anita Ekberg in *La Dolce Vita* (1960)

Fontana dei Cavalli Marini

(the tortoise fountain) has been in the tiny Piazza Mattei since 1581, and by Santa Maria in Domnica is the **Fontana della Navicella** (little boat), created out of an ancient Roman sculpture in the 16th century. In the forecourt of **Santa Sabina** (map 8 D2) water gushes from a huge mask set in an ancient basin. The **Pantheon Fountain** (map 4 F4), from 1575, is by Jacopo della Porta. **Le Quattro Fontane** (four fountains) have stood at the Quirinal hill crossroads since 1593.

Fountains in parks and gardens include the **Galleon Fountain** (1620–21) at the Vatican, and the **Fontana dei Cavalli Marini** (seahorses), of 1791, at Villa Borghese. The somewhat decayed 16th-century terraced gardens of the **Villa d'Este**, with their display of over 500 fountains, are still worth the journey.

Piazza Navona with Fontana dei Fiumi, by Pannini (1691–1765)

The Ovato Fountain at Villa d'Este

OBELISKS

T HE MOST ANCIENT and tallest of Rome's obelisks is the **Obelisk of Piazza di San Giovanni in Laterano**. Built of red granite, 31 m (100 ft) high, it came from the Temple of Ammon at Thebes, erected in the 15th century BC. It was brought to Rome in AD 357 by the order of Constantine II and put up in the Circus Maximus. In 1587 it was rediscovered, broken into three pieces, and was re-erected in the following year. Next in age is the obelisk in **Piazza del Popolo**, from the 12th or 13th century BC. It was brought to Rome in the

time of Augustus and also erected in the Circus Maximus. The slightly smaller **Obelisk of Piazza Montecitorio** was another of Augustus's trophies.

Other obelisks, such as the one at the top of the Spanish Steps, are Roman imitations of Egyptian originals. The **Obelisk of Piazza dell' Esquilino** and the one in **Piazza del Quirinale** (map 5 B4) first stood at the entrance to the Mausoleum of Augustus. When re-erected, most obelisks were mounted on decorative bases, often with statues and fountains at their foot. Others became parts of sculptures. Bernini was the creator of the marble elephant balancing the Egyptian **Obelisk of Santa Maria sopra Minerva** on its back, and the **Fontana dei Fiumi**, with an obelisk

Obelisk in Piazza del Popolo

from the Circus of Maxentius. Another obelisk was added to the remodelled Pantheon Fountain in 1711. The obelisk in **Piazza San Pietro** is Egyptian but does not have the usual hieroglyphics.

The **Obelisk of Axum** was brought by Mussolini's army from Ethiopia in 1937 as a war trophy. It now stands by the UN Food and Agriculture Organization building near the Circus Maximus.

Wall fountain at Villa d'Este

Celebrated Visitors and Residents

Rome exerts a powerful fascination and foreigners thoughout history have succumbed to its charms, often staying for long periods or even taking up permanent residence. The list of famous visitors is almost endless: painters, sculptors and architects from Rome's very earliest days; writers, poets, musicians, exiles, pilgrims, religious teachers, philosophers, aesthetes, archaeologists – all have passed through. Their orchestral works, operas, paintings, drawings, drama and literary journals testify to Rome's inspirational effect.

Martin Luther *(1483–1546)*
The religious reformer from Germany came to the convent at Santa Maria del Popolo in 1511. His horror at the corruption he saw led to the Reformation.

J W von Goethe *(1749–1832)*
The German poet, philosopher, artist, playwright, botanist and courtier lived at No. 20 Via del Corso, now a museum.

Vatican

Piazza d Popolo

Piazza della Roton

Piazza Navona

Sant'Ignazio di Loyola *(1491–1556)*
He came to Rome from Spain in 1537 and founded the Jesuits near what is now the Gesù, the first Jesuit church.

Janiculum

Campo de' Fior

Trastevere

Queen Christina *(1626–89)*
The Swedish queen abdicated in 1654, and came to live in Palazzo Corsini on Via Lungara.

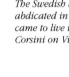

St Dominic *(1170–1221)*
Founder of the Dominican order, St Dominic was born in Spain. The order's headquarters were at Santa Sabina on the Aventine.

Jean Auguste Ingres *(1780–1867)*
The 19th-century French painter, leader of the Neo-Classical tradition, lived in Rome from 1806 until 1820. He returned in 1834 as director of the French Academy at Villa Medici.

Pauline Borghese
(1780–1825)
Napoleon's sister was the subject of scandal in 1805, when she posed semi-nude for a statue by Canova, which is now in Museo Borghese.

Via Veneto

The Exiled Stuarts
James Stuart (1688–1766), unsuccessful claimant to the British throne, came to Rome as an exile. He was presented with Palazzo Balestra by Pope Clement XI and died here.

Quirinal

Esquiline

pitol

Forum

Palatine

Lateran

Caracalla

Lord Byron *(1788–1824)*
Though the English poet's stay in the city was brief, the influence on his work was long-lasting. Stanzas in Childe Harold's Pilgrimage *and* Manfred *were inspired by seeing the Colosseum in moonlight.*

Aventine

| 0 metres | 500 |
| 0 yards | 500 |

Percy Bysshe Shelley
(1792–1822)
The great English Romantic poet wrote his drama Prometheus Unbound *in the calm of the ruined Baths of Caracalla in 1819.*

Artists and Writers Inspired by Rome

Aᴿᴛɪsᴛs ᴀɴᴅ ᴡʀɪᴛᴇʀs have been attracted to Rome since Classical times. Many came to work for the emperors; the poets Horace, Virgil and Ovid, for example, all enjoyed the patronage of Emperor Augustus. Later on, especially in the Renaissance and Baroque periods, the greatest artists and architects came to Rome to compete for commissions from the popes. However, patronage was not the only magnet. Since the Renaissance, Rome's Classical past and its picturesque ruins have drawn artists, architects and writers from all over Italy and abroad.

The prolific love poet Ovid (43 BC–AD 17)

Self-portrait by the 18th-century artist Angelica Kauffmann, c 1770

PAINTERS, SCULPTORS AND ARCHITECTS

Diego Velázquez, one of many great 17th-century artists to visit Rome

Iɴ ᴛʜᴇ ᴇᴀʀʟʏ 16th century, artists and architects were summoned from all parts of Italy to realize the grandiose building projects of the popes. From Urbino came Bramante (1444–1514) and Raphael (1483–1520); from Perugia Perugino (1450–1523); from Florence Michelangelo (1475–1564) and many others. They worked in the Vatican, on the new St Peter's and the decoration of the Sistine Chapel. Artists were often well rewarded, but they also lived in dangerous times. Florentine sculptor and goldsmith Benvenuto Cellini (1500–71) helped defend Castel Sant' Angelo (see pp248–9) during the Sack of Rome (1527), but was later imprisoned there and made a dramatic escape. His memoirs tell the story.

Towards the end of the 16th century church patronage was generous to the

Milanese-born Caravaggio (1571–1610) despite his violent character and unruly life. The Carracci family from Bologna also flourished – especially brothers Annibale (1560–1609) and Agostino (1557–1602).

The work of Gian Lorenzo Bernini (1598–1680) can be seen all over Rome. He succeeded Carlo Maderno (1556–1629) as architect of St Peter's, and created its great bronze baldacchino, the splendid colonnade (see pp230–31) and numerous fountains, churches and sculptures. His rival for the title of leading architect of the Roman Baroque was Francesco Borromini (1599–1667), whose highly original genius can be appreciated in many Roman churches and palazzi.

In the 17th century it became more common for artists from outside Italy to come and work in Rome. Diego Velázquez (1599–1660), King Philip IV of Spain's court painter, came in 1628 to study

the art treasures of the Vatican. Rubens (1577–1640) came from Antwerp to study, and carried out various commissions. The French artists Nicolas Poussin (1594–1665) and Claude Lorrain (1600–82) lived here for many years.

The Classical revival of the 18th century attracted artists to Rome in unprecedented numbers. From Britain came the Scottish architect Robert Adam (1728–92) and the Swiss artist Angelica Kauffmann (1741–1807), who settled here and was buried with great honour in Sant'Andrea delle Fratte. After the excesses of the Baroque, sculpture also turned to the simplicity of Neo-Classicism. A leading exponent of this movement was Antonio Canova (1757–1821). Sculptors from all over Europe were influenced by him, including the Dane Bertel Thorvaldsen (1770–1844) who lived in Rome for many years.

Claude Lorrain's view of the Forum, painted in Rome in 1632

WRITERS

Dante (1262–1321) visited Rome during his exile from Florence and in the *Inferno* describes the great influx of pilgrims for the first Holy Year (1300). The poet Petrarch (1304–74), born in Arezzo, came to the city in much happier circumstances to be crowned with laurels on the Capitol in 1341. The poet Torquato Tasso (1544–95), from Sorrento, was invited to receive a similar honour, but died soon after his arrival. He is buried in Sant'Onofrio *(see p219)* on the Janiculum. Two of the first writers from abroad to visit Rome were the French essayist Montaigne (1533–92) and English poet John Milton (1608–74). Then, by the early 18th century, writers seemed to flock to Rome. Edward Gibbon (1737–94) was inspired to write *Decline and Fall of the Roman Empire* when he heard the monks singing the Angelus outside Santa Maria in Aracoeli *(see p69)*. German visitors included J J Winckelmann (1717–68)

Torquato Tasso

who wrote influential studies of ancient art, and the poet J W von Goethe (1749–1832).

In the Romantic period Rome teemed with English writers: poets Keats, Shelley and Byron, followed by the Brownings and the novelist Charles Dickens. Travel writers in the 19th century included Augustus Hare (1834–1903) and the German historian Ferdinand Gregorovius (1821–91). Much of *The Portrait of a Lady* by American Henry James (1843–1916) is set in Rome.

Modern life in Rome is brilliantly captured by the Roman-born novelist and short-story writer Alberto Moravia (1907–90).

MUSICIANS

Giovanni Luigi da Palestrina (1525–94), from the town of that name, became choirmaster and organist to the Vatican and composed some of the greatest unaccompanied choral music ever written. In 1770 the 14-year-old Mozart heard Gregorio Allegri's unpublished *Miserere* in the Sistine Chapel and wrote it down from memory. Arcangelo

Portrait of the poet John Keats painted by his friend Joseph Severn in 1819

Corelli (1653–1713), the great violinist and composer of the Baroque age, worked in Rome under the patronage of Cardinal Ottoboni. One of his first commissions was to provide a festival of music for Queen Christina of Sweden.

During the 19th century the Prix de Rome brought many French musicians to study here at the Villa Medici *(see p135)*. Hector Berlioz (1803–69) owed the inspiration for his popular *Roman Carnival*, the overture to his opera *Benvenuto Cellini*, to his two-year stay in Rome. Georges Bizet (1838–75) and Claude Debussy (1862–1918) were also Prix de Rome winners. Franz Liszt (1811–86), after his 50th year, settled in Rome, took minor orders and became known as Abbé Liszt. He wrote *Fountains of the Villa d'Este* while staying at the villa in Tivoli.

Giacomo Puccini

More recent, 20th-century musical associations with Rome include the popular works by Ottorino Respighi (1870–1936): *The Fountains of Rome* and *The Pines of Rome*, while Giacomo Puccini (1858–1924) used Roman settings when creating his dramatic, tragic opera *Tosca*.

ROMAN CINEMA

The Cinecittà studios, built in 1937 just outside Rome, are most famous for the films made here in the 1940s, classics of Italian Neo-Realism such as Roberto Rossellini's *Roma Città Aperta* and Vittorio De Sica's *Sciùscià* and *Ladri di Bicicletta*. In the 1950s Cinecittà became a centre for international productions, including the epics *Ben Hur* and *Spartacus*.

The director most strongly associated with Roman cinema is Federico Fellini, whose films *La Dolce Vita* (1960) and *Roma* (1972) present a highly idiosyncratic portrait of the follies of the city. Perhaps the most famous film-maker associated with Rome is the controversial writer Pier Paolo Pasolini (1922–75), who became internationally known with his films *Teorema* (1968) and *Il Decamerone* (1971).

Pier Paolo Pasolini

ROME THROUGH THE YEAR

THE BEST TIMES to visit Rome are spring and autumn when the weather is usually warm, and sometimes even hot enough to sunbathe and swim at the beaches and lakes outside the city. November is best avoided as the weather tends to be grey and extremely rainy, while in high summer, most people (including Romans, who leave the city in their droves) find the heat unbearable.

Easter and Christmas are obviously very special in Rome, but there are other religious festivals worth seeing at other times in the year, as well as some enjoyable secular events like the Festa de Noantri in Trastevere and the Flower Festival in Genzano. In villages outside Rome, local celebrations are held to welcome new crops such as strawberries and beans in the spring, and grapes and truffles in the autumn.

SPRING

EASTER, falling in March or April, marks the official beginning of the tourist season in Rome. Catholics from all over the world flock into the city to make their pilgrimages to the main basilicas and to hear the pope's Easter Sunday address outside St Peter's, while the less devout come simply to take advantage of the mild weather. Meanwhile, Romans pile into their cars and head for the coast and countryside, so you can expect the roads, beaches, and the restaurants of the Castelli Romani and Lake Bracciano to be busy.

Temperatures tend to be around 18° C (66° F), but can hit 28° C (82° F), so by mid-May it's usually possible to lunch and dine outside. However, there can still be sudden downpours and temperature swings, so do bring warm clothes and an umbrella.

Crowds gathering in St Peter's square at Easter

In April tubs full of colourful azaleas are ranged on the Spanish Steps and along Via Veneto, and once the roses start to flower in the city's Rose Garden overlooking the Circus Maximus, it is opened to the public.

For a fortnight from mid-May Via dei Coronari is lit by candles, lined with plants and hung with banners for the street's antiques fair, while Via Margutta hosts an outdoor art show. In the first week of May the International Horse Show is held in the Villa Borghese, and towards the end of the month many world-class tennis players flock to Rome to compete in the International Tennis Championships held at the Foro Italico.

EVENTS

Festa di Santa Francesca Romana *(9 March)*, Santa Francesca Romana. Blessing of the city's cars, buses and trams *(see p87)*.
Festa di San Giuseppe *(19 March)*, in the Trionfale area. St Joseph's (and Father's) Day celebrated with street stalls, cream puffs and music.
Good Friday *(March/April)*, Colosseum. Procession of the Cross at 9pm led by the pope.
Easter Sunday *(March/April)*, St Peter's square. Address made by the pope *(see p231)*.
Rome's Birthday *(Sunday before 21 April)*, Piazza del Campidoglio.
Festa della Primavera *(March/April)*, Spanish Steps and Trinità dei Monti. Azaleas in the street and concerts.
Art exhibition *(April/May)*, Via Margutta *(see p339)*.
International Horse Show *(early May)*, Villa Borghese *(see p350)*.
Antiques Fair *(mid–late May)*, Via dei Coronari *(see p324)*.
International Tennis Championships *(late May)*, Foro Italico *(see p350)*.

International Horse Show in Villa Borghese in May

AVERAGE DAILY HOURS OF SUNSHINE

Hours

10
8
6
4
2
0

Jan Feb Mar Apr May Jun Jul Aug Sep Oct Nov Dec

Sunshine Chart
Rome is famous for its light. June is the sunniest month; but it is also very dry, and without the odd shower the bright heat can feel intense. In autumn, Rome's southerly position means that the sun can still be enjoyably warm at midday.

SUMMER

IN JUNE a summer season of concerts begins, with performances in some of the city's most beautiful palaces, churches and courtyards. In July and August opera and classical drama is staged at Ostia Antica and in various outdoor locations. Throughout the summer there are also contemporary cultural events – film, music of all kinds, dance and theatre – staged as part of the Cineporto and Massenzio film festivals (*see p346*) and RomaEuropa. On midsummer evenings there are stalls and amusements on the Tiber embankments by Castel Sant'Angelo, while in the last two weeks of July

Flower-carpeted streets in Genzano

Summer vegetables

Trastevere becomes an open-air party as the Noantri festival is celebrated with trinket stalls, dining in the street and fireworks. Mid-July is good for shoppers as the sales (*saldi*) begin.

Many Romans leave the city at the end of June, when schools close, but as June and July are peak tourist months, hotels, cafés, restaurants and sights are packed. In August,

when the temperature often soars to over 40° C (104° F), virtually all Romans flee the city for the seaside, and many cafés, shops and restaurants close for the month.

EVENTS

Flower Festival (*June, the Sunday after Corpus Domini*), Genzano, Castelli Romani, south of Rome. Streets are carpeted with flowers.
Festa di San Giovanni (*23–24 June*), Piazza di Porta San Giovanni. Celebrated with meals of snails in tomato sauce, suckling pig, a fair and firework display.
RomaEuropa (*late June–autumn*). Films, dance, theatre and concerts in venues around Rome (*see p341*).
Festa di San Pietro (*29 June*), many churches. Celebrations mark the feast of St Peter.

Tevere Expo (*end June–mid-July*), along the Tiber. Arts and crafts, food and wine stalls, folk music and fireworks (*see p339*).
Festa de Noantri (*last two weeks in July*), the streets of Trastevere. Feasting, processions and entertainment (*see p339 and p341*).
Estate Romana (*July/August*), Villa Ada, Ostia Antica, in parks, by the Tiber. Outdoor opera, concerts, drama, dance performances and film (*see p341*).
Festa della Madonna della Neve (*5 August*), Santa Maria Maggiore. Legendary 4th-century fall of snow re-enacted with showers of white flower petals (*see p172*).
Ferragosto (*15 August*), Santa Maria in Trastevere. Midsummer Roman holiday. Almost everything closes down. Celebrations are held for the Feast of the Assumption.

The heat of an August afternoon in front of St Peter's

AVERAGE MONTHLY RAINFALL

Rainfall Chart
Autumn is Rome's rainiest season, with heavy downpours, sometimes lasting for days, especially in November. Rain in summer tends to come in violent – but often extremely refreshing – storms. In winter and early spring expect a few dull, drizzly days.

AUTUMN

SEPTEMBER AND OCTOBER are the best – and among the most popular – months to visit Rome. The fiery heat of July and August will have cooled a little, but midday can be very hot, and you can still eat and drink outside without feeling chilly until late at night. Visiting Rome in November is not recommended: it is the wettest month of the year and Roman rainstorms are often very strong and heavy.

At the beginning of October an artisans' fair is held on Via dell'Orso and adjacent streets, while nearby the antiques galleries of Via dei Coronari hold open house. There are also October antiques fairs in Orvieto and Perugia, two of the loveliest Umbrian hill towns, which are about an hour's drive north of Rome. In November, there's yet another prestigious antiques fair at the papal palace of Viterbo, 65 km (40 m) north of Rome *(see p271)*.

Autumn is, of course, the season of harvest festivals, and it can be fun to head out to the small towns around Rome to sample delicacies such as local cheeses,

A roast chestnut stall in autumn

sausages, chestnuts and mushrooms. Another reason for taking a trip out of Rome is the wine festival in Marino, which is located in the Castelli Romani, south of Rome. There are plenty of opportunities to sample the wines of this region that was once the home to luxurious 16th- and 17th-century country residences but now is renowned particularly for its white wines.

Throughout the autumn and winter in Rome, freshly roasted chestnuts can be bought from vendors on street corners, and there is usually a stand on Campo de' Fiori where you can sample the new season's wine, *vino novello*, for free.

On All Souls and All Saints days, which fall on 1 and 2 November respectively, the Romans make pilgrimages to the tombs of relatives who are buried in the cemeteries of Prima Porta and Verano. Chrysanthemums are then traditionally placed on their graves and for this reason they should definitely not be given to friends, hosts and hostesses as thank you presents for their hospitality.

On a much happier note, the classical concert and opera seasons begin again in October and November. Details of performances can be found in listings magazines such as *Trovaroma* and *Roma c'è* *(see p340)* and on posters dotted around the city.

EVENTS

Art fair *(September)*, Via Margutta *(see p339)*.
Crafts fair *(last week September/first week October)*, Via dell'Orso, near Piazza Navona *(see p339)*.
Marino Wine Festival *(first Sunday in October)*, Marino. Celebrations include tastings and street entertainment.
Antiques Fair *(mid-October)*, Via dei Coronari *(see p339)*.
All Souls and All Saints Days *(1, 2 November)*, Prima Porta and Verano cemetaries. Witness the Pope usually celebrating Mass in the extensive Verano cemetary.
Festa di Santa Cecilia *(22 November)*, Santa Cecilia in Trastevere and Catacombs of San Callisto.
Vino Novello tasting *(late November)*, Campo de' Fiori.

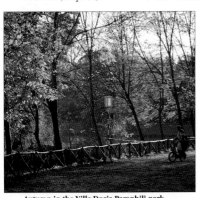

Autumn in the Villa Doria Pamphilj park

AVERAGE MONTHLY TEMPERATURE

Temperature Chart
The chart shows the average minimum and maximum monthly temperatures. July and August can be unbearably hot, making sightseeing a chore. The fresher days of spring and autumn are ideal to visit Rome, but there are some dull and rainy spells.

WINTER

DURING THE WINTER Rome is bracingly chilly but the temperature rarely drops below freezing. Not all buildings are centrally heated so if you're staying in a small hotel bring warm clothes and request extra blankets as soon as you arrive, as they can be in short supply. Warm up in cafés with hot chocolate and cappuccino.

The run-up to Christmas is great fun in Rome, especially if you have children. Manger scenes, *presepi*, are set up in many churches, piazzas and public places and from mid-December to Twelfth Night

Rome during one of its rare snowfalls

Market on Piazza Navona

Piazza Navona hosts a market where you can buy manger scenes, decorations and toys. Unless you have friends in Rome, Christmas itself can be rather lonely, as it is very much a family event. On New Year's Eve, however, everyone is out on the street to drink sparkling wine and let off fireworks.

Befana, on 6 January, is a traditional holiday when a witch, called La Befana, delivers sweets to children.

The Carnival season runs from late January through to February, celebrated largely by children with fancy-dress

parties and parades along Via Nazionale, Via Cola di Rienzo and the Pincio. Keep out of the way of teenagers with shaving cream spray cans and water-filled balloons.

EVENTS

Festa della Madonna Immacolata *(8 December)*, Piazza di Spagna. Firemen climb up a ladder to place a wreath on the statue of the Virgin Mary.
Christmas Market *(mid-December – mid-January)*, Piazza Navona. Christmas and children's market *(see p120)*.
Nativity scenes *(mid-December – mid-January)*, many churches. Life-size scene in St Peter's square, collection at Santi Cosma e Damiano.
Midnight Mass *(24 December)*, at most churches.
Christmas Day *(25 December)*, St Peter's square. Blessing by the pope.
New Year's Eve *(31 December)*, all over city. Firework displays, furniture thrown out.
Befana *(6 January)*, all over city. Parties for children.

PUBLIC HOLIDAYS
New Year's Day (1 Jan)
Epiphany (6 Jan)
Easter Monday
Liberation Day (25 Apr)
Labour Day (1 May)
SS Peter and Paul's Day (29 Jun)
Ferragosto (15 Aug)
All Saints (1 Nov)
Immaculate Conception (8 Dec)
Christmas Day (25 Dec)
Santo Stefano (26 Dec)

Via Condotti at Christmas

ROME AREA
BY AREA

CAPITOL

THE TEMPLE OF JUPITER on the Capitol, the southern summit of the Capitoline hill, was the centre of the Roman world. Reached by a zig-zag path up from the Forum, the temple was the scene of all the most sacred religious and political ceremonies. The hill and its temple came to symbolize Rome's authority as *caput mundi*, head of the world, and the concept of a "capital" city is derived from the Capitol. Throughout the city's history, the Capitol, or Campidoglio as it is called in Italian, has remained the seat of municipal government.

Hand of colossal statue in Palazzo dei Conservatori

Today's city council, the Comune di Roma, meets in the Renaissance splendour of Palazzo Senatorio. Rome's position as a modern capital is forcefully expressed in the enormous white Victor Emmanuel Monument, which unfortunately blots out the view of the Capitol from Piazza Venezia. The present arrangement of the buildings on the hill dates from the 16th century, when Michelangelo created a beautiful piazza reached by a dramatic flight of steps, the Cordonata. Two of the three buildings around the piazza are now home to the Capitoline Museums.

SIGHTS AT A GLANCE

Churches and Temples
Santa Maria in Aracoeli ❼
Temple of Jupiter ❽
San Marco ⓬

Museums and Galleries
Capitoline Museums:
Palazzo Nuovo pp70–71 ❶
Capitoline Museums:
Palazzo dei Conservatori
pp72–3 ❷
Palazzo Venezia
and Museum ⓫

Historic Buildings
Roman Insula ❺

Historic Streets and Piazzas
Piazza del Campidoglio ❸
Cordonata ❹
Aracoeli Staircase ❻

Ancient Sites
Tarpeian Rock ❾

Monuments
Victor Emmanuel
Monument ❿

GETTING THERE
All the sights in this area are within walking distance of Piazza Venezia. Bus routes converge here from all parts of the city, as do many thousands of motorists. From Termini station you can catch the 64, 70, 75 or 170; from Piazza Barberini the 56, 60 or 492. From St Peter's and the Vatican the only bus is the 64. Other useful routes include the 44, 46, and 628.

KEY
▨ Street-by-Street map

0 metres   200
0 yards   200

Statue of Marcus Aurelius on Michelangelo's Piazza del Campidoglio

Street-by-Street: The Capitol and Piazza Venezia

THE CAPITOL, citadel of ancient Rome, is a must for every visitor. A broad flight of steps (the Cordonata) leads up to Michelangelo's spectacular Piazza del Campidoglio. This is flanked by the Palazzo Nuovo and Palazzo dei Conservatori, housing the Capitoline Museums with their fine collections of sculpture and paintings. The absence of cars makes the hill a welcome retreat from the squeal of brakes below, but you should brave the traffic to visit Palazzo Venezia and its museum.

Victor Emmanuel Monument
This huge white marble monument to Italy's first king was completed in 1911 ❿

PIAZZA VENEZIA

PIAZZA VENEZIA

VIA DEL TEATRO DI MARCELLO

San Marco
The church of the Venetians in Rome has a fine 9th-century apse mosaic ⓬

Palazzo Venezia
The museum's finest exhibits, such as this 13th-century gilded angel decorated with enamel, date from the late Middle Ages ⓫

Roman Insula
This is a ruined apartment block dating from Imperial Rome ❺

Aracoeli Staircase
When it was built in 1348, the staircase became a centre for political debate ❻

Cordonata
Michelangelo's great staircase changed the orientation of the Capitol towards the west ❹

KEY

– – – Suggested route

0 metres   75
0 yards   75

★ **Palazzo dei Conservatori**
In this part of the Capitoline Museums a fine series of reliefs from the Temple of Hadrian (see p106) is displayed in the courtyard ❷

Santa Maria in Aracoeli
The treasures hidden behind the church's brick facade include this 15th-century fresco of the Funeral of St Bernardino *by Pinturicchio* **7**

LOCATOR MAP
See Central Rome Map pp12–13

★ Palazzo Nuovo
This bust of Augustus in the Hall of the Emperors is one of many fine Classical sculptures in the Capitoline Museums **1**

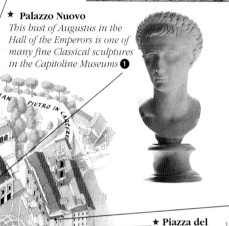

Palazzo Senatorio was used by the Roman Senate from about the 12th century. It now houses the offices of the mayor.

★ Piazza del Campidoglio
Michelangelo designed both the geometric paving and the facades of the buildings **3**

Temple of Jupiter
This artist's impression shows the gold and ivory statue of Jupiter that stood in the temple **8**

Tarpeian Rock
In ancient Rome traitors were thrown to their death from this cliff on the Capitol **9**

STAR SIGHTS

- **★ Piazza del Campidoglio**
- **★ Palazzo dei Conservatori**
- **★ Palazzo Nuovo**

Capitoline Museums: Palazzo Nuovo **❶**

See pp70–71.

Capitoline Museums: Palazzo dei Conservatori **❷**

See pp72–3.

Piazza del Campidoglio **❸**

Map 5 A5 & 12 F5. 🚌 *See **Getting There** p65.*

WHEN EMPEROR Charles V visited Rome in 1536, Pope Paul III Farnese was so embarrassed by the muddy state of the Capitol that he asked Michelangelo to draw up plans for repaving the piazza, and for renovating the façades of the Palazzo dei Conservatori and Palazzo Senatorio.

Michelangelo proposed adding the Palazzo Nuovo to form a piazza in the shape of a trapezium, embellished with Classical sculptures chosen for their relevance to Rome. Building started in 1546 but progressed so slowly that Michelangelo only lived to oversee the double flight of steps at the entrance of Palazzo Senatorio. The piazza was completed in the 17th

century, the design remaining largely faithful to the original. Pilasters two storeys high and balustrades interspersed with statues link the buildings thematically. The piazza faces west towards St Peter's, the Christian equivalent of the Capitol. At its centre stands a replica of a statue of Marcus Aurelius. The original is in the Palazzo Nuovo *(see pp70–71).*

Cordonata **❹**

Map 5 A5 & 12 F5. 🚌 *See **Getting There** p65.*

FROM PIAZZA VENEZIA, the Capitol is approached by a gently rising, subtly widening ramp – the Cordonata. At the foot is a pair of granite Egyptian lions, and on the left a 19th-century monument to Cola di Rienzo, close to where the dashing 14th-century tyrant was executed. The top of the ramp is guarded by restored Classical statues of the Dioscuri, Castor and Pollux.

Roman Insula **❺**

Piazza d'Aracoeli. **Map** 5 A5 & 12 F4. ☎ 06-67 10 30 65. 🚌 *See **Getting There** p65.* **Open** by appt only: permit needed (see p367).

TWO THOUSAND YEARS ago the urban poor of Rome used to make their homes in *insulae* – apartment blocks.

One of the statues of the Dioscuri at the top of the Cordonata

These were often badly maintained by landlords, and expensive to rent in a city where land costs were high. This 2nd-century AD tenement block, of barrel-vault construction, is the only survivor in Rome from that era. The fourth, fifth and part of the sixth storey remain above current ground level.

In the Middle Ages, a section of these upper storeys was converted into a church; its bell tower and 14th-century Madonna in a niche are visible from the street.

During the Fascist years, the area was cleared, and three lower floors emerged. Some 380 people may have lived in the tenement, in the squalid conditions described by the 1st-century AD satirical writers Martial and Juvenal. The latter mentions that he had to climb 200 steps to reach his garret.

This *insula* may once have had more storeys. The higher you lived, the more dismal the conditions, as the poky spaces of the building's upper levels testify.

The Cordonata in an 18th-century painting by Antonio Canaletto

Aracoeli Staircase ❻

Piazza d'Aracoeli. **Map** 5 A5 & 12 F4.
🚌 *See **Getting There** p65.*

THE ARACOELI Staircase numbers 124 marble steps (122 if you start from the right) and was completed in 1348, some say in thanks for the passing of the Black Death, but probably in view of the 1350 Holy Year.

The 14th-century tribune-turned-tyrant Cola di Rienzo used to harangue the masses from the Aracoeli Staircase; in the 17th century foreigners used to sleep on the steps, until Prince Caffarelli, who lived on the hill, scared them off by rolling barrels filled with stones down them.

Popular belief has it that by climbing the steps on your knees you can win the national lottery. From the top there is a good view of Rome, with the domes of Sant' Andrea della Valle and St Peter's slightly to the right.

Aracoeli Staircase

Santa Maria in Aracoeli ❼

Piazza d'Aracoeli (entrances via Aracoeli Staircase and door behind Palazzo Nuovo). **Map** 5 A5 & 12 F4.
📞 06-679 81 55. 🚌 *See **Getting There** p65.* **Open** *7am–6.30pm daily.*

DATING FROM AT LEAST the 6th century, the church of Santa Maria in Aracoeli, or St Mary of the Altar in the Sky, stands on the northern summit of the Capitoline, on the site of the ancient temple

Ceiling commemorating Battle of Lepanto in nave of Santa Maria in Aracoeli

to Juno. Its 22 columns were taken from various ancient buildings; the inscription on the third column to the left tells us that it comes *"a cubiculo Augustorum"* – from the bedroom of the emperors.

The church of the Roman senators and people, Santa Maria in Aracoeli has been used to celebrate many triumphs over adversity. Its ceiling, with naval motifs, commemorates the Battle of Lepanto (1571), and was built under Pope Gregory XIII Boncompagni, whose family crest, the dragon, can be seen towards the altar end.

Many other Roman families and individuals are honoured by memorials in the church. To the right of the entrance door, the tombstone of archdeacon Giovanni Crivelli, rather than being set into the floor of the church, stands eternally to attention, partly so that the signature "Donatelli" (by Donatello) can be read at eye-level.

The frescoes in the first chapel on the right, painted by Pinturicchio in the 1480s in the beautifully clear style of the early Renaissance, relate the life and death of St Bernardino of Siena. On the left-hand wall, the perspective of *The Burial of the Saint* actually slants to the right, taking into account the position of the viewer standing just outside the chapel.

The church is most famous, however, for an icon with apparently miraculous powers, the *Santo Bambino*, a 15th-century olive-wood figure of the Christ child which was carved out of a tree from the garden of Gethsemane. Its powers are said to include resurrecting the dead, and it is sometimes summoned to the bedsides of the gravely ill. The original figure was stolen in 1994 but has been replaced by a replica.

At Christmas the Christ Child takes its place in the centre of a picturesque crib (second chapel to the left) but is usually to be found in the sacristy, as is the panel of the *Holy Family* from the workshop of Giulio Romano.

The miraculous olive-wood Christ Child at Santa Maria in Aracoeli

Capitoline Museums: Palazzo Nuovo ❶

A COLLECTION of Classical statues has been kept on the Capitoline hill since the Renaissance. The first group of bronze sculptures was given to the city by Pope Sixtus IV in 1471 and more additions were made by Pope Pius V in 1566. The Palazzo Nuovo was designed by Michelangelo as part of the renovation of the Piazza del Campidoglio, and after its completion in 1655, a number of the statues were transferred there. In 1734 Pope Clement XII decreed that the building be turned into the world's first public museum.

MUSEUM GUIDE
The two floors of the Palazzo Nuovo are devoted chiefly to sculpture. Most of the finest works, such as the Capitoline Venus, are Roman copies of Greek masterpieces. There are also two collections of busts assembled in the 18th century for visitors keen to identify all the philosophers and poets of ancient Greece and the rulers of ancient Rome. The price of entry includes admission to the Palazzo dei Conservatori, which is directly opposite.

Hall of the Philosophers
The hall contains a rich mix of portraits of Greek politicians, scientists and literary figures. They are Roman copies that decorated the libraries, villas and gardens of the wealthy in ancient times.

Portrait of a Flavian Lady
The woman wears the fanciful and elaborate hairstyle popular among the female aristocracy of the 1st century AD.

Capitoline Venus

First floor

Courtyard

★ **Marcus Aurelius**
This bronze equestrian statue of the emperor dates from the 2nd century AD. It used to stand on a pedestal in the centre of the Campidoglio, but has now been restored and is housed in the Palazzo Nuovo. A copy stands on the square.

Ground floor

The facade of Palazzo Nuovo was designed by Michelangelo, but the work was actually finished in 1655 by the brothers Carlo and Girolamo Rainaldi.

STAR SCULPTURES
* ★ Marcus Aurelius
* ★ Discobolus
* ★ Dying Galatian

KEY TO FLOORPLAN
☐ Non-exhibition space
☐ Exhibition space

Mosaic of the Doves
This charming, naturalistic mosaic once decorated the floor of Hadrian's Villa at Tivoli (see p269). It shows doves drinking water from a vase.

★ **Discobolus**
The twisted torso was part of a Greek statue of a discus thrower. An 18th-century French sculptor, Monnot, made the additions that turned him into a wounded warrior.

VISITORS' CHECKLIST

Musei Capitolini, Piazza del Campidoglio. **Map** 5 A5 & 12 F5.
(06-67 10 27 33. **▦** 44, 46, 56, 64, 70, 81, 95, 117, 715 and many other routes to Piazza Venezia. **Open** 9am–7pm Tue–Sun. **Closed** 1 Jan, 1 May, 25 Dec. **Adm charge** (free last Sun of month). Entrance ticket is also valid for Palazzo dei Conservatori. **NB** Altough open, the museum is currently undergoing restoration and reorganization during which exhibits might move around.

Stairs to ground floor

Stairs to first floor

Red Faun
Found at Tivoli, the famous red marble satyr is a 2nd-century AD version of a Greek original – an example of Hadrian's fondness for all things Greek.

★ **Dying Galatian**
Great compassion is conveyed in this Roman copy of an original Greek work of the 3rd century BC.

Main entrance

Alexander Severus as Hunter
In this marble of the 3rd century AD, the emperor's pose is a pastiche of Perseus, holding up the head of Medusa the Gorgon after he had killed her in her sleep.

Capitoline Museums: Palazzo dei Conservatori ❷

T HE PALAZZO DEI CONSERVATORI was the seat of the city's magistrates during the late Middle Ages. Its frescoed halls are still used occasionally for political meetings and the ground floor houses the municipal registry office. The palazzo was built by Giacomo della Porta who carried out Michelangelo's designs for the Piazza del Campidoglio in the mid-16th century. While much of the palazzo is given over to sculpture, the art galleries on the second floor hold works by Veronese, Guercino, Tintoretto, Rubens, Caravaggio, Van Dyck and Titian.

Facade of Palazzo dei Conservatori
Work began on this Michelangelo design in 1563, the year before his death.

MUSEUM GUIDE

The whole museum is now open after restoration, but is still being reorganized, why objects might move. The rooms on the first floor are remarkable for their original 16th- and 17th-century decoration and Classical statues. The second-floor gallery houses paintings and a collection of porcelain.

Burial and Glory of St Petronilla
This huge Baroque altar-piece was painted in 1622–3 by Guercino to hang in St Peter's.

Second-floor art gallery

Stairs to second floor

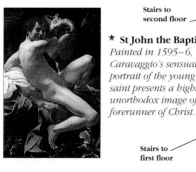

★ **St John the Baptist**
Painted in 1595–6, Caravaggio's sensual portrait of the young saint presents a highly unorthodox image of the forerunner of Christ.

Stairs to first floor

Courtyard

Main entrance

The Horatii and Curatii
D'Arpino's fresco was painted in 1613 and depicts a duel taken from early Roman legend.

KEY TO FLOORPLAN

☐ Garden
☐ Non-exhibition space
☐ Re-opened after restoration
☐ Exhibition space

Endymion
The youth doomed to sleep forever by the goddess Diana was painted by Pier Francesco Mola (1612–66) who studied under Cavalier d'Arpino.

VISITORS' CHECKLIST
See p71.

STAR EXHIBITS

★ She-Wolf

★ St John the Baptist by Caravaggio

★ Spinario

Braccio Nuovo

Esquiline Venus
The 1st-century BC figure was associated with the cult of Isis.

Museo Nuovo

Roman Garden

26
25
19

First floor

16
17
8
18
7
6

Constantine II
The head of a colossal 4th-century AD statue of the emperor has survived, along with a hand and other odd fragments.

★ **Spinario**
This is a charming bronze sculpture from the 1st century BC of a boy trying to remove a thorn from his foot.

★ **She-Wolf**
The Etruscan bronze of the wolf dates from the early 5th century BC. The legendary twins, Romulus and Remus (see pp16–17), were probably added in the 15th century.

Temple of Jupiter ❽

Via del Tempio di Giove. **Map** 5 A5 & 12 F5. ▦ See **Getting There** p65.

THE TEMPLE of Jupiter, the most important in ancient Rome, was founded in honour of the arch-god around 509 BC on the southern summit of the Capitoline hill. From the few traces that remain, archaeologists have been able to reconstruct the rectangular, Greek appearance of the temple as it once stood. In places you can see remnants of its particularly Roman feature, the podium. Most of this lies beneath the Museo Nuovo wing of the Palazzo dei Conservatori (see pp72–3).

By walking around the site, from the podium's south-western corner in Via del Tempio di Giove to its south-eastern corner in Piazzale Caffarelli, you can see that the temple was about the same size as the Pantheon.

Ancient coin showing the Temple of Jupiter

Tarpeian Rock ❾

Via di Monte Caprino and Via del Tempio di Giove. **Map** 5 A5 & 12 F5. ▦ See **Getting There** p65.

THE SOUTHERN TIP of the Capitoline is called the Tarpeian Rock (Rupe Tarpea), after Tarpeia, the young daughter of Spurius Tarpeius, defender of the Capitol in the 8th-century BC Sabine War.

The Sabines, bent on vengeance for the rape of their women by Romulus and

Sabine soldiers crushing the treacherous Tarpeia with their shields

his men, bribed Tarpeia to let them up on to the Capitol. As the Augustan historian Livy records, the Sabines used to wear heavy gold bracelets and jewelled rings on their left hands, and Tarpeia's reward for her treachery was to be "what they wore on their shield-arms".

The Sabines kept to the letter of the bargain if not to its spirit – they repaid Tarpeia not with their jewellery but by crushing her to death between their shields. Tarpeia was possibly the only casualty of her act of treachery – as the invading warriors met the Roman defenders, the Sabine women leapt between the two opposing armies, forcing a reconciliation. Traitors and other condemned criminals were subsequently executed by being thrown over the sheer face of the rock. The place has been considered dangerous and used to be fenced off, but restoration work is now under way.

Victor Emmanuel Monument ❿

Piazza Venezia. **Map** 5 A5 & 12 F4. ▦ See **Getting There** p65. **Open** for temporary exhibitions only.

KNOWN AS Il Vittoriano, this monument was begun in 1885 and inaugurated in 1925 in honour of Victor Emmanuel II of Savoy, the first king of a unified Italy. The king is depicted here in a gilt bronze equestrian statue, over-sized like the monument itself – the statue is 12 m (39 ft) long.

The edifice also contains a museum of the Risorgimento, the events that led to unification (see pp36–7). It has, however, been closed since the early 1980s. Built in austere white Brescian marble, the "wedding cake" or "typewriter" (two of the many insulting nicknames given to this unloved white elephant) will never mellow into the ochre tones of surrounding buildings. It is widely held to be the epitome of self-important, insensitive architecture.

Victor Emmanuel Monument in Piazza Venezia

Palazzo Venezia and Museum ⓫

Via del Plebiscito 118. **Map** 5 A4 & 12 E4. ☎ 06-679 88 65. 🚌 See **Getting There** p65. **Open** 9am–1.30pm Tue–Sat, 9am–12.30pm Sun (last adm: 30 mins before closing). **Closed** 1 Jan, 1 May, 25 Dec. **Adm charge**. ♿ **Temporary exhibitions**.

Palazzo Venezia with Mussolini's balcony in the centre

Pope Paul II

ONE OF THE first Renaissance civic buildings in Rome, the palazzo's arched windows and doors are so harmonious that the facade was once attributed to the great Humanist architect Leon Battista Alberti (1404–72). It was more probably built by Giuliano da Maiano, who is known to have carved the fine doorway on to the piazza.

Palazzo Venezia was built in 1455–64 for the Venetian cardinal Pietro Barbo, who later became Pope Paul II. It was at times a papal residence, but it also served as the Venetian Embassy to Rome before passing into French hands in 1797. Since 1916 it has belonged to the state; in the Fascist era Mussolini used it as his headquarters and addressed crowds from the central balcony.

The interior is best seen by visiting the Museo del Palazzo Venezia, Rome's most underrated museum. It holds first-class collections of early Renaissance painting; painted wood sculptures and Renaissance chests from Italy; tapestries from all of Europe; majolica; silver; Neapolitan ceramic figurines; Renaissance bronzes; arms and armour; Baroque terracotta sculptures by Bernini, Algardi and others; and 17th- and 18th-century Italian painting. There is a marble screen from the Aracoeli convent, destroyed to make way for the Victor Emmanuel Monument, and a bust of Paul II, showing him to rank with Martin V and Leo X among the fattest-ever popes. The building also hosts major temporary exhibitions.

San Marco ⓬

Piazza San Marco 48. **Map** 5 A4 & 12 F4. ☎ 06-679 52 05. 🚌 See **Getting There** p65. **Open** 8am–12.30pm, 4pm–7pm Tue, Thu–Sun, 4pm–7pm Mon, 8am–12.30pm Wed. ✝ 🚫

THE CHURCH of San Marco was founded in 336 by Mark, the then pope, in honour of St Mark the Evangelist. The relics of Pope Mark lie under the altar. The church was restored by Pope Gregory IV in the 9th century – the magnificent apse mosaics date from this period.

Further major rebuilding took place in 1455–71, when Pope Paul II Barbo made San Marco the church of the Venetian commu-

nity in Rome. The blue and gold coffered ceiling is decorated with Pope Paul's heraldic crest, the lion rampant, recalling the lion of St Mark, the patron saint of Venice. The appearance of the rest of the interior, with its colonnades of Sicilian jasper, was largely the creation of Filippo Barigioni in the 1740s. Complemented by an interesting array of funerary monuments in the aisles, the taste is typical of the late Roman Baroque. Leon Battista Alberti, whose name is also mentioned tentatively in connection with Palazzo Venezia, may have been the architect of the elegant travertine arcade and loggia of the facade.

Coat of arms of Pope Paul II

San Marco's apse mosaic of Christ, with Gregory IV on the far left

FORUM

THE FORUM was the centre of political, commercial and judicial life in ancient Rome. The largest buildings were the basilicas, where legal cases were heard. According to the playwright Plautus, the area teemed with "lawyers and litigants, bankers and brokers, shopkeepers and strumpets, good-for-nothings waiting for a tip from the rich". As

Figure of barbarian on the Arch of Constantine

Rome's population boomed, the Forum became too small. In 46 BC Julius Caesar built a new one, setting a precedent that was followed by emperors from Augustus to Trajan. As well as the Imperial Fora, emperors also erected triumphal arches to themselves, and just to the east Vespasian built the Colosseum, centre of entertainment after the business of the day.

SIGHTS AT A GLANCE

Churches and Temples
Temple of Saturn **5**
Temple of Castor and Pollux **8**
Temple of Vesta **9**
Temple of Antoninus and Faustina **11**
Temple of Romulus and Santi Cosma e Damiano **12**
Santa Francesca Romana **14**
Temple of Venus and Rome **17**

Historic Buildings
Basilica Aemilia **1**
Curia **2**
Basilica Julia **7**

House of the Vestal Virgins **10**
Basilica of Constantine and Maxentius **13**
Trajan's Markets pp88–9 **18**
Torre delle Milizie **20**
Casa dei Cavalieri di Rodi **21**
Mamertine Prison **24**
Colosseum pp92–5 **27**

Museums
Antiquarium Forense **15**

KEY

	Tour of the Forum maps
M	Metro station

Arches and Columns
Arch of Septimius Severus **4**
Column of Phocas **6**
Arch of Titus **16**
Column of Trajan **19**
Arch of Constantine **26**

Ancient Sites
Rostra **3**
Forum of Augustus **22**
Forum of Caesar **23**
Forum of Nerva **25**

GETTING THERE
The simplest way to reach the area is by Metro to Colosseo on line B. The main entrance to the Forum is on Via dei Fori Imperiali, served by buses 75, 85, 87, 117, 175, 186, 810 and 850. Many more routes go to Piazza Venezia. For Trajan's Markets, the best buses are the H, 64, 65 and 70 which stop in Via IV Novembre.

SEE ALSO
• *Street Finder*, maps 5, 8, 9, 12
• *Where to Stay* pp294–5
• *Triumphal Arches Walk* pp278–9

View of the Forum with the Colosseum rising behind the bell tower of Santa Francesca Romana

A Tour of the Roman Forum: West

To APPRECIATE THE LAYOUT of the Forum before visiting its confusing patchwork of ruined temples and basilicas, it is best to view the whole area from above, from the back of the Capitol. From there you can make out the Via Sacra (the Sacred Way), the route followed through the Forum by religious and triumphal processions towards the Capitol. Up until the 18th century when archaeological excavations began, the Arch of Septimius Severus and the columns of the Temple of Saturn lay half buried underground. Excavation of the Forum continues, and the ruins uncovered date from many different periods of Roman history.

The Temple of Vespasian was the point from where Piranesi made this 18th-century engraving of the Forum. Its three columns were then almost completely buried.

Temple of Saturn
The eight surviving columns of this temple stand close by the three columns of the Temple of Vespasian **5**

Temple of Concord

Portico of the Dii Consentes

Rostra
These are the ruins of the platform used for public oratory in the Forum **3**

Basilica Julia
Named after Julius Caesar, who ordered its construction, the basilica housed important law courts **7**

Column of Phocas
One of the very last monuments erected in the Forum, this single column dates from AD 608 **6**

★ **Arch of Septimius Severus**
A 19th-century engraving shows the arch after the Forum was first excavated ❹

Santi Luca e Martina was an early medieval church, but was rebuilt in 1635–64 by Pietro da Cortona.

The Forum included the area under Via dei Fori Imperiali. More parts have now been made public.

LOCATOR MAP
See Central Rome Map pp12–13

STAR SIGHTS

★ **Arch of Septimius Severus**

Curia
A copy stands on the site of the chamber of the Roman Senate ❷

KEY

Suggested route

0 metres   75

0 yards   75

Basilica Aemilia
This large meeting hall was razed to the ground in the 5th century AD ❶

Entrance to Forum

The Temple of Julius Caesar was erected in his memory by Augustus on the spot where Caesar's body was cremated after his assassination in 44 BC.

Julius Caesar

To Roman Forum: East
See pp80–81

Temple of Castor and Pollux
A temple to the twin sons of Jupiter stood on this spot from the 5th century BC. This section of cornice and the columns supporting it date from the rebuilding of AD 6 ❽

A Tour of the Roman Forum: East

THE EASTERN END of the Roman Forum is dominated by the massive barrel-vaulted ruins of the Basilica of Constantine. To picture the building as it was in the 4th century AD, you must imagine marble columns, floors and statues, and glittering tiles of gilt bronze. The remains of the other important buildings are scanty, though the garden and ponds in the centre of the House of the Vestal Virgins make it a very attractive spot. The two churches in this part of the Forum cannot be reached from within the archaeological area, but are accessible from the road outside.

The Regia was the office of the Pontifex Maximus, the chief priest of ancient Rome.

To Forum entrance

Temple of Antoninus and Faustina
The portico of this temple, built in AD 141, has been incorporated in the church of San Lorenzo in Miranda ⓫

An early Iron Age necropolis was found here in 1902. Finds from it, such as this burial urn, are on view in the Antiquarium.

VIA SACRA

Temple of Vesta
Partly reconstructed, this tiny temple to the goddess of the hearth was one of ancient Rome's most sacred shrines ❾

Temple of Romulus
This domed building from the 4th century AD has survived as part of the church of Santi Cosma e Damiano ⓬

★ **House of the Vestal Virgins**
The priestesses who tended the sacred flame in the Temple of Vesta lived here. The house was a large rectangular building around a central garden ❿

★ **Basilica of Constantine and Maxentius**
The stark remains of the basilica's huge arches and ceilings give some idea of the original scale and grandeur of the Forum's public buildings ⑬

LOCATOR MAP
See Central Rome Map pp12–13

Santa Francesca Romana
The church takes its name from a saint who cared for the Roman poor in the 15th century ⑭

Antiquarium Forense
A small museum houses archaeological finds made in the Forum. They include this frieze of Aeneas and the Founding of Rome *from the Basilica Aemilia* ⑮

Colonnade surrounding Temple of Venus and Rome

Temple of Venus and Rome
These extensive ruins are of a magnificent temple, built here in AD 121 by the Emperor Hadrian, largely to his own design ⑰

VIA DEI FORI IMPERIALI

VIA SACRA

To the Palatine

Ruined Baths

Arch of Titus
This 19th-century reconstruction shows how the arch may have looked when it spanned the flagstoned roadway of the Via Sacra ⑯

STAR SIGHTS

★ **Basilica of Constantine**

★ **House of the Vestal Virgins**

KEY

‐ ‐ ‐ Suggested route

0 metres   75
0 yards   75

VISITORS' CHECKLIST

Entrances: Largo Romolo e Remo and near the Arch of Titus on Via Sacra.
Map 5 B5 & 8 F1.
06-699 01 10.
81, 85, 87, 117, 175, 186.
Colosseo.
Open 9am–6pm Mon–Sat, 9am–1pm Sun.
Closed 1 Jan, 1 May, 25 Dec.

Melted coins embedded in the floor of the Basilica Aemilia

Basilica Aemilia ❶

See Visitors' Checklist.

ORIGINALLY this building was a rectangular colonnaded hall, with a multicoloured marble floor and a bronze-tiled roof. It was built by the consuls Marcus Aemilius Lepidus and Marcus Fulvius Nobilor in 179 BC. The two consuls, who were elected annually, exercised supreme power over the Republic.

Basilicas in ancient Rome served no religious purpose; they were meeting halls for politicians, moneylenders and *publicani* (businessmen contracted by the state to collect taxes). A consortium agreed to hand over a specified sum to the state, but its members were allowed to collect as much as they could and keep the difference. This is why tax-collectors in the Bible were so loathed.

The basilica was rebuilt many times; it was finally burned down when the Visigoths sacked Rome in AD 410. Business seems to have carried on until the last moment, for the pavement is splashed with tiny lumps of coins that melted in the fire.

Curia ❷

See Visitors' Checklist.

A MODERN REPLICA has been built over the ruins of the hall where Rome's Senate (chief council of state) used to meet. The first Curia stood on the site now occupied by the church of Santi Luca e Martina, but after the building was destroyed by fire in 52 BC, Julius Caesar built a new Curia at the edge of the Forum. This was restored by Domitian in AD 94 and, after another fire, rebuilt by Diocletian in the 3rd century. The replica you see today is based on Diocletian's Curia. Inside are two relief panels commissioned by Trajan to decorate the Rostra. One shows Trajan destroying records of unpaid taxes to free citizens from debt; in the other he sits on a throne receiving a mother and child.

Replica of the Curia

Rostra ❸

See Visitors' Checklist.

Ruins of the Imperial Rostra

SPEECHES WERE delivered from this dais, the most famous – thanks to Shakespeare – being Mark Antony's "Friends, Romans, Countrymen" oration after the assassination of Julius Caesar in 44 BC. Caesar himself had just reorganized the Forum and this speech was made from the newly-sited Rostra, where the ruins now stand. In the following year the head and hands of Cicero were put on show here after he had been put to death by the second Triumvirate (Augustus, Mark Antony and Marcus Lepidus). Fulvia, Mark Antony's wife, stabbed the great orator's tongue with a hairpin. It was also here that Julia, Augustus's daughter, was said to have played the prostitute – one of many scandalous acts that led to her banishment.

The dais took its name from the ships' prows *(rostra)* with which it was decorated. Sheathed in iron (for ramming enemy vessels), these came from ships captured at the Battle of Antium in 338 BC.

— Honorary statue

Relief panel in balustrade, showing Trajan's acts of charity

Prows of ships *(rostra)*

ROSTRA
This reconstruction shows the platform for public speaking in the Forum, as it looked in Imperial times.

Arch of Septimius Severus **4**

See Visitors' Checklist.

T HIS TRIUMPHAL ARCH, one of
the most striking and best
preserved monuments of the
Forum, was erected in AD 203
to celebrate the tenth
anniversary of the accession
of Septimius Severus. The
relief panels – largely eroded –
celebrate the emperor's
victories in Parthia (modern-
day Iraq and Iran) and Arabia.
Originally, the
inscription along
the top of the
arch was to
Septimius and
his two sons,
Caracalla and
Geta, but after
Septimius died
Caracalla
murdered Geta
and had his
brother's name
removed. Even
so the holes into
which the letters of his name
were pegged are still visible.

Barbarian captives, Arch of Severus

During the Middle Ages the
central arch, half buried in
earth and debris, was used to
shelter a barber's shop.

**Triumphal arch of the Emperor
Septimius Severus**

Temple of Saturn **5**

See Visitors' Checklist.

T HE MOST PROMINENT of the
ruins in the fenced-off area
between the Forum and the
Capitoline hill is the Temple
of Saturn. It consists of a high
platform, eight columns and a
section of entablature. There
was a temple dedicated to

Ionic capitals on the surviving columns of the Temple of Saturn

Saturn here as early as 497 BC,
but it had to be rebuilt many
times and the current remains
date only from 42 BC.

Saturn was the mythical
god-king of Italy, said to have
presided over a prosperous
and peaceful Golden Age
from which slavery, private
property, crime and war were
absent. As such, he appealed
particularly to the lower and
slave classes. Every year,
between 17 December and
23 December, Saturn's reign
was remembered in a week
of sacrifices and feasting,
known as the Saturnalia.

As long as the revels lasted,
the normal social order was
turned upside down. Slaves
were permitted to drink and
dine with (and sometimes even
be served by) their masters.
Senators and other high-
ranking Romans would
abandon the aristocratic togas
that they usually wore to
distinguish themselves from
the lower classes and wear
more democratic, loose-fitting
gowns. During the holidays,
all the courts of law and
schools in the city were
closed. No prisoner could be
punished, and no war could
be declared.

People also celebrated the
Saturnalia in their own homes:
they exchanged gifts, in
particular special wax dolls
and wax tapers, and played
light-hearted gambling games,
the stakes usually being nuts,
a symbol of fruitfulness. Much
of the spirit and many of the
rituals of the festival have
been preserved in the Christian
celebration of Christmas.

Column of Phocas **6**

See Visitors' Checklist.

T HIS COLUMN, 13.5 m (44 ft)
high, is one of the few to
have remained upright since
the day it was put up. Until
1816, when an inquisitive
Englishwoman, Lady Elizabeth
Foster, widow of the fifth
Duke of Devonshire, decided
to excavate its pedestal,
nobody knew what it was. It
turned out to be the youngest
of the Forum's monuments,
erected in AD 608 in honour
of the Byzantine emperor,
Phocas, who had just paid a
visit to Rome. The column
may have been placed here as
a mark of gratitude to Phocas
for giving the Pantheon to the
pope (*see pp110–11*).

Slender, fluted Column of Phocas

Remains of the Basilica Julia, a Roman court of civil law

Basilica Julia **7**

See Visitors' Checklist, p82.

THIS IMMENSE basilica, which occupied the area between the Temple of Saturn and the Temple of Castor and Pollux, was begun by Julius Caesar in 54 BC and completed after his death by his great nephew Augustus. It was damaged by fire almost immediately afterwards in 9 BC, but was subsequently repaired and dedicated to the emperor's grandsons, Gaius and Lucius.

After numerous sackings and pilferings, only the steps, pavement and column stumps remain. Nevertheless the ground plan is fairly clear. The basilica had a central hall, measuring 82 m by 18 m

(260 ft by 59 ft), surrounded by a double portico. The hall was on three floors, while the outer portico had only two.

The Basilica Julia was the seat of the *centumviri*, a body of 180 magistrates who tried civil law cases. They were split into four chambers of 45 men, and unless a case was particularly complicated they would all sit separately.

The four courts were, however, divided only by screens or curtains, and the voices of lawyers and cheers and boos of spectators in the upper galleries echoed through the building. Lawyers used to hire crowds of spectators, who would applaud every time the lawyer who was paying them made a point and jeer at his opponents. The clappers and booers must have had a good deal of time on their hands: scratched into the steps are chequerboards where they played dice and other gambling games to while away the time between cases.

TEMPLE OF VESTA
The temple preserved the shape of an original primitive structure made of wooden posts with a thatched roof.

Cella (sacred inner chamber)

Ring of Corinthian columns

Sacred flame

Temple of Castor and Pollux **8**

See Visitors' Checklist, p82.

THE THREE SLENDER fluted columns of this temple form one of the Forum's most beautiful ruins. The first temple here was probably dedicated in 484 BC in honour of the mythical twins and patrons of horsemanship, Castor and Pollux. During the battle of Lake Regillus (499 BC) against the ousted Tarquin kings, the Roman dictator Postumius promised to build a temple to the twins if the Romans were victorious. Some said the twins appeared on the battlefield, helped the Romans to victory and then materialized in the Forum – the temple marks the spot – to announce the news.

The temple, like most buildings in the Forum, was rebuilt many times. The three surviving columns date from the last occasion on which it was rebuilt – by the future Emperor Tiberius after a fire in 6 BC. For a long period the temple housed the city's office of weights and measures, and it was also used at times by a number of bankers.

Corinthian columns of the Temple of Castor and Pollux

Temple of Vesta **9**

See Visitors' Checklist, p82.

THE FORUM'S most elegant temple, a circular building originally surrounded by a ring of 20 fine fluted columns, dates from the 4th century AD, though there had been a temple on the site for far longer. It was partially reconstructed in 1930.

The cult of the Vestals was one of the oldest in Rome, and centred on six Vestal Virgins, who were required to keep alight the sacred flame of Vesta, the goddess of the hearth. This responsibility was originally entrusted to the daughters of the king, but it then passed to the Vestals, the only group of women priests in Rome. It was no easy task, as the flame was easily blown out. Any Vestal who allowed the flame to die was whipped by the high priest *(Pontifex Maximus)* and dismissed.

The girls, who had to belong to noble families, were selected when they were between six and ten years old. They served for 30 years: the first ten were spent learning their duties, the next ten performing them and the final ten teaching novices. They enjoyed high status and financial security, but had to remain virgins. The penalty for transgressing was to be buried alive, although only ten Vestals are recorded as ever having suffered this fate. The men concerned were whipped to death. When Vestals retired, they were free to live the rest of their lives as ordinary citizens. If they wished they could marry, but few ever did.

Another of the Vestals' duties was to guard the Palladium, a sacred statue of the goddess Pallas Athenae. The irreverent Emperor Heliogabalus burgled the temple in the 3rd century AD. He thought he had succeeded in stealing the Palladium, but the Vestals had been warned of his intention and had replaced it with a replica.

Honorary statue of a Vestal Virgin

Restored section

Central courtyard of the House of the Vestal Virgins

House of the Vestal Virgins ❿

See Visitors' Checklist, p82.

AS SOON AS a girl became a Vestal she came to live in the House of the Vestal Virgins. Originally this was an enormous complex with about 50 rooms on three storeys. The only substantial remains today are some of the rooms around the central courtyard. This space is perhaps the most evocative part of the Forum. Overlooking ponds of water lilies and plump goldfish is a row of eroded, and mostly headless, statues of senior Vestals, dating from the 3rd and 4th centuries AD. The better-preserved examples were transferred to the Museo Nazionale Romano *(see p163).* On one of the pedestals the inscription has been removed because the Vestal in question suffered some disgrace. It is thought she may have been a certain Claudia, known to have betrayed the cult by converting to Christianity.

Though many of the rooms surrounding the courtyard are well-preserved – some even retain flights of steps leading to an upper floor – you are not allowed inside them. If you peep into the series of rooms along the south side, however, you might be able to see the remains of a mill, used for grinding the grain with which the Vestals made a special sacrificial cake. The bakery was next door.

Temple of Antoninus and Faustina ⓫

See Visitors' Checklist, p82. **Church open** *10am– noon Thu; ring the bell.*

ONE OF THE FORUM'S oddest sights is the Baroque facade of the church of San Lorenzo in Miranda rising above the porch of a Roman temple. First dedicated in AD 141 by the Emperor Antoninus Pius to his late wife Faustina, the temple was rededicated to them both on the death of the emperor. In the 11th century it was converted into a church because it was believed that San Lorenzo (St Lawrence) had been condemned to death there. The current church dates from 1601.

Temple of Antoninus and Faustina

Temple of Romulus and Santi Cosma e Damiano ⑫

See Visitors' Checklist, p82. **Santi Cosma e Damiano** ☎ 06-699 15 40. **Open** Apr–Sep: 9am–1pm, 4–7pm daily; Oct–Mar: 7am–1pm, 3–7pm daily. **Crib** 9.30am–12.30pm, 3–6.30pm daily. **Adm charge** for crib. ⌂ ⟁

NO-ONE IS SURE to whom the Temple of Romulus was dedicated, but it was probably to Emperor Maxentius' son, and not to Rome's founder.

The temple is a circular brick building, topped by a cupola, with two rectangular side rooms and a concave porch. The heavy, dull bronze doors are original.

Since the 6th century the temple has acted as a vestibule to the church of Santi Cosma e Damiano, which itself occupies an ancient building – a hall in Vespasian's Forum of Peace. The entrance to the church is on Via dei Fori Imperiali. The beautiful carved figures of its 18th-century Neapolitan *presepio* (crib or

Nativity scene) are back on view now, and the church has a vivid Byzantine apse mosaic with Christ pictured against orange clouds.

Roof of the Temple of Romulus

Basilica of Constantine and Maxentius ⑬

See Visitors' Checklist, p82.

THE BASILICA'S three vast, coffered barrel vaults are powerful relics of what was the largest building in the Forum. Work began in AD 308 under the Emperor Maxentius. When he was deposed by Constantine after the Battle of the Milvian Bridge in AD 312, work on the massive project continued under the new regime. The building, which, like other Roman basilicas, was used for

the administration of justice and for carrying on business, is often referred to simply as the Basilica of Constantine.

The area covered by the basilica was roughly 100 m by 65 m (330 ft by 215 ft). It was originally designed to have a long nave and aisles running from east to west, but Constantine switched the axis around to create three short broad aisles with the main entrance in the centre of the long south wall. The height of the building was 35 m (115 ft). In the apse at the western end, where it could be seen from all over the building, stood

a 12-m (39-ft) statue of the emperor, made partly of wood and partly of marble. The giant head, hand and foot are on display in the courtyard of the Palazzo dei Conservatori *(see pp72–3)*. The roof of the basilica glittered with gilded tiles until the 7th century when they were stripped off to cover the roof of the old St Peter's.

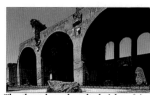

The three barrel-vaulted aisles of the basilica were used as law courts.

The octagonal coffers in the vaulted ceiling were originally faced with marble.

The main entrance was added by Constantine in AD 313.

The roof was supported by eight massive Corinthian columns. One now stands in Piazza Santa Maria Maggiore *(see p173)*.

Santa Francesca Romana 🄔

Piazza di Santa Francesca Romana.
Map 5 B5. 🄲 06-679 55 28. 🚌 85, 87, 117, 175, 673, 810. 🚇 30b. Ⓜ Colosseo. **Open** 9.30am–12.30pm, 3.30pm–7pm daily. 🄗 🄖

E VERY YEAR on 9 March devout Romans drivers try to park as close as possible to this Baroque church with a Romanesque bell tower. The aim of their pilgrimage is to have their vehicles blessed by Santa Francesca Romana, the patron saint of motorists. During the 15th-century, Francesca of Trastevere founded a society of pious women

Bell tower of Santa Francesca

devoted to helping the less fortunate. After her canonisation in 1608 the church, originally named Santa Maria Nova, was rededicated to Francesca.

The most curious sight inside the church is a flagstone with what are said to be the imprints of the knees of St Peter and St Paul. A magician, Simon Magus, decided to prove that his powers were superior to those of the Apostles by levitating above the Forum. As Simon was in mid-air, Peter and Paul fell to their knees and prayed fervently for God to humble him, and Simon immediately plummeted to his death.

Antiquarium Forense 🄕

See Visitors' Checklist, p82.

T HE FORMER CONVENT of Santa Francesca Romana is now occupied by the offices in charge of the excavations of the Forum and a small museum. The latter is currently being reorganized, and only a couple of rooms are open. They contain Iron Age burial urns, graves and their skeletal

Dedication to Titus and Vespasian on the Arch of Titus

occupants along with some ancient bric-a-brac exhumed from the Forum's drains. When the reorganization is complete you should be able to see fragments of statues, capitals, friezes and other architectural decoration taken from the Forum's buildings.

Frieze of Aeneas in the Antiquarium Forense

Arch of Titus 🄖

See Visitors' Checklist, p82.

T HIS TRIUMPHAL ARCH was erected in AD 81 by the Emperor Domitian in honour of the victories of his brother, Titus, and his father, Vespasian, in Judaea. In AD 68 the Jews, weary of being exploited by unscrupulous Roman officials, rebelled. A bitter war broke out which ended two years later in the fall of Jerusalem and the Jewish Diaspora.

Although the reliefs inside the arch are badly eroded, you can make out a triumphant procession of Roman soldiers carrying off spoils from the Temple of Jerusalem. The booty includes the altar, silver trumpets and a golden seven-branched candelabrum.

Temple of Venus and Rome 🄗

See Visitors' Checklist, p82.

T HE EMPEROR Hadrian designed this temple to occupy what had been the vestibule to Nero's Golden House. Many of the columns have been re-erected, and though there is no access, there is a good view as you leave the Forum and from the upper tiers of the Colosseum. The temple, was the largest in Rome, was dedicated to Roma, the personification of the city, and to Venus because she was the mother of Aeneas, father of Romulus and Remus. Each goddess had her own *cella* (shrine). When the architect Apollodorus pointed out that the seated statues in the niches were too big (had they tried to "stand" their heads would have hit the vaults), Hadrian had him put to death.

Statue of goddess   **Porphyry column**

Cross-section of Temple of Venus and Rome

Trajan's Markets ⑱

ORIGINALLY CONSIDERED among the wonders of the Classical world, Trajan's Markets now show only a hint of their former splendour. Emperor Trajan and his architect, Apollodorus of Damascus, built this visionary new complex of 150 shops and offices (probably used for administering the corn dole) in the early 2nd century AD. It was the ancient Roman equivalent of the modern shopping centre, selling everything from silks and spices imported from the Middle East to fresh fish, fruit and flowers.

The Markets Today
Above the facade stands the 13th-century Torre delle Milizie, built for defensive purposes.

Trajan
The emperor was a benevolent ruler and a successful general.

Cross vaulting

Main Hall
Twelve shops were built on two floors, and the corn dole was shared out on the upper storey. This was a free corn ration given to Roman men to prevent hunger.

Via Biberatica
The main street which runs through the market is named after the drinking inns which once lined it.

Small semicircle of shops

Staircase

TIMELINE

AD 100–112 Building of Trajan's Markets	**472** Invasion by Ricimer the Suevian. Some of his Germanic troops stationed here	**1200s** Torre delle Milizie built on top of the markets	**1572** Convent of Santa Caterina da Siena built over part of markets	**1924** Many medieval houses demolished	

AD 100	AD 500	1000	1300	1800	1950

AD 117 Death of Trajan	**552** Byzantine takeover of Rome. Markets occupied and fortified by the army		**1300s** Annibaldi and Caetani families vie for control of the area	**1828** First tentative excavations, but value of site not recognized	**1911–14** Convent demolished
AD 98 Trajan succeeds Nerva as emperor					**1930–33** Markets finally excavated

VISITORS' CHECKLIST

Mercati Traianei, Via IV Novembre.
Map 5 B4. 06-67 90 048.
64, 65, 70 to Via IV Novembre
and many routes to Piazza Venezia.
Open Apr–Sep: 9am–6.30pm
Tue–Sat, Oct–Mar: 9am–5pm
(last adm: 30 mins before closing).
Closed Mon, public hols. **Adm
charge**, except last Sun of month;
ticket incl Forum of Augustus.

The Markets in the 16th Century
*This fanciful fresco depicts a gladiatorial combat
taking place in front of the partly-buried remains
of Trajan's Markets.*

A Market Shop
*Shops were built with
arched entrances, with
jambs and lintels
creating rectangular
portals and windows.
A wooden mezzanine
was used for storage.*

Upper Corridor
*Shops on this upper level
were thought to have sold
wine and oil as a number
of storage jars were
discovered here.*

**Large hall with
semidomed
ceiling**

MARKET SHOPPING

Shops opened early and closed about
noon. The best ones were decorated
with mosaics of the goods they sold.
Almost all the shopping was done
by men, though women visited the
dressmaker and cobbler. The
tradesmen were almost all male.
In employment records for the
period AD 117–193, the only
female shopkeepers mentioned
are three wool-sellers, two
jewellers, a greengrocer
and a fishwife.

**Wall dividing
market area from
Forum of Trajan**

The terrace
over the archway
spanning Via
Biberatica has
a good view of
the Forum of
Trajan below.

Forum of Trajan, built in front
of the markets in AD 107–113,
was flanked by the Basilica
Ulpia. The basilica, measuring
170 m (558 ft) by 60 m (197
ft), was the largest in Rome.

Fish mosaic

Trajan's Markets ⓲

See pp88–9.

Column of Trajan ⓳

Via dei Fori Imperiali. **Map** 5 A4 &
12 F4. *See Visitors' Checklist for
Trajan's Markets, p89.*

Detail of Trajan's Column

THIS ELEGANT marble column
was inaugurated by Trajan
in AD 113, and celebrates his
two campaigns in Dacia
(Romania) in AD 101–3 and
AD 107–8. The column, base
and pedestal are 40 m (131 ft)
tall – precisely the same height
as the spur of the Quirinal hill
which was excavated to make
room for Trajan's Forum.
Spiralling up the column are
minutely detailed scenes from
the campaigns, beginning with
the Romans preparing for war
and ending with the Dacians
being ousted from their
homeland. The column is
pierced with small windows
to illuminate its internal spiral
staircase (closed to the public).
If you wish to see the reliefs
in detail there is a complete
set of casts in the Museo
della Civiltà Romana at EUR
(see p267).
　　When Trajan died in AD 117
his ashes, along with those of
his wife, Plotina, were placed
in a golden urn in the column's
hollow base. The column's
survival was largely thanks to
the intervention of Pope
Gregory the Great (reigned
590–604). He was so moved
by a relief showing Trajan
helping a woman whose son
had been killed that he
begged God to release the
emperor's soul from hell. God

duly appeared to the pope to
say that Trajan had been
rescued, but requested him
not to pray for the souls of
any more pagans.
　　According to legend, when
Trajan's ashes were exhumed
his skull and tongue were not
only intact, but his tongue
told of his release from hell.
The land around the column
was then declared sacred and
the column itself was spared.
The statue of Trajan remained
on top of the column until
1587, when it was replaced
with one of St Peter.

Torre delle Milizie ⓴

Mercati Traianei, Via IV Novembre.
Map 5 B4. ***Closed*** for restoration.

FOR CENTURIES this massive
brick tower was thought to
have been the one in which
Nero stood watching Rome
burn, after he had set it alight
in order to clear the city's
slums. It is uncertain whether
arson was among Nero's
crimes, but it is certain that he
did not watch the fire from
this tower – it was built in the
13th century.

Casa dei Cavalieri di Rodi ㉑

Piazza del Grillo 1. **Map** 5 B5.
⬤ 06-679 00 48. ▥ 85, 87, 115,
117, 175, 186. ***Open*** by appt only.

Loggia, Casa dei Cavalieri di Rodi

SINCE THE 12TH CENTURY the
crusading order, the Knights
of St John, also known as the
Knights of Rhodes (Rodi) or
Malta, have had their priorate
in this medieval house above
the Forum of Augustus. If you
are lucky enough to get
inside, ask to see the beautiful
Cappella di San Giovanni
(Chapel of St John).

Forum of Augustus ㉒

Piazza del Grillo 1. **Map** 5 B5 & 12 F5.
*See Visitors' Checklist for Trajan's
Markets, p89.*

**Podium of the Temple of Mars in
the Forum of Augustus**

THE FORUM of Augustus
was built to celebrate
Augustus's victory over Julius
Caesar's assassins, Brutus and
Cassius, at the Battle of
Philippi in 41 BC. The temple
in its centre was dedicated to
Mars the Avenger. The forum
stretched from a high wall at
the foot of the sleazy Suburra
quarter to the edge of the
Forum of Caesar. At least half
of it is now concealed below
Mussolini's Via dei Fori
Imperiali. The temple is easily
identified, with its cracked
steps and four Corinthian
columns. Originally it had a
statue of Mars which looked
very like Augustus. In case
anyone failed to notice the
resemblance, a giant statue of
Augustus himself was placed
against the Suburra wall.

Forum of Caesar ㉓

Via del Carcere Tulliano. **Map** 5 A5.
⬤ 06-67 10 30 65. ▥ 85, 87, 115,
117, 175, 186. ***Open*** by appt only;
permit needed (see p367).

THE FIRST of Rome's Imperial
fora was built by Julius
Caesar. He spent a fortune –
most of it booty from his
conquest of Gaul – buying up
and demolishing houses on
the site. Pride of place went
to a temple dedicated in 46
BC to the goddess Venus
Genetrix, from whom Caesar
claimed descent. The temple
contained statues of Caesar
and Cleopatra as well as of
Venus. All that remains of this
temple to vanity is a platform

and three Corinthian columns. The forum was enclosed by a double colonnade which sheltered a row of shops, but this burnt down in AD 80 and was rebuilt by Domitian and Trajan. Trajan also added the Basilica Argentaria (a financial exchange) and a heated public lavatory.

The forum is only open to the public by appointment, but parts are visible from above in Via dei Fori Imperiali.

Mamertine Prison ❷

Clivo Argentario 1. **Map** 5 A5.
📞 06-679 29 02. 🚌 85, 87, 115, 117, 175, 186. **Open** 9am–noon, 2–6pm daily. **Donation** expected. 🅿

19th-century engraving of guards visiting prisoners in the Mamertine

BELOW THE 16th-century church of San Giuseppe dei Falegnami (St Joseph of the Carpenters) is a dank dungeon in which, according to Christian legend, St Peter was imprisoned. He is said to have caused a spring to bubble up into the cell, and used the water to baptize his guards.

The prison, also known as Tullianum, was in an old cistern with access to the city's main sewer (the Cloaca Maxima). The lower cell was used for executions and bodies were thrown into the sewer. Among the enemies of Rome to be executed here was the Gaulish leader Vercingetorix, defeated by Julius Caesar in 52 BC.

17th-century view of the ruined Forum of Nerva

Forum of Nerva ❷

Piazza del Grillo 1 (reached through Forum of Augustus). **Map** 5 B5. 📞 06-67 10 30 65. 🚌 87, 186. **Closed** for excavations.

THE FORUM of Nerva was begun by his predecessor, Domitian, and completed in AD 97. Little more than a long corridor with a colonnade along the sides and a Temple of Minerva at one end, it was also known as the Forum Transitorium because it lay between the Forum of Peace built by the Emperor Vespasian in AD 70 and the Forum of Augustus. Vespasian's forum is almost completely covered by Via dei Fori Imperiali, as is much of the Forum of Nerva itself. Excavations have unearthed Renaissance shops and taverns, but only part of the forum can be seen, including the base of the temple and two columns that were part of the original colonnade. These support a relief of Minerva above a frieze of young girls learning to sew and weave.

Arch of Constantine ❷

Between Via di San Gregorio and Piazza del Colosseo. **Map** 8 F1.
🚌 81, 85, 87, 117, 175, 673, 810.
🚋 30b. Ⓜ Colosseo.

THIS TRIUMPHAL ARCH was dedicated in AD 315 to celebrate Constantine's victory three years before over his co-emperor, Maxentius. Constantine claimed he owed his victory to a vision of Christ, but there is nothing Christian about the arch – in fact, most of the medallions, reliefs and statues were scavenged from earlier monuments. There are statues of Dacian prisoners taken from Trajan's Forum and reliefs of Marcus Aurelius, including one where he distributes bread to the poor. Inside the arch are reliefs of Trajan's victory over the Dacians. These were probably by the artist who worked on the Column of Trajan.

Medallion on the Arch of Constantine

Colosseum ❷

See pp92–5.

North side of the Arch of Constantine, facing the Colosseum

Colosseum ㉗

ROME'S GREATEST amphitheatre was commissioned by the Emperor Vespasian in AD 72 on the marshy site of a lake in the grounds of Nero's palace, the Domus Aurea *(see p175)*. Deadly gladiatorial combats and wild animal fights were staged free of charge by the emperor and wealthy citizens for public viewing.

Outer Wall of the Colosseum
Stone plundered from the facade in the Renaissance was used to build several palaces, bridges and parts of St Peter's.

The Colosseum was built to a practical design, with its 80 arched entrances allowing easy access to 55,000 spectators, but it is also a building of great beauty. The drawing here shows how it looked at the time of its opening in AD 80. It was one of several similar amphitheatres built in the Roman Empire, and some survive at El Djem in North Africa, Nîmes and Arles in France and Verona in northern Italy. Despite being damaged over the years by neglect and theft, it remains a majestic sight.

The Founder of the Colosseum
Vespasian was a professional soldier who became emperor in AD 69, founding the Flavian dynasty.

The outer walls are made of travertine.

FLORA OF THE COLOSSEUM
By the 19th century the Colosseum was heavily overgrown. Different micro-climates in various parts of the ruin had created an impressive variety of herbs, grasses and wild flowers. Several botanists were inspired to study and catalogue them and two books were published, one listing 420 different species. **Borage, a herb**

The bollards anchored the velarium.

The velarium was a huge awning which shaded spectators from the sun. Supported on poles fixed to the upper storey of the building, it was then hoisted into position with ropes anchored to bollards outside the stadium.

TIMELINE

80 Vespasian's son, Titus, stages inaugural festival in the amphitheatre. It lasts 100 days

AD 70	100
72 Emperor Vespasian begins work on the Colosseum	**81–96** Amphitheatre completed in reign of Domitian

Internal Corridors
These were designed to allow the large and often unruly crowd to move freely and to be seated within ten minutes of arriving at the Colosseum.

VISITORS' CHECKLIST

Piazza del Colosseo. **Map** 9 A1.
☎ 06-700 42 61. 🚌 81, 85, 87, 117, 175, 673, 810. 🚎 30b to Piazza del Colosseo.
Ⓜ *Colosseo.* **Open** 9am–7pm (3pm in winter) Thu–Tue, 9am–1pm Wed & public hols. **Closed** 1 Jan, 1 May, 25 Dec. **Adm charge.** ♿ limited.

The vomitorium was the exit used from each numbered section.

Brick formed the inner walls.

The podium was a large terrace where the emperor and the wealthy upper classes had their seats.

Entry routes to take the spectators to their seats were reached by means of staircases to the various levels of the amphitheatre.

Corinthian columns

Ionic columns

Doric columns

Arched entrances, 80 in total, were all numbered to let in the vast crowds that attended the fights.

Colossus of Nero
The Colosseum may have acquired its name from this huge gilt bronze statue that stood near the amphitheatre.

200	400		1300	1500	1700	1900

230 Colosseum restored by Alexander Severus

404 Gladiatorial combats banned

A gladiator's shield

1200s Frangipane family turn Colosseum into a fortress

15th–16th centuries Ruins used as quarry. Travertine blocks recycled by popes

1870 All vegetation removed

8 Thousandth anniversary celebration of founding of Rome by Romulus and Remus

442 Building damaged in an earthquake

523 Wild animal fights banned

1312 Emperor Henry VII gives Colosseum to the Senate and people of Rome

1749 Colosseum dedicated to Passion of Jesus

1893–6 Structure below arena revealed

How Fights were Staged in the Arena

THE EMPERORS HELD shows here which often began with animals performing circus tricks. Then on came the gladiators, who fought each other to the death. When one was killed, attendants dressed as Charon, the mythical ferryman of the dead, carried his body off on a stretcher, and sand was raked over the blood ready for the next bout. A badly-wounded gladiator would surrender his fate to the crowd. The "thumbs up" sign from the emperor meant he could live, "thumbs down" that he die, and the victor became an instant hero. Animals were brought here from as far away as North Africa and the Middle East. The games held in AD 248 to mark the 1,000th anniversary of the founding of Rome saw the death of a host of lions, elephants, hippos, zebras and elks.

Beneath the Arena
Late 19th-century excavations exposed the network of underground rooms where the animals were kept.

Interior of the Colosseum
The stadium was built in the form of an ellipse, with tiers of seats around a vast central arena.

Emperor's box

Emperor's entrance

Layout of underground passages

Tiers of seats

Consul's box

Consul's entrance

Gladiators' entrance

A complex of rooms, passages and lifts lie underneath the arena.

Dramatic Entrances
Below the sand was a wooden floor through which animals, men and scenery appeared in the arena.

Roman Gladiators
These were usually slaves, prisoners of war or condemned criminals. Most were men, but there were a few female gladiators.

The Colosseum by Antonio Canaletto
This 18th-century view of the Colosseum shows the Meta Sudans fountain (now demolished). Water "sweated" from a metal ball on top of its brick cone.

Metal fencing kept animals penned in, while archers stood by just in case any escaped.

Seating was tiered, and different social classes were segregated.

A winch brought the animal cages up to arena level when they were due to fight.

A ramp and trap door enabled the animal to reach the arena after walking along a corridor.

Cages were like three-sided lifts which went up to the next level where the animals were released.

SEA BATTLES IN THE ARENA

The historian Dion Cassius, writing in the 4th century AD, relates how, 150 years earlier, the Colosseum's arena was flooded to stage a mock sea battle. Scholars now believe that he was mistaken. The spectacle probably took place in the Naumachia of Augustus, a water-filled arena situated across the Tiber in Trastevere.

PALATINE

ACCORDING TO LEGEND, Romulus and Remus were brought up here by a wolf in a cave. Traces of Iron Age huts, dating from the 10th century BC, have been found on the Palatine hill, providing archaeological support for the area's legendary links with the founding of Rome. The Palatine was a very desirable place to live, becoming home to some of the city's most famous inhabitants. The great orator Cicero had a house here, as did the lyric poet Catullus. Augustus was born on the hill and continued to live here in very modest circumstances even when he became emperor. The two buildings identified as the House of Augustus and the House of Livia, his wife, are among the best preserved here. The first emperor's example of frugality was ignored by his successors, Tiberius, Caligula and Domitian, who all built extravagant palaces here. The ruins of Tiberius's palace lie beneath the 16th-century Farnese Gardens. The most extensive ruins are those of the Domus Augustana and Domus Flavia, the two wings of Domitian's palace, and the later extension built by Septimius Severus.

Fresco of mask in the House of Augustus

SIGHTS AT A GLANCE

Temples
Temple of Cybele ❻

Historic Buildings
Domus Flavia ❶
Domus Augustana ❸
House of Livia ❺

Ancient Sites
Cryptoporticus ❷
Stadium ❹
Huts of Romulus ❼

Parks and Gardens
Farnese Gardens ❽

SEE ALSO

• *Street Finder*, map 8

GETTING THERE
There are two ways of getting on to the Palatine hill; either through the Roman Forum (from Via dei Fori Imperiali) or through the entrance in Via di San Gregorio. A separate ticket for the Palatine is needed, even if you come through the Forum.
The best buses are the 85, 87, 175; all stop in Via dei Fori Imperiali near the main entrance. Tram 30b and Colosseo Metro station *(see p77)* are also handy.

KEY

Tour of the Palatine map

0 metres 200
0 yards 200

Towering ruins of the Palace of Septimius Severus on the Palatine hill

A Tour of the Palatine

SHADED ON ITS LOWER SLOPES with pines, and scattered in spring with wild flowers, the Palatine is the most pleasant and relaxing of the city's ancient sites. You can reach the hill by walking up from the Roman Forum *(see pp76–7)*. The area is dominated by the ruins of the Domus Flavia and the Domus Augustana, two parts of Domitian's huge palace built at the end of the 1st century AD. What you are able to see depends on where excavations are taking place at the time.

Huts of Romulus
These are traces of a 9th-century BC village on the Palatine ❼

To Farnese Gardens
See p101

House of Augustus

Temple of Cybele
Also known as the Temple of the Magna Mater, this was the centre of an important fertility cult ❻

★**House of Livia**
Many of the wall paintings have survived in the house where Augustus lived with his wife Livia ❺

STAR SIGHTS

★ **Domus Flavia**

★ **House of Livia**

KEY

– – – Suggested route

0 metres   75

0 yards   75

★**Domus Flavia**
This oval fountain was designed to be seen from the dining hall of the palace ❶

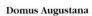

Domus Augustana
The Roman emperors lived in this part of the palace, while the Domus Flavia was used for public functions ❸

Cryptoporticus
In this long underground gallery, built by Nero, the stuccoes that decorated the walls and vault have been replaced with copies ❷

LOCATOR MAP
See Central Rome Map pp12–13

Octagonal fountain of the Domus Flavia

The Palatine Antiquarium is housed in a former convent, and houses artefacts from ancient Rome.

Stadium
Part of the Imperial palace, this enclosure may have been used by the emperors as a private garden ❹

Entrance

The exedra of the Stadium may have housed a balcony for emperors to view races.

Baths of Septimius Severus

The Palace of Septimius Severus (reigned AD 193–211) was an extension of the Domus Augustana. It projected beyond the hillside, requiring enormous arched supports.

Substructure of palace

Domus Flavia ❶

See Visitors' Checklist.

**Marble pavement in the courtyard
of the Domus Flavia**

IN AD 81 DOMITIAN, the third
of the Flavian dynasty of
emperors, decided to build a
splendid new palace on the
Palatine hill. But the western
peak, the Germalus, was
covered with houses and
temples, while the eastern
peak, the Palatium, was very
steep. So the emperor's
architect, Rabirius, flattened
the Palatium and used the
soil to fill in the cleft between
the two peaks, burying (and
preserving) a number of
Republican-era houses.

The palace had two wings –
one official (the Domus
Flavia), the other private (the
Domus Augustana). It was
the main Imperial palace for
300 years. At the front of the
Domus Flavia, the surviving
stubs of columns and fragments of walls trace the
shapes of three adjoining
rooms. In the first of these, the
Basilica, Domitian dispensed
his personal brand of justice.

The central Aula Regia was a
throne room decorated with
12 black basalt statues. The
third room (now covered
with corrugated plastic) was
the Lararium, a shrine for the
household gods known as
Lares (usually the owner's
ancestors). It may have been
used for official ceremonies
or by the palace guards.

Fearing assassination,
Domitian had the walls of the
courtyard covered with shiny
marble slabs designed to act
as mirrors so that he could
see anyone lurking behind
him. In the event, he was
assassinated in his bedroom,
possibly on the orders of his
wife, Domitia. The courtyard
is now a pleasant place to
pause; the flower beds in the
centre follow the maze pattern
of a sunken fountain pool.

Cryptoporticus ❷

See Visitors' Checklist.

THE CRYPTOPORTICUS, a series
of underground corridors,
was built by Nero to connect
his Golden House *(see p175)*
with the palaces of earlier
emperors on the Palatine. A
further branch leading to the
Palace of Domitian was added
later. Its vaults are decorated
with delicate stucco reliefs –
copies of originals now kept in
the Palatine's closed museum.

Domus Augustana ❸

See Visitors' Checklist.

THIS PART of Domitian's
palace was called the
Domus Augustana because it
was the private residence of
the "august" emperors. On
the upper level a high brick

wall remains, and you can
make out the shape of its two
courtyards. The far better
preserved lower level is closed
to the public, though you can
look down on its sunken
courtyard with the geometric
foundations of a fountain in
its centre. Sadly, you can't see
the stairs linking the two levels
(once lit by sunlight falling
on a mirror-paved pool), nor
the surrounding rooms,
paved with coloured marble.

Stadium ❹

See Visitors' Checklist.

Stadium viewed from the south

THE STADIUM on the Palatine
was laid out at the same
time as the Palace of Domitian.
It is not clear whether it was a
public stadium, a private track
for exercising horses, or
simply a large garden. The
alcove in the eastern wall
looks as though it may have
held a box from which the
emperor could have watched
races. It is, however, known
that the Stadium was used for
foot races by the Ostrogothic
king, Theodoric, in the 6th
century – he added the small
oval-shaped enclosure at the
southern end of the site.

Remains of the Domus Augustana and the Palace of Septimius Severus

House of Livia ❺

See Visitors' Checklist. If closed, apply to custodian.

Fresco in the House of Livia

THIS HOUSE dating from the 1st century BC is one of the best preserved on the Palatine. It was probably part of the house in which the Emperor Augustus and his wife Livia lived. Compared with later Imperial palaces, it is a relatively modest home. According to Suetonius, the biographer of Rome's early emperors, Augustus slept in the same small bedroom for 40 years on a low bed which had "a very ordinary coverlet". He wore home-made clothes (woven by Livia, his sister Octavia and daughter Julia), but he was vain enough to wear shoes with extremely thick soles to conceal the fact that he was rather short.

Detail of floor mosaic

The ground level of the Palatine is now above the house, so you walk down a flight of steps and along a mosaic-paved corridor into a courtyard. Its imitation marble wall frescoes have been detached in order to preserve them, but they still hang in situ. Though they are very faded, you can still make out the veining patterns. Leading off the courtyard are three small reception rooms. The frescoes in the central one include a faded scene of Hermes coming to the rescue of Zeus's beloved Io, who is guarded by the 100-eyed Argos. In the left-hand room you can make out frescoed figures of griffins and other beasts, while the decor in the right-hand room includes landscapes and cityscapes.

Temple of Cybele ❻

See Visitors' Checklist.

OTHER THAN a platform with a few column stumps and capitals, there is little to see of the Temple of Cybele, a popular fertility goddess imported to Rome from Asia. The priests of the cult castrated themselves in the belief that if they sacrificed their own fertility it would guarantee that of the natural world. The annual festival of Cybele, in early spring, culminated with frenzied eunuch-priests slashing their bodies to offer up their blood to the goddess, and the ceremonial castration of novice priests.

Statue of the goddess Cybele

Huts of Romulus ❼

See Visitors' Checklist.

ACCORDING TO LEGEND, after killing his brother Remus, Romulus founded a village on the Palatine. In the 1940s a series of holes was found filled with earth lighter in colour than the surrounding soil. Archaeologists deduced that these holes must originally have held the supporting poles of three Iron Age huts – the first foundations of Rome *(see pp16–17).*

Farnese Gardens ❽

See Visitors' Checklist.

IN THE MID-16TH century Cardinal Alessandro Farnese, grandson of Pope Paul III, bought the ruins of Tiberius's palace on the Palatine. He filled in the ruined building and had Vignola, architect of the interior of the Gesù church, design a garden for him. The result was one of the first botanical gardens in Europe, its terraces linked by steps stretching from the House of Vestal Virgins in the Forum to the Palatine's Germalus peak. The gardeners introduced a number of plants to Italy and Europe, among them *Acacia farnesiana.* Farnese was at the centre of a glittering set which included a number of courtesans, so the parties here are likely to have been somewhat unholy.

The area was dug up during the excavation of the Palatine and re-landscaped afterwards. Nevertheless the tree-lined avenues, rose gardens and glorious views still make it an ideal place to unwind.

Farnese pavilions, relics of the age when the Palatine was a private garden

PIAZZA DELLA ROTONDA

THE PANTHEON, one of the great buildings in the history of European architecture, has stood at the heart of Rome for nearly 2,000 years. The historic area around it has seen uninterrupted economic and political activity throughout that time. Palazzo di Montecitorio, built for Pope Innocent XII as a papal tribunal in 1694,

Bitter-style apéritif, popular in Roman cafés

is now the Italian parliament and many nearby buildings are government offices. This is also the main financial district of Rome with banking headquarters and the stock exchange. Not many people live here, but in the evenings, Romans stroll in the narrow streets and fill the lively restaurants and cafés that make this a focus for the city's social life.

SIGHTS AT A GLANCE

Churches and Temples
Temple of Hadrian **1**
Sant'Ignazio di Loyola **3**
Gesù pp114–15 **9**
Santa Maria sopra Minerva **11**
Pantheon pp110–11 **13**
Sant'Eustachio **14**
La Maddalena **15**
Santa Maria in Campo Marzio **18**
San Lorenzo in Lucina **20**

Historic Streets and Piazzas
Piazza di Sant'Ignazio **2**
Via della Gatta **7**

Historic Buildings
Palazzo del Collegio Romano **4**
Palazzo Doria Pamphilj **6**
Palazzo Altieri **8**
Palazzo Baldassini **17**
Palazzo Borghese **19**
Palazzo di Montecitorio **21**
Palazzo Capranica **24**

Columns, Obelisks and Statues
Pie' di Marmo **10**
Obelisk of Santa Maria sopra Minerva **12**
Obelisk of Montecitorio **22**
Column of Marcus Aurelius **23**

Fountains
Fontanella del Facchino **5**

Cafés and Restaurants
Caffè Giolitti **16**

KEY

▦	Street-by-Street map
P	Parking

GETTING THERE
The area has no Metro station, but is about 15 minutes' walk from Spagna or Barberini Metro stops. There are some convenient bus stops in Via del Plebiscito, served by the 56, 64, 70, 492 and many other routes. Piazza Colonna is served by the 56, 60, 85 and all buses that go up Via del Corso. The only bus that passes through the narrow streets of the area is the 116 electric minibus, which stops right outside the Pantheon.

0 metres 200
0 yards 200

SEE ALSO

Piazza della Rotonda seen through the granite columns of the Pantheon

Street-by-Street: Piazza della Rotonda

IF YOU WANDER THROUGH this area, sooner or later you will
emerge into Piazza della Rotonda with its jumble of
open-air café tables in front of the Pantheon. The refreshing
splash of the fountain makes it a welcome resting place. In
this warren of narrow streets, it can be hard to realize just how
close you are to some of Rome's finest
sights. The magnificent art collection of
Palazzo Doria Pamphilj and the Baroque
splendour of the Gesù are just a few
minutes' walk from the Pantheon. At night
there is always a lively buzz of activity, as
people dine in style or enjoy
the coffee and ice creams for
which the area is famous.

Temple of Hadrian
*The columns of this
Roman temple now
form the facade of the
stock exchange* ❶

**Piazza di
Sant'Ignazio**
*The square is a
rare example of
stylish domestic
architecture
from the early
18th century* ❷

La Tazza d'Oro enjoys a
reputation for the wonderful
coffee consumed on its
premises as well as for
its freshly-ground coffee
to take away. *(See p319.)*

PIAZZA DI SANT'IGNAZIO

VIA DI SANT' IGNAZIO

VIA DEL SEMINARIO

**Santa Maria
sopra Minerva**
*The rich decoration
of Rome's only Gothic
church was added in
the 19th century* ⓫

PIAZZA DELLA ROTONDA

★ **Pantheon**
*The awe-inspiring interior of
Rome's best-preserved ancient
temple is only hinted at
from the outside* ⓭

PIAZZA DELLA MINERVA

**Obelisk of Santa Maria
sopra Minerva**
*In 1667 Bernini dreamed up
the idea of mounting a recently
discovered obelisk on the back
of a marble elephant* ⓬

LOCATOR MAP
See Central Rome Map pp12–13

★ **Sant'Ignazio di Loyola**
Andrea Pozzo painted this glorious Baroque ceiling (1685) to celebrate St Ignatius and the Jesuit order ❸

Palazzo del Collegio Romano
Up until 1870, the college educated many leading figures in the Catholic Church ❹

Fontanella del Facchino
The water in this small 16th-century fountain spurts from a barrel held by a porter ❺

★ **Palazzo Doria Pamphilj**
Among the masterpieces in the art gallery of this magnificent family palazzo is this portrait of Pope Innocent X by Velázquez (1650) ❻

Via della Gatta
The street is named after the statue of a cat ❼

Palazzo Altieri
This enormous 17th-century palazzo is decorated with the arms of Pope Clement X ❽

★ **Gesù**
The design of the first-ever Jesuit church had a great impact on religious architecture ❾

Pie' di Marmo
This marble foot is a stray fragment from a gigantic Roman statue ❿

KEY

– – – Suggested route

0 metres   75

0 yards   75

STAR SIGHTS

★ **Pantheon**

★ **Palazzo Doria Pamphilj**

★ **Gesù**

★ **Sant'Ignazio di Loyola**

Temple of Hadrian ❶

La Borsa, Piazza di Pietra. **Map** 4 F3 &
12 E2. 🚌 *60, 81, 85, 116, 117 and
many other routes along Via del Corso.*
Not open to the public.

THIS TEMPLE honours the
Emperor Hadrian as a god
and was dedicated by his son
and successor Antoninus Pius
in AD 145. The remains of the
temple are visible on the
southern side of Piazza di
Pietra, incorporated in a 17th-
century building. This was
originally a papal customs
house, completed by Carlo
Fontana and his son in the
1690s. Today the building
houses the Roman stock
exchange (La Borsa).

Eleven marble Corinthian
columns 15 m (49 ft) high
stand on a base of *peperino*, a
volcanic rock quarried from
the Alban hills to the south of
Rome. The columns decorated
the northern flank of the
temple enclosing its inner
shrine, the *cella*. The *peperino*
wall of the *cella* is still visible
behind the columns, as is part
of the coffered portico ceiling.

A number of reliefs from
the temple, representing
conquered Roman provinces,
are now in the courtyard of
the Palazzo dei Conservatori
(see pp72–3). They reflect the
mostly peaceful foreign policy
of Hadrian's reign.

Remains of Hadrian's Temple

Piazza di Sant'Ignazio ❷

Map 4 F4 & 12 E3. 🚌 *60, 81, 85,
116, 117 and many other routes along
Via del Corso.*

ONE OF THE MAJOR works of
the Roman Rococo, the
piazza (1727–8) is Filippo
Raguzzini's masterpiece. It
offsets the imposing façade of
the church of Sant'Ignazio

Illusionistic ceiling in the crossing of Sant'Ignazio

with the intimacy of the houses
belonging to the bourgeoisie.
The theatrical setting, the cur-
vilinear design and the playful
forms of its windows, balconies
and balusters mark the piazza
as one of a highly distinct
group of structures. Along with
Palazzo Doria Pamphilj (1731),
the façade of La Maddalena
(1735) and the aristocratic
Spanish Steps (1723), it belongs
to the moment when Rome's
bubbly Rococo triumphed
over conservative Classicism.

Sant'Ignazio di Loyola ❸

Piazza di Sant'Ignazio. **Map** 4 F4 &
12 E3. 📞 *06-679 44 06.* 🚌 *60, 81,
85, 116, 117 and many other routes
along Via del Corso.* **Open** *7.30am–
12.30pm, 4–7.15pm daily.* ✝

THE CHURCH was built by
Pope Gregory XV in 1626
in honour of St Ignatius of
Loyola, founder of the Society
of Jesus and the man who
most embodied the zeal of
the Counter Reformation.

Together with the Gesù *(see
pp114–15)*, Sant'Ignazio forms
the centre of the Jesuit area in
Rome. Its vast interior, lined
with precious stones, marble,
stucco and gilt, creates a sense
of theatre. The church has a
Latin-cross plan, with an apse
and many side chapels.

A cupola was planned but
never built, so the space it
would have filled was covered
by a fake perspective painting.
The piers built to uphold the
cupola support the observatory
of the Collegio Romano.

Palazzo del Collegio Romano ❹

Piazza del Collegio Romano. **Map** 5 A4
& 12 E3. 🚌 *60, 81, 85, 116, 117 and
many other routes along Via del Corso.*
Not open to the public.

ON THE SAME BLOCK as the
church of Sant'Ignazio is
the palazzo used by Jesuits as
a college where many future
bishops, cardinals and popes
studied. The college was con-
fiscated in 1870 and turned
into an ordinary school. The
portals bear the coat of arms
of its founder, Pope Gregory
XIII of Boncompagni (reigned
1572– 85). The façade is also
adorned with a bell, a clock,
and two sundials. On the right
is a tower built
in 1787 as a
meteorological
observatory. Un-
til 1925 its time
signal regulated
all the clocks
within the city.

**Portal of the
Collegio Romano**

Fontanella del Facchino ❺

Via Lata. **Map** 5 A4 & 12 E3.
🚌 60, 64, 70, 81, 85, 117 and many other routes.

IL FACCHINO (the Porter), once in the Corso, now set in the wall of the Banco di Roma, was one of Rome's "talking statues" like Pasquino (see p124). Created around 1590, the fountain may have been based on a drawing by painter Jacopino del Conte. The statue of a man holding a barrel most likely represents a member of the Università degli Acquaroli (Fraternity of Water-carriers), though it is also said to be of Martin Luther, or of the porter Abbondio Rizzio, who died carrying a barrel.

The Facchino drinking fountain

Palazzo Doria Pamphilj ❻

Piazza del Collegio Romano 1/A.
Map 5 A4 & 12 E3. 📞 06-679 73 23.
🚌 56, 60, 62, 85, 95, 160, 492 and many other routes. **Open** 10am–5pm Fri–Wed. **Closed** 15–30 Aug, public hols. **Adm charge.** ♿ limited. 📷 compulsory for private apartments, otherwise ask. 📷

PALAZZO DORIA PAMPHILJ is a great island of stone in the heart of Rome, the oldest parts dating from 1435. Through the Corso entrance you can see the 16th-century porticoed courtyard with the coat of arms of the della Rovere family. The Aldobrandini were the next owners. Between 1601 and 1647 the mansion acquired a second courtyard and flanking wings at the expense of a public bath that stood nearby.

When the Pamphilj family took over, they completed the Piazza del Collegio Romano facade and the Via della Gatta wing, a splendid chapel and a theatre inaugurated by Queen Christina of Sweden in 1684.

In the first half of the 18th century, Gabriele Valvassori created the gallery above the courtyard and a new facade along the Corso, using the highly decorative style of the period known as the barocchetto, which now dominates the building. The stairways and salons, the Mirror Gallery and the picture gallery all radiate a joyous sense of light and space.

The family collection in the Doria Pamphilj gallery has over 400 paintings dating from the 15th to the 18th century, including the famous portrait of Pope Innocent X Pamphilj by Velázquez. There are also important works by Titian, Caravaggio, Lorenzo Lotto, Guercino and Claude Lorrain. The rooms in the private apartment have many of their original furnishings on display, including splendid Brussels and Gobelins tapestries.

Via della Gatta ❼

Map 5 A4 & 12 E3. 🚌 56, 60, 62, 85, 95, 160, 492 and many other routes along Corso Vittorio Emanuele II.

THIS NARROW STREET runs between the Palazzo Doria Pamphilj and the smaller Palazzo Grazioli. The ancient marble sculpture of a cat (gatta) that gives the street its name is on the first cornice on the corner of Palazzo Grazioli.

Via della Gatta's marble cat

Palazzo Altieri ❽

Via del Gesù 93. **Map** 4 F4 & 12 E3.
🚌 46, 56, 60, 64, 70, 81, 186 and many other routes along Corso Vittorio Emanuele II. 🚊 8.

THE ALTIERI FAMILY is first mentioned in Rome's history in the 9th century. This palazzo was built by the last male heirs, the brothers Cardinal Giambattista di Lorenzo Altieri and Cardinal Emilio Altieri, later Pope Clement X (reigned 1670–76). Many surrounding houses had to be demolished, but an old woman called Berta refused to leave, so her hovel was incorporated in the palazzo. Its windows are still visible on the west end of the building. Part of the palazzo is occupied by Mirabilia, a ticket agency (see p341).

Gesù ❾

See pp114–15.

Caravaggio's Rest during the Flight into Egypt in Palazzo Doria Pamphilj

Marble foot from a Roman statue

Pie' di Marmo ⑩

Via di Santo Stefano del Cacco. **Map** 4 F4 & 12 E3. 🚌 60, 64, 70, 81, 85, 116 and other routes along Via del Corso and Corso Vittorio Emanuele II.

IT WAS POPULARLY believed in the Middle Ages that half the population of ancient Rome was made up of bronze, gold and marble statues. Fragments of these giants, usually gods or emperors, are scattered over the city. This piece, a marble foot (pie' di marmo), comes from an area dedicated to the Egyptian gods Isis and Serapis and was probably part of a statue in one of the temples. These statues were painted and covered with jewels and clothes given by the faithful – a great fire hazard with unattended burning tapers.

Santa Maria sopra Minerva ⑪

Piazza della Minerva 42. **Map** 4 F4 & 12 E3. 📞 06-679 39 26. 🚌 116 and many routes along Via del Corso and Corso Vittorio Emanuele II. **Open** 7am–7pm daily. **Cloister open** 8.30am–1pm, 4–7.30pm Mon–Sat, ask in the church. 🔲 🔲 **Concerts**.

FEW OTHER CHURCHES display such a complete and impressive record of Italian art. Dating from the 13th century, the Minerva is one of the few examples of Gothic architecture in Rome. It was the traditional strong-hold of the Dominicans, whose anti-heretical zeal earned them the nickname of Domini Canes (the hounds of the Lord).

Built on ancient ruins, supposed to have been the Temple of Minerva, the simple T-shaped vaulted building acquired rich chapels and works of art by which its

many patrons wished to be remembered. Note the Cosmatesque 13th-century tombs and the exquisite works of 15th-century Tuscan and Venetian artists. Native Roman talent of the period can be admired in Antoniazzo Romano's Annunciation, featuring Cardinal Juan de Torquemada, uncle of the infamous Spanish Inquisitor.

The more monumental style of the Roman Renaissance is well represented in the tombs of the 16th-century Medici popes, Leo X and his cousin Clement VII, and in the richly decorated Aldobrandini Chapel. Near the steps of the choir is the celebrated sculpture of the Risen Christ, started by Michelangelo but completed by Raffaele da Montelupo in 1521.

There are also splendid works of art from the Baroque period, including a tomb and a bust by Bernini. The church is visited not only for its art, but also because it contains the tombs of many famous Italians: St Catherine of Siena, who died here in 1380; the Venetian sculptor Andrea Bregno (died 1506); the Humanist Cardinal Pietro Bembo (died 1547); and Fra Angelico, the Dominican friar and painter, who died in Rome in 1455.

Obelisk of Santa Maria sopra Minerva ⑫

Piazza della Minerva. **Map** 4 F4 & 12 D3. 🚌 116 and routes along Via del Corso and Corso Vittorio Emanuele II.

ORIGINALLY MEANT to decorate Palazzo Barberini as a joke, this exotic elephant and obelisk sculpture is typical of Bernini's inexhaustible imagination. (The elephant was actually sculpted by Ercole Ferrata to Bernini's design.) When the ancient obelisk was found in the garden of the monastery of Santa Maria sopra Minerva, the friars wanted the monument erected in their piazza. The elephant was provided with its enormous saddle-cloth because of a friar's insistence that the gap under the animal's abdomen would undermine its stability. Bernini knew better: you need only look at the Fontana dei Fiumi (see p120) in Piazza Navona to appreciate his use of empty space. The elephant, an ancient symbol of intelligence and piety, was chosen as the embodiment of

Bernini's Egyptian obelisk and marble elephant

the virtues on which Christians should build true wisdom.

Nave of Santa Maria sopra Minerva

Pantheon ⑬

See pp110–11.

Sant'Eustachio ⑭

Piazza Sant'Eustachio. **Map** 4 F4 & 12 D3. 06-686 53 34. 116 and many routes along Corso Vittorio Emanuele II. **Open** 4pm–8pm daily.

THE ORIGINS of this church date to early Christian times, when it offered relief to the poor. In medieval times, many charitable brotherhoods elected Sant'Eustachio as their patron and had chapels here.

The Romanesque bell tower is one of the few surviving remains of the medieval church, which was completely redecorated in the 17th and 18th centuries.

Nearby is the excellent Caffè Sant'Eustachio *(see p319)*.

Bell tower of Sant'Eustachio

La Maddalena ⑮

Piazza della Maddalena. **Map** 4 F3 & 12 D2. 06-679 77 96. 116 and many routes along Via del Corso and Corso Vittorio Emanuele II. **Open** 7.30am–noon, 5–7.30pm daily.

SITUATED IN a small piazza near the Pantheon, the Maddalena's Rococo facade, built in 1735, epitomizes the love of light and movement of the late Baroque. Its curves are reminiscent of Borromini's San Carlo alle Quattro Fontane *(see p161)*. The facade has been lovingly restored, despite the protests of diehard Neo-Classicists who dismiss its painted stucco as icing sugar.

The small size of the Maddalena did not deter the

The old-fashioned *salone* of the Caffè Giolitti

17th- and 18th-century decorators who filled the interior with ornaments from the floor to the top of the elegant cupola. The organ loft and choir are particularly powerful examples of the Baroque's desire to fire the imagination of the faithful.

Many of the paintings and sculptures adopt the Christian imagery of the Counter Reformation. In the niches of the nave, the statues are personifications of virtues such as Humility and Simplicity. There are also scenes from the life of San Camillo, who died in the adjacent convent in 1614. The church belonged to his followers, the Camillians, a preaching order active in Rome's hospitals. Like the Jesuits, they commissioned powerful works of art to convey the force of their religious message.

La Maddalena's stuccoed facade

Caffè Giolitti ⑯

Via degli Uffici del Vicario 40. **Map** 4 F3 & 12 D2. 06-699 12 43. 116 and many routes along Via del Corso and Corso Rinascimento. **Open** 7am–1.30am Tue–Sun.

FOUNDED IN 1900, the Caffè Giolitti is the heir to the *Belle Époque* cafés that lined the nearby Corso in Rome's first days as capital of the new Italian state. Its *salone* holds tourists in summer and Roman families at weekends, while on weekdays it is frequented by office workers, construction workers and officials from the nearby parliament *(see p112)*.

Palazzo Baldassini ⑰

Via delle Coppelle 35. **Map** 4 F3 & 12 D2. 116 and many routes along Via del Corso and Corso Rinascimento. **Not open** to the public.

MELCHIORRE BALDASSINI commissioned Antonio da Sangallo the Younger to build his home in Florentine Renaissance style in 1514–20. With its cornices marking the different floors and wrought-iron window grilles, this is one of the best examples of an early 16th-century Roman palazzo. It stands in the part of Rome still known as the Renaissance Quarter, which flourished around the long straight streets such as Via di Ripetta and Via della Scrofa built at the time of Pope Leo X (reigned 1513–21).

Pantheon ⓱

IN THE MIDDLE AGES the Pantheon, the Roman "temple of all the gods", became a church; in time this magnificent building with its awe-inspiring domed interior became a symbol of Rome itself. The rectangular portico screens the vast hemispherical dome: only from inside can its true scale and beauty be appreciated. The rotunda's height and diameter are equal: 43.3 m (140 ft). The hole at the top of the dome, the *oculus*, provides the only light. We owe this marvel of Roman engineering to the Emperor Hadrian (AD 118–125), who designed it to replace an earlier temple built by Marcus Agrippa, son-in-law of Augustus. The shrines that now line the wall of the Pantheon range from the Tomb of Raphael to those of the kings of modern Italy.

★ **Interior of Dome**
The dome was cast by pouring concrete mixed with tufa and pumice over a temporary wooden framework.

The walls of the drum supporting the dome are 6 m (19 ft) thick.

The portico, enclosed by granite columns

The immense portico is built on the foundations of Agrippa's temple.

STAR FEATURES

★ **Interior of Dome**

★ **Tomb of Raphael**

Bell Towers
This 18th-century view by Bernardo Bellotto shows Bernini's much-ridiculed turrets, which were removed in 1883.

Floor Patterning
The marble floor, restored in 1873, preserves the original Roman design.

RAPHAEL AND LA FORNARINA

Raphael, at his own request, was buried here when he died in 1520. He had lived for years with his model, La Fornarina (see p210), seen here in a painting by Giulio Romano, but she was excluded from the ceremony of his burial. On the right of his tomb is a memorial to his fiancée, Maria Bibbiena, niece of the artist's patron, Cardinal Dovizi di Bibbiena.

VISITORS' CHECKLIST

Piazza della Rotonda. **Map** 4 F4 & 12 D3. 06-68 30 02 30. 116 and many routes along nearby Via del Corso, Corso del Rinascimento and Corso Vittorio Emanuele II. **Open** 9am–6.30pm daily. **Closed** 1 Jan, 1 May, 25 Dec. Concerts.

Oculus

Coffering
Constructing the dome from hollow decorative coffers reduced its weight.

Relieving Arches
Brick arches embedded in the structure of the wall act as internal buttresses, distributing the weight of the dome.

★ **Tomb of Raphael**
The artist's body rests below a Madonna by Lorenzetto (1520).

TIMELINE

27–25 BC Marcus Agrippa builds first Pantheon	*Inscription on pediment* MAGRIPPA	**735** Gregory III roofs the Pantheon in lead	**1305–77** While papal seat is in Avignon, Pantheon is used as fortress and poultry market	**1888** Tomb of King Vittorio Emanuele II completed	
30 BC	**AD 100**	**600**	**1100**	**1600**	
AD 118 Hadrian builds new Pantheon	**609** Pope Boniface IV consecrates Pantheon as church of Santa Maria ad Martyres	**663** Byzantine Emperor Constans II strips gilded tiles from the roof	**1632** Urban VIII melts down bronze from portico for Bernini's baldacchino in St Peter's		

Bernini's curving southern facade of Palazzo di Montecitorio

Santa Maria in Campo Marzio ⓲

Piazza in Campo Marzio 45. **Map** 4 F3 & 12 D2. 🚌 116 and many routes on Via del Corso and Corso Rinascimento. **Closed for renovation.**

AROUND the courtyard through which you enter the church, there are fascinating remnants of medieval houses, once the property of the original monastery. The church itself was rebuilt in 1685 by Antonio de Rossi, using a square Greek-cross plan with a cupola. Above the altar is a 12th-century painting of the Madonna, which gives the church its name.

Palazzo Borghese ⓳

Largo della Fontanella di Borghese. **Map** 4 F3 & 12 D1. 🚌 70, 81, 117, 492, 628. **Not open** to the public.

THE PALAZZO was acquired in about 1605 by Cardinal Camillo Borghese, just before he became Pope Paul V. Flaminio Ponzio was hired to enlarge the building and give it the grandeur appropriate to the residence of the pope's family. He added a wing overlooking Piazza Borghese and the delightful porticoed courtyard inside. Subsequent enlargements included the building and decoration of a great *nympheum* known as the Bath of Venus. For more than two centuries this palazzo housed the Borghese family's renowned collection of paintings, which was bought

by the Italian state in 1902 and transferred to the Galleria Borghese *(see pp260–61).*

Pope Paul V, who commissioned Palazzo Borghese for his family

San Lorenzo in Lucina ⓴

Via in Lucina 16A. **Map** 4 F3 & 12 E1. 🎧 06-687 14 94. 🚌 81, 115, 117, 492, 628. **Open** 8am–noon, 5–7.30pm daily. 🔔 📷 last Sat of each month at 4.30pm (phone to book).

THE CHURCH is one of Rome's oldest Christian places of worship, and was probably built on a well sacred to Juno, protectress of women. It was rebuilt in the 12th century, and today's external appearance is typical of

the period: a portico with re-used Roman columns, crowned by medieval capitals, a plain triangular pediment and a Romanesque bell tower with coloured marble inlay.

The interior was totally rebuilt in 1856–8. The old basilical plan was destroyed and the two side naves were replaced by Baroque chapels. Don't miss the fine busts in the Fonseca Chapel, designed by Bernini, or the *Crucifixion* by Guido Reni above the main altar. There is also a 19th-century monument honouring French painter Nicolas Poussin, who died in Rome in 1655 and was buried in the church.

Palazzo di Montecitorio ㉑

Piazza di Montecitorio. **Map** 4 F3 & 12 E2. 🚌 56, 60, 62, 81, 95, 116, 117, 160 and many other routes. **Not open** to the public (visits 10am–4.30pm 1st Sun each month can be booked in adv 🎧 06-67601).

THE PALAZZO'S first architect, Bernini, got the job after he presented a silver model of his design to the wife of his patron, Prince Ludovisi. The building was completed in 1694 by Carlo Fontana and became the Papal Tribunal of Justice. In 1871 it was chosen to be Italy's new Chamber of Deputies and by 1927 it had doubled in size with a second grand facade. The 630 members of parliament are elected by a majority system with proportional representation.

The church of San Lorenzo in Lucina

Emperor Augustus's obelisk

Obelisk of Montecitorio ②

Piazza di Montecitorio. **Map** 4 F3 & 12 E2. 🚌 *56, 60, 62, 81, 95, 116, 117, 160 and many other routes.*

THE MEASUREMENT of time in ancient Rome was always a rather hit-and-miss affair: for many years the Romans relied on an imported (and therefore inaccurate) sundial, a trophy from the conquest of Sicily. In 10 BC the Emperor Augustus laid out an enormous sundial in the Campus Martius. Its centre was roughly in today's Piazza di San Lorenzo in Lucina. The shadow was cast by a huge granite obelisk that he had brought back from Heliopolis in Egypt. Unfortunately this sundial too became inaccurate after only 50 years, possibly due to subsidence.

The obelisk was still in the piazza in the 9th century, but then disappeared until it was rediscovered lying under medieval houses in the reign of Pope Julius II (1503–13). The pope was intrigued, because Egyptian hieroglyphs were thought to hold the key to the wisdom of Adam before the Fall, but it was only under Pope Benedict XIV (reigned 1740–58) that the obelisk was finally unearthed. It was erected in its present location in 1792 by Pope Pius VI.

Column of Marcus Aurelius ②

Piazza Colonna. **Map** 5 A3 & 12 E2. 🚌 *56, 60, 62, 81, 95, 116, 117, 160 and many other routes.*

CLEARLY AN IMITATION of the Column of Trajan (see p90), this monument was erected after the death of Marcus Aurelius in AD 180 to commemorate his victories over the barbarian tribes of the Danube. The 80-year lapse between the two works produced a great artistic change: the wars of Marcus Aurelius are rendered with simplified pictures in stronger relief, sacrificing Classical proportions for the sake of clarity and immediacy. The spirit of the work is more akin to the 4th-century Arch of Constantine (see p91) than to Trajan's monument. Gone are the heroic qualities of the Roman soldiers, by now mostly barbarian mercenaries, and a sense of respect for the vanquished. A new emphasis on the supernatural points to the end of the Hellenistic tradition and the beginning of Christianity.

Composed of 28 drums of marble, the column was restored in 1588 by Domenico Fontana on the orders of Pope Sixtus V. The emperor's statue on the summit was replaced by a bronze of St Paul. The 20 spirals of the low relief chronicle the German war of AD 172–3, and (above) the Sarmatic war of AD 174–5. The column is almost 30 m (100 ft) high and 3.7 m (12 ft) in diameter. An internal spiral staircase leads to the top. The easiest way to appreciate the sculptural work, however, is to visit the Museo della Civiltà Romana at EUR (see p267) and study the casts of the reliefs.

Palazzo Capranica ②

Piazza Capranica. **Map** 4 F3 & 12 D2. 🚌 *56, 60, 62, 81, 95, 116, 117, 160 and many other routes.*

Windows of Palazzo Capranica

ONE OF ROME'S small number of surviving 15th-century buildings, the palazzo was commissioned by Cardinal Domenico Capranica both as his family residence and as a college for higher education. Its fortress-like appearance is a patchwork of subsequent additions, not unusual in the late 15th century, when Rome was still hovering between medieval and Renaissance taste. The Gothic-looking windows on the right of the building show the cardinal's coat of arms and the date 1451 is inscribed on the doorway underneath. The palazzo is now a shell housing a popular cinema.

Relief of the emperor's campaigns on the Column of Marcus Aurelius

Gesù **❾**

DATING FROM BETWEEN 1568 and 1584, the Gesù was the first Jesuit church to be built in Rome. Its design epitomizes Counter Reformation Baroque architecture and has been much imitated throughout the Catholic world. The layout proclaims the church's two major functions: a large nave with side pulpits for preaching to great crowds, and a main altar as the centrepiece for the celebration of the mass. The illusionistic decoration in the nave and dome was added a century later. Its message is clear and confident: faithful, Catholic worshippers will be joyfully uplifted into the heavens while Protestants and other heretics are flung into hell's fires.

★ **Chapel of Sant'Ignazio**
Above its altar is a statue of the saint, framed by gilded lapis lazuli columns. The chapel was built in 1696–1700 by Andrea Pozzo, a Jesuit artist.

Triumph of Faith Over Idolatry
This vivid Baroque allegory sculpted by Théudon illustrates the great ambition of Jesuit theology.

ST IGNATIUS AND THE JESUIT ORDER

Spanish soldier Ignatius Loyola (1491–1556) joined the Church after being wounded in battle in 1521. He came to Rome in 1537 and founded the Jesuits, sending missionaries and teachers all over the world to win souls for Catholicism.

Main entrance

STAR FEATURES

- ★ **Nave Ceiling Decorations**
- ★ **Chapel of Sant'Ignazio**
- ★ **Tomb of San Roberto Bellarmino**

Allegorical Figures
Antonio Raggi made these stuccoes, which were designed by Il Baciccia to complement the figures on his own nave frescoes.

Madonna della Strada
This 15th-century image, the Madonna of the Road, was originally displayed on the facade of Santa Maria della Strada which once stood on this site.

VISITORS' CHECKLIST

Piazza del Gesù. **Map** 4 F4 & 12 E4. 06-69 70 01. H, 44, 46, 56, 60, 62, 64, 70, 75, 81, 87, 170, 492, 628, 719 and other routes. 8.
Open 6am–12.30pm, 4–7.15pm daily.

★ **Tomb of San Roberto Bellarmino**
Bernini captured the forceful personality of this anti-Protestant theologian, who died in 1621.

The Chapel of St Francis Xavier is a memorial to the great missionary who died alone on an island off China in 1552.

Cupola Frescoes
The cupola was completed by della Porta to Vignola's design. The frescoes, by Il Baciccia, feature Old Testament figures.

★ **Nave Ceiling Decorations**
The figures in Il Baciccia's astonishing fresco of the Triumph of the Name of Jesus spill out on to the coffered vaulting of the nave.

TIMELINE

1500	1600	1700
1540 Founding of the Society of Jesus (the Jesuits)	**1571** Giacomo della Porta's design chosen for the facade	**1696–1700** The Chapel of Sant' Ignazio is designed by Andrea Pozzo, a Jesuit artist
	1584 Church's consecration	**1773** Pope Clement XIV orders the suppression of the Jesuit order
1545–63 Council of Trent defines the new Catholic orthodoxy	**1568–71** Vignola builds the church up to the crossing under the patronage of Cardinal Alessandro Farnese	**1670–83** Giovanni Battista Gaulli (Il Baciccia) paints the nave vault, dome and apse
1556 Death of Ignatius	**1622** Ignatius Loyola is canonized	

PIAZZA NAVONA

THE FOUNDATIONS of the buildings surrounding the elongated oval of Piazza Navona were the ruined grandstands of the vast Stadium of Domitian. The piazza still provides a dramatic spectacle today with the ob-elisk of the Fontana dei Quattro Fiumi in front of the church of Sant' Agnese in Agone as its focal

Lion on Fontana dei Quattro Fiumi

point. The predominant style of the area is Baroque, many of its finest buildings dating from the reign of Innocent X Pamphilj (1644–55), patron of Bernini and Borromini. Of special interest is the complex of the Chiesa Nuova, headquarters of the Filippini, the order founded by San Filippo Neri, the 16th-century "Apostle of Rome".

SIGHTS AT A GLANCE

Churches and Temples
Sant'Agnese in Agone **4**
Santa Maria dell'Anima **5**
Santa Maria della Pace **6**
San Luigi dei Francesi **7**
Sant'Ivo alla Sapienza **9**
Sant'Andrea della Valle **10**
Chiesa Nuova **15**
Oratorio dei Filippini **16**
San Salvatore in Lauro **20**

Museums
Palazzo Braschi **12**
Museo Napoleonico **21**

Historic Buildings
Palazzo Pamphilj **3**
Palazzo Madama **8**
Palazzo Massimo
alle Colonne **11**
Torre dell'Orologio **17**
Palazzo del Banco
di Santo Spirito **18**
Palazzo Altemps **23**

Fountains and Statues
Fontana dei Quattro Fiumi **1**
Pasquino **13**

Historic Streets and Piazzas
Piazza Navona **2**
Via del Governo Vecchio **14**
Via dei Coronari **19**

Restaurants
Hostaria dell'Orso **22**

SEE ALSO

• *Street Finder*, maps 4, 11, 12

• *Where to Stay* pp294–5

• *Restaurants* pp310–11

GETTING THERE
This central area is within walking distance of many parts of the city. Much of the area itself is closed to traffic, but it is easily reached by bus. The principal routes along Corso Vittorio Emanuele II are the 64 from Termini station to St Peter's and the 46. Corso del Rinascimento, which runs parallel to Piazza Navona, is served by several useful routes, including the 70, 81, 116, 186 and 492.

KEY

Street-by-Street map

P Parking

0 metres 200
0 yards 200

Piazza Navona, with the Fontana del Moro and church of Sant'Agnese in Agone

Street-by-Street: Piazza Navona

Nᴏ ᴏᴛʜᴇʀ ᴘɪᴀᴢᴢᴀ in Rome can rival the theatricality of Piazza Navona. Day and night there is always something going on in the pedestrian area around its three flamboyant fountains. The Baroque is also represented in many of the area's churches. To discover an older Rome, walk along Via del Governo Vecchio to admire the facades of its Renaissance buildings and browse in the fascinating antiques shops.

Oratorio dei Filippini
The musical term oratorio comes from this place of informal worship ⓰

Torre dell' Orologio
This clock tower by Borromini (1648) is part of the Convent of the Filippini ⓱

Chiesa Nuova
This church was rebuilt in the late 16th century for the order founded by San Filippo Neri ⓯

To Corso Vittorio Emanuele II

Via del Governo Vecchio
This street preserves a large number of fine Renaissance houses ⓮

Santa Maria della Pace
The medallion shows Pope Alexander VII, who had the church restored by Pietro da Cortona in 1656 ❻

Pasquino
Romans hung satirical verses and dialogues on this weatherbeaten statue ⓭

Palazzo Pamphilj
This grand town house was built for Pope Innocent X and his family in the mid-17th century ❸

Palazzo Braschi
A late 18th-century building with a splendid balcony, the palazzo houses the Museo di Roma ⓬

Palazzo Massimo alle Colonne
The magnificent curving colonnade (1536) is by Baldassarre Peruzzi ⓫

VIA DEL CORALLO

VIA DEL GOVERNO VECCHIO

VIA DI PARIONE

CORSO VITTORIO EMANUELE II

PIAZZA DI PASQUINO

PIAZZA DI SAN PANTALEO

Sᴛᴀʀ Sɪɢʜᴛꜱ

★ Sant'Andrea della Valle

★ San Luigi dei Francesi

★ Piazza Navona

Kᴇʏ

– – –   Suggested route

| 0 metres | 75 |
| 0 yards | 75 |

Sant'Agnese in Agone
Borromini's startling concave facade (1657) dominates one side of Piazza Navona ❹

LOCATOR MAP
See Central Rome Map pp12–13

Santa Maria dell'Anima
For four centuries this has been the German church in Rome ❺

Palazzo Madama
A spread-eagled stone lionskin decorates the central doorway of the palazzo, now the Italian Senate ❽

Fontana dei Quattro Fiumi
This fountain supporting an Egyptian obelisk was designed by Bernini ❶

★ **San Luigi dei Francesi**
An 18th-century statue of St Louis stands in a niche in the facade ❼

★ **Piazza Navona**
This unique piazza owes its shape to a Roman race track and its stunning decor to the genius of the Roman Baroque ❷

The Fontana del Moro was remodelled in 1653 by Bernini, who designed the central sea god.

Sant'Ivo alla Sapienza
This tiny domed church is one of Borromini's most original creations. He worked on it between 1642 and 1650 ❾

★ **Sant'Andrea della Valle**
The church, with its grandiose facade by Carlo Rainaldi (1665), has gained fame outside Rome as the setting of the first act of Puccini's Tosca ❿

To Campo de' Fiori

Fontana dei Quattro Fiumi ❶

Piazza Navona. **Map** 4 E4 & 11 C3. 🚌
46, 62, 64, 70, 81, 87, 116, 492, 628.

Built for pope Innocent X Pamphilj, this magnificent fountain in the centre of Piazza Navona was unveiled in 1651. The pope's coat of arms, the dove and the olive branch, decorate the bold pyramid rock formation supporting the Roman obelisk, which once stood in the Circus of Maxentius on the Appian Way. Bernini designed the fountain, which was paid for by means of highly unpopular taxes on bread and other staples. The great rivers then known – the Ganges, the Danube, the Nile and the River Plate – are represented by four giants.

The Nile's veiled head symbolizes the river's unknown source, but there is also a legend that the veil conveys Bernini's dislike for the nearby Sant'Agnese in Agone, designed by his rival Borromini. Similarly, the

View of Palazzo Pamphilj across Piazza Navona

athletic figure of the River Plate, cringing with arm upraised, is supposed to express Bernini's fear that the church will collapse. Sadly these widely-believed stories can have no basis in fact: Bernini had completed the fountain before Borromini started work on the church.

Piazza Navona ❷

Map 4 E3 & 11 C2. 🚌 *46, 62, 64, 70, 81, 87, 116, 492, 628.*

Rome's most beautiful Baroque piazza follows the shape of Domitian's Stadium, which once stood on this site – some of its arches are still visible below the church of Sant'Agnese in Agone. The *agones* were athletic contests held in the 1st-century stadium, which could seat 33,000. The word "Navona" is thought to be a corruption of *in agone*. The piazza's unique appearance and atmosphere were created in the 17th century with the addition of the Fontana dei Quattro Fiumi. The

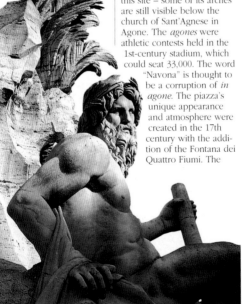

Symbolic figure of the River Ganges in the Fontana dei Quattro Fiumi

other fountains, the Fontana di Nettuno and the Fontana del Moro, date from the previous century but have been altered several times since. The figure known as Il Moro was designed by Bernini.

Up until the 19th century, Piazza Navona was flooded during August by stopping the fountain outlets. The rich would splash around in carriages, while street urchins paddled after them. Today the piazza is a favourite in all seasons, especially in winter when it fills with colourful stalls selling toys and sweets for the feast of the Befana.

Palazzo Pamphilj ❸

Piazza Navona. **Map** 4 E4 & 11 C3. 🚌 *46, 62, 64, 70, 81, 87, 116, 492, 628.* **Not open** to the public.

Family dove and olive branch on facade of Palazzo Pamphilj

In 1644 Giovanni Battista Pamphilj became Pope Innocent X. During his 10-year reign, he heaped riches on his own family, especially his domineering sister-in-law, Olimpia Maidalchini. The "talking statue" Pasquino *(see p124)* gave her the nickname "Olim-Pia", Latin for "formerly virtuous". She lived in the grand Palazzo Pamphilj, which has frescoes by Pietro da Cortona and a gallery by Borromini. The building is now the Brazilian embassy and cultural center.

Sant'Agnese in Agone ❹

Piazza Navona. **Map** 4 E4 & 11 C3.
📞 06-679 44 35. 🚌 46, 62, 64, 70, 81, 87, 116, 492, 628. **Open** 4.30pm–6.30pm Mon–Sat, 10am–noon Sun & religious hols. ♿ ♿

THE CHURCH IS believed to have been founded on the site of the brothel where, in AD 304, the young St Agnes was exposed naked to force her to renounce her faith. A marble relief in the crypt shows the miraculous growth of her hair, which fell around her body to protect her modesty. She was martyred on this site and is buried in the catacombs that bear her name along the Via Nomentana *(see p264)*.

Today's church was commissioned by Pope Innocent X in 1652. The first architects were father and son, Girolamo and Carlo Rainaldi, but they were replaced by Borromini who worked on the church from 1653 to 1657. He stuck more or less to the Rainaldi scheme except for the concave facade designed to emphasize the dome. A statue of St Agnes on the facade is said to be reassuring the Fontana dei Quattro Fiumi's statue of the River Plate that the church is stable.

Statue of St Agnes on facade of Sant' Agnese in Agone

Carlo Saraceni's *Miracle of St Benno and the Keys of Meissen Cathedral*

Santa Maria dell'Anima ❺

Via della Pace 24. **Map** 4 E4 & 11 C2.
📞 06-682 81 81. 🚌 46, 62, 64, 70, 81, 87, 116, 492, 628. **Open** 8am–7pm Mon–Sat, 8am–1pm, 3pm–7pm Sun. ♿ ♿

POPE ADRIAN VI (reigned 1522–3), son of a shipbuilder from Utrecht, was the last non-Italian pope before John Paul II. He would have disapproved of his superb tomb by Baldassarre Peruzzi in Santa Maria dell'Anima. It stands to the right of Giulio Romano's damaged altarpiece and is redolent of the pagan Renaissance spirit the pope had so condemned during his brief, rather gloomy reign, when patronage of the arts ground to a halt. Santa Maria dell'Anima is the German church in Rome and some of its paintings, such as the *Miracle of St Benno* by Carlo Saraceni (1618), illustrate events connected with the history of Germany.

Santa Maria della Pace ❻

Vicolo del Arco della Pace 5. **Map** 4 E3 & 11 C2. 📞 06-686 11 56. 🚌 46, 62, 64, 70, 81, 87, 116, 492, 628. **Closed** for restoration. ♿ ♿ 2 steps.

A DRUNKEN SOLDIER allegedly pierced the breast of a painted Madonna on this site, causing it to bleed. Pope Sixtus IV della Rovere (reigned 1471–84) placated the Virgin by ordering Baccio Pontelli to build her a church if she would bring the war with Turkey to an end. Peace was restored and the church was named Santa Maria della Pace (St Mary of Peace).

The cloister was added by Bramante in 1504. As in his famous Tempietto *(see p219)* he scrupulously followed Classical rules of proportion to produce a thoroughly original result, achieving a monumental effect in a relatively small space.

Pietro da Cortona may have had Bramante's Tempietto in mind when he added the church's charming semicircular portico in 1656. The interior, a short nave ending under an octagonal cupola, houses Raphael's famous frescoes of four *Sybils*, and four *Prophets* by his pupil Timoteo Viti, painted for the banker Agostino Chigi in 1514. Baldassarre Peruzzi also did some work in the church (fresco in the first chapel on the left), as did the architect Antonio da Sangallo the Younger, who designed the second chapel on the right.

San Luigi dei Francesi ❼

Via Santa Giovanna d'Arco.
Map 4 F4 & 12 D2. 📞 *06-688 27 1.*
🚌 *70, 81, 87, 116, 492, 628.* **Open**
8am–12.30pm, 3.30–7pm daily.
Closed *Thu pm.* 🚹 🏛

THE FRENCH national church was founded in 1518, but it took until 1589 to complete, with contributions by Giacomo della Porta and Domenico Fontana. The church serves as a last resting place for many illustrious French people, including Chateaubriand's lover Pauline de Beaumont.

Three Caravaggios hang in the fifth chapel on the left, all dedicated to St Matthew. Painted between 1597 and 1602, these were Caravaggio's first great religious works: the *Calling of St Matthew*, the *Martyrdom of St Matthew* and *St Matthew and the Angel*. The first version of this last painting was rejected because of its vivid realism; never before had a saint been shown as a tired old man with dirty feet. All three works display very disquieting realism and a highly dramatic use of light.

Caravaggio, whose paintings of St Matthew hang in San Luigi dei Francesi

Shield linking symbols of France and Rome on facade of San Luigi

Palazzo Madama ❽

Corso del Rinascimento. **Map** 4 F4 & 12 D3. 📞 *06-670 61.* 🚌 *70, 81, 87, 116, 186, 492, 628.* **Open** *10am–6pm first Sat of month.*

THIS 16TH-CENTURY palazzo was built for the Medici family, who had owned a bank here in the previous century. It was the residence of the Medici cardinals and cousins, Giovanni and Giuliano. Both later became popes: Giovanni as Leo X and Giuliano as Clement VII. Caterina de' Medici, Clement VII's niece, also lived here before she was married to Henry, son of King Francis I of France in 1533.

The palazzo takes its name from Madama Margherita of Austria, illegitimate daughter of Emperor Charles V, who married Alessandro de' Medici and, after his death, Ottavio Farnese. Thus part of the art collection of the Florentine Medici family was inherited by the Roman Farnese family.

The spectacular facade was built in the 17th century by Paolo Maruccelli. He gave it an ornate cornice and whimsical decorative details on the roof. Since 1871 the palazzo has been the seat of the upper house of the Italian parliament.

Cornice of Palazzo Madama

Sant'Ivo alla Sapienza ❾

Corso del Rinascimento 40.
Map 4 F4 & 12 D3. 📞 *06-686 49 87.*
🚌 *46, 64, 70, 81, 87, 116, 186, 492, 628.* **Open** *for mass 9am–noon Sun.* **Closed** *Jul, Aug.* 🚹

THE CHURCH's lantern is crowned with a cross on top of a dramatic twisted spiral – a highly distinctive landmark from Rome's roof terraces. Seen from close by, this Borromini church is even more striking. No other Baroque church is quite like it. Based on a ground design of astonishing geometrical complexity, the walls are a breathtaking combination of concave and convex surfaces. The church stands in the small courtyard of the Palazzo della Sapienza, seat of the old University of Rome from the 15th century until 1935.

Lantern and spire of Sant'Ivo

Sant'Andrea della Valle ⓾

Piazza Sant'Andrea della Valle. **Map** 4 E4 & 12 D4. 📞 06-686 13 39. 🚌 H, 46, 56, 60, 62, 64, 70, 75, 81, 87, 116, 170, 492, 628. 🚊 8. **Open** 8.30am– noon, 4.30– 7pm daily. ✝

Dome of Sant'Andrea della Valle

T HE CHURCH is the scene of the first act of Puccini's opera *Tosca*, though opera fans will not find the Attavanti chapel, a poetic invention. The real church has much to recommend it – the recently restored facade shows the flamboyant Baroque style at its best. Inside, a golden light filters through high windows, showing off the gilded interior. Here lie the two popes of the Sienese Piccolomini family: on the left of the central nave is the tomb of Pius II, the first Humanist pope (reigned 1458–64); Pope Pius III lies opposite – he reigned for less than a month in 1503.

The church is famous for its beautiful dome, the largest in Rome after St Peter's. It was built by Carlo Maderno in 1622–5 and was painted with splendid frescoes by Domenichino and Giovanni Lanfranco. The latter's extravagant style, to be seen in the dome fresco *Glory of Paradise*, won him most of the commission, and the jealous Domenichino is said to have tried to kill his colleague. He failed, but Domenichino's jealousy was unnecessary, as shown by his two beautiful paintings of scenes from the life of St Andrew around the apse and altar. In the Strozzi Chapel, built in the style of Michelangelo, the altar has copies of the *Leah* and *Rachel* by Michelangelo in San Pietro in Vincoli *(see p170).*

Palazzo Massimo alle Colonne ⓫

Corso Vittorio Emanuele II 141. **Map** 4 F4 & 11 C3. 🚌 46, 62, 64, 70, 81, 87, 116, 186, 492, 628. **Chapel open** 7am–noon 16 Mar every year.

Roman column, Palazzo Massimo

D URING THE LAST two years of his life, Baldassarre Peruzzi built this palazzo for the Massimo family, whose home had been destroyed in the Sack of Rome in 1527. Peruzzi displayed great ingenuity in dealing with an awkwardly shaped site. The previous building had stood on the ruined Theatre of Domitian, which created a curve in the great processional Via Papalis. Peruzzi's convex colonnaded facade follows the line of the street. His originality is also evident in the small square upper windows, the courtyard and the stuccoed vestibule. The Piazza de' Massimi entrance has a Renaissance-style, frescoed facade. A single column from the theatre has been set up in the piazza.

The Massimo family traced its origins to Quintus Fabius Maximus, conqueror of Hannibal in the 3rd century BC, and their proud coat of arms is borne by an infant Hercules. Over the years the family produced many great Humanists, and in the 19th century, it was a Massimo who negotiated peace with Napoleon. On 16 March each year the family chapel opens to the public to commemorate young Paolo Massimo's resurrection from the dead by San Filippo Neri in 1538.

Palazzo Braschi ⓬

Piazza San Pantaleo 10. **Map** 4 E4 & 11 C3. 📞 06-687 53 45. 🚌 46, 62, 64, 70, 81, 87, 116, 186, 492, 628. 🚊 8. *Reopens after restoration spring 2000 – phone for opening hours.*

O N ONE SIDE of Piazza San Pantaleo is the last Roman palazzo to be built for the family of a pope. Palazzo Braschi was built in the late 18th century for Pope Pius VI Braschi's nephews by the architect Cosimo Morelli. He gave the building its imposing facade which looks out on to the piazza.

The palazzo now houses the municipal Museo di Roma. It holds collections of pictures, drawings and everyday objects illustrating life in the city from medieval times until the 19th century.

Angel with raised wing by Ercole Ferrata, flanking the facade of Sant'Andrea della Valle

Pasquino ⑬

Piazza di Pasquino. **Map** 4 E4 &
11 C3. 🚌 46, 62, 64, 70, 81, 87,
116, 492, 628.

Pasquino, the most famous of
Rome's satirical "talking statues"

THIS ROUGH CHUNK of marble
is all that remains of a
Hellenistic group, probably
representing the incident in
Homer's *Iliad* in which
Menelaus shields the body of
the slain Patroclus. For years
it lay as a stepping stone in a
muddy medieval street until it
was erected on this corner in
1501, near the shop of an
outspoken cobbler named
Pasquino. Freedom of speech
was not encouraged in papal
Rome, so the cobbler wrote
out his satirical comments on
current events and attached
them to the statue.
 Other Romans were quick
to follow suit, hanging their
maxims and verses by the
statue by night to escape
punishment. Despite the wrath
of the authorities, the sayings
of the "talking statue" (renamed
Pasquino) were part of popular
culture right up until the 19th
century. Other statues started to
"talk" in the same satirical vein;
Pasquino used to conduct dialogues with the statue Marforio
in Via del Campidoglio (now
in the courtyard of Palazzo
Nuovo, *see pp70–71*) and
with the Babuino in Via del
Babuino (*see p135*). One of
Rome's few English-
language cinemas is named
after Pasquino (*see p347*).

Via del Governo Vecchio ⑭

Map 4 E4 & 11 B3. 🚌 46, 62, 64.

THE STREET TAKES its name
from Palazzo del Governo
Vecchio, the seat of papal
government in the 17th and
18th centuries. Once part of
the Via Papalis, which led
from the Lateran to St Peter's,
the street is lined with 15th-
and 16th-century houses and
small workshops. Particularly
interesting are the 15th-
century houses at No. 104
and No. 106. The small
palazzo at No. 123 was once
thought to have been the
home of Bramante.
Opposite is Palazzo del
Governo Vecchio. It is
also known as Palazzo
Nardini, from the name of
its founder, which is inscribed
on the first-floor windows
along with the date 1477.

Via del Governo Vecchio

Chiesa Nuova ⑮

Piazza della Chiesa Nuova.
Map 4 E4 & 11 B3. ☎ 06-687 52 89.
🚌 46, 62, 64. **Open** 7.30am–noon,
4.30pm–7pm daily. ✝

Facade of the Chiesa Nuova

SAN FILIPPO NERI (St Philip
Neri) is the most appealing
of the Counter Reformation
saints. A highly unconventional
reformer, he required his
noble Roman followers to
humble themselves in public.
He made aristocratic young
men parade through the
streets of Rome in rags or even
with a fox's tail tied behind
them, and set noblemen to
work as labourers building
his church. With the help of
Pope Gregory XIII, his church
was built in place of an old
medieval church, Santa Maria
in Vallicella, and it has been
known ever since as the
Chiesa Nuova (new church).
 Begun in 1575 by Matteo da
Città di Castello and continued
by Martino Longhi the Elder,
it was consecrated in 1599
(although the facade, by Fausto
Rughesi, was only finished
in 1606). Against San Filippo's
wishes, the interior was
decorated after his death;
Pietro da Cortona frescoed the
nave, dome and apse, taking
nearly 20 years. There are
also three paintings by Rubens:
Madonna and Angels above
the altar, *Saints Domitilla,
Nereus and Achilleus* on the
right of the altar, and *Saints
Gregory, Maurus and Papias*
on the left. San Filippo is
buried in his own chapel, to
the left of the altar.

Borromini's facade of the Oratorio

Oratorio dei Filippini ⑯

Piazza della Chiesa Nuova. **Map** 4 E4 & 11 B3. [icon] 06-686 93 74. [icon] 46, 62, 64. **Open** by appt only; phone the caretaker. [icon] **Concerts.**

W ITH THE ADJOINING church and convent, the oratory formed the centre of Filippo Neri's religious order, founded in 1575. Its members are commonly known as Filippini. The musical term "oratorio" (a religious text sung by solo voices and chorus) derives from the services held here.

Filippo Neri came to Rome aged 18 to work as a tutor. The city was undergoing a period of religious strife and an economic slump after the Sack of Rome in 1527. There was also an outbreak of the plague. It was left to newcomers like Neri and Ignazio di Loyola to revive the spiritual life of the city.

Neri formed a brotherhood of laymen who worshipped together and helped pilgrims and the sick *(see Santissima Trinità dei Pellegrini p146).* He founded the Oratory as a centre for religious discourse. Its conspicuous curving brick facade was built by Borromini in 1637–43.

Torre dell' Orologio ⑰

Piazza dell'Orologio. **Map** 4 E4 & 11 B3. [icon] 46, 62, 64.

B ORROMINI BUILT this clock tower to decorate one corner of the Convent of the Oratorians of San Filippo Neri in 1647–9. It is typical of Borromini in that the front and rear are concave and the

sides convex. The mosaic of the Madonna beneath the clock is by Pietro da Cortona, while on the corner of the building is a small tabernacle to the Madonna flanked by angels in the style of Bernini.

Pietro da Cortona (1596–1669)

Palazzo del Banco di Santo Spirito ⑱

Via del Banco di Santo Spirito. **Map** 4 D4 & 11 A2. [icon] 46, 62, 64. **Open** normal banking hours.

F ORMERLY THE MINT of papal Rome, this palazzo is often referred to as the Antica Zecca (old mint). The upper storeys of the facade, built by Antonio da Sangallo the Younger in the 1520s, are in the shape of a Roman triumphal arch. Above it stand two Baroque statues symbolizing Charity and Thrift, and in the centre of the arch above the main entrance an inscription records the founding of the Banco di Santo Spirito by Pope Paul V Borghese in 1605.

Pope Paul was a very shrewd financier and he encouraged Romans to deposit their money at the bank by offering the vast estates of the Hospital of Santo Spirito *(see p226)* as security. The system catered only for the rudimentary banking requirements of the population, but business was brisk as people deposited money here safe in the knowledge that they could get it out simply by presenting a chit. The hospital coffers also gained from the system. The Banco di Santo Spirito still exists, but is now part of the Banca di Roma.

Facade of the Banco di Santo Spirito, built to resemble a Roman arch

Via dei Coronari ⓳

Map 4 D3 & 11 B2. ➡ 46, 62, 64,
70, 81, 87, 115, 116, 186, 280, 492.

LARGE NUMBERS of medieval
pilgrims making their way
to St Peter's walked along this
street to cross over the Tiber
at Ponte Sant'Angelo. Of the
businesses that sprang up to
try to part the pilgrims from
their money, the most enduring
was the selling of rosaries, and
the street is still named after
the rosary sellers *(coronari)*.
The street followed the
course of the ancient Roman
Via Recta (straight street),
which originally ran from
today's Piazza Colonna to the
Tiber.

Making one's way through
the vast throng of people in
Via dei Coronari could be
extremely hazardous. In the
Holy Year of 1450, some 200
pilgrims died, crushed by the
crowds or drowned in the
Tiber. Following the tragedy,
Pope Nicholas V demolished
the Roman triumphal arch
that stood at the entrance to
Ponte Sant'Angelo. In the late
15th century, Pope Sixtus IV
encouraged the building of
private houses and palaces
along the street.

Although the rosary sellers
have been replaced by
antiques dealers, the street
still has many original
buildings from the 15th and
16th centuries. One of the
earliest, at Nos. 156–7, is
known as the House of
Fiammetta, the mistress of
Cesare Borgia.

Antiques shop, Via dei Coronari

Cloister, San Salvatore in Lauro

San Salvatore in Lauro ⓴

Piazza San Salvatore in Lauro 15.
Map 4 E3 & 11 B2. 🎫 06-687 51 87.
➡ 70, 81, 87, 115, 116, 186, 280.
Open 8.30am– noon Mon, Wed,
Sat, Sun, 4–7pm (summer: 5–8pm)
daily. ⓵

THE CHURCH is named "in
Lauro" after the laurel
grove that grew here in
ancient times. The church
standing here today was
constructed at the end of the
16th century by Ottaviano
Mascherino. The bell tower
and sacristy were 18th-
century additions by Nicola
Salvi, famous for the Trevi
Fountain *(see p159)*.

The church contains the
first great altarpiece by the
17th-century artist Pietro da
Cortona, *The Birth of Jesus*, in
the first chapel to the right.

The adjacent convent of San
Giorgio convent, to the left,
has a pretty Renaissance
cloister, a frescoed refectory
and the monument to Pope
Eugenius IV (reigned
1431–47), moved here when
old St Peter's was pulled
down. An extravagant
Venetian, Eugenius would
willingly spend thousands
of ducats on his gold tiara,
but requested a "simple,
lowly burial place" near his
predecessor Pope Eugenius
III. His portrait, painted by
Salviati, hangs in the refectory.

In 1669 the church became
the seat of a pious association,
the Confraternity of the Piceni,
inhabitants of the Marche
region. Fanatically loyal to
the pope, the Piceni were
traditionally employed as papal
soldiers and tax-collectors.

Museo Napoleonico ㉑

Piazza di Ponte Umberto 1. **Map** 4 E3
& 11 C1. 🎫 06-68 80 62 86. ➡ 70,
81, 87, 116, 186, 280, 492. **Open**
9am– 7pm Tue–Sat, 9am–1.30pm
Sun. **Closed** 1 Jan, 1 May, 25 Dec.
Adm charge. 🚫

THIS MUSEUM contains
memorabilia and portraits
of Napoleon Bonaparte and
his family. Personal relics of
Napoleon himself include an
Indian shawl he wore during
his exile on St Helena.

After his death in 1821, the
pope allowed many of the
Bonaparte family to settle in
Rome, including his mother
Letizia, who lived in Palazzo
Misciattelli on Via del Corso,
and his sister Pauline who
married the Roman Prince
Camillo Borghese. The
museum has a cast of her
right breast, made by Canova
in 1805 as a study for his
statue of her as a reclining
Venus, now in the Museo
Borghese *(see p261)*. Portraits
and personal effects of other
members of the family are on
display, including uniforms,
court dresses, and a penny-
farthing bicycle that belonged
to Prince Eugène, the son of
Emperor Napoleon III.

The last male of the Roman
branch of the family was
Napoleon Charles, portrayed
in a late 19th-century painting
by Guglielmo de Sanctis. The
collection was assembled in
1927 by the Counts Primoli,
the sons of Charles's sister,
Carlotta Bonaparte.

Facade of San Salvatore in Lauro

The palace next door, in Via Zanardelli, houses the Racolta Praz, an impressive selection of over 1,000 *objets d'art*, paintings and pieces of furniture. Dating from the 17th and 18th century, they were collected by the art historian Mario Praz, who died in 1981.

Side relief of the Ludovisi Throne, Palazzo Altemps

Entrance to Museo Napoleonico

Hostaria dell'Orso ㉒

Via dei Soldati 25. **Map** 4 E3 & 11 C2. 🚌 70, 81, 87, 116, 186, 280, 492, 628. **Not open** to the public.

THIS ANCIENT INN has a 15th-century portico and loggia built with columns taken from Roman ruins. Legend has it that Dante once stayed here. Later visitors to Rome known to have used the inn include the 16th-century French writers Rabelais and Montaigne.

Palazzo Altemps ㉓

Via di Sant'Apollinare 44. **Map** 4 E3 & 11 C2. 📞 06-683 37 59. 🚌 70, 81, 87, 115, 116, 280, 492, 628. **Open** 9am–10pm Tue–Sat, 9am–2pm Sun. **Adm charge**.

AN EXTRAORDINARY collection of Classical sculpture is housed in this branch of the Museo Nazionale Romano.

Restored as a museum during the 1990s, the palazzo was originally built for Girolamo Riario, nephew of Pope Sixtus IV in 1480. The Riario coat of arms can still be seen in the janitor's room. In the popular uprising that followed the pope's death in 1484, the building was sacked and Girolamo fled the city.

In 1568 the palazzo was bought by Cardinal Marco Sittico Altemps. His family was of German origin – the name is an Italianization of Hohenems – and influential in the church. The palazzo was renovated by Martino Longhi the Elder in the 1570s. He added the great belvedere, crowned with obelisks and a marble unicorn.

The Altemps family were ostentatious collectors; the courtyard and its staircase are lined with ancient sculptures. These form part of the museum's collection, together with the Ludovisi collection of ancient sculptures, which was previously housed in the Museo Nazionale Romano in the Terms of Diocletian *(see p163)*. Located on the ground floor is the Greek statue of Athena Parthenos and the Dionysious group, a Roman copy of the Greek original. On the first floor, at the far end of the courtyard, visitors can admire the beautifully decorated Painted Loggia, dating from 1595. The Ludovisi throne, a Greek original

carved in the 5th century BC, is located on the same floor.

It is decorated with reliefs, one of which shows a young woman rising from the sea, who is thought to represent Aphrodite. In the room which is known as the Salone del Camino is the powerful statue *Galata's Suicide*, a marble copy of a group originally made in bronze. Nearby is the Ludovisi Sarcophague, dating from the 3rd century AD.

Galata's Suicide in the Palazzo Altemps

PIAZZA DI SPAGNA

B Y THE 16th century, the increase in numbers of visiting pilgrims and ecclesiastics was making life in Rome's already congested medieval centre unbearable. A new triangle of roads was built, still in place today, to help channel pilgrims as quickly as possible from the city's north gate, the Porta del Popolo, to the Vatican. By the 18th century hotels had sprung up all over

Lion fountain in Piazza del Popolo

the district. Today this attractive area offers much more: the superb works of Renaissance and Baroque art in Santa Maria del Popolo and Sant' Andrea delle Fratte, the magnificent reliefs of the restored Ara Pacis, art exhibitions in the Villa Medici, fine views of the city from the Spanish Steps and the Pincio Gardens and Rome's most famous shopping streets, centred around Via Condotti.

SIGHTS AT A GLANCE

Churches
Sant'Andrea delle Fratte ❶
Trinità dei Monti ❿
All Saints ⓬
Santa Maria dei Miracoli and Santa Maria in Montesanto ⓮
Santa Maria del Popolo pp138–9 ⓱
San Rocco ㉑
Santi Ambrogio e Carlo al Corso ㉒

Museums and Galleries
Keats-Shelley Memorial House ❼
Casa di Goethe ⓭

Historic Buildings
Palazzo di Propaganda Fide ❷
Villa Medici ⓫

Arches, Gates and Columns
Colonna dell'Immacolata ❸
Porta del Popolo ⓲

Historic Streets and Piazzas
Via Condotti ❹
Piazza di Spagna ❻

Spanish Steps ❾
Piazza del Popolo ⓰

Monuments and Tombs
Ara Pacis ⓳
Mausoleum of Augustus ⓴

Parks and Gardens
Pincio Gardens ⓯

Cafés and Restaurants
Caffè Greco ❺
Babington's Tea Rooms ❽

GETTING THERE

For Piazza di Spagna and the shops around Via Condotti, Spagna Metro station on line A is more convenient than the main bus routes along Via del Corso and Via del Tritone. Stay on until Flaminio Metro if you wish to visit Piazza del Popolo. For getting around locally, the 117 minibus, which goes up Via del Babuino, is very handy.

KEY

▦	Street-by-Street map
Ⓜ	Metro station
🅿	Parking
—	City Wall

SEE ALSO

- *Street Finder*, maps 4, 5
- *Where to Stay* pp294–5
- *Restaurants* pp310–11
- *Shops* pp322–37

The Spanish Steps leading up to the church of Trinità dei Monti

Street-by-Street: Piazza di Spagna

THE NETWORK of narrow streets between Piazza di Spagna and Via del Corso is one of the liveliest areas in Rome, drawing throngs of tourists and Romans to its discreet and elegant shops. In the 18th century the area was full of hotels for frivolous English aristocrats doing the Grand Tour, but there were also artists, writers and composers, who took the city's history and culture more seriously.

Caffè Greco
Busts and portraits recall the café's former artistic patrons ❺

★ **Piazza di Spagna**
For almost three centuries the square with its curious Barcaccia fountain in the centre has been the chief meeting place for visitors to Rome ❻

Via delle Carrozze took its name from the carriages of wealthy tourists that used to queue up there for repairs.

Via Condotti
This shadowy, narrow street has the smartest shops in one of the smartest shopping areas in the world ❹

Bulgari sells very expensive jewellery behind an austere shopfront in Via Condotti.

0 metres	75
0 yards	75

KEY

– – – Suggested route

Ⓜ Metro station

Trinità dei Monti
This 16th-century church has a spectacular setting and some of the finest views in Rome ⑩

Babington's Tea Rooms
English tourists are catered for in the style of the 1890s ⑧

LOCATOR MAP
See Central Rome Map pp12–13

Colonna dell'Immacolata
A Roman column supports a statue of the Virgin Mary ③

Palazzo di Propaganda Fide
This facade (1665) was one of the last works of the great Francesco Borromini ②

Sant'Andrea delle Fratte
Pasquale Marini painted The Redemption *to decorate the interior of Borromini's high dome in 1691* ①

★ **Keats-Shelley Memorial House**
The library is part of the small museum established in the house where the English poet Keats died in 1821 ⑦

★ **Spanish Steps**
Even obscured by crowds, the steps are one of the glories of late Baroque Rome ⑨

STAR SIGHTS

★ Piazza di Spagna

★ Keats-Shelley Memorial House

★ Spanish Steps

Sant'Andrea delle Fratte ❶

Via Sant'Andrea delle Fratte 1.
Map 5 A3. 06-679 31 91. 117.
Spagna. **Open** 6.30am–12.30pm, 4pm–7pm daily.

WHEN SANT'ANDREA delle Fratte was built in the 12th century, this was the northernmost edge of Rome. Though the church is now firmly embedded in the city, its name (*fratte* means thickets) recalls its original setting.

The church was completely rebuilt in the 17th century, partly by Borromini. His bell tower and dome, best viewed from the higher ground further up Via Capo le Case, are remarkable for the complex arrangement of concave and convex surfaces. The bell tower is particularly fanciful, with angel caryatids, flaming torches, and exaggerated

Angel by Bernini, Sant'Andrea delle Fratte

scrolls like semi-folded hearts supporting a spiky crown.

In 1842, the Virgin Mary appeared in the church to a Jewish banker, who promptly converted to Christianity and became a missionary. Inside, the chapel of the Miraculous Madonna is the first thing you notice. The church is better known, however, for the angels that Borromini's rival, Bernini, carved for the Ponte Sant'Angelo. Pope Clement IX declared they were too lovely to be exposed to the weather, so they remained with Bernini's family until 1729, when they were moved to the church.

Palazzo di Propaganda Fide ❷

Via di Propaganda 1. **Map** 5 A2.
06-69 88 01 01. 116, 117.
Spagna. **Open** by appt; write to Mons. Mottola, Piazza di Spagna 48.

THE POWERFUL JESUIT Congregation for the Propagation of the Faith was founded in 1622. Their headquarters had to be a remarkable building, and Bernini was commissioned. But Innocent X, who became pope in 1644, preferred the style of Borromini who was asked to continue. His extraordinary west facade facade, completed in 1662, must have outstripped everyone's expectations. It is striped with broad pilasters, between which the first-floor windows bend in, and the central bay bulges. A rigid band divides its floors, and the cornice above the convex central bay swerves inwards. The more you look at it, the more restless it seems; a sign perhaps of the increasing unhappiness of the architect who committed suicide in 1667.

Entrance to the Jesuit College

Colonna dell'Immacolata ❸

Piazza Mignanelli. **Map** 5 A2.
116, 117, 492. Spagna.

INAUGURATED IN 1857, the column commemorates Pope Pius IX's proclamation of the doctrine of the Immaculate Conception, holding that the Virgin Mary was the only human being ever to have been born "without the stain of original sin". The column itself dates from ancient, pagan Rome but is crowned with a statue of the Virgin Mary.

On the 8 December the fire brigade places a wreath at the foot of the column *(see p61)*.

Portrait of Pope Pius IX (reigned 1846–78)

Via Condotti ❹

Map 5 A2. 🚌 *81, 115, 116, 117.* Ⓜ *Spagna. See **Shops and Markets** pp322–33.*

NAMED AFTER the conduits that carried water to the Baths of Agrippa near the Pantheon, Via Condotti is now home to the most traditional of Rome's designer clothes shops. Stores selling shoes and other leather goods are also well represented. The street is extremely popular for early evening strolls, when elegant, perfumed ladies and men in immaculate suits and trench coats mingle with tourists in shorts and trainers.

Slightly younger designers such as Laura Biagiotti, Gianfranco Ferrè and the Fendi sisters have shops on the parallel Via Borgognona, while Valentino and Giorgio Armani both have shops on Via Condotti itself. Valentino has a second branch on Via Bocca di Leone, which crosses Via Condotti just below Piazza di Spagna, and Versace also has a shop here. Giorgio Armani has a second store on nearby Via del Babuino, among the discreet art galleries, exclusive antique shops and furnishing stores.

View along Via Condotti towards the Spanish Steps

Caffè Greco ❺

Via Condotti 86. **Map** 5 A2. 📞 *06-679 17 00.* 🚌 *117.* Ⓜ *Spagna. **Open** 8am–8.30pm daily. **Closed** 1 Jan, 1 May, two weeks in August, 25–26 Dec.* ♿

THIS CAFE was opened by a Greek (hence *greco*) in 1760, and throughout the 18th century was a favourite

The 230-year-old Caffè Greco

meeting place for foreign artists. Writers such as Keats, Byron and Goethe and composers like Liszt, Wagner and Bizet all breakfasted and drank here. So too did Casanova, and mad King Ludwig of Bavaria.

Today, Italians stand in the crowded foyer to sip a quick espresso coffee, and foreigners sit at tables in a cosy back room, against walls studded with the many portraits of the café's more illustrious customers.

Piazza di Spagna ❻

Map 5 A2. 🚌 *117.* Ⓜ *Spagna.*

SHAPED LIKE a crooked bow tie and surrounded by tall shuttered houses painted in muted shades of ochre, cream and russet, Piazza di Spagna (Spanish square) is crowded all day and (in summer) most of the night. It is the most famous square in Rome, and has long been the haunt of foreign visitors and expatriates.

In the 17th century Spain's ambassador to the Holy See had his headquarters on the square, and the area around it was deemed to be Spanish territory. Foreigners who unwittingly trespassed were liable to be dragooned into the Spanish army. In the 18th and 19th centuries Rome was almost as popular with visitors as it is today, and the

square stood at the heart of the city's main hotel district. Some of the travellers came in search of knowledge and artistic inspiration, but most were more interested in gambling, collecting ancient statues to adorn their family homes, and conducting love affairs with Italian women.

Not surprisingly, the wealthy travellers attracted hordes of beggars, who were usually supplied with tear-jerking letters by scribes who worked in the square.

The Fontana della Barcaccia in the square is the least showy of Rome's Baroque fountains, and it is often completely screened from view by people resting on its rim. It was designed either by the famous Gian Lorenzo Bernini or by his father Pietro. Because the pressure from the aqueduct that feeds the fountain is

Pope Urban VIII's arms, with the Barberini bees

extremely low there are no spectacular cascades or spurts of water. Instead, Bernini constructed a leaking boat – *barcaccia* means useless, old boat – which lies half submerged in a shallow pool.

The bees and suns that decorate the Fontana della Barcaccia are taken from the family coat of arms of Pope Urban VIII Barberini, who commissioned the fountain.

The Fontana della Barcaccia at the foot of the Spanish Steps

Bust of Shelley by Moses Ezekiel

Keats-Shelley Memorial House ⑦

Piazza di Spagna 26. **Map** 5 A2.
📞 06-678 42 35. 🚌 117.
Ⓜ Spagna. **Open** 9am–1pm,
3pm–6pm (Oct–Mar: 2.30pm–
5.30pm) Mon–Fri. **Closed** public
hols, 10 days in Aug. **Adm charge**.
🚫 📷 book in advance. ▯

I N NOVEMBER 1820 the English
poet John Keats came to
stay with his friend, the
painter Joseph Severn, in a
dusty pink house, the Casina
Rossa, on the corner of the
Spanish Steps. Suffering from
consumption, Keats had been
sent to Rome by his doctor, in
the hope that the mild, dry
climate would help the young
man's recovery. Depressed
because of scathing criticism
of his work and tormented by
his unrequited love for a
young girl named Fanny
Brawne, Keats died the
following February aged 25.

His death inspired his friend
and fellow poet, Percy Bysshe
Shelley, to write the poem
Mourn not for Adonais. In
July 1822 Shelley himself was
drowned in a boating accident
in the Gulf of La Spezia off
the coast of Liguria. Keats,
Shelley and Severn are all
buried in Rome's Protestant
Cemetery *(see p205)*.

In 1906 the house was
bought by an Anglo-American
association and preserved as
a memorial and library in
honour of English Romantic

poets. The relics include a
lock of Keats's hair, some
fragments of Shelley's bones
in a tiny urn and a garish
carnival mask picked up by
Lord Byron as a souvenir of a
trip to Venice. You can visit
the room where Keats died,
though all the original
furniture was burnt after his
death, on papal orders.

Babington's Tea Rooms ⑧

Piazza di Spagna 23. **Map** 5 A2.
📞 06-678 60 27. 🚌 117.
Ⓜ Spagna. **Open** 9am–8.30pm
daily. **Closed** 25 Dec. ♿

T HESE AUGUST, old-fashioned
tea rooms were opened in
1896 by two Englishwomen,
Anna Maria and Isabel Cargill
Babington, to serve homesick
British tourists with scones,
jam and pots of Earl Grey tea.
The food remains homely –
shepherd's pie and chicken
supreme for lunch, muffins
and cinnamon toast for tea –
although these days the menu
offers pancakes with maple
syrup for breakfast as well as
the traditional bacon and egg.

Purveyors of English breakfasts to
homesick exiles since 1896

Spanish Steps ⑨

Scalinata della Trinità dei Monti,
Piazza di Spagna. **Map** 5 A2. 🚌 117.
Ⓜ Spagna.

I N THE 17TH century the
French owners of Trinità dei
Monti decided to link the
church with Piazza di Spagna
by building a magnificent
new flight of steps. They also
planned to place an equestrian
statue of King Louis XIV at the
top. Pope Alexander VII Chigi
was not too happy at the

The Spanish Steps in spring with azaleas in full bloom

prospect of erecting a statue of a French monarch in the papal city, and the arguments continued until the 1720s when an Italian architect, Francesco de Sanctis, produced a design that satisfied both parties. The steps, completed in 1726, combine straight sections, curves and terraces to create one of the city's most dramatic and distinctive landmarks.

When the Victorian novelist Charles Dickens visited Rome, he reported that the Spanish Steps were the meeting place for artists' models, who would dress in colourful traditional costumes, hoping to catch the attention of a wealthy artist. The steps are now a popular place to sit, write postcards, take photos, flirt, busk or watch the passers-by, but eating there is not allowed.

Trinità dei Monti ⑩

Piazza della Trinità dei Monti. **Map** 5 A2. 📞 06-679 41 79. 🚌 117. Ⓜ Spagna. **Open** 7am–7pm daily (4–8pm in summer). ✝

Trinità dei Monti's bell towers

THE VIEWS of Rome from the platform in front of the twin bell towered facade of Trinità dei Monti are so beautiful that the church itself is often ignored. It is, however, unusual for Rome, for it was founded by the French in 1495, and although it was later badly damaged, there are still traces of attractive late Gothic latticework in the vaults of the transept. The interconnecting side chapels are decorated with Mannerist paintings, including two fine works by Daniele da Volterra.

19th-century engraving of the inner facade of the Villa Medici

A pupil of Michelangelo, Volterra had to paint clothes on the nudes in the *Last Judgment* in the Sistine Chapel, in response to the objections of Pope Pius IV.

Michelangelo's influence is obvious in the powerfully muscled bodies shown in the *Deposition* (second chapel on the left). The circles of gesturing figures and dancing angels surrounding the Virgin Mary in the *Assumption* (third chapel on the right), have more in common with the graceful style of Raphael.

Villa Medici ⑪

Accademia di Francia a Roma, Viale della Trinità dei Monti 1. **Map** 5 A2. 📞 06-676 11. 🚌 117. Ⓜ Spagna. **Accademia and gardens open** spring & autumn: Sun am. Otherwise variable, so phone first. **Exhibitions, concerts. Adm charge.** 📷

SUPERBLY POSITIONED on the Pincio hill above Piazza di Spagna, this 16th-century villa has kept the name it assumed when Cardinal Ferdinando de' Medici bought it in 1576. From the terrace you can look across the city to Castel Sant'Angelo, from where Queen Christina of Sweden is said to have fired the large cannon ball which now sits in the basin of the fountain.

The villa is now home to the French Academy. This was founded by Louis XIV in 1666 to give a few select painters the

Fontana del Sileno, on Via del Babuino since 1957

chance to study in Rome. Nicolas Poussin was one of the first advisers to the Academy, Ingres was a director and ex-students include Fragonard and Boucher.

After 1803 when the French Academy moved to the Villa Medici, musicians were also admitted; both Berlioz and Debussy came to Rome as students of the Academy.

All Saints ⑫

Via del Babuino 153B. **Map** 4 F2. 📞 06-360 01 881. 🚌 117. **Open** 9am–noon, 5.30–6.30pm daily (phone to check). ✝

IN 1816 THE POPE gave English residents and visitors the right to hold Anglican services in Rome, but it wasn't until the early 1880s that they acquired a site to build their own church. The architect was G E Street, best known in Britain for his Neo-Gothic churches and the London Law Courts. All Saints is also built in Victorian Neo-Gothic, and the interior, though splendidly decorated with different coloured Italian marbles, has a very English air. Street also designed St-Paul's-within-the-Walls in Via Nazionale, whose interior is a jewel of British Pre-Raphaelite art.

The street on which All Saints stands got its name from the Fontana del Sileno, known as Babuino (baboon) due to the sad condition in which it was found.

Casa di Goethe ⑬

18–20 Via del Corso. **Map** 4 F1. 📞
06-32 65 04 12. 🚌 95, 117, 490, 495,
628, 926. 🚊 225. Ⓜ Flaminio.
Open 11am–6pm Wed–Mon. **Adm
charge**. 📷

T HE GERMAN POET, dramatist
and novelist Johann
Wolfgang von Goethe (1749–
1832) lived in this house from
1786 until 1788 and worked
on a journal that eventually
formed part of his travel book
The Italian Journey. Rome's
noisy street life irritated him,
especially during Carnival time.
He was a little perturbed by
the number of murders in his
neighbourhood, but Rome
energised him and his book
became one of the most influential ever written about Italy.

Santa Maria dei Miracoli and Santa Maria in Montesanto ⑭

Piazza del Popolo. **Map** 4 F1. 🚌 95,
117, 490, 495, 628, 926. 🚊 225. Ⓜ
Flaminio. **Santa Maria dei Miracoli**
📞 06-361 02 50. **Open** 6am–1pm,
5–7.30pm Mon–Sat, 8.30am–
1.30pm, 5–8pm Sun & public hols.
⛪ & **Santa Maria in Montesanto**
📞 06-361 05 94. **Open** Jul–Sep
5–7pm daily. ⛪

T HE TWO CHURCHES at the
south end of Piazza del
Popolo were designed by the
architect Carlo Rainaldi
(1611–91), proof that he could
be as ingenious as his peers,
Bernini and Borromini. To
provide a focal point for the
piazza, the churches had to
look symmetrical, but
the site on the

Portrait of Goethe in the Roman countryside by Tischbein (1751–1821)

left was narrower than that on
the right. Rainaldi solved the
problem by giving Santa Maria
dei Miracoli (on the right) a
circular dome and Santa Maria
in Montesanto an oval one,
cleverly squeezing it into the
narrower site, while the sides
of the supporting drums that
face the piazza are identical.

Pincio Gardens ⑮

Il Pincio. **Map** 4 F1. 🚌 95, 117, 490,
495, 628, 926. 🚊 225. Ⓜ Flaminio.
♿

T HE PINCIO GARDENS lie
above Piazza del Popolo
on a hillside that has been so
skilfully terraced and richly
planted with trees that, from
below, the zig-zagging road
climbing to the gardens is
virtually invisible. In ancient
Roman times, there were
magnificent gardens on the
Pincio hill, but the present
gardens were designed
in the early 19th century
by Giuseppe Valadier
(who also
redesigned
the Piazza

The Pincio Gardens water clock

del Popolo). The broad
avenues, lined with umbrella
pines, palm trees and
evergreen oaks soon became
a fashionable place to stroll,
and even this century such
diverse characters as Gandhi
and Mussolini, Richard Strauss
and King Farouk of Egypt
patronized the Casina
Valadier, an exclusive café
and restaurant in the grounds.
 From the Pincio's main
square, Piazzale Napoleone I,
the panoramic views of Rome
stretch from the Monte Mario
to the Janiculum. For full
effect, approach the gardens
from the grounds of Villa
Borghese *(see pp258–9)*
above the Pincio, or along
Viale della Trinità dei Monti.

The twin churches of Santa Maria di Montesanto (left) and Santa Maria
dei Miracoli in a 19th-century view of Piazza del Popolo

The panorama is particularly beautiful at sunset, the traditional time for tourists to take a stroll in the gardens.

One of the most striking features of the park itself is an Egyptian-style obelisk which Emperor Hadrian erected on the tomb of his favourite, the beautiful male slave Antinous. After the slave's premature death (according to some accounts he died saving the emperor's life), Hadrian deified him.

The 19th-century water clock on Via dell'Orologio was designed by a Dominican monk. It was displayed at the Paris Exhibition of 1889.

Traditional carnival band in Piazza del Popolo

The Casina Valadier restaurant in the Pincio Gardens

Piazza del Popolo ⑯

Map 4 F1. 🚌 95, 117, 490, 495, 628, 926. 🚋 225. Ⓜ Flaminio.

A VAST COBBLED OVAL standing at the apex of the triangle of roads known as the Trident, Piazza del Popolo forms a grand symmetrical antechamber to the heart of Rome. Twin Neo-Classical facades stand on either side of the Porta del Popolo; an Egyptian obelisk rises in the centre; and the matching domes and porticoes of Santa Maria dei Miracoli and Santa Maria di Montesanto flank the beginning of Via del Corso.

Although it is now one of the most unified squares in Rome, Piazza del Popolo evolved gradually over the centuries. In 1589 the great town-planning pope, Sixtus V, had the obelisk erected in the centre by Domenico Fontana.

Over 3,000 years old, the obelisk was originally brought to Rome by Augustus to adorn the Circus Maximus after the conquest of Egypt. Almost a century later Pope Alexander VII commissioned Carlo Rainaldi to build the twin Santa Marias.

In the 19th century the piazza was turned into a grandiose oval by Giuseppe Valadier, the designer of the Pincio Gardens. He also encased Santa Maria del Popolo in a Neo-Classical shell to make its south facade fit in better with the overall appearance of the piazza.

In contrast to the piazza's air of ordered rationalism, many of the events staged here were barbaric. In the 18th and 19th centuries, public executions were held in Piazza del Popolo, often as part of the celebration of Carnival. Condemned men were sometimes hammered to death by repeated blows to the temples. The last time a criminal was executed in this way was in 1826, even though the guillotine had by then been adopted as a more scientific means of execution.

The riderless horse races from the piazza down Via del Corso were scarcely more humane: the performance of the runners was enhanced by feeding the horses stimulants, wrapping them in nail-studded ropes, and letting off fireworks at their heels.

Santa Maria del Popolo ⑰

See pp138–9.

Porta del Popolo ⑱

Between Piazzale Flaminio and Piazza del Popolo. **Map** 4 F1. 🚌 95, 117, 490, 495, 628, 926. 🚋 225. Ⓜ Flaminio.

T HE VIA FLAMINIA, built in 220 BC to connect Rome with Italy's Adriatic coast, enters the city at Porta del Popolo, a grand 16th-century gate built on the orders of Pope Pius IV Medici. The architect, Nanni di Baccio Bigio, modelled it on a Roman triumphal arch. The outer face has statues of St Peter and St Paul on either side and a huge Medici coat of arms above.

A century later, Pope Alexander VII commissioned Bernini to decorate the inner face to celebrate the arrival in Rome of Queen Christina of Sweden. Lesser visitors were often held up while customs officers rifled their luggage. The only way to speed things up was with a bribe.

Porta del Popolo's central arch

Santa Maria del Popolo ⑰

O NE OF ROME'S greatest stores of artistic
treasures, this early Renaissance
church was commissioned by Pope
Sixtus IV della Rovere in 1472. Among
the artists who worked on the building
were Andrea Bregno and Pinturicchio.
Later additions were made by Bramante
and Bernini. Many illustrious families
have chapels here, all decorated with
appropriate splendour. The Della Rovere
Chapel has delightful Pinturicchio frescoes,
the Cerasi Chapel has two Caravaggio
masterpieces, the *Conversion of St Paul*
and the *Crucifixion of St Peter*, but the
finest of all is the Chigi Chapel designed
by Raphael for his patron,
the banker Agostino
Chigi. The most
striking of the
church's many
Renaissance
tombs are the
two by Andrea
Sansovino behind
the main altar.

★ Chigi Chapel
*Raphael designed
this chapel, which
has an altarpiece
by Sebastiano del
Piombo. Niches on
either side of the
altar house sculp-
tures by Bernini
and Lorenzetto.
Mosaics in the
dome show God as
creator of the seven
heavenly
bodies.*

Kneeling Skeleton
*This floor mosaic of
the figure of death
was added to the
Chigi Chapel in the
17th century.*

NERO'S GHOST
Nero lived on in the imagination of
the people long after the fall of the
Roman Empire. In the Middle Ages
a legend arose that a walnut tree
growing here on the spot where his
ashes were buried was haunted by
the emperor. Ravens roosting in the
tree were thought to be demons
tormenting him for his hideous crimes.
When the first church
was built here in
1099 by Pope
Paschal II, the
tree was cut
down, supposedly
putting an end to
the supernatural
events that had
terrified local people.

Entrance

Cybo
Chap

STAR FEATURES

★ Chigi Chapel

★ Caravaggio Paintings
in Cerasi Chapel

★ Delphic Sibyl

**Della Rovere
Chapel**
*Pinturicchio painted
the frescoes in the
lunettes and the
Nativity above the
altar in 1490.*

The altarpiece of *The Assumption* is by Annibale Carracci (1540–1609).

★ **Caravaggio Paintings in Cerasi Chapel**
One of two Caravaggios in the Cerasi Chapel, The Crucifixion of St Peter uses dramatic foreshortening to highlight the sheer effort involved in turning the saint's crucifix upside down.

Stained Glass
In 1509 French artist Guillaume de Marcillat was invited to provide Rome's first two stained-glass windows.

The Tomb of Ascanio Sforza, who died in 1505, is by Andrea Sansovino.

★ **Delphic Sibyl**
This is one of a series of frescoes by Pinturicchio, some Classical and others Biblical, painted in 1508–10 to decorate the ceiling of the apse.

The altar houses the 13th-century painting known as the *Madonna del Popolo*.

The Tomb of Giovanni della Rovere (1483) is by pupils of Andrea Bregno.

TIMELINE

1090	1200	1300	1400	1500

1213–27 Church enlarged under Gregory IX

Pinturicchio (c1454–1513)

1485–9 Della Rovere Chapel painted by Pinturicchio

1513–16 Raphael designs and executes Chigi Chapel

1099 Paschal II builds chapel over tombs of the Domitia family (which included Nero) in honour of the Madonna

Pope Paschal II (reigned 1099–1118)

1472–8 Sixtus IV builds church (one of the first Renaissance churches in Rome)

1473 Main altar built

1530–34 Chigi Chapel altarpiece built by Sebastiano del Piombo

Ara Pacis ⓳

Via di Ripetta. **Map** 4 F2.
Ⓒ 06-68 80 68 48. 🚌 70, 81, 115,
186. **Open** 9am–4.30pm Tue–Sat,
9am–1pm Sun. **Adm charge**.

Frieze on south wall showing procession with the family of Augustus

RECONSTRUCTED at great
expense over a period of
many years, the Ara Pacis
(Altar of Peace) is one of the
most significant monuments
of ancient Rome. It celebrates
the peace created throughout
the Mediterranean area by
Emperor Augustus after his
victorious campaigns in Gaul

Marcus Agrippa (right)

and Spain. The monument was
commissioned by the Senate
in 13 BC and completed four
years later. It was positioned so
that the shadow of the huge
obelisk sundial on Campus
Martius (see p113) would fall
upon it on Augustus' birthday.
It is a square enclosure on a
low platform with the altar in
the centre. All surfaces are
decorated with magnificent
friezes and reliefs carved
in Carrara marble, most
likely by Greek craftsmen.
The reliefs on the north
and south walls depict a
procession that took
place on 4 July 13 BC,

in which the members of the
emperor's family can be
identified, ranked by their
position in the succession.
The heir apparent at the time
was Marcus Agrippa, husband
of Augustus's daughter Julia.
All the portraits in the relief
are carved with extraordi-
narily effective realism, even
the innocent toddler clinging
to his mother's skirts.
  The tale of the rediscovery
of the Ara Pacis dates back to
the 16th century, when the
first panels were unearthed.
One section ended up in
Paris, another in Florence.
Further discoveries were
made in the late 19th century,

when archaeologists finally
realized just what they had
found. What we see today
has all been pieced together
since 1938, in part original, in
part facsimile. In 1999 works
began to further organize the
whole archeological area.

**Livia (right), Augustus's wife and
the mother of Tiberius, with an
unidentified member of the family**

South wall

East wall

The altar was used
once a year for a
sacrifice on the
anniversary of the
monument's
inauguration.

West wall

North wall

An acanthus frieze
runs around the
lower half of the
outside wall.

**Augustus's young
grandson, Lucius**

Mausoleum of Augustus 20

Piazza Augusto Imperatore.
Map 4 F2. 🚌 *32, 81, 117, 492, 628, 913, 926.* **Open** *by appt only: permit needed (see p367).*

NOW JUST a weedy mound ringed with cypresses and sadly strewn with litter, this was once the most prestigious burial place in Rome. Augustus had the mausoleum built in 28 BC, the year he became sole ruler, as a tomb for himself and his descendants. The circular building was 87 m (270 ft) in diameter with two obelisks (now in Piazza del Quirinale and Piazza dell'Esquilino) at the entrance.

Inside were four concentric passageways linked by corridors where the urns containing the ashes of the Imperial family were placed. The first to be buried there was Augustus's favourite nephew, Marcellus, who had married Julia, the emperor's daughter. He died in 23 BC, possibly poisoned by Augustus's second wife Livia, who felt that her son, Tiberius, would make a more reliable emperor. When Augustus died in AD 14, his ashes were placed in the mausoleum, Tiberius duly became emperor, and dynastic poisonings continued to fill the family vault with urns.

This sinister monument was later used as a medieval fortress, a vineyard, a private garden, and even, in the 18th century, as an auditorium and a theatre.

Augustus, the first Roman emperor

Madonna, San Rocco and Sant'Antonio with Victims of the Plague by Il Baciccia (1639–1709)

San Rocco 21

Largo San Rocco 1. **Map** 4 F2.
📞 *06-689 64 16.* 🚌 *32, 81, 117, 492, 628, 913, 926.* **Open** *7.30am–9am, 5–7.45pm Mon–Sat, 9am–1pm, 5–7.45pm Sun.* **Closed** *17–31 Aug.* 🔲

THIS CHURCH, with a restrained Neo-Classical facade by Giuseppe Valadier, the designer of Piazza del Popolo, began life as the chapel of a 16th-century hospital with beds for 50 men – San Rocco was a healer of the plague-stricken. A maternity wing was added for the wives of Tiber bargees to save them from having to give birth in the insanitary conditions of a boat. The hospital came to be used by unmarried mothers, and one section was set aside for women who wished to be unknown. They were even permitted to wear a veil for the duration of their stay. Unwanted children were sent to an orphanage, and if any mothers or children died they were buried in anonymous graves. The hospital was abandoned in the early 20th century, and demolished in the 1930s during the excavation of the Mausoleum of Augustus.

In the church sacristy is an interesting Baroque altarpiece (c.1660) by Il Baciccia, the artist who decorated the ceiling of the Gesù *(see pp114–15).*

Santi Ambrogio e Carlo al Corso 22

Via del Corso 437. **Map** 4 F2.
📞 *06-687 83 35.* 🚌 *32, 81, 117, 492, 628, 913, 926.* **Open** *7.30am–12.30pm, 5–7pm (Oct–Mar: 7.30pm) daily. Ring porter's door to left of church if closed.* 🚫

THIS CHURCH belonged to the Lombard community in Rome, and is dedicated to two canonized bishops of Milan, Lombardy's capital. In 1471, Pope Sixtus IV gave the Lombards a church which they dedicated to Sant'Ambrogio, who died in 397. Then in 1610, when Carlo Borromeo was canonized, the church was rebuilt in his honour. Most of the new church was the work of father and son, Onorio and Martino Longhi, but the fine dome is by Pietro da Cortona. The altarpiece by Carlo Maratta (1625–1713) is the *Gloria dei Santi Ambrogio e Carlo.* An ambulatory leads behind the altar to a chapel housing the the heart of San Carlo in a richly decorated reliquary.

Statue of San Carlo by Attilio Selva (1888–1970) behind the apse of Santi Ambrogio e Carlo

CAMPO DE' FIORI

BETWEEN Corso Vittorio Emanuele II and the Tiber, the city displays many distinct personalities. The open-air market of Campo de' Fiori preserves the lively, bohemian atmosphere of the medieval inns that once flourished here, while the area also contains Renaissance palazzi, such as Palazzo Farnese and Palazzo Spada, where powerful Roman families built

18th-century Madonna in Campo de' Fiori

their fortress-like houses near the route of papal processions. Close by, overlooking the picturesque Tiber Island, lies the former Jewish Ghetto, where many traces of daily life from past centuries can still be seen. The Portico of Octavia and the Theatre of Marcellus are spectacular examples of the city's many-layered history, built up over the half-ruined remains of ancient Rome.

SIGHTS AT A GLANCE

Churches and Temples
Santissima Trinità dei Pellegrini **5**
Santa Maria dell'Orazione e Morte **7**
San Girolamo della Carità **9**
Sant'Eligio degli Orefici **10**
Santa Maria in Monserrato **11**
San Carlo ai Catinari **18**
Santa Maria in Campitelli **20**
San Nicola in Carcere **21**
San Giovanni dei Fiorentini **29**

Museums and Galleries
Palazzo Spada **6**
Piccola Farnesina **14**
Burcardo Theatre Museum **15**

Historic Buildings
Palazzo Pio Righetti **2**
Palazzo del Monte di Pietà **3**
Palazzo Farnese **8**
Palazzo Ricci **12**
Palazzo della Cancelleria **13**
Casa di Lorenzo Manilio **25**
Palazzo Cenci **26**

Fountains
Fontana delle Tartarughe **19**

Historic Streets and Piazzas
Campo de' Fiori **1**
Tiber Island **27**
Ghetto and Synagogue **24**
Via Giulia **28**

Famous Theatres
Teatro Argentina **16**

Ancient Sites
Sotterranei di San Paolo alla Regola **4**
Area Sacra dell'Argentina **17**
Theatre of Marcellus **22**
Portico of Octavia **23**

GETTING THERE
Only bus 116 can manage the narrow streets around Campo de' Fiori, but many routes, including the 46, 56, 60 and 64, and tram 8, converge on Largo Argentina. This is a useful starting point for exploring the area. Only the 46, 62 and 64 run along the full length of Corso Vittorio Emanuele II while 23 and 280 run along Lungotevere.

SEE ALSO

KEY
Street-by-Street map

P Parking

Fruit stalls beneath the statue of Giordano Bruno in the Campo de' Fiori market

Street-by-Street: Campo de' Fiori

THIS FASCINATING PART of Renaissance Rome is also an exciting area for shopping and night life, centred on the market square of Campo de' Fiori. Its stalls supply many nearby restaurants and young people shop for clothes in Via dei Giubbonari. Popular reasonably-priced restaurants and pizzerias keep the area alive late into the night. By day there are great buildings to admire, though few are open to the public. Two exceptions are the Piccola Farnesina with its collection of Classical statues and Palazzo Spada, home to many important paintings.

Sant'Eligio degli Orefici
A small Renaissance church designed by Raphael is concealed behind a later facade ⑩

Palazzo Ricci
Painted Classical scenes were a favourite form of decoration for the facades of Renaissance houses ⑫

San Girolamo della Carità
The chief attraction of this church is Borromini's fabulous Spada Chapel ⑨

Santa Maria in Monserrato
This church, which has strong connections with Spain, houses a Bernini bust of Cardinal Pedro Foix de Montoya ⑪

Santa Maria dell'Orazione e Morte
A pair of dramatic winged skulls flank the doorway to this church dedicated to the burial of the dead ⑦

Palazzo Farnese
Michelangelo and other great artists helped create this monumental Renaissance palazzo ⑧

KEY

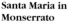

– – – Suggested route

0 metres   75

0 yards   75

Palazzo della Cancelleria
The papal administration ran the affairs of the church from this vast building ⑬

Piccola Farnesina
This plaque honours Giovanni Barracco. His sculpture collection is housed in the palazzo ⑭

LOCATOR MAP
See Central Rome Map pp12–13

★ **Campo de' Fiori**
The colourful market makes this one of the city's most entertaining squares ❶

Palazzo Pio Righetti
Heraldic eagles stare down from the pediments of the palazzo's windows ❷

Palazzo del Monte di Pietà
This was a papal institution, where the poor pawned their possessions in order to borrow small sums of money ❸

Sotterranei di San Paolo alla Regola
Remains of a Roman house have survived in the basement of an old palace ❹

★ **Palazzo Spada**
The picture gallery houses a collection started by two wonderfully eccentric 17th-century cardinals ❻

Santissima Trinità dei Pellegrini
The principal role of this church was one of charity, looking after poor pilgrims arriving in Rome ❺

STAR SIGHTS

★ Campo de' Fiori

★ Palazzo Spada

Campo de' Fiori ❶

Piazza Campo de' Fiori. **Map** 4 E4 & 11 C4. 🚌 *116 and routes to Largo di Torre Argentina. See **Markets** p338.*

T HE CAMPO DE' FIORI (field of flowers), once a meadow, occupies the site of the open space facing the Theatre of Pompey. Cardinals and noblemen used to rub shoulders with fishmongers and foreigners in the piazza's market, making it one of the liveliest areas of medieval and Renaissance Rome. Today's market retains much of the traditional lively atmosphere.

In the centre of the square is a statue of the philosopher Giordano Bruno, who was burnt at the stake for heresy on this spot in 1600. The hooded figure is a grim reminder of the executions that were held here.

The piazza was surrounded by inns for pilgrims and other travellers. Many of these were once owned by the successful 15th-century courtesan, Vannozza Catanei, mistress of Pope Alexander VI Borgia. On the corner between the piazza and Via del Pellegrino you can see Catanei's shield, which she had decorated with her own coat of arms and those of her husband and her lover, the Borgia pope.

Market stalls in Campo de' Fiori

Palazzo Pio Righetti ❷

Piazza del Biscione 89. **Map** 4 E5 & 11 C4. 🚌 *116 and routes to Largo Torre Argentina.* **Not open to the public.**

T HE VAST 17th-century Palazzo Pio Righetti was built over the ruined Theatre of Pompey. The windows of

Window pediment with heraldic lion and pine cones, Palazzo Pio Righetti

the palazzo are decorated with lions and pine cones from the coat of arms of the Pio da Carpi family who lived here.

The curve of the Theatre of Pompey, completed in 55 BC, is followed by Via di Grotta Pinta. This was Rome's first permanent theatre built of stone and concrete. In places, for example the basement of the Pancrazio restaurant, you can see early examples of *opus reticulatum* – small square blocks of tufa (porous rock) set diagonally as a facing for a concrete wall.

Palazzo del Monte di Pietà ❸

Piazza del Monte di Pietà 33. **Map** 4 E5 & 11 C4. 📞 *06-51 72 66 10.* 🚌 *116 and routes to Largo di Torre Argentina.* 🚇 *8.* **Chapel open** *7.40am–2pm Tue–Fri.* **Closed** *public hols.* **Adm** *by appt or on request to porter.*

T HE MONTE, as it is known, is a public institution, founded in 1539 by Pope Paul III Farnese as a pawnshop to staunch the usury then rampant in the city. The building still has offices and auction rooms for the sale of unredeemed goods.

The stars with diagonal bands on the huge central plaque decorating the facade are the coat of arms of Pope Clement VIII Aldobrandini, added when Carlo Maderno enlarged the palace in the 17th century. The clock on the left was added later.

Within, the chapel is a jewel of Baroque architecture, adorned with gilded stucco, marble panelling and reliefs. The decoration makes a perfect setting for the sculptures by Domenico Guidi – a bust of San Carlo Borromeo and a

relief of the *Pietà*. There are also splendid reliefs by Giovanni Battista Théudon and Pierre Legros of Biblical scenes illustrating the charitable nature of the institution.

Relief by Théudon of *Joseph Lending Grain to the Egyptians* in Palazzo del Monte di Pietà

Sotterranei di San Paolo alla Regola ❹

Via di San Paolo alla Regola. **Map** 11 C5. 📞 *06-67 10 38 19.* 🚌 *23, 116, 280 and routes to Largo di Torre Argentina.* 🚇 *8.* **Adm** *by request in advance to Ripartizione del Comune di Roma (06-67 10 38 19).*

A N OLD PALACE hides the perfectly conserved remains of an ancient Roman house, dating from the 2nd–3rd centuries. Restoration works are being carried out in order to open this site to the public, but at present it is only possible to visit by special arrangement.

A ramp leads down well below today's street level, to reveal the locations of shops of the time. One level above is the Stanza della Colonna, at one time an open courtyard, with traces of frescoes and mosaics on its walls.

Guido Reni's *Holy Trinity*, in Santissima Trinità dei Pellegrini

Santissima Trinità dei Pellegrini ⑤

Piazza della Trinità dei Pellegrini. **Map** 4 E5 & 11 C5. ◖ 06-686 84 51. ▭ 23, 116, 280 and routes to Largo di Torre Argentina. ▦ 8. **Currently closed** for restoration; phone to check.

THE CHURCH WAS donated in the 16th century to a charitable organization founded by San Filippo Neri to care for the poor and sick, in particular the thousands of paupers who flocked in pilgrimage to Rome during the special holy years known as Jubilees.

The 18th-century facade has niches with statues of the Evangelists by Bernardino Ludovisi. The interior, with Corinthian columns, ends in a horseshoe vault and apse, dominated by Guido Reni's striking altarpiece of the *Holy Trinity* (1625). The frescoes in the lantern are also by Reni.

Other interesting paintings include *St Gregory the Great Freeing Souls from Purgatory*, by Baldassarre Croce (third chapel to the left); Cavalier d'Arpino's *Virgin and Saints* (second chapel to the left); and a painting by Borgognone (1677) of the Virgin and recently canonized saints, including San Carlo Borromeo and San Filippo Neri. In the sacristy are depictions of the nobility washing the feet of pilgrims, a custom which was started by San Filippo.

Palazzo Spada ⑥

Piazza Capo di Ferro 13. **Map** 4 E5 & 11 C4. ◖ 06-686 11 58. ▭ 23, 116, 280 and routes to Largo di Torre Argentina. ▦ 8. **Gallery open** 9am–7pm Tue–Sat, 9am–1.30pm Sun. **Adm charge**. ⊘ ◖ ▢ **Adm** to other rooms on written request to Ufficio Personale, Consiglio di Stato (at Palazzo Spada). ⊘

THIS MAJESTIC PALAZZO, built around 1550 for Cardinal Capo di Ferro, has an elegant stuccoed courtyard and facade decorated with reliefs evoking Rome's glorious past.

Cardinal Bernardino Spada, who lived here in the 17th century with his brother Virginio (also a cardinal), hired Bernini and Borromini to work on the building. The brothers' whimsical delight in false perspectives resulted in a colonnaded gallery by Borromini that appears four times longer than it really is.

The cardinals also amassed a superb private collection of paintings. These are now displayed in the Galleria Spada together with some Classical statues and 18th-century furniture. The wide range of artists represented includes Rubens, Dürer and Guido Reni. Works to look out for by lesser artists include *The Visitation* by Andrea del Sarto (1486–1530), *Cain and Abel* by Giovanni Lanfranco (1582–1647) and *The Death of Dido* by Guercino (1591–1666).

Santa Maria dell'Orazione e Morte ⑦

Via Giulia. **Map** 4 E5 & 11 B4. ◖ 06-68 80 27 15. ▭ 23, 116, 280. **Open** for mass 6pm Sun, public hols. ✠

A PIOUS CONFRATERNITY was formed here in the 16th century to collect the bodies of the unknown dead and give them a Christian burial. The theme of death is stressed in this church, dedicated to St Mary of Prayer and Death. The doors and windows of Ferdinando Fuga's dramatic Baroque facade are decorated with winged skulls. Above the central entrance there is a *clepsydra* (an ancient hourglass) – symbolic of death.

Offertory box in Santa Maria dell'Orazione e Morte

Palazzo Farnese ⑧

Piazza Farnese. **Map** 4 E5 & 11 B4. ▭ 23, 116, 280 and routes to Largo di Torre Argentina. ▦ 8. **Not open** to the public.

THE PROTOTYPE for many princely palaces, the imposing Palazzo Farnese was originally built for Cardinal Alessandro Farnese (who became Pope Paul III in 1534). He commissioned the greatest artists to work on it, starting with Antonio da Sangallo the Younger as architect in 1517. Michelangelo, who took over after him, contributed the great cornice and central window of the main facade, and the third level of the courtyard.

Michelangelo had a plan for the Farnese gardens to be connected by a bridge to the Farnese home in Trastevere, Villa Farnesina *(see pp220–21)*. The elegant arch spanning Via Giulia belongs to this sadly unrealized scheme. The palazzo was completed in 1589, on a less ambitious scale, by Giacomo della Porta. It is now the home of the French Embassy, which moved in already in 1635.

Majestic facade of Palazzo Farnese

Spada Chapel in San Girolamo

San Girolamo della Carità **9**

Via di Monserrato 62A. **Map** 4 E5 & 11 B4. **(** 06-687 97 86. **[bus]** 23, 46, 62, 64, 116, 280. **Open** 10am–noon Wed, 10.30am–11.30am Sun. **[†]**

THE CHURCH was built on the site of the home of San Filippo Neri, the 16th-century saint from Tuscany. This warm, patient character renewed Rome's spiritual and cultural life by his friendly, open approach to religion. He would have loved the frolicking putti shown surrounding his statue, in his chapel, reminding him of the Roman urchins he had cared for during his lifetime.

The breathtaking Spada Chapel was designed by Borromini, and is unique both

Statue of San Filippo Neri by Pierre Legros

as a work of art and as an illustration of the spirit of the Baroque age. All architectural elements are concealed so that the space of the chapel's interior is defined solely by decorative marblework and statues. Veined jasper and precious multicoloured marbles are sculpted to imitate flowery damask and velvet hangings. Even the altar rail is a long swag of jasper drapery held up by a pair of kneeling angels with wooden wings.

Although there are memorials to former members of the Spada family, oddly there is no indication as to which of the Spadas was responsible for endowing the chapel. It was probably art-lover Cardinal Virginio Spada, a follower of San Filippo Neri.

Sant'Eligio degli Orefici **10**

Via di Sant'Eligio 8A. **Map** 4 D4 & 11 B4. **(** 06-686 82 60. **[bus]** 23, 46, 62, 64, 116, 280. **Open** 10.30am–noon Mon, Tue, Wed & Fri (phone to check). **Closed** Aug & Sep. **[†]**

THE NAME of the church still records the fact that it was commissioned by a rich corp-oration of goldsmiths (orefici) in the early 16th century. The original design was by Raphael, who, like his master Bramante, had acquired a sense of the grandiose from the remains of Roman antiquity. The influence of some of Bramante's works, such as the choir of Santa Maria del Popolo (see p138–9), is evident in the simple way the arches and pilasters define the structure of the walls.

The cupola of Sant' Eligio is attributed to Baldassarre Peruzzi, while the facade was added in the early 17th century by Flaminio Ponzio. Among the various 16th-century painters who decorated the interior was Taddeo Zuccari, who worked on Palazzo Farnese (see p147).

Santa Maria in Monserrato **11**

Via di Monserrato. **Map** 4 E4 & 11 B3. **(** 06-686 58 61. **[bus]** 23, 46, 62, 64, 116, 280. **Closed** to the public except by special permission: apply to the rector at Via Giulia 151. **[†]**

An early bust by Bernini of Cardinal Pedro Foix de Montoya

THE ORIGINS of the Spanish national church in Rome go back to 1506, when a hospice for Spanish pilgrims was begun by a brotherhood of the Virgin of Montserrat in Catalonia. Inside is Annibale Carracci's painting San Diego de Alcalà and, in the third chapel on the left, a copy of a Sansovino statue of St James. Some beautiful 15th-century tombs by Andrea Bregno and Luigi Capponi are in the court-yard and side chapels. Don't miss Bernini's bust of Pedro Foix de Montoya, the church's benefactor, in the annexe.

San Diego by Annibale Carracci

Palazzo Ricci ⑫

Piazza de' Ricci. **Map** 4 D4 & 11 B4.
🚌 23, 46, 62, 64, 116, 280, 870.
Not open to the public.

Palazzo Ricci was famous for its frescoed facade – now rather faded – originally painted in the 16th century by Polidoro da Caravaggio, a follower of Raphael.

In Renaissance Rome it was common to commission artists to decorate the outsides of their houses with heroes of Classical antiquity. A fresco by a leading artist such as Polidoro, reputedly the inventor of this style of painting, was a conspicuous status symbol, in the nobility's attempts to outshine each-other with their palazzi.

Part of the frescoed facade of Palazzo Ricci

Palazzo della Cancelleria ⑬

Piazza della Cancelleria. **Map** 4 E4 & 11 C3. 📞 06-69 88 48 16. 🚌 46, 62, 64, 70, 81, 87, 116, 492. **Open** with permit from Vatican only.

The palazzo, a supreme example of the confident architecture of the Early Renaissance, was begun in 1485. It was financed partly with the gambling winnings of Cardinal Raffaele Riario. Roses, the emblem of the Riario family, adorn the vaults and capitals of the beautiful Doric courtyard. The palazzo's interior was decorated after the Sack of Rome in 1527. Giorgio Vasari boasted that he had completed work on one enormous room in just 100 days; Michelangelo allegedly retorted: "It looks like it." Other Mannerist artists, Perin del Vaga and Francesco Salviati, frescoed the rooms of the cardinal in charge of the Papal Chancellery, the office that gave the palazzo its name when it was installed here by Pope Leo X. On the right of the main entrance is the unobtrusive and rather quaint church of San Lorenzo in Damaso, founded by Pope Damasus who reigned 366–384. It was reconstructed in 1495 and although Bernini made alterations to the transept and apse in 1638, it was later restored to its 15th-century lines.

Its surrounding porticoes housed libraries which held the first Papal Archives.

Piccola Farnesina ⑭

Corso Vittorio Emanuele II 166. **Map** 4 E4 & 11 C3. 📞 06-68 80 68 48. 🚌 46, 62, 64, 70, 81, 87, 116, 492. **Open** 9am–7pm Tue–Sat, 9am–1pm Sun & public hols. **Closed** 1 Jan, 1 May, 25 Dec. **Adm charge.** 🚫

This delightful miniature palazzo acquired its name from the lilies decorating its cornices. These were mistakenly identified as part of the Farnese family crest. In fact they were part of the coat of arms of a French clergyman, Thomas Le Roy, for whom the palazzo was built in 1523.

The entrance is in a new facade built to overlook Corso Vittorio Emanuele II when the road was constructed at the turn of the century. The original facade on the left of today's entrance is attributed to Antonio da Sangallo the Younger. Note the asymmetrical arrangement of its windows and ledges. The elegant central courtyard also retains its original appearance. The Piccola Farnesina now houses the Museo Barracco, a collection of ancient sculpture assembled during the last century by the politician Baron Giovanni Barracco. A bust of the baron

Lily on facade of the Piccola Farnesina

can be seen in the courtyard. The collection includes an ancient Egyptian relief of the scribe Nofer, some Assyrian artifacts and, among the Etruscan exhibits, a delicate ceramic female head. On the first floor is the Greek collection with a head of Apollo.

Inner courtyard, Piccola Farnesina

Burcardo Theatre Museum ⑮

Via del Sudario 44. **Map** 4 F4 & 12 D4. 📞 06-681 94 71. 🚌 46, 56, 60, 62, 64, 70, 81, 186, 492. 🚋 8. **Closed** for restoration until further notice. **Library open** 9am–4pm Tue & Thu, 9am–1.30pm Mon, Wed & Fri.

This late 15th-century house belonged to Johannes Burckhardt, chamberlain to Pope Alexander VI Borgia and author of a diary of Rome under the Borgias. His house now holds Rome's most complete collection of theatre literature, plus Chinese puppets and comic masks from the various regions of Italy.

Teatro Argentina ⑯

Via di Torre Argentina. **Map** 4 F4 &
12 D4. ☎ 06-68 40 00 11. 🚌 46,
56, 60, 62, 64, 70, 81, 87, 186, 492.
🚋 8. **Plays** performed Oct–Jun.
See **Entertainment** pp346–7.

Oᴺᴇ ᴏғ ʀᴏᴍᴇ'ѕ most
important theatres was
founded by the powerful
Sforza Cesarini family in 1732,
though the facade dates from
a century later. Many famous
operas were first performed
here. In 1816, for example,
the theatre saw the ill-fated
début of Rossini's *Barber of
Seville*, during which the
composer insulted the
unappreciative audience, who
then pursued him, enraged,
through the streets of Rome.
Many of Verdi's masterpieces
were first produced here.

Detail of facade, Teatro Argentina

Area Sacra dell'Argentina ⑰

Largo di Torre Argentina. **Map** 4 F4 &
12 D4. 🚌 46, 56, 60, 62, 64, 70,
81, 87, 186, 492. 🚋 8. **Open** by
appt only: permit needed (see p367).

Tʜᴇ ʀᴇᴍᴀɪɴѕ of four temples
were discovered here
during rebuilding in the 1920s.
Dating from the Republican
era, they are among the oldest
to have been found in Rome.
They are known as A, B, C
and D. The oldest (temple C)
dates from the early 3rd
century BC. It was placed on
a high platform preceded by
an altar and is typical of Italic
temple plans as opposed to
the Greek model. Temple A
is from later on in the 3rd
century BC. In medieval times
the small church of San Nicola
de' Cesarini was built over its
podium. The remains of its
two apses are still visible.

San Carlo at Prayer by Guido Reni

The north column stumps
belonged to a great portico,
the Hecatostylum (portico of
100 columns). In Imperial
times two marble lavatories
were built here – the remains
of one are visible behind
temple A. Behind temples B
and C are remains of a great
platform of tufa blocks. These
have been identified as part of
the Curia of Pompey, a rectangular building with a statue
of Pompey, where the Senate
met and Julius Caesar was
murdered on 15 March 44 BC.

**Area Sacra, with circular ruins of
temple B in the foreground**

San Carlo ai Catinari ⑱

Piazza B Cairoli. **Map** 4 F5 & 12 D4.
☎ 06-689 38 74. 🚌 see Area Sacra.
🚋 8. **Open** 7.30am–noon, 4.30–7pm
Mon–Sat (opens 8.30am Sun). ⛪

Iɴ 1620, ʀᴏᴍᴇ'ѕ Milanese
congregation decided to
honour Cardinal Carlo
Borromeo, with this great
church. It is called "ai
Catinari" on account of the
bowl-makers' *(catinari)*
shops in the area. The
solemn travertine facade
was completed in 1638 by
the Roman architect Soria.
The 16th-century basilican
plan is flanked by
chapels. The St Cecilia
chapel was designed and
decorated by Antonio
Gherardi, who added a
family portrait.
The church's paintings and
frescoes by Pietro da Cortona
and Guido Reni are confident,
mature works of the Counter
Reformation, depicting the
life and acts of the recently
canonized San Carlo. Make
sure you also see the ornate
crucifix, inlaid with marble,
glass and mother-of-pearl, by
the 16th-century sculptor
Algardi on the sacristy altar.

Sacristy altar, San Carlo ai Catinari

Fontana delle Tartarughe ⑲

Piazza Mattei. **Map** 4 F5 & 12 D4.
🚌 H, 23, 56, 60, 280. 🚋 8.

Tʜᴇ ᴅᴇʟɪɢʜᴛғᴜʟ Fontana
delle Tartarughe –
tartarughe are tortoises – was
commissioned by the Mattei
family to decorate "their"
piazza between 1581 and
1588. The design was by
Giacomo della Porta, but the
fountain owes much of its
grace and charm to the four
slender bronze youths each
resting one foot on the head
of a dolphin, sculpted by
Taddeo Landini. Nearly a
century later an unknown

Della Porta's graceful Fontana delle Tartarughe

sculptor was inspired to add the struggling tortoises to complete the composition.

Santa Maria in Campitelli ⓴

Piazza di Campitelli. **Map** 4 F5 & 12 E5. 📞 06-68 80 39 78. 🚌 44, 81, 95, 160, 628, 715, 716, 780. **Open** 7am–noon, 4pm–7pm daily. 🚹 🚻

I N 17TH-CENTURY ROME the plague could still strike fiercely and there were no reliable, effective remedies. Many Romans simply prayed for a cure to a sacred medieval icon of the Virgin, the Madonna del Portico. When a particularly lethal outbreak of plague abated in 1656, popular gratitude was so strong that a new church was built to house the icon in appropriate splendour.

Lavish altar tabernacle in Santa Maria in Campitelli

The church, designed by a pupil of Bernini, Carlo Rainaldi, was completed in 1667. The main elements of the lively Baroque facade are the graceful columns, symbolizing the supporters of the true faith.

Inside the church stands a fabulously ornate, gilded altar tabernacle with spiral columns which was designed by Giovanni Antonio de Rossi to contain the image of the Virgin. The side chapels are decorated by some of Rome's finest Baroque painters: Sebastiano Conca, Giovanni Battista Gaulli (known as Il Baciccia) and Luca Giordano.

Facade and medieval bell tower of San Nicola in Carcere

San Nicola in Carcere ⓴

Via del Teatro di Marcello 46. **Map** 5 A5 & 12 E5. 📞 06-68 30 71 98. 🚌 44, 81, 95, 160, 170, 628, 715, 716, 780. **Open** 7am–noon, 4pm–7pm Mon–Sat, 9.30am–1pm Sun & public hols. **Closed** Aug. 🚹

T HE MEDIEVAL CHURCH of San Nicola in Carcere stands on the site of three Roman temples of the Republican era which were converted into a prison (*carcere*) in the Middle Ages. The temples of Juno, Spes and Janus faced a city gate leading from the Forum Holitorium, the city's vegetable and oil market, to the road down to the port on the Tiber. The columns embedded in the walls of the church belonged to two flanking temples whose platforms are now marked by

grass lawns. The church was rebuilt in 1599 and restored in the 19th century, but the bell tower and Roman columns are part of the original design.

The Theatre of Marcellus by Thomas Hartley Cromek (1809–73)

Theatre of Marcellus ⓴

Via del Teatro di Marcello. **Map** 4 A5 & 12 E5. 📞 06-481 48 00. 🚌 23, 44, 81, 95, 160, 170, 280, 628, 71, 716, 780. **Closed** except for *concerts. See Entertainment p343.*

T HE CURVED OUTER WALL of this vast amphitheatre has supported generations of Roman buildings. It was built by the Emperor Augustus (27 BC–AD 14), who dedicated it to Marcellus, his nephew and son-in-law, who had died aged 19 in 23 BC.

The Middle Ages were a turbulent time of invasions and local conflicts (*see p28*) and by the 13th century the theatre had been converted into the fortress of the Savelli family. In the 16th century Baldassarre Peruzzi built a great palace on the theatre ruins for the Orsini family, including a garden facing the Tiber. The lower arches were later occupied by humble dwellings and workshops.

Close to the theatre stand three beautiful Corinthian columns and a section of frieze. These are from the Temple of Apollo, which housed many great works of art that the Romans had plundered from Greece in the 2nd century BC.

Portico of Octavia ❷❸

Via del Portico d'Ottavia. **Map** 4 F5 & 12 E5. 🚌 *23, 44, 81, 95, 160, 280, 628, 715, 716, 780.*

BUILT IN HONOUR of Octavia, (the sister of Augustus and the abandoned wife of Mark Antony) this is the only surviving portico of what used to be the monumental piazza of Circus Flaminius. The rectangular portico enclosed temples dedicated to Jupiter and Juno, decorated with bronze statues. The part we see today is the great central atrium originally covered by marble facings.

In the Middle Ages a great fish market and a church, Sant'Angelo in Pescheria, were built in the ruins of the portico. As the church was associated with the fishing activities of the nearby river port, aquatic flora and fauna feature in many of its inlays. Links with the Tiber are also apparent in the stucco facade on the adjacent Fishmonger's Oratory, built in 1689. The church has a fresco of the Madonna and angels by the school of Benozzo Gozzoli.

Narrow lane in the Jewish Ghetto

Ghetto and Synagogue ❷❹

Synagogue, Lungotevere dei Cenci. **Map** 4 F5 & 12 E5. 📞 *06-68 40 06 61.* 🚌 *23, 44, 56, 60, 160, 170, 186, 280, 710, 774, 780.* 🚊 *8.* **Open** *9am– 4.30pm Mon–Thu, 9am–1.30pm Fri, 9am–12.30pm Sun.* **Closed** *public hols.* **Adm charge.** 🚫 🎫 📷 **Ghetto**, main street is Via del Portico d'Ottavia.

THE FIRST Jews came to Rome as traders in the 2nd century BC and there has been a Jewish community in Rome ever since. Jews were much appreciated for their financial

Synagogue overlooking the Tiber

and medical skills during the time of the Roman Empire.

Systematic persecution began in the 16th century. From 25 July 1556 all Rome's Jews were forced to live inside a high-walled enclosure erected on the orders of Pope Paul IV. The Ghetto was in an unhealthy part of Rome. Inhabitants were only allowed out during the day, and on Sundays they were driven into the Church of Sant'Angelo in Pescheria to listen to Christian sermons – a practice abolished only in 1848.

Persecution started again in 1943 with the German occupation. Although many Jews were helped to escape or hidden by Roman citizens, thousands were deported to German concentration camps.

Today many Jews still live in the former Ghetto and the medieval streets, with shops selling typical Roman kosher food, retain much of their old character. The imposing Synagogue on Lungotevere was completed in 1904. It houses a Jewish museum which describes the history of the community through plans, torahs and other artifacts.

Casa di Lorenzo Manilio ❷❺

Via del Portico d'Ottavia 1D. **Map** 4 F5 & 12 D5. 🚌 *See Ghetto.* **Not open** to the public.

BEFORE THE RENAISSANCE, most Romans had only vague, confused ideas of their city's glorious past, but after the 15th-century revival of interest in the philosophy and arts of antiquity, some were even building houses to recall the splendour of ancient Rome. In 1468 a certain Lorenzo Manilio built a great house for his family, decorating it with an elegant Classical plaque. The

Latin inscription dates the building according to the ancient Roman method – 2,221 years after the foundation of the city – and mentions the owner's name. Original reliefs are embedded in the facades as well as a fragment of an ancient sarcophagus.

The Piazza Costaguti facade features windows patriotically inscribed with the legend *Ave Roma* (Hail Rome).

Balcony of Palazzo Cenci

Palazzo Cenci ❷❻

Vicolo dei Cenci. **Map** 4 F5 & 12 D5. 🚌 *See Ghetto.* **Not open** to the public.

PALAZZO CENCI belonged to the family of Beatrice Cenci, who was accused, together with her brothers and stepmother, of witchcraft and the murder of her tyrannical father. She was condemned to death and beheaded at Ponte Sant'Angelo in 1599.

Row of Roman busts decorating the Casa di Lorenzo Manilio

Tiber Island, with Ponte Cestio linking it to Trastevere

Most of the original medieval palazzo has been demolished, and the building you see today dates back to the 1570s, though its rather forbidding appearance seems medieval. Heraldic half-moons decorate the main facade on Via del Progresso while pretty balconies open on the opposite side where a medieval arch joins the palace to Palazzetto Cenci, designed by Martino Longhi the Elder. Inside is a traditional courtyard with an Ionic-style loggia; many of the rooms retain the original 16th-century decoration that the unfortunate Beatrice would have known as a child.

Tiber Island ㉗

Isola Tiberina. **Map** 8 D1 & 12 D5. H, 23, 44, 280. 8.

IN ANCIENT TIMES the island, which lay opposite the city's port, had large structures of white travertine at either end built to resemble the stern and prow of a ship.

Since 293 BC, when a temple was dedicated here to Aesculapius, the god of healing and protector against the plague, the island has been associated with the sick and there is still a hospital here.

San Bartolomeo all'Isola, the church in the island's central piazza, was built on the ruins of the Temple of Aesculapius in the 10th century. Its Romanesque bell tower is, clearly visible from across the river.

From the Ghetto area you can reach the island by a footbridge, the Ponte Fabricio. The oldest original bridge over the Tiber still in use, it was built in 62 BC. In medieval times the Pierleoni,

and then the Caetani, two powerful families, controlled this strategic point by means of a tower, still in situ. The other bridge to the island, the Ponte Cestio, is inscribed with the names of the Byzantine emperors associated with its restoration in AD 370.

Via Giulia ㉘

Map 4 D4 & 11 A3. 23, 116, 280.

THIS PICTURESQUE street was laid out by Bramante for Pope Julius II della Rovere. Lined with aristocratic palazzi dating from the 16th–18th centuries, as well as fine churches and antique shops, Via Giulia makes a fascinating walk *(see pp276–7)*.

Mask fountain in Via Giulia

San Giovanni dei Fiorentini ㉙

Via Acciaioli 2. **Map** 4 D4 & 11 A2. 06-68 89 20 59. 23, 46, 62, 64, 116, 280, 870. **Open** 8am–8pm daily.

THE CHURCH of St John of the Florentines was built for the large Florentine community living in this area. Pope Leo X wanted it to be an expression of the cultural superiority of Florence over Rome. Started in the early 16th century, the church took over a century to build. The principal architect was Antonio da Sangallo the Younger, but many others contributed before Carlo Maderno's elongated cupola was finally completed in 1620. The present facade was added in the 18th century.

The church was decorated mainly by Tuscan artists. One interesting exception is the 15th-century statue of San Giovannino by the Sicilian Mino del Reame in a niche above the sacristy. The spectacular high altar houses a marble group by Antonio Raggi, the *Baptism of Christ*. The altar itself is by Borromini, who is buried in the church along with Carlo Maderno.

This and San Lorenzo in Lucina *(see p112)* are the only churches in Rome which admit animals: the faithful can bring their pets, and an Easter lamb-blessing takes place.

Antonio Raggi's *Baptism of Christ* in San Giovanni dei Fiorentini

QUIRINAL

O NE OF THE original seven hills of Rome, the Quirinal was a largely residential area in Imperial times. To the east of the hill were the vast Baths of Diocletian, still standing in front of what is now the main rail station. Abandoned in the Middle Ages, the district returned to favour in the late 16th century. The prime

1st-century BC stucco in the Museo Nazionale Romano

site was taken by the popes for Palazzo del Quirinale. Great families such as the Colonna and the Aldobrandini had their palazzi lower down the hill. With the end of papal rule in 1870, the surrounding area, especially Via Nazionale, was redeveloped as the Quirinal became the residence of the kings of Italy, then of the President.

SIGHTS AT A GLANCE

Churches
Santi Apostoli **4**
San Marcello al Corso **5**
Santa Maria in Trivio **7**
Santi Vincenzo e Anastasio **9**
Sant'Andrea al Quirinale **11**
San Carlo alle Quattro Fontane **12**
Santa Maria degli Angeli **16**
Santa Maria dei Monti **20**
Sant'Agata dei Goti **21**
Santi Domenico e Sisto **23**

Museums and Galleries
Accademia Nazionale di San Luca **8**
Museo Nazionale Romano **17**
Museo delle Paste Alimentari **10**
Palazzo delle Esposizioni **19**

Historic Piazzas
Piazza della Repubblica **18**

Historic Buildings
Palazzo del Quirinale **2**
Palazzo Colonna **3**
Baths of Diocletian **15**

Fountains and Statues
Castor and Pollux **1**
Trevi Fountain **6**
Le Quattro Fontane **13**
Moses Fountain **14**

Parks and Gardens
Villa Aldobrandini **22**

GETTING THERE
The area has Metro stops at Repubblica and Cavour. Useful buses include the 64, 65 and 70 along Via Nazionale and the 71, 115 and 117, which go under the Quirinal through the Traforo Umberto I tunnel. Many buses run along Via del Tritone but there is no bus to the top of the Quirinal. You have to walk up Via XXIV Maggio.

KEY

- ▦ Street-by-Street map
- Ⓜ Metro station
- Ⓟ Parking

0 metres   300

0 yards   300

SEE ALSO
- **Street Finder**, maps 5, 6, 12
- **Where to Stay** pp294–5
- **Restaurants** pp310–11
- **Bernini Walk** pp282–3

Fontana delle Naiadi in Piazza della Repubblica

Street-by-Street: The Quirinal Hill

Even though Palazzo del Quirinale is closed to the public, it is well worth walking up the hill to the palace to see the giant Roman statues of Castor and Pollux in the piazza and enjoy fine views of the city below. Come down the hill by way of the narrow streets and stairways that lead to one of Rome's unforgettable sights, the Trevi Fountain. Many small churches lie hidden away in the back streets. Towards Piazza Venezia there are grand palazzi, including that of the Colonna, one of Rome's most ancient and powerful families.

Santa Maria in Via is famous for its medieval well and miraculous 13th-century icon of the Madonna.

Santa Maria in Trivio
The attractive facade of this tiny church conceals a rich Baroque interior **7**

Accademia Nazionale di San Luca
The art academy has works by famous former members, such as Canova and Angelica Kauffmann **8**

★ **Trevi Fountain**
Rome's grandest and best-known fountain almost fills the tiny Piazza di Trevi **6**

Santi Vincenzo e Anastasio
The grand facade of this small Baroque church is on a corner facing the Trevi Fountain **9**

San Marcello al Corso
This stark Crucifixion *by Van Dyck hangs in the sacristy of the church* **5**

Palazzo Odescalchi has a Bernini facade from 1664, with a balustrade and richly decorated cornice. The building faces Santi Apostoli.

Museo delle Cere, a wax museum opened in 1953, places its emphasis on horror.

To Piazza Venezia

Museo delle Paste Alimentari
All worth knowing about pasta is explained in this museum ⓾

LOCATOR MAP
See Central Rome Map pp12–13

PIAZZA DI SPAGNA   VIA VENETO

QUIRINAL

CAPITOL   FORUM   ESQUILINE

Palazzo del Quirinale
The old papal palace is now the home of the president of Italy. Palace guards in colourful dress uniform can often be seen outside ❷

Castor and Pollux
The statues are grouped with an obelisk and a fountain ❶

Piazza della Pilotta is dominated by the imposing facade of the Gregorian University.

Santi Apostoli
The figures of Christ and the Apostles on the balustrade were added by Carlo Rainaldi in 1681 ❹

Palazzo Colonna
One of the art gallery's finest old masters is Annibale Carracci's The Bean Eater ❸

STAR SIGHTS

★ Trevi Fountain

KEY

– – – Suggested route

0 metres   75

0 yards   75

Castor and Pollux ❶

Piazza del Quirinale. **Map** 5 B4.
🚌 H, 64, 70, 170, 640 and many
routes along Via del Tritone.

**Quirinal fountain and obelisk with
Roman statues of Castor and Pollux**

CASTOR AND POLLUX – the
patrons of horsemanship –
and their prancing horses
stand in splendour in the
Piazza del Quirinale. Over
5.5 m (18 ft) high, these
statues are huge Roman
copies of 5th-century BC
Greek originals. They once
stood at the entrance to the
nearby Baths of Constantine.
Pope Sixtus V had them
restored and placed here in
1588. Formerly known as the
"horse tamers", they gave the
square its familiar name of
Monte Cavallo (horse hill).

The obelisk which stands
between them was brought
here in 1786 from the
Mausoleum of Augustus. In
1818 the composition was
completed by the addition of
a massive granite basin, once
a cattle trough in the Forum.

Palazzo del Quirinale ❷

Piazza del Quirinale. **Map** 5 B3.
☎ 06-469 91. 🚌 H, 64, 70, 170,
175, 640 and many routes along Via
del Tritone. **Open** 8.30am–12.30pm
2nd and 4th Sun of each month.

BY THE 1500s, the Vatican
had a reputation as an unhealthy location because of the
high incidence of malaria, so
Pope Gregory XIII chose this

superb site on the highest of
Rome's seven hills as a papal
summer residence. Work began
in 1573. Piazza del Quirinale
has buildings on three sides
while the fourth is open, with a
splendid view of the city to the
great dome of St Peter's.

Many great architects
worked on the palace
before it assumed its
present form in the
1730s. Domenico
Fontana designed the
main facade, Carlo
Maderno the huge
chapel and Bernini
the narrow wing
that runs the
length of Via
del Quirinale.

Following the
unification of
Italy in 1870,
it became
the official
residence of the king, then, in
1947, of the president of the
republic. For security reasons,
the palace and gardens are
closed to the public apart from
two Sundays each month.

**Palazzo del Quirinale, official
residence of the president of Italy**

Palazzo Colonna ❸

Via della Pilotta 17. **Map** 5 A4 &
12 F3. ☎ 06-679 43 62. 🚌 H, 64,
70, 170, 640 and many routes to
Piazza Venezia. **Open** 9am–1pm Sat
only (last adm: noon). **Closed** Aug &
public hols. **Adm charge.** 🚫

POPE MARTIN V Colonna
(reigned 1417–31) began
building the palazzo, but most
of the structure dates from the
18th century. The art gallery,
built by Antonio del Grande
between 1654 and 1665, is the
only part open to the public.
The pictures are numbered but
unlabelled, so pick up a guide
on the way in. Go up the stairs

**Canova's monument to Pope Clement XIV in Santi
Apostoli, with figures of Humility and Modesty**

and through the antechamber
leading to a series of three
gleaming marble rooms with
prominent yellow columns,
the Colonna family emblem
(*colonna* means column).

The ceiling frescoes celebrate
Marcantonio Colonna's victory
over the Turks at the Battle of
Lepanto (1571). On the walls
are 16th- to 18th-century
paintings, including Annibale
Carracci's *Bean Eater (see
p157)*. The room of landscape
paintings, many by Poussin's
brother-in-law Gaspare
Dughet, reflects the 18th-
century taste of Cardinal
Girolamo Colonna. Beyond is
a room with a ceiling fresco
of the *Apotheosis of Martin V*.
The throne room has a chair
reserved for visiting popes and
a copy of Pisanello's portrait
of Martin V. The gallery also
offers a fine view of the
private palace garden, site of
the ruined Temple of Serapis.

Santi Apostoli ❹

Piazza dei Santi Apostoli. **Map** 5 A4
& 12 F3. ☎ 06-679 40 85. 🚌 64,
65, 70, 170 and many other routes to
Piazza Venezia. **Open** 6.30am–noon,
4pm–7.15pm daily. 🕇

THE ORIGINAL 6th-century
church on this site was
rebuilt in the 15th century by
Popes Martin V Colonna and

Sixtus IV della Rovere, whose oak tree crest decorates the capitals of the late 15th-century portico. Inside the portico on the left is Canova's 1807 memorial to the engraver Giovanni Volpato. The church itself contains a much larger monument by Canova, his Tomb of Clement XIV (1789).

The Baroque interior by Francesco and Carlo Fontana was completed in 1714. Note the 3-D effect of Giovanni Odazzi's painted *Rebel Angels*, who really look as though they are falling from the sky. A huge 18th-century altarpiece by Domenico Muratori shows the martyrdom of the Apostles James and Philip, whose tombs are in the crypt.

Detail of Triton and sea-horse at Rome's grandest fountain, the Trevi

San Marcello al Corso ❺

Piazza San Marcello 5. **Map** 5 A4 & 12 F3. 06-69 93 01. 56, 60, 62, 70, 81, 85, 95, 117, 492, 628. **Open** 8.30am–noon, 4–6pm Mon–Sat, 8.30am–11am, 4–6pm Sun.

THIS CHURCH was originally one of the first places of Christian worship in Rome, which were known as *tituli*. A later Romanesque building burned down in 1519, and was rebuilt by Jacopo Sansovino with a single nave and many richly-decorated private chapels on either side. The imposing travertine facade was designed by Fontana in late Baroque style.

The third chapel on the right has fine frescoes of the Virgin Mary by Francesco Salviati. The decoration of the next chapel was interrupted by the Sack of Rome in 1527. Raphael's follower Perin del Vaga fled, leaving the ceiling frescoes to be completed by Daniele da Volterra and Pellegrino Tibaldi when peace returned to the city. In the nave stands a splendid Venetian-style double tomb by Sansovino, a memorial to Cardinal Giovanni Michiel (victim of a Borgia poisoning in 1503) and his nephew, Bishop Antonio Orso.

Trevi Fountain ❻

Fontana di Trevi. **Map** 5 A3 & 12 F2. 52, 53, 58, 60, 61, 62, 71, 95, 116, 492 and many other routes along Via del Corso and Via del Tritone.

MOST VISITORS gathering around the coin-filled fountain assume that it has always been there, but by the standards of the Eternal City, the Trevi is a fairly recent creation. Nicola Salvi's theatrical design for Rome's largest and most famous fountain *(see p52)* was completed only in 1762. The central figures are Neptune, flanked by two Tritons. One struggles to master a very unruly "sea-horse", the other leads a far more docile animal. These symbolize the two contrasting moods of the sea.

The site originally marked the terminal of the Aqua Virgo aqueduct built in 19 BC. One of the first-storey reliefs shows a young girl (the legendary virgin after whom the aqueduct was named) pointing to the spring from which the water flows.

Chapel in San Marcello al Corso, decorated by Francesco Salviati

Facade of Santa Maria in Trivio

Santa Maria in Trivio ❼

Piazza dei Crociferi 49. **Map** 5 A3 & 12 F2. 📞 06-678 96 45. 🚌 52, 53, 56, 58, 60, 61, 62, 71, 95, 115, 116, 160, 175, 492, 628. **Open** 8am– 12.30pm, 3.30–7.30pm daily. 🔒

IT HAS BEEN SAID that Italian architecture is one of facades, and nowhere is this clearer than in the 1570s facade of Santa Maria in Trivio, delightfully stuck on to the building behind it. Note the false windows. There is illusion inside too, particularly in the ceiling frescoes, which show scenes from the New Testament by Antonio Gherardi (1644–1702).

The name of the tiny church probably means "St Mary-at-the-meeting-of-three-roads".

Accademia Nazionale di San Luca ❽

Piazza dell'Accademia di San Luca 77. **Map** 5 A3 & 12 F2. 📞 06-679 88 50. 🚌 52, 53, 56, 58, 60, 61, 62, 71, 95, 115, 116, 160, 175, 492, 628. **Open** 10am–1pm Mon, Wed, Fri & last Sun of month (last adm: 12.15pm). **Closed** Jul, Aug, public hols & Mon after last Sun of month.

ST LUKE IS supposed to have been a painter, hence the name of Rome's academy of fine arts. Appropriately, the gallery contains a painting of *St Luke Painting a Portrait of the Virgin* by Raphael and his followers. The academy's heyday was in the 17th and

18th centuries, when many members gave their work to the collection. Canova donated a model for his famous marble group, the *Three Graces*.

Of particular interest are three fascinating self-portraits by women: the 17th-century Italian Lavinia Fontana; the 18th-century Swiss Angelica Kauffmann, whose painting is copied from a portrait of her by Joshua Reynolds; and Elisabeth Vigée-Lebrun, the French painter of the years before the 1789 Revolution.

Santi Vincenzo e Anastasio ❾

Vicolo dei Modelli 73. **Map** 5 A3 & 12 F2. 📞 06-678 30 98. 🚌 52, 53, 56, 58, 60, 61, 62, 71, 95, 115, 116, 160, 175, 492, 628. **Open** 7.30am– 12.30pm, 3.30pm–7.30pm daily. 🔒

OVERLOOKING the Trevi Fountain is one of the most over-the-top Baroque facades in Rome. Its thickets of columns are crowned by the huge coat of arms of Cardinal Raimondo Mazzarino, who commissioned Martino Longhi the Younger to build the church in 1650. The female

bust above the door is of one of the cardinal's famous nieces, either Louis XIV's first love, Maria Mancini (1639–1715), or her younger sister, Ortensia. In the apse, memorial plaques record the popes whose *praecordia* (a part of the heart) are enshrined behind the wall. This gruesome tradition was started at the end of the 16th century by Pope Sixtus V and continued until Pius X stopped it in the early 20th century.

Museo delle Paste Alimentari ❿

Piazza Scanderberg 117. **Map** 5 A3 & 12 F2. 📞 06-699 11 19. 🚌 52, 53, 56, 58, 60, 61, 62, 71, 95, 115, 116, 160, 175, 492, 628. **Open** 9am–6pm daily. **Closed** public hols.

THE ROLE OF PASTA in Italian cuisine cannot be exaggerated, and this entertaining museum presents everything there is to know about the beloved staple. Its rooms focus on various aspects, such as the history of pasta, how it is made and the background of the different shapes, while others exhibits photography and art with a pasta theme.

Self-portrait by Lavinia Fontana in the Accademia Nazionale di San Luca

Interior of Bernini's oval Sant'Andrea al Quirinale

Sant'Andrea al Quirinale ⓫

Via del Quirinale 29. **Map** 5 B3.
06-489 031 87. 71, 115, 116T, 117. **Open** 9am–noon, 4–7pm Wed–Mon (closed in the afternoon in August). **Gratuity** expected by sacristan for showing St Stanislas's rooms.

KNOWN AS the "Pearl of the Baroque" because of its beautiful roseate marble interior, Sant'Andrea was designed by Bernini and executed by his assistants between 1658 and 1670. It was built for the Jesuits, hence the many IHS emblems (*Iesus Hominum Salvator* – Jesus Saviour of Mankind).

The site for the church was wide but shallow, so Bernini pointed the long axis of his oval plan not towards the altar, but towards the sides; he then leads the eye round to the altar end. Here he ordered works of art in various media which function not in isolation, but together. The crucified St Andrew (Sant' Andrea) of the altarpiece looks up at a stucco version of himself, who in turn ascends towards the lantern and the Holy Spirit.

Do not miss the rooms of St Stanislas Kostka in the adjacent convent. The quarters of the Jesuit novice, who died in 1568 aged 19, reflect not his own spartan taste, but the richer style of the 17th-century Jesuits. The Polish saint has been brilliantly immortalized in marble by Pierre Legros (1666–1719).

San Carlo alle Quattro Fontane ⓬

Via del Quirinale 23. **Map** 5 B3.
06-488 32 61. 116T and many routes to Piazza Barberini. **Open** 9.30am–12.30am daily.

IN 1634, the Spanish Trinitarians, an order whose role was to pay the ransom of Christian hostages to the Arabs, commissioned Borromini to design a church and convent at the Quattro Fontane crossroads. The church, so small it would fit inside one of the piers of St Peter's, is also known as "San Carlino".

Although dedicated to Carlo Borromeo, the 16th-century Milanese cardinal canonized in 1620, San Carlo is as much a monument to Borromini. Both the facade and the interior employ bold, fluid curves that give light and life to a small, cramped site. The oval dome and tiny lantern are particularly ingenious. The undulating lines of the facade are decorated with angels and a statue of San Carlo. Finished in 1667, the facade is one of Borromini's very last works.

There are further delights in the playful inverted shapes in the cloister and the stucco work in the refectory (now the sacristy), which houses a painting of San Carlo by Orazio Borgianni (1611).

In a small room off the sacristy hangs a portrait of Borromini himself wearing the Trinitarian cross. Borromini committed suicide in 1667, and in the crypt (which may soon be opened to the public) a small curved chapel reserved for him remains empty.

Dome of San Carlo alle Quattro Fontane, lit by concealed windows

Fountain of Strength (or Juno)

Le Quattro Fontane ⓭

Intersection of Via delle Quattro Fontane and Via del Quirinale. **Map** 5 B3. 🚌 116T and many routes to Piazza Barberini. Ⓜ Barberini.

THESE FOUR small·fountains are attached to the corners of the buildings at the intersection of two narrow, busy streets. They date from the great redevelopment of Rome in the reign of Sixtus V (1585–90). Each fountain has a statue of a reclining deity. The river god accompanied by the she-wolf is clearly the Tiber; the other male figure may be the Arno. The female figures represent Strength and Fidelity or the goddesses, Juno and Diana.

The crossroads is at the highest point of the Quirinal hill and commands splendid views of three distant landmark

obelisks: those placed by Sixtus V in front of Santa Maria Maggiore and Trinità dei Monti, and the one that stands in Piazza del Quirinale.

Moses Fountain ⓮

Fontana dell'Acqua Felice, Piazza San Bernardo. **Map** 5 C2. 🚌 60, 61, 62, 136, 137, 492. Ⓜ Repubblica.

OFFICIALLY KNOWN as the Fontana dell'Acqua Felice, this fountain owes its popular name to the grotesque statue of Moses in the central niche. The massive structure with its three elegant arches was designed by Domenico Fontana to mark the terminal of the Acqua Felice aqueduct, so-called because it was one of the many great improvements commissioned by Felice Peretti, Pope Sixtus V. Completed in 1587, it brought clean piped water to this quarter of Rome for the first time.

The notorious statue of Moses striking water from the rock is larger than life and the proportions of the body are obviously wrong. Sculpted either by Prospero Bresciano or Leonardo Sormani, it is a clumsy attempt at recreating the awesome appearance of Michelangelo's Moses in the church of San Pietro in Vincoli (see p170). As soon as it was unveiled, it was said to be frowning at having been brought into the world by such an inept sculptor.

Fontana's Moses Fountain

The side reliefs also illustrate water stories from the Old Testament: Aaron leading the Israelites to water and Joshua pointing the army towards the Red Sea. The fountain's four lions are copies of Egyptian originals (now in the Vatican Museums), which Sixtus V had put there for public "convenience" and "delight".

Gold coin with head of the Emperor Diocletian (AD 285–305)

Baths of Diocletian ⓯

Terme di Diocleziano, Piazza della Repubblica. **Map** 6 D3. 🚌 H, 60, 61, 62, 70, 115, 136, 137, 170, 175, 492, 640, 910. Ⓜ Repubblica, Termini.

BUILT IN AD 298–306 under the infamous Emperor Diocletian, who murdered thousands of Christians, the baths (see pp22–3) occupied well over a hectare (2.5 acres) of ground between the present Piazza dei Cinquecento and Piazza della Repubblica. The baths, the most extensive in Rome, could accommodate up to 3,000 bathers at a time.

Fidelity (or Diana) with her attendant dog, one of the Quattro Fontane

Part of the Museo Nazionale Romano, the baths include a former Carthusian monastery which has a cloister designed by Michelangelo.

Part of the Museo Nazionale Romano in the Baths of Diocletian

Santa Maria degli Angeli ⑯

Piazza della Repubblica. **Map** 5 C3.
📞 06-488 08 12. 🚌 H, 60, 61, 62, 70, 115, 136, 137, 170, 175, 492, 640, 910. Ⓜ Repubblica, Termini. **Open** 8am–12.30pm, 4pm–7pm (6.30pm in winter).

🏛 ♿ 🚻

PARTS OF THE RUINED Baths of Diocletian provided both building material and setting for this church, constructed by Michelangelo in 1563. The church was so altered in the 18th century by Luigi Vanvitelli it unfortunately has lost most of its original character.

The most striking works of art inside are a fresco of the *Martyrdom of St Sebastian* by Domenichino and a gigantic statue of St Bruno by Jean-Antoine Houdon.

An exhibition in the sacristy gives a detailed account of Michelangelo's original design.

Museo Nazionale Romano ⑰

Palazzo Massimo, Piazza dei Cinquecento. **Map** 6 D3. 📞 06-481 75 45. 🚌 H, 3, 36, 38, 38b, 64, 115, 170, 175 and many other routes to Piazza dei Cinquecento. Ⓜ Repubblica, Termini. **Open** 9am–10pm Tue–Sat, 9am–8pm Sun. **Closed** 1 Jan, 1 May, 25 Dec. **Adm charge.** ♿

FOUNDED IN 1889, the Museo Nazionale Romano holds most of the antiquities found in Rome since 1870 as well as pre-existing collections, and is one of the world's leading museums of Classical art. During the 1990s it underwent a major reorganization and it now has three branches; one in the Palazzo Altemps (see p127), one in its original site, occupying the part of the Baths of Diocletian not taken up by the church of Santa Maria degli Angeli, and one in the nearby Palazzo Massimo. The palace, built in 1883–7 on the site of a 16th-century villa which belonged to Sixtus V, used to be a Jesuit college. In 1981–97 it was restored to house a significant proportion of the museum's collections.

The exhibits in Palazzo Massimo, displayed on three floors, are originals dating from the 2nd century BC to the end of 4th century AD.

On the ground floor, Room 1 has a statue known as the *Generale de Tivoli*, by a Greek artist, which depicts a Roman soldier from the period of the Asian wars. Room 2 is devoted to funeral steles while a coin collection is in Room 3. Room 4 represents the golden period of the Imperial era with portraits of Octavian (Augustus), Drusus and Tiberius. Room 5, dedicated to Augustus, displays the famous statue of the emperor found on Via Labicana, and a series of frescoes from a grave on the Esquiline showing scenes from the history of Rome. Rooms 6, 7 and 8 display statues of Greek origins, including a splendid Niobid and the muse Melpomene.

The statues on the first floor date from the era of the successors of the Augustan dynasty, including a portrait of Vespasian in Room 1. In room 6 is the Discobolos Ex-Lancelotti and other athletes, while following rooms focus on divinities, mythology, historical celebrations and theatre.

The second floor display concentrates on decorations from public buildings, including beautiful frescoes and exquisitely detailed mosaics such as the Quattro Aurighe mosaics found in a villa in Baccano in northern Rome.

One of the Quattro Aurighe mosaics, Museo Nazionale Romano

Piazza della Repubblica ⑱

Map 5 C3. 🚌 *60, 61, 62, 64, 115, 170, 175, 492, 640, 910.*
Ⓜ *Repubblica.*

Romans often refer to the piazza by its old name, Piazza Esedra, so-called because it follows the shape of an *exedra* (a semicircular recess) that was part of the Baths of Diocletian. The piazza was part of the great redevelopment undertaken when Rome became capital of a unified Italy. Under its sweeping 19th-century colonnades there were once elegant shops, but they have been ousted by banks, travel agencies and cafés.

In the middle of the piazza stands the Fontana delle Naiadi. Mario Rutelli's four naked bronze nymphs caused something of a scandal when they were unveiled in 1901. Each reclines on an aquatic creature symbolizing water in its various forms: a seahorse for the oceans, a water snake for rivers, a swan for lakes, and a curious frilled lizard for subterranean streams. The figure in the middle, added in 1911, is of the sea god Glaucus, who represents man victorious over the hostile forces of nature.

Piazza della Repubblica and the Fontana delle Naiadi

Palazzo delle Esposizioni ⑲

Via Nazionale 194 (second entrance in Via Milano). **Map** 5 B4. (*06-474 59 03.* 🚌 *64, 70, 170, 175, 640.* **Open** *10am–9pm Wed–Mon (last adm: 8.30pm).* **Closed** *1 Jan, 1 May, 25 Dec.* **Adm charge**. 🚫 🚻 *from Via Piacenza entrance only.* **Concerts, lectures, films**. See **Entertainment** *pp346–7.* 🍴 🖥 🛍

Facade of the Palazzo delle Esposizioni

This somewhat grandiose building, with wide steps, Corinthian columns and statues, was designed as an exhibition centre by the architect Pio Piacentini and built by the city of Rome in 1882 during the reign of Umberto I. The main entrance looks like a triumphal arch.

The palazzo is still used to house exhibitions today and the exhibition space has recently been modernized. The exhibitions are changed every three months and include a variety of sculpture and paintings. Live performances, films and lectures also take place here. Foreign films are usually shown in the original language.

Santa Maria dei Monti ⑳

Via Madonna dei Monti 41. **Map** 5 B4. (*06-48 55 31.* 🚌 *64, 70, 75, 170, 175, 640.* Ⓜ *Cavour.* **Open** *7am–12.30pm, 4.30–8pm daily.* ✝ ♿

Designed by Giacomo della Porta, this church, dating from 1580, has a particularly splendid dome. Over the high altar is a medieval stunning painting of the Madonna, patroness of this quarter of Rome. The altar in the left transept houses the tomb and effigy of the unworldly French saint Benoit-Joseph Labre, who died here in 1783, having spent his life as a solitary pilgrim. He slept rough in the ruins of the Colosseum, gave away any charitable gifts he received, and came regularly to Santa Maria dei Monti to worship. His faith could not sustain his body: still in his mid-thirties, he collapsed and died outside the church. The foul rags he wore are preserved.

One of the bronze nymphs of the fountain in Piazza della Repubblica

Sant'Agata dei Goti ㉑

Via Mazzarino 16 and Via Panisperna. **Map** 5 B4. ☎ 06-488 80 61. ▦ 64, 70, 75, 170, 175. **Open** 7–9am, 5–7pm Mon–Fri, 10.30am–12.30pm, 4.30–7pm Sat, 8.30am–12.30pm, 4.30–7pm Sun. ✚ ♿

T HE GOTHS who gave their name to this church (*Goti* are Goths) occupied Rome in the 6th century AD. They were Arian heretics who denied the divinity of Christ. The church was founded between AD 462 and 470, shortly before the main Gothic invasions, and the beautiful granite columns date from this period. The main altar has a well-preserved 12th-century Cosmatesque tabernacle, but the most delightful part of the church is the charming 18th-century courtyard built around an ivy-draped well.

Villa Aldobrandini ㉒

Via Panisperna. Entrance to gardens: Via Mazzarino 1. **Map** 5 B4. ▦ 64, 70, 75, 115, 170. **Gardens open** *dawn–dusk daily.* **Villa not open** *to the public.*

B UILT IN the 16th century for the Dukes of Urbino and acquired for his family by Pope Clement VIII Aldobrandini (reigned 1592–1605), the villa is now government property and houses an international law library.

The villa itself, decorated with the family's six-starred coat of arms, is closed to the public, but the gardens and terraces, hidden behind a high wall that runs along Via Nazionale, can be reached through an iron gate in Via Mazzarino. Steps lead up past 2nd-century AD ruins into the recently renovated gardens, highly recommended as an oasis of tranquillity in the centre of the city. Gravel paths lead between formal lawns and clearly marked specimen trees, and benches are provided for the weary. Since the garden is raised some 10 m (30 ft) above street level, the views are excellent.

18th-century courtyard of Sant'Agata dei Goti

Santi Domenico e Sisto ㉓

Largo Angelicum 1. **Map** 5 B4. ☎ 06-670 22 08. ▦ 64, 70, 75, 170, 175. **Open** *by appt only.* **Closed** *Jul–Sep.*

Chapel in Santi Domenico e Sisto

T HE CHURCH has a tall, slender Baroque facade rising above a steep flight of steps. This divides into two curving flights that sweep up to the terrace in front of the entrance. The pediment of the facade is crowned by eight flaming candlesticks.

The interior has a vaulted ceiling with a large fresco of the *Apotheosis of St Dominic* by Domenico Canuti (1620–84). The first chapel on the right was decorated by Bernini, who may also have designed the sculpture of Mary Magdalene meeting the risen Christ in the Garden of Gethsemane. This fine marble group was executed by Antonio Raggi (1649). Above the altar is a 15th-century terracotta plaque of the Madonna and Child. On the left over a side altar is a large painting of the Madonna from the same period, attributed to Benozzo Gozzoli (1420–97), a pupil of Fra Angelico.

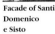

Facade of Santi Domenico e Sisto

ESQUILINE

THE ESQUILINE is the largest and highest of Rome's seven hills. In Imperial Rome the western slopes overlooking the Forum housed the crowded slums of the Suburra. On the eastern side there were a few villas belonging to wealthy citizens like Maecenas, patron of the arts and adviser to Augustus. The essential character of the place has persisted through two millennia; it is still one of the poorer quarters

Michelangelo's Rachel in San Pietro in Vincoli

of the city. The area is now heavily built up, except for a rather seedy park on the Colle Oppio, a smaller hill to the south of the Esquiline, where you can see the remains of the Baths of Titus, the Baths of Trajan and Nero's Golden House. The area's main interest, however, lies in its churches. Many of these were founded on the sites of private houses where Christians met to worship secretly in the days when the religion was banned.

SIGHTS AT A GLANCE

Churches
San Martino ai Monti ❶
San Pietro in Vincoli ❷
Santa Pudenziana ❸
Santa Maria Maggiore pp172–3 ❹
Santa Prassede ❺
Santa Bibiana ❼

Museums
Museo Nazionale d'Arte Orientale ❾

Historic Piazzas
Piazza Vittorio Emanuele II ❽

Ancient Sites
Auditorium of Maecenas ❿
Nero's Golden House ⓬
Sette Sale ⓫

Arches
Arch of Gallienus ❻

GETTING THERE
This area is close to Termini station and has several other Metro stops: Vittorio Emanuele and Manzoni on line A, Cavour and Colosseo on line B. Bus routes here are a little confusing. Among the most useful are the 4, 9, 16 and 75 from Stazione Termini. Tram 30b runs along Via Labicana.

SEE ALSO
• *Street Finder*, maps 5, 6
• *Restaurants* pp310–11
• *Mosaics Walk* pp280–81

KEY

	Street-by-Street map
FS	Railway station
M	Metro station
P	Parking

0 metres   300
0 yards   300

Southern facade of Santa Maria Maggiore by night

Street-by-Street: The Esquiline Hill

THE SIGHT that draws most people to this rather scruffy part of Rome is the great basilica of Santa Maria Maggiore. But it is also well worth searching out some of the smaller churches on the Esquiline: Santa Pudenziana and Santa Prassede with their celebrated mosaics, and San Pietro in Vincoli, home to one of Michelangelo's most famous sculptures. To the south, in the Colle Oppio park, are the scattered remains of the Baths of Trajan.

Santa Pudenziana
The apse of this ancient church has a magnificent 4th-century mosaic of Christ surrounded by the Apostles ❸

Piazza dell'Esquilino
was furnished with an obelisk in 1587 by Pope Sixtus V. This helped to guide pilgrims coming from the north to the important church of Santa Maria Maggiore.

To the Colosseum

★ **San Pietro in Vincoli**
The church's treasures include Michelangelo's Moses *and the chains that bound St Peter* ❷

Baths of Trajan (*p.*109) were the first to be built on the massive scale later used in the Baths of Diocletian and of Caracalla

★ **Santa Maria Maggiore**
This imposing rear facade was added by Baroque architect Carlo Rainaldi in 1673. Santa Maria's interior is one of the most richly decorated in Rome ❹

LOCATOR MAP
See Central Rome Map pp12–13

The Tomb of Pius V (died 1572) by Domenico Fontana stands in this less well-known Sistine Chapel, under the northeast dome of Santa Maria Maggiore.

Arch of Gallienus
This was built in the 3rd century AD to replace an entrance in the old Servian Wall ❻

To Vittorio Emanuele Metro

★ **Santa Prassede**
The 9th-century mosaics in the Chapel of San Zeno are among the finest in Rome ❺

The Torre dei Capocci, a restored medieval tower, is one of the area's most distinctive landmarks.

KEY

− − − Suggested route

0 metres 75
0 yards 75

San Martino ai Monti
The frescoes include 17th-century Roman landscapes and scenes from the life of Elijah by Gaspare Dughet ❶

STAR SIGHTS

★ **Santa Maria Maggiore**

★ **San Pietro in Vincoli**

★ **Santa Prassede**

San Martino ai Monti ❶

Viale del Monte Oppio 28. **Map** 6 D5.
█ 06-487 31 66. ▦ 4, 9, 16, 70,
71, 714. Ⓜ Cavour, Vittorio
Emanuele. **Open** 7.30am–11.30am,
4.30pm–6.30pm Mon–Sat, 8.30am–
12.30pm, 6pm–7.30pm Sun. ⬆ ⬇

Fresco of old San Giovanni in Laterano in San Martino ai Monti

Cᴴʀɪꜱᴛɪᴀɴꜱ have been worshipping on the site of this church since the 3rd century, when they used to meet in the house of a man named Equitius. In the 4th century, after Constantine had legalized Christianity, Pope Sylvester I built a church, one of very few things he did during his pontificate. In fact he was so insignificant that in the 5th century a more exciting life was fabricated for him – which included tales of him converting Constantine, curing him of leprosy and forcing him to close all pagan temples. Pope Sylvester's fictional life was further enhanced in the 8th century, with the forgery of a document in which Constantine offered him the Imperial crown.

Pope Sylvester's church was replaced in about AD 500 by St Symmachus, rebuilt in the 9th century and then transformed completely in the 1630s. The only immediate signs of its age are the ancient Corinthian columns dividing the nave and aisles. The most interesting interior features are a series of frescoed landscapes of the Campagna (the countryside around Rome) by the 17th-century

French artist Gaspare Dughet, Poussin's brother-in-law, in the right aisle. The frescoes by Filippo Gagliardi, at either end of the left aisle, show old St Peter's and the interior of San Giovanni in Laterano before Borromini's redesign. If you can find the sacristan, you can go beneath the church to see the remains of Equitius's house.

San Pietro in Vincoli ❷

Piazza di San Pietro in Vincoli 4A.
Map 5 C5. █ 06-488 28 65. ▦
75, 115, 117. Ⓜ Cavour, Colosseo.
Open 7am–12.30pm, 3.30pm–7pm
(Oct–Mar: 6pm) daily. ⬆ ⬇ ⬆

Aᴄᴄᴏʀᴅɪɴɢ ᴛᴏ ᴛʀᴀᴅɪᴛɪᴏɴ, the two chains (vincoli) used to shackle St Peter while he was being held in the depths

Reliquary with St Peter's chains

of the Mamertine Prison (see p91) were subsequently taken to Constantinople. In the 5th century, Empress Eudoxia deposited one in a church in Constantinople and sent the other to her daughter Eudoxia in Rome. She in turn gave hers to Pope Leo I, who had this church built to house it. Some years later the second chain was brought to Rome, where it linked miraculously with its partner.

The chains are still here, displayed below the high altar, but the church is now best known for Michelangelo's Tomb of Pope Julius II. When it was commissioned in 1505, Michelangelo spent eight months searching for perfect blocks of marble at Carrara in Tuscany, but Pope Julius became more interested in the building of a new St Peter's and the project was laid aside. After the pope's death in 1513, Michelangelo resumed work on the tomb, but had only finished the statues of Moses and the Dying Slaves when Pope Paul III persuaded him to start work on the Sistine Chapel's Last Judgment. Michelangelo had planned a vast monument with over 40 statues, but the tomb that was built – mainly by his pupils – is simply a facade with six niches for statues. The Dying Slaves are in Paris and Florence, but the tremendous bearded Moses is here. The horns on Moses' head should really be beams of light – they are the result of the Hebrew original from the Old Testament being wrongly translated.

Michelangelo's Moses in San Pietro

Santa Pudenziana ❸

Via Urbana 160. **Map** 5 C4.
☎ 06-481 46 22. 🚍 4, 9, 16, 70,
71, 714. **M** Cavour. **Open**
8am–noon, 3pm–6pm daily. ⛪

Apse mosaics in Santa Prassede, showing the saint with St Paul

CHURCHES tend to be dedicated to existing saints, but in this case, the church, through a linguistic accident, created a brand new saint. In the 1st century AD a Roman senator called Pudens lived on this site and, according to legend, allowed St Peter to lodge with him. In the 2nd century a bath house was built on this site and in the 4th century a church was established inside the baths, known as the *Ecclesia Pudentiana* (the church of Pudens). In time it was assumed that "Pudentiana" was a woman's name and a life was created for her – she became the sister of Prassede and was credited with caring for Christian victims of persecution. In 1969 both saints were declared invalid, though their churches both kept their names.

The 19th-century facade of the church retains an 11th-century frieze depicting both Prassede and Pudenziana dressed as crowned Byzantine empresses. The apse has a remarkable 4th-century mosaic, clearly influenced by Classical pagan art in its use of subtle colours. The Apostles are represented as Roman senators in togas. Unfortunately, a clumsy attempt at restoration in the 16th century destroyed two of the Apostles and left other figures without their legs.

Santa Maria Maggiore ❹

See pp172–3.

Santa Prassede ❺

Via Santa Prassede 9A. **Map** 6 D4.
☎ 06-488 24 56. 🚍 4, 9, 16, 70,
71, 714. **M** Vittorio Emanuele.
Open 7.30am– noon, 4pm–6.30pm
daily. ⛪ ♿

THE CHURCH was founded by Pope Paschal II in the 9th century, on the site of a 2nd-century oratory. Although the interior has been altered and rebuilt, the structure of the original design of the 9th-century church is clearly visible. Its three naves are separated by rows of granite columns. In the central nave, there is a round stone slab covering the well where, according to the legend, St Prassede would have buried the remains of 2,000 martyrs.

Artists from Byzantium decorated the church with glittering, jewel-coloured mosaics. Those in the apse and choir depict stylized white-robed elders, the haloed elect looking down from the gold and blue walls of heaven, spindly-legged lambs, feather-mop palm trees and bright red poppies.

In the apse, Santa Prassede and Santa Pudenziana stand on either side of Christ, with the fatherly arms of St Paul and St Peter on their shoulders. Beautiful mosaics of saints, the virgin and Christ and the Apostles also cover the walls and vault of the Chapel of St Zeno, built as a mausoleum for Pope Paschal's mother, Theodora. Part of a column brought back from Jerusalem, allegedly the one to which Christ was bound and flogged, also stands here.

11th-century frieze and medallions on the facade of Santa Pudenziana

Santa Maria Maggiore ❹

O F ALL THE GREAT Roman basilicas, Santa Maria has the most successful blend of different architectural styles. Its colonnaded triple nave is part of the original 5th-century building. The Cosmatesque marble floor and delightful Romanesque bell tower, with its blue ceramic roundels, are medieval. The Renaissance saw a new coffered ceiling, and the Baroque gave the church twin domes and its imposing front and rear facades. The mosaics are Santa Maria's most famous feature. From the 5th century come the Biblical scenes in the nave and the spectacular mosaics on the triumphal arch. Medieval highlights include a 13th-century enthroned Christ in the loggia.

★ Cappella Paolina
Flaminio Ponzio designed this richly decorated chapel (1611) for Pope Paul V Borghese.

Obelisk in Piazza dell'Esquilino
The Egyptian obelisk was erected by Pope Sixtus V in 1587 as a landmark for pilgrims.

LEGEND OF THE SNOW

In 356, Pope Liberius had a dream in which the Virgin told him to build a church on the spot where he found snow. When it fell on the Esquiline, on the morning of 5 August in the middle of a baking Roman summer, he naturally obeyed. The miracle of the snow is commemorated each year by a service during which thousands of white petals float down from the ceiling of Santa Maria. Originally roses were used, but nowadays the petals are more usually taken from dahlias.

Coffered Ceiling
The gilded ceiling, possibly by Giuliano da Sangallo, was a gift of Alexander VI Borgia at the end of the 15th century. The gold is said to be the first brought from America by Columbus.

TIMELINE

300 AD	600	900	1200	1500	1800
356 Virgin appears to Pope Liberius			**1347** Cola di Rienzo crowned Tribune of Rome in Santa Maria	**1673** Carlo Rainaldi rebuilds apse	
	432–40 Sixtus III completes church	*Pope Gregory VII*			
420 Probable founding date	**1075** Pope Gregory VII kidnapped by opponents while reading Christmas mass in Santa Maria		**1288–92** Nicholas IV adds apse and transepts	**1743** Ferdinando Fuga adds main facade on orders of Benedict XIV	
		Coat of arms of Gregory VII			

★ **Coronation of the Virgin Mosaic**
*This is the central image of a series
of wonderful apse mosaics of the
Virgin by Jacopo Torriti (1295).*

Baldacchino *(1740s)*
*Its columns of red
porphyry and bronze
were the work of
Ferdinando Fuga.*

★ **Tomb of
Cardinal
Rodriguez**
*The Gothic
tomb (1299)
contains
magnificent
Cosmatesque
marblework.*

★ **Cappella Sistina**
*The chapel was built for
Pope Sixtus V (1584–87) by
Domenico Fontana and
houses the pope's tomb.*

**Column in Piazza
Santa Maria Maggiore**
*A bronze of the Virgin and Child was
added to this ancient marble column
in 1615. The column came from the
Basilica of Constantine in the Forum.*

STAR FEATURES

★ **Cappella Sistina**

★ **Coronation of the
Virgin Mosaic**

★ **Cappella Paolina**

★ **Tomb of Cardinal
Rodriguez**

Arch erected in memory of Emperor Gallienus

Arch of Gallienus ⑥

Via Carlo Alberto. **Map** 6 D4. 🚌 *4, 9, 16, 71.* Ⓜ *Vittorio Emanuele.*

SQUASHED between two buildings just off Via Carlo Alberto is the central arch of an originally three-arched gate erected in memory of Emperor Gallienus, who was assassinated by his Illyrian officers in AD 262. It was built on the site of the old Esquiline Gate in the Servian Wall, parts of which are visible nearby.

Santa Bibiana ⑦

Via Giovanni Giolitti 154. **Map** 6 F4. 🄲 *06-446 10 21.* 🚌 *70, 71, 105.* Ⓜ *Vittorio Emanuele.* **Open** *7am–10am, 4.30pm–7.30pm daily (phone first).* 🚹 🚻

THE DECEPTIVELY simple facade of Santa Bibiana was Bernini's first foray into architecture. It is a clean, economic design with superimposed pilasters and deeply shadowed archways. The church itself was built on the site of the palace belonging to Bibiana's family. This is where the saint was buried after being flogged to death with leaded cords during the brief persecution of the Christians that took place in the reign of Julian the Apostate (361–3). Just inside the church is a small column against which Bibiana is said to have been whipped. Her remains, along with those of her mother Dafrosa and her sister Demetria, who also suffered martyrdom, are preserved in an alabaster urn below the altar. In a niche above the altar stands a statue of Santa Bibiana by Bernini – the first fully-clothed figure he ever sculpted. He depicts her standing beside a column, holding the cords with which she was whipped, apparently on the verge of a deadly swoon.

Early sculpture by Bernini of the martyr Santa Bibiana (1626)

Piazza Vittorio Emanuele II ⑧

Map 6 E5. 🚌 *4, 9, 71.* 🚊 *14, 516.* Ⓜ *Vittorio Emanuele. See **Markets** p338.*

PIAZZA VITTORIO, as it is called for short, is one of the city's main open-air food markets. The arcaded square was built in the urban development undertaken after the unification of Italy in 1870. It was named after Italy's first king, but there is nothing regal about its appearance today. The shabby stalls selling cheap shoes and clothes are however about to be moved.

However, the garden area in the centre of the square has recently been restored. It contains a number of mysterious ruins, including a large mound, part of a Roman fountain from the 3rd century AD and the Porta Magica, a curious 17th-century doorway inscribed with alchemical signs and formulae.

Museo Nazionale d'Arte Orientale ⑨

Via Merulana 248. **Map** 6 D5. 🄲 *06-487 44 15.* 🚌 *16, 70, 71, 714.* Ⓜ *Vittorio Emanuele.* **Open** *9am–7pm Tue–Thu, 9am–2pm Fri, Sat & Mon, 9am–1pm Sun.* **Closed** *1st & 3rd Mon of month.* **Adm charge.**

THE MUSEUM occupies part of the late 19th-century Palazzo Brancaccio, home of the Italian Institute of the Middle and Far East since 1957. The collection ranges from prehistoric Iranian ceramics, sculpture from Afghanistan, Nepal, Kashmir and India to 18th-century Tibetan paintings on vellum. From the Far East there are collections of Japanese screen paintings and Chinese jade.

The most unusual exhibits are the finds from the Italian excavation of the ancient civilization of

4th-century relief from Kashmir

Nepalese Bodhisattva in the Museo Nazionale d'Arte Orientale

Swat in northeast Pakistan. This fascinating Gandhara culture lasted from the 3rd century BC to about the 10th century AD. Its wonderfully exotic, sensual reliefs show an unusual combination of Hellenistic, Buddhist and Hindu influences.

Auditorium of Maecenas ⑩

Largo Leopardi. **Map** 6 D5.
🚌 16, 71, 714. Ⓜ *Vittorio Emanuele.* **Open** 9am– 1.30pm Sun. 🚫 ♿

MAECENAS, fop, gourmet and patron of the arts, was also an astute adviser and colleague of the Emperor Augustus. He was fabulously rich, and spent some of his wealth creating a fantastic villa and gardens on the Esquiline hill, most of which has long disappeared beneath the modern city. The partially reconstructed auditorium, isolated on a traffic island, is all that remains.

Inside, a semicircle of tiered seats suggests that it may have been a place for readings and performances. If it was, then Maecenas would have been entertained here by his protégés, the lyric poet Horace and Virgil, author of the *Aeneid*, reading their latest works. However, water ducts have also been discovered and it may well have been a *nympheum* – a kind of summerhouse – with

fountains. Traces of frescoes remain on the walls: you can make out garden scenes and a procession of miniature figures – including one of a characteristically drunken Dionysus (the Greek god of wine) being propped upright by a satyr.

Sette Sale ⑪

Via delle Terme di Traiano. **Map** 5 C5.
📞 06-67 10 38 19. 🚌 85, 87, 117, 186, 850. 🚋 30b. Ⓜ *Colosseo.* **Open** only by request; phone in advance.

NOT FAR FROM Nero's Golden House is the cistern of the Sette Sale. It was built there to supply the enormous quantities of water needed for the Baths of Trajan. These were built for Emperor Trajan in AD 104 on parts of the Golden House damaged by a fire.

A set of stairs leads down into the cistern, well below street level. There is not much to see there now, but a walk through the huge, echoing cistern where light rays illuminates the watery surfaces is still an evocative experience. The nine sections, 30 m (98 ft) long and 5 m (16 ft) wide, had a capacity of 8 million litres.

Nero's Golden House ⑫

Domus Aurea, Via Labicana 136.
Map 5 C5. 📞 06-699 01 10.
🚌 85, 87, 117, 186, 850. 🚋 30b.
Ⓜ *Colosseo.* **Closed** for restoration; phone the Soprintendenza Archeologica at the above number (8am–1.30pm) to arrange a visit.

AFTER ALLEGEDLY setting fire to Rome in AD 64, Nero decided to build himself an outrageous new palace. It occupied part of the Palatine, and most of the Celian and Esquiline hills – an area approximately 25 times the size of the Colosseum. The vestibule on the Palatine side of the complex contained a colossal gilded statue of Nero. There was an artificial lake, with gardens and woods

where imported wild beasts were allowed to roam free. According to Suetonius in his life of Nero, the palace walls were adorned with gold and mother-of-pearl, rooms were designed with ceilings that showered guests with flowers or perfumes, the dining hall rotated and the baths were fed with both sulphurous water and sea-water.

Tacitus described Nero's debauched garden parties, with banquets served on barges and lakeside brothels serviced by aristocratic women, though as Nero killed himself in AD 68, he did not have long to enjoy his new home.

Nero's successors, anxious to distance themselves from the monster-emperor, did their utmost to erase all traces of the palace. Vespasian drained the lake and built the Colosseum *(see pp92–5)* in its place, Titus and Trajan each erected a complex of baths over the palace, and Hadrian placed the Temple of Venus and Rome *(see p87)* over the vestibule.

Rooms from one wing of the palace have survived, buried beneath the ruins of the Baths of Trajan on the Oppian hill. Recent excavations have revealed large frescoes and mosaics which are thought be a panorama of Rome from a birds-eye perspective. Hopefully it will open to the public when considered safe from landslides.

Frescoed room in the ruins of Nero's Golden House

LATERAN

I N THE MIDDLE AGES the Lateran Palace was the residence of the popes, and the basilica of San Giovanni beside it rivalled St Peter's in splendour. After the return of the popes from Avignon at the end of the 14th century, the area declined in importance. Pilgrims still continued to visit San Giovanni and Santa

Cherub from San Giovanni in Laterano

Croce in Gerusalemme, but the area remained sparsely inhabited. Ancient convents slumbered amid gardens and vineyards until Rome became capital of Italy in 1870 and a network of residential streets was laid out here to house the influx of newcomers. Archaeological interest lies chiefly in the Aurelian Wall and the ruins of the Aqueduct of Nero.

SIGHTS AT A GLANCE

Churches
San Giovanni in Laterano
pp182–3 **1**
Santa Croce
in Gerusalemme **5**
Santi Quattro Coronati **11**
San Clemente pp186–7 **12**
Santo Stefano Rotondo **13**

Shrines
Scala Santa and Sancta
Sanctorum **2**

Arches and Gates
Porta Asinaria **3**
Porta Maggiore **7**

Ancient Sites
Amphiteatrum Castrense **4**
Baker's Tomb **8**
Aqueduct of Nero and
the Freedmen's Tombs **9**

Museums
Museum of Musical
Instruments **6**

Historic Buildings
Villa Wolkonsky **10**

SEE ALSO

• **Street Finder**, maps 6, 9, 10

• **Restaurants** pp310–11

• **Mosaics Walk** pp280–81

GETTING THERE
San Giovanni Metro station on line A is just outside the city wall, but handy for many of the sights in the area. The 16, 81, 87 and 186 are among the many buses to Piazza di San Giovanni in Laterano. This can also be reached by the 30b tram. This is slow, but its route makes it useful for exploring this part of Rome.

| 0 metres | 300 |
| 0 yards | 300 |

KEY

  Street-by-Street map

— City Wall

M Metro station

P Parking

15th-century apse fresco in Santa Croce in Gerusalemme

Street-by-Street: Piazza di San Giovanni

BOTH THE BASILICA of San Giovanni and the Lateran Palace look out over a huge open area, the Piazza di San Giovanni, laid out at the end of the 16th century with an Egyptian obelisk, the oldest in Rome, in the centre. Sadly the traffic streaming in and out of the city through Porta San Giovanni tends to detract from its grandeur. Across the square is the building housing the Scala Santa (the Holy Staircase), one of the most revered relics in Rome and the goal for many pilgrims. The area is also a venue for political rallies, and the feast of St John on 23 June is celebrated with a fair at which Romans consume roast *porchetta* (see p59).

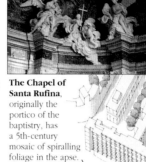

The Chapel of Santa Rufina, originally the portico of the baptistry, has a 5th-century mosaic of spiralling foliage in the apse.

The Cloister of San Giovanni fortunately survived the two fires that destroyed the early basilica. A 13th-century masterpiece of mosaic work, the cloister now houses fragments from the medieval basilica.

Piazza di San Giovanni in Laterano boasts an ancient obelisk and parts of Nero's Aqueduct. This 18th-century painting by Canaletto shows how the piazza once looked.

STAR SIGHTS

★ **San Giovanni in Laterano**

KEY

— — — Suggested route

0 metres   75

0 yards   75

The Chapel of San Venanzio is decorated with a series of 7th-century mosaics on a gold background. This detail from the apse shows one of the angels flanking the central figure of Christ. San Venanzio was an accomplished 6th-century Latin poet.

LOCATOR MAP
See Central Rome Map pp12–13

The Lateran Palace, residence of the popes until 1309, was rebuilt by Domenico Fontana in 1586.

★ **San Giovanni in Laterano**
Borromini's interior dates from the 17th century, but the grand facade by Alessandro Galilei, with its giant statues of Christ and the Apostles, was added in 1735 ❶

Scala Santa
This door at the top of the holy stair-case leads to the Sancta Sanctorum ❷

Porta Asinaria
This minor gateway, no longer in use, is as old as the Aurelian Wall, dating back to the 3rd century AD ❸

The Triclinio Leoniano is a piece of wall and a mosaic from the dining hall of 8th-century Pope Leo III.

San Giovanni in Laterano ❶

See pp182–3.

Scala Santa and Sancta Sanctorum ❷

Piazza di San Giovanni in Laterano 14.
Map 9 C1. 📞 06-70 49 44 89. 🚌
16, 81, 85, 87, 186 and other routes
to Piazza di San Giovanni in Laterano.
🚋 30b. Ⓜ San Giovanni. **Open**
6.30am–11.50am, 3.30pm–6.45pm
(Oct–Mar: 3pm–6.45pm) daily. ✝

**Devout Christians climbing the
Scala Santa on their knees**

ON THE EAST SIDE of Piazza
di San Giovanni in
Laterano, a building designed
by Domenico Fontana (1589)
houses two surviving parts of
the old Lateran Palace. One is
the Sancta Sanctorum, the other
the holy staircase, the Scala
Santa. The 28 steps, said to be
those that Christ ascended in
Pontius Pilate's house during
his trial, are supposed to have
been brought from Jerusalem
by St Helena, mother of the
Emperor Constantine. This
belief, however, cannot be
traced back any earlier than
the 7th century.

The steps were moved to
their present site by Pope
Sixtus V (1585–90) when the
old Lateran Palace was
destroyed. No foot may touch
the holy steps, so they are
covered by wooden boards.
They may only be climbed by
the faithful on their knees, a
penance that is performed
especially on Good Friday. In
the vestibule there are various

19th-century sculptures
including an *Ecce Homo* by
Giosuè Meli (1874).

The Scala Santa and two side
stairways lead to the Chapel
of St Lawrence or Sancta
Sanctorum (Holy of Holies),
built by Pope Nicholas III in
1278. Decorated with fine
Cosmatesque marble-work, the
chapel contains many important relics, the most precious
being an image of Jesus – the
Acheiropoeton or "picture
painted without hands", said to
be the work of St Luke, with
help of an angel. It was taken
on procession in medieval
times to ward off plagues.

On the walls and in the
vault, restoration work has
revealed 13th-century frescoes
which for 500 years had been
covered by later paintings.
The frescoes, representing
the legends of St Nicholas, St
Lawrence, St Agnes and St
Paul, show signs of the style
that would characterize the
frescoes of Giotto in Assisi,
made a few years later.

Porta Asinaria ❸

Between Piazza di Porta San Giovanni
and Piazzale Appio. **Map** 10 D2.
🚌 4, 16, 81, 85, 87, 850. 🚋 30b.
Ⓜ San Giovanni. See **Markets** p339.

THE PORTA ASINARIA (Gate of
the Donkeys) is one of the
minor gateways in the Aurelian
Wall *(see p196)*. Twin circular

Porta Asinaria from inside the wall

towers were added and a small
enclosure built around the
entrance; the remains are still
visible. From outside the walls
you can see the gate's white
travertine facade and two rows
of small windows, giving light
to two corridors built into the
wall above the gateway. In
AD 546 treacherous barbarian
soldiers serving in the Roman
army opened this gate to the
hordes of the Goth Totila,
who mercilessly looted the
city. In 1084 the Holy Roman
Emperor Henry IV entered
Rome via Porta Asinaria with
the antipope Guibert to oust
Pope Gregory VII. The gate
was badly damaged in the
conflicts that followed.

The area close to the gate,
especially in the Via Sannio,
is the home of a popular flea-
market *(see p339)*.

Amphiteatrum Castrense ❹

Between Piazza di Santa Croce in
Gerusalemme and Viale Castrense.
Map 10 E1. 🚌 9. 🚋 13, 30b.
Not open to the public.

**Columns and bricked-up arches of
the Amphiteatrum Castrense**

THIS SMALL 3rd-century
amphitheatre was used for
games and baiting animals. It
owes its preservation to the
fact that it was incorporated
in the Aurelian Wall *(see
p196)*, which included several
existing high buildings in its
fortifications. The graceful
arches framed by brick
semicolumns were blocked
up. The amphitheatre is best
seen from outside the walls,
from where there is also a
good view of the bell tower of
Santa Croce in Gerusalemme.

Discovery and Triumph of the Cross, **attributed to Antoniazzo Romano, in Santa Croce in Gerusalemme**

Santa Croce in Gerusalemme ❺

Piazza di Santa Croce in Gerusalemme 12. **Map** 10 E1. **(** 06-701 47 69. 🚌 9. 🚋 30b. **Open** 6.30am– 12.30pm, 3.30pm–7.30pm daily. 🔹🔹

Emperor Constantine's mother St Helena founded this church in AD 320 in the grounds of her private palace. Although the church stood at the edge of the city, the relics of the Crucifixion that St Helena had brought back from Jerusalem made it a

18th-century statue of St Helena on the facade of Santa Croce

centre of pilgrimage. Most important were the pieces of Christ's Cross (*croce* means cross) and part of Pontius Pilate's inscription in Latin, Hebrew and Greek: "Jesus of Nazareth King of the Jews".

In the crypt is a Roman statue of Juno, found at Ostia (*see pp270–71*), transformed into a statue of St Helena by replacing the head and arms and adding a cross. The 15th-century apse fresco shows the medieval legends that arose around the Cross. Helena is shown holding it over a dead youth and restoring him to life. Another episode shows its recovery from the Persians by the Byzantine Emperor Heraclitus after a bloody battle. In the centre of the apse is a magnificent tomb by Jacopo Sansovino made for Cardinal Quiñones, Emperor Charles V's confessor (died 1540).

Museum of Musical Instruments ❻

Museo degli Strumenti Musicali, Piazza di Santa Croce in Gerusalemme. **Map** 10 E1. **(** 06-701 47 96. 🚌 9. 🚋 30b. **Open** 9am–2pm Tue–Sun. **Closed** 1 Jan, 1 May, 25 Dec. **Adm charge**.

One of Rome's lesser-known museums, the building stands on the site of the Sessorianum, the great

Imperial villa belonging to Empress St Helena, later included in the Aurelian Wall. Opened in 1974, the museum has a collection of over 3,000 instruments from all over the world. It includes instruments typical of the various regions of Italy, and wind, string and percussion instruments of all ages (including Egyptian, Greek and Roman). There are also sections dedicated to church and military music.

The greater part of the collection is composed of Baroque instruments: don't miss the gorgeous Barberini harp, remarkably well-preserved, on the first floor in Room 13. There are spinets, harpsichords and clavichords of many different kinds, and one of the first pianos ever made, dating from 1722.

Art Nouveau entrance to the Museum of Musical Instruments

San Giovanni in Laterano ➊

EARLY IN THE 4th century, the Laterani family were disgraced and their land taken by Emperor Constantine to build Rome's first Christian basilica. Today's church retains the original shape, but has been destroyed by fire twice and rebuilt several times. Borromini undertook the last major rebuild of the interior in 1646, and the main facade is an 18th-century addition. Before the pope's move to Avignon in 1309, the adjoining Lateran Palace was the official papal residence, and until 1870 all popes were crowned in the church. The pope is the Bishop of Rome and here in the city's main cathedral he celebrates Maundy Thursday mass and attends the annual blessing of the people.

Cappella di San Venanzio
This chapel is attached to the baptistry and is decorated with 7th-century mosaics.

Entrance to museum

Apse

Papal Altar
Only the Pope can celebrate mass at this altar. The Gothic baldacchino, decorated with frescoes, dates from the 14th century.

★ **Cloisters**
Built by the Vassalletto family in about 1220, the cloisters are remarkable for their twisted twin columns and inlaid marble mosaics.

TIMELINE

AD 313 Constantine gives Laterani site to Pope Melchiades for a church	**896** Church damaged in earthquake	**1144** Church dedicated to San Giovanni in Laterano	**1377** Return of popes from Avignon	**1646** Borromini rebuilds interior
314–18 Five-aisled basilica church is built		**1309** Papacy moves to Avignon		

AD 300	800	1000		1400

324 Basilica consecrated by Pope Sylvester I and dedicated to the Redeemer	**904–911** Church rebuilt under Pope Sergius III	**1300** First Holy Year proclaimed	**1360** Church burnt down for second time	**1586** Domenico Fontana builds north facade
		1308 Church destroyed by fire	**1730–40** Alessandro Galilei constructs main facade	

★ Baptistry

Though much restored, the domed baptistry dates back to Constantine's time. It assumed its present octagonal shape in AD 432 and the design has served as the model for baptistries throughout the Christian world.

STAR FEATURES

★ Baptistry

★ Cloisters

North Facade

This was added by Domenico Fontana in 1586. The pope gives his blessing from the upper loggia.

The original Lateran Palace was almost destroyed by the fire of 1308 which devastated San Giovanni. Pope Sixtus V commissioned Fontana to replace it in 1586.

Statues of Christ and the Apostles

Boniface VIII Fresco

This fragment showing the pope proclaiming the Holy Year of 1300 is attributed to Giotto.

A side door is opened every Holy Year.

The main entrance's bronze doors originally came from the Curia *(see p82).*

TRIAL OF A CORPSE

Fear of rival factions led the early popes to extraordinary lengths. An absurd case took place at the Lateran Palace in 897 when Pope Stephen VI tried the corpse of his predecessor, Formosus, for disloyalty to the Church. The corpse was found guilty, its right hand was mutilated and it was thrown into the Tiber.

Pope Formosus

Corsini Chapel

This chapel was built in the 1730s for Pope Clement XII. The altarpiece is a mosaic copy of Guido Reni's painting of Sant'Andrea Corsini.

Porta Maggiore **7**

Piazza di Porta Maggiore. **Map** 6 F5.
🚌 *105, 516, 517.* 🚊 *14, 19, 30b.*

ORIGINALLY the two arches
of Porta Maggiore were
not part of the city wall, but
part of an aqueduct built by
the Emperor Claudius in AD
52. They carried the water of
the Aqua Claudia over the Via
Labicana and Via Prenestina,
two of ancient Rome's main
southbound roads. You can
still see the original roadway
beneath the gate. In the large
slabs of basalt – a hard
volcanic rock used in all old
Roman roads – note the great
ruts created by generations of
cartwheels. On top of the
arches separate conduits
carried the water of two
aqueducts: the Aqua Claudia,
and its offshoot, the Aqueduct
of Nero. They bear inscriptions from the time of the
Emperors Claudius, Vespasian
and Titus, who restored them
in AD 71 and AD 81. In all,
six aqueducts from different
water sources entered the city
at Porta Maggiore.

The Aqua Claudia was 68
km (43 miles) long, with
more than 15 km (9 miles)
above ground. Its majestic
arches are a distinctive feature
of the Roman countryside, and
a popular brand of mineral
water still bears its name.
One stretch of the Aqua
Claudia had its arches bricked
up when it was incorporated
into the 3rd-century Aurelian
Wall *(see p196).*

Relief showing breadmaking on the tomb of the baker Eurysaces

Baker's Tomb **8**

Piazzale Labicano. **Map** 6 F5. 🚌 *105,*
516, 517. 🚊 *14, 19, 30b.*

IN THE MIDDLE of the tram
junction near Porta
Maggiore stands the tomb of
the rich baker Eurysaces
and his wife Atistia, built
in 30 BC. Roman custom
forbade burials within
city walls, and the roads
leading out of cities
became lined with tombs
and monuments for the
middle and upper classes.
This tomb is shaped like a
baking oven: a low-relief
frieze at the top shows
Eurysaces presiding over
his slaves in the various
phases of breadmaking.
The inscription proudly
asserts his origins and reveals
him as a freed slave, probably
of Greek origin. Many men
like him saved money from
their meagre slave salaries to
earn their freedom and set up
businesses, becoming the
backbone of Rome's economy.

Aqueduct of Nero and the Freedmen's Tombs **9**

Intersection of Via Statilia and Via di
Santa Croce in Gerusalemme.
Map 10 D1. 🚌 *9, 105, 516, 517.*
🚊 *14, 19, 30b.* **Open** *by appt only:
permit needed (see p367).*

THE AQUEDUCT was built by
Nero in the 1st century AD
as an extension of the Aqua
Claudia to supply Nero's

**Relief on the Tomb of
the Statilii freedmen**

Golden House *(see p175).* It
was later extended to the
Imperial residences on the
Palatine. Partly incorporated
into later buildings, the imposing arches make their way via
the Lateran to the Celian hill.
Along the first section of the
aqueduct, in
Via Statilia, is a
small tomb in
the shape of a
house, dating
from the 1st
century BC,
bearing the
names and like-
nesses of a
group of freed
slaves. Their
name, Statilii,
indicates that
they had been
freed by the Statilii, the family
of Claudius's notorious wife
Messalina. Servants of families
often pooled funds in this way
to pay for a dignified burial in
a common resting place.

**Porta Maggiore, a city gate formed
by the arches of an aqueduct**

**Well-preserved section of Nero's
Aqueduct near San Giovanni**

Villa Wolkonsky ⑩

Via Conte Rosso. **Map** 10 D1.
🚌 *4, 81, 590.* 🚋 *30b.* **Not open to**
the public.

NOW THE RESIDENCE of the
British ambassador, the
villa has a beautiful garden
strewn with Roman remains,
including arches of the Aqua
Claudia and a columbarium,
or collective grave, of the 2nd
century AD. Sadly, garden
parties for British residents
are no longer given here on
the Queen's official birthday.

Santi Quattro Coronati ⑪

Via dei Santi Quattro Coronati 20.
Map 9 B1. 📞 *06-70 47 54 26.*
🚌 *81, 85, 87, 117, 175, 673, 810.*
🚋 *30b.* **Open** *9.30am–noon,*
3.30pm–6pm daily. 🚻 ♿

Cloister of Santi Quattro Coronati

THE NAME of this fortified
convent (Four Crowned
Saints) refers to four Christian
soldiers martyred after they
refused to worship a pagan
god. For centuries it was the
bastion of the pope's
residence, the Lateran Palace.
Its high apse still looms over
the houses below, while a
Carolingian tower dominates
the entrance. Erected in the
4th century AD, it was rebuilt
after the invading Normans
set fire to the neighbourhood
in 1084. Hidden within is the
garden of the delightful inner
cloister (admission on request),
one of the earliest of its kind,
built around 1220.
   The remains of medieval
frescoes can be seen in the
Chapel of Santa Barbara, but
the convent's main feature is
the Chapel of St Sylvester – its
remarkable frescoes (1246)
recount the legend of the
conversion to Christianity of

the Emperor Constantine by
Pope Sylvester I (reigned 314–
35), then living as a hermit on
Monte Soratte, north of Rome.
   Stricken by the plague,
Constantine is prescribed a
bath in children's blood, to
the horror of the matrons of
Rome. Unable to bring himself
to obey, Constantine is
visited in a dream by St Peter
and St Paul. They advise him
to find Sylvester, who cures
him and baptizes him. The
final scene shows the emperor
kneeling before the pope.
The implied idea of the pope
as heir to the Roman Empire
would affect the whole course
of medieval European history.

San Clemente ⑫

See pp186–7.

Santo Stefano Rotondo ⑬

Via di Santo Stefano Rotondo 7.
Map 9 B2. 📞 *06-70 49 37 17.*
🚌 *81, 117, 673.* **Open** *9am–1pm,*
3.30pm–6pm (summer), 9am–noon,
2pm–4pm (winter). 🚫

ONE OF ROME'S earliest
Christian churches, Santo
Stefano Rotondo was built
between 468 and 483. It has an
unusual circular plan with four
chapels in a cruciform. The

Distinctive circular outline
of Santo Stefano Rotondo

round inner area was
surrounded by concentric
corridors with 22 Ionic
supporting columns. The high
drum in the centre is 22 m (72
ft) high and just as wide. It is
lit by 22 high windows, a few
of them restored or blocked by
restorations carried out under
Pope Nicholas V (reigned
1447–55), who consulted the
Florentine architect Leon
Battista Alberti. The archway
in the centre of the church
may have been added during
this period, when the outer
corridor was eliminated.
   In the 16th century the
church walls were frescoed
by Niccolò Pomarancio, with
particularly gruesome
illustrations of the martyrdom
of innumerable saints. Some
of the medieval decor remains
in the chapels: in the first
chapel to the left of the
entrance is a 7th-century
mosaic of Christ with San
Primo and San Feliciano.

Fresco of St Sylvester and Constantine in Santi Quattro Coronati

San Clemente ⑫

San Clemente provides an opportunity to travel back through three layers of history. At street level, there is a 12th-century church; underneath this lies a 4th-century church; and below that are ancient Roman buildings, including a Temple of Mithras. Mithraism, an all-male fertility cult imported from Persia in the 1st century BC, was a rival to Christianity during the age of Imperial Rome.

The upper levels are dedicated to St Clement, the fourth pope, who was exiled to the Crimea and martyred by being tied to an anchor and drowned. His life is illustrated in some of the frescoes in the 4th-century church. The site was taken over in the 17th century by Irish Dominicans, who still continue the excavating work begun by Father Mullooly in 1857.

Entrance to the church is through a door in Via di San Giovanni in Laterano.

Paschal Candlestick
This 12th-century spiralling candlestick, striped with glittering mosaic, is a magnificent example of Cosmati work.

18th-Century Facade
Twelfth-century columns were used in the arcade.

★ **Cappella di Santa Caterina**
The restored frescoes by the 15th-century Florentine artist, Masolino da Panicale, show scenes from the life of the martyred St Catherine of Alexandria.

12th-century church

4th-century church

Piscina
This deep pit was discovered in 1967. It could have been used as a font or fountain.

1st–3rd-century temple and buildings

TIMELINE

2nd century Site possibly used for secret Christian worship

Late 2nd century Temple of Mithras built

867 Reputed transfer of remains of San Clemente to Rome

1108 New church built over 4th-century church

1857 Original 4th-century church rediscovered by Father Mullooly

AD 10	500	1000	1500	1900

90–99 Papacy of St Clement

4th century First church built over courtyard of earlier Roman building

1667 Church and convent given to Irish Dominicans

AD 64 Nero's fire destroys area

1084 Church destroyed during Norman invasion led by Robert Guiscard

1861 Church is excavated. Roman ruins discovered

★Apse Mosaic
The 12th-century
Triumph of the
Cross *includes
beautifully detailed
animals and
acanthus leaves.*

Schola Cantorum
*The 6th-century
enclosure for the
choir was retained
for the new church,
built in 1108.*

**Temple of
Mithras**

**★ Triclinium and
Altar of Mithras**
*The altar, with a
relief of Mithras
slaying the bull,
stands in the
triclinium, a room
used for ritual
banquets.*

**★ 11th-
Century
Frescoes**
*Commissioned by
the de Rapiza family,
one shows the story of a boy
found alive in St Clement's
tomb beneath the Black Sea.*

Catacomb
*Discovered in
1938 and dating
from the 5th or 6th
century, it contains
16 wall tombs
known as* loculi.

VISITORS' CHECKLIST

Via di San Giovanni in Laterano.
Map 9 B1. 06-70 45 10 18.
85, 87, 117, 186, 850.
30b. Colosseo. **Open**
9am–12.30pm, 3.30pm–6.30pm
(Oct–Mar: 6pm) Mon–Sat, 10am–
12.30pm, 3.30pm–6.30pm Sun.
Adm charge to excavations.

STAR FEATURES

★ Apse Mosaic

★ Cappella di Santa
Caterina

★ 11th-Century
Frescoes

★ Triclinium and Altar
of Mithras

IOVINVSALVMNVS

CARACALLA

THE CELIAN HILL over-looks the Colosseum, and takes its name from Caelius Vibenna, the legendary hero of Rome's struggle against the Tarquins *(see pp16–17)*. In Imperial Rome this was a fashionable place to live, and some of its vanished splendour is still apparent in the vast ruins of the Baths of Caracalla. Today, thanks to

Capital from ruins of Baths of Caracalla

the Archaeological Zone established at the turn of the century, it is a delight-fully peaceful area, a green wedge from the Aurelian Wall to the heart of the city. Through it runs the cobbled Via di Porta San Sebastiano, part of the old Via Appia. This road leads to Porta San Sebastiano, one of the best-preserved gates in the ancient city wall.

SIGHTS AT A GLANCE

Churches
Santi Giovanni e Paolo ❶
San Gregorio Magno ❷
Santa Maria in Domnica ❹
San Sisto Vecchio ❻
Santi Nereo e Achilleo ❼
San Cesareo ❽
San Giovanni a Porta Latina ❾
San Giovanni in Oleo ❿
Santa Balbina ⓰

Arches and Gates
Arch of Dolabella ❸
Arch of Drusus ⓭
Porta San Sebastiano
and the Aurelian Wall ⓮
Sangallo Bastion ⓯

Historic Buildings
UN Food and Agriculture
Organization ⓱
Baths of Caracalla ⓲

Tombs
Columbarium of
Pomponius Hylas ⓫
Tomb of the Scipios ⓬

Parks and Gardens
Villa Celimontana ❺

GETTING THERE
Circo Massimo Metro station is handy if you are visiting the churches and parks on the Celian hill. For the Baths of Caracalla and other sights closer to Porta San Sebastiano, take the 628 or 760 along Viale delle Terme di Caracalla.

SEE ALSO
• *Street Finder*, maps 8, 9
• *Where to Stay* pp294–5
• *Restaurants* pp310–11

0 metres 300
0 yards 300

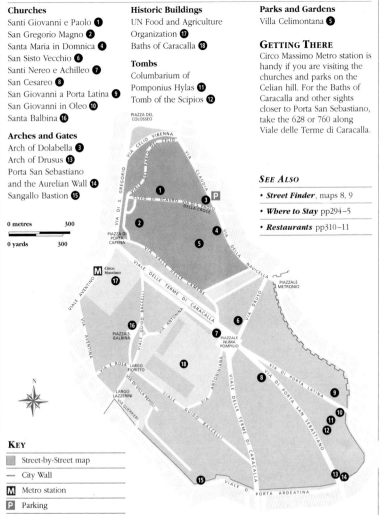

KEY
Street-by-Street map
— City Wall
Ⓜ Metro station
Ⓟ Parking

Mosaic of an athlete from the Baths of Caracalla

Street-by-Street: The Celian Hill

IN THE COURSE OF A MORNING exploring the green slopes of the Celian hill, you will see a fascinating assortment of archaeological remains and beautiful churches. A good starting point is the church of San Gregorio Magno, from where the Clivo di Scauro leads up to the top of the hill. The steep narrow street passes the ancient porticoed church of Santi Giovanni e Paolo with its beautiful Romanesque bell tower soaring above the surrounding medieval monastery buildings. Of the parks on the hill, the best kept and most peaceful is the Villa Celimontana with its formal walks and avenues. It is a good place for a picnic, as there are few bars or restaurants in the area.

Clivo di Scauro, the Roman *Clivus Scauri*, leads up to Santi Giovanni e Paolo, passing under the flying buttresses that support the church.

VIA DI SAN GREGORIO

CLIVO DI SCAURO

To Circo Massimo Metro

La Vignola is a delightful Renaissance pavilion, reconstructed here in 1911 after it had been demolished during the creation of the Archaeological Zone around the Baths of Caracalla.

San Gregorio Magno
A monastery and chapel were founded here by Pope Gregory the Great at the end of the 6th century ❷

★ **Santi Giovanni e Paolo**
The nave of the church, lit by a blaze of chandeliers, has been restored many times, assuming its present appearance in the 18th century ❶

★ **Villa Celimontana**
The delightful 16th-century villa built for the Mattei family is now the centre of a public park ❺

Trams passing over the Celian hill from the Colosseum rumble up a picturesque narrow track through the Parco del Celio.

LOCATOR MAP
See Central Rome Map pp12–13

Ruins of the Temple of Claudius are visible over a large area of the Celian hill. These travertine blocks have been incorporated in the base of the bell tower of Santi Giovanni e Paolo.

The gateway of San Tommaso in Formis is decorated with a wonderful 13th-century mosaic showing Christ with two freed slaves, one white, one black.

Arch of Dolabella
Built in the 1st century AD, probably as an entrance to the city, this archway was later incorporated in Nero's aqueduct to the Palatine ❸

STAR SIGHTS

★ **Santi Giovanni e Paolo**

★ **Santa Maria in Domnica**

★ **Villa Celimontana**

★ **Santa Maria in Domnica**
This church is famed for its 9th-century mosaics. These Apostles appear on the triumphal arch above the apse, flanking a medallion containing the figure of Christ ❹

KEY

– – – Suggested route

0 metres   75

0 yards   75

Santi Giovanni e Paolo ❶

Piazza Santi Giovanni e Paolo 13. **Map** 9 A1. [📞] 06-700 57 45. [🚌] 75, 81, 175, 673. [🚋] 30b. [Ⓜ] Colosseo or Circo Massimo. **Open** 8.30am–noon, 3.30pm–7pm (Oct–Mar: 6.30pm) daily (for Roman House, phone in adv). [🚻] [♿] church only.

SANTI GIOVANNI E PAOLO is dedicated to two martyred Roman officers whose house stood on this site. Giovanni (John) and Paolo (Paul) had served the first Christian emperor, Constantine. When they were later called to arms by the pagan emperor, Julian the Apostate, they refused and were beheaded in their own house in AD 362.

Built towards the end of the 4th century, the church retains many elements of its original structure. The Ionic portico dates from the 12th century, and the apse and bell tower were added by Nicholas Breakspeare, the only English pope, who reigned as Adrian IV (1154–9). The base of the superb 13th-century bell tower was part of the Temple of Claudius that stood on this site. In common with many Romanesque bell towers, it has inlaid marble and ceramic roundels decorating the brickwork.

The interior, remodelled in 1718, has granite piers and columns. A tomb slab in the nave marks the burial place of the martyrs, whose relics are preserved in an urn under the high altar. In a tiny room near the altar, a magnificent 13th-century fresco depicts the figure of Christ flanked by his Apostles (ask the sacristan to unlock the door for you).

Excavations beneath the church have revealed two Roman houses, of the 2nd and 3rd centuries, united and used as a Christian burial place. The two-storeyed construction, with 20 rooms and a labyrinth of corridors, has well-preserved pagan and Christian paintings. The arches to the left of the church were part of a 3rd-century street of shops.

Fresco of Christ and the Apostles in Santi Giovanni e Paolo

San Gregorio Magno ❷

Piazza di San Gregorio. **Map** 8 F2. [📞] 06-700 82 27. [🚌] 75, 81, 175, 673. [🚋] 30b. [Ⓜ] Circo Massimo. **Open** 8.30am–12.30pm, 1.45–6.30pm daily. [🚻]

Facade of San Gregorio Magno

TO THE ENGLISH, this is one of the most important churches in Rome, for it was from here that St Augustine was sent on his mission to convert England to Christianity. The church was founded in AD 575 by San Gregorio Magno (St Gregory the Great), who turned his family home on this site into a monastery. It was rebuilt in medieval times and restored in 1629–33 by Giovanni Battista Soria. The church is reached via a flight of steps from the street.

The forecourt contains some interesting tombs. To the left is that of Sir Edward Carne, who came to Rome several times between 1529 and 1533 as King Henry VIII's envoy to gain the pope's consent to the annulment of Henry's marriage to Catherine of Aragon.

The interior, remodelled by Francesco Ferrari in the mid-18th century, is Baroque, apart from the fine mosaic floor and some ancient columns. At the end of the right aisle is the chapel of St Gregory. Leading off it, another small chapel, believed to have been the saint's own cell, houses his episcopal throne – a Roman chair of sculpted marble. The Salviati Chapel on the left contains a picture of the Virgin said to have spoken to St Gregory.

Outside, amid the cypresses to the left of the church, stand three small chapels, dedicated to St Andrew, St Barbara and St Sylvia (Gregory the Great's mother). Recently restored, they contain frescoes by Domenichino and Guido Reni.

Marble throne of Gregory the Great from the 1st century BC

Arch of Dolabella ❸

Via di San Paolo della Croce.
Map 9 A2. 🚌 81, 117, 673.
🚋 30b. Ⓜ Colosseo.

THE ARCH was built in AD 10 by consuls Caius Junius Silanus and Cornelius Dolabella, possibly on the site of one of the old Servian Wall's gateways. It was made of travertine blocks and later used to support Nero's extension of the Claudian aqueduct, built to supply the Imperial palace on the Palatine hill.

The restored Arch of Dolabella

Santa Maria in Domnica ❹

Piazza della Navicella 12. **Map** 9 A2.
🎔 06-700 15 19. 🚌 81,117, 673.
🚋 30b. Ⓜ Colosseo. **Open**
9am–noon, 3.30–7pm (Oct–Mar:
6pm) daily. 🚻 ♿

THE CHURCH overlooks the Piazza della Navicella (little boat) and takes its name from the 16th-century fountain.

Dating from the 7th century, the church was made from an ancient stone galley which was probably a temple offering of a Roman traveller for his safe return to the city. In the 16th century Pope Leo X added the portico and the coffered ceiling.

In the apse behind the modern altar is a superb 9th-century mosaic commissioned by Pope Paschal I. Wearing the square halo of the living, the pope appears at the feet of the Virgin and Child. The Virgin, surrounded by a throng of angels, holds a handkerchief like a fashionable lady at a Byzantine court.

Villa Celimontana ❺

Piazza della Navicella. **Map** 9 A2.
🚌 81, 117, 673. **Park open**
7am–dusk daily.

THE DUKES OF MATTEI bought this land in 1553 and transformed the vineyards that covered the hillside into a formal garden. As well as palms and other exotic trees, the garden even has its own Egyptian obelisk. Villa Mattei, built in the 1580s, is now known as Villa Celimontana and houses the Italian Geographical Society.

The Mattei family used to open the park to the public on the day of the Visit of the Seven Churches, an annual event instituted by San Filippo Neri in 1552. Starting from the Chiesa Nuova (see p124), Romans went on foot to the city's seven major churches.

When they reached Villa Mattei, they were given a meal of bread, wine, salami, cheese, an egg and two apples. The garden, now owned by the city of Rome, still makes an ideal place for a picnic.

Park of Villa Celimontana

San Sisto Vecchio ❻

Piazzale Numa Pompilio 8.
Map 9 A3. 🎔 06-77 20 51 74.
🚌 628, 760, 714. **Open** by appt
only. **Closed** Aug. 🚫

THIS SMALL CHURCH is of great historical interest as it was granted to St Dominic in 1219 by Pope Honorius III. The founder of the Dominican order soon moved his own headquarters to Santa Sabina (see p204), San Sisto becoming the first home of the order of Dominican nuns. The church, with its 13th-century bell tower and frescoes, is also a popular church for weddings.

Apse mosaic of the Virgin and Child in Santa Maria in Domnica

Santi Nereo e Achilleo 𝟕

Via delle Terme di Caracalla 28.
Map 9 A3. ☎ 06-575 79 96.
🚌 160, 628, 760. **Open** 10am–
noon, 4–6pm Sat–Thu. ♿

ACCORDING to legend, St
Peter, after escaping
from prison, was
fleeing the city
when he lost a
bandage from
his wounds. The
original church
was founded
here in the 4th
century on the
spot where the
bandage fell, but
later on it was
rededicated to
the 1st-century
AD martyrs St
Nereus and St Achilleus.

**Detail of mosaic,
Santi Nereo e Achilleo**

Restored at the end of the
16th century, the church has
retained many medieval
features, including some fine
9th-century mosaics on the
triumphal arch. A magnificent
pulpit rests on an enormous
porphyry pedestal which was
found nearby in the Baths
of Caracalla. The walls of the
side naves are decorated
with a series of rather grisly
16th-century frescoes by
Niccolò Pomarancio, showing
in clinical detail how each of
the Apostles was martyred.

**Fresco by Niccolò Pomarancio of the *Martyrdom
of St Simon* in Santi Nereo e Achilleo**

San Cesareo 𝟖

Via di Porta San Sebastiano. **Map** 9
A3. ☎ 06-58 23 01 40. **Open** by
appointment 9am–1pm Sun.

THIS SPLENDID old church,
built over Roman ruins of
the 2nd century AD, has been
closed since 1988. You can
still admire Giacomo della
Porta's fine Renaissance
facade, but by phoning
ahead to book a visit,
you can also see
Cosmatesque mosaic
work and carving to
rival that of any
church in Rome. The
episcopal throne, altar
and pulpit are decorated
with delightful birds
and beasts. The church
was restored in the
16th century by Pope
Clement VIII, whose coat of
arms decorates the ceiling.

San Giovanni a Porta Latina 𝟗

Via di San Giovanni a Porta Latina.
Map 9 B3. ☎ 06-70 49 17 77.
🚌 4, 218, 628. **Open** 7am–noon,
3–7pm daily. ♿ ♿

THE CHURCH of "St John
at the Latin Gate" was
founded in the 5th century,
rebuilt in 720 and restored in
1191. This is one of the most
picturesque of
the old Roman
churches. Classical
columns support
the medieval
portico, and the
12th-century bell
tower is superb.
A tall cedar tree
shades an ancient
well standing in
the forecourt.
The interior has
recently been
restored, but it
preserves the rare
simplicity of its
early origins with
ancient columns
of varying styles
lining the aisles.
Traces of early
medieval frescoes
can still be seen.
There are 12th-
century frescoes
showing 46 different biblical
scenes from both the Old
and New Testaments, which
are among the finest of their
kind in Rome.

Fresco, San Giovanni a Porta Latina

San Giovanni in Oleo 𝟏𝟎

Via di Porta Latina. **Map** 9 C4. 🚌 4.
Adm ask at S. Giovanni a Porta Latina.

Frieze of San Giovanni in Oleo

THE NAME of this charming
octagonal Renaissance
chapel means "St John in Oil".
The tiny building marks the
spot where, according to
legend, St John was boiled in
oil – and came out unscathed,
or even refreshed. An earlier
chapel is said to have existed
on the site; the present one
was built in the early 16th
century. The design has been
attributed to Baldassare Peruzzi
or Antonio da Sangallo the
Younger. It was restored by
Borromini, who altered the
roof, crowning it with a cross
supported by a sphere
decorated with roses. He also
added a terracotta frieze of
roses and palm leaves. The
wall paintings inside the
chapel include one of St John
in a cauldron of boiling oil.

Niches for funerary urns in the Columbarium of Pomponius Hylas

Columbarium of Pomponius Hylas ⓫

Via di Porta Latina 10. **Map** 9 B4.
🚌 *4, 218, 628.* **Open** *by appt only: permit needed (see p367).*

KNOWN AS a columbarium because it resembles a dovecote (*columba* is the Latin word for dove), this kind of vaulted tomb was usually built by rich Romans to house the cremated remains of their freedmen. Many similar tombs have been uncovered in this part of Rome, which up until the 3rd century AD lay outside the city wall. This one, excavated in 1831, dates from the 1st century AD. An inscription informs us that it

is the Tomb of Pomponius Hylas and his wife, Pomponia Vitalinis. Above her name is a "V" which indicates that she was still living when the inscription was made. The tomb was probably a commercial venture. Niches in the interior walls of the columbarium were sold to people who could not afford to build vaults of their own.

Tomb of the Scipios ⓬

Via di Porta San Sebastiano 9.
Map 9 B4. 📞 *06-70 49 00 53.*
🚌 *218.* **Closed** *for restoration.*

THE SCIPIOS were a family of conquering generals. Southern Italy, Corsica, Algeria, Spain and Asia Minor all fell to their victorious Roman armies. The most famous of these generals was Publius Cornelius Scipio Africanus, who defeated the great Carthaginian general Hannibal at the Battle of Zama in 202 BC *(see p21)*. Scipio Africanus himself was not buried here in the family tomb, but at Liternum near Naples, where he owned a favourite villa.
  The Tomb of the Scipios was discovered in 1780. It contained various sarcophagi,

statues and niches with terracotta burial urns. Many of the originals have now been moved to the Vatican Museums and copies stand in their place.
  The earliest sarcophagus was that of Cornelius Scipio Barbatus, consul in 298 BC, for whom the tomb was built. Members of his illustrious family continued to be buried here up to the middle of the 2nd century BC. Excavations in the area have revealed many other archaeological finds: a columbarium similar to that of Pomponius Hylas, a Christian catacomb and a three-storey house dating from the 3rd century AD, which was built over the Tomb of the Scipios.

Arch of Drusus ⓭

Via di Porta San Sebastiano.
Map 9 B4. 🚌 *218.*

Arch of Drusus, part of the Aqua Antoniniana aqueduct

ONCE MISTAKENLY identified as a triumphal arch, the so-called Arch of Drusus merely supported the branch aqueduct that supplied the Baths of Caracalla. It was built in the 3rd century AD, so had no connection with Drusus, a stepson of the Emperor Augustus. Its monumental appearance was due to the fact that it carried the aqueduct across the important route, Via Appia. The arch still spans the old cobbled road, just 50 m (160 ft) short of the gateway Porta San Sebastiano.

Mosaic inscription in the Columbarium of Pomponius Hylas

Fortified gateway of Porta San Sebastiano

Porta San Sebastiano and the Aurelian Wall ⓮

Museo delle Mura, Via di Porta San Sebastiano 18. **Map** 9 B4. 🚌 *218*. 📞 *06-70 47 52 84.* **Open** *9am–7pm Tue–Sun (last adm: 30 mins before closing).* **Closed** *public hols.*
Adm charge. Ø

MOST OF the Aurelian Wall, begun by the Emperor Aurelian (AD 270–75) and completed by his successor Probus (AD 276–82), has survived. Aurelian ordered its construction as a defence against marauding Germanic tribes, whose raids were penetrating deeper and deeper into Italy. Some 18 km (11 miles) round, with 18 gates and 381 towers, the wall took in all the seven hills of Rome. It was raised to almost twice its original height by Maxentius (AD 306–12).

Porta San Sebastiano, the gate leading to the Via Appia Antica (*see p284*), is the largest and best-preserved gateway. It was rebuilt by the Emperor Honorius in the 5th century AD. Originally the Porta Appia, in Christian times it gradually became known as the Porta San Sebastiano, because the Via Appia led to the Basilica and Catacombs of San Sebastiano, which were popular places of pilgrimage.

It was at this gate that the last triumphal procession to enter the city by the Appian Way was received in state – that of Marcantonio Colonna after the victory of Lepanto over the Turkish fleet in 1571. Today the gate's towers house a museum containing prints and models illustrating the walls' history. From here you can take a short walk along the restored walls. The views are spectacular, especially out over the Via Appia.

The wall continued to be Rome's main defence until 1870, when it was breached by Italian artillery just by Porta Pia, close to today's British Embassy. Many of the gates are still in use, and although the city has spread, most of its noteworthy historical and cultural sights still lie within the walls.

Sangallo Bastion ⓯

Viale di Porta Ardeatina. **Map** 9 A4. 🚌 *160, 218, 671, 714.* **Closed** *for restoration.*

Pope Paul III Farnese

HAUNTED BY the memory of the Sack of Rome in 1527 and fearing attack by the Turks, Pope Paul III asked Antonio da Sangallo the Younger to reinforce the Aurelian Wall. Work on the huge projecting bastion began in 1537. For the moment its massive bulk can be admired from outside.

Santa Balbina ⓰

Piazza di Santa Balbina 8. **Map** 8 F3. 📞 *06-578 02 07.* 🚌 *81, 160, 175, 628, 673.* 🚋 *30b.* Ⓜ *Circo Massimo.* **Open** *8am–6pm daily.* 🕈

OVERLOOKING the Baths of Caracalla, this isolated church framed by cypresses is dedicated to Santa Balbina, a 2nd-century virgin martyr. Dating back to the 4th century, this is one of the city's oldest churches. Inside stands the magnificent sculpted and inlaid tomb of Cardinal Stefanus de Surdis, signed by Giovanni di Cosma (1303).

UN Food and Agriculture Organization ⓱

Viale delle Terme di Caracalla. **Map** 8 F2. 🚌 *81, 160, 175, 628, 673.* 🚋 *30b.* Ⓜ *Circo Massimo.* **Not open** to the public.

Obelisk of Axum (4th century AD)

THE FOOD and Agriculture Organization of the United Nations is based here in a modern building completed in 1952. Before it stands the obelisk of Axum, looted from Ethiopia by Mussolini, who commissioned the building originally to house the Ministry of Italian Africa.

Baths of Caracalla ⓲

Viale delle Terme di Caracalla 52.
Map 9 A3. 📞 *06-575 86 26.* 🚌 *81, 160, 175, 628, 673.* 🚋 *30b.* Ⓜ *Circo Massimo.* **Open** *Apr–Sep: 9am–6pm; Oct–Mar: 9am–1pm.* **Closed** *1 Jan, 1 May, 25 Dec.* **Adm charge.**

COMPLETED by the Emperor Caracalla in AD 217, the baths functioned for about 300 years, until the plumbing was destroyed by invading Goths. Over 1,600 bathers at a time could enjoy the facilities. A Roman bath was a long and complicated business, beginning with a sort of Turkish bath, followed by a spell in the *calidarium*, a large hot room with pools of water to moisten the atmosphere. Then came the lukewarm *tepidarium*, a visit to the large central meeting place, known as the *frigidarium*, and finally a plunge into the *natatio*, an open-air swimming pool. For the rich, this was followed by a rub-down with scented woollen cloth. As well as the baths, there were spaces for exercise, libraries, art galleries and gardens – a true leisure centre. Most of the rich marble decorations of the baths were removed by the Farnese family in the 16th century to adorn the interior of Palazzo Farnese *(see p147).*

Fragment of mosaic pavement

Part of one of the gymnasia in the Baths of Caracalla

Until recently, open-air operas were staged here – the vocal exertions of the performers are now thought to pose a threat to the structure of this ancient monument.

KEY

- ▨ Calidarium (very hot)
- ▨ Tepidarium (lukewarm)
- ▫ Frigidarium (cold)
- ▫ Natatio (pool)
- ▫ Garden

Greek and Latin libraries

Water tanks

Stadium

Conference and meeting rooms

Front entrance

Changing rooms

Gymnasia

Storage room for oils and perfumes

Conference and meeting room

Gymnasium

AVENTINE

THIS IS ONE of the most peaceful areas within the walls of the city. Although it is largely residential, there are some unique historic sights. From the top of the Aventine hill, crowned by the magnificent basilica of Santa Sabina, there are fine views across the river to Trastevere and St Peter's. At the

Mask fountain in courtyard of Santa Sabina

foot of the hill, ancient Rome is preserved in the two tiny Temples of the Forum Boarium and the Circus Maximus. The liveliest streets are in Testaccio, which has shops, restaurants and clubs, while to the south, beside Rome's solitary pyramid, the Protestant Cemetery is another oasis of calm.

SIGHTS AT A GLANCE

Churches and Temples
Santa Maria in Cosmedin ❶
San Giorgio in Velabro ❸
San Teodoro ❹
Santa Maria della Consolazione ❺
San Giovanni Decollato ❻
Temples of the Forum Boarium ❽
Santa Sabina ❾
Santi Bonifacio e Alessio ❿
San Saba ⓯

Historic Buildings
Casa dei Crescenzi ❼

Arches
Arch of Janus ❷

Historic Streets and Piazzas
Piazza dei Cavalieri di Malta ⓫

Ancient Sites
Monte Testaccio ⓬
Circus Maximus ⓰

Monuments and Tombs
Protestant Cemetery ⓭
Pyramid of Caius Cestius ⓮

GETTING THERE
The quickest way is by Metro line B to Piramide or Circo Massimo. For a more interesting trip, take tram 30b. Several buses go down Viale Aventino to Piramide, and the 23, 81, 160, 628 and 810 travel up the Aventine hill.

KEY

▦	Street-by-Street map
—	City Wall
Ⓜ	Metro station
Ⓟ	Parking

SEE ALSO

- **Street Finder**, maps 7, 8, 12
- **Where to Stay** pp294–5
- **Restaurants** pp310–11

Pines and orange trees on the Aventine hill with dome of St Peter's in the distance

Street-by-Street: Piazza della Bocca della Verità

T HE AREA ATTRACTS VISITORS eager to place their hands inside the Bocca della Verità (the Mouth of Truth) in the portico of Santa Maria in Cosmedin. There are many other sights to see in this quiet corner of the city beside the Tiber, which was the site of ancient Rome's first port and its busy cattle market. Substantial Classical remains include two small temples from the Republican age and the Arch of Janus from the later Empire. In the 6th century the area became home to a Greek community from Byzantium, who founded the churches of San Giorgio in Velabro and Santa Maria in Cosmedin.

Sant'Omobono, a late 16th-century church, now stands in isolation in the middle of an important archaeological site. The remains of sacrificial altars and two temples from the 6th century BC have been discovered.

Casa dei Crescenzi
This 11th-century building used columns and capitals from ancient Roman temples **7**

Ponte Rotto, as this forlorn ruined arch in the Tiber is called, means simply "broken bridge". Built in the 2nd century BC, its original name was the Pons Aemilius.

★ **Temples of the Forum Boarium**
The tiny round Temple of Hercules and its neighbour, the Temple of Portunus, are the best preserved of Rome's Republican temples **8**

PONTE PALATINO

KEY

– – –   Suggested route

0 metres   75

0 yards   75

STAR SIGHTS

★ **Santa Maria in Cosmedin**

★ **Temples of the Forum Boarium**

★ **Santa Maria in Cosmedin**
This medieval church has a fine marble mosaic floor and a Gothic baldacchino **1**

Santa Maria della Consolazione
This 16th-century church used to serve a hospital nearby **5**

San Teodoro
The 15th-century portal of this ancient round church is decorated with the arms of Pope Nicholas V **4**

LOCATOR MAP
See Central Rome Map pp12–13

San Giovanni Decollato
The plain Renaissance facade was completed in about 1504 **6**

San Giorgio in Velabro
The simple 12th-century portico of Ionic columns was destroyed by a bomb in 1993 but has been restored **3**

Arch of Janus
This square structure with arches on each side dates from the 4th century AD **2**

The Arco degli Argentari, dedicated to the Emperor Septimius Severus in AD 204, is decorated with scenes of religion and war.

The Fontana dei Tritoni by Carlo Bizzaccheri was built here in 1715. The style shows the powerful influence of Bernini.

Bocca della Verità

Santa Maria in Cosmedin ❶

Piazza della Bocca della Verità 18. **Map** 8 E1. 📞 06-678 14 19. 🚌 23, 44, 75, 81, 160, 175, 280, 628, 715. **Open** 9am–1pm, 2.30pm–6pm (5pm winter) daily. (Phone to check first). 🚻 👥 📷

Tᴴɪꜱ ʙᴇᴀᴜᴛɪꜰᴜʟ unadorned church was built in the 6th century on the site of the ancient city's food market. The elegant Romanesque bell tower and portico were added during the 12th century. In the 19th century a Baroque facade was removed and the church restored to its original simplicity. It contains many fine examples of Cosmati work, in particular the mosaic pavement, the raised choir, the bishop's throne and the canopy over the main altar.

Set into the wall of the portico is the Bocca della Verità (Mouth of Truth). This may have been a drain cover, dating back to before the 4th century BC. Medieval tradition had it that the formidable jaws would snap shut over the hand of those who told lies – a useful trick for testing the faithfulness of spouses.

Arch of Janus ❷

Via del Velabro. **Map** 8 E1. 🚌 23, 44, 75, 81, 160, 175, 280, 628, 715.

Pʀᴏʙᴀʙʟʏ ᴅᴀᴛɪɴɢ from the reign of Constantine, this imposing four-faced marble arch stood at the bustling crossroads on the edge of the Forum Boarium, near the ancient docks. Merchants and

customers did business in its shade. On the keystones above the four arches you can see small figures of the goddesses Roma, Juno, Ceres and Minerva. In medieval times the arch used to form the base of a tower fortress. It was restored to its original shape in 1827.

San Giorgio in Velabro ❸

Via del Velabro 19. **Map** 8 E1. 📞 06-683 29 30. 🚌 23, 44, 75, 81, 160, 175, 280, 628, 715. **Open** 10am–12.30pm, 4.30–7pm Tue–Fri.

San Giorgio in Velabro after its restoration in 1999

Iɴ ᴛʜᴇ ʜᴏʟʟᴏᴡ of the street named after the Velabrum, the swamp where Romulus and Remus are said to have been found by the she-wolf, is a small church dedicated to St George, whose bones lie under the altar.

The 7th-century basilica has suffered over the centuries from periodic floods, and in 1993 a bomb caused exten-

sive damage to the front of the church. Careful restoration has however returned it to its original appearance.

A double row of assorted granite and marble columns (taken from ancient Roman temples) divide the triple nave. The austerity of the cool grey interior is relieved by golden frescoes in the apse (attributed to Pietro Cavallini, 1295). The facade and the bell tower date from the 12th century.

San Teodoro ❹

Via di San Teodoro. **Map** 8 E1. 📞 06-678 66 24. 🚌 81, 95, 160, 175, 204, 628. **Open** 9.30am–6.30pm daily (to 5.30pm in winter).

Iꜰ ʏᴏᴜ ʜᴀᴘᴘᴇɴ to be in the area on a Sunday morning, you will find this small round 6th-century church at the foot of the Palatine a truly delightful place to visit for a weekly mass. Inside, the 6th-century mosaics in the apse are breathtaking, as is the Florentine cupola (1454). The fetching outer courtyard was designed by Carlo Fontana in 1705.

The church of San Teodoro, one of Rome's hidden treasures

The Arch of Janus, where cattle dealers sheltered from the midday sun

Facade of Santa Maria della Consolazione

Santa Maria della Consolazione ❺

Piazza della Consolazione 84.
Map 5 A5. ☎ 06-678 46 54.
🚌 44, 81, 95, 160, 170, 628, 715.
Open 6am– noon, 3.30pm–6.30pm
(6pm winter) daily. ✝ ♿

THE CHURCH STANDS near the foot of the Tarpeian Rock, the site of public execution of traitors since the time of the Sabine War.

In 1385, Giordanello degli Alberini, a condemned nobleman, paid two gold florins for an image of the Virgin Mary to be placed here, to provide some small consolation to prisoners in their final moments. Hence the name of the church that was built here in 1470. It was reconstructed between 1583 and 1600 by Martino Longhi who provided the early Baroque facade.

The church's 11 side-chapels are owned by noble families and local crafts guild members. In the presbytery is the famed image of Mary, attributed to Antoniazzo Romano.

San Giovanni Decollato ❻

Via di San Giovanni Decollato 22.
Map 8 E1. ☎ 06-699 07 28.
🚌 44, 81, 95, 160, 170, 628, 715.
Open by appointment only.

THE MAIN ALTAR is dominated by Giorgio Vasari's *Beheading of St John* (1553) from which the church takes its name, San Giovanni Decollato. In 1490 Pope Innocent VIII gave this site to build a church for a very specialized Florentine confraternity. Ghoulishly attired in black robes and hoods, their task was to encourage condemned prisoners to repent and to give them a decent burial after they had been hanged. In the cloisters there are seven manholes (one of them reserved for women), which received the bodies.

The oratory contains a cycle of frescoes describing the life of St John the Baptist by the leading Florentine Mannerists, Jacopino del Conte and Francesco Salviati. In style the figures resemble some of those in the Sistine Chapel.

Casa dei Crescenzi ❼

Via Luigi Petroselli. **Map** 8 E1.
🚌 44, 81, 95, 160, 170, 628, 715.

STUDDED WITH archaeological fragments, the house is what remains of an 11th-century tower fortress. It was built by the powerful Crescenzi family in order to keep an eye on the old docks of Rome (today the site of the Anagrafe or Public Records Office) and on the bridge where the family collected a toll.

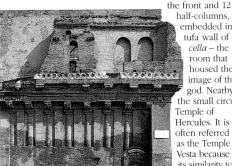

Ancient Roman fragments in the Casa dei Crescenzi

Temples of the Forum Boarium ❽

Piazza della Bocca della Verità. **Map** 8 E1. 🚌 44, 81, 95, 160, 170, 628, 715.

Temple of Portunus

THESE MIRACULOUSLY well-preserved Republican temples are particularly appealing by moonlight, in their grassy enclave under the umbrella pines beside the Tiber. They date from the 2nd century BC and were saved for posterity when they were reconsecrated as Christian churches in the Middle Ages. They offer rare examples of combined elements from Greek and Roman architecture.

The rectangular temple (formerly known as the Temple of Fortuna Virilis) was in fact dedicated to Portunus, the god of rivers and ports – a reference to the nearby port of ancient Rome. Set on a podium, it has four Ionic travertine columns fluted at the front and 12 half-columns, embedded in the tufa wall of the *cella* – the room that housed the image of the god. Nearby is the small circular Temple of Hercules. It is often referred to as the Temple of Vesta because of its similarity to the one in the Forum.

Luminous interior of Santa Sabina

Santa Sabina 🟐

Piazza Pietro d'Illiria 1. **Map** 8 E2. 🄲
06-574 35 73. 🚌 23, 44, 81, 95, 160,
170, 628. Ⓜ Circo Massimo. **Open**
10am–noon, 3.30–5.30pm daily. ♿

HIGH ON the Aventine stands
an early Christian basilica,
founded by Peter of Illyria in
AD 425 and restored to its
original simplicity in the early
20th century. Light filters
through 9th-century windows
upon a wide nave framed by
white Corinthian columns
supporting an arcade decorated
with a marble frieze. Over the
main door is a 5th-century blue
and gold mosaic dedicatory
inscription. The pulpit, carved
choir and bishop's throne date
from the 9th century.

The church was given to the
Dominicans in the 13th century
and in the nave is the magnificent mosaic tombstone of one
of the first leaders of the order,
Muñoz de Zamora (died 1300).

The side portico has 5th-
century panelled doors carved
from cypress wood, representing scenes from the Bible,
including one of the earliest
Crucifixions in existence.

Santi Bonifacio e Alessio 🟑

Piazza di Sant'Alessio 23. **Map** 8 D2.
🄲 06-574 34 46. 🚌 23, 44, 81, 95,
160, 170, 628, 715. Ⓜ Circo
Massimo. **Open** 8.30am–noon, 3.30–
6.30pm (Nov–Mar: 5pm) daily. ♿

THE CHURCH is dedicated to
two early Christian martyrs,
whose remains lie under the
main altar. Legend has it that

Alessio, son of a rich senator
living on the site, fled East to
avoid an impending marriage
amd become a pilgrim.
Returning home after many
years, he died as a servant,
unrecognized, under the stairs
of the family entrance hall,
clutching the manuscript of
his story for posterity.

The original 5th-century
church has undergone many
changes over time. Noteworthy
are the 18th century facade
with its five arches, the restored
Cosmati doorway and pave-
ment, and the magnificent
Romanesque five-storey bell
tower (1217).

An 18th-century Baroque
chapel by Andrea Bergondi
houses part of the famous
staircase. Other relics include
the well from Alessio's family
home and the glowing
Byzantine Madonna of the
Intercession brought from
Damascus to Rome at the end
of the 10th century.

Piazza dei Cavalieri di Malta 🟑

Map 8 D2. 🚌 23, 44, 81, 95, 160,
170, 628. Ⓜ Circo Massimo.

SURROUNDED BY cypress trees,
this ornate walled piazza
decorated with obelisks and
military trophies was designed
by Piranesi in 1765. It is named
after the Order of
the Knights of
Malta (Cavalieri di
Malta), whose
priory (at No. 3) is
famous for the
bronze keyhole
through which
there is a miniature
view of St Peter's,
framed by a tree-
lined avenue. The
priory church, Santa
Maria del Priorato,
was restored in
Neo-Classical style
by Piranesi in the
18th century. To
visit the church,
ask permission in
person at the
Order's building at
48 Via Condotti. At
the southwest cor-
ner of the square is
Sant'Anselmo,

the international Benedictine
church, where Gregorian
chants may be heard on
Sundays at 9.30am.

**Doorway of the Priory of the
Knights of Malta**

Monte Testaccio 🟑

Via Galvani. **Map** 8 D4. 🚌 23, 44, 75,
280. 🚋 30b. **Not open** to the public.

FROM ABOUT 140 BC to AD
250 this hill was created
by the dumping of millions of
testae (hence Testaccio) –
fragments of the amphorae
used to carry goods to the
nearby warehouses. The
artificial hill is 36 m (120 ft)
high, but its full archaeological
significance was not realized
until the late 18th century.

Facade of Santi Bonifacio e Alessio

Protestant Cemetery ⑬

Cimitero Acattolico, Via Caio Cestio 6.
Map 8 D4. 06-574 19 00. 23, 280, 716. 30b. **M** Piramide.
Open 9am–6pm (Oct–Mar: 5pm)
Tue–Sun (last adm 30 mins before closing). **Donation** expected.

T HE PEACE of this well-tended cemetery beneath the Aurelian Wall is profoundly moving. Non-Catholics, mainly English and German, have been buried here since 1738.

In the oldest part are the graves of John Keats (died 1821), whose epitaph reads: "Here lies One Whose Name was writ in Water", and his friend Joseph Severn (died 1879); not far away are the ashes of Percy Bysshe Shelley (died 1822). Goethe's son Julius is also buried here.

Tombstone of John Keats

Pyramid of Caius Cestius ⑭

Piazzale Ostiense. **Map** 8 E4. 23, 280. 30b. **M** Piramide.

Memorial pyramid of Caius Cestius

C AIUS CESTIUS, a wealthy praetor (senior Roman magistrate), died in 12 BC. His one claim to fame is his tomb, an imposing pyramid faced in white marble set in the Aurelian Wall near Porta San Paolo. It stands 36 m (118 ft) high and, according to an inscription, took 330 days to build. Unmistakable as a landmark, it must have looked almost as incongruous when it was built as it does today.

Detail of carving on sarcophagus in the portico of San Saba

San Saba ⑮

Via di San Saba. **Map** 8 F3.
06-574 33 52. 75, 673.
30b. **Open** 7am–noon, 4–7pm daily.

T UCKED AWAY in a residential street on the Little Aventine hill, San Saba began life as an oratory for Palestinian monks fleeing from Arab invasions in the 7th century. The existing church dates from the 10th century and has undergone much restoration. The portico houses a fascinating collection of archaeological remains.

The church has three naves in the Greek style and a short fourth 11th-century nave to the left with vestiges of 13th-century frescoes of the life of St Nicholas of Bari. Particularly intriguing is a scene of three naked young ladies lying in bed, who are saved from penury by the gift of a bag of gold from St Nicholas, the future Santa Claus. The beautiful marble inlay in the main door, the floor and the remains of the choir are all 13th-century Cosmati work.

Circus Maximus ⑯

Via del Circo Massimo. **Map** 8 F2.
75, 81, 160, 175, 628, 715, 716.
30b. **M** Circo Massimo.

W HAT WAS ONCE ancient Rome's largest stadium is today little more than a long grassy esplanade. Set in the valley between the Palatine and Aventine hills, the Circus Maximus was continually embellished and expanded from the 4th century BC until AD 549 when the last races were held. The grandstands held some 300,000 spectators, cheering wildly at the horse and chariot races, athletic contests and wild animal fights, betting furiously throughout.

The Circus had a central dividing barrier (spina) with seven large egg-shaped objects on it used for counting the laps of a race. These were joined in 33 BC by seven bronze dolphins that served a similar purpose. In 10 BC Augustus built the Imperial box under the Palatine and decorated the spina with the obelisk that now stands in the centre of Piazza del Popolo (see p137). A second obelisk, which was added in the 4th century by Constantius II, is now in Piazza di San Giovanni in Laterano (see pp178–9).

Reconstruction of the Circus Maximus in its heyday

TRASTEVERE

THE PROUD and aggressively independent inhabitants of Trastevere, the area "across the Tiber", consider themselves the most authentic Romans. In one of the most picturesque old quarters of the city, it is still possible to glimpse scenes of everyday life that seem to belong to bygone centuries. There are, however, signs that much of the earthy, proletarian character of the place may soon be destroyed by the proliferation of fashionable restau-

Romanesque bell tower

rants, clubs and boutiques. Some of Rome's most fascinating medieval churches lie hidden away in the patchwork of narrow, cobbled backstreets, the only clue to their location an occasional glimpse of a Romanesque bell tower. Santa Cecilia was built on the site of the martyrdom of the patron saint of music, San Francesco a Ripa commemorates St Francis of Assisi's visit to Rome, and Santa Maria in Trastevere is the traditional centre of the spiritual and social life of the area.

SIGHTS AT A GLANCE

Churches
Santa Maria della Scala ❸
Santa Maria in Trastevere
pp212–13 ❺
San Crisogono ❻
Santa Cecilia in Trastevere ❽
San Francesco a Ripa ❿

Museums and Galleries
Sant'Egidio and Museo
del Folklore ❹

Historic Buildings
Casa della Fornarina ❶
Caserma dei Vigili della
VII Coorte ❼
San Michele a Ripa Grande ❾

Bridges
Ponte Sisto ❷

Parks and Gardens
Villa Sciarra ⓫

SEE ALSO
• *Street Finder*, maps 4, 7, 8, 11
• *Where to Stay* pp294–5
• *Restaurants* pp310–11
• *Tiber Walk* pp274–5

KEY
▦ Street-by-Street map
— City Wall
🅿 Parking

GETTING THERE
The most convenient way is to take tram 8 which starts from Largo di Torre Argentina, crosses the river and runs along the broad, busy Viale di Trastevere. The H bus follows the same route but starts at Stazione Termini. From the Vatican it is best to take a 23 or 280 along Lungotevere. The 44 and 75 cross over to Trastevere at Porta Portese and run along Via Dandolo.

0 metres   300
0 yards   300

A typical *vicolo* (**narrow alleyway**) between the densely-packed buildings of Trastevere

Street-by-Street: Trastevere

$\mathbf{A}$LL YEAR ROUND TRASTEVERE is a major attraction both for its restaurants, clubs and cinemas, and for its picturesque maze of narrow cobbled alleyways. On summer evenings the streets are packed with jostling groups of pleasure-seekers, especially during the noisy local festival, the Festa de Noantri *(see p59)*. Everywhere café and restaurant tables spill out over pavements, especially around Piazza di Santa Maria in Trastevere and outside the pizzerias along Viale di Trastevere. There are also kiosks selling slices of watermelon and *grattachecca*, a mixture of syrup and grated ice. It is usually easier to appreciate the antique charm of Trastevere's narrow streets in the more tranquil atmosphere of the early morning.

Casa della Fornarina
Raphael's beautiful mistress is said to have lived here. There is now a flourishing restaurant in the back garden ❶

Santa Maria dei Sette Dolori
This church (1643) is a minor work by Borromini

Santa Maria della Scala
The church's unassuming façade conceals a rich Baroque interior ❸

Sant'Egidio and Museo del Folklore
This 17th-century fresco of Sant' Egidio by Pomarancio decorates the left-hand chapel in the church. The convent next door is a museum of Roman life and customs ❹

★ **Santa Maria in Trastevere**
The church is famous for its mosaics by Pietro Cavallini but it also has earlier works such as this mosaic of the prophet Isaiah to the left of the apse ❺

STAR SIGHTS

★ Santa Maria in Trastevere

KEY

- - - Suggested route

0 metres   75
0 yards   75

The fountain of Piazza di Santa Maria in Trastevere by Carlo Fontana (1692) is a popular meeting place. At night it is floodlit and dozens of young people sit on the steps around its octagonal base.

Ponte Sisto
This bridge was built on the orders of Sixtus IV in 1474 to link Trastevere to central Rome **2**

LOCATOR MAP
See Central Rome Map pp12–13

Piazza Belli is named after Giuseppe Gioacchino Belli (1791–1863), who wrote satirical sonnets in Roman dialect rather than academic Italian. At the centre of the piazza stands a statue of the poet (1913).

Vicolo del Piede is one of the picturesque narrow streets lined with restaurant tables leading off Piazza di Santa Maria in Trastevere.

The Torre degli Anguillara (13th century) is the only survivor of the many medieval towers that once dominated the Trastevere skyline.

Caserma dei Vigili della VII Coorte
The courtyard of this antique Roman fire station still stands **7**

San Crisogono
The Romanesque bell tower dates from the early 12th century. The plain portico is a later addition (1626), but is in keeping with the spirit of this ancient church **6**

Casa della Fornarina ●

Via di Santa Dorotea 20. **Map** 4 D5 & 11 B5. 🚌 *23, 280. See* ***Restaurants** p316.*

Not much is known about Raphael's model and lover, La Fornarina, yet over the centuries she has acquired a name, Margherita, and even a biography. Her father was a Sienese baker (*La Fornarina* means the baker's girl) and his shop was here in Trastevere near Raphael's frescoes in the Villa Farnesina *(see pp220–21)*.

Margherita earned a reputation as a "fallen woman" and Raphael, wishing to be absolved before dying, turned her away from his deathbed. After his death she took refuge in the convent of Santa Apollonia in Trastevere.

She is assumed to have been the model for Raphael's famous portrait *La Donna Velata* in the Palazzo Pitti in Florence.

Ponte Sisto ●

Map 4 E5 & 11 B5. 🚌 *23, 280.*

Named after Pope Sixtus IV della Rovere (reigned 1471–84), who commissioned it, this bridge was built by Baccio Pontelli to replace an ancient Roman bridge. The enterprising pope also built the Sistine Chapel *(see pp244–7)*, the Hospital of Santo Spirito *(see p226)* and restored many churches and monuments. This put him in great financial difficulties and he had to sell personal collections in order to finance his projects.

Another method of financing projects was to levy a tax on the city's prostitutes. Several popes are known to have resorted to this unpopular form of taxation.

Pope Sixtus IV

Gilded Baroque altar of Santa Maria della Scala

Santa Maria della Scala ●

Via della Scala. **Map** 4 D5 & 11 B5. 📞 *06-580 62 33.* 🚌 *23, 280.* **Church open** *7–8am, 5.30–6.30pm daily.* ✝ *7am, 5pm daily, 7am, 11.30am, 5pm Sun.*

This church belongs to a time of great building activity that lasted about 30 years from the end of the 16th to the early 17th century. Its rather simple facade contrasts with a rich interior decorated with multicoloured marbles and a number of spirited Baroque altars and reliefs.

Sant'Egidio and Museo del Folklore ●

Piazza Sant'Egidio 1. **Map** 7 C1. 🚌 *H, 23, 280.* 🚋 *8.* **Museo del Folklore** 📞 *06-589 59 45.* **Open** *9am–1pm Tue–Sun, also 5–7pm Tue & Thu.* **Church open** *for services only.* ✝ *8.30pm daily.*

Built in 1630, Sant'Egidio was the church of the adjoining Carmelite convent, one of many founded in the area to shelter the poor and destitute. The convent is now a folklore museum, containing a wealth of material relating to the festivals, pastimes, superstitions and customs of the Romans when they lived under papal rule.

There are old paintings and prints of the city and tableaux showing scenes of everyday life in 18th- and 19th-century Rome, including reconstructions of shops and a tavern.

The museum also has manuscripts by the much-loved poets Belli and Trilussa who wrote in local dialect..

Watercolour of public scribe (1880) in the Museo del Folklore

Santa Maria in Trastevere ●

See pp212–13.

San Crisogono ●

Piazza Sonnino 44. **Map** 7 C1. 📞 *06-581 82 25.* 🚌 *H, 23, 280.* 🚋 *8.* **Open** *7am–11am, 4pm–7pm Mon–Sat, 8am–1pm Sun.* **Adm charge** *for excavations.* ✝ &

This church was built on the site of one of the city's oldest *tituli* (private houses used for Christian worship). An 8th-century church with 11th-century frescoes can still be seen beneath the present church. This dates from the early 12th century, a period of intense building activity in the popular quarters of Rome. San Crisogono was decorated

Apse mosaic in San Crisogono

by Pietro Cavallini – the apse mosaic by his school remains.

Most of the columns were taken from previous buildings, including the great porphyry ones of the triumphal arch. The mosaic floor is the result of recycling precious marble from various Roman ruins.

Caserma dei Vigili della VII Coorte **7**

Via della VII Coorte. **Map** 7 C1.
(06-67 10 38 19. 🚌 23, 44, 280.
🚊 8. **Open** on request – phone first.

NOT ALL ROMAN RUINS are Imperial villas or grand temples; there are also those illustrating the daily life of a busy city. One of these is the barracks of the guards of the VII Coorte, the Roman fire brigade. It was built under Augustus' reign, in the 1st century AD, and the excavated courtyard seen today is where the men would rest while waiting for an alarm.

Santa Cecilia in Trastevere **8**

Piazza di Santa Cecilia. **Map** 8 D1.
(06-589 92 89. 🚌 H, 23, 280.
🚊 8. **Open** 10am–noon, 4–5.15pm daily. **Adm charge** for excavations. **Cavallini fresco** can be seen 10am–11.30am Tue & Thu only.

ST CECILIA, ARISTOCRAT and patron saint of music, was martyred here in AD 230. After an attempt at scalding her to death, she was beheaded. A church was founded – perhaps in the 4th century – on the site of her house (still to be seen beneath the church, with the remains of a Roman tannery). For a long time her body went missing, but it turned up in the Catacombs of San Callisto (*see p265*). In the 9th century it was reburied here by Pope Paschal I, who rebuilt the church. A fine apse mosaic survives from this period.

The altar canopy by Arnolfo di Cambio and the fresco of *The Last Judgment* by Pietro Cavallini, reached through the adjoining convent, date from the 13th century, one of the few periods when Rome had

Detail of 13th-century fresco by Pietro Cavallini in Santa Cecilia

a distinctive artistic style of its own. In front of the altar is a statue of St Cecilia by Stefano Maderno, who used her miraculously preserved remains as a model when she was briefly disinterred in 1599.

San Michele a Ripa Grande **9**

Via di San Michele. **Map** 8 D2.
(06-584 31. 🚌 23, 44, 75, 280.
Open for special exhibitions only.

THIS HUGE, IMPOSING complex, now housing the Ministry of Culture, stretches 300 m (985 ft) along the river Tiber. It was built on the initiative of Pope Innocent XII and contained a home for the elderly, a boys' reform school, a woollen mill

and various chapels. Today contemporary exhibitions are often held here.

San Francesco a Ripa **10**

Piazza San Francesco d'Assisi 88.
Map 7 C2. **(** 06-581 90 20. 🚌 23, 44, 280. 🚊 8. **Open** 7.30am–noon, 4pm–7pm daily. 🚻 🚹

ST FRANCIS OF ASSISI lived here in a hospice when he visited Rome in 1219 and his stone pillow and crucifix are preserved in his cell. The church was rebuilt by his follower, the nobleman Rodolfo Anguillara, who is portrayed on his tombstone wearing the Franciscan habit.

Entirely rebuilt in the 1680s by Cardinal Pallavicini, the church is rich in sculptures. Particularly flamboyant are the 18th-century Rospigliosi and Pallavicini monuments in the transept chapel.

Not to be missed in the Paluzzi-Albertoni chapel (fourth on the left, along the nave) is Bernini's breathtaking sculpture, the *Ecstasy of Beata Ludovica Albertoni*.

Villa Sciarra **11**

Via Calandrelli 35. **Map** 7 B2. 🚌 44, 75. **Park open** 9am–sunset daily. **House closed** for restoration. 🚹

IN ROMAN TIMES the site of this small, attractive public park was a nymph's sanctuary. It is especially picturesque in spring when its wisterias are in full bloom. The paths through the park are decorated with Romantic follies, fountains and statues, and there are splendid views of the city over Janiculum's bastions.

Bernini's *Ecstasy of Beata Ludovica Albertoni* (1674) in San Francesco a Ripa

Santa Maria in Trastevere ❻

PROBABLY THE FIRST official Christian place of worship to be built in Rome, this basilica became the focus of devotion to the Virgin Mary. According to legend, the church was founded by Pope Callixtus I in the 3rd century, when Christianity was still a minority cult. Today's church is largely a 12th-century building, remarkable for its mosaics, in particular those by Pietro Cavallini. The 22 granite columns in the nave were taken from the ruins of ancient Roman buildings. Despite some 18th-century Baroque additions, Santa Maria has retained its medieval character. This friendly church has strong links with the local community.

Piazza Santa Maria in Trastevere
The piazza in front of the church is the traditional heart of Trastevere. Today it is surrounded by lively bars and restaurants. Carlo Fontana built the octagonal fountain in the late 17th century.

The floor, relaid in the 1870s, is a recreation of the Cosmatesque mosaic floor of the 13th century.

The bell tower was built in the 12th century. At the top is a small mosaic of the Virgin.

★ Facade Mosaics
The 12th-century mosaic shows Mary feeding the baby Jesus and ten women holding lamps. Eight of the lamps are lit, symbolizing virginity; the veiled women whose lamps have gone out are probably widows.

STAR FEATURES

★ **Cavallini Mosaics**

★ **Facade Mosaics**

MODEST DONORS

Many of Rome's mosaics include a portrait of the pope or cardinal responsible for the building of the church. Often the portrait is dwarfed by the rest of the picture, which glorifies the saint to whom the church is dedicated. On the facade of Santa Maria, two tiny unidentified figures kneel at the Virgin's feet. Were they to stand up, the men would barely reach her knees.

Facade mosaic, detail

The portico was remodelled in 1702 by Carlo Fontana. Statues of four popes decorate the balustrade above.

Front entrance

15th-century wall tabernacle by Mino del Reame

Apse Mosaic
The 12th-century mosaic in the basin of the apse shows the Coronation of the Virgin. She sits on Christ's right hand, surrounded by saints.

★ **Cavallini Mosaics**
The details in the six mosaics of the Life of the Virgin (1291) display a touching realism.

Madonna della Clemenza
The life-size icon probably dates from the 7th century. A replica is displayed above the altar of the Cappella Altemps.

Tomb of Cardinal Pietro Stefaneschi
The last of his line, Pietro Stefaneschi died in 1417. His tomb is by an otherwise unknown sculptor called Paolo.

TIMELINE

AD 217–22 Church founded by Pope Callixtus I	*Pope Innocent II*	**1291** Pietro Cavallini adds mosaics of scenes from the life of the Virgin for his patron, Bertoldo Stefaneschi	**1617** Domenichino designs coffered ceiling with octagonal panel of the Assumption of the Virgin	

30 BC	AD 200	1150	1400	1650	1900

38 BC Jet of mineral oil spouts from the ground on this site. Later interpreted as a portent of the coming of Christ

c1138 Pope Innocent II starts rebuilding the church

1580 Martino Longhi the Elder restores church and builds family chapel for Cardinal Marco Sittico Altemps

1702 Pope Clement XI has portico rebuilt

1866–77 Church restored by Virginio Vespignani

JANICULUM

OVERLOOKING THE TIBER on the Trastevere side of the river, the Janiculum hill has often played its part in the defence of the city. The last occasion was in 1849 when Garibaldi held off the attacking French troops. The park at the top of the hill is filled with monuments to Garibaldi and his men. A popular place for walks, the park provides a welcome escape from the densely-packed streets of Trastevere.

Puppets in the park at the top of the Janiculum hill

You will often find puppet shows and other kinds of amusements for children. In medieval times most of the hill was occupied by monasteries and convents. Bramante built his miniature masterpiece, the Tempietto, in the convent of San Pietro in Montorio. The Renaissance also saw the development of the riverside area along Via della Lungara, where the rich and powerful built beautiful houses such as the Villa Farnesina.

SIGHTS AT A GLANCE

Churches and Temples
Sant'Onofrio **6**
San Pietro in Montorio **7**
Tempietto **8**

Museums and Galleries
Palazzo Corsini and Galleria Nazionale d'Arte Antica **2**

Historic Buildings
Villa Farnesina pp220–21 **1**

Fountains
Fontana dell'Acqua Paola **9**

Monuments
Garibaldi Monument **5**

Arches and Gates
Porta Settimiana **3**

Parks and Gardens
Botanical Gardens **4**

SEE ALSO
- *Street Finder*, maps 3, 4, 7, 11
- *Where to Stay* pp294–5
- *Restaurants* pp310–11

GETTING THERE
The Janiculum (Il Gianicolo) is not the easiest part of Rome to reach by public transport. It can be approached either from the Vatican area *(see p223)* or from Trastevere *(see p207)*. There is only one bus, the 870, that goes up to the top of the hill, but the 44 or 75 will take you from Piazza Venezia to Via Giacinto Carini from where start your walk up. For sights along Via della Lungara, take the 23 or 280, which go along Lungotevere.

0 metres   300

0 yards   300

KEY

Tour of the Janiculum map

— City Wall

The staircase fountain in the Botanical Gardens

A Tour of the Janiculum

THE LONG HIKE to the top of the Janiculum is rewarded by wonderful views over the city. The park's monuments include a lighthouse and statues of Garibaldi and his wife Anita. There is also a cannon which is fired off at noon each day. In Via della Lungara, between the Janiculum and the Tiber, stand Palazzo Corsini with its national art collection and the Villa Farnesina, decorated by Raphael for his friend and patron, the fabulously wealthy banker Agostino Chigi.

Tasso's Oak is a memorial to the poet Torquato Tasso, who liked to sit here in the days before he died in 1595. The tree was struck by lightning in 1843.

The Manfredi Lighthouse, built in 1911, was a gift to the city of Rome from Italians in Argentina.

The Monument to Anita Garibaldi by Mario Rutelli was erected in 1932. The great patriot's Brazilian wife lies buried beneath the statue.

The view from Villa Lante, a beautiful Renaissance summer residence, gives a magnificent panorama of the whole city.

Garibaldi Monument
The inscription on the base of the equestrian statue means "Rome or Death" ❺

ROMA O MORTE

Botanical Gardens
These were established in 1883 when part of the grounds of Palazzo Corsini was given to the University of Rome ④

★ **Palazzo Corsini**
This 15th-century triptych by Fra Angelico hangs in the Galleria Nazionale d'Arte Antica ②

LOCATOR MAP
See Central Rome Map pp12–13

★ **Villa Farnesina**
The suburban villa of the banker Agostino Chigi is celebrated for its frescoes by Raphael, Baldassarre Peruzzi and other Renaissance masters ①

Porta Settimiana
Looking through this Renaissance gateway from Via della Lungara, you catch a glimpse of Trastevere's warren of narrow streets ③

KEY

– – – Suggested route

0 metres 75
0 yards 75

STAR SIGHTS

★ Villa Farnesina

★ Palazzo Corsini and Galleria Nazionale d'Arte Antica

Villa Farnesina ❶

See pp220–21.

Palazzo Corsini and Galleria Nazionale d'Arte Antica ❷

Via della Lungara 10. **Map** 4 D5 &
11 A5. **☎** 06-68 80 23 23. **🚌** 23,
280. **Open** 9am–7pm Tue–Fri,
9am–2pm Sat, 9am–1pm Sun &
public hols (last adm: 30 mins before
closing). **Closed** 1 May, 15 Aug, 25
Dec & 1 Jan. **Adm charge.** ⊘ ♿ 📷

**Queen Christina's bedroom in the
Palazzo Corsini**

T HE HISTORY of Palazzo
Corsini is intimately
entwined with that of Rome.
Built for Cardinal Domenico
Riario in 1510–12, it has
boasted among its many
distinguished guests Bramante,
the young Michelangelo,
Erasmus and Queen Christina
of Sweden, who died here in
1689. The old palazzo was
completely rebuilt for Cardinal
Neri Corsini by Ferdinando
Fuga in 1736. As Via della
Lungara is too narrow for a
good frontal view, Fuga
designed the facade so it could
be viewed from an angle.
Palazzo Corsini now houses
the Galleria Nazionale d'Arte
Antica. This outstanding
collection includes paintings
by Rubens, Van Dyck, Murillo,
Caravaggio and Guido Reni,
together with 17th- and 18th-
century Italian regional art.
The palazzo is also home to
the Accademia dei Lincei, a
learned society founded in

1603, which once included
Galileo among its members.
In 1797 Palazzo Corsini was
the backdrop to momentous
events: French General Duphot
(the fiancé of Napoleon's
sister Pauline) was killed here
in a skirmish between papal
troops and Republicans. The
consequent French occupation
of the city and the deportation
of Pope Pius VI led to the
proclamation of a short-lived
Roman Republic (1798–9).

Porta Settimiana ❸

Between Via della Scala and Via della
Lungara. **Map** 4 D5 & 11 B5.
🚌 23, 280.

T HIS GATE was built in 1498
by Pope Alexander VI
Borgia to replace a minor
passageway in the Aurelian
Wall. The Porta Settimiana
marks the start of Via della
Lungara, a long straight road
built in the early 16th century.

Botanical Gardens ❹

Largo Cristina di Svezia 24, off Via
Corsini. **Map** 4 D5. **☎** 06-686 41 93.
🚌 23, 280. **Open** 9am–6.30pm
(Oct–Mar: 5.30pm) Mon–Sat. **Closed**
public hols & Aug. **Adm charge**.

S EQUOIAS, PALM TREES and
splendid collections of
orchids and bromeliads are
housed in Rome's Botanical
Gardens *(Orto Botanico)*. The
gardens contain more than
7,000 plant species from all
over the world. Indigenous
and exotic species are grouped

to illustrate their botanical
families and their adaptation
to different climates and
eco-systems. There are also
several interesting examples
of plants like the gingko that
have survived virtually
unchanged from earlier eras.
The gardens were originally
part of the Palazzo Corsini,
but since 1983 have belonged
to the University of Rome.

Garibaldi Monument ❺

Piazzale Giuseppe Garibaldi.
Map 3 C5. **🚌** 870.

Base of the Garibaldi Monument

T HIS HUGE equestrian statue
is part of a commemorative
park, recalling the heroic
events witnessed on the
Janiculum when the French
army attacked the city in 1849.
Garibaldi's Republicans fended
off the greatly superior French
forces for weeks, until the
Italians were overwhelmed.
Garibaldi and his men escaped.
The monument, erected in
1895, was the work of Emilio
Gallori. Around the pedestal
are four smaller sculptures in
bronze showing battle scenes
and allegorical figures.

Steps and tiered fountains at the Botanical Gardens

Courtyard of Sant'Onofrio

Sant'Onofrio ❻

Piazza di Sant'Onofrio 2. **Map** 3 C4.
📞 06-686 44 98. 🚌 870.
Open 10am–noon Sun & public hols.
Closed Aug, except saint's feast
day on 12 Aug. 🏛 **Museum
open** by appt only.

BEATO NICOLA da Forca
Palena, whose tombstone
guards the entrance, founded
this church in 1419 in honour
of the hermit Sant'Onofrio. It
retains the flavour of the 15th
century in the simple shapes
of the portico and the cloister.
In the early 17th century the
portico was decorated with
frescoes by Domenichino.
    The monastery next to the
church houses a small museum
dedicated to the 16th-century
poet Torquato Tasso, who
died here in one of the cells.

San Pietro in Montorio ❼

Piazza San Pietro in Montorio 2.
Map 7 B1. 📞 06-581 39 40. 🚌 44,
75. **Open** 7.30am–noon, 4–6pm
daily. If closed, ring bell at door to
right of church. 🏛

SAN PIETRO IN MONTORIO – the
church of St Peter on the
Golden Hill – was founded in
the Middle Ages near the spot
where St Peter was presumed
to have been crucified. It was
rebuilt by order of Ferdinand
and Isabella of Spain at the
end of the 15th century, and
decorated by outstanding
artists of the Renaissance.
    The facade is typical of a
time when clean, geometric
shapes derived from Classical
architecture were in vogue.
The single nave ends in a
deep apse that once contained

Raphael's *Transfiguration*,
now in the Vatican. Two wide
chapels, one on either side of
the nave, were decorated by
some of Michelangelo's most
famous pupils. The left-hand
chapel was designed by one
of the few artists Michelangelo
openly admired, Daniele da
Volterra, also responsible for
the altar painting, the *Baptism
of Christ*. The chapel on the
right was the work of Giorgio
Vasari, who included a self-
portrait (in black, on the left)
in his altar painting, the
Conversion of St Paul.
    The first chapel to the right
of the entrance contains a
powerful *Flagellation*, by the
Venetian artist Sebastiano del
Piombo (1518); Michelangelo
is said to have provided the
original drawings. Work by
Bernini and his followers can
be seen in the second chapel
on the left and in the flanking
De Raymondi tombs.

Tempietto ❽

Piazza San Pietro in Montorio (in
courtyard). **Map** 7 B1.
📞 06-581 39 40. 🚌 44, 75.
Open 9am–noon, 4–6pm daily. See
The History of Rome pp30–31.

AROUND 1502 Bramante completed what many consider
to be the first true Renaissance building in Rome – the
Tempietto. The name means
simply "little temple". Its
circular shape echoes early
Christian *martyria*,
chapels built on
the site of a saint's
martyrdom. This
was believed to be
the place where St
Peter was crucified.
    Bramante chose
the Doric order for
the 16 columns
surrounding the
domed chapel.
Above the columns
is a Classical frieze
and a delicate
balustrade. Though
the scale of the
Tempietto is tiny,
Bramante's masterly
use of Classical
proportions creates
a satisfyingly
harmonious whole.

The Tempietto illustrates the
great Renaissance dream that
the city of Rome would once
again relive its ancient glory.

Fontana dell'Acqua Paola ❾

Via Garibaldi. **Map** 7 B1. 🚌 44, 75.

Fontana dell'Acqua Paola

THIS MONUMENTAL FOUNTAIN
commemorates the
reopening in 1612 of an
aqueduct originally built by
Emperor Trajan in AD 109.
The aqueduct was renamed
"dell'Acqua Paola" after Paul V,
the Borghese pope who
ordered its restoration. When
it was first built, the fountain
had five small basins, but in
1690 Carlo Fontana altered the
design, adding the huge basin
you can see today. Despite
many laws intended to deter
them, generations of Romans
used this convenient pool of
fresh water for bathing and
washing their vegetables.

Bramante's round chapel, the Tempietto

Villa Farnesina ❶

THE WEALTHY SIENESE BANKER Agostino Chigi, who had established the headquarters of his far-flung financial empire in Rome, commissioned the villa in 1508 from his compatriot Baldassarre Peruzzi. The simple, harmonious design, with a central block and projecting wings, made this one of the earliest true Renaissance villas. The decoration was carried out between 1510 and 1519 and this has recently been restored. Peruzzi frescoed some of the interiors himself. Later, Sebastiano del Piombo, Raphael and his pupils added more elaborate works. The frescoes illustrate Classical myths, and the vault of the main hall, the Sala di Galatea, is adorned with astrological scenes showing the position of the stars at the time of Chigi's birth. Artists, poets, cardinals, princes and the pope himself were entertained here in magnificent style by their wealthy and influential host. In 1577 the villa was bought by Cardinal Alessandro Farnese. Since then, it has been known as the Villa Farnesina.

North Facade
The Loggia of Cupid and Psyche looks out on formal gardens that were used for parties and putting on plays.

Entrance

The Wedding of Alexander and Roxanne by Sodoma
Cherubs are shown helping the bride Roxanne to prepare for her marriage.

★ **Triumph of Galatea by Raphael**
The beautiful sea nymph Galatea was one of the 50 daughters of the god Nereus.

The Gabinetto delle Stampe sometimes holds exhibitions of rare prints.

Frescoes in the Room of Galatea
Perseus beheads Medusa in a scene from one of Peruzzi's series of mythological frescoes.

THE ARCHITECT

Baldassarre Peruzzi, painter and architect, arrived in Rome from Siena in 1503 aged 20 and became Bramante's chief assistant. Although his architectural designs were typical of Classicism, his painting owes more to Gothic influences, as his figurework is very highly stylized. On Raphael's death, he became Head of Works at St Peter's, but was captured in the Sack of Rome (*see p31*), exiled to Siena until 1535, and died in 1536.

Baldassarre Peruzzi

★ **Salone delle Prospettive**
Peruzzi's frescoes create the illusion of looking out at views of 16th-century Rome through a marble colonnade.

VISITORS' CHECKLIST

Via della Lungara 230. **Map** 4 D5 & 11 A5. 🚌 *23, 280 to Lungotevere Farnesina.* 📞 *06-68 80 17 67.* **Open** *9am–1pm Mon–Sat.* 🚫 💳 🏛 **Adm charge.** **Gabinetto delle Stampe** *(rare print collection)* 📞 *06-68 98 02 30.* **Open** *9am–1pm Tue–Sat for occasional exhibitions.* 🚫

Fresco from the Salone delle Prospettive
This scene shows the Torre delle Milizie (see p90) as it looked in the 1500s.

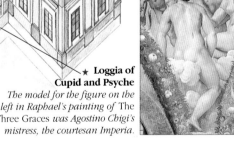

★ **Loggia of Cupid and Psyche**
The model for the figure on the left in Raphael's painting of The Three Graces *was Agostino Chigi's mistress, the courtesan Imperia.*

Lunette in the Room of Galatea
This giant monochrome head by Peruzzi was once attributed to Michelangelo.

STAR FEATURES

★ **Triumph of Galatea by Raphael**

★ **Loggia of Cupid and Psyche**

★ **Salone delle Prospettive**

VATICAN

AS THE SITE where St Peter was martyred and buried, the Vatican became the residence of the popes who succeeded him. Decisions taken here have shaped the destiny of Europe, and the great basilica of St Peter's draws pilgrims from all over the Christian world. The papal palaces beside St Peter's house the Vatican Museums. With the added attractions of Michelangelo's Sistine Chapel and the Raphael Rooms, their wonderful

Nuns in St Peter's Square

collections of Classical sculpture make them the finest museums in Rome. The Vatican's position as a state within a state was guaranteed by the Lateran Treaty of 1929, marked by the building of a new road, the Via della Conciliazione. This leads from St Peter's to Castel Sant' Angelo, a monument to a far grimmer past. Built originally as the Emperor Hadrian's mausoleum, this papal fortress and prison has witnessed many fierce battles for control of the city.

SIGHTS AT A GLANCE

Churches and Temples
St Peter's pp230–33 **1**
Santo Spirito in Sassia **4**
Santa Maria in Traspontina **9**

Museums and Galleries
Vatican Museums pp234–47 **2**

Historic Buildings
Hospital of Santo Spirito **5**
Palazzo del Commendatore **6**
Palazzo dei Convertendi **7**
Palazzo dei Penitenzieri **8**

Palazzo Torlonia **12**
Castel Sant'Angelo pp248–9 **13**
Palazzo di Giustizia **14**

Gates
Porta Santo Spirito **3**

Historic Streets and Piazzas
The Borgo **10**
Vatican Corridor **11**

GETTING THERE
The quickest way to reach the area is by Metro line A to Ottaviano. This is especially convenient when visiting the Vatican Museums. The 64 bus runs regularly from Piazza dei Cinquecento, in front of Termini station. Other routes that serve the area include the 81 and 492, which stop in Piazza del Risorgimento. There is a regular shuttle bus between St Peter's and the Vatican Museums.

0 metres   400
0 yards   400

KEY
▨   Tour of the Vatican map
—   City Wall
🅿   Parking

SEE ALSO

Dome of St Peter's dominating the Vatican skyline

A Tour of the Vatican

THE VATICAN, a centre of power for Catholics all over the world and a sovereign state since February 1929, is ruled by the pope. About 1,000 people live here, staffing the Vatican's facilities. There is a post office and shops, Vatican radio, broadcasting to the world in over 20 languages, a daily newspaper (*l'Osservatore Romano*), Vatican offices and a publishing house.

The Madonna of Guadalupe shows the miraculous image of the Madonna which appeared on the cloak of a Mexican Indian in 1531.

Papal heliport

The Grotto of Lourdes is a replica of the grotto in the southwest of France, where in 1858 the Virgin appeared to St Bernadette.

The Vatican Railway Station, opened in 1930, connects with the line from Rome to Viterbo, but is now used only for freight.

Radio Vatican is broadcast from this tower, part of the Leonine Wall built in 847.

The Papal Audience Chamber, by Pier Luigi Nervi, was opened in 1971. It seats up to 12,000.

The information office gives details of tours of the Vatican Gardens.

★ **St Peter's**
The Chapel of St Peter is in the Grottoes under the basilica. The rich marble decoration was added by Clement VIII at the end of the 16th century ❶

Piazza San Pietro was laid out by Bernini between 1656 and 1667. The narrow space in front of the church opens out into an enormous ellipse flanked by colonnades.

The obelisk was erected here in 1586 with the help of 150 horses and 47 winches.

STAR SIGHTS

★ **St Peter's**

★ **Vatican Museums**

The Eagle Fountain was built to celebrate the arrival of water from the Acqua Paola aqueduct at the Vatican. The eagle is the Borghese crest.

LOCATOR MAP
See Central Rome Map pp12–13

The Casina of Pius IV is a delightful summerhouse in the Vatican Gardens built by Pirro Ligorio in the mid-16th century.

Entrance to Vatican Museums

★ **Vatican Museums**
Raphael's Madonna of Foligno (1513) is just one of the Vatican's many Renaissance masterpieces ②

The Galleon Fountain is a perfect scale model of a 17th-century ship in lead, brass and copper. It was made by a Flemish artist for Pope Paul V.

The Cortile della Pigna is mostly the work of Bramante. The niche for the pine cone, once a Roman fountain, was added by Pirro Ligorio in 1562.

KEY

– – –	Suggested route

0 metres   75

0 yards   75

To Via della Conciliazione

St Peter's ❶

See pp230–33.

Vatican Museums ❷

See pp234–47.

Porta Santo Spirito ❸

Via dei Penitenzieri. **Map** 3 C3.
🚌 34, 46, 46b, 62, 98, 870, 881, 982.

THIS GATE stands at what was the southern limit of the "Leonine City", the area enclosed within walls by Pope Leo IV as a defence against the Saracens who had sacked Rome in AD 845. The walls measure 3 km (2 miles) in circumference.

Work on the walls started in AD 846. Pope Leo supervised the huge army of labourers personally, and thanks to his encouragement, the job was completed in four years. He then led a solemn procession to consecrate his massive feat of construction.

Since the time of Pope Leo the walls have needed much reinforcement and repair. The gateway visible today at Porta Santo Spirito was built by the architect Antonio da Sangallo the Younger in 1543–4. It is framed by two huge bastions that were added in 1564 by

Pope Pius IV Medici. Sadly, Sangallo's design for a monumental entrance to the Vatican was never completed; the principal columns come to an end somewhat abruptly in a modern covering of cement.

Santo Spirito in Sassia ❹

Via dei Penitenzieri 12. **Map** 3 C3.
📞 06-687 93 10. 🚌 23, 34, 62, 64, 982. **Open** 7am–noon, 3–8pm daily.
🚻 ♿

Nave of Santo Spirito in Sassia

BUILT ON THE SITE of a church erected by King Ine of Wessex, who died in Rome in the 8th century, the church is the work of Antonio da Sangallo the Younger. It was rebuilt (1538–44) after the

Sack of Rome had left it in ruins in 1527. The facade was added under Pope Sixtus V (1585–90). The nave and side chapels are decorated with a series of light, lively frescoes. The pretty bell tower is earlier, dating from the reign of Sixtus IV (1471–84). It was probably the work of the pope's architect Baccio Pontelli, who also built the nearby Hospital of Santo Spirito, and the Ponte Sisto *(see p210)* further down the River Tiber.

Sixtus V's arms over door of Santo Spirito

Hospital of Santo Spirito ❺

Borgo Santo Spirito 2. **Map** 3 C3.
🚌 34, 46, 46b, 62, 98, 870, 881, 982. **Octagonal chapel open** 8.30am–2pm daily.

THE OLDEST HOSPITAL in Rome, this is said to have been founded as a result of a nightmare experienced by Pope Innocent III (1198–1216). In the dream, an angel showed him the bodies of Rome's unwanted babies dredged up from the Tiber River in fishing nets. As a result, the pope hastened to build a hospice for sick paupers.

Fresco of an angel in the octagonal chapel of the Hospital of Santo Spirito

In 1475 the hospital was reorganized by Pope Sixtus IV to care for the poor pilgrims expected for the Holy Year. Sixtus's hospital was a radical building. Cloisters divided the different types of patients; one area is still reserved for orphans and their nurses.

Unwanted infants were passed through a revolving barrel-like contraption called the *rota,* still visible to the left of the central entrance in Borgo Santo Spirito, to guarantee anonymity. Martin Luther, who visited in 1511, was shocked by the number of abandoned children he saw, believing them to be "the sons of the pope himself".

In the centre, under the hospital's conspicuous drum, is an octagonal chapel, where mass was said for patients. This room can be visited while the rest of the building still functions as a hospital.

Rusticated doorway of the Palazzo dei Convertendi

The *rota* of Santo Spirito, where mothers left unwanted babies

Palazzo del Commendatore ❻

Borgo Santo Spirito 3. **Map** 3 C3. 🚌 *34, 46, 46b, 62, 64, 98, 870, 881, 982.* **Courtyard only open** to the public.

AS DIRECTOR of the Hospital of Santo Spirito, the Commendatore not only ran the hospital, he was also responsible for its estates and revenues. This important post was originally given to members of the pope's family.

The palazzo, built next door to the hospital, has a spacious 16th-century frescoed loggia appropriate to the dignity and sobriety of its owners. The frescoes represent the story of the founding of the Hospital of Santo Spirito. To the left of the entrance is the Spezieria, or Pharmacy. This still has the wheel used for grinding the bark of the cinchona tree to produce the drug quinine, first introduced here in 1632 by Jesuits from Peru as a cure for malaria.

Above the courtyard is a splendid clock (1827). The dial is divided into six; it was not until 1846 that the familiar division of the day into two periods of 12 hours was introduced in Rome by Pope Pius IX.

Palazzo dei Convertendi ❼

Via della Conciliazione 43. **Map** 3 C3. 🚌 *34, 46, 46b, 62, 64, 98, 870, 881, 982.* **Not open** to the public.

WITH THE BUILDING of Via della Conciliazione in the 1930s, Palazzo dei Convertendi was taken down and later moved to this new site nearby. The house, which is partly attributed to the architect Bramante, is where the artist Raphael died in 1520.

Palazzo dei Penitenzieri ❽

Via della Conciliazione 33. **Map** 3 C3. 📞 *06-682 81 21.* 🚌 *34, 46, 46b, 62, 64, 98, 881.* See **Where to Stay** p295.

THE PALAZZO owes its name to the fact that the place was once home to the confessors *(penitenzieri)* of St Peter's. Today, their places have been taken by tourists, as the building has been converted into the Hotel Columbus. Originally built by Cardinal Domenico della Rovere in 1480, the palazzo still bears the family's coat of arms, the oak tree *(rovere* means oak), on its graceful courtyard well-head. On the cardinal's death, the palazzo was acquired by Cardinal Francesco Alidosi, Pope Julius II della Rovere's favourite. Suspected of treason, the cardinal was murdered in 1511 by the pope's nephew, the Duke of Urbino, who also took possession of his palazzo. A few of the rooms still contain beautiful frescoes.

Della Rovere arms

View of the Tiber and the Borgo between Castel Sant'Angelo and St Peter's by Gaspare Vanvitelli (1653–1736)

Santa Maria in Traspontina ⑨

Via della Conciliazione 14.
Map 3 C3. 06-68 80 64 51.
23, 34, 62, 64, 870, 982. **Open**
6.30am–noon, 4pm–7.30pm
daily.

The facade of the Carmelite church of Santa Maria in Traspontina

THE CHURCH occupies the site of an ancient Roman pyramid, believed in the Middle Ages to have been the Tomb of Romulus. The pyramid was destroyed by Pope Alexander VI Borgia, but representations of it survive in the bronze doors at the entrance to St Peter's and in a Giotto triptych in the Vatican Pinacoteca *(see p240)*.

The present church was begun in 1566 to replace an earlier one which had been in the line of fire of the cannons defending Castel Sant'Angelo during the Sack of Rome in 1527. The papal artillery officers insisted that the dome of the new church should be as low as possible, so it was built without a supporting drum. The first chapel to the right is dedicated to the gunners' patron saint, Santa Barbara, and is decorated with warlike motifs. In the third chapel on the left are two columns, said to be those to which St Peter and Paul were bound before martyrdom.

The Borgo ⑩

Map 3 C3. 23, 34, 64, 982.

THE WORD BORGO derives from the German *burg*, meaning town. Rome's Borgo is where the first pilgrims to St Peter's were housed in hostels and hospices, often for quite lengthy periods. The first of these foreign colonies, called "schools", was founded in AD 725 by a Saxon, King Ine of Wessex, who wished to live a life of penance and to be buried near the Tomb of St Peter. These days hotels and

hostels have made the Borgo a colony of international pilgrims once again. Much of the area's character was destroyed by redevelopment in the 1930s, but it is still enjoyable to explore the old narrow streets on either side of Via della Conciliazione.

Vatican Corridor ⑪

Castel Sant'Angelo to the Vatican.
Map 3 C3. 23, 34, 64, 982.

Clement VII, who used the Vatican Corridor to evade capture in 1527

LOCALLY KNOWN as the Passetto (small corridor), this long passageway was built into the fortifications during medieval times. Meant to link the Vatican with the fortress of Castel Sant'Angelo, it constituted a fortified escape route which could also be used to control the strategic Borgo area. Arrows and other missiles could be fired from its bastions on to the streets and houses below. The corridor was used in 1494 by Pope Alexander VI Borgia when Rome was invaded by King Charles VIII of France. In 1527 it enabled Pope Clement VII to take refuge in Castel Sant'Angelo, as the troops commanded by the Constable of Bourbon began the Sack of Rome.

Palazzo Torlonia (1496), unaffected by changes to the surrounding area

Palazzo Torlonia ⑫

Via della Conciliazione 30. **Map** 3 C3.
🚌 23, 34, 64, 982. **Not open** to the public.

THE PALAZZO was built in the late 15th century by the wealthy Cardinal Adriano Castellesi, in a style closely resembling Palazzo della Cancelleria *(see p149)*. The cardinal was a much-travelled rogue, who collected vast revenues from the bishopric of Bath and Wells which he was given

Pope Leo X

by his friend King Henry VII of England. In return he gave Henry his palazzo for use as the seat of the English ambassador to the Holy See. Castellesi was finally stripped of his cardinalate by Pope Leo X Medici and disappeared from history.

Since then the palazzo has had many owners and tenants. In the 17th century it was rented for a time by Queen Christina of Sweden. The Torlonia family, who acquired the building in 1820, owed its fortune to the financial genius of shopkeeper-turned-banker Giovanni Torlonia. He lent money to the impoverished Roman nobility and bought up their property during the Napoleonic Wars.

Castel Sant'Angelo ⑬

See pp248–9.

Palazzo di Giustizia ⑭

Piazza Cavour. **Map** 4 E3. 🚌 32, 34, 49, 70, 87, 186, 280, 492, 913, 926, 990. **Not open** to the public.

THE MONUMENTAL Palazzo di Giustizia (Palace of Justice) was built between 1889 and 1910 to house the national

law courts. Its riverside facade is crowned with a bronze chariot and fronted by giant statues of the great men of Italian law.

The building was supposed to embody the new order replacing the injustices of papal rule, but it has never endeared itself to the Romans. It was soon dubbed the Palazzaccio (roughly, "the ugly old palazzo") both for its appearance and for the nature of its business. By the 1970s the building was collapsing under its own weight, but it has now been restored.

The ornate travertine facade of the Palazzo di Giustizia

St Peter's ❶

THE CENTRE of the Roman Catholic faith, St Peter's draws pilgrims from all over the world. Few are disappointed when they enter the sumptuously decorated basilica beneath Michelangelo's vast dome.

A shrine was erected on the site of St Peter's tomb in the 2nd century and the first great basilica, ordered by the Emperor Constantine, was completed around AD 349. By the 15th century it was falling down, so in 1506 Pope Julius II laid the first stone of a new church. It took more than a century to build and all the great architects of the Roman Renaissance and Baroque had a hand in its design.

★ **Dome of St Peter's**
Designed by Michelangelo, though not finished in his lifetime, the spectacular cupola, 136.5 m (448 ft) high, gives unity to the majestic interior of the basilica.

The nave's total lenght is 218 m (715 ft).

Papal Altar
The present altar dates from the reign of Clement VIII (1592–1605). The plain slab of marble found in the Forum of Nerva stands under Bernini's baldacchino, over-looking the well of the confessio, the crypt where St Peter's body is reputedly buried.

Baldacchino
This magnificent canopy of gilded bronze, supported on spiral columns 20 m (66 ft) high, was designed by Bernini in the 17th century.

TIMELINE

AD 61 Burial of St Peter		1506 Julius II lays first stone	1547 Michelangelo named as chief architect of St Peter's		1626 New basilica of St Peter's consecrated
324 Constantine builds basilica	1452 Nicholas V plans restoration			1593 Dome completed	

AD 60	800	1500	1550	1600	
200 Altar built marking grave of St Peter	1503 Pope Julius II chooses Bramante as architect for new basilica	1538 Antonio da Sangallo the Younger made director of works	1606 Carlo Maderno extends basilica	1614 Maderno finishes the facade	
800 Charlemagne crowned Holy Roman Emperor in St Peter's		1514 Raphael director of works	1564 Death of Michelangelo		

★ **View from the Dome**
The superb symmetry of Bernini's colonnade can be appreciated from the dome.

The two minor cupolas at the corners of the transept are by Vignola.

Pope Urban VIII's Keys
At the base of the columns of the baldacchino, the coat of arms of Pope Urban VIII features the keys to the Kingdom of Heaven.

Facade by Carlo Maderno (1614)

Stairs to the dome

Filarete Door
Finished in 1445, Antonio Averulino's bronze door came from the original basilica.

Entrances

STAR FEATURES

★ **Dome of St Peter's**

★ **View from the Dome**

Piazza San Pietro
On Sundays and religious occasions the pope blesses the crowds from his balcony above the square.

A Guided Tour of St Peter's

T HE VAST BASILICA'S 187-m (615-ft) long, marble-encrusted interior contains 11 chapels and 45 altars in addition to a wealth of precious works of art. Some were salvaged from the original basilica and others commissioned from late Renaissance and Baroque artists, but much of the elaborate decoration is owed to Bernini's work in the mid-17th century. The two side aisles are 76 m (250 ft) long and converge under Michelangelo's enormous dome. The central focus of the building is the Papal Altar beneath Bernini's great baldacchino, filling the space between four massive piers which support the dome. From the basilica you can visit the Grottoes, the Treasury and St Peter's Sacristy, or climb up to the terrace for panoramic views.

⑤ **Baldacchino by Bernini**
Commissioned by Pope Urban VIII in 1624, the extravagant Baroque canopy dominates the nave and crowns the Papal Altar, at which only the pope may celebrate mass.

Bernini's Monument to Urban VIII

④ **Throne of St Peter in Glory**
In the domed apse, look up to the window above Bernini's Baroque sculpture of 1656–65. It lights the image of the Holy Spirit, shown as a dove amid clouds, rays of sunlight and flights of angels.

Entrance to Treasury and Sacristy

Entrance to Necropolis

HISTORICAL PLAN OF THE BASILICA OF ST PETER'S

St Peter was buried in AD 64 in a necropolis near his crucifixion site at the Circus of Nero. Constantine built a basilica on the burial site in AD 324. In the 15th century the old church was found to be unsafe and had to be demolished. It was rebuilt in the 16th and 17th centuries. By 1614 the facade was ready, and in 1626 the new church was consecrated.

KEY

▨ Circus of Nero

▨ Constantinian

▨ Renaissance

▨ Baroque

③ **Monument to Pope Alexander VII**
Bernini's last work was finished in 1678 and is in an alcove on the left of the transept. The pope sits among the figures of Truth, Justice, Charity and Prudence.

② **Monument to Leo XI**
On the left beneath the aisle arch is Alessandro Algardi's white marble 1650 monument to Leo XI, whose reign as pope lasted only 27 days.

KEY

– – – Tour route

⑥ **Angelo della Navicella**
A fragment of Giotto's beautiful 13th-century mosaic, salvaged from the old basilica, is now in the Grottoes. A later copy of the entire mosaic of Jesus and St Peter fishing on Lake Tiberias decorates the atrium.

⑦ **St Peter**
Until recently this famous 13th-century statue, now attributed to Arnolfo di Cambio, was thought to be a late Roman work. Situated at the end of the nave, it is sculpted in bronze with a delicate filigree halo.

Entrance to Grottoes

The Tabernacle by Bernini is made of gilt bronze in the shape of a temple.

Chapel of St Sebastian

Stuart Monument by Canova

The Porta Santa (Holy Door) is opened only in Holy Years. The Pope knocks on it with a bronze hammer, it is unlocked and remains open throughout the Holy Year.

⑧ **Pietà**
This famous marble sculpture was finished in 1499 when Michelangelo was only 25. It stands in a chapel to one side of the nave, protected by glass since being damaged in 1972.

Filarete Door

Navicella Mosaic

Atrium by Carlo Maderno

① **Tomb of Maria Clementina Sobieski**
Near the entrance is Filippo Barigioni's sentimentally expressive 18th-century monument to Maria Clementina, the wife of James Stuart, the Old Pretender.

Vatican Museums ②

THE BUILDINGS that house one of the world's most important art collections were originally papal palaces built for Renaissance popes such as Sixtus IV, Innocent VIII and Julius II. The long courtyards and galleries, linking Innocent VIII's Belvedere Palace to the other buildings, are by Donato Bramante and were commissioned for Julius II in 1503. Most of the later additions to the buildings were made in the 18th century, when priceless works of art accumulated by earlier popes were first put on show. This complex of museums also houses the Sistine Chapel and the Raphael Rooms, and should not be missed.

★ **Atrium of the Four Gates**
Built by Camporese in 1792–3, this vast domed edifice was the original entrance to the Vatican Museums.

The Belvedere Palace was commissioned in the late 15th century by Pope Innocent VIII.

★ **Cortile della Pigna**
This huge bronze pine cone, part of an ancient Roman fountain, once stood in the courtyard of old St Peter's. Its niche was designed by Pirro Ligorio.

Cortile della Biblioteca

Cortile del Belvedere

Apartment of Pius V

Sistine Chapel

Borgia Tower

Borgia Apartment

Raphael Loggia

Cortile di San Damaso

STAR FEATURES

★ **Cortile della Pigna**

★ **Atrium of the Four Gates**

★ **Bramante Stairway**

Spiral Ramp
The spectacular stairway up to the museums from the street was designed by Giuseppe Momo in 1932.

Entrance

VISITORS' CHECKLIST

Città del Vaticano. Entrance in Viale Vaticano. Map 3 B2. 06-69 88 44 66. 49 to entrance, 23, 81, 492, 982 to Piazza del Risorgimento or 64 to St Peter's. Connecting bus between St Peter's and museums. M Ottaviano. 19 to Piazza del Risorgimento. **Open** Mar–Oct: 8.45am–3.45pm Mon–Fri, 8.45am–12.45pm Sat; Nov–Feb: 8.45am–12.45pm Mon–Sat. **Closed** public & religious hols. Special permit needed for Raphael Loggia, Vatican library, Lapidary Gallery & Vatican Archives. **Adm charge**, free last Sun of month. special routes. **Temporary exhibitions, lectures.**

Simonetti Stairway
Built in the 1780s with a vaulted ceiling, the stairs were part of the conversion of the Belvedere Palace into the Pio-Clementine Museum.

Cortile Ottagonale
The inner court of the Belvedere Palace was given its octagonal shape in 1773.

★ Bramante Stairway
Pope Julius II built the spiral staircase within a square tower as an entrance to the palace. The staircase could be ridden up on horseback in case of emergency.

Braccio Nuovo

TIMELINE

1198 Innocent III creates papal palace	1503 Bramante lays out Belvedere Courtyard	1655 Bernini designs Scala Regia	1756 Foundation of Christian Museum	1800–23 Chiaramonti Museum founded	1837 Etruscan Museum founded
	1509 Raphael begins work on Rooms				

1000	1500	1600	1700	1800
1473 Pope Sixtus IV builds Sistine Chapel	1503–13 Pope Julius II starts Classical sculpture collection	*Bramante (1444–1514)*	1758 Museum of Pagan Antiquities founded	1822 Braccio Nuovo is opened
			1776–84 Pius VI enlarges museum	1970 Pope Paul VI opens Gregorian Museum of Pagan Antiquities

Exploring the Vatican Museums

FOUR CENTURIES of papal patronage and connoisseurship have resulted in one of the world's great collections of Classical and Renaissance art. The Vatican houses many of the great archaeological finds of central Italy including the *Laocoön* group, discovered in 1506 on the Esquiline, the *Apollo del Belvedere* and the Etruscan bronze known as the *Mars of Todi*. During the Renaissance, parts of the museums were decorated with wonderful frescoes commissioned for the Sistine Chapel, the Raphael Rooms and the Borgia Apartment.

Mars of Todi

Gallery of the Candelabra
Once an open loggia, this gallery of Greek and Roman sculpture has a fine view of the Vatican Gardens.

Roo
the

Gallery of Tapestries

**Etruscan
Museum**

Siege of Malta
The Gallery of Maps is an important record of 16th-century history and cartography.

Upper floor

**Modern
Religious Art**

**Raphael
Loggia**

**Sistine
Chapel**

**Raphael
Rooms**

GALLERY GUIDE

Visitors have to follow a one-way system. It is best to concentrate on a single collection or to choose one of the suggested itineraries. These are colour-coded so that you can follow them throughout the museums. They vary in length from 90 minutes to five hours. If you are planning a long visit, make sure you allow plenty of time for resting. Conserve your stamina for the Sistine Chapel and the Raphael Rooms; they are 20–30 minutes' walk from the entrance, without allowing for any viewing time along the way.

Sala dei Misteri
This is one of the rooms of the Borgia Apartment, richly decorated with Pinturicchio frescoes.

Gregorian Profane Museum

Pio-Christian Museum

St Jerome
Leonardo da Vinci's unfinished work, lost then rediscovered in the 19th century, shows the artist's mastery of anatomy.

Entrance

Round Room

Pinacoteca

Pio-Clementine Museum

Room of the Busts
This contains portraits of emperors and other notable Romans.

Greek Cross Room

Stairs up

Stairs down

Egyptian Museum

Braccio Nuovo

Chiaramonti Museum

Laocoön
This 1st-century AD marble group depicts the Trojan priest Laocoön and his sons struggling with two snakes.

Vatican Library

Lapidary Gallery

Lower floor

Room of the Animals
Roman mosaics, like these delightful ducks, decorate the walls and floor of this room of animal sculptures.

Apollo del Belvedere
This Roman copy of a Greek statue of the sun god Apollo perfectly embodies the ideals of Classical beauty.

KEY TO FLOORPLAN

- Egyptian and Assyrian art
- Greek and Roman art
- Etruscan and Italic art
- Early Christian and medieval art
- 15th- to 19th-century art
- Modern Religious art
- Non-exhibition space
- Open by special permit only

Exploring the Vatican's Collections

T HE VATICAN'S GREATEST TREASURES are its Greek and
Roman antiquities. These have been on display
since the 18th century. The 19th century saw the
addition of exciting discoveries from Etruscan tombs
and excavations in Egypt. In the Pinacoteca (art gallery)
there is a small, choice collection of paintings, including
works by Raphael, Titian and Leonardo. Works by great
painters and sculptors are also on view throughout the
older parts of the museums in the form of sumptuous
decorations commissioned by the Renaissance popes.

Coloured bas-relief from an Egyptian tomb (c2400 BC)

EGYPTIAN AND ASSYRIAN ART

T HE EGYPTIAN COLLECTION
contains finds from 19th-
and 20th-century excavations
in Egypt and statues which
were brought to Rome in
Imperial times. There are also
Roman imitations of Egyptian
art from Hadrian's Villa (see
p269) and from the Campus
Martius district of ancient
Rome. Egyptian-style statuary
from Hadrian's Villa was used
to decorate the Greek Cross
Room, the entrance to the
new wing built in 1780 by
Michelangelo Simonetti.

The genuine Egyptian works,
exhibited on the lower floor of
the Belvedere Palace, include
statues, mummies, mummy
cases and funerary artefacts.
There is also a large collection
of documents written on
papyrus, the paper the ancient
Egyptians made from reeds.
Among the main treasures is a
colossal granite statue of
Queen Tuia, the mother of
Rameses II, found on the site
of the Horti Sallustiani gardens

(see p251) in 1714. The statue,
which dates from the 13th
century BC, may have been
brought to Rome by the
Emperor Caligula (reigned
AD 37–41), who had an
unhealthy interest in
pharaohs and in his own
mother, Agrippina.

Also noteworthy are
the head of a statue of
Mentuhotep IV (21st
century BC), the
beautiful mummy
case of Queen
Hetep-heret-es,
and the tomb of
Iri, the guardian
of the Pyramid of
Cheops (22nd
century BC).

The Assyrian
Stairway is
decorated with
fragments of
reliefs from
the palaces of
the Kings of
Nineveh (8th century BC).
These depict the military
exploits of King Sennacherib
and his son Sargon II, and
show scenes from Assyrian
and Chaldean mythology.

ETRUSCAN AND OTHER PRE-ROMAN ART

T HIS COLLECTION comprises
artefacts from pre-Roman
civilizations in Etruria and
Latium, from Neolithic times
to the 1st century BC, when
these ancient populations were
assimilated into the Roman
state. Pride of place in the
Gregorian Etruscan Museum
goes to the objects found in
the Regolini-Galassi tomb,
excavated in 1836 at the
necropolis of Cerveteri (see
p271). The tomb was found
intact and yielded numerous
everyday household objects,
plus a throne, a bed and a
funeral cart, all cast in bronze,
dating from the 7th century
BC. Beautiful black vases,
delightful terracotta figurines
and bronze statues such as
the famous Mars of Todi,
displayed in the Room of the
Bronzes, show the Etruscans
to have been a highly civilized,
sophisticated people.

A number of Greek vases
that were found in Etruscan
tombs are on display in the
Vase Collection. The Room of
the Italiot Vases contains only
vases produced locally in the
Greek cities of Southern Italy
and in Etruria itself. These
date from the 3rd to the 1st
century BC.

Etruscan
gold clasp
(fibula)
from the 7th
century BC

Head of an athlete in mosaic from the Baths of Caracalla

GREEK AND ROMAN ART

THE GREATER PART of the Vatican Museums is dedicated to Greek and Roman art. Exhibits line connecting corridors and vestibules; walls and floors display fine mosaics; and famous sculptures decorate the main courtyards.

The first serious organization of the collection took place in the reign of Julius II (1503–13) around Bramante's Belvedere Courtyard. The prize pieces form the nucleus of the 18th-century Pio-Clementine Museum. In the pavilions of the Octagonal Courtyard and in the surrounding rooms are sculptures considered among the greatest achievements of Western art. The *Apoxyomenos* (an athlete wiping his body after a race) and the *Apollo del Belvedere* are high-quality Roman copies of Greek originals of about 320 BC. The magnificent *Laocoön*, sculpted by three artists from Rhodes, had long been known to exist from a description by Pliny the Elder. It was rediscovered near the ruins of Nero's Golden House *(see p175)* in 1506. Classical works such as these had a profound influence on Michelangelo and other Renaissance artists.

The much smaller Chiaramonti Museum, named after Pope Pius VII Chiaramonti, was laid out by Canova in the early 19th century. It includes a striking colossal head of the goddess Athene. The Braccio Nuovo, an extension of the Chiaramonti, decorated with Roman floor mosaics, contains a statue of Augustus from the villa of his wife Livia at Prima Porta. Its pose is based on the famous *Doryphoros* by the Greek sculptor Polyclitus, of which there is a Roman copy on display opposite.

Exhibits in the Vase Rooms range from the Greek geometric style (8th century BC) to black-figure vases from Corinth, such as the famous vase by Exekias, with Achilles and Ajax playing a game similar to draughts (530 BC), and the later red-figure type, such as the *kylix* (a wide shallow cup) with Oedipus and the Sphinx from the 5th century BC. A stairway links this section to the Gallery of the Candelabra and the Room of the Biga (a two-horse chariot). The horses and harness were added in the 18th century.

The Gregorian Profane Museum, housed in a new wing, charts the evolution of Roman art from dependence upon Greek models to a recognizably Roman style.

The *Doryphoros* or spear-carrier, a Roman copy in marble of an original Greek bronze

Original Greek works include large marble fragments from the Parthenon in Athens. There is also a Roman copy of *Athene and Marsyas* by Myron, which was part of the decoration of the Parthenon. Totally Roman in character are two reliefs known as the Rilievi della Cancelleria, because they were discovered beneath the Palazzo della Cancelleria *(see p149)* in the 1930s. They show military parades of the Emperor Vespasian and his son Domitian. This section also has fine Roman floor mosaics. There are two from the Baths of Caracalla *(see p197)*, depicting athletes and referees. They date from the 3rd century AD. Most striking of all is a mosaic that creates the impression of an unswept floor, covered with debris after a meal. Away from the main Classical collections, in one of the rooms of the Vatican Library, is the *Aldobrandini Wedding*, a beautiful Roman fresco of a bride being prepared for her marriage, dating from the 1st century AD.

Marble relief of the Emperor Vespasian

Floor mosaic from the Baths of Otricoli in Umbria, in the Round Room

Detail from Giotto's *Stefaneschi Triptych*

EARLY CHRISTIAN AND MEDIEVAL ART

THE MAIN COLLECTION of early Christian antiquities is in the Pio-Christian Museum, founded in the last century by Pope Pius IX and formerly housed in the Lateran Palace. It contains inscriptions and sculpture from catacombs and early Christian basilicas. The sculpture consists chiefly of reliefs decorating sarcophagi, though the most striking work is a free-standing 4th-century statue of the *Good Shepherd*. The sculpture's chief interest lies in the way it blends Biblical episodes with pagan mythology. Christianity adopted Classical images so that its doctrines could be understood in clear visual terms. The idealized pastoral figure of the shepherd, for example, became Christ himself, while bearded philosophers turned into the Apostles. At the same time, Christianity laid claim to be the spiritual and cultural heir of the Roman Empire.

The first two rooms of the Pinacoteca are dedicated to late medieval art, mostly wooden panels painted in tempera which served as altarpieces. The outstanding work is Giotto's altarpiece dating from about 1300, known as the *Stefaneschi Triptych*. It expresses much the same theme as the early Christian works: the continuity between the Classical world of the Roman Empire and the new order of Christian Europe. The crucifixion of St Peter takes place between two landmarks of ancient Rome, the Pyramid of Caius Cestius *(see p205)*, and the pyramid known in the Middle Ages as the Tomb of Romulus, which stood near the Vatican. The triptych, which decorated the main altar of old St Peter's, includes portraits of Pope St Celestine V (reigned 1294–6), and of the donor, Cardinal Jacopo Stefaneschi, shown offering the triptych to St Peter.

The Vatican Library has a number of medieval treasures exhibited rather haphazardly in showcases; these include woven and embroidered cloths, reliquaries, enamels and icons. One of the aims of the 18th-century reorganization of the Vatican collections was to glorify Christian works by contrasting them with earlier pagan creations. In the long Lapidary Gallery over 3,000 stone tablets with Christian and pagan inscriptions are displayed on opposite walls. The world's greatest collection of its kind, it may be visited only with special permission.

15TH- TO 19TH-CENTURY ART

THE RENAISSANCE POPES, many of whom were cultured connoisseurs of the arts, considered it their duty to sponsor the leading painters, sculptors and goldsmiths of

Pietà by the Venetian artist Giovanni Bellini (1430–1516)

the age. The galleries around the Cortile del Belvedere were all decorated by great artists between the 16th and the 19th centuries. The Gallery of Tapestries is hung with tapestries woven in Brussels to designs by students of Raphael; the Apartment of Pope Pius V has beautiful 15th-century Flemish tapestries; and the Gallery of Maps is frescoed with 16th-century maps of ancient and contemporary Italy. When you go to visit the Raphael Rooms *(see pp242–3),* you should not overlook the nearby Room of the Chiaroscuri and Pope Nicholas V's tiny private chapel, frescoed by Fra Angelico between 1447 and 1451. Similarly, before reaching the Sistine Chapel *(see pp244–7),* visit the Borgia Apartment, frescoed in a decorative, flowery style by Pinturicchio and his students in the 1490s. The contrast with Michelangelo's Sistine Chapel ceiling, begun in 1508, could hardly be greater. Another set of fascinating frescoes decorates the Loggia of Raphael, but this requires special permission to visit.

Many important works by Renaissance masters are on show in the Pinacoteca (art gallery). Highlights among the works by 15th-century painters are a fine *Pietà* by the Venetian Giovanni Bellini and Leonardo da Vinci's unfinished *St Jerome.* Of the

great 16th-century works, do not miss the fine altarpiece by Titian, the *Crucifixion of St Peter* by Guido Reni, the *Deposition* by Caravaggio and the *Communion of St Jerome* by Domenichino. Raphael has a whole room dedicated to his work. It contains the beautiful *Madonna of Foligno* and the *Transfiguration* as well as eight tapestries made to his designs.

Lunette of the *Adoration of the Magi* by Pinturicchio in the Room of the Mysteries in the Borgia Apartment

MODERN RELIGIOUS ART

MODERN ARTISTS exhibited in the Vatican Museums face daunting competition from the great works of the past. Few modern works are displayed conspicuously, the exceptions being Momo's spiral staircase of 1932, which greets visitors as they enter the museums, and Giò Pomodoro's abstract sculpture in the centre of the Cortile della Pigna.

In 1973 a contemporary art collection was inaugurated by Pope Paul VI. Housed in the Borgia Apartment, it includes over 800 exhibits by modern artists from all over the world, donated by collectors or the artists themselves. Works in a great variety of media show many contrasting approaches to religious subjects. There are paintings, drawings, engravings and sculpture by 19th- and 20th-century artists, as well as mosaics, stained glass, ceramics and tapestries. Well-known modern painters such as Georges Braque, Paul Klee, Edvard Munch and Graham Sutherland are all represented. There are also drawings by Henry Moore, ceramics by Picasso and stained glass by Fernand Léger. Projects for modern church ornaments include Matisse's decorations for the church of St Paul de Vence, Luigi Fontana's models for the bronze doors of Milan cathedral, and Emilio Greco's panels for the doors of Orvieto cathedral.

***Town with Gothic Cathedral* by Paul Klee (1879–1940)**

Raphael Rooms

POPE JULIUS II'S PRIVATE APARTMENTS were built above those of his hated predecessor, Alexander VI, one of the Borgias, who died in 1503. Julius was impressed with Raphael's work and chose him to redecorate the four rooms *(stanze)*. Raphael and his pupils began the task in 1508, replacing existing works by several better-known artists, including Raphael's own teacher, Perugino. The work took over 16 years and Raphael himself died before its completion. The frescoes express the religious and philosophical ideals of the Renaissance. They quickly established Raphael's reputation as an artist in Rome, putting him on a par with Michelangelo, then working on the ceiling of the Sistine Chapel.

Detail from *The Expulsion of Heliodorus from the Temple*, showing Pope Julius II watching the scene from his litter

Cortile del Belvedere

KEY TO FLOORPLAN

① Hall of Constantine

② Room of Heliodorus

③ Room of the Segnatura

④ Room of the Fire in the Borgo

HALL OF CONSTANTINE ①

THE FRESCOES in this room were started in 1517, three years before Raphael's death, but Raphael himself probably had little hand in their execution. As a result they are not held in the same high regard as those in the other rooms. The work was completed in 1525 in the reign of Pope Clement VII by Giulio Romano and two other former pupils of Raphael, Giovanni Francesco Penni and Raffaellino del Colle.

The theme of the decoration is the triumph of Christianity over paganism. The four major frescoes show scenes from the life of Constantine and include his *Vision of the Cross* and his victory over his rival Maxentius at *The Battle of the Milvian Bridge*, for which Raphael had provided a preparatory sketch. In both *The Baptism of Constantine* and *The Donation of Constantine*, the figure of Pope Sylvester *(see p170)* was given the features of Clement VII.

ROOM OF HELIODORUS ②

THIS PRIVATE antechamber was decorated by Raphael between 1512 and 1514. The main frescoes show the miraculous protection granted to all the Church's ministers, doctrines and property. The room's name refers to the fresco on the right, *The Expulsion of Heliodorus from the Temple*. This shows a story from Jewish history, in which a thief called Heliodorus is felled

Swiss guards waiting with papal chair in *The Mass at Bolsena*

by a horseman as he tries to make off with the treasure from the Temple of Jerusalem. The scene is witnessed by the pope, borne on a litter by courtiers. The incident is also a thinly-veiled reference to Julius II's success in driving foreign armies out of Italy. In *The Meeting of Leo I and Attila* Raphael pays a similar compliment to the pope's political skill. Pope Leo was originally given the face of Julius II, but after his death, Raphael substituted the features of Julius's successor, Leo X.

The Mass at Bolsena depicts a miracle that occurred in 1263. A priest

***The Battle of the Milvian Bridge*, completed by one of Raphael's assistants**

The Liberation of St Peter, a three-part composition, shows the saint asleep in his cell in the middle section, led out of prison by an angel on the right, while, on the left, the prison guards cower in terror

who doubted that the bread and wine really were the body and blood of Christ suddenly saw the host bleed while he was celebrating mass. Julius II appears in this fresco, accompanied by a colourful group of Swiss guards.

Julius appears yet again as St Peter in *The Liberation of St Peter*. This fresco is remarkable for its dramatic lighting effects, achieved despite the painting's awkward shape and its position above a window.

ROOM OF THE SEGNATURA ③

THE NAME is derived from a special council which met in this room to sign official documents. The frescoes here were completed between 1508 and 1511. The scheme Raphael followed was dictated by Pope Julius II. It reflects the Humanist belief that there could be perfect harmony between Classical culture and Christianity in their mutual search for truth.

The Dispute over the Holy Sacrament, the first fresco completed by Raphael for Pope Julius, represents the triumph of religion and spiritual truth. The conse-crated host is shown at the centre of the painting. This links the group of learned scholars, who discuss its significance, to the Holy Trinity and the saints floating on clouds up above.

On the opposite wall, *The School of Athens (see p30)* is a bustling scene

centred around the debate on the search for truth between Greek philosophers Plato and Aristotle. It also features portraits of many of Raphael's contemporaries, including Leonardo da Vinci, Bramante and Michelangelo. The other works include a portrait of the bearded Pope Julius II, who in 1511 vowed not to shave until he managed to rid Italy of all usurpers.

ROOM OF THE FIRE IN THE BORGO ④

THIS WAS ORIGINALLY the dining room, but when the decoration was completed under Pope Leo X, it became a music room. All the frescoes exalt the reigning pope by depicting events in the lives of his namesakes, the 9th-century popes Leo III and IV. The main frescoes were finished by two of Raphael's assistants between 1514 and 1517,

following their master's own plans. The most famous, *The Fire in the Borgo*, was painted from Raphael's designs and reflects his maturity as an artist. It celebrates the miracle that took place in 847, when Pope Leo IV extinguished a fire raging in the Borgo *(see p228)* by making the sign of the cross. The incident is likened to the flight of Aeneas from Troy described by Virgil. The figure of Aeneas appears in the foreground carrying his father on his back. This borrowing of an event from Classical legend shows a new willingness to experiment on the part of Raphael. Sadly, his pupils did not always follow his designs faithfully and this, combined with some poor restoration, has spoilt the work.

Detail from *The Fire in the Borgo*, showing Aeneas, the Trojan hero, with his father on his back, fleeing from the fire

The Dispute over the Holy Sacrament, the first fresco completed in the Rooms

Sistine Chapel: The Walls

THE MASSIVE WALLS of the Sistine Chapel, the main chapel in the Vatican Palace, were frescoed by some of the finest artists of the 15th and 16th centuries. The 12 paintings on the side walls, by artists including Perugino, Ghirlandaio, Botticelli and Signorelli, show parallel episodes from the life of Moses and of Christ. The decoration of the chapel walls was completed between 1534 and 1541 by Michelangelo, who added the great altar wall fresco, the *Last Judgment*.

KEY TO THE FRESCOES: ARTISTS AND SUBJECTS

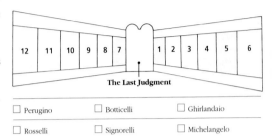

| 12 | 11 | 10 | 9 | 8 | 7 | | 1 | 2 | 3 | 4 | 5 | 6 |

The Last Judgment

☐ Perugino   ☐ Botticelli   ☐ Ghirlandaio

☐ Rosselli   ☐ Signorelli   ☐ Michelangelo

1 Baptism of Christ in the Jordan
2 Temptations of Christ
3 Calling of St Peter and St Andrew
4 Sermon on the Mount
5 Handing over the Keys to St Peter
6 Last Supper

7 Moses's Journey into Egypt
8 Moses Receiving the Call
9 Crossing of the Red Sea
10 Adoration of the Golden Calf
11 Punishment of the Rebels
12 Last Days of Moses

THE LAST JUDGMENT BY MICHELANGELO

REVEALED IN 1993 after a year's restoration, the *Last Judgment* is considered to be the masterpiece of Michelangelo's mature years. It was commissioned by Pope Paul III Farnese, and required the removal of some earlier frescoes and two windows over the altar. A new wall was erected which slanted inwards to stop dust settling on it. Michelangelo worked alone on the fresco for seven years, until its completion in 1541.

The painting depicts the souls of the dead rising up to face the wrath of God, a subject that is rarely used for an altar decoration. The pope chose it as a warning to Catholics to adhere to their faith in the turmoil of the Reformation. In fact the work conveys the artist's own tormented attitude to his faith. It offers neither the certainties of Christian orthodoxy, nor the ordered view of Classicism.

In a dynamic, emotional composition, the figures are caught in a vortex of motion. The dead are torn from their graves and hauled up to face Christ the Judge, whose athletic, muscular figure is the focus of all the painting's movement.

Christ shows little sympathy for the agitated saints around him, clutching the instruments of their martyrdom. Neither is any pity shown for the damned, hurled down to the demons in hell. Here Charon, pushing people off his boat into the depths of Hades, and the infernal judge Minos, are taken from Dante's *Inferno*. Minos has ass's ears, and is a portrait of courtier Biagio da Cesena, who had objected to the nude figures in the fresco. Michelangelo's self-portrait is on the skin held by the martyr St Bartholomew.

Souls meeting the wrath of Christ in Michelangelo's *Last Judgment*

WALL FRESCOES

Detail from Botticelli's fresco
Temptations of Christ

WHEN THE Sistine Chapel was built, the papacy was a strong political power with vast accumulated wealth. In 1475 Pope Sixtus IV was able to summon some of the greatest painters of his day to decorate the chapel. Among the artists employed were Perugino, who was Raphael's master and is often credited with overseeing the project, Sandro Botticelli, Domenico Ghirlandaio, Cosimo Rosselli and Luca Signorelli. Their work on the chapel's frescoes took from 1481 to 1483.

Although frequently overlooked by visitors who concentrate on Michelangelo's work, the frescoes along the side walls of the chapel include some of the finest works of 15th-century Italian art. The two cycles of frescoes represent scenes from the lives of Moses and Christ. Above them in the spaces between the windows are portraits of the earliest popes, painted by various artists, including Botticelli.

The fresco cycles start at the altar end of the chapel, with the story of Christ on the right-hand wall and that of Moses on the left. Originally there were two paintings, *The Birth of Christ* and *The Finding of Moses*, on the wall behind the altar, but these were both destroyed to make way for Michelangelo's *The Last Judgment*.

The final paintings of the two cycles are also lost. They were on the entrance wall, which collapsed during the 16th century. When the wall was restored, they were replaced with poor substitutes.

As was customary at the time, each fresco contains a series of scenes, linked thematically to the central episode. Hidden meanings and symbols connect each painting with its counterpart on the opposite wall, and there are also many allusions to contemporary events.

The elaborate architectural details in the frescoes include familiar Roman monuments. The Arch of Constantine *(see p91)* provides the backdrop for the *Punishment of the Rebels* by Botticelli, the fifth panel in the cycle of Moses, in which the artist himself appears as the last figure but one on the right. Two similar arches appear in the painting opposite, Perugino's *Handing over the Keys to St Peter*.

Moses was both spiritual and temporal leader of his people. He called down the wrath of God on those who challenged his decisions, thus

The crowd of onlookers in the *Calling of St Peter and St Andrew* by Ghirlandaio

setting a precedent for the power exercised by the pope. In *Handing over the Keys to St Peter*, Christ confers spiritual

and temporal authority on St Peter by giving him the keys to the Kingdoms of Heaven and Earth. The golden-domed building in the centre of the vast piazza represents both the Temple of Jerusalem and the Church, as founded by Peter, the first pope. The fifth figure on the right is thought to be a self-portrait by Perugino.

Botticelli's *Temptations of Christ* includes a view of the

The central episode in Botticelli's *Punishment of the Rebels*

Hospital of Santo Spirito, rebuilt in 1475 by Sixtus IV *(see p226)*. Here the devil is disguised in the habit of a Franciscan monk. Portraits of both Botticelli and Filippino Lippi are visible in the left hand corner. A portrait of the pope's nephew, Girolamo Riario, appears in the painting of the *Crossing of the Red Sea* by Rosselli, in which the sea is literally red. This painting also commemorates the papal victory at Campomorto in 1482.

Perugino's *Handing over the Keys to St Peter*

Sistine Chapel: The Ceiling

MICHELANGELO FRESCOED the ceiling for Pope Julius II between 1508 and 1512, working on specially designed scaffolding. The main panels, which chart the Creation of the World and Fall of Man, are surrounded by subjects from the Old and New Testaments – except for the Classical Sibyls who are said to have foreseen the birth of Christ. In the 1980s the ceiling was restored revealing colours of an unsuspected vibrancy.

Libyan Sibyl
The pagan prophetess reaches for the Book of Knowledge. Like most female figures Michelangelo painted, the beautiful Libyan Sibyl was probably modelled on a man.

Illusionistic
architecture

Creation of the Sun and Moon
Michelangelo depicts God as a dynamic but terrifying figure commanding the sun to shed light on the earth.

KEY TO CEILING PANELS

GENESIS: 1 God Dividing Light from Darkness; **2** Creation of the Sun and Moon; **3** Separating Waters from Land; **4** Creation of Adam; **5** Creation of Eve; **6** Original Sin; **7** Sacrifice of Noah; **8** The Deluge; **9** Drunkenness of Noah.

ANCESTORS OF CHRIST: 10 Solomon with his Mother; **11** Parents of Jesse; **12** Rehoboam with Mother; **13** Asa with Parents; **14** Uzziah with Parents; **15** Hezekiah with Parents; **16** Zerubbabel with Parents; **17** Josiah with Parents.

PROPHETS: 18 Jonah; **19** Jeremiah; **20** Daniel; **21** Ezekiel; **22** Isaiah; **23** Joel; **24** Zechariah.

SIBYLS: 25 Libyan Sibyl; **26** Persian Sibyl; **27** Cumaean Sibyl; **28** Erythrean Sibyl; **29** Delphic Sibyl.

OLD TESTAMENT SCENES OF SALVATION: 30 Punishment of Haman; **31** Moses and the Brazen Serpent; **32** David and Goliath; **33** Judith and Holofernes.

Original Sin
This shows Adam and Eve tasting the forbidden fruit from the Tree of Knowledge, and their expulsion from Paradise. Michelangelo represents Satan as a snake with the body of a woman.

The Ignudi are athletic male nudes whose significance is uncertain.

RESTORATION OF THE SISTINE CEILING

Restorers used computers, photography and spectrum analysis to inspect the fresco before cleaning began. They were therefore able to detect and remove the changes previous restorers had made to Michelangelo's original work. Analysis showed that the ceiling had been cleaned with materials ranging from bread to retsina wine. The restoration then revealed the familiarly

A restorer cleaning the Libyan Sibyl

dusky, eggshell-cracked figures to have creamy skins, lustrous hair and to be dressed in brightly-coloured, luscious robes: "a Benetton Michelangelo" mocked one critic, claiming that a layer of varnish which the artist had added to darken the colours had been removed. However, after examining the work, most experts agreed that the new colours probably matched those painted by Michelangelo.

The lunettes are devoted to frescoes of the ancestors of Christ, like Hezekiah.

Castel Sant'Angelo ⑬

THE MASSIVE FORTRESS of Castel Sant'Angelo takes its name from the statue of the Archangel Michael on its summit. It began life in AD 139 as the Emperor Hadrian's mausoleum. Since then it has had many roles: as part of the Emperor Aurelian's city wall, as a medieval citadel and prison, and as the residence of the popes in times of political unrest. From the dank cells in the lower levels to the fine apartments of the Renaissance popes above, a 58-room museum covers all aspects of the castle's history.

Mausoleum of Hadrian
This artist's impression shows the tomb before Aurelian fortified its walls in AD 270–75.

Courtyard of Honour
Heaps of stone cannonballs decorate the courtyard, once the castle's ammunition store.

The Treasury was probably the original site of Hadrian's burial chamber.

Hall of the Columns

Loggia of Paul III

Hall of the Library

PROTECTING THE POPE

The Vatican Corridor leads from the Vatican Palace to Castel Sant'Angelo. It was built in 1277 to provide an escape route when the pope was in danger. The pentagonal ramparts built around the castle during the 17th century improved its defences in times of siege.

The Rooms of Clement VIII are inscribed with the family crest of the Aldobrandini pope (1592–1605).

The Hall of Justice is decorated with a fresco of *The Angel of Justice* by Domenico Zaga (1545).

The spiral ramp was the entrance to the mausoleum.

■ Walls and fortifications
□ Vatican Corridor

★**View from Terrace**
The castle's terrace, scene of the last act of Puccini's Tosca, *offers splendid views in every direction.*

The Chamber of the Urns housed the ashes of members of Hadrian's family.

STAR FEATURES

★ **Sala Paolina**

★ **View from Terrace**

★ **Staircase of Alexander VI**

VISITORS' CHECKLIST

Lungotevere Castello (entrance through gardens to the right of building). **Map** 4 D3 & 11 A1.
 06-681 91 11. 23, 34, 64, 280 to Lungotevere Castello; 34,49, 64, 70, 186, 926, 990 to Piazza Cavour. Lepanto.
Open 9am–10pm Tue–Sat, 9am–8pm Sun. **Closed** public hols, 2nd & 4th Tue of month.
Adm charge.
  Exhibitions.

Bronze Angel
The gigantic statue of the Archangel Michael is by the 18th-century Flemish sculptor Pieter Verschaffelt.

The Round Hall houses the original model from which Verschaffelt's angel was cast.

★ **Sala Paolina**
The illusionistic frescoes by Perin del Vaga and Pellegrino Tibaldi (1546–8) include one of a courtier entering the room through a painted door.

Hall of Apollo
The room is frescoed with scenes from mythology attributed to the pupils of Perin del Vaga (1548).

Ventilation shaft

★ **Staircase of Alexander VI**
This staircase cuts right through the heart of the building.

Bridge

TIMELINE

AD 100	500	1000	1500
AD 139 Mausoleum completed by Antoninus Pius	**590** Legendary date of appearance of Archangel Michael above the castle	**1493** Pope Alexander VI restores Vatican Corridor	*Facade of Castel Sant'Angelo*
		1390 Pope Boniface IX remodels the castle	
271 Tomb is incorporated into Aurelian Wall and fortified		**1527** Castle withstands siege during Sack of Rome	**1557** Ramparts built to protect the castle
AD 130 Hadrian begins family mausoleum	*Cannonballs in the Courtyard of Honour*	**1542–9** Sala Paolina and apartments built for Pope Paul III	**1870** Castle used as barracks and military prison

VIA VENETO

IN IMPERIAL ROME, this was a suburb where rich families owned luxurious villas and gardens. Ruins from this era can be seen in the excavations in Piazza Sallustio, named after the most extensive gardens in the area, the Horti Sallustiani.

Film director Federico Fellini

After the Sack of Rome in the 5th century, the area reverted to open countryside. Not until the 17th century did it recover its lost splendour, with the building of Palazzo Barberini and the now-vanished Villa Ludovisi.

When Rome became capital of Italy in 1870, the Ludovisi sold their land for development. They kept a plot for a new house, but tax on the profits from the sale was so high, they had to sell that too. By 1900, Via Veneto had become a street of smart modern hotels and cafés. It featured prominently in Fellini's 1960 film *La Dolce Vita*, a scathing satire on the lives of film stars and idle rich, but since then has lost its position as the meeting place of the famous.

SIGHTS AT A GLANCE

Churches and Temples
Santa Maria della Concezione ❸
Santa Susanna ❼
Santa Maria della Vittoria ❽

Historic Buildings
Casino dell'Aurora ❷
Palazzo Barberini ❻

Famous Streets
Via Veneto ❶

Fountains
Fontana delle Api ❹
Fontana del Tritone ❺

SEE ALSO

0 metres   200
0 yards   200

GETTING THERE
This is one of the easiest parts of Rome to reach by public transport. Barberini and Repubblica Metro stations on line A are very handy, and Stazione Termini is only 10–15 minutes' walk away. The Via Veneto itself starts at Piazza Barberini, well served by buses from all parts of the city. The 95 goes the whole length of Via Veneto to Porta Pinciana. Other useful routes include the 52, 53, 56, 58 and 116 along Via del Tritone.

KEY

▨	Street-by-Street map
—	City Wall
Ⓜ	Metro station
Ⓟ	Parking

The onset of autumn in Via Veneto

Street-by-Street: Via Veneto

THE STREETS AROUND VIA VENETO, though within the walls of ancient Rome, contain little dating from before the unification of Italy in 1870. With its hotels, restaurants, bars and travel agencies, the area is the centre of 20th-century tourism in the way that Piazza di Spagna was the hub of the tourist trade in the Rome of the 18th-century Grand Tour. However, glimpses of the old city can be seen among the modern streets. These include Santa Maria della Concezione, the church of the Capuchin friars, whose convent once stood in its own gardens. In the 17th century Palazzo Barberini was built here for the powerful papal family. Bernini's Fontana del Tritone and Fontana delle Api have stood in Piazza Barberini since it was the meeting place of cart tracks entering the city from surrounding vineyards.

Casino dell'Aurora
A pavilion is all that remains of the great Ludovisi estate that once occupied most of this quarter of Rome ❷

Santa Maria della Concezione
This church is best known for the macabre collection of bones in its crypt ❸

Fontana delle Api
Bernini's drinking fountain is decorated with bees, emblem of his Barberini patrons ❹

Fontana del Tritone
Bernini's muscular sea god has been spouting water skywards for 350 years ❺

★ **Palazzo Barberini**
Pietro da Cortona worked on his spectacular ceiling fresco The Triumph of Divine Providence *between 1633 and 1639* ❻

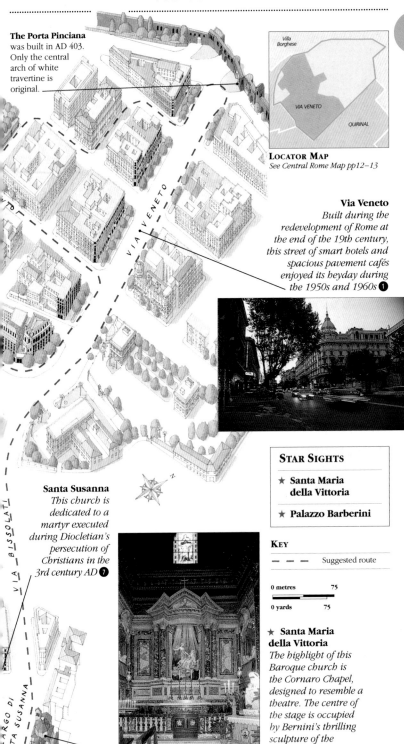

The Porta Pinciana
was built in AD 403.
Only the central
arch of white
travertine is
original.

LOCATOR MAP
See Central Rome Map pp12–13

Via Veneto
*Built during the
redevelopment of Rome at
the end of the 19th century,
this street of smart hotels and
spacious pavement cafés
enjoyed its heyday during
the 1950s and 1960s* ❶

Santa Susanna
*This church is
dedicated to a
martyr executed
during Diocletian's
persecution of
Christians in the
3rd century AD* ❼

STAR SIGHTS

★ **Santa Maria
della Vittoria**

★ **Palazzo Barberini**

KEY

– – – Suggested route

0 metres   75

0 yards   75

★ **Santa Maria
della Vittoria**
*The highlight of this
Baroque church is
the Cornaro Chapel,
designed to resemble a
theatre. The centre of
the stage is occupied
by Bernini's thrilling
sculpture of the
Ecstasy of St Teresa* ❽

Pavement café in Via Veneto

Via Veneto **❶**

Map 5 B1. 🚌 52, 53, 56, 58, 58b,
95, 116, 490, 495 and many routes
to Piazza Barberini. Ⓜ Barberini.

VIA VENETO descends in a
lazy curve from the Porta
Pinciana to Piazza Barberini,
lined in its upper reaches with
exuberant turn-of-the-century
hotels and canopied pavement
cafés. It was laid out in 1879
over a large estate sold by the
Ludovisi family in the great
building boom of Rome's first
years as capital of Italy. Palazzo
Margherita, intended to be the
new Ludovisi family palazzo,
was completed in 1890. It now
houses the American embassy.

In the 1960s this was the
most glamorous street in Rome,
its cafés patronized by film
stars and plagued by the
paparazzi. Most of the people
drinking in the cafés today are
tourists, as film stars now seem
to prefer the livelier bohemian
atmosphere of Trastevere.

Palazzo Margherita, the US embassy

Casino dell'Aurora **❷**

Via Lombardia 46. **Map** 5 B2.
📞 06-48 39 42. 🚌 52, 53, 56, 58,
58b, 95, 116. Ⓜ Barberini.
Open by appt only.

THE CASINO (a stately country
residence) was a summer-
house on the grounds of the
Ludovisi palace. It was built

by Cardinal Ludovisi in
the 17th century, and
frescoed by Guercino.
The ceiling fresco's
subject is Aurora, the
goddess of dawn. It is a
dizzying work creating
the impression that the
Casino has no roof, but
lies open to a cloudy
sky, across which
horses pull Aurora's
carriage from the darkness of
night towards the light of day.

Santa Maria della Concezione **❸**

Via Veneto 27. **Map** 5 B2.
📞 06-487 11 85. 🚌 52, 53, 56, 58,
58b, 60, 61, 62, 95, 116, 175.
Ⓜ Barberini. **Open** 7am–noon,
3.45pm–7.30pm daily. **Crypt open**
9am–noon, 3pm–6pm Fri–Wed.
Donation expected. ✝

POPE URBAN VIII's brother,
Antonio Barberini was
a cardinal and a Capuchin
friar. In 1626 he founded this
plain, unassuming church at
what is now the foot of the
Via Veneto. When he died he
was buried not, like most
cardinals, in a grand marble
sarcophagus, but below a
simple flagstone close to
the altar, where you can
read the bleak epitaph
in Latin: "Here lies dust,
ashes, nothing".

The grim reality of death
is illustrated even more
graphically in the crypt beneath
the church, where generations
of Capuchin friars have
decorated the walls of the five
vaulted chapels with the bones
and skulls of their departed
brethren. In all, some 4,000
skeletons were used to create
this macabre *memento mori*.
Some of the bones are wired
together to form Christian
symbols such as crowns of
thorns, sacred hearts and
crucifixes. There are
also a number of
complete skeletons,
including one of a
Barberini princess who
died as a child. At the
exit, an inscription
in Latin reads:
"What you are, we
used to be. What
we are, you will be." **Pope Urban VIII**

Fontana delle Api **❹**

Piazza Barberini. **Map** 5 B2. 🚌 52,
53, 56, 58, 58b, 60, 61, 62, 95, 116,
175. Ⓜ Barberini.

THE FOUNTAIN of the bees –
api are bees, symbol of
the Barberini family – is one
of Bernini's more modest
works. Tucked away in a
corner of Piazza Barberini, it
is quite easy to miss. Dating
from 1644, it pays homage to
Pope Urban VIII Barberini,
and features rather crab-like
bees which appear to be
sipping the water as it dribbles
down into the basin. A Latin
inscription informs us that
the water is for the use of the
public and their animals.

Bernini's Fontana delle Api

Fontana del Tritone **❺**

Piazza Barberini. **Map** 5 B3. 🚌 52,
53, 56, 58, 58b, 60, 61, 62, 95, 116,
175. Ⓜ Barberini.

IN THE CENTRE of busy Piazza
Barberini is one of Bernini's
liveliest fountains, the Triton
Fountain. It was created for
Pope Urban VIII Barberini
in 1642, shortly after the
completion of his palace
on the ridge above.
Acrobatic dolphins stand
on their heads, twisting
their tails together to
support a huge scallop
shell on which the
sea god Triton kneels,
blowing a spindly
column of water up into

the air through a conch shell. Entwined artistically among the dolphins' tails are the papal tiara, the keys of St Peter and the Barberini coat of arms.

The Triton and his conch shell in Bernini's Fontana del Tritone

Palazzo Barberini **6**

Via delle Quattro Fontane 13. **Map** 5 B3. [06-481 45 91. 52, 53, 56, 58, 58b, 60, 61, 62, 95, 116, 175, 492, 590. [M] Barberini. **Open** 9am–7pm Tue–Sat, 9am–1pm Sun and public hols (last adm: 30 mins before closing). **Adm charge**.

WHEN MAFFEI BARBERINI became Pope Urban VIII in 1623 he decided to build a grand palace for his family. The site he chose was then on the fringes of the city, over-looking a ruined temple. The architect, Carlo Maderno, designed it as a typical rural villa, with wings extending into the surrounding gardens. Maderno died in 1629, shortly after the foundations had been laid, and Bernini took over, assisted by Borromini. The peculiar pediments on some of the top floor windows, and the oval staircase inside, are almost certainly by Borromini.

Of the many sumptuously decorated rooms, the most striking is the Gran Salone, with a dazzling illusionistic ceiling fresco by Pietro da Cortona. The palazzo also houses paintings from the 13th to the 16th centuries, part of the Galleria Nazionale d'Arte

Antica, with important works by Filippo Lippi, El Greco and Caravaggio. There is also a Holbein portrait of King Henry VIII of England dressed for his wedding to Anne of Cleves. Of greater local significance are Guido Reni's *Beatrice Cenci*, the young woman executed for planning her father's murder *(see p150)*, and *La Fornarina*, traditionally identified as a portrait of Raphael's mistress, although not painted by him.

Santa Susanna **7**

Via XX Settembre 14. **Map** 5 C2. [06-488 27 48. 60, 61, 62, 175, 492. [M] Repubblica. **Open** 9am–noon, 4pm–7pm daily.

Facade of Santa Susanna

SANTA SUSANNA'S most striking feature is its vigorous Baroque facade by Carlo Maderno, finished in 1603. Christians have worshipped on the site since at least the 4th century. In the nave, there are four huge frescoes by Baldassarre Croce (1558–1628), painted to resemble tapestries. These depict scenes from the life of Susanna, an obscure Roman saint who was martyred here, and the rather better-known life of the Old Testament Susanna, who was spotted bathing in her husband's garden by two lecherous judges.

Santa Susanna is the Catholic church for Americans in Rome and holds services in English every day.

Santa Maria della Vittoria **8**

Via XX Settembre 17. **Map** 5 C2. [06-482 61 90. 37, 60, 61, 62, 175, 492, 910. [M] Repubblica. **Open** 6.30am–noon, 4.30–7pm daily.

SANTA MARIA della Vittoria is an intimate Baroque church with a lavishly decorated candlelit interior. It contains one of Bernini's most ambitious sculptural works, the *Ecstasy of St Teresa* (1646), centrepiece of the Cornaro Chapel, built to resemble a miniature theatre. It even has an audience: sculptures of the chapel's benefactor, Cardinal Federico Cornaro, and his ancestors sit in boxes, as if watching and discussing the scene occurring in front of them.

Visitors may be shocked or thrilled by the apparently physical nature of St Teresa's ecstasy. She lies on a cloud, her mouth half open and her eyelids closed, with rippling drapery covering her body. Looking over her with a smile, which from different angles can appear either tender or cruel, is a curly-haired angel holding an arrow with which he is about to pierce the saint's body for a second time. The marble figures are framed and illuminated by rays of divine light materialized in bronze.

Bernini's astonishing *Ecstasy of St Teresa*

FURTHER AFIELD

THE MORE INQUISITIVE visitor to Rome may wish to try a few excursions to the large parks and some of the more isolated churches on the outskirts of the city. With a day to spare, you can explore the villas of Tivoli and the ruins of the ancient Roman port of Ostia. Traditional haunts of the

Dish (3rd century BC) in Villa Giulia

Grand Tour *(see p130)*, such as the catacombs and the ruined aqueducts of Parco Appio Claudio, still offer glimpses of the rapidly vanishing Campagna, the country-side around Rome. More modern sights include the suburb of EUR, built in the Fascist era, and the memorial at the Fosse Ardeatine.

SIGHTS AT A GLANCE

Towns and Areas
EUR ⑭
Tivoli ⑱

Historic Roads
Via Appia Antica ⑧

Churches
Santa Costanza ⑤
Sant'Agnese fuori le Mura ⑥
San Lorenzo fuori le Mura ⑦
San Paolo fuori le Mura ⑮

Museums and Galleries
Museo e Galleria Borghese pp260–61 ②
Villa Giulia pp262–3 ③
Galleria Communale d'Arte Moderna ④
Centrale Montemartini ⑯

Ancient Sites
Hadrian's Villa ㉑
Ostia Antica ㉒

Parks and Gardens
Villa Borghese ①
Villa Doria Pamphilj ⑰
Villa d'Este ⑲
Villa Gregoriana ⑳

Tombs and Catacombs
Catacombs of San Callisto ⑨
Catacombs of San Sebastiano ⑩
Catacombs of Domitilla ⑪
Fosse Ardeatine ⑫
Tomb of Cecilia Metella ⑬

KEY

Main sightseeing areas

Motorway

0 kilometres 2

0 miles 1

Caryatids beside the canal of the Canopus at Hadrian's Villa

Villa Borghese ❶

Map 2 E5. 🚌 *3, 52, 53, 56, 95,116, 490, 495.* 🚊 *19, 30b.*
Park open *dawn to sunset.*
Bioparco *Viale del Giardino Zoologico.*
Map 2 E4. 📞 *06-321 65 64.*
🚌 *3, 52.* 🚊 *19, 19b, 30b.*
Open *daily Mar–Oct: 9.30am–7pm; Nov–Feb: 9.30am–5pm.*
Closed *1 May.* ♿ 🍴 🖥 📷
Galleria Nazionale d'Arte Moderna *Viale delle Belle Arti 131.*
Map 2 D4. 📞 *06-322 981.*
🚊 *19, 19b, 30b.* **Open** *9am–7pm Tue–Sat, 9am–5pm Sun & public hols.* ♿ 📷 🖥 📷

British School at Rome, designed by Edwin Lutyens in 1911

T HE VILLA and its park were designed in 1605 for Cardinal Scipione Borghese, nephew of Pope Paul V. The park was the first of its kind in Rome. It contained 400 newly-planted pine trees, garden sculpture by Bernini's father, Pietro, and dramatic waterworks built by Giovanni Fontana. The layout of the formal gardens was imitated by other prominent Roman families at Villa Ludovisi and Villa Doria Pamphilj, but the cardinal's 18th-century successors preferred a more natural-looking park.

In the early 19th century Prince Camillo Borghese assembled the family's magnificent art collection in the Casino Borghese, now the home of the Galleria and Museo Borghese.

In 1901 the park became the property of the Italian state. Within its 6-km (4-mile) circumference there are now museums and galleries, foreign academies and schools of archaeology, a zoo, a riding school, a grassy amphitheatre, an artificial lake, an aviary and an array of summer houses, fountains, Neo-Classical statuary and exotic follies.

There are several ways into the park, including a monumental entrance on Piazzale Flaminio, built for Prince Camillo Borghese in 1825 by Luigi Canina. Other conveniently-sited entrances are at Porta Pinciana at the end of Via Veneto and from the Pincio Gardens *(see p136).* The main attraction of Italian gardens in hot weather is shade, so the long avenues are lined with hedges and trees. Piazza di Siena, a pleasantly open, grass-covered amphitheatre surrounded by tall umbrella pines, was the inspiration for Ottorino Respighi's famous symphonic poem *The Pines of Rome,* written in 1924. Near Piazza di Siena are the so-called Casina di Raffaello, said to have been owned by Raphael, and the

Statue of the English poet Byron by Thorvaldsen

18th-century Palazzetto dell'Orologio. These were summerhouses from which people enjoyed the beautiful vistas across the park. Many buildings in the park were originally surrounded by formal gardens: the Casino Borghese and the nearby 17th-century Casino della Meridiana and its aviary (the Uccelliera) have both kept their geometrical flowerbeds. Throughout the park the intersections of paths and avenues are marked by fountains and statues. West of Piazza di Siena is the Fontana dei Cavalli Marini (the Fountain of the Seahorses) added during the villa's 18th-century remodelling. Walking through the park you will encounter statues of Byron, Goethe and Victor Hugo, and a gloomy equestrian King Umberto I.

Dotted about the park are picturesque temples made to look like ruins, including a circular Temple of Diana between Piazza di Siena and Porta Pinciana, and a Temple of Faustina, wife of Emperor Antoninus Pius, on the hill north of Piazza di Siena. The nearby medieval-looking Fortezzuola by Canina contains the works of the sculptor Pietro Canonica, who lived in the building and died there in 1959. In the garden stands Canonica's *Monument to the Alpino and his Mule,* which honours the humblest

Neo-Classical Temple of Diana

Ionic temple dedicated to Aesculapius, built on the lake island

protagonists in Italy's alpine battles against Austria in World War I.

In the centre of the park is the Giardino del Lago, its main entrance marked by an 18th-century copy of the Arch of Septimius Severus.

The garden has an artificial lake complete with an Ionic Temple to Aesculapius, the god of health, by the 18th-century architect Antonio Asprucci. Rowing boats and ducks make the lake a favourite with children, banana trees and bamboo grow around the shore, and clearings are studded with sculptures.

Surrounded by flowerbeds south of the lake is the Art Nouveau Fontana dei Fauni, one of the garden's prettiest sculptures. In a clearing close to the entrance on Viale Pietro Canonica are the original Tritons of the Fontana del Moro in Piazza Navona *(see p120)* – they were moved here and replaced by copies in the 19th century.

From the northwest the park is entered by the Viale delle Belle Arti, where the Galleria Nazionale d'Arte Moderna houses a modest collection of 19th- and 20th-century paintings. The Art Nouveau character of the area dates from the International Exhibition held here in 1911, for which pavilions were built by many nations, the most impressive being the British School at Rome, by Edwin Lutyens, with a facade adapted from the upper west portico of St Paul's Cathedral in London. Originally a School of Archaeology, the school now teaches literature, fine arts and history. The diverse statues close by include Simon Bolivar and other liberators of Latin America, and the great Persian poet Firdusi.

In the northeastern corner of the park lie the Museo Zoologico and a small re-developed Zoo, known as the Bioparco, where the emphasis is on conservation. Nearby the pretty 16th-century Villa Giulia houses a world-famous collection of Etruscan and

Bioparco symbol

other pre-Roman remains. Another Renaissance building of importance is the Palazzina of Pius IV, close to the Via Flaminia entrance. Designed by the architect Vignola in 1552, it later became an elegant apartment for Pius IV's nephew Carlo Borromeo. It now houses the Italian Embassy to the Holy See.

Museo e Galleria Borghese ❷

See pp260–61.

Villa Giulia ❸

See pp262–3.

A stone lion guarding the ornate entrance to the Zoo

Museo e Galleria Borghese ❷

THE VILLA AND PARK were laid out by Cardinal Scipione Borghese, favourite nephew of Paul V, who had the house designed for pleasure and entertainment. The hedonistic cardinal was also an extravagant patron of the arts and he commissioned sculptures from the young Bernini which now rank among his most famous works. Scipione also opened his pleasure park to the public. Today the villa houses the superb private Borghese collection of sculptures and paintings in the Museo and Galleria Borghese.

Facade of the Villa Borghese
This painting (1613) by the villa's Flemish architect Jan van Santen shows the highly ornate facade of the original design.

MUSEUM GUIDE

The museum is divided into two sections: the sculpture collection (Museo Borghese) occupies the entire ground floor and the picture gallery (Galleria Borghese) is on the upper floor. The Galleria Borghese has reopened to the public after extensive restoration work.

★ Rape of Proserpine
One of Bernini's finest works shows Pluto (Hades) abducting his bride. The sculptor's amazing skill with marble can be seen clearly in the twisting figures.

Sleeping Hermaphrodite
Dated around 150 BC, this is a bronze Roman copy of the Greek original by Polycles. The head and mattress were added by Andrea Bergondi in the 17th century.

The Egyptian Room
Frescoes show episodes in Egyptian history and Egyptian motifs.

TIMELINE

1613 15-year-old Bernini sculpts *Aeneas and Anchises*	**Early 1800s** Statues and reliefs are considered too ornate and stripped from the villa's facade	**1809** Much of the collection is sold by Prince Camillo Borghese to France and goes to Louvre	**1902** Villa, grounds and collection bought by the state
1621–5 Bernini sculpts *Pluto and Persephone*			
1625	1725	1825	
1622–5 Bernini sculpts *Apollo and Daphne*		**1805** Canova sculpts the semi-nude, reclining Pauline Borghese	**Early 1900s** Balustrade round the forecourt is bought by Lord Astor for the Cliveden estate in England
1613–15 The Flemish architect Jan van Santen designs and builds Villa Borghese			

Daphne's fingers turning into leaves

Rear entrance

★ **Apollo and Daphne**
Bernini's most famous masterpiece depicts the nymph Daphne fleeing the sun god Apollo at the moment of Daphne's dramatic transformation into a tree.

David is captured the moment before he slew Goliath in the sculpture by Bernini, who modelled his face on his own.

VISITORS' CHECKLIST

Villa Borghese, Piazzale Scipione Borghese 5. **Map** 2 F5.
06-84 24 16 07. 52, 53, 116, 910 to Via Pinciana, 3, 4 to Via Po. 19, 30b to Viale delle Belle Arti.
Open 9am–10pm Tue–Sat, 9am–8pm Sun. Advance reservation advisable for visits on Tue–Fri and obligatory for visits on Sat & Sun. **Closed** public hols. **Adm charge.**
no flash.

★ **Galleria Borghese**
The gallery has old master paintings, such as Titian's Sacred and Profane Love *(detail) dating from 1514.*

★ **Pauline Borghese**
Napoleon's sister Pauline posed as Venus for this scupture. Once the statue was finished, her husband locked it away, even from its sculptor Canova.

Front entrance

Gladiator Mosaic
The floor is decorated with the fragments of a 4th-century AD mosaic from a villa in Torrenova.

STAR SCULPTURES

★ **Pauline Borghese by Canova**

★ **Apollo and Daphne by Bernini**

★ **Rape of Proserpine by Bernini**

★ **Galleria Borghese**

KEY TO FLOORPLAN

☐ Exhibition space

☐ Non-exhibition space

Villa Giulia ❸

THIS VILLA was built as a country retreat for Pope Julius III, and was designed for entertaining rather than as a permanent home. It once housed an impressive collection of statues – 160 boatloads were sent to the Vatican after the pope died in 1555. The villa, gardens, pavilions and fountains were designed by exceptional architects: Vignola (designer of the Gesù), Vasari and the sculptor Ammannati. Michelangelo also contributed. The villa's main features are its facade, the courtyard and garden and the *nympheum*. Since 1889 Villa Giulia has housed the Museo Nazionale Etrusco, with its outstanding collection of pre-Roman antiquities from central Italy.

Faliscan Crater of the Dawn
This ornate vase, painted in the free style of the 4th century BC, shows Dawn rising in a chariot.

Chigi Oinochoe
Battle and hunting scenes adorn this Corinthian vase from the 6th century BC

First floor

★ **Husband and Wife Sarcophagus**
This 6th-century BC masterpiece, from Cerveteri, shows a dead couple at the eternal banquet.

MUSEUM GUIDE
This is the most important Etruscan museum in Italy, housing artefacts from most of the major exca-vations in Tuscany and Lazio. Rooms 1–10 and 23–34 are arranged by site and include Vulci, Todi, Veio and Cerveteri, while private collections are in rooms 11–22.

Votive Offering
The religious Etruscans made artefacts, such as this model of a boy feeding a bird, in their gods' honour.

TIMELINE

1550	1650	1750	1850	1950
1550 Work begins on Villa Giulia under Pope Julius III	**1655** Queen Christina of Sweden stays in villa as Vatican guest		**1889** Etruscan museum founded	**1919** Castellani private collection donated to museum
		Late 1700s First large-scale studies of Etruscan artefacts		

Late 1500s First, chance finds of Etruscan artefacts raise some scholastic interest

1555 Villa completed

Corner decoration of bronze chariot used to burn incense

1908 Barberini private collection bought by the state

1972 Pesciotti private collection bought by the state

Facade
The villa's facade dates from 1552–3. The entrance is designed in the form of a triumphal arch.

VISITORS' CHECKLIST

Piazzale di Villa Giulia 9.
Map 1 C4. ☎ 06-322 65 71.
🚌 52, 926 to Viale Bruno Buozzi, 95, 490, 495 to Viale Washington. 🚋 19, 30b to Piazza Thorwaldsen. **Open** 9am–7pm Tue–Sat, 9am–1pm Sun. **Closed** 1 Jan, 1 May, 25 Dec. **Adm charge.** ♿ 🎧 with seven days notice. **Concerts:** "Notturno Etrusco" evenings held at the Ninfeo (Nympheum) on Saturdays throughout July & August. **Lectures, films.**
📷 🎬

★ Reconstruction of an Etruscan Temple
Count Adolfo Cozza built the Temple of Alatri here in 1891. He based his design on the accounts of Vitruvius and 19th-century excavations.

Nympheum
Literally, the "area dedicated to the nymphs", this is a sunken courtyard decorated with Classical mosaics, statues and fountains.

STAR EXHIBITS

★ **Husband and Wife Sarcophagus**

★ **Ficoroni Cist**

★ **Reconstruction of an Etruscan Temple**

Main entrance

Ground floor

★ Ficoroni Cist
Engraved and beautifully illustrated, this fine bronze marriage coffer dates from the 4th century BC.

KEY TO FLOORPLAN

☐ Ground floor
▨ First floor
☐ Non-exhibition space

Galleria Communale d'Arte Moderna **4**

Via Cagliari 29. **[** 06-474 28 48.
36, 36b, 38, 38b, 58, 58b, 60, 136,
137, 490. **Open** 9am–6.30pm
Tue–Sat, 9pm–1.30pm Sun.
Adm charge.

THE OLD Peroni beer factory
has been restored and
transformed to house the art
collections of the Comune di
Roma. The paintings are not
as "modern" as the name
might imply; most date from
the 19th century and include
works by Rodin, Ximenes,
Balla, De Pissis, Guttuso and
Carrà. There will also be a
cinematheque and videotheque
showing films about art.

Interior of Santa Costanza

Santa Costanza **5**

Via Nomentana 349. **[** 06-861 08 40.
36, 36b, 37, 60, 62, 136, 137.
Open 9am–noon, 4pm–6pm
Tue–Sat, 4pm–6pm Sun, 9am–noon
Mon. **Adm charge**. &

THE ROUND CHURCH of Santa
Costanza was first built as
a mausoleum for Emperor
Constantine's daughters
Constantia and Helena, in the
early 4th century. The dome
and its drum are supported
by a circular arcade resting on
12 magnificent pairs of granite
columns. The ambulatory that
runs around the outside of

Part of the 4th-century mosaic in the ambulatory of Santa Costanza

the central arcade has a barrel-
vaulted ceiling decorated with
wonderful 4th-century mosaics
of flora and fauna and
charming scenes of a Roman
grape harvest. In a niche on
the far side of the church from
the entrance is a replica of
Constantia's ornately carved
porphyry sarcophagus. The
original was moved to the
Vatican Museums in 1790.
 Constantia's sanctity is de-
batable – she was described
by the historian Marcellinus
as a fury incarnate, constantly
goading her equally unpleasant
husband Hannibalianus to
violence. Her canonization
was probably the result of
some confusion with a saintly
nun of the same name.

Sant'Agnese fuori le Mura **6**

Via Nomentana 349. **[** 06-861 08 40.
36, 36b, 37, 60, 62, 136, 137.
Open 9am–noon, 4pm–6pm Tue–Sat,
4pm–6pm Sun, 9am–noon Mon.
Adm charge to catacombs. &

THE CHURCH OF Sant'Agnese
stands among a group of
early Christian buildings which
includes the ruins of a covered

cemetery, some extensive
catacombs and the crypt
where the 13-year-old martyr
St Agnes was buried in AD
304. Agnes was exposed
naked by order of Emperor
Diocletian, furious that she
should have rejected the
advances of a young man at
his court, but her hair
miraculously grew to protect
her modesty.
 The church is said to have
been built at the request of
the Emperor Constantine's
daughter, Constantia, after
she had prayed at the Tomb
of St Agnes for delivery
from leprosy.
 Though much altered over
the centuries, the form and
much of the structure of the
4th-century basilica remain
intact. In the 7th-century apse
mosaic St Agnes appears as a
bejewelled Byzantine empress
in a stole of gold and a violet
robe. According to tradition
she appeared like this eight
days after her death holding a
white lamb. Every year on 21
January two lambs are blessed
on the church altar and a
vestment called the *pallium* is
woven from their wool. Every
newly-appointed archbishop
is sent a *pallium* by the pope.

Apse mosaic in Sant'Agnese, showing the saint flanked by two popes

Cloister, San Lorenzo fuori le Mura

San Lorenzo fuori le Mura ❼

Piazzale del Verano 3. ☎ 06-49 15 11. 🚌 71, 163, 448, 492. 🚋 19, 30b. **Open** 7am–noon, 4pm–5.30pm (7.30pm in summer) daily. ♿

JUST OUTSIDE the eastern wall of the city stands the church of San Lorenzo. Roasted slowly to death in AD 258, San Lorenzo was one of the most revered of Rome's early Christian martyrs. The first basilica erected over his burial place by Constantine was largely rebuilt in 576 by Pope Pelagius II. Close by stood a 5th-century church dedicated to the Virgin Mary. The intriguing two-levelled church we see today is the result of these two churches being knocked into one. This process, started in the 8th century, was completed in the 13th century by Pope Honorius III, when the nave, the portico and much of the decoration were added. The remains of San Lorenzo are in the choir of the 6th-century church (beneath the 13th-century high altar).

Romanesque bell tower of San Lorenzo

Via Appia Antica ❽

🚌 218, 760. See **Walks** pp284–5.

THE FIRST PART of the Via Appia was built in 312 BC by the Censor Appius Claudius Caecus. When it was extended to the ports of Benevento, Taranto and Brindisi in 190 BC, the road became Rome's link with its expanding empire in the East. It was the route taken by the funeral processions of the dictator Sulla (78 BC) and Emperor Augustus (AD 14) and it was along this road that St Paul was led a prisoner to Rome in AD 56.

Gradually abandoned during the Middle Ages, the road was restored in the mid-16th century by Pope Pius IV. It is lined with ruined family tombs and the collective burial places known as columbaria, while beneath the fields on either side lies a vast maze of catacombs. Today the road starts at Porta San Sebastiano (see p196). Major Christian sights include the church of Domine Quo Vadis?, built on the spot where St Peter is said to have met Christ while fleeing from Rome, and the Catacombs of San Callisto and San Sebastiano. Among the tombs lining the road are those of Cecilia Metella (see p266) and of Romulus, son of the Emperor Maxentius, who died in AD 309.

Catacombs of San Callisto ❾

Via Appia Antica 110. ☎ 06-513 67 25. 🚌 218, 660, 760. **Open** 8.30am– noon, 2.30pm–5.30pm (Oct–Mar: 5pm) Thu–Tue. **Closed** Feb; 1 Jan, Easter Sun & 25 Dec. **Adm charge.** 🔲 ∅ 🔲 🔲 🔲

IN BURYING their dead in underground cemeteries out-side the city walls, the early Christians were simply obeying the laws of the time. They were not forced to use them because of persecution. So many saints were buried that the catacombs became shrines and places of pilgrimage.

The vast Catacombs of San Callisto are on four different

levels and only partly explored. The rooms and connecting passageways are hewn out of volcanic tufa. The dead were placed in niches, known as *loculi*, which held two or three bodies. The most important rooms were decorated with stucco and frescoes. The area that can be visited includes the Crypt of the Popes, where many of the early popes were buried, and the Crypt of Santa Cecilia, where the saint's body was discovered in 820 before being moved to her church in Trastevere (see p211).

Catacombs of San Sebastiano ❿

Via Appia Antica 136. ☎ 06-785 03 50. 🚌 218, 660, 760. **Open** 9am–noon, 2.30pm–5.30pm Fri–Wed. **Closed** Nov. **Adm charge.** 🔲 🔲 🔲

THE 17TH-CENTURY church of San Sebastiano, above the catacombs, occupies the site of a basilica from the age of Constantine. Preserved at the entrance to the catacombs is the *triclia*, a building that once stood above ground and was used by mourners for taking funeral refreshments. Its walls are covered with graffiti invoking St Peter and St Paul, whose remains may have been moved here during one of the periods of persecution.

Cypresses lining part of the Roman Via Appia Antica

Catacombs of Domitilla ⓫

Via delle Sette Chiese 282.
📞 06-511 03 42. 🚌 218, 660, 760.
Open 8.30am–noon, 2.30pm–
5.30pm (Oct–Mar: 5pm) Tue–Sun.
Closed Jan. **Adm charge.** 🚫 🎦

THIS NETWORK of catacombs is the largest in Rome. Many of the tombs from the 1st and 2nd centuries AD have no Christian connection. In the burial chambers there are frescoes of both Classical and Christian scenes, including one of the earliest depictions of Christ as the *Good Shepherd*. Above the catacombs stands the basilica of Santi Nereo e Achilleo. After rebuilding and restoration, little remains of the original 4th-century church.

Bronze entrance gates to the Fosse Ardeatine by Mirko Basaldella

Fosse Ardeatine ⓬

Via Ardeatina 174. 📞 06-513 67 42.
🚌 218. **Open** 8.15am–5.15pm daily
(from 8.45 Sun). Last adm: 30 mins
before closing. **Closed** public hols.

ON THE EVENING of 24 March 1944, Nazi forces took 335 prisoners to this abandoned quarry south of Rome and shot them at point blank range. The execution was in reprisal for a bomb attack that had killed 32 German soldiers. The victims included various political prisoners, 73 Jews and ten other civilians, among them a priest and a 14-year-old boy. The Germans blew up the tunnels where the massacre had taken place, but a local peasant had witnessed the scene and later helped

find the corpses. The site is now a memorial to the values of the Resistance against the Germans, which gave birth to the modern Italian Republic. A forbidding bunker-like monument houses the rows of identical tombs containing the victims.

Beside it is a museum of the Resistance. Interesting works of modern sculpture include *The Martyrs*, by Francesco Coccia, and the gates shaped like a wall of thorns by Mirko Basaldella.

Tomb of Cecilia Metella ⓭

Via Appia Antica, km 3.
📞 06-780 24 65. 🚌 660, 770.
Open 9am–4pm Tue–Sat (6pm in
summer), 9am–12.30pm Mon & Sun.
Closed public hols.

ONE OF THE most famous landmarks on the Via Appia Antica is the huge drum-shaped tomb built for the noblewoman Cecilia Metella. Her father and husband were rich patricians and successful generals of late Republican Rome, but hardly anything is known about the woman herself. Byron muses over her unknown destiny in his poem *Childe Harold*.

In 1302 Pope Boniface VIII donated the tomb to his family, the Caetani. They incorporated it in a fortified castle that blocked the Via Appia, allowing them to control the traffic on the road and exact high tolls.

The marble facing of the tomb was pillaged by another pope, Sixtus V, at the end of the 16th century.

Fragments of marble relief on the Tomb of Cecilia Metella

EUR's Palazzo della Civiltà del Lavoro, the "Square Colosseum"

EUR ⓮

🚌 671, 703, 708, 714, 717, 762 and
other routes . Ⓜ EUR Fermi, EUR
Palasport. **Museo della Civiltà
Romana** Piazza G. Agnelli. 📞 06-
592 6041. **Open** 9am–7pm Tue–Sat,
9am–1pm Sun and public hols.
Closed 1 Jan, 1 May, 25 Dec. **Adm**

THE ESPOSIZIONE Universale di Roma (EUR), a suburb to the south of the city, was built originally for an international exhibition, a kind of "Work Olympics", that was planned for 1942, but never took place because of the war. The architecture was intended to glorify Fascism and to modern eyes the style of the public buildings is very overblown and rhetorical. The eerie shape of the Palazzo della Civiltà del Lavoro (the Palace of the Civilization of Work) is an unmistakable landmark for people arriving from Fiumicino airport.

The scheme was completed in the 1950s. In terms of town planning, EUR has been quite successful and people are still keen to live here. The great marble halls house a number of government offices and museums. The Museo della Civiltà Romana displays a vast scale model of Rome at the time of Constantine and casts of the reliefs on the Column of Trajan.

To the south is a lake and park, and the huge domed Palazzo dello Sport built for the 1960 Olympics.

San Paolo fuori le Mura ⑮

Via Ostiense 186. ☏ 06-541 03 41.
🚌 23, 128, 170, 670, 702, 707,
761, 766. Ⓜ San Paolo.
Open 7.30am–6.40pm daily
(last adm: 15 mins before closing).
🚹 ♿ 📷

T ODAY'S CHURCH IS a faithful
if somewhat soulless
reconstruction of the great 4th-
century basilica destroyed by
fire on 15 July 1823. Few fragments of the original church
survived. The triumphal arch
over the nave is decorated on
one side with restored 5th-
century mosaics. On the other
side are mosaics by Pietro
Cavallini, originally on the
facade. The splendid Venetian
apse mosaics (1220) depict the
figures of Christ with St Peter,
St Andrew, St Paul and St Luke.

The fine marble canopy over
the high altar is signed by the
sculptor Arnolfo di Cambio
(1285) "together with his partner Pietro", who may have
been Pietro Cavallini. Below
the altar is the *confessio*, the
tomb of St Paul. To the right
is an impressive Paschal
candlestick by Nicolò di
Angelo and Pietro Vassalletto.

The cloister of San Paolo,
with its pairs of colourful inlaid

19th-century mosaic on facade of San Paolo fuori le Mura

columns supporting the
arcade, was spared completely
by the fire. Completed around
1214, it is considered one of
the most beautiful in Rome.

Centrale Montemartini ⑯

Via Ostiense 106. ☏ 06-57991.
🚌 23, 702. **Open** 10am–6pm
Tue–Fri, 10am–7pm Sat–Sun.
Closed public hols. **Adm charge.**
🚹 ♿

A N ENORMOUS old industrial
site has been restored to
house the ACEA art centre.
Originally, the building was
used as the first Roman power

station and its two huge
generators still occupy the
central machine room and
create an intriguing contrast
to the exhibitions.

The display of Greek and
Roman statues belongs to the
Capitoline Museums (see
pp70–73) and found in
excavation in the late 19th
and early 20th cen-turies but
have been kept in storage,
and never before exhibited
to the public.

Casino del Bel Respiro, summer residence in Villa Doria Pamphilj

Villa Doria Pamphilj ⑰

Via di San Pancrazio. 🚌 44, 75, 710,
870. **Park open** dawn–dusk daily.

O NE OF ROME'S largest public
parks, the Villa Doria
Pamphilj was laid out in the
mid-17th century for Prince
Camillo Pamphilj. His uncle
Pope Innocent X paid for the
magnificent summer residence,
the Casino del Bel Respiro,
fountains and summerhouses,
some of which still survive.
Today the park is a popular
with joggers and dog lovers.

Statue in Centrale Montemarini, former power plant turned art cenre

Day Trips around Rome

Tivoli, a favourite place to escape the heat of the Roman summer

Tivoli ⑱

Town is 31 km (20 miles) northeast of Rome. ⒡⒮ *from Roma Termini or Tiburtina.* ⛴ *COTRAL from Rebibbia (on Metro line B).*

TIVOLI HAS BEEN a popular summer resort since the days of the Roman Republic. Among the famous men who owned villas here were the poets Catullus and Horace, Caesar's assassins Brutus and Cassius, and the Emperors Trajan and Hadrian. Tivoli's main attractions were its clean air and beautiful situation on the slopes of the Tiburtini hills, its healthy sulphur springs and the waterfalls of the Aniene – the Emperor Augustus said these had cured him of insomnia. The Romans' luxurious lifestyle was revived in Renaissance times by the owners of the Villa d'Este,

Detail of Fontana dell'Organo at Villa d'Este

the town's most famous sight.

In the Middle Ages Tivoli suffered frequent invasions as its position made it an ideal base for an advance on Rome. In 1461 Pope Pius II built a fortress here, the Rocca Pia, declaring: "It is easier to regain Rome while possessing Tivoli, than to regain Tivoli while possessing Rome."

After suffering heavy bomb-damage in 1944, Tivoli's main buildings and churches were speedily restored. The town's cobbled streets are still lined with medieval houses. The Duomo (cathedral) houses a beautiful 13th-century life-size wooden group representing the *Deposition from the Cross.*

Villa d'Este ⑲

Piazza Trento, Tivoli. ⒞ *0774-31 20 70.* Ⓜ *COTRAL from B Rebibbia.* **Open** *winter: 9am–4pm Tue–Sun; summer: 9am–6.30pm Tue–Sun.* **Closed** *1 Jan, 1 May, 25 Dec.* **Adm charge.** ▯

THE VILLA OCCUPIES the site of an old Benedictine convent. In the 16th century the estate was developed by Cardinal Ippolito d'Este, son of Lucrezia Borgia. A palace was designed by Pirro Ligorio to make the most of its hilltop situation, but the villa's fame rests more on the terraced gardens and fountains laid out by Ligorio and Giacomo della Porta.

The gardens have suffered from neglect, but the grottoes and fountains still give a vivid impression of the great luxury which the princes of the church enjoyed. From the great loggia of the palace you descend through the privet-lined paths to the Grotto of Diana and Bernini's Fontana del Bicchierone. Below to the right is the Rometta (little Rome), a model of Tiber Island with allegorical figures and the legendary she-wolf.

The Rometta is at one end of the Viale delle Cento Fontane. Its 100 fountains are in the shape of grotesques, obelisks, ships and the eagles of the d'Este coat of arms, now overgrown with moss. Other fountains have also lost much of their former glory. The Fontana dell'Organo was a water-organ, in which the force of the water pumped air through the pipes, but it has long been silent. The garden's lowest level has flower beds, fountains and splendid views out over the plain below.

Terrace of 100 Fountains in the gardens of Villa d'Este

Villa Gregoriana ⑳

Largo Massimo, Tivoli. ⒡⒮ *Tivoli, then short walk.* **Open** *9.30am–1 hr before sunset daily.* **Adm charge.**

THE MAIN ATTRACTIONS of this steeply sloping wooded park are the beautiful waterfalls and grottoes created over the centuries by the River Aniene. The park is named after Pope Gregory XVI, who in the 1830s ordered the building of a tunnel as a way of eradicating the danger of flooding. This created a new waterfall, the Grande Cascata, which plunges a full 160 m (525 ft) into the valley behind the town.

The Canopus, extensively restored, with replicas of its original caryatids lining the bank of the canal

Hadrian's Villa ㉑

Villa Adriana, Via Tiburtina. Site is 6 km (4 miles) southwest of Tivoli. ▮ 0774-53 02 03. ▯ Tivoli, then local bus No. 4. ▮ COTRAL from Rebibbia (on Metro line B). **Open** winter: 9am–4pm Tue–Sun; summer: 9am–6.30pm Tue–Sun. **Closed** 1 Jan, 1 May, 25 Dec. **Adm charge.** ▯ ▯

BUILT AS a private summer retreat between AD 118 and 134, Hadrian's Villa was a vast open-air museum of the finest architecture of the Roman world. The grounds of the Imperial palace covered an area of 120 hectares (300 acres) and were filled with full-scale reproductions of the emperor's favourite buildings from Greece and Egypt. Although excavations began in the 16th century, many of the ruins lying scattered in the surrounding fields have yet to be identified with any certainty. The grounds of the villa make a very picturesque site for a picnic, with scattered fragments of columns lying among olive trees and cypresses.

For an idea of how the whole complex would have looked in its heyday, study the scale model in the building beside the car park. The most important buildings are signposted and several have been partially restored or reconstructed. One of the most impressive is the so-called Maritime Theatre. This is a round pool with an island in the middle, surrounded by columns. The island, reached by means of a swing bridge, was probably Hadrian's private studio, where he withdrew from the cares of the Empire to indulge in his two favourite pastimes, painting and architecture. There were also theatres, Greek and Latin libraries, two bath houses, extensive housing for guests and the palace staff, and formal gardens with fountains, statues, pools.

Hadrian also loved Greek philosophy. One part of the gardens is thought to have been Hadrian's reproduction of the Grove of Academe, where Plato lectured to his students. He also had a replica made of the Stoà Poikile, a beautiful painted colonnade in Athens, from which the Stoic philosophers took their name. This copy enclosed a great piazza with a central pool. The so-called Hall of the Philosophers close to the Poikile was probably a library.

The most ambitious of Hadrian's replicas was the Canopus, a sanctuary of the god Serapis near Alexandria. For this a canal 119 metres (130 yards) long was dug and Egyptian statues were imported to decorate the temple and its grounds. This impressive piece of engineering has been restored and the banks of the canal are lined with caryatids.

Another picturesque spot in the grounds is the Vale of Tempe, the legendary haunt of the goddess Diana with a stream representing the river

Pair of Ionic columns in the vaulted baths of Hadrian's Villa

Peneios. Below ground the emperor even built a fanciful recreation of the underworld, Hades, reached through underground tunnels, of which there were many linking the various parts of the villa.

Plundered by barbarians who camped here in the 6th and 8th centuries, the villa fell into disrepair. Its marble was burnt to make lime for cement and Renaissance antiquarians contributed even further to its destruction. Statues unearthed in the grounds are on show in museums around Europe. The Vatican's Egyptian Collection (see p238) has many fine works that were found here.

Fragment of marble mosaic pavement in the Imperial palace

Ostia Antica ㉒

Viale dei Romagnoli 717. Site is 25 km
(16 miles) southwest of Rome. ☎ *06-
56 35 80 99.* Ⓜ *Magliana on line B,
then train to Ostia Antica.* **Excavations
open** *winter: 9am–4pm Tue–Sun;
summer: 9am–6pm Tue–Sun.* **Closed**
1 Jan, 1 May, 25 Dec. **Museum open**
9am–1pm daily. **Closed** *public hols.*
Adm charge.

Ruins of shops, offices and houses near Ostia's theatre

I N REPUBLICAN TIMES Ostia was
Rome's main commercial
port and a military base
defending the coastline and
the mouth of the Tiber. The
port continued to flourish
under the Empire, despite the
development of Portus, a new
port slightly to the northwest,
in the 2nd century AD. Ostia's
decline began in the 4th
century, when a reduction
in trade was combined with
the gradual silting up of the
harbour. Worse was to come
when malaria became endemic
in the area and the city, whose
population is reckoned to
have been nearly 100,000 at its
peak, was totally abandoned.

Buried for centuries by
sand, the city is remarkably
well preserved. The site is
less spectacular than Pompei
or Herculaneum because
Ostia died a gradual death,
but it gives a more complete
picture of life under the
Roman Empire. People of all
social classes and from all
over the Mediterranean lived
and worked here.

Visitors can understand the
layout of Ostia's streets almost
at a glance. The main road
through the town, the
Decumanus Maximus, would
have been filled with hurrying
slaves and citizens, avoiding
the jostling carriages and
carts, while tradesmen

pursued their business under
the porticoes lining the street.
The floorplans of the public
buildings along the road are
very clear. Many were bath
houses, such as the Baths of
the Cisiarii (carters) and the
grander Baths of Neptune,
named after their fine black-
and-white floor mosaics.
Beside the restored theatre,
three large masks, originally
part of the decoration of the
stage, have been mounted
on large blocks of tufa.
Beneath the great brick
arches that supported the
semicircular tiers of seats
were taverns and shops.
Classical plays are put on
here in the summer.

The Tiber's course has
changed considerably since
Ostia was the port of Rome. It
once flowed past just to the
north of Piazzale delle

Corporazioni, the square
behind the theatre. The
corporations were the guilds
of the various trades involved
in fitting out and
supplying ships:
tanners and rope-
makers, ship
builders and
timber merchants,
ships' chandlers
and corn weighers.
There were some
60 or 70 offices
around the square.
Mosaics showing
scenes of everyday
life in the port and
the names and
symbols of the
corporations can
still be seen.

**Mask decorating
the theatre**

There were also offices used
by ship-owners and their
agents from places as far apart
as Tunisia and the south of
France, Sardinia and Egypt. In
one office, belonging to a
merchant from the town of
Sabratha in North Africa,
there is a delightful mosaic
of an elephant.

The main cargo coming into
Rome was grain from Africa.
Much of this was distributed
free to prevent social unrest.
Although only men received
this *annona* or corn dole, at
times over 300,000 were
eligible. In the centre of the
square was a temple, probably

Mural from Ostia of merchant ship being loaded with grain

dedicated to Ceres, goddess of the harvest. Among the buildings excavated are many large warehouses in which grain was stored before it was shipped on to Rome.

The Decumanus leads to the Forum and the city's principal temple, erected by Hadrian in the 2nd century AD and dedicated to Jove, Juno and Minerva. In this rather romantic, lonely spot, it is hard to imagine the Forum as a bustling centre, where justice was dispensed and officials

Floor mosaic of Nereid and sea monster in the House of the Dioscuri

Detail of floor mosaic in the
Piazzale delle Corporazioni

met to discuss the city's affairs. In the 18th century it was used as a sheepfold.

Away from the main street are the buildings where Ostia's inhabitants lived. The great majority were housed in rented apartments in blocks three or four storeys high known as *insulae*. These varied considerably in their comfort and decoration. The House of Diana was one of the smarter ones, with a balcony around the second floor, a private bath house and a central courtyard with a cistern where tenants came to collect their water. Around the ground floor of the block were shops, taverns and bars selling snacks and drinks. In the bar at the House of Diana you can see the marble counter used by customers buying their

sausages and hot wine sweetened with honey.

For the wealthy there were detached houses *(domus)* such as the House of the Dioscuri, which has fine mosaics, and the House of Cupid and Psyche, named after a statue there. This is now in the site's Museo Ostiense, near the Forum, along with other sculptures and reliefs found in Ostia.

Among the houses and shops there are other fascinating buildings including a laundry and the firemen's barracks. The religions practised in Ostia reflect the cosmopolitan nature of the port. There are also no fewer than 18 temples dedicated to the Persian god Mithras, as well as a Jewish Synagogue dating from the 1st century AD and a Christian basilica. A plaque records the death of St Augustine's mother in a hotel here in AD 387.

ALSO WORTH SEEING

Anagni FS *from Termini (c50 min).*
Picturesque hill-town with papal palace and famous Romanesque cathedral.

Bracciano FS *from Termini or Tiburtina (c90 min).* 🚌 *from Lepanto, on Metro line A (bus c90 min).*
Volcanic lake with villages and wooded hills. Nice for walks or a visit to Orsini Castle. Swimming in summer.

Cerveteri FS *from Termini, Tiburtina or Ostiense to Cerveteri-Ladispoli, then local bus (c70 min).* 🚌 *from Via Lepanto, on Metro line A (bus c80 min).*
One of the greatest Etruscan cities. Necropolis with complete streets and houses.

Nemi 🚌 *from Anagnina, on Metro line A (bus c60 min).*
Charming village at volcanic lake in the Castelli Romani. Famous for its wine and strawberries.

Palestrina 🚌 *from Rebibbia, on Metro line B (bus c70 min).*
Impressive Roman sanctuary to goddess Fortuna. Museum and the Mosaic of the Nile.

Pompei FS *to Naples, then change to local train (c170 min).* 🚌 *Special bus tours from tourist agents.*
Excavations of the wealthy and bustling Roman city where the busy daily life was put to a sudden end by the eruption of Vesuvius in AD 79.

Subiaco 🚌 *from Rebibbia, on Metro line B (bus c120 min).*
Birthplace of St Benedict. Two monasteries to visit.

Tarquinia FS *from Termini or Ostiense (c180 min).* 🚌 *from Via Lepanto, on Metro line A. Change at Civitavecchia (c150 min).*
Outstanding collection of Etruscan objects and frescoes from Tarquinia's necropolis.

Viterbo FS *from Termini (c90 min) or COTRAL train from Roma Nord, Piazzale Flaminio, on Metro line A (c120 min).* 🚌 *from Saxa Rubra reached by the COTRAL train above (bus c90 min).*
Medieval quarter, papal palace and archaeological museum within 13th-century walls.

SIX GUIDED WALKS

ROME IS an excellent city for walking. The distances between major sights in the historic centre are easily covered on foot and many streets are pedestrianized. When you get tired, there are plenty of pavement cafés in wonderful settings, such as Piazza Navona and Campo de' Fiori. If you are interested in archaeology, then a walk across the Forum *(see pp76–87)* and over the Palatine *(see pp96–101)* takes you away from the roaring traffic of modern Rome to a different world of scattered ruins and shady pine trees.

The first of the six suggested walks takes in picturesque quarters on either side of the Tiber, the river that has played such an important part in the city's development. The second walk, along the perfectly straight Via

Bernini angel on Ponte Sant'Angelo

Giulia, gives a vivid impression of the Renaissance city. The next three walks each follow a particular theme. For visitors who wish to savour the glory of ancient Rome, there is a walk taking in the surviving triumphal arches of the emperors. For those who prefer the Middle Ages, there is a tour of early Christian churches with well-preserved mosaics, and for those who enjoy the Roman Baroque there is a walk concentrating on the great contribution of Bernini to the appearance of the city.

The Romans were famous for the straightness of their roads. The final walk is outside the central sightseeing area along the best-known of all Roman roads, the Via Appia Antica, parts of which are still intact after more than 2,000 years of use.

CHOOSING A WALK

Via Giulia
(pp276–7)

Bernini
(pp282–3)

The Six Walks
The routes of the first five walks are marked on the larger map, which also shows the main sightseeing areas of Rome. The smaller inset map shows the location of the Via Appia walk in relation to the central area.

Mosaics
(pp280–81)

Tiber
(pp274–5)

Triumphal Arches
(pp278–9)

N

KEY

··· Walk routes

— City Wall

| 0 kilometres | 1 |
| 0 miles | 0.5 |

Via Appia Antica
(pp284–5)

Pedestrians strolling across Ponte Sant'Angelo

A Two-Hour Walk by the River Tiber

ROME OWES ITS VERY EXISTENCE to the Tiber; the city grew up around an easy fording point where a market place developed. The river could also be a hazard; shallow and torrent-like, it flooded the city every winter up to 1870, when work began on the massive Lungotevere embankments that run along both sides of the river. These provide many fine views from points along their avenues of plane trees. The walk also explores the neighbourhoods along the riverside, in particular the Jewish Ghetto and Trastevere, which have preserved much of their character from earlier periods in the colourful history of Rome.

From the old port of Rome to Via dei Funari

Starting from the church of Santa Maria in Cosmedin ① *(see p202)*, cross the piazza to the Temples of the Forum Boarium ② *(see p203)*. This was the cattle market that stood near the city's river port. The river here has preserved two less obvious structures from ancient Rome: the mouth of the Cloaca Maxima ③, the city's great sewer, and one arch of a ruined bridge, known as the Ponte Rotto ④. In Via Petroselli stands the rather extraordinary medieval Casa dei Crescenzi ⑤ *(see p203)*, decorated with fragments of Roman temples. Passing the modern Anagrafe (public records office) ⑥, built on the site of the old Roman port, you come to San Nicola in Carcere ⑦ *(see p152)*.

You are now in the Foro Olitorio, Rome's ancient vegetable market. To the east stand the ruins of a Roman portico and the medieval house of the Pierleoni family. Head for the massive Theatre

Santa Maria in Cosmedin ①

of Marcellus ⑧ *(see p151)*, and look for the three Corinthian columns of the Temple of Apollo beside it. Turn into Piazza Campitelli and walk up to Santa Maria in Campitelli ⑨ *(see p151)*. The church honours a miraculous image of the Virgin credited with halting the plague in 1656. The 16th-century piazza was the home of Flaminio Ponzio, its architect, who lived at No. 6. Take Via dei Delfini to Piazza Margana where you should look up at the 14th-century tower of the Margani family ⑩. Retrace your steps, then go up Via dei Funari (Street of the Ropemakers) to the 16th-century facade of Santa Caterina dei Funari ⑪.

The Ghetto

From Piazza Lovatelli take Via Sant'Angelo in Pescheria, which

leads to the ruined Portico of Octavia ⑫ *(see p151)* in the Jewish Ghetto *(see p152)*. The Roman portico, once Rome's fish market, houses the church of Sant'Angelo in Pescheria. Find the marble plaque on the facade: fish longer than this slab were given to the city's *conservatori* (governors). Turn into the Ghetto: two column stumps belonging to the Portico stand in front of a patched-up doorway made of fragments of Roman sculpture. The cramped buildings and streets around Via del Portico

Arch of the Ponte Rotto ④

Main altar of Santa Maria in Campitelli ⑨

d'Ottavia are typical of old Rome: see the Casa di Lorenzo Manilio ⑬ *(see p153)*, and turn down Via delle Cinque Scole, past Palazzo Cenci ⑭ *(see p152)*, towards the river. On Lungotevere walk past the Synagogue ⑮ *(see p152)* to the small church of San Gregorio ⑯. Here stood the gates of the Ghetto, which were locked at sundown.

Across the river to Trastevere

Crossing to Tiber Island *(see p152)* by Ponte Fabricio, with its two ancient

Classical relief of Medusa above the doorway of Palazzo Cenci ⑭

much of the spirit of old Trastevere. Walk up to the start of Viale di Trastevere at Piazza Belli. After crossing the road look back

Santa Maria in Trastevere, don't miss the old-fashioned chemist's shop at No. 7. The piazza itself, in front of the magnificent church of Santa Maria in Trastevere ㉒ *(see pp212–13)*, has a cheerful atmosphere, and the fountain steps are a favourite meeting place. Go back a little way to Via del Moro. This leads to Piazza Trilussa, dominated by the fountain of the Acqua Paola ㉓, where you emerge on to the bank of the river again. Note the life-like statue, near the fountain, of Roman poet Trilussa, who wrote in the local dialect. From Ponte Sisto ㉔ *(see p210)*, look back to Tiber Island and, beyond it, to the medieval bell tower of Santa Maria in Cosmedin, set against the pine trees on the summit of the Palatine.

The western tip of Tiber Island

0 metres	250
0 yards	250

TIPS FOR WALKERS

Starting point: *Piazza della Bocca della Verità.*
Length: *3.5 km (2 miles).*
Getting there: *The 23, 44, 75, 81, 160, 280, 628 and 810 buses stop near Santa Maria in Cosmedin.*
Best time for walk: *This walk can be very romantic in the evenings, but is enjoyable at any time.*
Stopping-off points: *Piazza Campitelli and Piazza Margana have typical Roman restaurants, and Via del Portico d'Ottavia has restaurants and a bakery. Tiber Island has a bar and the famous Sora Lella restaurant (see p314). In Viale Trastevere there are a variety of bars and pizzerias. Piazza Santa Maria in Trastevere has lively bars and restaurants with outdoor tables.*

stone heads on the parapet, you can enjoy a good view of the river in both directions. On the island itself, you should not miss the Pierleoni Tower ⑰ or the church of San Bartolomeo all'Isola ⑱.

Trastevere

As you cross into Trastevere, you can see the medieval house of the powerful Mattei family ⑲, with its fragments of ancient sculpture. Beyond it, Piazza in Piscinula and the surrounding streets retain

KEY

— Walk route

᠁ Good viewing point

at the medieval tower of the Anguillara ⑳ and the statue honouring the poet Gioacchino Belli ㉑ *(see p209)*. As you go down Via della Lungaretta to Piazza

Piazza in Piscinula, old Trastevere

A One-Hour Walk along Via Giulia

LAID OUT BY BRAMANTE for Pope Julius II in the early 16th century, Via Giulia was one of the first Renaissance streets to slice through Rome's jumble of medieval alleys. The original plan included new law courts in a central piazza, but this project was abandoned for lack of cash. The street now is dominated by antiques shops and furniture restorers. On summer evenings, hundreds of oil lamps light the street while cloisters and courtyards provide romantic settings for a special season of concerts.

Baroque capital on the facade of Sant'Eligio degli Orefici ⑦

From Lungotevere to Largo della Moretta

Starting from Lungotevere dei Tebaldi ① at the eastern end of Via Giulia, you will see ahead of you an archway ② spanning the road. This was the start of Michelangelo's unrealized project linking Palazzo Farnese and its gardens (see p147) with the Villa Farnesina (see pp220–21) on the other side of the river.

Just before you reach the archway, you will see to your left the curious Fontana del Mascherone ③, in which an ancient grotesque mask and granite basin were combined to create a Baroque fountain.

Beyond the Farnese archway on the left is the lively Baroque facade of the church of Santa Maria dell'Orazione e Morte ④ (see p147). A bit further along on the same side of the road stands Palazzo Falconieri ⑤, enlarged by Borromini in 1650. Note its two stone falcons glowering at each other across the width of the facade. On the other side of the road you pass the yellowish facade of Santa Caterina da Siena ⑥, church of the Sienese colony in Rome, which has pretty 18th-century reliefs. The figures of Romulus and Remus symbolize Rome

Relief of Romulus and Remus on Santa Caterina da Siena ⑥

and Siena – there is a legend that the city of Siena was founded by the less fortunate of the twins. After passing the short street that leads down to Sant'Eligio degli Orefici ⑦ (see p148) and the facade of Palazzo Ricci ⑧ (see p149), you come to an area of half-demolished buildings around the ruined church of San Filippo Neri ⑨, called Vicolo della Moretta. If you look to the left down to the river, you can see

Fontana del Mascherone ③

Ponte Mazzini and the huge prison of Regina Coeli on the other side of the Tiber. At this point you may like to make a small detour to the right to the beginning of Via del Pellegrino, where there is an inscription ⑩, defining the *pomerium*, or boundary, of the city in the time of the Emperor Claudius.

From Largo della Moretta to the Sofas of Via Giulia

Further on, facing the narrow Vicolo del Malpasso are the imposing prisons, the Carceri

Nuove ⑪, built by Pope Innocent X Pamphilj in 1655. When first opened, they were a model of humane treatment of prisoners, but were replaced by the Regina Coeli prison across the river at the end of the 19th century. The buildings now house offices of the Ministry of Justice and a small Museum of Crime.

At the corner of Via del Gonfalone, a small side street running down to the river,

KEY

— Walk route

⁂ Good viewing point

0 metres	250
0 yards	250

Farnese archway across Via Giulia, built to a design by Michelangelo ②

Plaque honouring Antonio da Sangallo on Palazzo Sacchetti ⑮

the traditional distribution of bread to the poor that took place on the saint's feast day.

On the corner there are more travertine blocks belonging to the foundations of Julius II's projected law courts, known because of their curious shape as the "Sofas of Via Giulia".

The Florentine Quarter

Your next stop should be the imposing Palazzo Sacchetti at No. 66 ⑮. Originally this was the house of Antonio da Sangallo the Younger, the architect of Palazzo Farnese, but it was greatly enlarged by later owners. The porticoed courtyard houses a 15th-century Madonna and a striking Roman relief of the 3rd century AD. Just opposite Palazzo Sacchetti, note the beautiful late Renaissance portal of Palazzo Donarelli ⑯. The 16th-century house at No. 93 is richly decorated with stuccoes and coats of arms ⑰. No. 85 is another typical Renaissance palazzo with a heavily rusticated ground floor ⑱. There is a tradition

that, like many houses of the period, it once belonged to Raphael. Palazzo Clarelli ⑲ was built by Antonio da Sangallo the Younger as his own house. The inscription above the doorway bears the name of Duke Cosimo II de' Medici, whose family later bought the palazzo.

This whole area used to be inhabited by a flourishing Florentine colony, which had its own water-mills built on pontoons along the Tiber. Their national church is San Giovanni dei Fiorentini ⑳ (see p153), the final great landmark at the end of Via Giulia. Many Florentine artists and architects had a hand in its design, including Sangallo and Jacopo Sansovino.

Coat of arms of Pope Paul III Farnese on the facade of Via Giulia No. 93 ⑰

you can see part of the foundations of Julius II's planned law courts. Just down the street stands the small Oratorio di Santa Lucia del Gonfalone ⑫, which is often used for concerts.

The next interesting facade is Carlo Rainaldi's 17th-century Santa Maria del Suffragio ⑬ on the left. On the same side is San Biagio degli Armeni ⑭, the Armenian church in Rome. It is often referred to by local people as San Biagio della Pagnotta (of the loaf of bread). The nickname originates from

Detail on the side of the door of Santa Maria del Suffragio ⑬

TIPS FOR WALKERS

Starting point: Lungotevere dei Tebaldi, by Ponte Sisto.

Length: 1 km (1,100 yds).

Getting there: The 116 goes to and along Via Giulia, or you can take 46, 62 or 64 to Corso Vittorio Emanuele II, then walk down Via dei Pettinari or a 23, 65 or 280 along Lungotevere.

Best time for walk: On summer evenings oil lamps light the street. At Christmas, there are cribs on display in many shop windows.

Stopping-off points: There are bars in Via Giulia, at Nos. 21 and 84. Campo de' Fiori has better bars, with outdoor tables, and a wide choice of places to eat. These include a fried fish restaurant in Piazza Santa Barbara dei Librai (closed Sun).

A 90-Minute Tour of Rome's Triumphal Arches

ROME'S GREATEST GIFT to architecture was the arch and the Roman people's highest tribute to its victorious generals was the triumphal arch. In Imperial times, arches were erected to honour an emperor's campaign victories almost as a matter of course, promoting his personal cult and ensuring his subsequent deification. Spectacular processions passed through these arches. Conquering generals, cheered by rapturous crowds, rode in their chariots to the Capitol, accompanied by their legions bearing spoils from their campaigns.

Part of the Via Sacra, once spanned by the Arch of Augustus ③

Arches of the Forum

This walk through the Forum and around the base of the Palatine takes in Rome's three great surviving triumphal arches and two arches of more

Relief of barbarian captives on the Arch of Septimius Severus ①

humble design that were used simply as places of business. It starts from the Arch of

Emperor Septimius Severus ① and his sons Geta and Caracalla *(see p83)* in the Forum. Erected in AD 203, it celebrates a successful campaign in the Middle East. Eight years later when Caracalla had his brother killed, all mention of Geta was removed from the inscription.

Look up at the reliefs showing phases of the campaigns. Set in tiers, they are probably the sculptural counterparts of the paintings illustrating the general's feats that were borne aloft in the triumphal procession. On the right, the inhabitants of a fortified city surrender to the Romans' siege machines. Below are smaller friezes showing the triumphal procession itself.

Heading east, make your way through the Forum to the ruins of the Temple of Julius Caesar ②. The temple was built by Augustus in 29 BC, on the site where Caesar's body was cremated after Mark Antony's famous funerary oration. A nearby sign marks the ruins of one of the arches dedicated to Augustus ③, spanning the Via Sacra between the Temple of Castor and Pollux ④ *(see p84)* and the Temple of Caesar. This arch, erected after Augustus had defeated Mark Antony and Cleopatra, was finally demolished in 1545, and its

Capital from Temple of Castor and Pollux ④

materials were used in the new St Peter's. From here, proceed uphill towards the elegant Arch of Titus ⑤ *(see p87)*. Compared with Septimius Severus's arch, it shows an earlier, simpler style. Look up at the beautiful lettering of the inscription before

TIPS FOR WALKERS

Starting point: The Roman Forum, entrance Largo Romolo e Remo, on Via dei Fori Imperiali.
Length: 2.5 km (1½ miles).
Getting there: The nearest Metro stations is Colosseo on line B. Buses 85, 87, 117, 175, 186, 850 stop in Via dei Fori Imperiali, near the Forum entrance.
Best time for walk: Any time of day during Forum opening hours (see p82) is suitable.
Stopping-off points: Several bars and restaurants overlook the Colosseum. There is a small bar in Via dei Cerchi and a smarter one behind San Giorgio in Velabro, in Piazza San Giovanni Decollato (closed Sun). For a meal, try Alvaro al Circo Massimo (closed Mon) in Via di San Teodoro.

KEY

— Walk route

☆ Good viewing point

M Metro station

0 metres   250

0 yards   250

Arch of Titus in a 19th-century watercolour by the English artist Thomas Hartley Cromek ⑤

excavated in the 18th and 19th centuries. Many of the carts that passed through the arch would have been carrying building materials quarried from the Forum's many ruined monuments.

Arch of Constantine

Leave the Forum by heading down the hill towards the Colosseum ⑥ *(see pp92–5)* and the nearby Arch of Constantine ⑦ *(see p91)*. This arch, hastily built to commemorate the emperor's victory over his rival Maxentius in AD 312, is a patchwork of reliefs from different periods. Stand on the Via di San Gregorio side and compare

Arches of Domitian's extension to the Claudian Aqueduct ⑨

the earlier panels at the top (AD 180– 193) with the hectic battle scenes just above the smaller arches, sculpted in AD 315. In the curious dwarf-like soldiers, you can see the transition from Classicism to a cruder medieval style of sculpture.

Now take Via di San Gregorio, which runs the length of the valley between the Palatine and Celian hills. This was the ancient route taken by most triumphal processions. Passing the entrance to the Palatine ⑧ and the well-preserved arches of the Claudian Aqueduct ⑨

on the right, you come to Piazza di Porta Capena ⑩, named after the gate that stood here to mark the beginning of the Via Appia *(see p284)*. After rounding the back of the Palatine, follow Via dei Cerchi, which runs alongside the grassy area that preserves, in an oval outline, all that remains of the Circus Maximus ⑪ *(see p205)*.

Arches of the Forum Boarium

When you reach the church of Sant'Anastasia ⑫, turn right up Via di San Teodoro, then first left down Via del Velabro. Straddling the street is the four-sided Arch of Janus ⑬ *(see p202)*, erected in the 3rd century AD. This is not a triumphal arch but a covered area where merchants could take shelter from the sun or rain when discussing business. Like the Arch of Titus, it became part of a fortress built by the Frangipane family during the Middle Ages.

Tucked away beside the nearby church of San Giorgio in Velabro ⑭ *(see p202)* is what looks like a large rectangular doorway. This is the Arco degli Argentari, or Moneychangers' Arch ⑮. Look up at the inscription, which says that it was erected by local silversmiths in honour of Septimius Severus and his family in AD 204. As in the emperor's triumphal arch, the name of Geta has been obliterated by his brother and murderer, Caracalla. Geta's figure has also been removed from among the portraits on the panels inside the arch. Triumph in Imperial Rome could be very short-lived.

you examine the inner bas-reliefs. These show Roman legionaries carrying the spoils looted from the conquest of Jerusalem, heralds holding plaques with the names of vanquished peoples and cities, and Titus riding in triumph in his chariot.

The medieval Frangipane family turned the Colosseum into a vast impregnable stronghold and incorporated the Arch of Titus into their fortifications. Notice the wheelmarks scratched on the inside walls of the arch by generations of carts; they indicate the steady rise in the level of the Forum floor before it was eventually

Four-sided Arch of Janus in the Forum Boarium ⑬

A Three-Hour Tour of Rome's Best Mosaics

IN IMITATION of the audience chambers of Imperial palaces, Rome's early Christian churches were decorated with colourful mosaics. These were pieced together from cubes of marble, coloured stone and fragments of glass. To create a golden background, gold leaf was placed between pieces of glass. These were then heated so that they fused. The glorious colours and subjects portrayed gave the faithful a glimpse of the heavenly court of the King of Kings. This walk concentrates on a few of the churches decorated in this wonderful medium.

Apse mosaic in the Chapel of Santa Rufina ③

San Giovanni
Start from Piazza di Porta San Giovanni, where you can visit the heavily-restored mosaic of the Triclinio Leoniano *(see p179)*. Originally in the banqueting hall of Pope Leo III (reigned 795–816) ①, it shows Christ among the Apostles. On the left are Pope Sylvester and the Emperor Constantine, on the right, Pope Leo and Charlemagne

Obelisk and side facade of San Giovanni in Laterano ②

just before he was crowned Holy Roman Emperor in AD 800. Inside the church of San Giovanni in Laterano ② *(see pp182–3)*, the 13th-century apse mosaic shows Christ as he appeared miraculously during the consecration of the church. In the panels by the windows, look for the small figures of two Franciscan friars; these are the artists Jacopo Torriti (left) and Jacopo de

Camerino (right). Leave by the exit on the right near the splendid 16th-century organ and head for the octagonal Baptistry of San Giovanni ③, where the Chapel of Santa Rufina has a beautiful apse mosaic, dating from the 5th century. In the neighbouring Chapel of San Venanzio, there are golden 7th-century mosaics, showing the strong influence of the Eastern Church at this time.

Santo Stefano Rotondo to San Clemente
Leave the piazza by the narrow road that leads to the round church of Santo Stefano Rotondo ④ *(see p185)*. One of its chapels contains a 7th-century Byzantine mosaic honouring two martyrs buried here. Further on, in Piazza della Navicella, is the church of Santa Maria in Domnica ⑤ *(see p193)*. It houses the superb mosaics commissioned by Pope Paschal I, who gave new impetus to Rome's mosaic production in the 9th century. He is represented kneeling beside the Virgin. On leaving the church, notice the facade of San Tommaso in Formis ⑥, which has a charming mosaic of Christ flanked by two freed slaves, one black and one white, dating from the 13th

Ceiling mosaic, Baptistry of San Giovanni ③

Interior of Baptistry of San Giovanni ③

century. From here, head up the steep hill, past the forbidding apse of Santi Quattro Coronati ⑦ (see p185), to the fascinating church of San Clemente ⑧ (see pp186–7). Its 12th-century apse mosaic shows the cross set in a swirling pattern of acanthus leaves. San Clemente also has a fine 12th-century Cosmatesque mosaic floor.

The Colle Oppio
Passing the old entrance to the church, cross Via Labicana and walk up the hill to the small Colle Oppio park ⑨. This has fine views of the Colosseum and contains the ruins of Nero's Golden House ⑩ (see p175) and the Baths of Trajan ⑪. Across the park lie San Martino ai Monti ⑫ (see p170), which has a 6th-century mosaic portrait of Pope St Sylvester near the crypt, and Santa Prassede ⑬ (see p171). Here the Chapel of St Zeno contains the most important Byzantine mosaics in Rome, reminiscent of the fabulous mosaics of Ravenna. Pope Paschal I erected the chapel as a mausoleum for his mother

14th-century facade mosaics by Filippo Rusuti. Inside, the 5th-century mosaics in the nave depict Old Testament stories, while the triumphal arch has scenes relating to the birth of Christ, including one of the Magi wearing striped stockings. In the apse there is a Coronation of the Virgin by Jacopo Torriti (1295).

On leaving Santa Maria, pass the obelisk ⑮ in the piazza behind the church and go downhill to Via Urbana and Santa Pudenziana ⑯ (see p171). The figures in the apse mosaic, one of the oldest in Rome (AD 390), are remarkable for their naturalism. The two women with crowns are traditionally identified as Santa Prassede and Santa Pudenziana. When you leave the church, you can either retrace your steps to Santa Maria Maggiore or walk down Via Urbana to Via Cavour Metro station.

Mosaic saint in Santa Prassede ⑬

11th-century frieze above the doorway of Santa Pudenziana ⑯

PIAZZA DI S. GIOVANNI IN LATERANO

PIAZZA DI PORTA S. GIOVANNI

San Giovanni Ⓜ

mother Theodora. The apse and triumphal arch of the church itself also have fine mosaics. When you move on to Santa Maria Maggiore ⑭ (see pp172–3), go to the column in the centre of the piazza in front of the church to see the beautiful

KEY

— Walk route

— City Wall

⁑ Good viewing point

Ⓜ Metro station

0 metres   250
0 yards   250

TIPS FOR WALKERS

Starting point: Piazza di Porta San Giovanni.
Length: 3.5 km (2 miles).
Getting there: The nearest Metro station is San Giovanni, on line A, in Piazzale Appio, just outside Porta San Giovanni. The 81, 85, 87, 650, and 850 buses and the 30b tram stops in front of San Giovanni in Laterano, while 117, 218 and 650 stop around the corner on Piazza San Giovanni in Laterano.
Best time for walk: Go in the morning, in order to to appreciate the mosaics in the best light.
Stopping-off points: The bars and restaurants in Piazza del Colosseo are popular with tourists. In the Parco del Colle Oppio there is a café kiosk with tables. There are several bars around Santa Maria Maggiore, some with outdoor tables.

A Two-Hour Walk around Bernini's Rome

GIAN LORENZO BERNINI (1598–1680) is the artist who probably left the strongest personal mark on the appearance of the city of Rome. Favourite architect, sculptor and town-planner to three successive popes, he turned Rome into a uniquely Baroque city. This walk traces his enormous influence on the development and appearance of the centre of Rome. It starts from the busy Largo di Santa Susanna just north of Termini station, at the church of Santa Maria della Vittoria.

Facade of Santa Maria in Via ⑬

Quirinale. The long wing of the Palazzo del Quirinale ⑦ *(see p158)*, nicknamed the Manica Lunga (long sleeve), is by Bernini. On the other side of the road is the facade of Sant'Andrea al Quirinale ⑧ *(see p161)*, one of Bernini's greatest churches. When you reach the Piazza del Quirinale ⑨, note the doorway of the palazzo, attributed to Bernini. From the piazza, go down the

composer Donizetti lived at No. 77 and turn into Via Santa Maria in Via, where the church ⑬ has a fine Baroque

Bernini's Fontana del Tritone ②

Through Piazza Barberini
Santa Maria della Vittoria ① *(see p255)* houses the Cornaro Chapel, the setting for one of Bernini's most revolutionary and controversial sculptures, the *Ecstasy of St Teresa* (1646). From here take Via Barberini to Piazza Barberini. In its centre is Bernini's dramatic Fontana del Tritone ② *(see p254)* and at one side stands the more modest Fontana delle Api ③ *(see p254)*. As you go up Via delle Quattro Fontane, you catch a glimpse of Palazzo Barberini ④ *(see p255)* built by Bernini and several other artists for Pope Urban VIII. The gateway and cornices are decorated with the bees that made up part of the Barberini family crest. Next make your way to the crossroads, decorated by Le Quattro Fontane ⑤ *(see p162)*, to enjoy the splendid views in all four directions.
  Passing the diminutive San Carlo alle Quattro Fontane ⑥ *(see p161)*, built by Bernini's rival Borromini, take Via del

stairs to Via della Dataria, and into Vicolo Scanderbeg which leads to a small piazza with the same name ⑩. Scanderbeg was the nickname of the Albanian prince Giorgio Castriota (1403–68), the "Terror of the Turks". His portrait is preserved on the house where he lived.

The Trevi Fountain
Go along the narrow Vicolo dei Modelli ⑪, where male models waited to be chosen by artists, then turn towards the Trevi Fountain ⑫ *(see p159)*. Its energy is clearly inspired by Bernini's work, a tribute to his lasting influence on Roman taste. Leave the piazza along Via delle Muratte where the

Neptune Fountain at the north end of Piazza Navona ⑱

facade by Bernini's follower Carlo Rainaldi. At the top of this street, turn left down to Via del Corso. On the other side of the road, you will see the towering Column of Marcus Aurelius ⑭ *(see p113)* in Piazza Colonna. Beyond this is Palazzo Montecitorio ⑮, begun in 1650 by Bernini and now the home of the Italian parliament *(see p112)*.

Pantheon to Piazza Navona

Via in Aquiro leads you to the Pantheon ⑯ *(see pp110–11)*. Refusing Pope Urban VIII's request for him to redecorate

Collegio Innocenziano by Borromini and Fontana di Moro by Bernini

the dome, Bernini said that although St Peter's had a hundred defects, the Pantheon did not have any. From the Pantheon, make a small detour to Piazza della Minerva where you can see the bizarre Bernini obelisk, supported by a small elephant, by the church of Santa Maria sopra Minerva ⑰ *(see p108)*. Then retrace your steps and take Salita dei Crescenzi to

Quattro Fiumi *(see p120)*, was by Bernini, though the figures symbolic of the four rivers were sculpted by other artists. The central figure in the Fontana del Moro, however, is by Bernini himself. Bernini's contemporaries were fascinated by the innovative use of shells, rocks and other natural forms in his fountains, and his expert handling of water to create constant movement.

An extended walk

More energetic walkers may like to head towards the river to see the Ponte Sant'Angelo and its Bernini angels; and then on to St Peter's *(see pp230–33)* where they can admire Bernini's great colonnaded piazza in front of the church, the papal tombs, his altar decorations and the bronze baldacchino.

KEY

— Walk route

✢ Good viewing point

Ⓜ Metro station

0 metres 250

0 yards 250

Angel on Ponte Sant'Angelo

reach the fabulous Piazza Navona ⑱ *(see p120)* which was remodelled by Bernini for Pope Innocent X Pamphilj. The design for the central fountain, the Fontana dei

---

**Map labels:**

N

VIA BISSOLATI
LARGO DI SANTA SUSANNA ①

VIA BARBERINI

Barberini Ⓜ ③
PIAZZA BARBERINI ②
④

RITONE

QUATTRO FONTANE
VIA D.

⑤
⑥

VIA XX SETTEMBRE

Repubblica Ⓜ

VIA DEL QUIRINALE

⑦
⑧

⑩

LLA DATARIA

PIAZZA DEL QUIRINALE ⑨

VIA D. CONSULTA

VIA XXIV MAGGIO

TIPS FOR WALKERS

Starting point: *Largo di Santa Susanna.*
Length: *3.5 km (2 miles).*
Getting there: *Take Metro line A to Repubblica or any bus to Termini, then walk. Buses 60, 61, 62 and 492 stop in Via Barberini.*
Best time for walk: *Go either between 9am and noon for good lighting conditions in the churches, or between 4pm and 7pm.*
Stopping-off points: *The Piazza Barberini and Fontana di Trevi areas have lots of bars and pizzerias for tourists. The many elegant cafés en route include the famous Caffè Giolitti (see p109) and there is a vast choice of outdoor cafés and restaurants around Piazza della Rotonda and Piazza Navona.*

A 90-Minute Walk along the Via Appia Antica

LINED WITH CYPRESSES AND PINES as it was when the ancient Romans came here by torchlight to bury their dead, the Via Appia is wonderfully atmospheric. The fields are strewn with ruined tombs set against the picturesque background of the Alban hills to the south. Although the marble or travertine stone facings of most tombs have been plundered, a few statues and reliefs survive or have been replaced by copies.

Tomb of Sixtus Pompeus the Righteous ⑨

Capo di Bove

Start from the Tomb of Cecilia Metella ① (see p266). In the Middle Ages this area acquired the name Capo di Bove (ox head) from the frieze of festoons and ox heads still visible on the tomb. On

Gothic windows in the church of San Nicola ②

the other side of the road you can see the ruined Gothic church of San Nicola ②, which, like the Tomb of Cecilia Metella, was part of the medieval fortress of the Caetani family.

Proceed to the crossroads ③, where there are still many original Roman paving slabs, huge blocks of extremely durable volcanic basalt. Just

The ruined church of San Nicola ②

past the next turning (Via Capo di Bove), you will see on your left the nucleus of a great mausoleum overgrown with ivy, known as the Torre di Capo di Bove ④. Beyond it,

on both sides of the Appia, are other tombs, some still capped with the remains of the medieval towers that were built over them. On the right after passing some private villas, you come to a military zone around the Forte Appio ⑤, one of a series of forts built around the city in the 19th century. On the left, a little further on, stand the ruins of the Tomb of Marcus Servilius ⑥, showing fragments of reliefs excavated in 1808 by the Neo-Classical sculptor Antonio Canova. He was one of the first to work on the principle that excavated tombs and their inscriptions and reliefs should be allowed to remain in situ. On the other side of the road stands a tomb with a relief of a man, naked except for a short cape, known as the

"Heroic Relief" ⑦. On the left of the road are the ruins of the so-called Tomb of Seneca ⑧. The great moralist Seneca owned a villa near here, where he committed suicide in AD 65 on the orders of Nero.

The next major tomb is that of the family of Sixtus Pompeus the Righteous, a freed slave of the 1st century AD ⑨. The verse inscription records the father's sadness at having to bury his own children, who died young.

Artist's impression of how the mausoleums and tombs lining the Via Appia looked in the 2nd century AD

Section of the Via Appia Antica, showing original Roman paving stones

From Via dei Lugari to Via di Tor Carbone

Just past Via dei Lugari on the right, screened by trees, is the Tomb of Pope St Urban (reigned 222–230) ⑩. Set back from the road on the left stands a large ruined podium, probably part of a Temple of Jupiter ⑪. The next stretch was excavated by the architect Luigi Canina early in the 19th century. On the right is the Tomb of Caius Licinius ⑫, followed by a smaller Doric tomb ⑬ and the imposing Tomb of Hilarius

Fuscus ⑭, with five portrait busts in relief of members of his family. Next comes the Tomb of Tiberius Claudius Secondinus ⑮, where a group of freedmen of the Imperial household were buried in the 2nd century AD.

Passing a large ruined columbarium, you reach the Tomb of Quintus Apuleius ⑯ and the reconstructed Tomb of the Rabirii freed slaves (1st century BC) ⑰. This has a frieze of three half-length figures above an inscription.

The figure on the right is a priestess of Isis. Behind her you can see the outline of a *sistrum*, the metal rattle used at ceremonies of the cult.

The majority of the tombs are little more than shapeless stacks of eroded brickwork. Two exceptions in the last stretch of this walk are the Tomb of the Festoons ⑱, with its reconstructed frieze of festive putti, and the Tomb of the Frontispiece ⑲, which has a copy of a relief with four portraits. The two central figures are holding hands.

When you reach Via di Tor Carbone, the Via Appia still stretches out ahead of you in a straight line and, if you wish to extend your walk, there are many more tombs and ruined villas to visit along the way.

KEY

— Walk route

⁎⁎ Good viewing point

0 metres	250
0 yards	250

Figure on the Tomb of the Heroic Relief ⑦

TIPS FOR WALKERS

Starting point: *Tomb of Cecilia Metella.*

Length: *3 km (2 miles).*

Getting there: *Taking a taxi is the easiest way to reach the tomb. Alternatively, take the 760 from Circo Massimo (Sundays and public holidays only) or the 660 from Colli Albani on Metro Line A.*

Best time for walk: *Go fairly early, before it gets too hot.*

Stopping-off points: *There is a bar near the church of Domine Quo Vadis?, before the start of the walk, but it is best to bring your own refreshment. There are also several well-established restaurants on the first stretch of the Appia, including the Cecilia Metella, Via Appia Antica 125/127, tel 06-513 67 43 (closed Mon).*

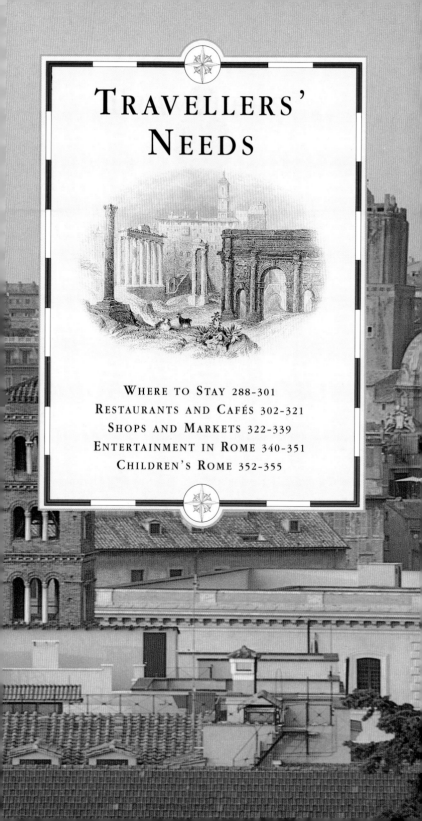

TRAVELLERS' NEEDS

WHERE TO STAY

ROME HAS BEEN a major tourist centre since the Middle Ages, when pilgrims from all over Europe came to visit the home of Catholicism and its relic-packed churches. The nostalgic can still sleep in a 15th-century hotel, or stay around the Campo de' Fiori market, where visiting ecclesiastics were entertained by courtesans in the Renaissance era. Those who prefer their history a little less raffish could opt for an ex-monastery or convent, or stay in a still-functioning religious house. Romantics could sleep in the house once occupied by Keats, while stargazers could stay

Porter at the Majestic Hotel

in former palaces graced by celebrities of the past and present. Rome can offer the full range of accommodation, mostly in historical buildings, very little purpose-built. *Pensione* (guesthouse) is no longer an official category, but in practice many retain the name and more personal character that has made them so popular with travellers. Other possibilities include hostels, residential hotels and self-catering accommodation.

The 72 hotels we have selected are organized in the *Choosing a Hotel* chart *(pp294–5)* and in the listings *(pp296–301)* according to their price category and area.

WHERE TO LOOK

AROUND the Spanish Steps and Piazza di Spagna lies the traditional heartland of foreign visitors, with some of the most exclusive smaller hotels. Similar places can be found all over the centre, to the west of Via del Corso.

While moderately priced accommodation is rare in central Rome, the advantages of staying right on the doorstep of the city's many ancient sights cannot be over-estimated; you can walk to the major areas of interest and easily return at midday for a shower and siesta. If the

less expensive hotels we have recommended in the centre are full, try the Borgo – close to the Vatican – or the lively quarter of Trastevere.

Those in search of glamour should head for Via Veneto, which has many grand and luxurious hotels.

If you're looking for a peaceful retreat, try the area around the Aventine, or one of the high-class hotels next to the Villa Borghese park.

Although many of the streets immediately around Termini station are rather seedy, the area is nonetheless a convenient stopover for travellers and there's a

concentration of cheap hotels, with some decent (if basic) ones among them. The hotels recommended lie in a fairly safe area on the east side of the station. The approach to the centre from Termini has a number of good hotels that are particularly suitable for the business traveller.

HOTEL PRICES

ROME MAY STILL have more cheap accommodation than London or New York, but rates for comparable establishments have caught up. Prices are set by the state, and hotels are supposed to display the official rate on the door of each room. VAT is usually included, and has been taken into account in the price categories on p291.

Hotels in Rome generally have low and high season rates, so it is often worth bargaining as you will inevitably be quoted the official rate, even in the winter months before and after Christmas, when competition is less strong. Discounts for long-stay visitors and groups are often negotiable.

Rooms without a bathroom can cost about 30% less. Single travellers are badly catered for, and though it is possible to find a single room for 60% of the price of a double, on average you'll

The Verdi Room in Via Veneto's Majestic Hotel *(see p301)*

The Plaza Minerva *(see p296)*

pay 70%, and occasionally 90%. Where breakfast is included in the quoted price, you can ask for the relevant amount to be deducted from your bill if you don't want it.

HIDDEN EXTRAS

EVEN IF the price of your room includes service, you are often still expected to give a tip for room service or for bellboys.

Hotels will often add hefty surcharges to international phone calls, and may charge extra for parking and air conditioning. The cost of drinks in minibars can be high – you can buy a cheaper supply from local shops.

FACILITIES

HOTEL STANDARDS have improved of late – you can expect air conditioning and some bathrooms with hair dryers in middle-range establishments and direct-dial phones in middle to lower price rooms, although budget travellers staying in cheaper hotels shouldn't expect much more than a clean room.

Because most hotels occupy historic buildings, room sizes can vary dramatically even within the same establishment (and this is often reflected in the

The Portoghesi Hotel *(see p296)*

pricing), so don't be afraid to ask to see your room before you check in. For the same reason, swimming pools are few and far between, but roof terraces or gardens are common across the range.

Top-class hotels will usually have some soundproofing; otherwise noise levels can be dreadful, in which case ask for a room facing away from the road. The chart on pages 294–5 indicates which hotels have a quiet location – this covers both peaceful neighbourhoods and certain quiet streets in busy areas which don't have a constant stream of traffic.

Parking in central Rome is a problem, though a few hotels have a limited number of parking spaces of their own.

Business visitors to the capital are well catered for, with hotel facilities ranging from fax machines to meeting rooms *(see pp294–5)*.

HOW TO BOOK

THE ITALIAN postal service tends to be unreliable, so it is safer to book by phone or fax. You should do this at least two months in advance if you want a particular hotel in May, June, September or October; Easter and Christmas are also busy.

If a deposit is required you can pay by credit card or international money order. Under Italian law a booking is valid as soon as the deposit is paid, so you're likely to lose money if you pull out. If you arrive by train, touts may descend on you at the station with offers of accommodation. They can be of some use if you are looking for a budget hotel, but you should exercise the usual caution. A better bet if you haven't booked anywhere in advance is to head for one of the tourist board offices. Here, staff will reserve you a room within the price range you specify.

Villa San Pio garden *(see p299)*

CHECKING IN AND OUT

ITALIAN HOTELIERS are legally obliged to register you with the police, which is the reason they always ask for your passport. They usually hold on to it for a few hours, but you need it if you're going to change money. Everyone in Italy is supposed to carry with them some sort of identification.

In some of Rome's cheaper *pensioni*, don't be surprised if you are asked to pay in advance. To speed up the checking out process, mention in advance if you intend to pay by credit card.

The Locarno *(see p297)*

TOURIST BOARDS

PROVINCIAL and state tourist boards can provide advice on accommodation. There is also a free booking service.

Rome Provincial Tourist Board (EPT)
Via Parigi 11, 00185. **[** 06-48 89 91. *Open 8.15am–7.15pm Mon–Fri, 8.15am–1.30pm Sun.*

Leonardo da Vinci Airport, Fiumicino, 00054. **[** 06-65 95 44 71 or 06-65 95 60 74. *Open 8.15am–7pm daily.*

Termini Station, Piazza dei Cinquecento, 00185. **[** 06-482 40 78 or 06-487 12 70. *Open 8.15am–7.15pm daily.*

Booking Service
[06-699 10 00. *Open 7am–10pm daily.*

The reception area of the Regina Hotel Baglioni *(see p301)*

DISABLED TRAVELLERS

PROVISION for disabled
travellers is very poor.
Small hotels that occupy parts
of buildings sometimes only
start their rooms up several
flights of stairs, whereas
certain establishments can
accommodate disabled guests
on the ground floor, or only
have a couple of rooms
which are appropriate.
Ramps, wide doorways and
bathroom handrails are rare.

Our entries for wheelchair
access in the listings below
rely on the establishments'
own assessments; any specific
requirements should be
checked before booking.

There is a private organization, Associazione Nazionale
degli Handicappati at Corso
Vittorio 154, which advises
disabled travellers. They can be
contacted on 06-68 21 91 68,
9am–6pm Mon–Fri.

TRAVELLING WITH CHILDREN

ITALIANS LOVE CHILDREN and
they are usually welcome
across the range of hotels.
Facilities, however, tend to be
unimpressive on paper. Most
hotels can provide cots or
small beds, but high chairs,
children's meals and baby-
sitting services are rare.
In practice, though, many
establishments – especially
smaller, family-run ones – go
out of their way to be helpful.

Many hotels do not have
any special rates for children,
especially in high season, and
charge a standard rate if you
require an extra bed in a

room, whether it's for a baby
or an adult, which can add
anything from a few thousand
lire to 40% on to the price of
a double room. For a family
with older children, two-room
suites are sometimes to be
found. For hotels providing
children's facilities, see
Choosing a Hotel *(pp294–5)*.

BED & BREAKFAST

A FAIRLY NEW option for
visitors to Rome is bed
& breakfast accommodation.
Roman hosts offer their spare
rooms to visitors, generally
for a much lower price than
an equivalent hotel room.
The **Bed & Breakfast
Association of Rome** is the
organization to contact for an
attractive selection of rooms
and apartments. **Rome Bed &
Breakfast**, based in the US,
also has a good range of
rooms available.

**Bed & Breakfast
Association of Rome**
Piazza del Teatro di Pompeo 2.
[FAX 06-687 73 48.

Rome Bed & Breakfast
[1-619-238 60 76.
FAX 1-619-531 16 86.

RESIDENTIAL HOTELS

IF YOU WANT the comfort
and privacy of your own
apartment coupled with the
services of a hotel, you could
opt to stay in a *residenza*.
Prices range from around
L500,000 to over L6 million
for a week in a two-bedded
room, though some *residenze*
are only available for fort-

nightly or monthly lets. A full
list is available from tourist
board offices *(see p289)*; the
following are some of the
most central:

Residence Babuino
Via del Babuino 172, 00187.
[06-361 16 63.

Di Ripetta
Via di Ripetta 231, 00186.
[06-323 11 44.
FAX 06-320 39 59.

In Trastevere
Vicolo Moroni 35–36, 00153.
[06-581 27 68.

Vittoria
Via Vittoria 60, 00187.
[FAX 06-679 75 33.

RELIGIOUS INSTITUTIONS

IF YOU DON'T MIND an early
curfew when the rest of
Rome is still swinging, quite a
few religious institutions take
in paying guests. You do
not have to be a practising
Catholic to stay in one of
these, but be sure to book
well in advance as all of the
following places cater for
groups of students and
pilgrims. **Domus Mariae** and
Istituto Madri Pie are near
the Vatican; **Congregazione
Suore dello Spirito Santo**
is further out of town, 6 km
(4 miles) west of the centre.
Prices are in the same range
as the cheapest hotels.

Domus Mariae
Via Aurelia 481, 00165.
[FAX 06-660 00 576, 06-663 88 23.

The Gregoriana *(see p297)*

Istituto Madri Pie
Via A. de Gasperi 4, 00165.
☎ 06-63 19 67 or 06-63 34 41.

Congregazione Suore dello Spirito Santo
Via della Pineta Sacchetti 227, 00168.
☎ FAX 06-305 31 01, 06-633 441.

Facade of the Excelsior *(see p301)*

BUDGET ACCOMMODATION

EVEN IF YOU'RE TRAVELLING on a shoestring, it's possible to find a clean, decent room in Rome. Dormitory accom-modation can be found at rock-bottom prices in simple establishments, such as the **Ottaviano.** Youth hostels are a good option – and not just for the young. At the **Ostello del Foro Italico** bed, break-fast and shower can all be had at a very reasonable price.

Women can get single, double or triple rooms at the **Young Women's Christian Association** (YWCA). Its location near Termini is convenient but insalubrious, so those arriving at night should take care. The **Protezione della Giovane** organization has a useful

information office for women under 25; they will try to find you somewhere to stay.

HOSTEL AND DORMITORY ADDRESSES

Ottaviano
Via Ottaviano 6, 00192.
☎ 06-39 73 72 53,
or 06-39 73 81 38.

Associazione Italiana Alberghi per la Gioventù
(Youth Hostel Association)
Via Cavour 44, 00184.
☎ 06-487 11 52. FAX 06-488 04 92.

Ostello del Foro Italico
Viale delle Olimpiadi 61, 00194.
☎ 06-323 62 79. FAX 06-324 26 13.

Residenza Universitaria de Lollis
Via Cesare de Lollis 20, 00185.
Rooms in August only. Details from Youth Hostel Association, above.

YWCA
Via C. Balbo 4, 00184.
☎ 06-488 39 17. FAX 06-487 10 28.

Protezione della Giovane
Via Urbana 158, 00184.
☎ 06-488 14 89.

CAMPING

MOST CAMPSITES are well out of town – suitable for an occasional excursion into Rome – with the exception of **Flaminio**, near the Olympic Village, 6 km (4 miles) north of the centre.

Flaminio
Via Flaminia Nuova 821, 00191.
☎ 06-333 26 04. FAX 06-333 06 53.

The pool in the Aldrovandi Palace garden *(see p301)*

Rome's Best: Hotels

ROMAN HOTELS RANGE from frescoed palaces and *fin-de-siècle* bastions of faded glamour, to family-run guesthouses. Most are within easy reach of restaurants, shops and transport. Whatever the price level, all the hotels shown on this map have something special to offer, whether it's a chic location, or a roof terrace with soaring views across the city. The only drawback is that these places and the others listed on pages 294–301 are exceptions to the many unremarkable hotels in the city, so you should book well in advance. The hotels shown here are the best in their particular style or price range.

Hotel Raphaël

Sole al Pantheon
The writers Jean Paul Sartre and Simone de Beauvoir stayed in this superbly located – and recently refurbished – 15th-century palazzo. (See p296.)

0 metres 500
0 yards 500

Raphael
Full of antiques and art, the Raphael offers a central location. (See p297.)

Piazza Spag

Pia d Rot

Vatican

Piazza Navona

Campo de Fiori

Janiculum

Trastevere

Campo de' Fiori
Central Rome's best bargain offers small, well-furnished rooms and terrific views from the sixth-floor roof terrace. (See p298.)

Crowne Plaza Minerva
Smart, post-modern interiors grace this international standard hotel. (See p296.)

Sant'Anselmo
To be sure of getting a room you need to book well in advance at this peacefully located Roman villa. An added bonus is the lovely secluded garden. (See p299.)

Hassler
Luxurious suites and an air of faded grandeur remind visitors of the Hassler's heyday. The roof-top restaurant is Rome's most famous. (See p298.)

Hotel Eden
One of the oldest and most exclusive hotels in Rome, the Eden offers elegant decor and truly innovative cuisine. (See p301.)

Carriage
The serene atmosphere makes this city-centre hotel a special haven. (See p297.)

Grand
Good service and extensive facilities are the main features of this old-fashioned, luxury hotel. (See p299.)

Via Veneto

Quirinal

Esquiline

Forum

Palatine

Caracalla

Lateran

Scalinata di Spagna
The prized location at the top of the Spanish Steps, and a large private terrace, make this hotel a popular choice with visitors. (See p298.)

Inghilterra
Sip a cocktail in the Inghilterra's club-like bar, once frequented by Ernest Hemingway. (See p298.)

Choosing a Hotel

THE 71 HOTELS listed in the following pages have all been inspected and assessed. This choosing chart shows some of the features which may affect your hotel choice. The hotels are listed alphabetically within their price category. For more detailed information, see pages 296–301.

Hotel	Price	Number of Rooms	Large Rooms	Business Facilities	Hotel Parking	Recommended Restaurant	Close to Shops and Restaurants	Quiet Location	24-Hour Room Service
FORUM *(see p296)*									
Forum	LLLL	76		■					●
PIAZZA DELLA ROTONDA *(see p296)*									
Abruzzi	LL	25					●		
Mimosa	LL	11					●	■	
Santa Chiara	LLLL	98					●		
Colonna Palace	LLLLL	110	●				●		
Holiday Inn Crowne Plaza Minerva	LLLLL	134	●	■			●	■	
Nazionale	LLLLL	87	●	■			●		
Sole al Pantheon	LLLLL	25					●		
PIAZZA NAVONA *(see p296)*									
Navona	LL	21					●	■	
Portoghesi	LLLL	28					●	■	
Due Torri	LLLL	26					●	■	
Genio	LLLLL	60					●	■	
Raphael	LLLLL	72					●	■	
PIAZZA DI SPAGNA *(see p297)*									
Jonella	L	5					●		
Margutta	LL	24					●	■	
Firenze	LLL	25	●				●		●
Homs	LLL	50					●	■	
Locarno	LLL	48		■	●				
Lydia	LLL	28					●		
Mozart	LLL	95					●	■	
Piazza di Spagna	LLL	16	●				●		
Suisse	LLL	12	●				●	■	
Carriage	LLLL	27	●				●		
Condotti	LLLL	16	●				●		
Gregoriana	LLLL	19					●	■	●
Manfredi	LLLL	18		■			●	■	●
Dei Borgognoni	LLLLL	50		■	●		●	■	
Hassler	LLLLL	100	●	■	●		●	■	
D' Inghilterra	LLLLL	105		■			●	■	●
Scalinata di Spagna	LLLLL	16					●		●
Valadier	LLLLL	45		■			●	■	●
CAMPO DE' FIORI *(see p298)*									
Campo de' Fiori	LL	27					●	■	
Della Lunetta	LL	35					●	■	
Piccolo	LL	15					●		
Pomezia	LL	24					●		
Smeraldo	LL	35					●		
Sole	LL	58		■	●		●	■	
Rinascimento	LLL	19			●		●	■	
Teatro di Pompeo	LLL	12		■	●		●	■	

Price categories for a double room per night, including breakfast, tax and service:
Ⓛ under L100,000
ⓁⓁ L100,000–L199,000
ⓁⓁⓁ L200,000–L299,000
ⓁⓁⓁⓁ L300,000–L399,000
ⓁⓁⓁⓁⓁ over L400,000.

HOTEL PARKING
Car parking facilities attached to the hotel or in the hotel complex.

CLOSE TO SHOPS AND RESTAURANTS
Within a 5-minute walk of a good area for shops, bars, cafés and restaurants.

BUSINESS FACILITIES
Message-taking service, fax machine for guest use, desk and telephone in each room and a meeting room which is available within the hotel

Hotel	Price	Number of Rooms	Large Rooms	Business Facilities	Hotel Parking	Recommended Restaurant	Close to Shops and Restaurants	Quiet Location	24-Hour Room Service
QUIRINAL *(see p299)*									
Le Grand Hotel	ⓁⓁⓁⓁⓁ	170	●	●		●			●
TERMINI *(see p299)*									
Katty	Ⓛ	12							
Restivo	Ⓛ	6							
Cervia	ⓁⓁ	28							
Mari	ⓁⓁ	21	●						
Canada	ⓁⓁⓁ	74	●	●					
Hotel Giuliana	ⓁⓁⓁ	21						●	
Venezia	ⓁⓁⓁ	61	●					●	
AVENTINE *(see p299)*									
Aventino	ⓁⓁ	23	●	●				●	
Domus Aventina	ⓁⓁⓁ	26	●	●				●	●
Sant'Anselmo	ⓁⓁⓁ	46		●				●	
Villa San Pio	ⓁⓁⓁ	59	●	●	●			●	
TRASTEVERE *(see p300)*									
Carmel	ⓁⓁ	10							
VATICAN *(see p300)*									
Alimandi	ⓁⓁ	35			●			●	
Amalia	ⓁⓁⓁ	30					●		
Atlante Star	ⓁⓁⓁⓁ	62	●	●	●		●		●
Columbus	ⓁⓁⓁⓁ	100		●	●				
Hotel dei Mellini	ⓁⓁⓁⓁⓁ	80		●	●			●	●
VIA VENETO *(see p300)*									
Merano	ⓁⓁⓁ	30					●		
Oxford	ⓁⓁⓁ	58		●					
Residenza	ⓁⓁⓁ	29	●		●		●		
Alexandra	ⓁⓁⓁⓁ	45					●		
Victoria	ⓁⓁⓁⓁ	108		●			●	●	●
Bernini Bristol	ⓁⓁⓁⓁⓁ	125	●	●			●		●
Eden	ⓁⓁⓁⓁⓁ	92	●	●		●	●	●	●
Excelsior	ⓁⓁⓁⓁⓁ	321	●	●	●		●		●
Imperiale	ⓁⓁⓁⓁ	96		●			●		●
Majestic	ⓁⓁⓁⓁⓁ	100			●		●		
Regina Hotel Baglioni	ⓁⓁⓁⓁⓁ	130	●	●	●		●		
Romantik Barocco	ⓁⓁⓁⓁ	28		●			●		
VILLA BORGHESE *(see p301)*									
Villa Borghese	ⓁⓁⓁⓁ	31			●				●
Aldrovandi Palace	ⓁⓁⓁⓁⓁ	137		●	●	●			
Lord Byron	ⓁⓁⓁⓁⓁ	37		●		●		●	●

FORUM

Forum

Via Tor de' Conti 25, 00184.
Map 5 B5. **C** 06-679 24 46.
FAX 06-679 67 72. **Rooms:** 76.
🛏 ♿ 24 TV ≋ ▤ 🔧 ⬜
Ⓨ 🍴 🏊 📶 AE, DC, MC, V, JCB.
ⓁⓁⓁⓁⓁ

Occupying a palace built out of
materials from the ruins of the
nearby Imperial Fora, the Forum
is an old-fashioned hotel, with
mellow, wood-panelled public
rooms, and a sunny roof-terrace
restaurant giving wonderful views
over the archaeological centre.

PIAZZA DELLA ROTONDA

Abruzzi

Piazza della Rotonda 69, 00186.
Map 4 F4 & 12 D3. **C** 06-679 20 21.
Rooms: 25. 1 ⓁⓁ

The Abruzzi provides clean, basic
rooms with terracotta-tiled floors
in an ochre-coloured palazzo overlooking the Pantheon. The rooms
at the back are not the best, but
quiet. No breakfast is served.

Mimosa

Via di Santa Chiara 61, 00186. **Map**
4 F4 & 12 D3. **C** 06-68 80 17 53.
FAX 06-683 35 57. **Rooms:** 11. 🛏 1.
1 ♿ ≋ 🔧 ⓁⓁ

The Mimosa is a clean, if slightly
scruffy, family-run hotel close to
the Pantheon. Rooms are cool and
the five communal bathrooms and
showers are immaculate. As the
hotel is popular with groups of
visiting students, book well ahead.

Santa Chiara

Via di Santa Chiara 21, 00186.
Map 4 F4 & 12 D3. **C** 06-687 29 79.
FAX 06-687 31 44. **Rooms:** 98. 🛏 1
♿ TV Ⓨ 🍴 🔧 🖼 AE, DC, MC,
V, JCB. ⓁⓁⓁⓁ

Conveniently located in the historic
centre, the Santa Chiara occupies
an apricot-washed palazzo. Public
rooms are cool, particularly the
marble reception area and the
lounge. Bedrooms are carpeted,
and have good-quality furnishings.

Colonna Palace

Piazza di Montecitorio 12, 00186.
Map 4 F3 & 12 E2. **C** 06-678 13 41.
FAX 06-678 90 04. **Rooms:** 110.
🛏 1 ♿ TV ≋ ▤ 🔧
Ⓨ 🍴 🖼 AE, DC, MC, V.
ⓁⓁⓁⓁ

The Colonna Palace stands on the
same piazza as Italy's Chamber
of Deputies, and so attracts
politicians as well as tourists.
Bedrooms are spacious, though
the bathrooms are small. Breakfast
is served in a basement room
livened up by frescoes. There are
lovely views from the impressive
roof garden where a jacuzzi has
recently been installed.

Holiday Inn Crowne Plaza Minerva

Piazza della Minerva 69, 00186.
Map 4 F4 & 12 D3. **C** 06-69 94
18 88. **FAX** 06-679 41 65. **Rooms:**
134. 🛏 1 ♿ TV Ⓨ ≋ ≋
🔧 🍴 🏊 📶 ▤ 🖼 AE,
DC, MC, V, JCB. ⓁⓁⓁⓁⓁ

Occupying Palazzo Fonseca
behind the Pantheon, this is
Rome's newest luxury hotel. The
interior was designed by Post-
Modern architect Portoghesi, and
its centrepiece is the lounge,
canopied in semi-translucent
Venetian glass, and presided over
by a statue of Minerva. The large
bedrooms are decorated in shades
of beige and coral. Views from the
roof terrace are magnificent,
stretching over the Pantheon, St
Peter's and the Janiculum hill.

Nazionale

Piazza di Montecitorio 131, 00186.
Map 4 F3 & 12 E2. **C** 06-69 50 01.
FAX 06-678 66 77. **Rooms:** 87. 🛏
1 ♿ TV Ⓨ ▤ 🔧
Ⓥ 🖼 AE, DC, MC, V.
ⓁⓁⓁⓁ

Home to Robert de Niro while he
was making *Godfather II*, the
Nazionale is usually frequented
by visiting tourists, businessmen
and politicians – it stands right
on the corner of the Chamber
of Deputies. Public rooms are
comfortable, particularly the
lounge, with its brocade sofas and
flower arrangements. Some of the
rooms are huge, and most are also
partially furnished with French
and Italian antiques.

Sole al Pantheon

Piazza della Rotonda 63, 00186.
Map 4 F4 & 12 D3. **C** 06-678
04 41. **FAX** 06-699 406 89.
Rooms: 25. 🛏 1 ♿ TV Ⓨ
▤ 🔧 Ⓥ 🖼 AE, DC, MC, V.
ⓁⓁⓁⓁ

A hotel since 1467, the Sole's
illustrious list of former guests
ranges from Renaissance writer
Ariosto to Jean-Paul Sartre and
Simone de Beauvoir. It is easy to
explain its attraction: its location
opposite the Pantheon is
unbeatable, and though it has
been modernized (60% of the

rooms now have jacuzzis) there
are still bedrooms with painted,
panelled ceilings.

PIAZZA NAVONA

Navona

Via dei Sediari 8, 00186. **Map** 4 F4 &
12 D3. **C** 06-686 42 03. **FAX** 06-68
80 38 02. **Rooms:** 21. 🛏 18. 1 ♿
≋ 📶 ⓁⓁ

A superb location – across the
road from Piazza Navona and five
minutes' stroll from the Pantheon
– means that it's hard to find a
room here unless you book well
in advance. The hotel is run
largely by the owners' Australian
son-in-law, who is extremely
helpful. Bedrooms are basic, but
some of them have bathrooms.
The restaurant opens for groups
of 15 or more.

Due Torri

Vicolo del Leonetto 23, 00186.
Map 4 E3 & 11 C1. **C** 06-687 69 83.
FAX 06-686 54 42. **Rooms:** 26. 🛏
1 ♿ TV Ⓨ ▤ 🔧 📶 🖼 AE,
DC, MC, V. ⓁⓁⓁ

This amiable hotel is a short walk
from both Piazza Navona and the
Spanish Steps, tucked into an
alleyway in the artisans' district
of the old town. Bedrooms vary:
some are stylish, others plain.
The lounge is both elegant and
homely, with swept back drapes,
statuettes, an immense gilt-framed
mirror and pink velvet sofas.

Portoghesi

Via dei Portoghesi 1, 00186.
Map 4 E3 & 11 C2. **C** 06-686 42 31.
FAX 06-687 69 76. **Rooms:** 28. 🛏
1 ♿ TV ▤ 🔧 📶 ⬜ 🖼 MC, V.
ⓁⓁⓁ

Ideally located on a cobbled street
a couple of minutes' walk from
Piazza Navona, the Portoghesi is
a fairly simple hotel, with slightly
dated bedrooms. The public
rooms, however, are elegant and
there's a roof terrace looking on
to the dome of the Portuguese
community's church next door.

Genio

Via Zanardelli 28, 00186. **Map** 4 E3 &
11 C2. **C** 06-683 37 81. **FAX** 06-68
30 72 46. **Rooms:** 60. 🛏 1 ♿ TV
Ⓨ ▤ 🔧 ⬜ 🖼 AE, DC, MC, V,
JCB. ⓁⓁⓁⓁ

On a fairly busy road just behind
Piazza Navona, the Genio's
bedrooms are ordinary, though
quite comfortable. The location,
however, and a roof terrace where
you can picnic with your own
food, make it worth considering.

Raphael

Largo Febo 2, 00186. **Map** 4 E3 & 11 C2. **[** 06-68 28 31. **FAX** 06-687 89 93. **Rooms**: 72. 🛏 [1] [TV] [Y] 🍽 🗐 [♣] 🎇 [Y] [¶] 🚹 🖊 🎜 *AE, DC, MC, V, JCB.* Ⓛ Ⓛ Ⓛ Ⓛ

The Raphael is curtained with ivy and situated on a cobbled street just off Piazza Navona. The big reception lounge has the air of an exhibition hall, being full of antique statues, modern sculpture and even a painted sled. There is a restaurant in the basement where pride of place goes to an ornate wine cabinet. Bedrooms are decorated with parquet floors, marbled walls and 18th-century-style furniture as well as paisley curtains. The rooms on the top floor have terrific views.

PIAZZA DI SPAGNA

Jonella

Via della Croce 41, 00187. **Map** 4 F2. **[** 06-679 79 66. **FAX** 06-446 23 68. **Rooms**: 5. [1] [♣] Ⓛ

The Jonella occupies an orange-coloured palazzo on one of the most attractive shopping streets in the Piazza di Spagna area. The décor is somewhat down-at-heel, but the location and low prices make it worth considering. The owner occasionally pops out to shop, so if you arrive when no-one's there, be patient and wait for their return.

Firenze

Via Due Macelli 106, 00187. **Map** 5 A2 & 12 F1. **[** 06-679 72 40. **FAX** 06-678 56 36. **Rooms**: 25. 🛏 [1] [♣] [24] [TV] 🗐 [♦] [Y] 🎜 *AE, MC, V.* Ⓛ Ⓛ Ⓛ

The Firenze lies a short distance from Piazza di Spagna on a busy main road. The owner has set her elegant stamp on the hotel: Chinese urns and gilt-framed mirrors greet you in the entrance hall, and the bedrooms are large and beautifully decorated. There is also a leafy terrace where you can take breakfast.

Homs

Via della Vite 71–72, 00187. **Map** 5 A3 & 12 F1. **[** 06-679 29 76. **FAX** 06-678 04 82. **Rooms**: 50. [1] [♣] [TV] [Y] 🗐 [♣] 🎇 [♦] [Y] 🎜 *AE, DC, MC, V.* Ⓛ Ⓛ Ⓛ

On one of the quieter, less pretentious shopping streets in the Piazza di Spagna area, the Homs has clean, pleasant rooms with dark-green carpets, white walls and white bathrooms. The breakfast room opens out on to a pleasant terrace.

Locarno

Via della Penna 22, 00186. **Map** 4 F1. **[** 06-361 08 41, 06-361 08 42. **FAX** 06-321 52 49. **Rooms**: 48. 🛏 [♣] [TV] [Y] 🗐 [♣] 🎇 [♦] [P] [♦] [Y] 🚹 🎜 *AE, DC, MC, V.* Ⓛ Ⓛ Ⓛ

Situated on a small, busy side-street near the Tiber, a brief walk from Piazza del Popolo, the Locarno is an attractive 1920s hotel with an Art Nouveau door and swags of lilac growing across its facade. Old-fashioned touches remain, with a grandfather clock and Tiffany lamp in the reception, and a marble-topped bar of polished wood. Outside, there's a patio packed with greenery and kept cool by a tiny fountain.

Lydia

Via Sistina 42, 00187. **Map** 5 B2. **[** 06-679 38 15. **FAX** 06-679 72 63. **Rooms**: 28. 🛏 6. [1] [♣] [♦] 🎇 🎜 *AE, DC, MC, V.* Ⓛ Ⓛ Ⓛ

The Lydia is a pleasant hotel, popular with students, on a busy road a few minutes' walk from the Spanish Steps. Rooms have pale blue walls and pastel bedcovers, and two retain their old ceiling frescoes. If you're not lucky enough to get one of these, content yourself with breakfasting in the chandelier-lit dining room, which is also decorated with beautiful frescoes. Some street-facing rooms can be noisy.

Margutta

Via Laurina 34, 00187. **Map** 4 F1. **[** 06-322 36 74. **FAX** 06-320 03 95. **Rooms**: 24. 🛏 [♣] [♦] 🎜 *AE, DC, MC, V.* Ⓛ Ⓛ Ⓛ

The Margutta sits on a quiet cobbled street just below the Piazza del Popolo. The scruffy facade and slightly grubby seats in the lobby are forgotten as soon as you get into your room, which has white walls and green wrought-iron bedsteads and candle-holders. If you wish to stay in one of the three attic rooms that share a pretty roof terrace, be sure to book well in advance.

Mozart

Via dei Greci 236, 00187. **Map** 4 F2. **[** 06-36 00 19 15. **FAX** 06-36 00 17 35. **Rooms**: 95. 🛏 [1] [TV] [Y] 🗐 [♦] [Y] 🎜 *AE, DC, MC, V, JCB.* Ⓛ Ⓛ Ⓛ

Located in a cobbled street between Piazza del Popolo and Piazza di Spagna, the Mozart is immediately appealing. Decor is attractively worn and includes a Venetian mirror. There's a breakfast room, as well as a bar-café, which opens off the stone-lagged reception. Rooms have ceramic-

tiled or parquet floors, and bathrooms tend to be small, most having only a shower.

Piazza di Spagna

Via Mario de' Fiori 61, 00187. **Map** 5 A2 & 12 F1. **[iv** 06-679 30 61, 06-679 64 12. **FAX** 06-679 06 54. **Rooms**: 16. 🛏 [1] [♣] [TV] [Y] 🗐 [♦] [Y] 🎜 *AE, MC, V.* Ⓛ Ⓛ Ⓛ

Close to the designer boutiques of Via Condotti, this attractive, small hotel has simple, but good-sized rooms, with tiled floors and a couple of bathrooms with jacuzzis. The breakfast room and bar are tiny, so most residents decide to take breakfast in their own rooms.

Suisse

Via Gregoriana 54–56, 00187. **Map** 5 A2 & 12 F1. **[** 06-678 36 49. **FAX** 06-678 12 58. **Rooms**: 12. 🛏 8. [1] [♣] [♦] Ⓛ Ⓛ Ⓛ

Occupying the third floor of a dusty palazzo (the entrance is at No. 54), the Suisse is a small, pleasant hotel with friendly staff. Chinese prints hang along the corridors and in the rooms. These also have polished floors, moulded ceilings and marble-topped dressers and tables.

Carriage

Via delle Carrozze 36, 00187. **Map** 5 A2. **[** 06-699 01 24. **FAX** 06-678 82 79. **Rooms**: 27. 🛏 [1] [TV] [Y] 🗐 [♦] [♦] 🎜 *AE, DC, MC, V, JCB.* Ⓛ Ⓛ Ⓛ

Situated in a street where noblemen used to park their carriages, this hotel's elegance is immediately evident in the reception area, with its panelling, candelabra and gilt-framed mirrors. The rooms live up to expectations, decorated in a serene shade of blue, with some antique furniture. Two rooms open on to the leafy, terracotta tiled terrace for all residents while two have their own private terraces.

Condotti

Via Mario de' Fiori 37, 00187. **Map** 5 A2 & 12 F1. **[** 06-679 46 61. **FAX** 06-679 04 57. **Rooms**: 16. 🛏 [1] [TV] [Y] 🗐 [♦] [Y] 🚹 🎜 *AE, DC, MC, V, JCB.* Ⓛ Ⓛ Ⓛ

Close to Piazza di Spagna and in the heart of the designer shopping district, the Condotti is a comfortable, welcoming hotel with an ambience and style all of its own. Rooms are medium to large and well decorated. One room has its own small terrace and three others share one.

For key to symbols *see p291*

Gregoriana

Via Gregoriana 18, 00187. **Map** 5 A2 & 12 F1. **(** 06-679 49 88.
FAX 06-678 42 58. **Rooms**: 19. 🛇
🔲 24 📺 👥 🔨 🔌 🐕 🔨 👔
Ⓛ Ⓛ Ⓛ Ⓛ

The Gregoriana is a stylish, congenial hotel, situated close to the Spanish Steps in a tree-lined, quiet street of elegant palazzi. The first- and third-floor corridors are papered with a leopard-spotted print, while that of the second floor is in the style of William Morris. The rooms are all the same: black lacquer doors, terracotta-coloured carpets, flowery wallpaper and 1920s drawings on the walls. Rather peculiarly, there are no public rooms, so breakfast and drinks are served in the bedrooms.

Manfredi

Via Margutta 61, 00187. **Map** 5 A2. **(** 06-320 76 76, 06-320 76 95.
FAX 06-320 77 36. **Rooms**: 18. 🛇
🔲 🏋 24 📺 👔 🐕 🔨 ↕ 👔
🔨 👔 AE, MC, V, JCB. Ⓛ Ⓛ Ⓛ Ⓛ

This pretty hotel is excellently located, just off Piazza di Spagna, in a cobbled street of art galleries and antique shops. The reception area and bar-breakfast room are paved with marble and decorated in soft pastels. The comfortable bedrooms are all soundproofed, with pale fabric wall coverings and co-ordinated furnishings.

Dei Borgognoni

Via del Bufalo 126, 00187. **Map** 5 A3 & 12 F1. **(** 06-69 94 15 05. **FAX** 06-69 94 15 01. **Rooms**: 50. 🛇 🔲 🏋
📺 👔 🐕 🔌 🔨 🔌 ↕ 👔
AE, DC, MC, V, JCB. Ⓛ Ⓛ Ⓛ Ⓛ

This elegant hotel is just off Piazza San Silvestro, five minutes from the Spanish Steps. In the public rooms, modern style is coupled with traditional oil paintings. The bedrooms – some of which have terraces – are exquisite and beautifully understated.

Hassler

Piazza Trinità dei Monti 6, 00187. **Map** 5 A2. **(** 06-69 93 40. **FAX** 06-678 99 91. **Rooms**: 100. 🛇 🔲 🏋 📺
👔 👥 🔨 🔌 🔨 🔌 🌐 👔
🔨 👔 👔 AE, DC, MC, V, JCB.
Ⓛ Ⓛ Ⓛ Ⓛ Ⓛ

Standing at the top of the Spanish Steps, with magnificent views of Rome from its roof terrace, restaurant (*see p313*) and suites, the Hassler was once host to royalty and the glitterati-of Europe and America. Its *dolce vita* days are over, but the lounges and

bedrooms lit by Venetian glass chandeliers, the wood-panelled bar and marble bathrooms retain the air of a more extravagant era.

D' Inghilterra

Via Bocca di Leone 14, 00187. **Map** 5 A2. **(** 06-69 9 81. **FAX** 06-69 92 22 43. **Rooms**: 105. 🛇 🔲 🏋 24 📺
👔 👔 👥 🔨 🔌 🔨 🔌 ↕ 👔
👔 AE, DC, MC, V. Ⓛ Ⓛ Ⓛ Ⓛ Ⓛ

Liszt and Hemingway are among the writers, artists and musicians who have stayed here. In the heart of Rome's designer shopping area and close to the Spanish Steps, it's still a desirable place to stay. The bedrooms are all individually decorated and furnished. The bar could have been lifted straight from a London gentlemen's club, and the restaurant walls, painted with views of gardens and the sky-frescoed ceiling create the illusion of dining in the open.

Scalinata di Spagna

Piazza Trinità dei Monti 17, 00187. **Map** 5 A2. **(** 06-67 93 006.
FAX 06-69 94 05 98. **Rooms**: 16. 🛇
🔲 🏋 24 📺 👔 👥 🔨 🔌 🔨 🔌 👔
AE, DC, MC, V. Ⓛ Ⓛ Ⓛ Ⓛ

This hotel occupies a small 18th-century villa at the top of the Spanish Steps. Breakfast is at a communal table under the gaze of a parrot. Some rooms retain their panelled ceilings. Book well ahead if you want to stay in one of the rooms that open out on to the large terrace.

Valadier

Via della Fontanella 15, 00187. **Map** 4 F1. **(** 06-361 23 44. **FAX** 06-320 15 58. **Rooms**: 45. 🛇 🔲 🏋 24
📺 👔 🐕 🔌 🔨 👔 ↕ 👔 👔 AE,
DC, MC, V, JCB. Ⓛ Ⓛ Ⓛ Ⓛ

Slickly decorated with shiny wood and marble, the Valadier styles itself as an intimate hideaway for those on a romantic visit to Rome. Public rooms are tailor-made for seduction, with low sofas, marble floors and oriental rugs. If you believe the hotel's publicity, the bizarre art selection is there to provide shy Casanovas with conversation openers.

CAMPO DE' FIORI

Campo de' Fiori

Via del Biscione 6, 00186. **Map** 4 E4 & 11 C4. **(** 06-68 80 68 65. **FAX** 06-687 60 03. **Rooms**: 27. 🛇 🏋 🏋
👥 🔨 🔨 👔 MC, V. Ⓛ Ⓛ

This very good value, mid-range hotel occupies a well-kept house,

just off the Campo de' Fiori market square. You enter the tiny reception area along a passageway, in which mirrors intriguingly repeat a series of columns into an illusory optical suggestion of infinity. The small bedrooms have beams and paisley furnishings, or sky-painted ceilings, lacy walls and frilly bedcovers. On the sixth floor a split-level roof garden gives vertiginous but aesthetically rewarding views over the Pantheon, the Victor Emmanuel monument and St Peter's.

Della Lunetta

Piazza del Paradiso 68, 00186. **Map** 4 E4 & 11 C4. **(** 06-686 10 80. **FAX** 06-689 20 28. **Rooms**: 35.
🛇 🏋 🔲 🏋 👔 Ⓛ Ⓛ

On a tiny, crumbling piazza, midway between Corso Vittorio Emanuele and Piazza Campo de' Fiori, the Lunetta is a popular, well-maintained little hotel with neat, clean rooms and a courtyard. More bathrooms are gradually being installed and a rooftop garden is being renovated. No breakfast is served.

Piccolo

Via dei Chiavari 32, 00186. **Map** 4 E4 & 11 C4. **(** 06-68 80 25 60. **Rooms**: 15. 🛇 🏋 🔲 🏋 👔 👔 AE, MC, V.
Ⓛ Ⓛ

Close to Piazza Campo de' Fiori, the Piccolo is a family-run hotel at the cheap end of its price band. There is, however, nothing cheap about the atmosphere. Cool and serene, with clean, simple rooms in a variety of sizes. The Piccolo also has a separate bar-breakfast room.

Pomezia

Via dei Chiavari 12, 00186. **Map** 4 E4 & 12 D4. **(** 06-686 13 71.
Rooms: 24. 🛇 🏋 🔲 🏋 👔 👔
AE, DC, MC, V. Ⓛ Ⓛ

In the heart of the lively Campo de' Fiori district, the Pomezia was renovated recently and now has spotless, simply decorated rooms and a bar in the reception area to welcome weary arrivals.

Smeraldo

Vicolo dei Chiodaroli 9, 00186. **Map** 4 F5 & 12 D4. **(** 06-687 59 29. **FAX** 06-68 80 54 95. **Rooms**: 35. 🛇 🏋 🔲 📺 👔 🔌 🔨 👔 👔 👔 AE, MC, V. Ⓛ Ⓛ

Situated in the heart of the bustling Campo de' Fiori quarter, the Smeraldo offers an oasis of serenity, with clean, simple rooms in an ochre-washed building with shutters over the windows.

Sole

Via del Biscione 76, 00186. **Map** 4 E4
& 11 C4. [06-68 80 52 58.
FAX 06-689 37 87. *Rooms*: 58. 🛏
31. 🛏 1 ⚏ 🔧 📺 ⬛ 🅿 🅿 🔒 Ⓛ Ⓛ

Possibly the oldest hotel in Rome,
this appealing establishment
occupies a palazzo just off the
central market square of Campo
de' Fiori. Rooms are furnished in a
slightly haphazard way, but with
some character. There are small
sitting areas and a leafy, sunny
terrace with a drink and snack
machine. No breakfast is served.

Rinascimento

Via del Pellegrino 122, 00186. **Map** 4
E4 & 11 B3. [06-687 48 13. FAX
06-683 35 18. *Rooms*: 19. 🛏 1
⚏ 📺 ⬛ 🔧 🔧 🅿 ℹ 🔒
AE, MC, V. Ⓛ Ⓛ Ⓛ

With an appealing location in the
Campo de' Fiori district, close to
artisans' workshops and a variety
of trattorias, the Rinascimento is
housed in an old palazzo with
stone arched windows. The
bedrooms, however, tend to be
slightly worn and have rather
cramped bathrooms.

Teatro di Pompeo

Largo del Pallaro 8, 00186. **Map** 4 E4
& 11 C4. [06-687 28 12.
FAX 06-68 80 55 31. *Rooms*: 12. 🛏
1 ⚏ 📺 ⬛ ☰ 🔧 🔧 🔧
🅿 ℹ 🔒 AE, DC, MC, V.
Ⓛ Ⓛ Ⓛ

This small, courteously run hotel
sits over the ruins of the first
permanent theatre in the city,
which was completed in 55 BC by
Pompey the Great. You can eat
breakfast among the original
theatre arches, and the bar has a
terracotta floor and marble tables.

Le Grand Hotel

Via V. E. Orlando 3, 00185. **Map** 5 C2.
[06-47 091. FAX 06-482 38 67.
Rooms: 170. 🛏 1 ⚏ 24 📺 🔧
☰ 🔧 🔧 🔧 🔧 ℹ 🔒 AE, DC,
MC, V, JCB. Ⓛ Ⓛ Ⓛ Ⓛ Ⓛ

To step into the Grand is to enter
another world. Cherubs cavort over
the reception area; flowers and
fruit are carved on the walls of the
lounge and rich pastel rugs lie on
the parquet floor. Facilities include
a sauna, beauty salon, hairdresser
and a restaurant renowned as one
of the most beautiful in the country.
The standard of bedrooms varies,
but you might find yourself sleeping
in an antique bed, reading by the
light of a genuine Venetian lamp.

Katty

Via Palestro 35, 00185. **Map** 6 E2.
[06-444 12 16. FAX 06-444 12 16.
Rooms: 12. 🛏 🔧 Ⓛ

The Katty has clean, basic rooms,
some of which have an occasional
piece of antique furniture. It's
extremely popular with British and
American students, so either book
in advance or turn up early,
ideally between 8am and 9am. No
breakfast is served.

Restivo

Via Palestro 55, 00185. **Map** 6 E2. [
06-446 21 72. *Rooms*: 6. 1 ⚏ Ⓛ

In the same building as the Mari,
the Restivo has six immaculately
maintained bedrooms. The elderly
lady owner has a hall full of gifts
and postcards from grateful guests
who often return again and again.

Cervia

Via Palestro 55, 00185. **Map** 6 E2.
[06-49 10 57. FAX 06-49 10 56.
Rooms: 28. 🛏 7. 1 ⚏ 🔒 AE,
DC, MC, V. Ⓛ Ⓛ

The Cervia is housed in the same
palazzo as the Mari and the Restivo.
Some of the rooms have been
refurbished with sponge-painted
walls and private bathrooms, and
these give excellent value. The rest,
however, tend to be a bit more
basic. The public areas are immaculate, and there is also a pleasant
up-to-date bar-breakfast room.

Mari

Via Palestro 55, 00185. **Map** 6 E2. [
06-446 21 37. FAX 06-482 83 13.
Rooms: 21. 🛏 11. 1 ⚏ 🔒 DC,
MC, V. Ⓛ Ⓛ

This friendly hotel run by three
women has clean, pleasant rooms
with no frills. If it's full, Mari 2
nearby at Via Calatafimi 38 (tel 06-
474 03 71) has more rooms (half
with bathrooms) and is also good
value. There is a 5% surcharge for
paying by credit card.

Canada

Via Vicenza 58, 00185. **Map** 6 E2.
[06-445 77 70. FAX 06-445 07 49.
Rooms: 74. 🛏 1 ⚏ 📺 ☰ ⬛
🔧 🔧 ℹ 🔒 AE, DC, MC, V.
Ⓛ Ⓛ Ⓛ

Outside the centre, behind Termini
station, the Canada is an above-
average, mid-range hotel. Rooms
are very comfortable, and there's a
pleasant lounge-bar with attractive
cane seats and squashy sofas. The
service is courteous.

Hotel Giuliana

Via Palermo 36, 00184. **Map** 5 C4.
[06-488 07 95. FAX 06-482 42 87.
Rooms: 21. 🛏 1 ⚏ 📺 🔧 ⬛
🔧 🔧 ℹ 🔒 AE, DC, V, JCB.
Ⓛ Ⓛ Ⓛ

Within walking distance of many
major sights, and 10 minutes from
Termini station, this small hotel
offers comfortable accommodation
at reasonable prices. Helpful,
English-speaking staff are happy
to offer advice on any aspect of
your visit, from transport tips to
restaurant recommendations.

Venezia

Via Varese 18, 00185. **Map** 6 E2.
[06-445 71 01. FAX 06-495 76 87.
Rooms: 61. 🛏 1 ⚏ 📺 🔧 🔧
🔒 AE, DC, MC, V, JCB. Ⓛ Ⓛ Ⓛ

One of the nicer mid-size hotels
near Termini station, the Venezia
is pleasantly decorated with antique
furniture and Murano glass chandeliers in the common areas. The
bedrooms are light and airy with
smart bathrooms. The hotel offers
an especially rich buffet breakfast.

Aventino

Via San Domenico 10, 00153. **Map**
8 D2. [06-574 51 74, 06-578 32
14. FAX 06-578 36 04. *Rooms*: 23. 🛏
1 ⚏ 🔧 🔧 🔧 🅿 ℹ 🔒 AE, DC,
MC, V. Ⓛ Ⓛ

Run by the owners of Villa San Pio
and Sant'Anselmo, the Aventino is
more modest, with large but fairly
simple rooms. However, its lush,
garden location is gorgeous, and
the breakfast room, with a
magnificent armoire and stained
glass, a reminder of headier days.

Domus Aventina

Via di Santa Prisca 11B, 00153. **Map**
8 E2. [06-574 61 35. FAX 06-57 30
00 44. *Rooms*: 26. 🛏 1 ⚏ 24
📺 🔧 🔧 🔧 🔒 ℹ 🔒
AE, DC, MC, V, JCB. Ⓛ Ⓛ Ⓛ

This immaculate hotel occupies a
14th-century convent situated at the
foot of the Aventine hill. Rooms are
large, and simply decorated in pastel
tones, and there are wonderful
views of the Celian hill from many
of the balconies – 18 rooms have
them – and from the huge terrace.

Sant'Anselmo

Piazza di Sant'Anselmo 2, 00153. **Map**
8 D2. [06-574 35 47. FAX 06-578
36 04. *Rooms*: 46. 🛏 1 ⚏ 🔧 🔧
🔧 🔒 ℹ 🔒 AE, DC, MC, V. Ⓛ Ⓛ Ⓛ

This pretty villa, among the gardens of the peaceful Aventine, is within walking distance of the Colosseum. The entrance hall ceiling is stencilled with flowers; there are chandeliers and corridors with floors of inlaid marble. The lounge looks on to the hotel's garden. Book well in advance.

Villa San Pio

Via di Sant'Anselmo 19, 00153.
Map 8 E3. 【 06-578 32 14, 06-574 35 47. FAX 06-578 36 04. Rooms: 59.
🛏 1 ♨ & 📺 🌂 📶 🅿 ⚡ ▮
🛈 📧 AE, DC, MC, V. Ⓛ Ⓛ Ⓛ

The Villa San Pio occupies a yellow and ochre villa set in a garden graced with statues. The elegant entrance hall is furnished with velvet and brocade chairs and an 18th-century Venetian tapestry. Some of the rooms are simple, others have flower-stencilled furniture; others open on to the garden. There are two bars. Breakfast or drinks can also be taken in the bedrooms or garden.

TRASTEVERE

Carmel

Via Mameli 11, 00153. **Map** 7 C2.
【 FAX 06-580 99 21. Rooms: 10.
🛏 9. 1 ♨ Ⓛ Ⓛ

The Carmel's most appealing feature is a terrace with its leafy canopy. A couple of rooms open off the terrace. All ten rooms are spotless, and most have bathrooms. The owner is not keen on having children to stay and you must book in advance as she closes the hotel if she thinks trade will be slack.

VATICAN

Alimandi

Via Tunisi 8, 00192. **Map** 3 B2. 【
06-39 72 39 48. FAX 06-39 72 39 43.
Rooms: 35. 🛏 26. 1 ♨ 📺 🌂
🅿 ⚡ 📧 AE, DC, MC, V. Ⓛ Ⓛ

On a quietish street just below the entrance to the Vatican Museums, the Alimandi is a simple pensione at the cheap end of its price band – hence its popularity with young travellers. Rooms are clean and adequate. Its outstanding feature is the lovely large roof terrace

Amalia

Via Germanico 66, 00192. **Map** 3 C2.
【 06-39 72 33 54, 06-39 72 33 56.
FAX 06-39 72 33 65. Rooms: 30. 🛏
20. 1 📺 🌂 🌂 🛈 📧 AE, DC, MC,
V, JCB. Ⓛ Ⓛ Ⓛ

Situated between the Ottaviano Metro station and the Vatican, the Amalia attracts mainly Italian guests. It has spotless rooms ranged on three floors and a lounge with bar.

Atlante Star

Via Vitelleschi 34, 00193. **Map** 3 C2.
【 06-687 32 33. FAX 06-687 23 00.
Rooms: 62. 🛏 1 ♨ 📻 📺 🌂 🌂
🌂 ⚡ 🌂 🌂 🌂 🅿 ⚡ ▮
▮ 🛈 📧 AE, DC, MC, V, JCB.
Ⓛ Ⓛ Ⓛ Ⓛ

This hotel is a good option for business travellers needing on-site office facilities. The rooftop restaurant has views of St Peter's, but both service and atmosphere leave much to be desired. Double rooms are modest in size and singles can be cramped, some of them with only a shower. Avoid street-facing rooms as they can be noisy.

Columbus

Via della Conciliazione 33, 00193. **Map** 3 C3. 【 06-686 54 35. FAX 06-686 48 74. Rooms: 100. 🛏 1 ♨ 📺
🌂 🌂 🌂 🌂 🌂 🌂 🌂 🌂 🅿 ⚡ ▮
📧 AE, DC, MC, V, JCB. Ⓛ Ⓛ Ⓛ

Perfect for anyone wishing to stay near the Vatican, the Columbus occupies an austere former monastery. Heavy wrought-iron light fittings hang in the reception hall; the magnificent upper lounge has a beamed ceiling and terracotta floor; the function room (the old refectory) has kept its frescoes, and there is a walled terrace garden.

Hotel dei Mellini

Via Muzio Clementi 81, 00193. **Map** 4 E2. 【 06-324 771. FAX 06-32 47 78 01. Rooms: 80. 🛏 1 ♨ 📻 📺
🌂 🌂 🌂 🌂 🌂 🌂 🌂 🅿 ⚡ 🌂 📧
AE, DC, MC, V. Ⓛ Ⓛ Ⓛ Ⓛ Ⓛ

Opened in 1996 in a converted late 19th-century building, this hotel has all the modern confort you could wish for but still feels charming and welcoming. It is located in a quiet residential area near Castel Sant'Angelo and only a short walk across the river from Via Condotti. The reception staff is very helpful and there is a small but nice bar in the lobby and a roof terrace.

VIA VENETO

Merano

Via Veneto 155, 00187. **Map** 5 B2.
【 06-482 17 96. FAX 06-482 18 10.
Rooms: 30. 🛏 1 ♨ 🌂 📶 🛈
📧 AE, DC, MC, V. Ⓛ Ⓛ Ⓛ

The Merano is a small, friendly pensione in a 19th-century palazzo. The décor is a little dated and

relatively high prices, for what is essentially a guesthouse, reflect the up-market location. The best feature is the sunny breakfast room.

Oxford

Via Boncompagni 89, 00187. **Map** 5 C1.
【 06-42 82 89 52. FAX 06-42 81 53 49. Rooms: 58. 🛏 1 📺 🌂 📶
🌂 📶 🛈 📧 AE, DC, MC, V, JCB. Ⓛ Ⓛ Ⓛ

On a quiet road off Piazza Fiume, about ten minutes' walk from Via Veneto, the Oxford has stylish public rooms: squashy sofas and modern pictures in the reception area; striped sofas and abstract art in the bar. The bedrooms are more dated, with hessian-covered walls and candlewick bedspreads.

Residenza

Via Emilia 22–24, 00187. **Map** 5 B2.
【 06-488 07 89. FAX 06-48 57 21.
Rooms: 29. 🛏 1 📺 🌂 🛈
🅿 📶 🛈 📧 AE, MC, V. Ⓛ Ⓛ Ⓛ

The Residenza is an elegant hotel that occupies a villa in a quiet road off Via Veneto. There is a canopied terrace with pine furniture, and a terracotta-tiled roof garden with potted plants. The bedrooms although less stylish than the public rooms, are comfortable, large and well-equipped.

Alexandra

Via Veneto 18, 00187. **Map** 5 B2.
【 06-488 19 43. FAX 06-487 18 04.
Rooms: 45. 🛏 1 ♨ 📺 🌂 🌂
🌂 🌂 📧 AE, DC, MC, V, JCB.
Ⓛ Ⓛ Ⓛ

One of the less expensive hotels on the up-market Via Veneto, the Alexandra has a pleasant conservatory-style breakfast room and a lounge decorated with chintz and brocade. All the bedrooms are different; some furnished with antiques, some with splash-painted walls. If you are a light sleeper ask for an internal room, as the windows do not block out all the traffic noise.

Victoria

Via Campania 41, 00187. **Map** 5 B1.
【 06-47 39 31. FAX 06-487 18 90.
Rooms: 108. 🛏 1 ♨ 📻 📺 🌂
🌂 🌂 🌂 🌂 🌂 🅿 ⚡ ▮ ▮
📧 AE, DC, MC, V. Ⓛ Ⓛ Ⓛ

Situated on a quiet road at the top of Via Veneto and overlooking the walls abutting the Porta Pinciana, the Victoria prides itself on being a "hotel for individuals", keeping its personal touch by refusing large group bookings. It is renowned for good service. There are stylish public rooms and an attractive roof terrace, but the bedrooms are rather small and uninspired.

Bernini Bristol

Piazza Barberini 23, 00187. **Map** 5 B3.
C 06-488 30 51. **FAX** 06-482 42 66.
Rooms: 125. 🛏 1 👥 24 TV ☕
⛱ 🏊 🦽 💇 🍴 🍽 📠
AE, DC, MC, V, JCB. ⓛⓛⓛⓛ

This unprepossessing brick building overlooks a busy piazza that has Bernini's Triton fountain as its centrepiece. The marble-laden hotel is comfortable, with a roof garden, but the décor is uninspiring and the atmosphere more conducive to work than pleasure. The central location and secretarial facilities ensure a steady stream of business visitors.

Eden

Via Ludovisi 49, 00187. **Map** 5 B2.
C 06-47 81 21. **FAX** 06-482 15 84.
Rooms: 92. 🛏 1 👥 TV 24 ☕
🍴 🦽 💇 🍽 🍴 📠
AE, DC, MC, V, JCB. ⓛⓛⓛⓛ

Historically one of Rome's most illustrious hotels, Eden has recently been restored to pristine condition. The roof garden is stunning, giving every justification for the hotel's name; like its biblical namesake, it has its temptations, not least the beautiful La Terrazza restaurant (see p317), which nestles on the roof like a beacon of refinement.

Excelsior

Via Veneto 125, 00187. **Map** 5 B1.
C 06-470 81. **FAX** 06-482 62 05.
Rooms: 321. 🛏 1 👥 24 TV
☕ 🍴 🦽 💇 🏊 ☕ 🍴 📠
🍴 AE, DC, MC, V, JCB.
ⓛⓛⓛⓛ

Exotically sculpted balconies supported by statues set the tone for this extravagant hotel, which houses boutiques, saunas, a restaurant and a famous piano bar. Public rooms are sumptuous, with marble walls and floors, rich carpets and brocade furnishings, and the corridors are panelled with silk or imitation marble. The bedrooms are elegant and spacious with chandeliers, painted and gilded wooden panelling and ornate, marble bathrooms.

Imperiale

Via Veneto 24, 00187. **Map** 5 B2.
C 06-482 63 51. **FAX** 06-478 25 43.
Rooms: 96. 🛏 1 👥 24 TV ☕
🍴 🦽 💇 🍴 🍽 📠 AE,
DC, MC, V. ⓛⓛⓛⓛ

One of the more reasonably priced Via Veneto hotels, the Imperiale

lacks the panache of its more glamorous neighbours, but the friendly staff make for a good relaxed atmosphere. The lounge is more of a place to wait than to spend an evening, but the bar is quite pleasant and the bedrooms are well decorated, with pretty co-ordinating furnishings and small marble bathrooms.

Majestic

Via Veneto 50, 00187. **Map** 5 B2.
C 06-48 68 41, 06-482 80 14.
FAX 06-488 56 57. **Rooms**: 100. 🛏
1 👥 TV ☕ 🦽 💇 📠 ☕
🍴 🍴 AE, DC, MC, V, JCB.
ⓛⓛⓛⓛ

Founded in 1889, the Majestic is the oldest of Via Veneto's hotels. Since its five-year refurbishment it has played host to international stars such as Madonna, Pavarotti and Stallone. Most of the furniture and much of the décor in the public rooms are original, down to the startling lime-green and gilt lounge. Bedrooms and corridors are decorated in a bold, fresh style, particularly on the fifth floor, where carpets with a zig-zag pattern provide the background to chintz and brocade.

Regina Hotel Baglioni

Via Veneto 72, 00187. **Map** 5 B2.
C 06-42 11 11. **FAX** 06-48 54 83.
Rooms: 130. 🛏 1 👥 TV ☕
🍴 🦽 💇 🏊 📠 🍴 🍴 📠
📠 AE, DC, MC, V. ⓛⓛⓛⓛ

The exuberance of the Baglioni's exterior – it is painted vanilla and strawberry pink and decorated with grimacing masks – continues in the reception area where a wrought-iron staircase is guarded by the statue of a sea god. The bedrooms are painted in vivid shades of coral, aqua and blue, and many are very spacious. Double glazing in the rooms overlooking Via Veneto cuts down on some of the traffic noise but light sleepers might still prefer to ask for a room at the back of the hotel when booking.

Romantik Barocco Hotel

Via della Purificazione 7, 00187. **Map** 5 B3. **C** 06-487 20 01. **FAX** 06-48 59 94. **Rooms**: 28. 🛏 1 👥 TV ☕ 🍴 🦽 💇 🍴 📠 🍴 AE, DC, MC, V, JCB. ⓛⓛⓛⓛ

Occupying a restored palazzo at the bottom of Via Veneto, the Barocco is ideal for anyone who prefers a small hotel. Bedrooms are pleasant with unobtrusive décor, and some have a working area. There are two small lounges (one with a bar) and a restaurant.

Villa Borghese

Via Pinciana 31, 00198. **Map** 2 F5.
C 06-841 41 00. **FAX** 06-841 41 00.
Rooms: 31. 🛏 1 👥 24 TV ☕
⛱ 🏊 🦽 💇 ☕ 🍴 🍴 AE, DC, MC, V, JCB. ⓛⓛⓛⓛ

This immediately likeable hotel occupies a villa close to Villa Borghese. Although the hotel is situated on a rather busy main road, the atmosphere is pleasant: more that of a private home than a hotel. Public rooms include an intimate, old-fashioned bar and a lounge with comfortable sofas and floral soft furnishings, and there is also a courtyard sheltered by a pretty ivy-covered pergola. The rooms are on the small side but they are tastefully decorated.

Aldrovandi Palace

Via Aldrovandi 15, 00197. **Map** 2 E4.
C 06-322 39 93. **FAX** 06-322 14 35.
Rooms: 137. 🛏 1 👥 TV ☕
⛱ 🏊 🦽 💇 ☕ 🍴 🍴
🍴 🍴 AE, DC, MC, V, JCB.
ⓛⓛⓛⓛ

Among the most restful luxury hotels in the city, the Aldrovandi is situated just outside the centre of Rome on a fairly busy road overlooking Villa Borghese. The reception lounge is elegant and decorated with rich soft furnishings, carpets, chandeliers and lots of vases of fresh flowers. The real highlight of the hotel, however, is the sunny garden with its attractive swimming pool, which is overlooked by an airy restaurant.

Lord Byron

Via de Notaris 5, 00197. **Map** 2 D4.
C 06-322 45 41. **FAX** 06-322 04 05.
Rooms: 37. 🛏 1 👥 24 TV ☕
🍴 🦽 💇 🏊 🍴 🍴 📠
📠 AE, DC, MC, V. ⓛⓛⓛⓛ

This small, refined hotel is housed in a dazzling white building in the residential district of Parioli. Although it was originally a monastery, there is nothing ascetic about its rooms today. The lounge is lavishly furnished with antiques and tapestry-seated chairs and the tiny sitting room has capacious sofas and old-fashioned portraits. The restaurant is decorated with plenty of chintz and fresh flowers and serves some of the best food in Rome. All the bedrooms have tapestry and floral soft furnishings with marble coffee tables. Each room is also provided with a full decanter of port, which comes with the compliments of the management.

For key to symbols see p291

RESTAURANTS AND CAFÉS

IN ROME, eating out can be both a joy and an entertainment. On warm summer evenings tables flow out into every conceivable open space and diners dedicate long hours to the popular social activity of people watching (and of being noticed and admired themselves) in a confusion of passers-by, buskers, rose sellers and traffic. Although Romans have always loved to linger at the table, the lavish feasts of ancient Rome have slimmed down and today's cooking is based on simplicity, freshness and good quality local raw ingredients in

Waiter at Alberto Ciarla
(see p316)

what is essentially a seasonal cuisine. Fast food is gradually arriving, but it is fundamentally alien to the Roman temperament and way of life.

The 66 restaurants reviewed in this chapter have been selected from the best that Rome can offer across all price ranges. The chart on pages 310–11 will help narrow down your selection, and the map on page 308 shows the highlights of the list. The section on *Light Meals and Snacks* featured on pages 318–21 has details of recommended cafés, pizzerias, wine bars and other places for more casual eating.

WHERE TO FIND GOOD RESTAURANTS

EVERY AREA of the city has its own culinary delights. True Roman cooking can be found in the old slaughterhouse area of Testaccio and in the Jewish quarter (the Ghetto) near Campo de' Fiori. Around the university, in San Lorenzo, northeast of the city centre, you will find lots of cheap pizzerias and trattorias.

Near Termini station there's a good selection of African – particularly Ethiopian and Eritrean – restaurants. For dining outdoors, which often means in beautifully secluded piazzas, or in impressively ancient parts of the city, try the restaurants in the narrow streets of Trastevere (the old

artists' quarter), around Campo de' Fiori, or along the old Via Appia Antica.

TYPES OF RESTAURANTS

IN GENERAL, a *trattoria* is an unassuming, family-run establishment with good home cooking, while a *ristorante* is more up-market, more elegant and thus more expensive.

Many eating places – where paper tablecloths give a clue to low prices – simply have no

Fresh artichokes, a Roman speciality

name. They offer an open doorway and, more often than not, excellent, basic home cooking. Some of them offer a great deal more than that, and your chances of finding authentic Roman cooking are higher in the best of these establishments than in expensive restaurants.

There will probably be times when you don't want a full-blown restaurant meal, and Rome offers a huge variety of places for more casual eating (*see pp318–21*). One type of place offering snacks or more

substantial dishes is the *enoteca,* which doubles as a well-stocked wine shop for browsers and connoisseurs.

The sign *vino e cucina* (wine and food), sadly fast disappearing, holds the same promise. Other places for a sit-down, informal lunch or dinner are *birrerie,* which are not only for beer drinkers, but which also offer pizzas or even four-course meals.

There's plenty of interesting takeaway food on sale throughout the day – *pizza al taglio* (pizza by the slice) is available all over the city. For full-size pizzas, places with wood stoves (*forno a legna*) for better results than from electric ovens. Other takeaways such as whole roast chicken, potatoes or *suppli* (fried rice croquettes) can be had from *rosticcerie*. A self-service *tavola calda* will serve an impressive array of hot food and is ideal for lunchtimes.

VEGETARIAN FOOD

PURELY VEGETARIAN restaurants are largely unknown in Rome, but everywhere you'll find pasta or rice dishes (risotto) using interesting combinations of vegetables, salads, artichokes cooked in different ways, or vegetables stuffed and then baked in the oven. Most menus are very adaptable.

The interior of Relais le Jardin *(see p317)*

The Price of a Meal

WHAT YOU PAY will clearly depend on your choice of establishment. In a *tavola calda* or Roman pizzeria, for example, you can often eat for as little as L15,000 a head. A local trattoria costs perhaps L25,000, whereas in a full-blown restaurant reckon on around L50,000 and up. Bottled wine, as opposed to a jug or carafe of house wine (*vino della casa*), commands higher prices but should offer a more interesting range of tastes (*see p306*). House wine is usually acceptable, though.

Reading the Menu

NOT EVERY restaurant automatically provides a menu – the waiter will often tell you the day's specialities (*piatti del giorno*), usually not mentioned on the standard menu but almost always worth ordering. If you are not sure about these, you can always ask for *la lista* (the menu) and then allow yourself to be guided. ·

A meal could begin with *antipasti* (appetizers) or *primi piatti* – the latter consisting of *pasta asciutta* (pasta with some kind of sauce), *pasta in brodo* (clear broth with pasta in it), *pasta al forno* (baked pasta), risotto or a substantial soup. You then move on to the *secondi*, the main meat or fish course, for which you'll need to order vegetables (*contorni*) separately if you would like them. Afterwards you have *formaggi* (cheeses), *frutta* (fruit) or *dolci* (desserts). Romans don't usually eat

One of many Trastevere cafés

Outdoor café life in the piazza outside Santa Maria in Trastevere

cheese as well as a sweet dish, but cheese often comes with fruit such as pears, figs or melon. Strong espresso coffee, and perhaps a liqueur (*amaro* or *digestivo*) rounds off the meal (*see p306*). You may want to skip the first course, or you may prefer to choose a salad or vegetable dish. Pasta alone tends not to be seen as a full meal.

Opening Times

RESTAURANTS are generally open from about noon to 3pm and from 8pm to 11pm or much later. The busiest times tend to be 9pm–9.30pm for dinner and 1pm–1.30pm at lunchtime. Dinner is generally the preferred time for dedicated, relaxed eating, particularly in summer, when it will begin and end late as the heat of the day subsides. Bars are open all day, often from the early hours, serving all kinds of drinks (alcohol can be sold at any time of day) and snacks. The quietest month is August, when many restaurant owners take their annual holiday (shown by *chiuso per ferie* signs).

Booking a Table

BOOKING (*prenotazione*) is generally advisable. Sunday is the main lunch date of the week when you should definitely book; the same usually goes for Saturday evening. Check the weekly closing day if you don't book. Many places are closed on Mondays, and Sunday evening can also be difficult.

In summer try to book a shady table outside, since air conditioning is not universal.

Wheelchair Access

ROME is becoming more solicitous towards those in wheelchairs, but a call to the restaurant in advance will help secure the right table.

Taking Children Along

CHILDREN are made very welcome, particularly in family-run places. You can usually order half-portions (but expect to pay more than half), or just ask for an extra plate. High chairs (*seggioline*) may also be available in some of the establishments.

Using the Listings

Key to symbols in the listings on pp312–17.

🍴	fixed price menus
🚭	non-smoking area
V	vegetarian dishes
🔆	child portions and sometimes high chairs
♿	wheelchair access
👔	jacket and tie required
🎵	live music
🌂	tables outside
🍷	exceptional wine list
★	highly recommended
💳	credit cards accepted
AE	American Express
DC	Diners Club
MC	Mastercard/Access
V	Visa
JCB	Japanese Credit Bureau

Price categories for a three-course meal for one, including a half bottle of house wine, cover charge, tax and service:

Ⓛ up to L35,000
ⓁⓁ L35,000–L55,000
ⓁⓁⓁ L55,000–L75,000
ⓁⓁⓁⓁ L75,000–L100,000
ⓁⓁⓁⓁⓁ over L100,000

What to Eat in Rome

Bulb of fresh garlic

THE TRADITIONAL *cucina romanesca* has always relied on local markets full of fresh seasonal vegetables, fruit, cheese and meat from the nearby countryside plus seafood from the Mediterranean. As in the rest of Italy, pasta is an important part of the menu; one popular dish is the famous *spaghetti alla carbonara*, which was devised in Rome. Many genuinely Roman meat dishes are based on the so-called *quinto quarto* (fifth quarter) – head, innards, tail, trotters and so on. Highly flavoured with olive oil, herbs, lard, bacon *(pancetta)* or pig's cheek *(guanciale)* they become a culinary delight. Fish from the Mediterranean is excellent. In season, mushrooms and artichokes may be served in dozens of different ways. *Mesticanza* is also good in season; it's a fresh mix of salad leaves including the peppery *rughetta* (rocket) and *puntarelle* (curly endive shoots, often served with anchovy dressing). For dessert you should not miss out on ice cream, or puddings like the classic *tiramisù*.

Maritozzi alla Panna
These soft buns with raisins and candied peel are filled with whipped cream.

Fresh basil · **Anchovies** · **Artichoke hearts** · **Roasted peppers** · **Baby octopus**

Antipasto
Italian appetizers may include olives, cured meats, seafood and grilled or preserved vegetables.

Bruschetta
Toasted bread is rubbed with garlic and olive oil; tomato can be added.

Supplì
Fried rice croquettes are stuffed with mozzarella and make a tasty snack.

Olive Oil and Vinegar
Always on the table, these are for dressing salads and flavouring antipasto.

Filetti di Baccalà
A Jewish speciality, deep-fried cod fillets are a typical Roman snack or first course.

Risotto alla Romana
Liver, sweetbreads, Marsala and pecorino cheese are used to make this risotto.

TYPICAL ITALIAN PASTA

Penne rigate (quills)

Farfalle (butterflies)

Fusilli (spirals)

Conchigliette (shells)

Cappelletti (small hats)

Bucatini all'Amatriciana
Pasta tubes are served with bacon, tomatoes and onion, with grated pecorino on top.

Spaghetti alla Carbonara
Chopped bacon, eggs and cheese are used to prepare this famous local dish.

Gnocchi alla Romana
Small semolina dumplings are served with tomato or just with butter.

Fiori di Zucca e Carciofi Fritti
Courgette flowers in batter and whole artichokes deep-fried are popular antipasti.

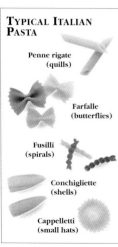

Coda alla Vaccinara
A traditional Roman dish, this is made from braised oxtail with tomatoes.

Saltimbocca alla Romana
Veal with Parma ham and sage, this tasty dish is also served rolled and skewered.

Fave al Guanciale
Fresh springtime broad beans are simmered with bacon and onion.

Crostata di Ricotta
This Roman cheesecake is filled with ricotta, Marsala and lemon.

Parmesan

Italian Cheeses
Parmesan is the best-known Italian cheese but Rome's classic is pecorino romano, made from ewe's milk. The mature, hard version is often used grated, but fresh pecorino can be eaten as a dessert cheese. Mild buffalo-milk mozzarella is the classic one for pizza.

Mozzarella

Tiramisù
Mascarpone cheese, coffee and chocolate are combined for this wonderful dessert.

What to Drink in Rome

Roman mosaic showing bird and vines

ITALY IS ONE OF Europe's most significant wine-producing countries, keeping up a tradition started in the hills around Rome over 2,000 years ago. Today, wine is usually drunk with meals as a matter of course, and knowing the difference between *rosso* (red) and *bianco* (white) may be all the vocabulary you need to get by. Beer is widely available too, as well as good ranges of apéritifs and digestifs. Rome's drinking water, another debt to the ancient Romans, is particularly good, fresh and sweet, and in abundant supply.

The vineyards of Frascati, southeast of Rome

WHITE WINE

Orvieto   Frascati

VINES THRIVE in the warm climate of Lazio, the region around Rome, producing abundant supplies of inexpensive dry white wine for the city's cafés and restaurants. It is usually sold by the carafe. Of local bottled wines, Frascati is the best-known, but Castelli Romani, Marino, Colli Albani and Velletri are very similar in style. All are made from one grape variety, the Trebbiano, though better quality versions contain a dash of Malvasia for perfume and flavour. Other central Italian whites worth trying are Orvieto and Verdicchio. Quality white wines from all over Italy, including fine whites from Friuli in the northeast, are widely available in Rome.

Calcaia comes from Barberani, a reliable producer of Orvieto.

Bigi produce good quality Orvieto, especially the single-vineyard Torricella.

Casal Pilozzo is an easy-drinking white wine from Frascati producers, Colli di Catone. Choose the youngest vintage.

Colle Gaio, with its rich, fruity flavour, stands out among the dry white Frascatis.

WINE TYPE	GOOD VINTAGES	GOOD PRODUCERS
WHITE WINE		
Friuli (Pinot Bianco, Chardonnay, Pinot Grigio, Sauvignon)	The most recent	Gravner, Jermann, Puiatti, Schiopetto, Volpe Pasini
Orvieto/ Orvieto Classico	The most recent	Antinori, Barberani, Bigi, Il Palazzone
RED WINE		
Chianti/ Chianti Classico/ Chianti Rufina	95, 90, 88, 85	Antinori, Castello di Ama, Castello di Cacchiano, Castello di Volpaia, Felsina Berardenga, Fontodi, Frescobaldi, Isole e Olena, Il Palazzino, Riecine, Rocca delle Macie, Ruffino, Vecchie Terre di Montefili, Villa Cafaggio
Brunello di Montalcino/ Vino Nobile di Montepulciano	95, 90, 88, 85	Altesino, Avignonesi, Biondi Santi, Caparzo, Case Basse, Lisini, Il Poggione, Poliziano, Villa Banfi
Barolo/ Barbaresco	95, 90, 89, 88, 85, 82, 78	Aldo Conterno, Altare, Ceretto, Clerico, Gaja, Giacomo Conterno, Giacosa, Mascarello, Ratti, Voerzio

RED WINE

THOUGH SOME local red wine is made, most of the bottled red wine in Rome comes from other parts of Italy. Regions like Tuscany and Piedmont produce very good everyday drinking as well as top-class wines like Barolo. Price should reflect quality – try Dolcetto, Rosso di Montalcino or Montepulciano for good value reds.

Tuscan table wine   Barolo

Montepulciano d'Abruzzo, a rich and juicy red wine, is always good value. It is produced in the Abruzzi region east of Rome.

Chianti Classico Riserva is older and stronger than a normal Chianti Classico.

Torre Ercolana is produced in small quantities and is generally regarded as one of Lazio's best red wines. It is made from Cesanese and Cabernet grapes and requires at least five years' ageing.

READING THE LABEL

ITALY has a two-tier system for labelling quality wine. DOC *(denominazione di origine controllata)* means you can be sure the wine is from the region declared on the label and is made from designated grape varieties. A higher classification – DOCG *(denominazione di origine controllata e garantita)* – is given to top wines such as the reds Barolo, Barbaresco, Chianti Classico and Brunello di Montalcino.

Chianti Classico

APÉRITIFS AND OTHER DRINKS

BITTER, herb-flavoured drinks like Martini, Campari or Aperol are the most popular apéritifs. (Ask for an *analcolico* if you prefer a non-alcoholic one.) Italians drink their apéritifs neat or with ice and soda. Strong, herby after-dinner drinks, known as *digestivi* or *amari*, are worth trying if you need to settle your stomach. Italian brandy and grappa can be very fiery. Italian beer, popular with pizza, is made in lager style.

Campari

SOFT DRINKS

ITALIAN FRUIT juices are good and most bars squeeze fresh orange juice *(spremuta)* on the spot. Iced tea and coffee are refreshing in summer, and fruit-flavoured tea, such as peach, is very popular.

Refrigerated storage for wine and beer

DRINKING WATER

Unlike many Mediterranean cities, Rome benefits from a constant supply of fresh drinking water, piped down from the hills through a system of pipes and aqueducts which has changed little from ancient Roman times. Only if there is a sign saying *acqua non potabile* is the water not safe to drink.

One of Rome's many fresh water drinking fountains

Coffee is almost more important to Roman life than wine. Take espresso for neat strong black coffee at any time of day, milky cappuccino for breakfast or mid-afternoon, caffelatte for extra milk.

Espresso

Cappuccino

Caffelatte

Rome's Best: Restaurants and Cafés

ROME IS NOT particularly known for luxury restaurants, but more for atmospheric places where the focus is on the social side of dining and on regional cooking. An amazing variety can be found. Many places specialize, priding themselves on being the best of their kind – whether they offer superb espresso, or traditional foods like deep-fried salted cod *(baccalà)*. Other restaurants can offer beautiful settings or are the best places to see and be seen. This selection shows some of the many highlights of a city where eating is taken very seriously.

Caffè Giolitti
This historic ice cream shop serves a variety of flavours, to eat in or take away. (See p320.)

Camponeschi
This stylish restaurant offers elegantly prepared dishes and outdoor tables on Piazza Farnese (See p314.)

Filetti di Baccalà
This small, crowded place serves tasty fried fillets of cod – one of Rome's most traditional dishes – and offers a truly Roman experience. (See p320.)

Alberto Ciarla
Fish dominate the exquisite dishes as well as the decor in this elegant restaurant. (See p316.)

Piperno
For over a century, traditional Roman Jewish cooking has been the speciality of Piperno, in the heart of the Jewish Ghetto. (See p314.)

Vatican

Piazza Nav

Campo de' Fiori

Janiculum

Trastevere

Babington's Tea Rooms
This old-fashioned, genteel establishment at the foot of the Spanish Steps serves English tea and cakes. (See p320.)

La Terazza
Gloriously situated in the roof garden of Hotel Eden, La Terazza offers some of the finest cuisine in Rome, with views to match. (See p317.)

Caffè Greco
Famous as the haunt of writers, artists and intellectuals in the 19th century, this café still retains the faded grandeur shown in this painting. (See p320.)

za di gna

Via Veneto

za a da

Quirinal

Capitol

Esquiline

Forum

Palatine

Caracalla   Lateran

Aventine

| 0 metres | 500 |
| 0 yards | 500 |

Sora Lella
This Roman trattoria is famous for its setting on the Isola Tiberina and for the fashionable crowd which it attracts. (See p314.)

Tazza d'Oro
This figure graces the facade of Tazza d'Oro, where you will find some of the best espresso in Rome. (See p320.)

Choosing a Restaurant

THE RESTAURANTS in this guide have been selected for their good value or exceptional food. This chart highlights some of the factors which may influence your choice. Entries are alphabetical within price category. For more details on the restaurants, see pages 312–17. Information on cafés and wine bars is on pages 318–21.

	Price	Fixed Price Menu	Vegetarian Dishes	Tables Outside	Seafood Specialities	Late Opening	Air Conditioning	Attractive Setting
PIAZZA DELLA ROTONDA (see p312)								
Il Bacaro	LL			●	▨	●		
Il Buco	LL			●			▨	
Le Due Colonne	LL		▨			▨	●	
Da Gino	LL							
Vecchia Locanda	LL		▨	●	▨	●	▨	●
Enoteca Capranica	LLLL	●	▨		▨			
Sangallo	LLLL						▨	
La Rosetta ★	LLLLL				▨	●	▨	
El Toulà	LLLL	●	▨		▨		▨	
PIAZZA NAVONA (see p312)								
La Taverna	LL	●		●			▨	●
Osteria dell'Antiquario	LLL			●			▨	●
Papà Giovanni	LLLL		▨			●	▨	
Il Convivio	LLLL	●			▨		▨	
PIAZZA DI SPAGNA (see p313)								
Al 34	LL		▨	●	▨		▨	
Birreria Viennese	LL	●				●	▨	
Mario alle Vite	LL			●			▨	
Nino	LLL							
Sogo-Asahi	LLL	●			▨		▨	
Porto di Ripetta	LLLL	●			▨		▨	
Hassler Roof Restaurant	LLLLL						▨	●
CAMPO DE' FIORI (see p313)								
Bella Shanghai	L	●	▨			●	▨	
Al Pompiere	LL							
Il Cardinale	LLL		▨		▨	●	▨	
Il Drappo	LLL			●		●	▨	
Le Maschere	LLL		▨	●		●	▨	
Sora Lella	LLL						▨	
Vecchia Roma	LLL		▨	●	▨	●	▨	●
Piperno	LLLL			●	▨			
Camponeschi	LLLLL			●	▨	●		●
QUIRINAL (see p314)								
Colline Emiliane	LL						▨	
Al Moro	LLL				▨	●	▨	
Il Posto Accanto	LLL		▨		▨		▨	
Quadrifoglio	LLL					●	▨	
TERMINI (see p314)								
Gemma alla Lupa	L	●	▨	●			▨	
Coriolano	LLLL		▨		▨		▨	
ESQUILINE (see p314)								
Trattoria Monti	LL							
Cicilardone	LLL					●		
La Tana del Grillo	LLL							
Agata e Romeo	LLLL	●					▨	

Price categories for a three-course meal for one, half a bottle of house wine, and all unavoidable extra charges such as cover, service, tax:
Ⓛ up to L35,000
ⓁⓁ L35–55,000
ⓁⓁⓁ L55–75,000
ⓁⓁⓁⓁ L75–100,000
ⓁⓁⓁⓁⓁ over L100,000.

★ Means highly recommended.

FIXED PRICE MENU
Restaurant offering *menu turistico* (tourist menu): usually three or four courses without wine or coffee, for a set price.

VEGETARIAN DISHES
Restaurant with a good selection of vegetarian dishes.

LATE OPENING
Last orders on or after 11.30pm.

ATTRACTIVE SETTING
Restaurant set in a pretty piazza or with a garden terrace, or with a lovely view.

	Fixed Price Menu	Vegetarian Dishes	Tables Outside	Seafood Specialities	Late Opening	Air Conditioning	Attractive Setting
LATERAN *(see p315)*							
Alfredo a Via Gabi ⓁⓁ						■	
Charly's Saucière ⓁⓁ					●		
Cannavota ⓁⓁⓁ				■		■	
AVENTINE *(see p315)*							
Perilli a Testaccio ⓁⓁ						■	
Checchino dal 1887 ★ ⓁⓁⓁⓁ				●			
TRASTEVERE *(see p316)*							
Da Lucia Ⓛ			●				
Fricandò ⓁⓁ		■	●		●		
La Cornucopia ⓁⓁⓁ	●		●	■		■	●
L'Isola Felice ⓁⓁⓁ			●				
Da Paris ⓁⓁⓁ			●	■		■	●
Romolo nel Giardino della Fornarina ⓁⓁⓁ			●		●	■	●
Alberto Ciarla ★ ⓁⓁⓁⓁ	●		●	●	●	■	
JANICULUM *(see p316)*							
Antico Arco ★ ⓁⓁ					●	■	
VATICAN *(see p316)*							
Macondo ⓁⓁ		■	●				
San Luigi ⓁⓁⓁ		■				■	
Les Etoiles ⓁⓁⓁⓁ			●	■			
VIA VENETO *(see p317)*							
Andrea ⓁⓁⓁ		■		■		■	
Tullio ⓁⓁⓁ				■		■	
Giovanni ⓁⓁⓁⓁ				■			
George's ★ ⓁⓁⓁⓁⓁ			●		●	■	●
Le Sans Souci ★ ⓁⓁⓁⓁⓁ				■	■	■	
La Terrazza ⓁⓁⓁⓁⓁ		■		■	●	■	
VILLA BORGHESE *(see p317)*							
Al Ceppo ⓁⓁⓁ		■	●	■		■	
Relais la Piscine ★ ⓁⓁⓁⓁ	●		●	■		■	●
Relais le Jardin ★ ⓁⓁⓁⓁⓁ				■		■	

PIAZZA DELLA ROTONDA

Il Bacaro

Via degli Spagnoli 27. **Map** 12 D2.
(06-686 41 10. **Open** 8pm–
midnight Mon–Sat. **Closed** 1 wk Jan
& 2 wks Aug. 🔲 🍷 🎴 DC, MC, V,
JCB. ⓁⓁ

Located in the historic centre of
the city, near the Pantheon, this
tiny restaurant serves meals
cooked in a minute kitchen. The
menu is very much based around
meat and fish dishes and includes
such main courses as fillet steak
with basil sauce. The superb
desserts include an excellent
chocolate mousse.

Il Buco

Via di Sant'Ignazio 8. **Map** 4 F4 &
12 E3. **(** 06-679 32 98, 06-678 44
67. **Open** 12.30pm–4pm, 7pm–
midnight Tue–Sun. **Closed** Aug &
Christmas. 🎴 ♿ 🔲 🎴 AE, DC,
MC, V. ⓁⓁ

Much has happened since the tiny
buco (hole) opened in 1891 – the
small osteria has become a large
restaurant, yet the calm atmosphere, unfailing courtesy and
formidable Tuscan menu remain.
From the traditional *crostini* (liver
pâté canapés), robust *ribollita*
(thick vegetable soup) and huge
Florentine steaks, to the final
tozzetti (almond biscuits) with vin
santo (dessert wine), this is a truly
Tuscan experience.

Le Due Colonne

Via del Seminario 122. **Map** 4 F4 &
12 D3. **(** 06-678 14 49. **Open**
noon–3pm, 7pm–midnight daily.
🍷 ♿ ♿ 🎴 AE, DC, MC, V, JCB.
ⓁⓁ

Evocative of ancient Rome, the
decor of this restaurant includes
two imperial columns, from which
it gets its name, and an ancient
fountain. The cuisine is rich in
Mediterranean flavours, and
includes both Italian and Spanish
dishes. The seafood dishes, such
as *calamari* stuffed with onions
and hard-boiled eggs and giant
prawns with *Pachino* tomatoes,
are particularly good.

Da Gino

Vicolo Rosini 4 (Piazza del Parlamento).
Map 4 F3 & 12 D1. **(** 06-687 34 34.
Open 12.45pm–3pm, 8pm–10.30pm
Mon–Sat. **Closed** Aug. ⓁⓁ

Journalists, politicians and the
initiated scramble for a seat under
the kitsch, frescoed pergola of this

ancient, ultra-Roman trattoria to
feast upon traditional daily dishes:
gnocchi and *osso buco* (Thursdays),
baccalà (Fridays), tripe (Saturdays),
plus classic sturdy soups and
delectable homemade *tiramisù*.

Vecchia Locanda

Vicolo Sinibaldi 2. **Map** 4 F4 & 12 D3.
(06-68 80 28 31. **Open** 12.30pm–
3pm, 7pm–midnight Mon–Sat.
Closed Christmas. 🍷 🔲 🍷
🎴 AE, DC, MC, V. ⓁⓁ

Visit this small, family-run Ligurian
restaurant in summer, when tables
line the secluded arched street.
Everything shows extreme care –
including the impeccable service.
An imaginative combination of
herbs and vegetables characterizes
the menu: risotto with courgette
flowers, *porcini* mushroom crêpes,
stuffed truffled rabbit and lots of
fresh fish. There's a good selection
of French and regional wines.

Enoteca Capranica

Piazza Capranica 99–100. **Map** 12 D2.
(06-69 94 09 92. **Open** noon–3pm,
7pm–11pm Mon–Fri, 7pm–11pm
Sat. **Closed** Aug. 🔲 🍷 🔲 ♿
🎴 AE, DC, V, JBC. ⓁⓁⓁⓁ

Housed in part of the impressive
15th-century Palazzo Capranica
(see p113), the Enoteca Capranica
offers an extensive menu, mostly
based around seafood and vegetable dishes. Starters include delights
such as lobster and mango salad,
while the exotic main courses
include unusual dishes like *risotto
con zucca e tartufo* (risotto with
pumpkin and truffle) and *spigola
al sale* (sea bass in a salt crust).

Sangallo

Vicolo della Vaccarella 11. **Map** 4 F3
& 12 D2. **(** 06-686 55 49. **Open**
12.30pm–2.30pm, 7.45pm–10.30pm
Tue–Sat, 12.30pm–2.30pm Mon.
Closed 2 wks Aug. ♿ 🎴 AE, DC,
MC, V. ⓁⓁⓁⓁ

This elegant fish restaurant has an
interesting menu complemented by
an impressive wine list. Antipasti
include *crostini con calamaretti al
radicchio* (baby squid and radicchio
on toast). First courses such as
*fettuccelle con gamberi, pomodori e
pecorino* (pasta with shrimps,
tomatoes and pecorino cheese)
are prepared delicately and simply.
Ask about the speciality of the day.

La Rosetta

Via della Rosetta 9. **Map** 4 F4 & 12 D2.
(06-68 30 88 41. **Open** 1pm–3pm,
7.30pm–11.30pm Mon–Fri, 7.30pm–
11.30pm Sat. **Closed** 3 wks Aug,
Christmas. ♿ 🍷 ★ 🎴 AE, DC,
MC, V, JCB. ⓁⓁⓁⓁⓁ

Despite the exorbitant prices,
people flock nightly (having
booked in advance) for a seat in
the elegant, tightly-packed rooms
of this restaurant. Fresh fish and
seafood are brought in daily from
Sicily and, cooked in the simplest
ways, achieve close to culinary
perfection. The enthusiastic
service and top-quality French
and Italian wines, particularly
the Sicilian whites, available do
justice to the cuisine.

El Toulà

Via della Lupa 29B. **Map** 4 F3 &
12 D1. **(** 06-687 34 98. **Open**
1pm–3pm, 8pm–11pm Tue–Fri,
8pm–11pm Mon, Sat. **Closed** Aug,
Christmas. 🍽 🍷 🍷 🎴 AE,
DC, MC, V, JCB. ⓁⓁⓁⓁ

El Toulà is justly renowned as
one of the most exclusive, traditional and luxurious restaurants
in Rome. The Venetian-inspired
cooking is serious and professional,
with forays into the realms of the
best classic international cuisine.
In dignified, sober surroundings
the service is exemplary and the
selection of wines superb.

PIAZZA NAVONA

La Taverna

Via del Banco di Santo Spirito 58.
Map 4 D3 & 11 A2. **(** 06-686 41
16. **Open** noon–3pm, 7pm–11pm
Tue–Sun. 🍽 ♿ 🎵 🔲 🎴 AE,
DC, MC, V, JCB. ⓁⓁ

Tourists and local residents mingle
in Giovanni's crowded Roman
trattoria to enjoy the family
atmosphere and traditional
regional cooking. Particularly
appreciated are the *rigatoni
all'amatriciana, coda alla
vaccinara* and, on Thursday,
Friday and Saturday respectively,
gnocchi, baccalà and tripe.

Osteria dell'Antiquario

Piazzetta San Simeone 27. **Map** 4 E3
& 11 B2. **(** 06-687 96 94. **Open**
12.30pm–2.30pm, 8pm–11pm
Tue–Sat, 8pm–11pm Mon. **Closed** 2
wks Aug & 2 wks Jan. 🔲 🍷 🎴 AE,
DC, MC, V. ⓁⓁⓁ

In the comfort of the elegantly
restructured rooms of an old
antique shop, Giorgio Nisti
offers an unusual menu dictated
by the whims of the chef and the
daily market. The largely
traditional dishes are creatively
adapted to contemporary health-
conscious tastes. There is an
impressive choice of regional,
French and Californian wines.

Papà Giovanni

Via dei Sediari 4. **Map** 4 F4 & 12 D3.
℡ 06-686 53 08. **Open** 1pm–3pm,
8pm–11.30pm Mon–Sat. 🎴 **V** **Y**
🍽 MC, V. ⓁⓁⓁ

Nearly 60 years have passed since
Papà Giovanni first sold his
country wines in Rome; the bottles
lining the walls are testimony to
the past and to the superb cellar of
Giovanni's son, Renato Sentuti.
Here diners sample the best of the
new lighter Roman cuisine.
Classics such as *cacio e pepe*, salt
cod and tripe live alongside exotic
salads and truffled dishes. Desserts
include ricotta soufflé with
strawberry sauce, hot chocolate
profiteroles and exquisite sorbets.

Il Convivio

Via dell'Orso 44. **Map** 4 E3 & 11 C2.
℡ 06-686 94 32. **Open** 1pm–
2.30pm, 8pm–10.30pm Tue–Sat,
8pm–10.30pm Mon. **Closed** 1 week
Aug. **🍽** 🖪 ★ 🍽 AE, DC, MC,
V. ⓁⓁⓁⓁ

An air of sophisticated tranquillity
pervades this intimate restaurant,
one of the very best specializing
in modern creative cookery. Its
young chef, one of the three
brother-owners from the Marches,
creates both subtle and unusual
combinations of flavours, and the
highly personalized menu evolves
with the seasons. The wine list is
extensive and service is discreet.

PIAZZA DI SPAGNA

Al 34

Via Mario de' Fiori 34. **Map** 5 A2.
℡ 06-679 50 91. **Open** 12.30pm–
3pm, 7.30pm–11pm Tue–Sun.
Closed 3 wks Aug. **V** 🖪 🖪
🍽 AE, DC, MC, V. ⓁⓁ

This busy, bustling restaurant is an
ideal choice if you're in a hurry, as
the service is speedy and efficient.
Predominantly featuring southern
Italian cooking, the extensive
menu offers an esoteric choice,
particularly where vegetables and
herbs are allied with pasta, meat
and fish. Given its location, the
prices are affordable.

Birreria Viennese

Via della Croce 21. **Map** 5 A2.
℡ 06-679 55 69. **Open** noon–
midnight daily. **🍽** 🖪 🍽 AE, DC,
MC, V, JCB. ⓁⓁ

The stained-glass entrance leads to
a long, crowded room where, for
more than 60 years, traditional
beers and Austrian specialities
have been sampled. Try sausages,
goulash, *Wienerschnitzel*,

sauerkraut, or the massive *piatto
di legno della Transilvania*
(wooden platter heaped with
delights, for two). Wine is
available, and the service is
extremely helpful and courteous.

Mario alla Vite

Via della Vite 55. **Map** 5 A3 & 12 E1.
℡ 06-678 38 18. **Open** 12.30pm–
3pm, 7.30pm–11pm Mon–Sat. **Closed**
Aug. 🖪 **🍽** AE, DC, MC, V. ⓁⓁ

Despite an exclusive address,
Mario has kept prices reasonable,
and his food is still simple Tuscan
fare. Elbow-to-elbow dining,
haphazard service and noisy
confusion seem inevitable.
Nevertheless, the food is usually
worth it – traditional *fagioli al
fiasco* (cannellini beans in oil),
ribollita (thick vegetable soup),
Florentine steaks and delicious
pastries are the attractions, along
with a wide selection of wines.

Nino

Via Borgognona 11. **Map** 5 A2 &
12 E1. **℡** 06-679 56 76. **Open**
12.30pm–2.30pm, 7.30pm–11pm
Tue–Fri, 7.30pm–11pm Sat. **🍽** AE,
DC, MC, V. ⓁⓁ

A reliable restaurant, located
among the fancy shops around
Piazza di Spagna, Nino has been
popular with visitors and local
alike since it opened in 1934. The
menu features mostly Tuscan
food, so there is always a hearty
soup on offer to go along with
other standards such as *bistecca
alla fiorentina* (grilled T-bone
steak). Save room for the desserts,
which are all home-made.

Sogo-Asahi

Via di Propaganda 16. **Map** 5 A2.
℡ 06-678 60 93. **Open** noon–
2.30pm, 6.30pm–10pm Mon–Sat.
🍽 🖪 🍽 AE, DC, MC, V, JCB.
ⓁⓁ

This luxury, top-quality restaurant
is a find for lovers of Japanese
cooking. Traditional Japanese
specialities are elegantly served by
helpful and knowledgeable
waiters: *sashimi* (raw fish) and
melt-in-the-mouth tempura are
accompanied by saké, Japanese
beer or a good Italian wine. The
special set menus are particularly
inexpensive at lunchtime. Sogo-
Asahi opens in August, when most
of Rome's restaurants are closed.

Porto di Ripetta

Via di Ripetta 250. **Map** 4 F2.
℡ 06-361 23 76. **Open** 12.45pm–
2.45pm, 8pm–11pm Mon–Sat.
Closed Aug. **🍽** 🖪 **Y** 🍽 AE,
DC, MC, V, JCB. ⓁⓁⓁⓁ

The fame of this restaurant
depends largely on the genius of
chef Maria Romani. With the fish
that arrives daily from her native
Marches she creates inspired
combinations such as fish and
broad bean soup or giant prawns
with artichokes. It is expensive,
but worth it; the business lunch
menu is much cheaper. There's a
selection of excellent wines.

Hassler Roof Restaurant

Piazza Trinità dei Monti 6. **Map** 5 A2.
℡ 06-69 93 47 26. **Open** 7am–
11am, noon–2.30pm, 7.30pm–
10.30pm Mon–Sat, 7am–11am,
12.30pm–3pm, 7.30pm–10.30pm
Sun. **🍽** 🎵 **Y** 🍽 AE, DC, MC, V,
JCB. ⓁⓁⓁⓁ

Perched on the sixth floor of the
Hotel Hassler, overlooking the
Spanish Steps, the roof restaurant
commands a breathtaking view of
Rome. Come for the gargantuan
and pricy Sunday brunch. The wine
list is excellent and the hovering
waiter service timely and discreet.
In the evening, when prices are
higher, there's piano music.

CAMPO DE' FIORI

Bella Shanghai

Corso Vittorio Emanuele II 333.
Map 4 E4 & 11 C3. **℡** 06-686 96 51.
Open 11am–3pm, 6pm–midnight
daily. **🍽** **V** 🍽 AE, DC, MC, V. ⓁⓁ

Centrally located and inexpensive,
this is the place to go for Chinese
food which is fairly standard, but
certainly not mundane. The menu
contains such unusual dishes as
strips of beef and bamboo cooked
in a curry sauce and served up in
a steaming pot, and aubergines
cooked with chopped carrots and
mincemeat. There are tables outside, the service is fast and
friendly, and there is a modest
selection of wines and beers.

Al Pompiere

Via S. M. dei Calderari 38. **Map** 4 F5
& 12 D5. **℡** 06-686 83 77. **Open**
noon–3pm, 7.30pm–11pm Mon–Sat.
Closed Aug. **Y** 🍽 MC, V. ⓁⓁ

In the heart of the Jewish Ghetto,
Al Pompiere occupies the first
floor of the 16th-century Palazzo
Cenci-Bolognetti. Under its
frescoed and open-beamed
ceilings, in a homely atmosphere,
all the classic dishes of the
substantial Roman cuisine are
expertly served: among them
fried courgette flowers with
anchovies, *rigatoni con la pajata*,
and baby lamb.

For key to symbols *see p291*

Il Cardinale

Via delle Carceri 6. **Map** 4 D4 & 11 B3.
(06-686 93 36. **Open** 12.45pm–
3pm, 7.30pm–11.30pm Mon–Sat.
V **&** **Ξ** *AE, DC, MC, V.* **Ⓛ****Ⓛ****Ⓛ**

For genuine regional cooking, using
the best local ingredients from the
Castelli Romani, this small, elegant
yet comfortable restaurant near
Via Giulia is highly recommended.
Dishes range from tasty robust
soups, to specialities such as
zucchine alla velletrana (baked
courgettes) and *crema al cocco*
(coconut *crème brûlée).* There are
some very good wines from Lazio.

Il Drappo

Vicolo del Malpasso 9. **Map** 4 D4 &
11 B3. **(** 06-687 73 65. **Open** 8pm–
midnight Mon–Sat. **Closed** 1 Jan, 2
wks Aug, Easter, 25 Dec. **&** **Ψ**
Ξ *AE, DC, MC, V, JCB.* **Ⓛ****Ⓛ****Ⓛ**

A small, intimate restaurant, with
ceiling drapes (hence the name),
plants and candlelight, Il Drappo
provides an authentic taste of
Sardinia – traditional dishes
imbued with flashes of culinary
creativity. Everything is evocative
of the island, including the wines,
particularly the *seada* (sweet
cheese-filled ravioli) for dessert.
Try the *mirto* liqueur at the end.

Le Maschere

Via Monte della Farina 29. **Map** 4 F5
& 12 D4. **(** 06-687 94 44. **Open**
7pm–12.30am Tue–Sun. **Closed**
Aug. **V** **Ψ** **▦** *AE, DC, MC, V,*
JCB. **Ⓛ****Ⓛ**

There is an agreeable sensation of
being in the country as you cross
the spacious tiled hall and descend
to the rustic indoor terrace with its
high reed-lined ceiling, a roofed
grill and eerily-lit wall masks.
Candles on the tables, and a
subdued conversational hum, lull
you in preparation for the fiery
Calabrian food to come. Charming
service and good Calabrian house
wine (plus a short list) ensure an
enjoyable evening.

Sora Lella

Via Ponte Quattro Capi 16, Isola
Tiberina. **Map** 8 D1. **(** 06-686 16 01.
Open 1pm–2.30pm, 8pm–10.40pm
Mon–Sat. **Closed** Aug. **&** **Ξ** *AE,*
DC, MC, V. **Ⓛ****Ⓛ****Ⓛ**

Founded by the exuberant Roman
actress Sora Lella, this small, bright
trattoria is a well-known place to
people-watch. Sora Lella is now
run by Lella's son Aldo. Dishes are
based on traditional Roman
cuisine, but prices are very high
for an essentially simple style of
cooking. Go instead for the

beautiful location on the Isola
Tiberina, the often glamorous
clientele, and the good service.

Vecchia Roma

Piazza Campitelli 18. **Map** 4 F5 &
12 E5. **(** 06-686 46 04. **Open**
1pm–3pm, 8pm–11.30pm Thu–Tue.
Closed 2 weeks Aug. **V** **&** **▦** **Ψ**
Ξ *AE, DC.* **Ⓛ****Ⓛ****Ⓛ**

Set in a quiet, atmospheric piazza,
this is one of the best places for a
summer evening. Reliable Roman
cooking is on offer, with tempting
antipasto, simply-cooked fish and
grilled meats, and a connoisseur's
wine list. Specialities are summer
salads and, in winter, numerous
variations on polenta. Added
pleasures are the 18th-century
interior and the excellent service.

Piperno

Via Monte de' Cenci 9. **Map** 4 F5 &
12 D5. **(** 06-686 11 13. **Open**
12.15pm–2.30pm, 8pm–11pm
Tue–Sat, 12.30pm–3pm Sun. **Closed**
Aug, Christmas, Easter. **V** **&** **▦**
Ξ *AE, DC, MC, V.* **Ⓛ****Ⓛ****Ⓛ****Ⓛ**

Piperno, at the heart of the Jewish
Ghetto, has been famed for over
a century for its traditional
Jewish/Roman dishes. Despite the
competition, the restaurant is still
unbeaten for lightly fried courgette
flowers, vegetable *fritto misto,*
carciofi alla giudia, tripe, and
superb fish, served in plain
surroundings. Service is familiarly
attentive and timely. The house
wine is excellent Frascati. Book
well in advance.

Camponeschi

Piazza Farnese 50. **Map** 4 E5 & 11 C4.
(06-687 49 27. **Open** 8pm–
12.30am Mon–Sat. **Closed** 10 days
Aug. **▦** **Ξ** *AE, DC, MC, V.*
Ⓛ**Ⓛ****Ⓛ****Ⓛ**

Camponeschi is set in one of the
most attractive piazzas in Rome,
especially beautiful in summer, and
booking in advance is necessary.
The extensive menu includes
modern and regional Italian
cooking, creative Mediterranean
fish and meat dishes, soufflés and
French specialities.

QUIRINAL

Colline Emiliane

Via degli Avignonesi 22. **Map** 5 B3.
(06-481 75 38. **Open** 12.45pm–
2.45pm, 7.45pm–10.45pm Sat–Thu.
Closed Aug. **&** **Ξ** *MC, V.* **Ⓛ****Ⓛ**

Regional dishes are the hallmarks
of this small family trattoria: one
unpretentious room presenting a

haven from the nearby Via del
Tritone. Enjoy food typical of the
northern province of Emilia
Romagna – salamis and cold meats,
homemade pastas (tagliatelle,
tortellini), boiled meats with *salsa*
verde (spinach, onion and
anchovy sauce) and strictly
Emilian wines.

Al Moro

Vicolo delle Bollette 13. **Map** 5 A3 &
12 F2. **(** 06-678 34 95. **Open**
1pm–3.30pm, 8pm–11.30pm
Mon–Sat. **Closed** Aug. **Ⓛ****Ⓛ****Ⓛ**

Franco Romagnoli's trattoria is a
reliable choice for traditional
Roman cooking, using fresh local
ingredients. Noisy and crowded,
its closely packed tables do not
encourage intimate dining. Classic
dishes are served: *bucatini*
all'amatriciana, spaghetti alla
Moro (special *carbonara),* fried
vegetables, excellent *baccalà alla*
Moro (salt cod), tripe, *abbacchio.*
There is a vast wine list.

Il Posto Accanto

Via del Boschetto 36 A. **Map** 5 B4.
(06-474 30 02. **Open** 12.30pm–
3pm Mon–Fri, 8pm–10pm Mon–Sat.
Closed Aug. **V** **Ψ** **&** **Ξ** *AE, DC,*
MC, V. **Ⓛ****Ⓛ****Ⓛ**

Tiny, intimate and elegant, this
family-run restaurant owes its
success to a short, carefully chosen
menu revolving around homemade
pasta (excellent *tagliolini con*
asparagi and *ravioli con zenzero*
– ginger), simply prepared fish
and meat, top-quality vegetables
and familiar desserts *(tiramisù),*
often prepared within sight of the
lucky diners. There is a range of
wines, as well as good grappas.

Quadrifoglio

Via del Boschetto 19. **Map** 5 B4.
(06-482 60 96. **Open** 7pm–
midnight Mon–Sat. **Closed** Aug. **Ψ**
Ξ *AE, DC, MC, V.* **Ⓛ****Ⓛ****Ⓛ**

Chef Pino Forlenza has researched
diligently to reproduce authentic,
skilfully prepared dishes from
Naples, Campania and the tip of
Africa, tailored to modern tastes by
the carefully selected raw
ingredients. These are delivered
with southern hospitality and
courteous service. Most of the
wines are from Campania, too.

TERMINI

Gemma alla Lupa

Via Marghera 39. **Map** 6 E3.
(06-49 12 30. **Open** noon–
3.30pm, 7pm–11pm Mon–Sat.
Closed 2 wks Aug. **Ψ⊙Ψ** **V** **▦** **Ⓛ**

Gemma's is a modest, family-run, typically Roman trattoria which serves up substantial portions of orthodox Roman cooking. Although the main features are its bustling atmosphere and speedy service, it represents an excellent choice if you want to eat well for a low price.

Coriolano

Via Ancona 14. **Map** 6 D1.
(06-44 24 98 63. **Open** noon–3pm, 7pm–11pm daily. **Closed** 3 wks Aug. **V** **&** **Y** **⊠** AE, DC, MC, V. **(L)(L)(L)(L)**

This small restaurant aims at perfection with its lacy tablecloths and crystal glasses. The Italian menu changes with the seasons and uses only the freshest of raw materials, including fish. Specialities include the home-made *ravioli di ricotta e spinaci*, *capretto* (kid) and creamy chocolate *zuppa del contadino*.

ESQUILINE

Trattoria Monti

Via di San Vito 13A. **Map** 6 D4.
(06-446 65 73. **Open** 12.30pm–3pm, 7.30pm–11pm Wed–Mon. **Closed** Easter, Aug & 3 wks Dec–Jan. **☆** **⊠** DC, MC, V. **(L)(L)**

This small, unpretentious local trattoria serves delicate, creative regional dishes from the Marches. Franca Camerucci cooks, while her husband Mario is attentive waiter and expert *sommelier*. Their specialities include fried stuffed olives, artichokes and *ciauscolo* (salami); *tortello al rosso d'uova* (fresh pasta stuffed with ricotta cheese, spinach and tomato); and *tacchino all'aceto balsamico* (lightly vinegared turkey slices). There's a good Verdicchio house wine and a commendable wine list.

Cicilardone

Via Farini 12. **Map** 6 D4.
(06-48 35 49. **Open** noon–3pm Tue–Sat, 8pm–midnight Mon–Sat. **Closed** mid 2 wks Aug. **⊠** AE, DC, MC, V. **(L)(L)(L)**

Ring at Cicilardone's door and your host – Domenico Lucia – will greet you like an old friend and converse about the gastronomic delights from the region of Basilicata. Try the *menu di assaggini* – a selection of dishes to give you an idea of the regional taste, including traditional pastas and hot chocolate profiteroles. There are some unusual southern wines available.

La Tana del Grillo

Via Alfieri 4. **Map** 6 E5.
(06-70 45 35 17. **Open** 12.30pm–2.30pm, 7.30pm–11pm Tue–Sat, 7.30pm–11pm Mon. **Closed** Aug. **☆** **&** **⊠** AE, DC, MC, V. **(L)(L)(L)**

Marisa Balboni runs an elegant and characteristically hospitable Emilian restaurant. Clients are pampered, from the cushioned chairs, restful prints and attractive tableware, to the wholesome food served with courtesy and care. Particularly recommended are the *polpettone all'emiliana* (meat loaf), *salame al sugo ferrarese* (Ferrarese salami), *cappellacci con la zucca* (pumpkin-stuffed pasta).

Agata e Romeo

Via Carlo Alberto 45. **Map** 6 D4.
(06-446 58 42. **Open** 1pm–3pm, 7pm–11pm Mon–Sat. **Closed** 2 wks Jan & 2 wks Aug. **⑩** **&** **Y** **⊠** AE, DC, MC, V, JCB. **(L)(L)(L)(L)**

One of the newer trattorie-turned-restaurants, its increasing prices sadly reflect recent popular acclaim. Nevertheless, Agata's skill in producing a changing menu of predominantly Roman and southern Italian dishes, and Romeo's impeccable service and range of carefully chosen wines, are hard to beat. Well-spaced, elegantly set tables are ideal for tranquil eating. The *menu degustazione* is recommended.

LATERAN

Alfredo a Via Gabi

Via Gabi 36. **Map** 10 D3.
(06-77 20 67 92. **Open** noon–3pm, 7.30pm–11pm Wed–Mon. **Closed** Aug. **(L)(L)**

This is a spacious local trattoria with a pavement pergola for outdoor eating. Specialities from Rome and the Marches – served in ample portions – include *tonnarelli ai sapori di bosco* (pasta with mushrooms), excellent *porcini* mushrooms (in season), *straccetti all'ortica* (meat in nettle sauce), and *panna cotta* (rich crème caramel) with fruit or chocolate. Service is cheerful and friendly.

Charly's Saucière

Via San Giovanni in Laterano 270. **Map** 9 B1. **(** 06-70 49 56 66.
Open 12.45pm–2.30pm, 8pm–11.15pm Tue–Fri, 8pm–midnight Mon & Sat. **Closed** 2 wks Aug. **&** **⊠** AE, MC, V, JCB. **(L)(L)**

An old-style, unsurprising and well-established French restaurant, this has scarcely altered over the years and is especially warm and

intimate on a winter evening. Diners choose from reassuring French and Swiss fare: pâtés, onion soup, cheese soufflé, fondues, *rösti*, steaks in a variety of sauces and crêpes, accompanied by a small but careful selection of wines. Service is professional and attentive.

Cannavota

Piazza San Giovanni in Laterano 20. **Map** 9 C1. **(** 06-77 20 50 07. **Open** 12.30pm–3pm, 7.45pm–11pm Thu–Tue. **Closed** 1–20 Aug. **⊠** AE, DC, MC, V. **(L)(L)(L)**

Join the enthusiastic regulars who crowd this friendly restaurant if you are feeling especially hungry. Portions are generous, the cooking is traditional Italian and the service is swift. Seafood – prawns, in particular – is excellent, but meat also features on the menu.

AVENTINE

Perilli a Testaccio

Via Marmorata 39. **Map** 8 D3.
(06-574 24 15. **Open** 12.30pm–3pm, 7.30pm–11pm Thu–Tue. **Closed** Aug. **&** **(L)(L)**

In the heart of Testaccio, this archetypal Roman trattoria is always packed with hungry regulars (and the occasional famous face). On offer are giant-size quantities of robust traditional fare – *rigatoni alla pajata*, *spaghetti alla carbonara* (served in king-size bowls), *coda alla vaccinara*, *carciofi alla romana* – helpfully and efficiently served. Ignore the noise and hideous murals – tuck in and enjoy yourself.

Checchino dal 1887

Via di Monte Testaccio 30. **Map** 8 D4.
(06-574 63 18. **Open** Oct–May: 12.30pm–3pm, 8pm–11pm Tue–Sat, 12.30pm–3pm Sun; Jun, Jul & Sep: 12.30pm–3pm, 8pm–11pm Tue–Sat. **Closed** Aug, 1 wk at Christmas. **&** **⊞** **Y** **★** **⊠** AE, DC, MC, V. **(L)(L)(L)(L)**

Historic home of Roman cuisine for over 100 years, Checchino specializes in authentic dishes using the *quinto quarto* (offal, intestines, tripe and tail), originally discarded by the old slaughterhouse opposite. At the old convent tables under vaulted ceilings, with an open fire in winter, Ninetta Mariani and her two *sommelier* sons offer traditional *rigatoni alla pajata*, *coda alla vaccinara*, *crostata di ricotta*, a superb cheese tray and an extraordinary wine selection. Carved into the artificial Monte de' Cocci (made from broken amphoras), its cool, natural wine cellar deserves a special visit.

TRASTEVERE

Da Lucia

Vicolo del Mattonato 2. **Map** 7 B1.
(06-580 36 01. **Open** 12.30pm–
3.30pm, 7.30pm–11pm Tue–Sun.
Closed 2 wks Aug, 1 wk Christmas.
🔒 🔥 🎫 Ⓛ

Head for this popular, well-worn
trattoria off Via Garibaldi if you
want to enjoy genuine Roman
cooking. You won't be disappointed by the *pasta e ceci,
baccalà, pollo con i peperoni*
(chicken with peppers), boiled
meats and, incongruously,
Milanese risotto. However, the
service is take it or leave it, and
the choice of wine is basic. The
outdoor tables make a more
attractive dining area in summer.

Fricandò

Vicolo del Leopardo 39A (off Vicolo del
Cedro). **Map** 7 B1. **(** 06-581 47 38.
Open 7pm–late Mon–Sat. **Closed**
16–20 Aug. Ⓥ 🔥 🔒 🎫 🗎 AE,
V. Ⓛ Ⓛ

This small, intimate restaurant
is situated in a narrow *vicolo*
(alleyway) reminiscent of a much
older Rome. Sit at one of the
tables outside, below the lines of
washing strung across the street,
and soak up the atmosphere. The
menu features simple Tuscan
dishes such as fettucine with
rabbit. The food is fresh and all
the pastas and cakes are made
on the premises.

La Cornucopia

Piazza in Piscinula 18. **Map** 8 D1.
(06-580 03 80. **Open** 12.30pm–
3pm, 8pm–11pm Mon–Sat. **Closed**
3 wks Aug–Sep & Christmas. 🍴
🎫 🗎 AE, MC, V. Ⓛ Ⓛ

One of the better fish restaurants
in Trastevere, La Cornucopia is
particularly recommended for its
candlelight, elegant place settings
and, in summer, its comfortable
tables outside in the piazza.
The dishes are predominantly
Mediterranean, with excellent
antipasto, unusual pasta, simply
cooked fish such as *spigola al
vapore* (steamed sea bass) and
selected meats. The Castelli house
white will soften the bill.

Da Paris

Piazza San Calisto 7A.
Map 7 C1. **(** 06-581 53 78.
Open 12.30pm–3pm, 8pm–
11pm Tue–Sat, 12.30pm–3pm
Sun. **Closed** Aug. 🎫 🏮
🗎 AE, DC, MC, V. Ⓛ Ⓛ Ⓛ

This classic Roman-Jewish restaurant is a firm favourite with
choosy diners in Trastevere. Jole
Cappellanti's homemade pasta
and traditional dishes are a must
and include *minestra di arzilla*
(skate) and *trippa* (tripe) *alla
romana*. The *fritto misto vegetale*
is extraordinary, the fish fresh.
There are good desserts and the
owner's personal choice of wines.

L'Isola Felice

Vicolo del Leopardo. **Map** 7 B4.
(06-581 738. **Open** noon–
2.30pm, 9pm–11pm Tue–Sun.
🔒 🔥 🎫 🗎 AE, DC, MC, V, JCB.
Ⓛ Ⓛ Ⓛ

This is the way the Romans spell
intimacy. Tucked away in a tiny
backstreet, L'Isola is a secret that
everyone should know about. The
cuisine blends modern Roman and
traditional rural. The starters are
truly excellent – almost a feast in
themselves – and the main courses
add pleasure upon pleasure.

Romolo nel Giardino della Fornarina

Via Porta Settimiana 8. **Map** 4 D5 &
11 B5. **(** 06-581 82 84. **Open**
noon–3pm, 7.30pm–midnight Tue–
Sun. **Closed** 3–26 Aug. 🔒 🎫 🗎
AE, DC, MC, V. Ⓛ Ⓛ Ⓛ See p210.

A Roman institution, this was said
to be the home of La Fornarina,
Raphael's celebrated mistress
and model, and is best enjoyed
for its atmosphere on a summer
evening. Eat out by candlelight
in the walled courtyard, to the
accompaniment of a melancholy
guitar. The food is Roman,
including fried *mozzarella alla
Fornarina* and *cervella e carciofi*
(brains and artichokes).

Alberto Ciarla

Piazza San Cosimato 40. **Map** 7 C1.
(06-581 86 68. **Open** 8pm–
midnight Mon–Sat. **Closed** 15 days
Aug, 15 days Jan. 🍴 🌿 🎵 🎫
🏮 ★ 🗎 AE, DC, MC, V, JCB.
Ⓛ Ⓛ Ⓛ Ⓛ

This is the quintessential restaurant for fish lovers – at least, those
who are prepared to splash out.
Elegant, dramatically dark decor
is relieved by candlelight. Perfectly executed dishes fluctuate
between the traditional and
inventive, always with an eye to
what's at its best in the market,
ranging from simple to elabo-
rately creative. A few innovatory
meat dishes can be had. Ciarla,
the president of the Italian
sommeliers, provides an exceptional wine list, with the emphasis
on French and Californian wines.

JANICULUM

Antico Arco

Piazzale Aurelio 7. **Map** 7 A1.
(06-581 52 74. **Open** 8pm–
midnight Tue–Sat, noon–3pm,
8pm–midnight Sun. 🏮 ★ 🗎 AE,
DC, MC, V. Ⓛ Ⓛ

Since changing management a few
years ago, the Antico Arco has
become one of Rome's best places
to eat innovative food and drink
excellent wines without spending
a fortune. Choose from a long list
of interesting wines from all over
Italy and France (with a few
dozen labels available by the
glass). The menu is based on
classic Roman dishes using
seasonal ingredients, but they
have been "revisited" and given a
modern flair. The low-key, bistro-
style decor makes it suitable for
an intimate meal as well as
convivial dining.

VATICAN

Macondo

Via Marianna Dionigi 37. **Map** 4 E2.
(06-321 26 01. **Open** 8pm–11pm
Mon–Sat. 🌿 Ⓥ 🎫 Ⓛ Ⓛ

This brightly decorated, friendly
little Caribbean restaurant is just
the place to visit if you fancy a
change from Italian cuisine, but
be warned, you'll be turned away
if you haven't made a reservation.
The food is fresh, light and
plentiful and is always beautifully
presented. The star dish is
pabellon criollo (strips of beef,
black beans, rice and fried
plantain). Try such starters as
patacones y guacamole (plantains
and avocado dip), remembering
to leave room for desserts such as
the banana cake soaked in banana
liquor. There is a good selection
of wines at various prices as well
as cocktails and Venezuelan rums.

San Luigi

Via Mocenigo 10. **Map** 3 B2.
(06-39 72 07 04. **Open**
noon–3pm, 8pm–11pm Mon–Sat.
Closed Aug. 🍴 Ⓥ 🎵 🗎 AE,
DC, MC, V. Ⓛ Ⓛ Ⓛ

If you have just spent hours in the
Vatican Museums, the pleasure
of a relaxing restaurant with 19th-
century decor and soft music will
soothe your aching limbs. A set
menu is on offer at lunchtime and
a choice of traditional Neapolitan
and creative dishes in the evening.
Pastas and desserts are particularly
successful. There's a choice of
good French and Italian wines.

Les Etoiles

Via Vitelleschi 34. **Map** 3 C2.
C 06-689 34 34. **Open** 12.30pm–
2.30pm, 7.30pm–10.30pm daily.
T ⊞ **Y** ⪒ 🖾 AE, DC, MC, V,
JCB. Ⓛ Ⓛ Ⓛ Ⓛ Ⓛ

Located at the top of the Atlante
Star hotel (see p300), this rooftop
restaurant was completely
renovated in 1992, and now
includes free valet parking and a
separate entrance with a lift
leading directly to the restaurant
levels. The restaurant and its
terraces offer panoramic views of
the Rome skyline, including St
Peter's. Speciality dishes include
snails with truffles on pecorino
cheese, quail's eggs on a bed of
rocket with mustard dressing, and
tagliolini (pasta) with clams and
finferli (mushrooms).

VIA VENETO

Andrea

Via Sardegna 28. **Map** 5 C1.
C 06-482 18 91, 06-474 05 57.
Open 12.30pm–3pm, 7.30pm–
11pm Mon–Fri, 7.45pm–11pm Sat.
Closed 2 wks Aug & Christmas.
V ⪒ **Y** 🖾 AE, DC, MC, V, JCB.
Ⓛ Ⓛ Ⓛ

This congenial, refined restaurant
offers a superb array of antipasto,
ranging from humble suppli (rice
croquettes) to regal lobster dishes
(try it in insalata catalana). Try
not to be completely seduced by
the starters; leave room for the
impressive seasonal first and
second courses, and for the
delicious desserts.

Tullio

Via San Nicola da Tolentino 26.
Map 5 B2. **C** 06-474 55 60. **Open**
12.30pm–3pm, 7.30pm–11pm
Mon–Sat. **Closed** Aug. ⪒ 🖾 AE,
DC, MC, V, JCB. Ⓛ Ⓛ Ⓛ

This genuine Tuscan restaurant
is frequented by an enthusiastic
clientele for its generous helpings
and fair prices. Typical dishes
include porcini mushrooms in
every possible form, pasta e
fagioli, grilled meat and fish
and Florentine steaks – served
in agreeable surroundings by
courteous, speedy waiters.

Giovanni

Via Marche 67. **Map** 5 B1.
C 06-482 18 34. **Open** 12.30pm–
3pm, 7.30pm–11pm Mon–Thu,
12.30pm–3pm Fri. **Closed** Aug &
Christmas. 🖾 AE, DC, MC, V.
Ⓛ Ⓛ Ⓛ

A throng of satisfied regulars
crowd this classic, well-established restaurant near Via Veneto.
The efficient, reliable service is
hard to beat. The place is run
along traditional lines by the
Sbrega family, with a strong
regional influence from Lazio
and the Marches. They serve
fresh pasta dishes such as tagliolini
all'amatriciana, vegetable soups,
boned chicken with rice, unbeatable roast lamb, osso buco,
fresh fish and millefeuilles. The
house wines are good.

George's

Via Marche 7. **Map** 5 B2.
C 06-42 08 45 75. **Open** 12.30pm–
3pm, 7.30pm–midnight (piano bar
2am) Mon–Sat. **Closed** Aug. **T** ♫
⊞ **Y** ★ 🖾 AE, DC, MC, V, JCB.
Ⓛ Ⓛ Ⓛ Ⓛ

Visit this slightly tarnished
survivor from the dolce vita era
for its nostalgic air of luxurious
elegance. The softly illuminated
rooms, garden terrace, tinkling
piano music and impeccable
service provide the perfect foil
for George's tempting and
expertly prepared international
dishes. There is also a good
selection of French and Italian
wines on offer.

Le Sans Souci

Via Sicilia 20–24. **Map** 5 C1.
C 06-482 18 14. **Open** 8pm–
midnight Tue–Sun. **Closed** Aug.
V **T** ♫ **Y** ★ 🖾 AE, DC, MC,
V, JCB. Ⓛ Ⓛ Ⓛ Ⓛ

This restaurant has overcome a
glitzy fame to emerge as a sound
exponent of elaborate French
and Italian cuisine. The decor is
black and gold throughout, with
17th-century gilt mirrors and
chandeliers. In the sophisticated
anteroom you can drink an
apéritif at your leisure and consult
the menu and magnificent wine
list. As you might expect, the
service is eagerly efficient.

La Terrazza

Via Ludovisi 49. **Map** 5 B2.
C 06-47 81 21. **Open** noon–3.30pm,
7pm–midnight Mon–Sat. **Closed** 2
wks Aug, 25 Dec–6 Jan. ⊞ 🖾 AE,
DC, MC, V, JCB. Ⓛ Ⓛ Ⓛ Ⓛ

Positioned in the roof garden of
the Eden Hotel (see p301), this
spacious establishment has gained
a reputation in its own right. The
menu is traditional Italian – in this
case a guarantee of quality – and
the kitchen is just about as
spotless as spotless gets. As you
might expect from its location, the
views of the city are peerless.

VILLA BORGHESE

Al Ceppo

Via Panama 2. **Map** 2 F3.
C 06-841 96 96. **Open** 12.30pm–
3pm, 8pm–11pm Tue–Sun. **Closed** 2
wks Aug. **V** ⪒ ⊞ **Y** 🖾 AE,
DC, MC, V. Ⓛ Ⓛ Ⓛ

In 20 years, two sisters from the
Marches, Cristina and Marisella
Milozzi, have won over an
affectionate following of regulars
in this exclusive, notoriously
diffident area of Rome, attracted
by the consistently reliable food
and a hospitable yet refined family
atmosphere. The strictly seasonal
menu concentrates on traditional
dishes with a touch of daily
invention, as well as excellent
grilled meats, homemade
desserts and Italian wines.

Relais la Piscine dell'Aldrovandi Palace Hotel

Via G Mangili 6. **Map** 2 D4.
C 06-321 61 26. **Open** 12.30pm–
3pm, 7.30pm–11pm daily. **|O|** ⪒
⪒ **T** **Y** ★ 🖾 AE, DC,
MC, V. Ⓛ Ⓛ Ⓛ Ⓛ

The autonomous restaurant of
the Aldrovandi Palace Hotel is
especially beautiful in summer
when tables are set outside on
the terrace by the pool. Jean Luc
Frenat, the young Breton chef,
produces an excellent, typically
Mediterranean nouvelle cuisine,
using prime meat and fish,
vegetables and herbs. This is
accompanied by meticulous
service, wonderful desserts and
a fully comprehensive wine list.
Business lunches are a speciality.

Relais le Jardin dell'Hotel Lord Byron

Via Giuseppe de Notaris 5. **Map** 2 D4.
C 06-322 04 04. **Open** 12.30pm–
2.30pm, 8pm–10.30pm Mon–Sat.
Closed Aug. **Y** ★ 🖾 AE, DC,
MC, V, JCB. Ⓛ Ⓛ Ⓛ Ⓛ

For many, this is Rome's greatest
restaurant, located in the quiet,
exclusive and green area of
Parioli. Diners here are undaunted
by absolutely top prices, high-
class, impeccably correct service,
and haute cuisine at its finest. The
inspired chef draws predominantly
on traditional Italian regional
cooking, with exceptionally
creative combinations of fruit,
herbs and vegetables as partners
to top-quality meats and fish.
To finish, there are homemade
desserts and pastries; the list of
French, Italian and Californian
wines is outstanding.

For key to symbols see p291

Light Meals and Snacks

WHERE SHOULD YOU GO for a casual bite to eat? Rome has the ability to satisfy the all-important stomach at most hours of the day and night. A sound network of *gelaterie, pasticcerie*, pizzerias, wine bars, *rosticcerie* and *tavole calde* mean that good food and drink are always just around the corner.

Start with a classic breakfast at your local stand-up bar: cappuccino and a hot *cornetto* (like a croissant). A heavy morning's sightseeing may leave you ready for an apéritif in one of Rome's elegant 19th-century bars, followed by lunch at a wine bar or Roman-style fast food. In the afternoon there are plenty of opportunities for coffee and cakes at a *pasticceria,* while the late-night bars, especially those with tables outside, are a source of endless entertainment, where you can sip a drink or linger over the final ice cream of the day.

PIZZERIAS

ROMAN PIZZERIAS are the natural choice for in-formal eating: they are noisy, convivial and fun. Most open only in the evening, when the wood ovens are lit and the embers glow reassuringly up until last orders. Look out for the *forno a legna* (wood-burning oven) sign – electric ovens simply don't produce the same results. In the best pizzerias you sit in view of the vast marble slabs where the *pizzaioli* flatten the dough and whip the pizzas in and out of the oven on long-handled pallets. The turnaround is fast, so you may not be encouraged to linger.

The running order is straightforward: you might have a *bruschetta* (toasted tomato or garlic bread) to start, some *suppli* (fried rice croquettes) or some fried courgette flowers. Alternatively, try some *filetti di baccalà* (battered cod fillets) or per-haps a plate of *cannellini* beans in oil. Follow this with a *calzone* (folded-over pizza) or the classic Roman pizza – round, thin and crunchy – with various toppings: the basic *margherita* (tomato, mozzarella), *napoletana* (tomato, anchovies, mozza-rella), *capricciosa* (ham, artichokes, eggs, olives) and anything else the *pizzaiolo* fancies. Draught beer is the classic thing to drink, but

wine is always available. You should expect to pay around L15,000 a head for a meal.

The most representative Roman pizzerias, from all points of view, are **Da Baffetto**, which can be located by looking for the queue outside, and its offspring, **La Montecarlo**. **Remo** in Testaccio and **Ivo** in Trastevere, where tables line the road in summer, are also typically Roman. Another place not to be missed is **Panattoni**, where a huge variety of customers patiently queue for a pave-ment seat on Viale Trastevere in summer, or clamour for one of the marble-topped tables (from which it gets its well-known nickname "the mortuary") inside.

ENOTECHE (WINE BARS)

ENOTECHE offer a fine selection of wines from Italy and around the world. They are usually run by experts, keen to share their knowledge and advise on the best combinations of wine and food. Some *enoteche* are simply shops for browsing. Others like **Achilli al Parlamento** and **Bevitoria Navona** offer the traditional *mescita* – wine and cham-pagne tasting by the glass, accompanied by snacks and canapés. Their prices are reasonable: about L1,500 for a glass on tap, L3,000 upwards for a quality wine, to about

L8,000 for champagne. **Vineria Reggio** in Campo de' Fiori is a typical spot for *mescita*, especially at night. Here business people, residents and tourists alike meet for an apéritif or to share a bottle at a table.

For more substantial food for as little as L20–25,000 a head, try the bistro- or restaurant-style *enoteche*, open at lunch and until late. Particularly recommended are the innovative **Cul de Sac**, **Trimani Wine Bar**, the tiny **Il Tajut** serving specialities from Friuli, and **Cavour 313**.

BIRRERIE (BEER HOUSES)

ROMAN BIRRERIE had their heyday in the early years of the 20th century and many have since closed. However, the few that have survived the competition from subsequent pizzerias and *enoteche* are some of the best: German-style beer houses where you can still enjoy beer and substantial snacks in traditional wood-panelled rooms. The permanently crowded **Fratelli Tempera**, serving classic beer-drinkers' fare, is worth a visit for its authentic, turn-of-the-century air of decadence. Another place which attracts Italians and foreigners alike is the **Birreria Viennese/Wiener Bierhaus** with its excellent Transylvanian specialities, which come heaped gener-ously on a wooden plate. If you eat here, or in the **Birreria Bavarese**, you'll spend around L30–50,000. Elsewhere will be cheaper if you want to concentrate more on drinking.

FAST FOOD

ROME HAS PLENTY of homespun fast food options for when you need something quick and inexpensive to eat. Slices of freshly baked pizza are available for a couple of thousand lire from *pizza al taglio* shops. Many of these places also sell spit-roasted chickens, *suppli* and other traditional pizzeria fare. *Rosticcerie* offer deliciously tasty roast chicken and potatoes as well as ready-made pasta dishes, cooked vegetables, salads and desserts – useful for picnics or for making a complete takeaway meal. For a similarly speedy but sit-down snack, bars with a *tavola calda* (hot table) have the same kind of selection, especially at lunchtime; one of the largest and most popular is **Il Delfino** at Largo Argentina. Vegetarians should seek out the **Centro Macrobiotico** near Piazza di Spagna. The **McDonald's** in Piazza di Spagna also offers a good range of fresh mixed salads.

Most *alimentari* (grocery shops) will make you up a *panino* (filled roll). Especially delicious are **Paladini's** hot plain pizza pockets stuffed with choices from the shop's counters, where you can also have a glass of wine. Try one of the region's specialities if you see the sign *porchetta*: whole aromatic roast pig with crackling, sliced into *rosette* (rolls) or thick country-bread sandwiches – there is a good stall selling these at the tram stop in Viale Carlo Felice opposite San Giovanni in Laterano. At the hole-in-the-wall **Er Buchetto** you can even sit down in relative comfort with a glass of wine. For a really typical Roman snack, make a late-afternoon detour to **Filetti di Baccalà** serving, as the name suggests, fried cod fillets and little else.

BARS, CAFÉS AND TEA ROOMS

ROMAN BARS are the city's lifeline: they are places to meet, eat, drink, pick up milk, buy coffee, make phone calls or find a toilet. Some of them are small, stand-up, basic one-counter bars for grabbing a quick *cornetto* and cappuccino and some may be more luxurious, grandiose affairs doubling as cake shop, ice cream parlour, tea room or *tavola calda*, or all of these in one. Most open early at around 7.30am and close late,

particularly at weekends, at around midnight or 2am. In summer, tables cover all the available outdoor space, and the fight for a place in the shade begins.

Traditionally elegant – and pricy – bars for people watching are the admirably located **Rosati** and **Doney**, as well as **Caffè Greco**, the 19th-century haunt of artists, writers and composers *(see p133)*, or the carefully restored **La Caffettiera** at the Pantheon. Another popular and well-established bar is the **Antico Caffè della Pace**. **Caffè Flores** (with piano music) and **Selarum** in Trastevere are recommended for late-night drinks, as is **Zodiaco** on Monte Mario for its panoramic views.

Earlier in the day Rome's favoured meeting places are its tea rooms. **Babington's** *(see p134)* is the place to go for an expensive cup of tea and cakes in genteel surroundings, while **Dolci e Doni** is more relaxed. Try a *gran caffè speciale* at the counters of **Sant'Eustachio**, or one of Rome's best espressos at **Tazza d'Oro**. **Ciampini al Café du Jardin** with its garden setting and roof-top views is unbeatable in summer, particularly at the apéritif hour, as is the **Bar Parnaso** in Parioli.

Museum cafés in Rome are seldom open, and even when they are, few are really worth a visit. A welcome exception however is the café of the **Palazzo delle Esposizioni** *(see p164)*, which is open throughout the day and serves an attractive selection of snacks and drinks.

PASTICCERIE (PASTRY SHOPS)

ON SUNDAY mornings you'll often see Romans emerging from the local *pasticceria* with a beautifully wrapped package. This can contain dainty individual pastries, whole cakes or tarts, traditional Easter *colombe* (doves) or Christmas *panettoni* – huge cakes with raisins and candied peel – all for consumption by large

gatherings of friends, relatives or family after lunch. The window displays of Rome's cake shops are often fantastic. These, and the aroma of brewing coffee, might tempt you in for a hot *cornetto* or a *brioche* in the early morning, a midday *pizzetta* or savoury tart, or choux pastry or fruit tart later in the afternoon.

GELATERIE (ICE CREAM PARLOURS)

ICE CREAM *(gelato)* is one of summer's particular delights, and nowhere more so than in Rome. Every well-equipped bar has its tubs of homemade ice cream, and in the *gelaterie* the choice is endless – water-ices made with a phenomenal variety of fruit; lemon and coffee *granite* (crushed ice); as well as more exotic ice cream specialities such as rice, *zuppa inglese* (English trifle), *zabaglione*, *tiramisù* and After Eight. Choose as many varieties as the size of your cone or cup will hold, topped with cream *(panna)* and then go for a stroll, or else take a break and be served with an ornate creation with all the trimmings at a table. *Gelaterie* are open all day until late at night, when they become evening entertainment.

Tre Scalini in Piazza Navona is a famous spot for enjoying the pricy, yet so heavenly, chocolate *tartufo*, while a summer evening in EUR, especially with children, nearly always ends in a trip to **Giolitti**, a historic ice cream name. Try also the strategically placed, crowded original near the Pantheon *(see p109)*, which serves coffee and pastries as well as ice cream. In the same area is the popular **Gelateria della Palma**.

Adults may prefer to pick their night-time treat at **Chalet del Lago**, again in EUR, while sitting beside the lake. If you come across a small kiosk bearing the sign *grattachecche* (most likely in Trastevere and Testaccio), try one of Rome's oldest traditions – ice grated on the spot and enlivened with a variety of classic flavourings.

DIRECTORY

FORUM

Pizzerias
Alle Carrette
Vicolo delle Carrette 19,
off Via della Madonna
dei Monti.
Map 5 B5.

PIAZZA DELLA ROTONDA

Pizzerias
Barroccio
Via dei Pastini 13.
Map 4 F4 & 12 D2.

Er Faciolaro
Via dei Pastini 123.
Map 4 F4 & 12 D2.

Wine Bars
Achilli al Parlamento
Via dei Prefetti 15.
Map 4 F3 & 12 D1.

Corsi
Via del Gesù 88.
Map 4 F4 & 12 E3.

Spiriti
Via di Sant'Eustachio 5.
Map 4 F4 & 12 D3.

Bars, Cafés and Tea Rooms
La Caffettiera
Piazza di Pietra 65.
Map 4 F3 & 12 E2.

Camilloni
Piazza Sant'Eustachio 54.
Map 4 F4 & 12 D3.

Ciampini
Piazza S. Lorenzo in
Lucina 29.
Map 4 F3 & 12 D1.

Sant'Eustachio
Piazza Sant'Eustachio 82.
Map 4 F4 & 12 D3.

Tazza d'Oro
Via degli Orfani 82/84.
Map 4 F4 & 12 D2.

Teichner
Piazza S. Lorenzo in
Lucina 17.
Map 4 F3 & 12 E1.

Ice Cream Parlors
Fiocco di Neve
Via del Pantheon 51.
Map 4 F4 & 12 D2.

Gelateria della Palma
Via della Maddalena 20.
Map 4 F3 & 12 D2.

Giolitti
Via Uffici del Vicario 40.
Map 4 F3 & 12 D2.

PIAZZA NAVONA

Pizzerias
Da Baffetto
Via del Governo
Vecchio 114.
Map 4 E4 & 11 B3.

Corallo
Via del Corallo 10.
Map 4 E4 & 11 B3.

La Montecarlo
Vicolo Savelli 12/13.
Map 4 E4 & 11 C3.

Wine Bars
Bevitoria Navona
Piazza Navona 72.
Map 4 E4 & 11 C2.

Cul de Sac
Piazza Pasquino 73.
Map 4 E4 & 11 C3.

Fast Food
Paladini
Via del Governo
Vecchio 28/29.
Map 4 E4 & 11 B3.

Bars, Cafés and Tea Rooms
Antico Caffè della Pace
Via della Pace 5.
Map 4 E4 & 11 C3.

Pastry Shops
Bella Napoli
Corso Vittorio
Emanuele II 246.
Map 4 E4 & 11 B3.

Ice Cream Parlors
Tre Scalini
Piazza Navona 28.
Map 4 E4 & 11 C3.

PIAZZA DI SPAGNA

Pizzerias
La Capricciosa
Largo dei Lombardi 8.
Map 4 F2.

Il Leoncino
Via del Leoncino 28.
Map 4 F2.

Wine Bars
Antica Enoteca di Via della Croce
Via della Croce 76 B.
Map 5 A2.

Buccone
Via di Ripetta 19.
Map 4 F1.

Beer Houses
Birreria Bavarese
Via Vittoria 47.
Map 5 A2.

Birreria Viennese/ Wiener Bierhaus
Via della Croce 21.
Map 5 A2.

Fast Food
Centro Macrobiotico
Via della Vite 14.
Map 5 A3.

Fior Fiore
Via della Croce 17/18.
Map 5 A2.

McDonald's
Piazza di Spagna 46.
Map 5 A2.

Bars, Cafés and Tea Rooms
Babington's Tea Rooms
Piazza di Spagna 23.
Map 5 A2.

Caffè Greco
Via Condotti 86.
Map 5 A2.

Ciampini al Café du Jardin
Viale Trinità dei Monti.
Map 5 A2.

Dolci e Doni
Via delle Carrozze 85 A.
Map 4 F2.

Rosati
Piazza del Popolo 5.
Map 4 F1.

CAMPO DE' FIORI

Wine Bars
Bottega del Vino da Bleve
Via Santa Maria del
Pianto 9 A/11.
Map 4 F5 & 12 D5.

Il Goccetto
Via dei Banchi Vecchi 14.
Map 4 D4 & 11 B3.

Vineria Reggio
Piazza Campo de' Fiori 15.
Map 4 E4 & 11 C4.

Fast Food
Il Delfino
Corso Vittorio
Emanuele II 67.
Map 4 F4 & 12 D4.

Filetti di Baccalà
Largo dei Librari 88.
Map 4 E5 & 11 C4.

Da Giovanni
Piazza Campo de' Fiori 39.
Map 4 E4 & 11 C4.

Bars, Cafés and Tea Rooms
Alberto Pica
Via della Seggiola 12.
Map 4 F5 & 12 D5.

Caffè Flores
Lungotevere dei
Vallati 25/27.
Map 4 E5 & 11 C5.

Pastry Shops
Bernasconi
Largo di Torre
Argentina 1.
Map 4 F4 & 12 D4.

La Dolceroma
Via del Portico
d'Ottavia 20B.
Map 4 F5 & 12 E5.

Il Forno del Ghetto
Via del Portico
d'Ottavia 2.
Map 4 F5 & 12 E5.

QUIRINAL

Pizzerias
Est! Est! Est!
Via Principe Amedeo 4A.
Map 6 D3.

I Rioni
Via dei SS. Quattro
Coronati 24.
Map 9 B1.

Wine Bars
Cavour 313
Via Cavour 313.
Map 5 B5.

Beer Houses
Fratelli Tempera
Via San Marcello 19.
Map 5 A4 & 12 F3.

Fast Food
Bar del Palazzo del
Yogobar
Via Mazzarino 8–10.
Map 5 B4.

Er Buchetto
Via del Viminale 2.
Map 5 C3.

McDonald's
Piazza della Repubblica
40. **Map** 5 C3.

Nadia e Davide
Via Milano 33.
Map 5 B4.

**Bars, Cafés and
Tea Rooms**
Palazzo delle
Esposizioni
Via Milano 9. **Map** 5 B4.

Pastry Shops
Dagnino
Via Vittorio Emanuele
Orlando 75. **Map** 5 C2.

TERMINI

Pizzerias
La Bruschetta
Via Sardegna 39.
Map 5 B1.

Formula Uno
Via degli Equi 13.
Map 6 F4.

Le Maschere
Via degli Umbri 16.
Map 6 F4.

Wine Bars
Trimani Wine Bar
Via Cernaia 37B.
Map 6 D2.

Beer Houses
Rive Gauchez
Via dei Sabelli 43.
Map 6 F4.

ESQUILINE

Beer Houses
Marconi
Via di Santa Prassede 9C.
Map 6 D4.

Fast Food
Cottini
Via Merulana 286.
Map 6 D4.

Palazzo del Freddo di
Giovanni Fassi
Via Principe Eugenio
65/67.
Map 6 E5.

**Bars, Cafés and
Tea Rooms**
Ristoro della Salute
Piazza del Colosseo 2.
Map 9 A1.

LATERAN

Fast Food
Viale Carlo Felice
Porchetta Stall
Viale Carlo Felice.
Map 10 D1.

Ice Cream Parlors
Premiate Gelaterie
Fantasia
Via La Spezia 100/102.
Map 10 E1.

AVENTINE

Pizzerias
Remo
Piazza Santa Maria
Liberatrice 44.
Map 8 D3.

Wine Bar
Palombi
Piazza Testaccio 48.
Map 8 D3.

TRASTEVERE

Pizzerias
Almacri
Via F. Benaglia 3.
Map 7 B4.

Dar Poeta
Vicolo del Bologna 45.
Map 4 E5 & 11 B5.

Ivo
Via di San Francesco a
Ripa 158.
Map 7 C1.

Panattoni
Viale Trastevere 53.
Map 7 C1.

Ar Popi Popi
Via delle Fratte di
Trastevere 45. **Map** 7 C1.
Piccola Montecarlo
Via Dandolo 26.
Map 7 C2.

Wine Bars
Il Cantiniere di Santa
Dorotea
Via di S. Dorotea 9.
Map 4 D5 & 11 B5.

Ferrara
Via del Moro 1/A.
Map 7 C1.

Fast Food
McDonald's
Piazza Sonnino 39/40.
Map 8 D1.

**Bars, Cafés and
Tea Rooms**
Selarum
Via dei Fienaroli 12.
Map 7 C1.

Pastry Shops
Valzani
Via del Moro 37B.
Map 7 C1.

Ice Cream Parlors
La Fonte della Salute
Via Cardinale Marmaggi
2/4/6. **Map** 7 C1.

Sacchetti
Piazza Santa Maria
Cosima 61. **Map** 7 C1.

VATICAN

Pizzerias
Pizzeria San Marco
Via Tacito 29. **Map** 4 D2.

Il Tempio della Pizza
Viale Giulio Cesare 91.
Map 3 C1.

Wine Bars
Il Simposio di Piero
Costantini
Piazza Cavour 16.
Map 4 E2.

Beer Houses
Penny Lane
Via dei Gracchi 35.
Map 3 C2.

VIA VENETO

Wine Bars
Semidivino
Via Alessandria 230.
Map 6 D1.

**Bars, Cafés and
Tea Rooms**
Doney
Via Veneto 145.
Map 5 B2.

EUR

Fast Food
McDonald's
Piazzale Don Luigi Sturzo
21/22.

**Bars, Cafés and
Tea Rooms**
Chalet del Lago
Lake, EUR.

Ice Cream Parlors
Giolitti
Casina dei Tre Laghi,
Viale Oceania 90.

FURTHER AFIELD

Wine Bars
Guerrini
Viale Regina Margherita
205/207.

Il Tajut
Via Albenga 44.
Map 10 E3.

Fast Food
Svizzera Siciliana
Piazza Pio XI 10/11.

**Bars, Cafés and
Tea Rooms**
Bar Parnaso
Piazza delle Muse 22.
Map 2 E2.

Il Cigno
Viale Parioli 16.
Map 2 E3.

Duse
Via Eleonora Duse 1E.
Map 2 F2.

Pannocchi
Via Bergamo 56.
Map 6 D1.

San Filippo
Via di Villa San Filippo
8/10. **Map** 2 F2.

Zodiaco
Viale Parco Mellini 90.

Pastry Shops
Euclide
Via F. Civinini 119.
Map 2 D3.

SHOPS AND MARKETS

ROME HAS BEEN a thriving centre for design and cosmopolitan shopping since ancient times. In the heyday of the Empire the finest craftsmen were drawn to Rome, and artefacts and produce of all kinds, including gold, furs, wine and slaves, were imported from far-flung corners of the Empire to service the needs of the wealthy Roman population.

Shopping in Rome today in many ways reflects this diverse tradition. Italian designers have

Window shopping in Rome, an absorbing pastime

an international reputation for their luxuriously chic style in fashion, knitwear and leather goods (especially shoes and handbags) as well as in interior design, fabrics, ceramics and glass. The artisan-craftsman tradition is strong and the love of good design filters through into the smallest items. It is not a city for bargains (though often better value than Florence or Milan), but the joys of window shopping here will offer plenty of compensation.

BEST BUYS

LEATHER GOODS of all kinds, including shoes and bags, are a strong point. Ready-to-wear Italian designer clothes are not cheap, but they are certainly less expensive than in other countries. Armani jeans are a good example *(see p327)*. You are also likely to find designer lighting fixtures, for example, at lower prices here. Both modern and traditional Italian ceramics and handicrafts can be very beautifully made and, if you have time to wander around the back streets, really unusual and individual gifts can often be found.

SALES

SALE TIME *(saldi)* is from mid-July to mid-September and the period from just before Christmas to the first week in March. Top designers

(see p326) slash prices by half, but their clothes are still very expensive even then. Good bargains can be found in the young designer wear shops *(see p327)* and good-quality large shoe sizes are sold off very cheaply (most Italians have small feet). Both of the Cesari shops *(see p327 and p333)* are well-known for their sales. In general, though, sales in Rome do not offer huge discounts.

Both the original and the sale price should be quoted on each reduced item. *Liquidazioni* (closing down sales) are usually genuine and can sometimes be worth investigating. However, other signs in shop windows such as *vendite promozionali* (special introductory prices) and *sconti* (discounts) are often only lures to get you into the shop. The sign on the door saying *entrata libera* means "browsers welcome".

Antiques at Acanto *(see p336)*

WHEN TO SHOP

SHOPS ARE GENERALLY open from 9am to 1pm and from 3.30pm to 7.30pm (4pm to 8pm in the summer months). Some of the shops in the centre stay open all day from 10.30am to 7.30pm.

Most shops are closed on Sunday (except immediately before Christmas). Shops are also closed on Monday morning, apart from most food stores, which close on Thursday afternoons in winter and Saturday afternoons in summer.

August brings the city to a virtual standstill as Roman families escape the heat to the sea or the mountains. Signs saying *chiuso per ferie* (closed for vacation) appear everywhere in the shops. Most shops close for at least two weeks around 15 August, the national holiday.

Flower stalls in Piazza Campo de' Fiori *(see p338)*

SHOPPING ETIQUETTE

APART FROM a few department stores, most Roman shops are small, specializing in just one field. Browsing at leisure may at first seem daunting if you are used to large shopping centres. Customers will almost always receive better attention if they dress smartly – the emphasis on *fare la bella figura* (making a good impression) is taken seriously.

Stylish leather gloves on display

Sizes are not always uniform, so it's wise to try clothes on if possible before buying, since refunds and exchanges are not usually given.

HOW TO PAY

MOST SHOPS now accept all the major credit cards, whose signs are displayed on the shop window. Some will also accept foreign currency, though the exchange rate may not be good. When you make a purchase you are bound by Italian law to leave the shop with a *scontrino fiscale* (receipt). You can try asking for a discount if paying cash and you may be lucky, though many shops have a *prezzi fissi* (fixed prices) sign.

VAT EXEMPTION

VALUE ADDED TAX – VAT (IVA in Italy) – ranges from 12% on clothing to 35% on luxury items such as jewellery and furs. Marked or advertised prices normally include the IVA. It is possible for non-European Union citizens to

Craftsmen near Piazza Navona

obtain an IVA refund for individual purchases that exceed L650,000, but be prepared for a long and bureaucratic process. The simplest method is to shop at a place displaying the "Euro Free Tax" sign. Present your passport when you make your purchase, and fill in a form from the shop; the shop then deducts the IVA, gives you a copy of the form, and sends their copy to the Euro Free Tax Organization in Milan which will then deal with the paperwork.

If you wish to buy something from a shop which is not part of the "Euro Free Tax" scheme, you must get the Italian customs to stamp the vendor's receipt at your departure, showing them the purchased article, and then post the stamped receipt back to the shop, who should then send you a refund.

Mercato delle Stampe *(see p338)*

DEPARTMENT STORES AND SHOPPING CENTRES

DEPARTMENT STORES, known as *grandi magazzini*, are few and far between in Rome. **La Rinascente** and **Coin** are good for ready-to-wear clothes, household linens and haberdashery, and have well-stocked perfume counters. La Rinascente give 10% discount to tourists on perfumes and cosmetics if you show your passport. The **Standa** and **Upim** chain stores offer moderately-priced medium-quality clothes and household goods.

Another alternative for the zealous shopper is to head for one of Rome's two shopping centres. **Cinecittà Due Centro Commerciale**, built in 1988, offers around a 100 shops plus bars, banks

Bargains in Via Sannio *(see p339)*

and restaurants within easy reach of the centre by Metro (line A to Cinecittà). An even bigger centre, called **I Granai**, has now opened in Via Laurentina, reachable by Metro (line B to Laurentina).

Cinecittà Due Centro Commerciale
Via Palmiro Togliatti 2.
[06-722 09 10.

Coin
Piazzale Appio 7. **Map** 10 D2.
[06-708 00 20.

I Granai
Via Rigamonti 100.
[06-51 95 57 77.

La Rinascente
Via del Corso 189. **Map** 5 A3 & 12 E2.
[06-679 76 91.

Piazza Fiume. **Map** 6 D1.
[06-884 12 31.

Standa
Via Cola di Rienzo 153. **Map** 4 D2.
[06-324 32 83.

Viale Trastevere 62. **Map** 7 C2.
[06-581 60 36.

Via Appia Nuova 181–3. **Map** 10 D2.
[06-702 48 96.

Upim
Via del Tritone 172. **Map** 5 A3.
[06-678 33 36.

Via Nazionale 211. **Map** 5 C3.
[06-48 45 02.

Via Gioberti 64. **Map** 6 D4.
[06-446 55 79.

Rome's Best: Shopping Streets and Markets

THE MOST INTERESTING shops in Rome are in the old centre, so shopping is easy to combine with sightseeing. The shops are often housed in medieval or Renaissance buildings and their window displays can be exquisite. Just like shopkeepers in past centuries, traders tend to specialize in one type of merchandise. Street names often refer to the old tradesmen: locksmiths in Via dei Chiavari, leather jerkin makers in Via dei Giubbonari and chairs in Via dei Sediari. Today, antique merchants have taken over from the rosary sellers on Via dei Coronari. The top names in fashion and modern design dominate the Via Condotti area, and the artisan-craftsman tradition is still strong around Campo de' Fiori and Piazza Navona.

Via dei Coronari
Art Nouveau and antiques enthusiasts will love browsing in the shops that line this charming street just northwest of Piazza Navona. But be prepared for high prices as most of the items are imported.

Via Cola di Rienzo
Situated close to the Vatican Museums, this long wide street has the finest food shops and is also good for clothes, books and gifts.

Via del Pellegrino
Book and art shops abound here next to working artisans in the historic centre. Don't miss the mirror-lined alley near Campo de' Fiori.

Via dei Cappellari
This narrow, medieval street is a great place for watching furniture restorers and other artisans plying their crafts in the open air.

Porta Portese
You can buy anything from antiques to a tin whistle at Trastevere's Sunday morning flea market. (See p339.)

Via Margutta
Up-market antique shops mix with genteel restaurants on this peaceful, cobbled street.

Via del Babuino
This street is renowned for designer furniture, lighting and glass, as well as interesting antique and fashion shops.

Via Veneto

Quirinal

Capitol

Forum

Esquiline

Palatine

Lateran

Caracalla

DESIGNER SHOPPING
All the well-known stars of the Italian fashion scene, plus exclusive jewellers, gift shops, shoe designers and tailors, are concentrated in this cluster of chic and stylish shopping streets by the Spanish Steps *(see pp326–31)*. Romans love to stroll here in the early evening.

MISSONI

GIORGIO ARMANI

TRUSSARDI

GUCCI

valentino

VIA CONDOTTI

VIA BORGOGNONA

VIA DEL CORSO

FENDI

VIA FRATTINA

PIAZZA DI SPAGNA

Max Mara

Via Borgognona
Crowds flock here to buy, or just gaze at, high-fashion clothes, shoes, leather bags and other accessories.

0 metres 500

0 yards 500

Testaccio Market
A visual feast of fruit and vegetables greets the eye in this lively market. (See p338.)

Men's and Women's Fashion

ITALY IS ONE of the leading lights in high-class fashion, or *alta moda*. Many of the most famous designers are based in Milan, but Rome is home to a cluster of sophisticated and internationally distinguished fashion houses. There is also a wonderful selection of *alta moda* shops. Boutiques displaying an eclectic mix of designer goods rub shoulders with showrooms devoted to single collections. But even for those of us unable to splash out on genuine designer-wear, much fun can be gained from a stroll down the exclusive streets that radiate out from the Piazza di Spagna, as some of the window displays are truly spectacular.

The "atelier" made-to-measure fashions are beyond most pockets, but the designers also offer ready-to-wear alternatives in their boutiques. These are not cheap, but cost far less than a tailor-made garment.

to go – its Roman showrooms have exclusive rights to the original couture collections of avant-garde stylists such as Dolce & Gabbana and Moschino, plus Europeans such as Jean-Paul Gaultier. **MaxMara** also has a number of branches here. Chic suits and separates are the main-stays of this popular label. The quality of fabric and finish is superb and, with suits available for around L1,000,000, its prices are much lower than other *alta moda* couture designers' ready-to-wear lines.

WOMEN'S HIGH FASHION

ROME'S MOST famous designer internationally is probably **Valentino**. However, one of the first houses to make a name for Roman fashion was **Sorelle Fontana**. This was *the* salon to be dressed by during the 1950s heyday of Rome's *dolce vita*. Sorelle Fontana has been dressing high society since the 1930s, and stocks a wide selection of ready-to-wear clothes and accessories.

Fendi occupies a large tract of the fashion street, Via Borgognona. Fendi made its name with high-fashion furs, then branched out into leather goods, accessories and ready-to-wear, collaborating with Karl Lagerfeld who designed the coveted double-F logo which emblazons its very collectable products. Third-generation family members design the younger, less expensive Fendissime line.

For well over a decade, **Laura Biagiotti** has reigned as Rome's queen of discreet, conservative couture. From her headquarters in a castle just outside Rome, she designs a range of timelessly elegant knitwear and silk separates for women who don't want to sacrifice style for comfort. She is famous for her use of cashmere and white as well as her creative use of fabrics and quality of finish. Her flagship showroom in Via Borgognona stocks her complete collection, which now includes hosiery,

perfumes, swimwear and leather goods. Her scarves make wonderful presents, and are often reduced in price during sales; other items from previous collections are available in the shop all year round at very good discounts.

Other internationally known Rome-based designers include **Renato Balestra**, who produces tailored suits and glamorous evening wear and **Roberto Capucci**, who uses wonderful textures and fabrics in classy suits. **Mila Schön's** speciality is dramatic evening wear.

Other luminaries of Italian fashion who have shops in Rome include **Giorgio Armani**, **Gianni Versace** and **Trussardi**. A rising star in ready-to-wear is **Genny**. Based in Ancona, the Genny design team produces some really classic, elegant and stylish collections.

If you're looking for clothes from more unconventional designers, **Gente** is the place

MEN'S TAILORS AND DESIGNER WEAR

ITALIAN MEN are every bit as fashion conscious as the women, and there is no shortage of choice in Rome for the well-dressed man. Suits generally begin at around L1,000,000, jackets L750,000 and trousers L250,000.

Most of the "star" designers of women's *alta moda* have a shop for men, like **Valentino Uomo**, **Gianfranco Ferrè** and **Versus by Versace**. The designs are generally less dramatic than the women's, with the accent on understated sophistication and casual sportiness. Valentino's distinctive monogrammed accessories are relatively affordable.

Battistoni is probably the most prestigious designer concentrating on menswear. Giorgio Battistoni and family's fine custom-made shirts and suits have been in demand with film stars and top society for 50 years. **Etro** sells

---

VALENTINO

One of the high priests of Italian fashion, **Valentino Garavani** opened the doors of his Roman studio in 1959 to a distinguished clientele which included Sophia Loren, Audrey Hepburn and Jackie Kennedy, and has never looked back. He has created some of the most dramatic and flattering evening dresses of the last

three decades. In the 1970s he began designing ready-to-wear lines for both men and women alongside his *alta moda* collections, and you can now find his very distinctive "V" logo on a wide range of accessories. Valentino's headquarters is in a huge palazzo in Piazza Mignanelli, and he also has a separate ready-to-wear boutique nearby (see p330).

classically cut clothes and accessories for men and women in exotic Italian-designed printed fabrics.

Ermenegildo Zegna is housed in a Baroque palazzo setting. It offers elegant ready-to-wear, and the master tailor Peppino Scarapazzi will also make to measure. **Davide Cenci** has been a mecca for those in search of the English country gentleman look since 1926. **Brioni** offers traditional tailor-made and own-label ready-to-wear men's clothing. **Trussardi** sells beautifully tailored classics, and **Polidori Uomo** offers sober classics made-to-measure or ready-to-wear from its own gorgeous tweeds and wools. **Testa** has impeccably tailored suits that appeal to younger Romans, and **Enzo Ceci** is popular for ready-to-wear *alta moda* designs. **Degli Effetti** stocks more avant-garde designers such as Romeo Gigli and Jean-Paul Gaultier.

YOUNG DESIGNER WEAR

THERE IS A HUGE choice for the young. Top designers Valentino and Armani offer their particular styles trans-lated into more affordable lines at **Oliver** and **Emporio Armani** (Armani jeans are very good value at around L100,000). Fendi has its Fendissime line, and Max Mara's Penny Black label can be found in its **Max & Co** branches. Targeted at the younger set, these are good places to pick up stylish, sporty numbers.

Timberland is another casual label very popular with young Italians. Average prices are in the region of L100,000 for a shirt, L400,000 for raincoats, L800,000 for suits.

Energie is a big hit and has some of the best window displays in Rome. Teenagers flock here for jeans and T-shirts, both the shop's own and other labels. **Aria**, **Diesel**, and **Box 233** are also very popular. **Eventi** represents the more avant-garde styles – *dark*, as they call it here – fusing Gothic, New Age and punk influences which can result in some outrageous

window creations. **Luna e L'altra** and **Maga Morgana** offer some unconventional designer clothes in a pleasant, friendly atmosphere.

HIGH STREET FASHION

ROME IS NOT a good place to look for everyday wear, since there is a distinct lack of mid-price shops bridging the huge gap between the dazzlingly priced *alta moda* designer exclusives and the ultra-cheap goods sold in markets *(see pp338–9)*. Lower-budget shops do exist, but quality is often poor. If you have the stamina, you may find a bargain along Via del Corso, Via del Tritone, Via Nazionale, Via Cavour, Via Cola di Rienzo, Via Ottaviano or the Via dei Giubbonari.

The most convenient places to shop are department stores like La Rinascente, Standa and Upim *(see p323)*. They may not sound exciting, but you can browse at leisure and find nice things. It's also worth trying shops mentioned under Young Designer Wear – particularly the *alta moda* designers' cheaper lines such as **Emporio Armani** and **Max & Co**. At **Discount dell'Alta Moda** and **Discount System** you can find end-of-season designer labels at 50% less than the boutique prices. **Scala Quattordici** is a good place to buy simple linen dresses made by the owner. And while you don't need to come all the way to Rome to shop at **Benetton**, there are many shops here, which sell the authentic garments in their universal colours.

KNITWEAR

KNITWEAR is a particular strength in Italian design, and in Rome there are plenty of specialist shops. **Laura Biagiotti** is celebrated for her luxurious cashmere separates, and **Missoni Sport** and **Missoni Uomo/Donna** for spectacular kaleidoscopic patterns and colours.

Krizia no longer has a shop in Rome but its sophisti-cated knitware can be purchased at **Liz**.

Choses de Cachemire has cashmere cardigans, pullovers and knitted suits. Other shops, such as the **Luisa Spagnoli** outlets, offer a wider selection, including lower-priced items.

LINGERIE

THIS IS ANOTHER Italian speciality excelling in both style and quality, with lines like La Perla exported world-wide. Lingerie is traditionally sold in top household linen shops *(see p333)* – **Cesari**, for example, is La Perla's main outlet in Rome. There are also boutiques specializing in lingerie and swimwear.

Liberti has a range of swim-wear that's ideal for Italian beaches, as well as lingerie and women's night attire. **Brighenti** is said to be where film stars go for their lingerie.

Tomassini has original designs by Luisa Romagnoli. **Schostal** has more traditional underwear with a very good men's section.

SECOND-HAND CLOTHES

THOSE WHO are willing to browse will find a wide variety of second-hand clothes, whether inspired by a collector's interest in vintage clothes or a low budget. Apart from Via Sannio and Porta Portese markets *(see p339)*, which have many second-hand clothes stalls, the mecca is Via del Governo Vecchio. Among the best shops in this ancient street off Campo de' Fiori are **Mai Visto**, with a range of leather jackets in every colour, as well as clothes from the 1970s onwards, and **Moon**, which has mostly 1920s dresses and some hats and jewellery.

Le Gallinelle offers a marvellous selection of period hats and sells both second-hand and vintage clothes. At **Via dei Chiavari 40** you can find smart clothes dating from the 1920s on-wards, and owner Solange also does some dressmaking on the premises and sells at reasonable prices. Via del Pellegrino is also a good street for shops selling second-hand clothes.

Shoes and Accessories

ITALY'S LEATHER INDUSTRY is renowned all over the world, and shoes, bags and belts are a good buy in Rome. Accessories in general are not just an afterthought but an integral part of an outfit for the well-dressed Roman. The choice of stylish jewellery, scarves, ties and other accessories is excellent.

SHOES

ROME IS FULL of shoe shops, ranging from high-quality stores in the Via Condotti area (where prices tend to start at L250,000) to the more economical shops around the Trevi fountain, and every big market has its bargain shoe stalls on its fringes.

Probably the best-known shop is **Ferragamo** – one of the world's top shoe shops. It stocks classic yet fashion-conscious shoes, as well as women's clothing and leather goods – the silk signature scarves are quite a feature.

Fratelli Rossetti is a close contender for the number one position. Founded by brothers Renzo and Renato more than 30 years ago, this company produces classic men's shoes and beautiful, dressy low-heeled shoes for women that reflect the most up-to-the-minute trends. Along with **Campanile** in Via Condotti it represents the epitome of elegance. Its prices, of course, are sky-high but why not buy something small, and at least you'll have the bag! **Bruno Magli**, Bologna's well-known star, has dressy patent-leather pumps and other classic styles.

Rome's own **Raphael Salato** has three extremely elegant, high-priced shops: his shoes are genuine masterpieces of craftsmanship, and many are made of intricately embroidered leather.

Carlotto Rio is one of the more long-lived shoe shops in Rome, having been in business for over a decade, but it can't compete with **Domus**, which opened in 1938. Carlotto Rio sells made-to-measure footwear for both men and women, particularly shoes for special occasions, and also makes bags to customers' specifications.

Domus sells a selection of high-quality footwear, specializing in classic shoes for women. They also stock a limited range of bags. **De Bach** has colourful shoe styles for women.

Via Frattina has several more moderately-priced shoe shops such as **Pollini**, which makes boots and bags for both men and women in trendy and imaginative styles. **Fausto Santini** stocks original, colourful designs for younger people at more reasonable prices. The same goes for **Cervone**, which specializes in highly colourful women's shoes. **Borino** stocks simple and elegant, low-heeled designs. The **Mr Boots** chain of shops stock a wide range of trendy boots and casual shoes for men and women, while **Dominici** sells witty, smart and affordable footware for women.

LEATHER BAGS AND ACCESSORIES

THE MOST FAMOUS of Rome's leather shops is the trendy to-the-nth **Gucci**, a dandy's paradise selling shoes, suitcases, handbags, wallets, belts and other accessories. It has a fashion boutique for men and women and is well-known for its silk ties and scarves. **Fendi** also has exquisite leather goods as well as some lower-priced lines in synthetic materials and a range of gift items. Although their famous "stripe" line of leather-finished synthetic handbags cost as much as L250,000 (and their all-leather ones start at L300,000), they are at least cheaper to buy here than abroad. **Skin** and **Ginocchi**, both situated in the Via Sistina area, are also quite pricey. Located a short walk to the south of Skin and Ginocchi, near the

Trevi Fountain, is **La Sella**. It sells all things leather, including a range of shoes, bags, purses and belts.

Valextra has high-quality, fairly traditional briefcases, handbags, wallets and purses from Milan.

Mandarina Duck's brightly coloured fabric bags and range of luggage are very much in fashion and make an attractive (and vegetarian) alternative to the more traditional leather styles.

There are also some great places to buy artisan leatherwork. **Sirni** is at the top end of the scale with elegant bags and briefcases made in a workshop at the back of the shop.

For a more unusual men's present, try **La Cravatta** in Trastevere. In addition to their selection of classy hand-made ties, they also manufacture ties to meet customers' specifications. You can choose the design, material, length and shape of the tie to create the perfect gift.

CLASSIC JEWELLERY

WHAT CARTIER is to Paris, Tiffany & Co is to New York and Asprey's is to London, **Bulgari** is to Rome. This internationally revered jeweller's has passers-by glued to the windows gazing at its large fat gemstones. These "windows" are rather curious small boxes inserted into a wall with one or two pieces of jewellery in each of them, which adds to the feeling of looking at precious items in a case at a museum. Bulgari's watches, especially the men's, are popular and very elegant, as are the famous mesh necklaces. It specializes in large, colourful stones in High Renaissance-style settings but also produces a selection of contemporary designs. This was one of Andy Warhol's favourite shops, and it is definitely the most palatial shop on Via Condotti. Inside, the shop's atmosphere is one of almost religious awe and contemplation.

Buccellati is an offshoot of the famous Florentine dynasty, which was begun by Mario Buccellati in the 1920s and patronized by the poet Gabriele D'Annunzio. Its delicately engraved designs are inspired by the Italian Renaissance, and are real classics, displaying superb craftsmanship.

Ansuini designs are fashionable yet classic with strong, imaginative themes being introduced for each new collection. **Massoni**, founded in 1790, is one of Rome's oldest jewellery houses. Its refined one-offs and brooches are quite outstanding. At **Moroni Gioielli** you will also find imaginative, unique pieces of the highest-quality workmanship. **Petocchi**, which was jeweller to the former Italian monarchy (1861–1946), the House of Savoy, has both traditional and contemporary styles on display.

Peroso is an old-fashioned shop which has been going since 1891 and specializes in antique jewellery and silverware. **Boncompagni Sturni** sells traditional designs with the emphasis on quality and craftsmanship. You have to ring the bell to be admitted to both of these shops, and they are extremely expensive.

COSTUME JEWELLERY

For less conventional tastes, there are several shops selling innovative, avant-garde pieces, often using semiprecious metals and stones. **Via dei Coronari 193** is worth trying. **Delettré** produces bold, unique designs influenced by Art Deco styles. You are as likely to find rock crystal here as diamonds. Their logo of a crescent moon and five stars was specially designed by Karl Lagerfeld.

Tempi Moderni has an interesting collection of Art Deco and Liberty period jewellery. You can also find some nice pieces from the 1920s and 1930s in Cose Così (see p336). **Bozart** is the place for trendy, flashy costume jewellery. **Siragusa** puts beautiful 3rd- and 4th-

century BC beads and coins into handmade gold chains, in a museum-like shop just off the Piazza di Spagna.

TRADITIONAL GOLDSMITHS AND SILVERSMITHS

THE MAINSTAY of Rome's jewellery industry is still the traditional artisan goldsmith and silversmith, working to order in tiny studio workshops. These are concentrated in the old Jewish Ghetto area, Campo de' Fiori, Ponte Sisto near Via Giulia, and Montepietà (where the pawnbrokers live). Artisan jewellery can also be found in Via dei Coronari, Via dell'Orso, Via del Pellegrino. The jewellers create individual pieces to their own designs and have often learned their profession from their parents and grandparents. They will

also do repair work, or take old gold jewellery, melt it down and make it into something to suit you. **Oddi e Seghetti** produces some traditional artisan jewellery and always works to customers' commissions.

GLOVES, HATS AND HOSIERY

IF YOU'RE LOOKING for top quality, you will find an expensive line of gloves and scarves at **Merola**. **Di Cori** and **Sermoneta** stock every imaginable kind of glove. **Catello d'Auria** specializes in gloves and hosiery. **Borsalino** is the place for hats. **Calza e Calze** has the best range of hosiery in Rome – the friendly staff will serve you with almost any colour or pattern of tights and stockings that you could wish for.

SIZE CHART

For Australian sizes follow British and American convention.

Children's clothing

Italian	2-3	4-5	6-7	8-9	10-11	12	14	14+ (years)
British	2-3	4-5	6-7	8-9	10-11	12	14	14+ (years)
American	2-3	4-5	6-6x	7-8	10	12	14	16 (size)

Children's shoes

Italian	24	25$\frac{1}{2}$	27	28	29	30	32	33	34
British	7	8	9	10	11	12	13	1	2
American	7$\frac{1}{2}$	8$\frac{1}{2}$	9$\frac{1}{2}$	10$\frac{1}{2}$	11$\frac{1}{2}$	12$\frac{1}{2}$	13$\frac{1}{2}$	1$\frac{1}{2}$	2$\frac{1}{2}$

Women's dresses, coats and skirts

Italian	38	40	42	44	46	48	50
British	8	10	12	14	16	18	20
American	6	8	10	12	14	16	18

Women's blouses and sweaters

Italian	81	84	87	90	93	96	99 (cms)
British	31	32	34	36	38	40	42 (inches)
American	6	8	10	12	14	16	18 (size)

Women's shoes

Italian	36	37	38	39	40	41
British	3	4	5	6	7	8
American	5	6	7	8	9	10

Men's suits

Italian	44	46	48	50	52	54	56	58 (size)
British	34	36	38	40	42	44	46	48 (inches)
American	34	36	38	40	42	44	46	48 (inches)

Men's shirts (collar size)

Italian	36	38	39	41	42	43	44	45 (cms)
British	14	15	15$\frac{1}{2}$	16	16$\frac{1}{2}$	17	17$\frac{1}{2}$	18 (inches)
American	14	15	15$\frac{1}{2}$	16	16$\frac{1}{2}$	17	17$\frac{1}{2}$	18 (inches)

Men's shoes

Italian	39	40	41	42	43	44	45	46
British	6	7	7$\frac{1}{2}$	8	9	10	11	12
American	7	7$\frac{1}{2}$	8	8$\frac{1}{2}$	9$\frac{1}{2}$	10$\frac{1}{2}$	11	11$\frac{1}{2}$

DIRECTORY

WOMEN'S HIGH FASHION

Fendi
Via Borgognona 39.
Map 5 A2.
06-679 76 41.

Genny
Piazza di Spagna 27.
Map 5 A2.
06-679 60 74.

Gente
Via del Babuino 81.
Map 4 F1.
06-320 76 71.
Also: Via Frattina 69.
Map 5 A2.
06-678 91 32.
Also: Via dei Due Macelli 62. **Map** 5 A3 & 12 F1.
06-679 27 27.

Gianni Versace
Via Bocca di Leone 26.
Map 5 A2.
06-678 05 21.

Giorgio Armani
Via Condotti 77.
Map 5 A2.
06-699 14 61.
Also: Via del Babuino 140.
Map 4 F1.
06-36 00 21 97.

Laura Biagiotti
Via Borgognona 43–44.
Map 5 A2.
06-679 12 05.

Max & Co
Via Condotti 46.
Map 5 A2.
06-678 79 46.

MaxMara
Via Frattina 28.
Map 5 A2.
06-679 36 38.

Mila Schön
Via Condotti 51–52.
Map 5 A2.
06-678 48 05.

Renato Balestra
Via Sistina 67. **Map** 5 A2.
06-679 55 37.

Roberto Capucci
Via Gregoriana 56.
Map 5 A2.
06-679 51 80.

Sorelle Fontana
Salita S. Sebastianello 5.
Map 5 A2.
06-679 86 52.

Trussardi
Via Condotti 49–50.
Map 5 A2.
06-679 21 51.

Valentino
Via Bocca di Leone 15.
Map 5 A2.
06-679 58 62.

MEN'S TAILORS AND DESIGNER WEAR

Battistoni
Via Condotti 61A.
Map 5 A2.
06-678 62 41.

Brioni
Via dei Condotti 21/A.
Map 5 A2.
06-678 36 35.

Davide Cenci
Via Campo Marzio 1–7.
Map 4 F3 & 12 D2.
06-699 06 81.

Degli Effetti
Piazza Capranica 79.
Map 4 F3 & 12 D2.
06-679 02 02.

Enzo Ceci
Via della Vite 52.
Map 5 A3 & 12 E1.
06-679 88 82.

Ermenegildo Zegna
Via Borgognona 7 E.
Map 5 A2.
06-678 91 43.

Etro
Via del Babuino 102.
Map 5 A2.
06-678 82 57.

Gianfranco Ferrè
Via Borgognona 6.
Map 5 A2.
06-679 74 45.

Polidori Uomo
Via Borgognona 4C.
Map 5 A2.
06-699 41 171.

Testa
Via Borgognona 13.
Map 5 A2.
06-679 61 74.
Also: Via Frattina 104.
Map 5 A2.
06-679 12 96.

Trussardi
See Women's High Fashion.

Valentino Uomo
Via Condotti 13.
Map 5 A2.
06-678 36 56.

Versus by Versace
Via Borgognona 34.
Map 5 A2.

YOUNG DESIGNER WEAR

Aria
Via Nazionale 239.
Map 5 C3.
06-48 44 21.

Box 233
Via Nazionale 233.
Map 5 C3.
06-481 45 18.

Diesel
Via del Corso 185.
Map 4 F3 & 12 E1.
06-678 66 41.

Emporio Armani
Via del Babuino 140.
Map 4 F1.
06-322 15 84.

Energie
Via del Corso 486–487.
Map 4 F2.
06-322 70 46.

Eventi
Via dei Serpenti 134.
Map 5 B4.
06-48 49 60.

Luna e L'Altra
Via del Governo Vecchio 105. **Map** 4 E4 & 11 B3.
06-68 80 49 95.

Maga Morgana
Via del Governo Vecchio 27. **Map** 4 E4 & 11 C3.
06-687 99 95.

Max & Co
Via Nazionale 56.
Map 5 C3.
06-48 90 31 10.
Also: Via Appia Nuova 201–203. **Map** 10 D2.
06-701 44 13.

Oliver
Via del Babuino 61.
Map 4 F1.
06-360 01 906.

Timberland
Via del Babuino 75.
Map 4 F1.
06-679 08 36.

HIGH STREET FASHION

Benetton
Via Condotti 59.
Map 5 A2.
06-679 79 82.

Discount dell'Alta Moda
Via di Gesù e Maria 16A.
Map 4 F2.
06-361 37 96.

Discount System
Via del Viminale 35.
Map 5 C3.
06-482 39 17.

Emporio Armani
See Young Designer Wear.

Max & Co
See Young Designer Wear.

Scala Quattordici
Via della Scala 14.
Map 4 D5 & 11 B5.

KNITWEAR

Choses de Cachemire
Via del Babuino 105.
Map 4 F1.
06-679 84 88.

Laura Biagiotti
See Women's High Fashion.

Liz
Via Appia Nuova 90.
Map 10 D2.
06-700 36 09.

Luisa Spagnoli
Via del Corso 385.
Map 5 A4 & 12 F3.
06-679 81 89.
Also: Via Vittorio Veneto 130. **Map** 5 B1.
06-420 11 81.
Also: Via Frattina 84B.
Map 5 A2.
06-699 17 06.

Missoni Sport
Via del Babuino 96A–97.
Map 4 F1.
06-679 79 71.

Missoni Uomo/Donna
Piazza di Spagna 78.
Map 5 A2.
06-679 25 55.

LINGERIE

Brighenti
Via Frattina 7–8. **Map** 5 A2.
06-679 14 84.

Cesari
Via del Babuino 195.
Map 5 B3.
06-361 34 51.

Liberti
Via del Tritone 101.
Map 12 F1.
06-488 22 46.

Schostal
Via del Corso 158.
Map 4 F3 & 12 E1.
06-679 12 40.

Tomassini
Via Sistina 119. **Map** 5 A2.
06-488 19 09.

SECOND-HAND CLOTHES

Le Gallinelle
Via del Boschetto 76.
Map 5 B4.
06-488 10 17.

Mai Visto
Via del Governo Vecchio
85. **Map** 11 C3.
06-687 20 26.

Moon
Via del Governo Vecchio
89 A. **Map** 4 E4 & 11 B3.

Via dei Chiavari 40
Via dei Chiavari 40.
Map 4 E4 & 11 C4.

SHOES

Borino
Via dei Pettinari 86–87.
Map 4 E5 & 11 C5.
06-687 56 70.

Bruno Magli
Via Vittorio Veneto 70A.
Map 5 B2.
06-488 43 55.

Campanile
Via Condotti 58.
Map 5 A2.
06-678 30 41.

Carlotto Rio
Via dell'Arco della
Ciambella 8. **Map** 12 D3.
06-687 23 08.

Cervone
Via del Corso 99.
Map 4 F2.
06-678 35 22.

De Bach
Via del Babuino 123.
Map 4 F1.
06-678 33 84.

Dominici
Via del Corso 14.
Map 12 E1.
06-361 05 91.

Domus
Via Belsiana 52.
Map 4 F2.
06-678 90 83.

Fausto Santini
Via Frattina 120.
Map 5 A2.
06-678 41 14.

Ferragamo
Via Condotti 73–74.
Map 5 A2.
06-679 15 65.
Also: Via Condotti 66.
Map 5 A2.
06-678 11 30.

Fratelli Rossetti
Via Borgognona 5 A.
Map 5 A2.
06-678 26 76.

Mr Boots
Piazza Trilussa 33.
Map 4 E5.
06-580 38 20.
Also: Piazza Re di Roma 10.
Map 10 D3.
06-77 20 86 72.
Also: Via A Brunetti 2.
Map 4F1.
06-321 57 33.

Pollini
Via Frattina 22–24.
Map 5 A2 & 12 E1.
06-678 90 28.

Raphael Salato
Via Veneto 149.
Map 5 B1.
06-482 18 16.

LEATHER GOODS

La Cravatta
Via Santa Cecilia 12.
Map 8 D1.
06-581 66 76.

Fendi
See Women's High
Fashion.

Ginocchi
Via Sistina 35.
Map 5 B2.
06-488 39 25.

Gucci
Via Condotti 8. **Map** 5 A2.
06-678 93 40.

Mandarina Duck
Via di Propaganda 1.
Map 5 A2.
06-69 94 03 20.

La Sella
Via del Lavatore 56.
Map 5 A3 & 12 F2.
06-679 66 54.

Sirni
Via della Stelletta 33.
Map 4 F3 & 12 D2.
06-68 80 52 46.

Skin
Via Capo le Case 41.
Map 5 A3 & 12 F1.
06-678 55 31.

Valextra
Via del Babuino 94.
Map 4 F1.
06-679 23 23.

CLASSIC JEWELLERY

Ansuini
Via del Babuino 150 D.
Map 4 F1.
06-322 10 72.

Boncompagni
Via del Babuino 115.
Map 4 F1.
06-678 32 39.

Buccellati
Via Condotti 31.
Map 5 A2.
06-679 03 29.

Bulgari
Via Condotti 10.
Map 5 A2.
06-679 38 76.

Massoni
Largo Carlo Goldoni 48.
Map 4 F2 & 12 E1.
06-678 01 82.

Moroni Gioielli
Via Belsiana 32 A.
Map 4 F2.
06-678 04 66.

Peroso
Via Sistina 29. **Map** 5 B3.
06-474 79 52.

Petocchi
Piazza di Spagna 23.
Map 5 A2.
06-679 39 47.

COSTUME JEWELLERY

Bozart
Via Bocca di Leone 4.
Map 5 A2.
06-678 10 26.

Delettré
Via Fontanella Borghese 39.
Map 4 F2.
06-678 19 12.

Siragusa
Via delle Carrozze 64.
Map 5 A2.
06-679 70 85.

Tempi Moderni
Via del Governo
Vecchio 108.
Map 4 E4 & 11 B3.
06-687 70 07.

Via dei Coronari 193
Via dei Coronari 193.
Map 4 E3 & 11 B2.
06-68 80 15 03.

TRADITIONAL GOLDSMITHS AND SILVERSMITHS

Oddi e Seghetti
Via del Cancello 20.
Map 4 E3 & 11 C2.
06-686 13 84.

GLOVES, HATS AND HOSIERY

Borsalino
Via IV Novembre 157B.
Map 5 A4 & 12 F3.
06-679 41 92.

Calza e Calze
Via della Croce 78.
Map 4 F2.
06-678 42 81.

Catello d'Auria
Via dei Due Macelli 55.
Map 5 A2 & 12 F1.
06-679 33 64.

Di Cori
Piazza di Spagna 53.
Map 5 A2.
06-678 44 39.

Merola
Via del Corso 143.
Map 4 F3 & 12 E1.
06-679 19 61.

Sermoneta
Piazza di Spagna 61.
Map 5 A2.
06-679 19 60.

Interior Design

ITALIAN DESIGN belongs to a long-established tradition based on the skills of the master craftsman, and some firms have a history going back hundreds of years. Rome's stylish interior design shops are worth seeking out, even if it's only to look around and enjoy the ambience. You might well pick up some design ideas for your home, as well as finding some interesting or unusual things to buy.

FURNITURE

ALTHOUGH THERE is no distinct area of Rome renowned for its furniture shops, most of the top stores are located to the north of the city centre. **Fontana Arte**, on Via Giulia, has some highly original furniture and lamps made almost entirely of glass.

Take a look at the nearby **Studio Punto Tre** if you want something different: it's packed with strangely painted chests of drawers, Egyptian-style artefacts and small bits and pieces that would make good presents.

Myricae dazzles with its sensible prices and its covetable Tuscan wrought iron and Venetian painted furniture in sun-drenched or delicate hues.

Spazio Sette, near Largo Argentina, has a spectacular showroom on three levels in the Palazzo Lazzaroni, a former cardinal's palace. It is one of Rome's premier home furnishing stores and, apart from furniture, it stocks items that would make interesting gifts. The furniture – modern, laminated, stack-up chairs and so forth, vases, glass, bowls, and kitchen equipment – is jumbled together in a fascinating display.

Nearby, on Via dei Chiavari, is **Paola Agostara**, another shop that stocks an impressive cornucopia of household objects. Items ranging from hand-painted furniture to glassware from Eastern Europe are on sale here, along with a collection of designer fabrics and furniture by Paola Agostara herself.

Magazzini Forma & Memoria is an innovative design studio located near the east bank of the Tiber. It displays the latest in furniture and design items from Italy and elsewhere. Also on sale are a range of designer clothes, accessories and toys.

Stildomus, situated approximately half an hour's drive out of the centre of the city, has a showroom displaying mainly very fine modern wood furniture.

LIGHTING FIXTURES

LIGHTING FIXTURES are one of the most popular and more easily transportable items, and there are a number of superb showrooms to visit.

Flos Arteluce is a merger of two design houses whose Roman showroom displays its lights as if they were museum exhibits. The design style is chic and minimalist, with plenty of black and white, chrome and steel.

Nearby **Artemide** is, like Flos Arteluce, a design house in its own right, and is similarly well-known abroad. Its Rome showroom is elegant, with expensive, hi-tech lighting design similar to Flos Arteluce. **Borghini** sells less famous names, and so is more economical.

Paolo Marj is a sculptor working in mixed media such as glass, wood and plastics to create lamps that are original works of art in themselves. Also on sale are a variety of original sculptures by the artist.

Italian lighting and other electrical equipment is designed for 220–240 volts. If you are going to use it in countries with lower voltages always ask the shop whether the product needs a transformer, as this can depend on the model. Lighting fixtures generally use screw-bulbs, although some designer models can be ordered with fittings for bayonet-bulbs.

KITCHENS AND BATHROOMS

ALTHOUGH YOU won't be able to take one home with you, you may like to take a look at a few of the ultra-modern hi-tech kitchens sold in Rome. For an overview of the latest designs, visit **La Residenza**, which has a selection of about 15 kitchen sets from about nine different Italian manufacturers. **Coas Tradizione Casa** in Piazza Cardelli has some interesting combinations in a centrally located showroom.

Italian bathroom shops concentrate almost entirely on modern design. **Odorisio** is the equivalent of La Residenza for bathrooms, and has some luxurious examples. **Ravasini**, nearby, has very decorative floral fixtures with some matching accessories. **Andreucci** also has a bathroom shop which sells all the latest styles.

TILES

THE ITALIAN ceramic tile tradition is an ancient one. A great variety of tiles is displayed in kitchen and bathroom showrooms, but there are also a number of specialist shops. The most beautiful, and the most expensive, of these is **Farnese**, looking ancient Roman in style with its mosaic tables. Di Donato uses old-fashioned methods to design and produce the tiles – hence the cost. He is influenced by Roman and Pompeian art but also produces modern one-off designs.

Ceramiche Musa specializes in modern tiles with decorative floral and ancient Roman motifs, which are popular with visitors.

GLASS

DECORATIVE GLASS objects are a popular buy in Rome. **Navona Venetian Glass**, just behind Piazzo Navona, sells Murano and other glass items at reasonable prices. This shop is one of the few that opens on Sundays – which can be useful for visitors on short trips to Rome. **Archimede Seguso** also specializes in Murano glass but includes smaller pieces and a range of gift-sized items.

Tupini, the Roman equivalent of the Harrods china department, has a variety of quality glass, china and silverware. **Arteque** is a very beautiful shop, with a more traditional flavour.

For less expensive gifts, try **Stilvetro**. It is the ideal place for pasta bowls, glass and ceramics.

Shipment home can usually be arranged at any of these glass establishments so you can make your purchase without worrying about transporting it home.

FABRICS

SUMPTUOUS furnishing fabrics are what **Cesari** in Via del Babuino is renowned for. It also has a linen and lingerie shop *(see p327)*. **Il Sigillo** offers fabrics and wallpapers to order from a rich assortment of samples. At **Galtrucco** you can choose material for a suit which they will make to measure so that your individual taste can be combined with their professional expertise.

If you are looking for worthwhile bargains, take a walk round the old Jewish quarter that runs from Largo Argentina down to the Tiber; it is full of cheaper fabric shops such as **Paganini**. At sale time, remnants *(scampoli)* can be really good value, and you could find just the right fabric at just the right price.

HOUSEHOLD LINENS AND KITCHENWARE

A SELECTION of lovely sheets can be found at **Frette**. If you enjoy designer kitchenware, don't miss **C.u.c.i.n.a.** in the cellars of No. 118 Via del Babuino. It stocks kitchen utensils from all over the world, as well as pots and pans in both rustic and hi-tech styles and countless space-saving accessories. **Single** specializes in stainless steel designs like Alessi, and also sells wooden breadboards and a selection of assorted containers.

For the budget conscious, there is also **Salvoni**, whose basement is well stocked with cut-price gift ideas. You'll find an array of household and kitchenware, including silver, china and crystal items.

DIRECTORY

FURNITURE

Fontana Arte
Via Giulia 98.
Map 4 D4 & 11 A3.
[06-686 75 43.

Magazzini Forma & Memoria
Passeggiata di Ripetta 19.
Map 4 E1.
[06-321 47 68.

Myricae
Via Frattina 36. **Map** 5 A2.
[06-679 53 35.

Paola Agostara
Via dei Chiavari 8.
Map 4 E4 & 11 C4.
[06-689 37 77.

Spazio Sette
Via dei Barbieri 7.
Map 4 F5 & 12 D4.
[06-68 80 42 61.

Stildomus
Via Laurentina km. 27.
Map 5 A2.
[06-914 51 44.

Studio Punto Tre
Via Giulia 145.
Map 4 E4 & 11 B4.
[06-686 43 21.

LIGHTING FIXTURES

Artemide
Via Margutta 107–108.
Map 4 F1.
[06-36 00 18 02.

Borghini
Via Belsiana 87–89.
Map 4 F2.
[06-679 06 29.

Flos Arteluce
Via del Babuino 84.
Map 5 A2.
[06-320 76 31.

Paolo Marj
Piazza del Fico 21a.
Map 11 B3.
[06-68 80 77 07.

KITCHENS AND BATHROOMS

Andreucci
Via Po 39. **Map** 2 F5.
[06-884 81 47.

Coas Tradizione Casa
Piazza Cardelli 5A.
Map 4 F3 & 12 D1.
[06-686 75 79.

La Residenza
Via Cola di Rienzo 36.
Map 4 E1.
[06-321 67 51.

Odorisio
Via Tomacelli 150.
Map 4 F2.
[06-687 82 35.

Ravasini
Via di Ripetta 71.
Map 4 F2.
[06-322 70 96.

TILES

Farnese
Piazza Farnese 52.
Map 4 E5 & 11 C4.
[06-687 47 92.

Ceramiche Musa
Via Campo Marzio 39.
Map 4 F3 & 12 D1.
[06-687 12 42.

GLASS

Archimede Seguso
Via dei Due Macelli 56.
Map 5 A2.
[06-679 17 81.

Arteque
Via Giulia 13.
Map 4 D4 & 11 A3.
[06-687 73 88.

Navona Venetian Glass
Corso Rinascimento 43.
Map 4 E3.
[06-687 51 16.

Stilvetro
Via Frattina 56.
Map 5 A2.
[06-679 02 58.

Tupini
Piazza San Lorenzo in Lucina 8.
Map 4 F3 & 12 E1.
[06-687 14 58.

FABRICS

Cesari
Via del Babuino 495.
Map 5 A2.
[06-361 14 41.

Galtrucco
Via del Tritone 23.
Map 5 A3 & 12 F1.
[06-678 90 22.

Paganini
Via delle Botteghe Oscure 51. **Map** 4 F5 & 12 E4.
[06-678 68 31.

Il Sigillo
Via Laurina 15. **Map** 4 F1.
[06-361 32 47.

HOUSEHOLD LINENS AND KITCHENWARE

C.u.c.i.n.a.
Via del Babuino 118 A.
Map 5 A2.
[06-679 12 75.

Frette
Piazza di Spagna 10.
Map 5 A2.
[06-679 06 73.

Salvoni
Via Arenula 39. **Map** 4 F5.
[06-68 80 67 70.

Single
Via Francesco Crispi 45–47.
Map 5 B2.
[06-679 07 13.

Books and Gifts

ROME OFFERS HUGE SCOPE for gift buying. There are products from all over Italy as well as locally-produced artisan wares. Seeking out the smaller shops can be an adventure in itself, as many are in attractive parts of the city that you might not otherwise visit.

Some of the artisan ceramics are very unusual; there are beautiful books on Italian art and architecture, and there are wonderful paper products. Foodie gifts and drinks are always welcome – especially if it is something really special such as a 20-year-old balsamic vinegar. As well as the usual souvenirs, there is an abundance of religious artefacts – for obvious reasons – and Michelangelo masterpieces are the number one icon for T-shirts, statuettes and postcards.

BOOKSHOPS

ROME IS RICH in bookshops, from the encyclopedic to the very specialized. Italian books, both hardback and softback, are generally very attractive but also tend to be quite expensive.

Rizzoli, Rome's largest bookshop, has a wide selection on art and cookery among other subjects, and many books in English and other foreign languages. **Feltrinelli** has three shops in the capital. The most important is situated in Largo Argentina and offers a wide selection of contemporary literature. Milanese **Franco Maria Ricci** offers very beautiful art books, as well as its own glossy magazine *FMR*. **Libreria Godel** is also good for browsing – it has a lot of books on Rome, great postcards, art calendars and some second-hand art books.

Remainder has half-price bargains and sells games for children too. There are lots of cut-price bargains as well as second-hand book stalls in Via delle Terme di Diocleziano and in Largo della Fontanella di Borghese.

MULTIMEDIA AND MUSIC

ROME'S BIGGEST music store is **Ricordi**. As well as records, cassettes and CDs, it sells musical instruments and musical scores in its four central outlets. By contrast, **Discoteca Frattina** is quite a small, handy music shop that also sells video cassettes. The multimedia shop **Mondadori** sells greetings cards, posters and videos, and has good map and music departments as well as stocking books.

STATIONERY AND PAPER CRAFTS

A WIDE SELECTION of pretty marbled notebooks, writing papers, and files and boxes in various sizes are on offer at **Laboratorio Scatole**. **Pineider**, stationery suppliers to the Roman gentry, will print sets of exquisite visiting cards for you. They also sell handsome leather-bound desk diaries. Just as classy, though less traditional, **Vertecchi** is filled with original paper gifts. These include boxes of every size and shape, paper napkins and table-cloths, wrapping paper and a dazzling range of Christmas decorations.

ARTISAN HANDICRAFTS

SPACIOUS and artistically rustic, **La Galleria** is filled with authentic artisan wares, including hand-woven textiles and beautiful ceramics that owner Clotilde Sambuco chooses from all parts of Italy. Domenico and Lavinia Sarti's **Bottega Artigiana** nearby is a small shop with ceramics made by the couple in their Anzio studio. You can buy vases and urns in unglazed terracotta and some attractive terracotta wall-light fittings. **Arti e Mestieri** is the workshop of a friendly mother and daughter who make original articles in wood and terracotta. **Arte in Città** is a cross between a shop and a gallery. It sells a variety of original craft works by around a hundred artists and artisans, along with a range of hand-made cards and postcards. Every month the shop holds an exhibition with a different theme.

For a really original gift, try **Opificio Romano**, a work-shop that reproduces ancient Roman and Pompeian mosaics, where they will recreate any design you choose to order.

SOUVENIRS AND RELIGIOUS ARTEFACTS

MOST OF the tobacconists in central Rome sell post-cards, stamps and a variety of souvenirs, and many cheap and sometimes appealingly kitsch souvenirs are sold by the mobile stalls around the major tourist attractions.

Bookshops near the main basilicas, such as **Libreria Belardetti**, sell souvenirs and religious mementos. Other shops specialize in religious articles for both the clergy and the layman. Facing the Vatican gates in Via di Porta Angelica there are several shops, such as **Al Pellegrino Cattolico**, selling mementos to visiting pilgrims.

FOOD

ONE OF THE unusual things about shopping in Rome is the absence of large-scale supermarkets in the centre. It has been local government policy to keep them out in order to protect the little *alimentari* or delicatessens. There are hundreds of these, not on the main shopping streets, but in small side streets running off them or in the "village" districts such as Monti, Trastevere, the Ghetto, Borgo and Campo de' Fiori. They are often crammed from floor to ceiling with all the irresistible delicacies that are typical of Italy.

Here you can buy, the day before your departure, your supply of parmesan and

pecorino romano cheese
(see p305), Parma ham or
prosciutto di montagna,
attractive bottles of dark-
green, extra-virgin unfiltered
olive oil, dried porcini
mushrooms and sun-dried
tomatoes to take home (but
check customs restrictions
first). Food is by no means
cheap, and most of the above
are considered luxury items.

Pietro Franchi is without
doubt the most exclusive
delicatessen in the city, and
its windows are a visual feast
of seafood platters, pâtés,
cheeses and cold meats. Next
door is the famous coffee
shop **Castroni**, which has
Rome's largest selection of
imported products from all
over the world. It also stocks
Italian olive oils, balsamic
vinegars, honeys and preserves,
and of course coffee.

Via della Croce deserves
a special mention for its good
selection of well-stocked
alimentari like **Fratelli
Fabbi**. Specialist food shops
like **Fior Fiore** sell exquisite
little almond and orange peel
cakes, ricotta cheese, and
piles of artichoke-, spinach-
and tomato-flavoured pasta,
as well as thin, crispy pizza
straight from the oven.

Cheese-lovers can usually
find plenty of Italian varieties
in any of the small *alimentari*
dotted around the city.
However, it's also well worth
trying the local cow, sheep
and buffalo milk cheeses that
are sold at the **Cisternino
Cooperativa fra Produttori
di Latte di Lazio**, situated
near Piazza Campo de' Fiori.

Boxes of chocolates and
traditional confectionery and
cakes such as *torrone* and
panettone can generally be
bought from good-quality
bars. **L'Albero del Pane** sells
wonderful wholemeal and
rye flour breads and other
health foods.

WINE

WINE IS GENERALLY sold in
alimentari and also in
supermarkets. There are,
however, many specialist
shops (look for the sign
Enoteca) with a huge stock
of wines and spirits. They
invariably have a little bar
where they serve wine and
light snacks or canapés. Here
you can find Italian wines,
and usually local wines,
mostly white, from the nearby
Frascati, Colli Albani and
Marino vineyards, on tap.
One of the most select is
Enoteca Buccone, which is
housed in an old coach-
house. Another well-known
one is **Antica Enoteca** which
has an old-world feeling to it.
The **Enoteca del Corso** is
more modern, with a good
selection of Italian grappa
and jars of marinated fruits.
Enoteca Corsi in Via del
Gesù is also worth a visit.

DIRECTORY

BOOKSHOPS

Feltrinelli
Largo Argentina 5 A.
Map 4 F4.
☎ 06-68 80 32 48.

Franco Maria Ricci
Via Borgognona 4D. **Map**
5 A2. ☎ 06-679 34 66.

Libreria Godel
Via Poli 46. **Map** 5 A3 &
12 F2. ☎ 06-679 87 16.

Remainder
Piazza San Silvestro 28.
Map 5 A3 & 12 E1.
☎ 06-679 28 24.

Rizzoli
Largo Chigi 15. **Map** 5 A3
& 12 E2. ☎ 06-679 66 41.

MULTIMEDIA
AND MUSIC

Discoteca Frattina
Via Frattina 50–51. **Map**
5 A2. ☎ 06-679 14 93.

Mondadori
Piazza Cola di Rienzo
81–83. **Map** 4 D2.
☎ 06-622 01 88.

Ricordi
Via Battisti 120.

Map 5 A4 & 12 F3.
☎ 06-679 80 22.

STATIONERY AND
PAPERCRAFT

Laboratorio Scatole
Via della Stelletta 27.
Map 4 F3 & 12 D2.
☎ 06-68 80 20 53.

Pineider
Via dei Due Macelli 68.
Map 5 A2 & 12 F1.
☎ 06-679 58 84;
Also: Via della Fontanella
Borghese 22. **Map** 4 F3 &
11 D1. ☎ 68 30 80 14.

Vertecchi
Via della Croce 70. **Map**
4 F2. ☎ 06-678 31 10

ARTISAN
HANDICRAFTS

Arte in Città
Corso Rinascimento 60.
Map 4 E3 & 11 C2.
☎ 06-68 80 88 78.

Arti e Mestieri
Via dei Cappellari 57.
Map 4 E4 & 11 C4.
☎ 06-683 25 21.

Bottega Artigiana
Via Santa Dorotea 21.
Map 4 D5 & 11 B5.
☎ 06-588 20 79.

La Galleria
Via della Pelliccia 30. **Map**
7 C1. ☎ 06-581 66 14.

Opificio Romano
Via dei Gigli d'Oro 10.
Map 4 E3 & 11 C2.
☎ 06-68 80 27 62.

SOUVENIRS
AND RELIGIOUS
ARTEFACTS

**Al Pellegrino
Cattolico**
Via di Porta Angelica 83.
Map 3 C2.
☎ 06-68 80 23 51.

Libreria Belardetti
Via della Conciliazione 4a.
Map 3 C2.
☎ 06-686 55 02.

FOOD

L'Albero del Pane
Via Santa Maria del Pianto
19–20. **Map** 4 F5 & 12 D5.
☎ 06-686 50 16.

**Cisternino
Cooperativa fra
Produttori di Latte
di Lazio**
Vicolo del Gallo 18–19.
Map 4 E5 & 11 C4.
☎ 06-687 28 75.

Castroni
Via Cola di Rienzo 196.
Map 4 D2.
☎ 06-687 43 83.

Fior Fiore
Via della Croce 17–18.
Map 5 A2.
☎ 06-679 13 86.

Fratelli Fabbi
Via della Croce 28.
Map 5 A2.
☎ 06-679 06 12.

Pietro Franchi
Via Cola di Rienzo 200.
Map 4 D2.
☎ 06-686 45 76.

WINE

Antica Enoteca
Via della Croce 76B.
Map 5 A2.
☎ 06-679 08 96.

Enoteca Buccone
Via di Ripetta 19. **Map**
4 F1. ☎ 06-361 21 54.

Enoteca Corsi
Via del Gesù 87–88.
Map 4 F4 & 12 E3.
☎ 06-679 08 21.

Enoteca del Corso
Corso Vittorio Emanuele II
293–295. **Map** 4 D4 &
11 A3. ☎ 06-68 80 15 94.

Art and Antiques

ROME'S ART and antique shops range from exclusive establishments to contemporary art galleries. In response to a fashion for collecting early-20th-century artefacts, new dealers and galleries are springing up throughout Rome – Venini's Murano glass is popular, as are lighting and furniture. Many more sell general bric-a-brac and jewellery. Copies of antique prints can be picked up for a fraction of the originals' price. Rome is not good for antique bargains, but it's worth looking in shops along Via dei Cappellari and Via del Pellegrino or going to the Porta Portese Sunday market *(see p339)*.

ANTIQUES AND OLD MASTER PAINTINGS

THERE ARE antique shops dotted all over the centre of Rome, though the cream tend to be concentrated in distinct areas. Discreet haggling in the shops is accepted practice, but even if you get a reduction in price, make sure the dealer provides you with the relevant export documents.

The famous Via del Babuino, and to a lesser extent Via Margutta, which is better known for its art galleries, are home to around 30 of Rome's grandest showrooms for antique furniture, Old Master paintings and *objets d'art*.

Apolloni is owned by top dealer Cesare Lampronti. Aided and complemented by his partner Carlo Peruzzi, he sells 16th- to 18th-century European paintings, with an emphasis on Roman and Italian works in general.

Amedeo di Castro, apparently no relation to the other four di Castros on this street, is a fourth-generation dealer in bas-relief sculptures and exquisite pieces from the 18th and early 19th centuries.

Claudio e Laura Moretti's small, narrow shop is full of antique and later copies of marble busts and statues.

Via Giulia *(see p153)* has over 20 high-quality antique shops to choose from. Definitely worth a visit is **Antichita Cipriani**, which is a temple to owner Paola Cipriani's love of simply elegant Neo-Classical furniture and paintings. She also sells the occasional modern piece.

Another shop not to miss on Via Giulia is **Antiquariato Valligiano**. It's the only place in Rome where you can find 19th-century Italian country furniture; a rustic antidote for those overpowered by the grandiose Baroque.

Via Monserrato, running parallel, is worth scouring for slightly lower-quality pieces at more attainable prices.

The area just to the north of Via Giulia is also a good potential hunting ground. **Mario Prilli**, on Via Banchi Nuovi, is tiny, but don't let that deter you. With every inch of space occupied by a wide variety of antiques, this fascinating shop is worth a look even if you are only browsing. Nearby is **Ad Antiqua Domus**, a treasure trove of antique Italian furniture. Pieces dating from ancient Rome though to the 19th century are on sale.

Via dei Coronari is almost exclusively devoted to antiques, with over 40 shops lining both sides of this picturesque street. Quality is very high – as are the prices. It is a good place for Baroque and Empire elaborate inlaid vases, secretaries and consoles.

L'Art Nouveau specializes in high-quality Art Nouveau (usually called *Liberty* here). The **Art Deco Gallery** sells furniture and sculpture from that period.

Piero Tagoni has a superb collection of lighting fixtures from the Baroque through to Art Deco periods.

Slightly further away lies Via della Stelletta, which is home to a handful of unusual and fascinating shops.

Acanto is an inexpensively priced Aladdin's cave with an eclectic mix of *objets d'art*. It is the perfect place to search for religious memorabilia, Italian curiosities and prints.

Bilenchi is yet another specialist, this time in exquisite, turn-of-the-century lamps.

Another relatively undiscovered area is Via del Boschetto and Via Panisperna. Shops around here tend to specialize in early-20th-century artefacts, with some English Victorian pieces thrown in.

Tad is a great place to come and browse, with a large collection of wierd and original design items from all around the world.

Of course there are many perennial favourites apart from these streets. The best way to discover them is through word of mouth or just by chance as you stroll along. **Cose Così**, in the north of the city, is a shop full of small decorative pieces from 1800–1940 (watches, silver, glass, frames, vases and jewellery), while **Galleria dei Cosmati** is one of the oldest antiques shops in Rome, and definitely one of the largest. It offers an impressive collection of European antiques.

Anticaja e Petrella has an eccentric collection of used junk and printed ephemera stored under Sant'Andrea della Valle *(see p123)*.

MODERN ART

ROME IS RICH in avant-garde galleries exhibiting paintings by recognized Modern Masters through to the up-and-coming generation of young, mainly Italian, artists.

Rome's art galleries are usually open 10am–1pm and 5pm–8pm Tue–Sat. Some open only in the afternoon; others also stay open on Monday afternoon. The best times to visit are afternoons and early evenings.

As with Rome's antique shops, the art galleries tend to be concentrated in a couple of distinct areas. The largest of these covers the triangular area between

Via del Babuino and Via di Ripetta and adjoining streets, known locally as the Trident.

The pioneering **Agenzia d'Arte Moderna**, founded in 1913, promoted Futurism from the start and other modern art movements as well. There are works by Burri and Kounellis always on show.

Sperone, under the owner-directorship of Gian Enzo Sperone, shows works by American artists such as Ray Smith, Jonathan Lasker and Julio Galan. Also on view are Italian artists like Gallo, Dessi, Bianchi, Paladino and Merzi.

Apollodoro, which sells interesting design artifacts, has an entrance modelled on Borromini's illusionistic perspective in the garden gallery of Palazzo Spada *(see p147).*

One of this area's highlights is the Via Margutta art fair *(see p339),* which usually takes place around Christmas and in springtime.

Via Giulia and its surroundings is the next area to investigate: **Galleria Giulia** is a gallery-cum-bookshop with work by artists such as Argeles, Boille, Cano, Cascella, Echaurren, Erba and Lionni, as well as by Bauhaus artists and German Expressionists. Fabio Sargentini at **L'Attico** follows the latest trends in Italian art from Del Giudice to Corsini and Fabiani.

Trastevere is possibly better for more innovative ventures: The **Galleria Bondho** (previously Alessandro Bonomo) spotlights young Italian and foreign painters such as Schifano, Boetti, Twombly, Nunzio, Tremlett, LeWitt, Dokoupil. In a stupendous villa situated quite a way out of Rome, **Mauro Vigneti** specializes in both Italian and international artists who are working in Rome.

ANTIQUE PRINTS AND PHOTOGRAPHS

THE JUSTIFIABLY celebrated **Nardecchia**, named after its cultivated owner Plinio, is the cream of Rome's print dealers. Look out for originals by the 18th-century engraver, Piranesi, and views of the city and ancient Roman life.

Another Roman institution, **Casali**, has been trading for over 100 years. The family now runs two shops specializing in 16th- to 19th-century drawings and engravings of Roman scenes ranging from museum-standard Piranesi down to relatively inexpensive unknown and delightfully decorative floral scenes.

The Florence-based **Alinari** family is renowned for its old sepia photographs of Italy from 1890 onwards, including shots of Rome at the turn of the century. At its Roman outlet, prices of photographs from the original plates start at around L30,000 and mounted prints at L500,000. Larger sizes can be mounted on wood or card.

Another place definitely worth heading for in search of that perfect print of old Rome and some enjoyable, relaxing and maybe persuasive browsing is the **Mercato delle Stampe** *(see p338).*

Street Markets

ROME'S OPEN-AIR MARKETS are essential to visit if you're interested in soaking up the bubbling exuberance and earthiness for which Romans are renowned. They are wonderfully vivid experiences too, as Italian stallholders have raised the display of even the humblest vegetable to an art form.

The city is dotted with popular, small local food markets, and there are several fascinating well-established markets near the centre, along with the famous flea market over in Trastevere.

It is important to keep your wits about you in markets because pickpockets work with lightning speed in the bustling crowds. But this said, Roman markets provide a vibrant source of entertainment and it would be a shame to let such caveats deter you from joining in the fun.

The street fairs that take place throughout the year are fun to go to, if they coincide with your visit, as they normally sell a good variety of local produce, handicrafts and clothes. Seasonal fairs also occur, especially around Christmas, when you can stock up on Italian specialities.

Campo de' Fiori

Piazza Campo de' Fiori. **Map** 4 E4 & 11 C4. ⊟ H, 46, 62, 64, 70, 81, 116, 492, 628. ⏲ 8. **Open** 7am–1.30pm Mon–Sat. See p146.

Right in the heart of the old city, Rome's most picturesque market is also its most historical. Its name, Campo de' Fiori, which translates as field of flowers, sometimes misleads people into expecting a flower market. In fact the name is said to derive from Campus Florae (Flora's square) – Flora being the lover of the great Roman general Pompey. A market has actually been held in this now rather shabby, but still beautiful, piazza for many centuries.

Every morning, except Sunday, the piazza is transformed by an array of stalls selling colourful fruit and vegetables, meat, poultry and fish. One or two stalls specialize in pulses, rice, dried fruit and nuts and there are also flower stalls situated near the fountain. But the huge open baskets of ready-stripped broccoli and spinach, chopped vegetables for minestrone and freshly prepared green salad mixes are the main attraction for visitors. They provide a real visual display as well as an edible feast.

The excellent delicatessen shops on the square, and bread shops nearby, complement the market. They make it a great place to stock up for an impromptu picnic if the weather turns out fine and you're tempted to do some *al fresco* dining in one of Rome's many attractive parks.

Mercato delle Stampe

Largo della Fontanella di Borghese. **Map** 4 F3 & 12 D1. ⊟ 81, 115, 117, 492, 628, 913, 926. **Open** 7am–1pm Mon–Sat.

This market is a veritable haven for lovers of old prints, books (both genuine antiquarian and less-exalted second-hand), magazines and other printed ephemera. The quality varies, but it is a good deal more specialized than the *banche* or stalls near Termini station which are a more obvious tourist trap. Italian-speaking collectors can enjoy a field day leafing through back issues of specialist magazines. Other visitors might prefer the wonderful selection of illustrated art books and old prints of Rome. It is a good place to pick up that Piranesi print of your favourite Roman vista, ruin or church – but be prepared to bargain hard.

Mercato dei Fiori

Via Trionfale. **Map** 3 B1. Ⓜ Ottaviano. ⊟ 23, 70. **Open** 10.30am–1pm Tue.

Essentially a trade market, the Flower Market, just north of Via Andrea Doria, is open to the public only on Tuesdays. Housed in a covered hall, it has two floors brimming over with cut flowers upstairs and all kinds of pot plants on the lower floor. Anyone who has an interest in flowers will enjoy this wonderful array of Mediterranean blooms, which are on sale at giveaway prices.

Mercato Andrea Doria

Via Andrea Doria. **Map** 3 B1. Ⓜ Ottaviano. ⊟ 23, 70. **Open** 7am–1.30pm Mon–Sat.

The market used to stretch the whole length of this wide avenue. It has now been reorganized on to a huge square of open ground between Via Santamaura and Via Tunisi. Apart from the magnificent displays of fruit and vegetables, it has numerous stalls selling meat, poultry, fish and groceries, as well as an interesting clothes and shoe section. Situated northwest of the Vatican Museums, it is a little off the normal beaten track and has remained very much a Roman market that caters for the needs of the large local population.

Mercato di Piazza Vittorio

Piazza Vittorio Emanuele II. **Map** 6 E5. Ⓜ Vittorio Emanuele. ⊟ 4, 9. **Open** 7am–2pm Mon–Sat. See p174.

Bustling Piazza Vittorio was, until recently, perhaps the most Roman of the city's larger markets.

Organized as a cramped corridor of stalls around a central garden, it is the place where bargain-hunting *popolari*, Rome's bustling shoppers, buy their food. Stallholders offer cheap prices if you buy by the kilo, but watch out for bad fruit.

Lately it has become more international and now features African and Asian food stalls.

Sadly, the market's days are numbered, as the city council says that it defaces the 19th-century square. Some stalls have moved to the new site in Via Giolitti; others won't go. The battle is on, but make a visit before a splash of Roman colour is lost for ever.

Mercato di Testaccio

Piazza Testaccio. **Map** 8 D3. Ⓜ Piramide. ⊟ 23, 75, 280. **Open** 7.30am–1.30pm Mon–Sat.

The covered market at Testaccio occupies the central area of its eponymous piazza. The few cheap clothing and shoe stalls skirting the outside are unremarkable, but the inside is well worth a visit. Lined with butchers, grocers and fishmongers, the whole central area is given over to fruit and vegetables – a theatre-set array of seductive colours and textures. Very popular with local residents, it offers super-fresh, high-quality produce and reasonable prices. Much of this market's charm for visitors lies in its compact size and relaxed, friendly atmosphere.

Porta Portese

Via Portuense & Via Ippolito Nievo.
Map 7 C3. 🚌 *H, 23, 75*. 🚋 *8*.
Open *6.30am–2pm Sun.*

The *mercato delle pulci* or flea market is a relatively new market in Roman terms. Established shortly after the end of World War II, it is said to have grown out of the thriving black market that operated at Tor di Nona opposite Castel Sant'Angelo during those lean years. Stallholders come from as far away as Naples and set up shop in the early hours of the morning – if you are strolling in that direction after a late night in Trastevere, it's well worth pausing just to watch them.

Anything and everything seems to be for sale, piled high on stalls in carefully arranged disorder – clothes, shoes, bags, luggage, camping equipment, linen, towels, pots, pans, kitchen utensils, plants, pets, spare parts, cassettes and CDs, old LPs and 78s.

Furniture stalls tend to be concentrated around Piazza Ippolito Nievo along with what they call "antiques", though you may have to sort through an awful lot of junk before finding a real one. And then you will have to bargain for it. The technique is to offer them half the asked price and then walk away. A lot of people go just for the fun of it and always end up buying something.

There are also second-hand clothes – leather or sheepskin coats and jackets go for L10,000 – with many of the Via Sannio stall holders relocating here for the Sunday trade. The stretch along Via Ippolito Nievo is monopolized by "*i Russi di Porta Portese*", immigrant Russian stallholders selling caviar, icons (authenticity uncertain), lace, other ethnic handicrafts, old cameras and binoculars. A must if you have a Sunday morning to spare.

Mercato di Via Sannio

Via Sannio. **Map** 9 C2. Ⓜ *San Giovanni*. 🚌 *16, 81, 87*. **Open** *8am–1pm Mon–Fri, 8am–6pm Sat.*

In the 1960s and 1970s this used to be Italy's answer to Carnaby Street. Today, at first glance, it doesn't seem to have anything very special to offer – random stalls selling inexpensive casual clothes, shoes, bags, belts, jewellery, toys, kitchen utensils and music cassettes. But towards the end of the street there is a large covered section which extends back to the Aurelian Wall *(see p196)* with many stalls piled high with second-hand clothes at very low prices for those who like to rummage. There is also a

section that sells military-style goods plus some camping and fishing equipment.

Some of these stalls move their wares to Porta Portese on a Sunday morning.

Local markets

Generally open *7am–1pm Mon–Sat.*

Piazza delle Coppelle (map 4 F3 & 12 D2), near the Pantheon, is probably the most picturesque of the food markets sprinkled around the city. A tiny market devoted to food and fruit and flowers, it

offers a charming splash of colour in the heart of the city.

Piazza San Cosimato (map 7 C1) in Trastevere hosts another lively local market with some tempting cheeses and salami.

There is a fairly big market on **Via Alessandria** (map 6 D1) in Nomentana, and other smaller ones in **Via della Pace** (map 4 E4 & 11 C3) near Piazza Navona, and in **Via Balbo** (map 5 C4) and **Via Milazzo** (map 6 E3) near Termini station. You can also visit the trade market, the **Mercato Generale** (map 8 D5), in Via Ostiense, which is open to the public after 8am.

ENTERTAINMENT IN ROME

T HERE'S A PARTICULAR excitement attached to Roman entertainment. Football and opera, for example, are both worth experiencing for sheer atmosphere alone, whether or not you are a fan. The jazz scene is especially good with international stars appearing alongside local talent. And concerts and films take on an added dimension when performances take place beneath the stars in the many open-air arenas spread across the city. Unexpectedly, given the general shutdown among shops, restaurants and museums, the summer remains Rome's liveliest time for live music and other cultural events. Rome's graceful Renaissance squares, vast parks, villa gardens, Classical ruins and other open spaces host various major arts festivals. If you prefer sport, or want to try out some Roman nightclubs, there's plenty on offer too.

Gregory Peck and Audrey Hepburn in *Roman Holiday*

PRACTICAL INFORMATION

A GOOD SOURCE of information about what's on is *Trovaroma*, the weekly Thursday supplement to *La Repubblica* newspaper. It has a day-by-day rundown of what's on and where, and covers music, exhibitions, theatre, cinemas,

Saxophonist at Alpheus *(see p344)*

guided tours, restaurants and children's entertainment. Two weekly listings magazines, *Città Aperta* and *Roma c'è*, have an English section covering the "Week in Rome" and there is a weekly *Time Out* in both Italian and English editions. Daily newspapers like *Il Messaggero, Il Manifesto, Paese Sera* and *La Repubblica* usually list that evening's entertainment.

Two fortnightly magazines, *Wanted in Rome* and *Metropolitan* (found at Via Veneto newsagents or English bookshops), provide less detailed listings in English. Also worth getting hold of is *Carnet di Roma*, available from the EPT *(see p359)*, which gives details in English of classical

music, festivals, theatre and exhibitions in the city and surroundings.

Punctuality is not what Italians are renowned for, so don't be surprised if some events start slightly later than advertised in listings.

BOOKING TICKETS

B OOKING in advance is not part of Italian lifestyle. Two ticket agencies that will book theatre tickets for you (for a small fee) are **Gesman** and **Box Office**. As a rule, theatres themselves do not accept telephone bookings – you have to visit the box office in person. They will charge you a *prevendita* supplement (about 10% of the normal price) for any tickets sold in advance. The price of a theatre ticket can be anything between L10,000 and L70,000.

Tickets for classical concerts are usually sold on the spot, and are sometimes for that night only, an arrangement that favours the last-minute

decision to go. Opera is the exception. Tickets are sold months in advance, with just a few held back until two days before the performance.

Stage at Caffè Latino *(see pp344-5)*

It is usually easier (and also cheaper) to get tickets for the Caracalla Festival which takes place in the summer.

The **Teatro dell'Opera** box office *(see p343)* handles sales for both summer and winter seasons, and they have a high-tech booking system, with a computer which colour-codes unsold seats.

Tickets for most big rock and jazz events can be bought at **Orbis**, **Prontospettacolo, Mirabilia** and at larger record shops such as **Rinascita**.

Remember that if you're trying to get hold of a ticket for a particular performance that has already sold out, you're extremely unlikely to be able to obtain one from

Member of contemporary dance group Momix *(see p343)*

unofficial sources – there are very few ticket touts in Rome, except at major football matches such as important finals.

REDUCED-PRICE TICKETS

THEATRES and concert venues tend not to offer discounts on tickets since performances are so often over-subscribed.

Cinemas, however, offer people aged over 60 and disabled people a 30% reduction on weekdays. Many cinemas also have cheaper ticket prices for weekday afternoon screenings and on for all shows on Wednesdays.

Some clubs at the beach resorts such as Fregene offer reductions: look out for *due per uno* coupons in local bars that allow two people entrance for the price of one.

FACILITIES FOR THE DISABLED

FEW ROMAN venues provide easy access for people with restricted mobility, and any disabled visitors and their companions are likely to find the lack of provision for them very frustrating.

The situation does improve a little in summer, however, when a great many performances in the city are held at open-air venues. The Baths of Caracalla have wheelchair access, as do the classical concerts held in the beautiful gardens of Villa Giulia *(see pp262–3)*.

For more general information on provision for the disabled, see page 359.

The Teatro dell'Opera *(see p342)*

Summer night outdoor performance among Roman ruins

OPEN-AIR ENTERTAINMENT

OPEN-AIR OPERA, cinema, classical music and jazz concerts fill the calendar from late June until the end of September. These performances outdoors can be wonderful, with spectacular settings and enthusiastic audiences. Some of them are grand affairs, but small events may be just as evocative – a guitar recital in the cloisters of Santa Maria della Pace *(see p342)*, for example, or jazz in the beautiful gardens of Villa Doria Pamphilj *(see p344)*.

Singers performing the *Barber of Seville*

Many cinemas roll back their ceilings in summer for open-air screenings, or else move to outdoor arenas, and there are also annual open-air cinema festivals. The Cineporto along the Tiber and the Festival di Massenzio offer films, food and small exhibitions in July and August. Theatre, too, moves outside in summer. Greek and Roman plays are staged at Ostia Antica *(see p270)* and other shows take place at the Anfiteatro del Tasso *(see p347)*.

Rome's most important, month-long summer festival is RomaEuropa, with main performances in the grounds of the Villa Medici. There are other, smaller festivals too, but times and venues change from year to year, so it's best to watch for posters around

the city for the most up-to-date information. More traditional is Trastevere's community festival, Festa de Noantri *(see p59)*, with music, fireworks and processions. This religious festival is on the Saturday after 16 July but celebrations continue well into August. The Festa dell' Unità, run by the PDS (the former Communist Party), but not limited to politics, is generally held in September. The programme includes games, stalls, food and drink.

Finally, if you like your entertainment less structured you can always do as the Romans do and take part in the *passeggiata* (early evening stroll) – the city's favourite spots are Piazza Navona *(see p120)* and along Via del Corso.

TICKET AGENCIES

Gesman
Via Angelo Emo 65. **Map** 3 A2.
Open *9am–1pm, 2pm–6pm Mon–Fri,
9am–1pm Sat.* 06-39 74 07 89.

Box Office
Viale Giulio Cesare 88. **Map** 3 C1.
*Box office tickets for classical music,
rock, pop and jazz concerts and some
sporting events.* 06-372 02 16.

Mirabilia
Corso Vittorio Emanuele (in Palazzo
Altieri). **Map** 4 F4 & 12 E4.
1478-82211.

Orbis
Piazza dell'Esquilino 37. **Map** 6 D4.
06-47 44 776.

Prontospettacolo
Telephone bookings only.
Open *10am–5pm Mon–Fri.*
06-39 38 72 97.

Classical Music and Dance

CLASSICAL CONCERTS take place in a surprising number of venues: tickets for opera premières may be hard to get, but soloists, groups or orchestras playing in gardens, churches, villas or ancient ruins are more accessible. World-renowned soloists and orchestras make appearances throughout the year; past visitors have included Luciano Pavarotti and Placido Domingo, Catherine Malfitano and prima ballerina Sylvie Guillem.

Programmes are generally international in scope but sometimes you will find a festival dedicated to one of Italy's own, like Palestrina, the great 16th-century master of polyphonic church music, or Arcangelo Corelli, inventor of the Baroque *concerto grosso*.

MUSIC IN CHURCHES

ONE OF ROME'S main attractions for classical music lovers is the rich repertoire that can be heard in the city's churches. Always sacred in theme (by decree of Pope John Paul II), music is mainly performed as concerts rather than during services.

Programmes are posted around the city and outside the churches. You will often find very good musicians playing in the main churches, while the smaller, out-of-the-way churches frequently play host to young musicians and amateur choirs as well.

St Peter's *(see p230)* hosts one major RAI (national broadcasting company) concert on 5 December attended by the pope and free for the general public. It has two established choirs. The Coro della Cappella Giulia sing at the 10.30am mass and 5pm vespers on Sunday. The Coro della Cappella Sistina sing when-ever the pope celebrates mass here, as on 29 June (St Peter and St Paul's day).

Important choral masses also take place on 25 January in **San Paolo fuori le Mura** *(see p267)*, when the pope attends, on 24 June in **San Giovanni in Laterano** *(p182)* and on 31 December at the **Gesù** *(pp114–5)* where the *Te Deum* is sung. The church of **Sant'Ignazio di Loyola** *(p106)* is another favourite venue for choral concerts.

Gregorian chant can be heard in **Sant'Apollinare** *(p127)* at 11am on Sundays and religious festivals. Easter and the Christmas festivities are a great time for cheap and chilly concerts: there is usually neither entrance fee nor heating!

ORCHESTRAL, CHAMBER AND CHORAL MUSIC

THE **Auditorium di Santa Cecilia**, the national broadcasting company's **Foro Italico** and **Teatro dell' Opera** are Rome's three main auditoriums, with their own resident orchestras and choirs. The Orchestra e Coro dell' Accademia di Santa Cecilia is the top orchestra but the Orchestra e Coro di Roma della RAI is also good. All three offer interestingly varied seasons which include visiting groups and soloists from all over the world.

The season at the **Teatro Olimpico** usually offers very good chamber music, some orchestral concerts and ballet with at least one concert a week. They are advertised on large yellow posters with red borders, easily identifiable in the streets and a hallmark for high-level performances.

Although a variety of classical concerts take place at the **Accademia Filarmonica Romana**, the emphasis is on chamber and choral music, with an internationally renowned series of concerts running from mid-October to mid-May. Performances take place in the Sala Casella, which seats around 180.

Ticket prices for classical concerts depend a lot on performers and venue. The **Auditorium del Foro Italico** sells tickets for most concerts for under L20,000; a ticket for the **Teatro Olimpico** costs between L25,000–L40,000, but seats for an important concert at **Teatro dell'Opera** may cost as much as L150,000.

The Associazione Musicale Romana organizes three annual festivals in the **Palazzo della Cancelleria** *(see p149):* the Festival Internazionale di Cembalo (harpsichord festival) in March; Musica al Palazzo in May; and the Festival Internazionale di Organo in September.

It's always worth checking which musicians are due to be playing at the **Teatro Ghione**, the **Oratorio del Gonfalone** or the **Aula dell' Università la Sapienza**.

OPEN-AIR SUMMER CONCERTS

IN THE SUMMER music lovers can enjoy concerts in cloisters, palazzo courtyards and ancient ruins. Concerts can be one-offs or part of a festival programme, regular fixtures or impromptu. Do as the Romans do, don't plan until the last moment and keep an eye on the posters and listings pages *(see p340)* for the latest details.

Open-air opera and dance once had their home in the majestic Baths of Caracalla, but this venue is no longer used. Classical concerts are often part of festivals like RomaEuropa *(see p341)* but there are also open-air festivals and concert series dedicated to classical music. Among the more interesting is the Stagione Estiva dell'Orche-stra dell'Accademia di Santa Cecilia held at the Ninfeo *(nympheum)* in the grounds of **Villa Giulia** *(see p263)*. Also listed as the Concerti a Villa Giulia, the concerts begin in July and tickets are under L20,000.

The Associazione Musicale Romana organizes Serenate in Chiostro – a lively and varied programme of concerts during July in the cloisters of **Santa Maria della Pace** *(see* *p121)* with tickets on sale for under L20,000. Estate al Tempietto (listed also as Concerti del Tempietto) is the Tempietto orchestra's summer treat with concerts every evening from July to September in the **Area Archeologica del Teatro di Marcello** *(see p151).* They're held in the adjacent basilica of San Nicola in Carcere if it rains.

Festival Villa Pamphilj in Musica, in July, is a series of concerts in the gardens of **Villa Doria Pamphilj** *(see p267).* Programmes range from comic opera to jazz and 20th-century classical music.

Brass bands can be heard in the **Pincio Gardens** *(see p136)* on Sunday mornings from the end of April until mid-July – they usually strike up at around 10.30am.

CONTEMPORARY MUSIC

THE **Auditorium del Foro Italico**, the **Auditorium di Santa Cecilia** and the Accademia Filarmonica Romana (usually at the **Teatro Olimpico**) sometimes include modern pieces in their programmes but these are generally less popular than the classics and there is no set venue with a regular contemporary programme.

International names appear on festival programmes and at one-off concerts. The most interesting festivals are Nuovi Spazi Musicali (now part of RomaEuropa) in the summer, with free concerts transmitted on Italian radio, and the Festival Nuova Consonanza in the autumn. Modern Italian composers are performed in the Rassegna Nuova Musica Italiana concert series two or three times a year. It's also worth keeping an eye out for performances by scholars of the French Academy at **Villa Medici** *(see p135).*

OPERA

ITALY AND OPERA are to many people synonymous. Critics will tell you (justifiably) that Rome's opera is nowhere near the standard of Milan's La Scala or Naples's San Carlo. But that doesn't mean it's not worth visiting – world-class singers do appear here *(see p38),* mainly in premières or solo recitals. However you judge the quality of the performances, the surroundings in which they take place are often incomparable. In summer the visual spectacle of *Aida,* say, performed in the open air, is simply magnificent.

The season starts late at **Teatro dell'Opera**, between November and January. In recent years programmes have concentrated on the great popular operas, rather than staging experimental productions or historical recoveries. Tickets range from L25,000 to L250,000.

Until recently the Teatro dell' Opera would move outdoors in July and August to stage opera and ballet in the ancient Baths of Caracalla. This celebrated tradition has now stopped as the vibrations caused by the basso profundos and by nimble corps de ballet were deemed to pose a threat to the structural integrity of the Baths.

BALLET AND DANCE

OPPORTUNITIES to watch ballet or contemporary dance are fairly limited in Rome. The opera house's resident company Corpo di Ballo del Teatro dell'Opera di Roma performs the great classics as well as Roland Petit-style modern choreographies. Performances are staged at **Teatro dell'Opera**.

Contemporary dance is best seen during summer festivals but foreign companies often perform at **Teatro Olimpico**. American modern dance groups of the Moses Pendleton school – Pilobolus, Momix, ISO and Daniel Ezralow – are popular visitors. **Teatro del Vascello** is another venue noted for its experimental dance performances. In summer, entertaining outdoor performances are organized by **RomaEuropa Festival**.

DIRECTORY			
For information about times or tickets for festivals and open-air concerts, see Trovaroma or similar listings (see p359).	**Auditorium di Santa Cecilia** Via della Conciliazione 4. **Map** 3 C3. 06-68 80 10 44 (for information); 06-39 38 72 97 (for credit card sales).	06-323 48 90 or 06-323 49 36. **Teatro dell'Opera** See below.	06-48 16 02 55 *(for tickets).* **BALLET AND DANCE**
ORCHESTRAL, CHAMBER AND CHORAL MUSIC	**Aula dell'Università la Sapienza** Piazzale Aldo Moro 5. 06-361 00 52.	**Teatro Ghione** Via delle Fornaci 37. **Map** 3 B4. 06-637 22 94.	**RomaEuropa Festival** Via XX Settembre 3. 06-48 90 40 24.
Accademia Filarmonica Romana Via Flaminia 118.**Map** 1 A1. 06-320 17 52.	**Oratorio del Gonfalone** Via del Gonfalone 32A. **Map** 4 D4 & 11 A3. 06-687 59 52.	**OPERA** **Teatro dell'Opera** Via Firenze 62 & Piazza Beniamino Gigli 8.	**Teatro dell'Opera** See above. **Teatro Olimpico** See above.
Auditorium del Foro Italico Piazza Lauro de Bosis 5. 06-36 86 56 25.	**Teatro Olimpico** Piazza Gentile da Fabriano 17.	**Map** 5 C3. 06-48 16 01 *(for information);*	**Teatro del Vascello** Via G Carini 72. **Map** 7 A2. 06-588 10 21.

Rock, Jazz, Folk and World Music

ROME'S NON-CLASSICAL MUSIC SCENE is unpredictable, but if you have the patience, you'll come across a huge variety of music at the many clubs, as well as open-air events with foreign stars such as Madonna, Michael Jackson and Dire Straits. Publicity is often disorganized, but the "Music Box" section of *Trovaroma* or *Roma c'è* (*see p340*) give an idea of what's on.

It's not possible to book tickets in advance at the smaller venues – just turn up with everyone else. You will need to buy a *tessera* (membership card) though, costing anything from L1,000 to L20,000. Well-known musicians may mean a further entrance fee, but local groups are generally included in the membership.

ROCK MUSIC

BIG ROCK CONCERTS are held at EUR in the **Palazzo dello Sport**, or in a stadium: the **Stadio Flaminio**, the **Stadio Olimpico**, or in out-of-the-way **Ippodromo Capannelle**. Get there at least an hour before the gates open for a good seat. Testaccio's **Villaggio Globale Il Mattatoio** (a converted abattoir) is a large-scale, stand-up venue for concerts and other events. The facilities are basic, and again, over-crowding means you should turn up early.

Rome also has several lively clubs and discos which play rock music. Loyal devotees head for the good clubs in large numbers. Some are unpretentious and friendly and some, which are rather sumptuous and stylish, are frequented by the rich and famous. Entrance for the top spots can cost up to to L40,000. **Frontiera** is one of Rome's largest venues; some nights it features pop groups, including big name bands, and others it becomes a huge disco. However, is not easy to get to using public transport as it is located well out of the centre towards the western end of Via Aurelia. **Horus** is the place to head for if you want to see US and English outfits who are just breaking big internationally.

Check what's on, too, at the **Antica Carboneria**, **Black Out**, with concerts held on Thursdays, or at **Mecca Dancing**, and, in the Vatican area, **Il Castello**, a converted cinema housing rock and jazz festivals and a club. **Forte Prenestino** is an interesting venue – a former prison, it was taken over by squatters a few years ago, and turned into a different kind of social centre, housing rock concerts, debates and art exhibitions. Nearer the centre one can find the more traditional establishments. **Big Mama**, the trendy **Palladium** and **Caffè Caruso** are well-known, popular venues for a great variety of live bands.

JAZZ

ROME'S TASTE for jazz has developed over the years as a result of visits from American and other foreign musicians. Miles Davis played one of his last concerts at the Roma Jazz Festival, for instance, and guitarist Pat Metheny, Sonny Rollins, Gil Evans' Band, the Lounge Lizards, Spyrogyra, and Joe Zawinul's Syndicate are frequent visitors. Roma Jazz takes place every year, generally in July, with performances at the **Foro Italico** (*see p351*), sometimes listed as the Stadio del Tennis in *Trovaroma*. Tickets, which cost around L35,000–40,000, are obtainable from Orbis (*see p341*) and other agents.

Outside festival times, the best jazz musicians play at **Palladium**, near San Paolo fuori le Mura, or at **Airport Café** and **Alpheus**. **Alpheus** is unique in offering separate concert halls and interesting festivals featuring high-quality jazz ensembles every night. Smaller venues, some of which encourage budding talent, include **Vicolo 49** where you are welcome to join in. Some of Rome's music schools also double as showcases for new performers – these include **Alexanderplatz**.

In summer, many of the music festivals take place outdoors at night. Jazz has featured in the Festival Villa Pamphilj in Musica in recent years, held every July and organized by I Concerti nel Parco. Tickets, costing around L15,000, are available from the Villa Pamphilj itself.

In winter, try the pub-style venue **Stardust**, which opens until late. It offers jazz on Tuesdays, and a pianist on other nights. Or check what's on at **Caffè Latino**, **Caffè Caruso** and **Fonclea**.

Pianist Antonello Salis plays a mix of jazz and Caribbean rhythms. The quaintly named Crystal White and the Super-naturals are a resident Roman jazz funk formation. Guitar lovers may enjoy Eddie Palermo's fusion, and the major names to be aware of in jazz groups are Roberto Gatto, Maurizio Gianmarco, Massimo Moriconi and Massimo Urbani. Rome's other well-known bands include Orizzonte degli Eventi (fusion), Sestetto Swing di Roma (swing) and Area 2 (not strictly Roman) who play jazz-rock.

FOLK MUSIC

AT THE FOREFRONT of folk music in Rome for 30 years, **Folkstudio** in Trastevere is well worth a visit. Founded back in the 1960s, its cramped rooms have an informal, friendly, participatory atmosphere which welcomed up-and-coming stars such as Bob Dylan – a fact which is remembered here with fondness and pride. Irish folk music, and American country and western are much in demand, as well as the regional strains of Italian folk music. No drinks are sold, so bring your own. You'll need to buy a membership card to enter, costing around L10,000.

A recent arrival on Rome's folk music scene is the **Shamrock** in the Colosseum area offering country and blue-grass music. If you want to eat too, head for **Fonclea** near St Peter's, but check in *Trovaroma* to see who's playing – country music only features on some nights.

Visit some of Rome's Irish pubs and you may be lucky to find some spontaneous music-making going on. Places to try are the **Fiddler's Elbow** and **Druid's Den**, both in the Santa Maria Maggiore area. Also look out for where the Kay McCarthy Ensemble, or Square Dance are performing.

WORLD MUSIC

A STRONG Latin American colony has made its home in Rome since the 1970s. Latin American music is no passing fad for poseurs and culture-hoppers here; Romans customarily dance the night away together with the many Brazilian, Argentinian and Peruvian residents and merengue, salsa and soca are all very popular. For the last few years an open-air summer Caribe festival has taken place in Villa Borghese with live music and other attractions. It's by no means a certain annual event, but worth keeping an eye out for.

Many venues offer similar opportunities to enjoy Latin American music throughout the year: **El Charango** offers South American food as well as music and a small dance area. Also look out for resident Brazilian musicians Brenazil, Carlos de Lima and Alvinho, and local salsa band Xenaya, or check what's on at the **Caffè Latino** and **K.K.** in the Ghetto, at **Caffè Caruso** in Testaccio and the **Bossa Nova** in Trastevere. If you want to get in touch with your inner cha-cha-cha, Latin rhythms pulsate seductively against an r'n'b backbeat in Cuba's Roman sub-branch, **St Louis Music City**. Or try **Berimbau**, where you can enjoy some cocktails along with the Brazilian music.

Other regional musical styles have less of a presence in the city, but exist nevertheless. Lovers of African music should look out for performances by Sanganà or Akwaba. African and Italian musicians often play together to wonderful effect in Pietro dall'Oglio's group at various venues in the city.

DIRECTORY

Airport Café
Via di Porta Castello 44.
Map 4 D3.
06-686 83 28.

Akab
Via di Monte Testaccio 69.
Map 8 D4.
06-574 41 54.

Alexanderplatz
Via Ostia 9.
Map 3 B1.
06-39 74 21 71.

Alpheus
Via del Commercio 36–8.
Map 8 D5.
06-574 78 26.

Berimbau
Via dei Fienaroli 30.
Map 7 C1.
06-581 32 49.

Big Mama
Vicolo S. Francesco a Ripa 18.
Map 7 C2.
06-581 25 51.

Black Out
Via Saturnia 18.
Map 9 C3.
06-70 49 67 91.

Bossa Nova
Via degli Orti di Trastevere 43.
Map 7 C2.
06-581 61 21.

Caffè Caruso
Via di Monte Testaccio 36.
Map 8 D4.
06-574 50 19.

Caffè Latino
Via di Monte Testaccio 96.
Map 8 D4.
06-57 28 83 84.

El Charango
Via di Sant'Onofrio 28.
Map 3 C4.
06-687 99 08.

Druid's Den
Via S. Martino ai Monti 28.
Map 6 D4.
06-488 02 58 .

Fiddler's Elbow
Via dell'Olmata 43.
Map 6 D4.
06-487 21 10.

Folkstudio
Via Frangipane 42.
Map 5 B5.
06-487 10 63.

Fonclea
Via Crescenzio 82 A.
Map 3 C2.
06-689 63 02.

Forte Prenestino
Via F. del Pino.
06-259 70 37.

Frontiera
Via Aurelia 1051.
Map 3 A3.
06-669 28 78.

Horus Club
Corso Sempione 21.
06-86 89 91 81.

Ippodromo Capannelle
Via Appia Nuova km.12.
06-718 31 43.

K.K.
Piazza in Piscinula 20.
Map 8 D1.
06-589 64 21.

Mecca Dancing
Via Tagliamento 9.
06-855 53 98.

Palazzo dello Sport
Viale dell'Umanesimo.
06-592 51 07.

Palladium
Piazza B. Romano 8.
06-511 02 03.

Shamrock
Via Capo d'Africa 26 D.
Map 9 A1.
06-700 25 83.

Stadio Flaminio
Via dello Stadio Flaminio.
Map 1 B2.
06-323 65 39.

Stadio Olimpico
Viale dei Gladiatori.

Stardust
Vicolo de Renzi 4.
Map 7 C1.

St Louis Music City
Via Cardello 13.
Map 5 B5.
06-4745 076.

Vicolo 49
Vicolo dei Soldati 47.
Map 4 E3 & 11 C2.
06-687 54 40.

Villaggio Globale Il Mattatoio
Lungotevere Testaccio.
Map 8 D4.
06-57 30 03 29.

Cinema and Theatre

CINEMA-GOING IS A POPULAR pastime in Rome, with around 40 films on show on an average weekday, while theatre-goers have far less choice.

The great majority of Roman cinemas are *prima visione* (first run) and show the latest international films in dubbed version. The smaller art cinemas are more likely to show subtitled versions of foreign films.

Theatre productions are performed in Italian whether the plays are national classics or by foreign playwrights. The main theatres offer a selection by great Italian playwrights. There are also performances of traditional cabaret, avant-garde theatre and dance theatre. Theatre tickets cost between L10,000 and L70,000 and can generally only be booked in advance by visiting the theatre box office in person, or through agencies such as **Gesman** and **Box Office** *(see p341)*.

PRIMA VISIONE

THERE ARE OVER 80 *prima visione* cinemas in the city. The best cinemas for decor and comfort are the **Fiamma** (two screens), **Barberini** (three screens) and **Rivoli**.

Foreign films are dubbed rather than subtitled (Italian dubbers are among the best in the world) but the **Alcazar** and **Pasquino** have showings in the original language – mainly English – on Mondays.

Tickets for new films generally cost around L13,000 but a few cinemas listed as *prima visione* charge less, namely **Capranichetta** and **Cinema Roma**. Over 60s and disabled people are normally entitled to a 30% reduction on weekdays. Tickets are reduced for all on weekday afternoons and on Wednesdays. Check the newspaper or listings magazines such as *Trovaroma* or *Roma c'è* for accurate details *(see p340)*.

ART CINEMAS

THERE ARE TWO main types of art cinema in Rome: the *cine-clubs* and the *cinema d'essai*. Both of these are good if you're interested in catching older classics and new foreign films as well as films by some of the contemporary Italian directors.

The *d'essai* cinemas now and then show films in the original language (indicated by *v.o.* for *versione originale* in the listings). Try the

Azzurro Scipioni (one of the few to remain open throughout summer) or the **Nuovo Sacher**. Some of the smaller cinemas like the **Labirinto** are called *cine-clubs* and require membership.

The multi-media arts centre **Palazzo delle Esposizioni** usually shows interesting series of international films in the Sala Rossellini (prior booking is advised).

Cartoons and children's favourites are shown at **Dei Piccoli**. The evening showings for adults, often in the original language, are listed as Dei Piccoli Sera.

The **Tibur** is a small cinema with a varied programme and one of the few places where students get a reduction.

ENGLISH-LANGUAGE FILMS

IN ADDITION TO occasional undubbed showings of British, American and Australasian films in art cinemas and the **Alcazar**, Rome has its own English-language cinema, the **Pasquino**, in Trastevere. Titles change every few days (tickets cost around L12,000).

SUMMER CINEMA

MANY ROMAN cinemas have roll-back ceilings which are in use during the summer, while the others close down. The **Nuovo Sacher** has an outdoor arena which also is used for summer screenings.

Rome also has two summer cinema festivals: Cineporto and Massenzio. These show several films each night from 9pm until the small hours, with food and drinks on sale and often live music to keep patrons entertained during the intervals. Cineporto (every night, July–September) has a fixed venue in the Parco della Farnesina but Massenzio moves around (see listings).

It's also worth keeping an eye on the listings pages *(see p340)* for retrospectives or avant-garde film seasons at the **Azzurro Scipioni** and the open-air arts festivals like RomaEuropa *(see p341)* and Festa dell'Unità *(see p341)*. Sci-fi enthusiasts should keep an antenna out for the Fantafestival (early June), a science fiction, fantasy and horror film festival.

MAINSTREAM THEATRE

THE BACKBONE of Rome's theatrical repertoire are Luigi Pirandello's dramas and comedies by 18th-century Venetian Carlo Goldoni and 20th-century Neapolitan Eduardo de Filippo. Major foreign playwrights are also performed from time to time.

The best classic productions are staged at the **Teatro Argentina**, **Teatro Quirino**, **Teatro Valle**, **Teatro Eliseo** and **Teatro Piccolo Eliseo**. **Teatro Argentina**, originally an opera house, is state-owned and home of Rome's permanent theatre company. The **Quirino** and **Valle** host productions from other Italian cities. The **Valle** alternates between productions of great Italian classics by famous companies and lesser known modernist works. Plays at the **Quirino** often feature famous Italian actors. The **Eliseo** and **Piccolo Eliseo** are among the best of the private theatres. Agatha Christie and Alfred Hitchcock are often on at the **Teatro Stabile del Giallo** which specializes in crime and detective thrillers, while **Teatro Vittoria** goes in for Noël Coward or Raymond Queneau. The programme at

Teatro Sistina usually includes musicals by visiting foreign companies and shows by popular Italian actors.

CONTEMPORARY THEATRE

THE HOME OF contemporary theatre is the **Tordinona**, **Politecnico**, **Ateneo** (inside the university) and in a host of small theatres, ingeniously rigged up in cellars, garages, small apartments or tents. The **Colosseo** hosts some alternative fringe-type productions (known here as *teatro off*) while the **Tordinona**, the **Ateneo** and the **Politecnico** tend to stage works by contemporary authors and occasional avant-garde productions. Some of them, like the **Teatro dei Cocci**, put on drama school productions.

FOLK, CABARET AND PUPPET THEATRE

ROMAN AND Neapolitan folk songs and cabaret can be enjoyed in one of Trastevere's traditional lively cabaret restaurants like **Ciceruacchio**, **Fantasie di Trastevere** or **Meo Patacca**.

Puppet theatre is another Roman tradition. Shows generally take place early in the evening at weekends, and sometimes during the week, at **Teatro Verde**, **Teatro Mongiovino** and the **English Puppet Theatre**. Puppeteers at the **English Puppet Theatre** will recite in English if there is enough demand. In the summer, travelling Neapolitan and Sicilian marionette companies give one-off performances.

OPEN-AIR THEATRE

THE OPEN-AIR summer theatre season usually features Greek and Roman plays at **Ostia Antica** *(see pp270–71)*.

The **Anfiteatro Quercia del Tasso** in the Janiculum park takes its name from the oak tree under which 16th-century poet Tasso used to sit. Comedy shows are staged here in July to September, when the weather permits. In winter the company performs at the **Teatro Anfitrione**.

Nearby is a permanent Neapolitan street puppet theatre booth featuring *Pulcinella* (the Italian original of Punch). Shows are usually on in the afternoons, with morning shows on Sundays; children love them.

DIRECTORY

PRIMA VISIONE

Alcazar
Via Card. Merry del Val 14. **Map** 7 C1.
06-588 00 99.

Barberini
Piazza Barberini 52. **Map** 5 B3. 06-482 77 07.

Capranichetta
Piazza di Montecitorio 125. **Map** 4 F3 & 12 E2.
06-679 69 57.

Cinema Roma
Piazza Sonnino 37. **Map** 7 C1. 06-581 28 84.

Fiamma
Via Bissolati 47. **Map** 5 C2.
06-482 71 00.

Rivoli
Via Lombardia 23. **Map** 5 B2. 06-488 08 83.

ART CINEMAS

Azzurro Scipioni
Via degli Scipioni 82. **Map** 3 C2. 06-39 73 71 61.

Dei Piccoli
Viale della Pineta 15. **Map** 5 B1.
06-855 34 85.

Labirinto
Via di Pompeo Magno 27. **Map** 4 D1.
06-321 62 83.

Nuovo Sacher
Largo Ascianghi 1. **Map** 7 C2. 06-581 81 16.

Palazzo delle Esposizioni
Via Milano 9A. **Map** 5 B4.
06-488 54 65.

Tibur
Via degli Etruschi 36.
06-495 77 62.

ENGLISH-LANGUAGE

Alcazar
See left.

Pasquino
Vicolo del Piede 19. **Map** 7 C1. 06-580 36 22.

MAINSTREAM THEATRE

Teatro Argentina
Largo Argentina 56.
Map 4 F4 & 12 D4.
06-68 80 46 01.

Teatro Eliseo
Via Nazionale 183. **Map** 5 B4. 06-474 34 31.

Teatro Piccolo Eliseo
Via Nazionale 183.
Map 5 B4.
06-488 50 95.

Teatro Quirino
Via M. Minghetti 1.
Map 5 A4 & 12 F2.
06-679 45 85.

Teatro Sistina
Via Sistina 129. **Map** 5 B2.
06-482 68 41.

Teatro Stabile del Giallo
Via Cassia 871C.
06-30 31 13 35.

Teatro Valle
Via Teatro Valle 23 A.
Map 4 F4 & 12 D3.
06-68 80 37 94.

Teatro Vittoria
Piazza S. Maria Liberatrice 8. **Map** 8 D3.
06-574 01 70.

CONTEMPORARY THEATRE

Teatro Anfitrione
Via di San Saba 24. **Map** 8 E3. 06-575 08 27.

Teatro Ateneo
Viale delle Scienze 3. **Map** 6 F3. 06-49 91 44 35.

Teatro Colosseo
Via Capo d'Africa 5 A. **Map** 9 A1. 06-700 49 32.

Teatro dei Cocci
Via Galvani 69. **Map** 8 D3.
06-578 35 02.

Teatro Politecnico
Via Tiepolo 13 A. **Map** 1 B3. 06-361 15 01.

Teatro Tordinona
Via degli Acquasparta 16. **Map** 4 E3 & 11 C2.
06-68 80 58 90.

FOLK, CABARET, PUPPET THEATRE

Ciceruacchio
Via del Porto 1. **Map** 8 D2.
06-580 60 46.

English Puppet Theatre
Piazza di Satiri.
06-589 62 01.

Fantasie di Trastevere
Via di Santa Dorotea 6.
Map 4 D5.
06-588 16 71.

Meo Patacca
Piazza dei Mercanti 30.
Map 8 D1.
06-581 61 98.

Teatro Mongiovino
Via Genocchi 15.
06-513 94 05.

Teatro Verde
Circonvall. Gianicolense 10.
Map 7 B4.
06-588 20 34.

OPEN-AIR THEATRE

Anfiteatro Quercia del Tasso
Passeggiata del Gianicolo.
Map 3 C5.
06-575 08 27.

Nightclubs

THE CENTRE OF ROMAN NIGHT LIFE used to be the Via Veneto area so effectively portrayed by Fellini in his film *La Dolce Vita*. The place still offers plenty of venues, but new, less formal and more affordable clubs have emerged, with a more vibrant atmosphere and appealing to a younger and more diverse crowd.

With the new clubs come new areas. The picturesque narrow streets in Trastevere, the Piazza Navona and the Pantheon areas are becoming more popular. Testaccio too has become a new mecca for Roman clubbers.

WHAT'S ON

AS IN ANY OTHER major city, Rome's nightlife is constantly changing. Roman club-goers are an extremely varied group and most clubs arrange different nights to appeal to different tastes – so it's essential to keep up-to-date on what's happening by checking in a magazine like *Roma C'E'*, on newsstands every Thursday.

For a more direct source of information, head for the bars around the Piazza Navona and Campo de' Fiori areas. At about 10.30pm the narrow streets and piazzas swarm with people and any interesting event will soon become common knowledge. *Buoni* (free or reduced price tickets) may be handed out.

PRACTICALITIES

PREFERRED CLUBBING nights for Romans are Thursday, Friday and, of course, Saturday, when you should expect to pay around L35,000 for entrance. Queues for the most popular places can be long but provided you arrive before midnight you'll avoid the crush.

Some clubs require a *tessera* (membership card) which you can buy on the spot and which usually replaces the entrance fee. Your ticket or *tessera* usually includes a free first drink; your second could well be expensive – as much as L20,000 in some of the plusher clubs.

In these smarter places how you look is all important: a jacket and tie are a must and usually you need an invitation or a personal introduction to get in. It should not be difficult to gain entrance to the traditional discos as long as you dress in designer casual wear, but choose your clothes with care – a black T-shirt could make you too *alternativo*. All-male groups are never welcome, and in more exclusive clubs neither are unaccompanied men.

CLUBS AND BARS

AN ELEGANT NIGHT out could start in one of the re-fined piano bars such as **Le Cornacchie**, **Giulio Passami l'Olio** frequented by the English-speaking community, or the intimate **Tartarughino**, popular with politicians and financiers. Livelier places include American-style bars such as **Hemingway**. If you prefer the arts world, head for **Bar del Fico**, **Café les Folies** and **La Vetrina**.

To continue, head for **Gilda**, a favourite with the Roman jet set, with two elegant restaurants, a large glitzy dancefloor and many VIPs. The famous nightclub of the 1960s, **Jackie O**, has been revamped in lavish style, with a lush interior and expensive restaurant. In a similar vein, and not to be missed, are **Open Gate** and **Club 84**.

The hottest club among the younger and trendier is **Alien**. This club offers house, techno and hip-hop, along with stages, wild lighting effects and "happenings". A smaller dance floor offers a more mellow music selection. Equally funky is **Heaven** which also offers soul and dance music. At **Groove**, acid jazz, rap and soul dominate on Wednesday, Thursday and Friday nights.

An unforgettable place for dancing in a blitzkrieg of beat is **Radio Londra**, designed to look like a World War II bunker, where hard dance music and free entrance attract huge crowds of jive bombers. **Black Out** is one of the few clubs in Rome offering punk and British rock music, with the occasional live concert.

The more traditional disco is at its best at **Mecca Dancing**, the oldest and biggest Roman disco which totally revamps its interior every season. It's especially popular with the younger crowd, as is **Smile**. **Qube** is a huge disco laid out on several floors with various dance floors playing mainly rave music. There are some disco bars worth noting too, like **B-Side** and **DDT**.

To find out about events in the more unusual Roman venues, start the evening at the **Vineria**. The old abattoir *(il Mattatoio)* at Testaccio is the setting for **Villaggio Globale**, a social centre hosting concerts, shows, discos and parties. **Circolo degli Artisti** is another social centre with a large dance floor, bar, theatre and video room, situated in the old milk centre. In the southern suburbs, two larger venues offer a variety of concerts and events – the converted cinema **Palladium** and **Alpheus**.

GAY

THE GAY SCENE is well served. Many clubs have fixed gay nights and one-offs are arranged, especially during the Maratona Gay festival in May. The most famous gay club is **Alibi**, where the music is a mixture of underground and 1970s hits. **Angelo Azzurro** offers hi-energy and house in Post-Modern surroundings, but is only open at weekends. Listen out for events organized by **Circolo Mario Mieli di Cultura Omosessuale**, or go to bars such as **Hangar** for ideas of what's on. For gay women **Angelo Azzurro** has a women-only night on Thursdays, and **New Jolie Coeur** often has them on Saturdays.

Jazz, Salsa and African

There are plenty of jazz venues *(see p344)* from which to choose while spending time in Rome. The following clubs combine live music with dancing and drinking. **Caffè Latino** (membership club) is best to visit at the weekend. For South American style music try **Yes Brazil**, which has live bands and lots of people. **Alpheus** is a four-roomed venue where different kinds of music events take place at the same time.

African clubs like **Fantasy**, which is free on Fridays, are lively, friendly and cheap.

Clubbing in Summer

In summer when everything closes down in the city, head for the Roman seaside resorts. At Fregene, for instance, there are 13 clubs; all pretty much the same, with a dress-code of designer-label casuals. Take along your swimsuit too as much of the fun takes place in and around the swimming pools. The clubs include **Gilda on the Beach** and **Miraggio** – the latter is popular with a younger crowd. Most of these seaside clubs have restaurants attached to them as well.

Late Clubs

Most roman clubs stay open until 3am or 4am. However, it is possible to find one or two clubs that remain open until dawn. Before finally heading off to bed, join other die-hard clubbers at any of the city's 24-hour bars for a final drink and make for one of the early-morning bakers to buy sweet *cornetti* straight from the oven.

DIRECTORY

Alibi
Via di Monte Testaccio 44.
Map 8 D4.
06-574 34 48.

Alien
Via Velletri 13. **Map** 6 D1.
06-841 22 12.

Alpheus
Via del Commercio 36/8.
Map 8 D5.
06-574 78 26.

Angelo Azzurro
Via Card. Merry del Val 13.
Map 7 C1.
06-580 04 72.

Antico Caffè della Pace
Via della Pace 3–7.
Map 4 E4 & 11 C2.
06-686 12 16.

Bar del Fico
Piazza del Fico 26/8.
Map 11 B2.
06-686 52 05.

Black Out
Via Saturnia 18.
Map 9 C3.
06-70 49 67 91.

B-Side
Via dei Funari 21A.
Map 12 E5.
06-68 83 32 32.

Cafe' les Folies
Via San Francesco a Ripa 165.
Map 7 C1.
06-588 59 08.

Caffè Latino
Via di Monte Testaccio 96.
Map 8 D4.
06-574 40 20.

Circolo degli Artisti
Via Lamarmora 28.
Map 6 E5.
06-70 30 56 84.

Circolo Mario Mieli di Cultura Omosessuale
Via Ostiense 202.
06-541 39 85.

Club 84
Via Emilia 84.
Map 5 B2.
06-482 75 38.

Le Cornacchie
Piazza Rondanini 53.
Map 4 F4 & 12 D2.
06-68 80 45 50.

DDT
Via dei Sabelli 2.
Map 6 F4.

Fantasy
Via Alba 42. **Map** 10 F3.
06-701 67 41.

Gilda
Via Mario de' Fiori 97.
Map 5 A2 & 12 F1.
06-678 48 38.

Giulio Passami l'Olio
Via di Monte Giordano 2.
Map 11 B2.
06-68 80 32 88.

Groove
Vicollo Savelli 10.
Map 11 C3.
06-687 24 27.

Hangar
Via in Selci 69. **Map** 5 C5.
06-488 13 97.

Heaven
Viale di Porta Ardeatina 118A. **Map** 9 B5.
06-574 37 72.

Hemingway
Piazza delle Coppelle 10.
Map 4 F3 & 12 D2.
06-686 44 90.

Jackie O
Via Boncompagni 11.
Map 5 B2.
06-42 88 54 57.

Mecca Dancing
Via Tagliamento 9.
06-841 44 59.

New Jolie Coeur
Via Sirte 5.
06-86 21 58 27.

Open Gate
Via San Nicola da Tolentino 4. **Map** 5 C2.
06-42 00 08 48.

Palladium
Piazza B. Romano 8.
06-511 02 03.

Qube
Via di Portonaccio 212.
06-438 10 05.

Radio Londra
Via Monte Testaccio 65/b.
Map 8 D4.
06-575 00 44.

Safari
Via Aurelia 601.
06-66 41 63 09.

Smile
Via Schiaparelli 29–31.
Map 2 D3.
06-322 12 51.

Tartarughino
Via della Scrofa 1.
Map 4 F3 & 12 D2.
06-686 41 31.

La Vetrina
Via della Vetrina 20.
Map 4 E3 & 11 B2.
06-68 80 84 44.

Villaggio Globale
Lungotevere Testaccio.
Map 8 D4.
06-57 30 03 29.

Vineria Reggio
Campo de' Fiori 5.
Map 4 E4 & 11 C4.
06-68 80 32 68.

Yes Brazil
Via S. Francesco a Ripa 103.
Map 7 C2.
06-581 62 67.

Summer Clubs

Gilda on the Beach
Lungomare di Ponente 11.
06-66 56 06 49.

Miraggio
Lungomare di Ponente 95.
06-66 56 03 69.

Sport

DON'T BE SURPRISED if the peace of a Sunday afternoon in Rome is interrupted by the honking of cars and people shouting. It simply means that one of the home football teams has won at the stadium and the whole city will vibrate with the excitement.

Football is Italy's national sport but other sports also attract a large following and Roman sports fans are never at a loss for varied events and activities.

You'll find times and venues for most spectator sports listed in *Trovaroma* or *Roma c'è (see p340)*, as well as the local sections of *La Gazzetta dello Sport* or *Corriere dello Sport*.

FOOTBALL

AN ITALIAN SOCCER MATCH is an experience not to be missed for the quality of the play, the excitable crowds and fun atmosphere. Football hooligans are rare.

Rome has two teams, Roma and Lazio, and they take it in turns to play at the **Stadio Olimpico** on a Sunday afternoon at 3pm, in the Campionato Italiano (Italian championship league). Seats can be scarce so get tickets in advance from the stadium (L15,000 to L150,000). The cheapest tickets are in the Le Curve stand; middle-range and most expensive are in Le Gradinate and La Tribuna respectively.

On Wednesday evenings there are international competitions – the Coppa delle Coppe (European Cup Winners Cup), the UEFA cup and the Coppa dei Campioni (European Championship Cup). In between these, teams battle it out for the national Coppa Italia.

TENNIS

A MAJOR EVENT, the International Championships go on at **Foro Italico** for two weeks in May. The world's top tennis stars thrash it out on clay courts at 1pm and 8.30pm from Tuesday to Friday, and at 1pm only at weekends. Buy tickets in advance either directly from the Foro Italico or from a ticket agency.

If you wish to play yourself, there are now over 350 tennis clubs in Rome. It is often essential to book at least a week in advance and there's usually a moderate court fee.

Clubs where membership is not required include **Tennis Lazio** and the **Circolo della Stampa** in northern Rome and the **Oasis di Pace**, just off the Via Appia Antica. The big hotels offer tennis for a reasonable price. **St Peter's Holiday Inn** requires a small annual membership fee on top of the court price, which includes the gym and the pool (in the summer).

HORSE-RACING, TROTTING AND LEISURE-RIDING

IMPORTANT RACES include the Derby in June and the Premio Roma in November. There are trotting races at the **Ippodromo di Tor di Valle** and both flat races and steeplechases at **Concorso Ippico** and the **Ippodromo delle Capannelle**.

The International Horse Show is held at the end of April and the beginning of May in Piazza di Siena, Villa Borghese *(see p258)*. It is one of the most important social and sporting events in the calendar, and the setting makes it a great attraction.

It may be possible to find a riding club that will take you on a hack in the countryside around Rome, but most do not accept short-term members.

GOLF

EVEN THE MOST ELITE golf clubs will accept a touring golfer with a home membership and handicap. Most clubs are shut on Mondays and at the weekend when they host competitions, and when guests cannot play. Prices range from L50,000–80,000.

The **Olgiata Golf Club** is open to everybody from Tuesday to Thursday, and to guests accompanied by a member Friday to Sunday. **Country Club Castel Gandolfo** is the newest club and **Circolo Golf Roma** the oldest and most prestigious. Within the city ring road is the course at the **Sheraton Hotel** (closed Tuesday).

Two of the many important competitions on the various golf courses around Rome are the National Championships in October and the Rome Masters in April.

CAR AND MOTORBIKE RACING

FORMULA 1 and Formula 3 races take place on Sundays at **Vallelunga**; be prepared for some relatively expensive entrance fees. Frequently on Saturdays official trials are open to spectators, and on some non-racing Sundays Italy's car designers show new models.

GREYHOUND RACING

THE **Cinodromo** track has shed its sleazy image, and the entrance fee and bets are inexpensive. There is usually a lively, animated crowd of all ages in attendance. Races are run every Wednesday and Thursday at 6.30pm and on Sundays at 10.15am.

ROWING

IN MID-JUNE an Oxbridge crew challenges the historic Aniene crew to a race taking place alternately on the Thames and the Tiber. The best place to view this from is between the Margherita and the Sant'Angelo bridges. The race usually starts at around 6pm. Another event is the battle between the Roma and Lazio crews, from Ponte Milvio to Ponte Flaminio, on the same variable date as the Roma-Lazio football Derby.

SWIMMING

SWIMMING POOLS are few and definitely not geared to the short-term visitor. You often have to pay an expensive membership and on top of that a monthly tariff. It's also essential, in most pools, to produce a medical certificate assuring your good health.

The state-owned pools can be slightly cheaper, but you still have to pay an initial membership fee.

It's better to try the outdoor pools, often part of the big hotels. The **Shangri-La Hotel** opens its pool to non-residents from July to September. For a higher entrance fee, swim at the **Hilton Hotel** which also opens its pool in summer. The best deal is on a Sunday when the sports club and swimming pool **La Margherita** opens to non-members 10am–1pm, for a reasonable entrance charge. **Piscina delle Rose** in EUR is an Olympic-sized pool (often deserted in the morning) open from June to September 9am–5.30pm during the week, 9am–7pm at weekends.

HEALTH CLUBS

LIKE THE swimming pools, Roman health clubs usually require both a membership fee and monthly payments. For just a short stay in Rome, it would be much more sensible to try the facilities in your hotel, or, if you are willing to pay, head for one of the private clubs. Use of club facilities may well be negotiable – you could possibly be lucky and find that you are waved through for the price of a guest pass.

The **Roman Sports Centre** welcomes daily members for a reasonable price and you can use the swimming pools, the gym and the sauna. The facilities are open 9am–10pm. Be sure to wear lycra, as shorts made from other materials are not allowed.

JOGGING AND CYCLING

ROME'S PERFECT climate and stunning scenery attract thousands of well-dressed joggers and cyclists into the city's many parks. Early on week-day mornings or at any time on a Sunday you'll find the more popular locations looking rather more like a high-speed fashion show than sweat tracks.

Villa Doria Pamphilj (see p267) is an extensive park situated above the Janiculum, where you can choose among three tracks, plenty of open spaces and a network of paths. **Villa Borghese** (see p258) is another vast popular place with a running track.

Alternatively, jog away your cares under the acacia trees and palms at Villa Torlonia, on the spot-lit track at Villa Glori, or combine sport with culture, by running the **Via Appia Antica** (see p265) branching off into Parco Caffarella. Other favourite places for inviting exhaustion are Viale delle Terme di Caracalla, Circo Massimo, Parco degli Aquedotti and Parco di Colle Oppio.

All of the above are also ideal for cyclists, and you can hire bikes from many places including **Collalti**, **Via del Corso** and **I Bike Roma**.

Organized bike trips are advertised in *Trovaroma*.

CHILDREN'S ROME

ITALIANS LOVE HAVING children around, and you can be sure yours will be made welcome wherever they go. But there are few special facilities for children, and the heat, crowds and lack of clean public loos mean that Rome is not an ideal city for a holiday with babies or under-sevens. It does, however, have plenty to offer slightly older children, especially those who are keen on

**Renaissance cherub
from the
Villa Farnesina**

history or art. The temptation may be to wear yourself and your children out by packing too many sights into one day. Plan in advance and leave plenty of time to wander around the city: looking at the quirkier fountains and monuments, watching knife-grinders at work in the markets, and spending hours agonizing over the choice of ice cream flavours and special pizza toppings.

PRACTICAL ADVICE

IF YOU ARE bringing your children to Rome, try to come in early spring or late autumn, when the weather is good, but not too hot. Easter is best avoided, as the city is more crowded than usual, and you're constantly jostled on packed buses and streets. Where you stay is crucial. A hotel near the Villa Borghese park will give your children plenty of chance to relax and let off steam, though you may end up spending a lot of time and money to get to and from the town centre. A hotel in the old centre is ideal, as you can easily pop back during the day for a rest and a clean bathroom.

**Jogging in
Villa Borghese**

As hygienic toilets and changing facilities are rare within the city, it is really not advisable to bring a baby to Rome unless you are visiting friends or family. As with many historic cities, Rome may not instantly appeal to all children, but there is plenty to inspire their imaginations. Use this book to make the buildings and history come alive. Children might also enjoy learning a few Italian words and phrases so they can order food and buy things by themselves.

If lingering over drinks on the café terraces is what you enjoy best, bring your offspring something to keep them busy once they have finished with their treat: crayons and paper, a computer game or a Walkman. Alternatively, most other adults are very tolerant of children running around and making a noise while they relax and, if yours are reasonably outgoing, they could join in with the local children playing ball games in early evenings on piazzas like Campo de' Fiori.

If you feel the need for a total break, most hotels will be able to provide a baby-sitter or help you to contact a qualified childminding agency.

In the event of bad luck, see pages 360–61 for information on what to do and a list of emergency numbers.

Fairground in the Villa Borghese park

GETTING AROUND

BUMPY COBBLES, narrow streets without pavements and overcrowded buses make pushing children around in pushchairs tiring work. You will, however, inevitably find some people willing to help you haul a pram up steps in a Metro station or on to a bus. Mothers with young children are usually allowed to jump queues, and may even be offered seats on buses. The Metro is often less crowded. Kids under 1 m (3 ft 3 in) tall travel free on public transport.

Although the city is not good for cyclists, families with older children could hire bikes to ride along the Via Appia Antica, or to take on a regional train into the country. The bike hire hut in the Pincio gardens has free baby seats.

Anyone over the age of 14 can ride a scooter under 50 cc, although Rome is not the best place for novices (see p378).

A hire bike with free baby seat

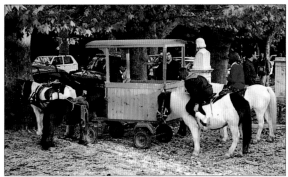
Pony-pulled trains in the Villa Borghese park

EATING OUT

C HILDREN ARE normally warmly welcomed in neighbourhood pizzerias and trattorias, and high chairs are often available for toddlers and babies. If there's no high chair, be prepared for the waiters to improvise for you with armloads of cushions or telephone directories. Most places are perfectly happy to serve half portions, or to let children share meals.

In trattorias it can sometimes be difficult to be exactly sure what a certain dish contains (especially when there is no menu and the dishes of the day are reeled off, usually at top speed, by the waiter), so faddy eaters are likely to be happier in pizzerias *(see pp318–21)*. Here they can choose their own topping (remember that *prosciutto*, which is usually translated in menus as ham, is cured). The most entertaining pizzerias for kids are the old-fashioned ones where they can watch the chefs pound, stretch and flip the pizza dough. The best places get busy from around 8.30pm, so it is wise to go early to avoid having to queue. If all else fails, there are many branches of McDonald's.

PICNICS

P ICNICS IN THE parks are ideal, and shopping for the food is often half the fun. There's no problem finding small cartons of fruit juice and branded canned drinks, but these are expensive unless you go to a supermarket – the branch of Standa on Viale Trastevere is the most convenient. Water from the drinking fountains is hygienic, so it's worth carrying plastic cups around.

As well as picnic food from bakeries and markets, there are lots of scrumptious takeaway foods. Many of them are appealingly messy, so it's wise to bring paper tissues. Try deep-fried fruit and vegetables from Cose Fritte on Via di Ripetta and *supplì al telefono*, rice croquettes with a gooey string of mozzarella inside, from *pizza al taglio* outlets. A *tramezzino* comes quite close to an English sandwich and if your kids are miserable without Marmite or peanut butter, you can find them (and other foreign foods) at Ruggieri on Campo de' Fiori.

Feeding pigeons on Piazza Navona

ICE CREAM

R OME, OF COURSE, is famous for ice cream; you and your children are likely to be tempted at every turn. Real ice cream fans may even want to plan their day's sight-seeing round one of the best *gelaterie (see pp319–21)*. It's far cheaper to buy either a cone or tub of ice cream to eat in the street, but in some of the more traditional places it's worth paying to sit down. At Fassi, they have an old-fashioned ice cream-making machine on display and at Giolitti, you can enjoy gargan-tuan sundaes in the elegant parlour *(see p109)*.

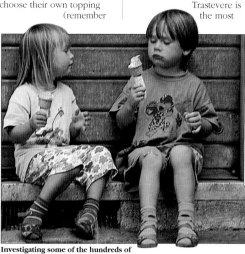
Investigating some of the hundreds of Italian ice cream flavours

Sightseeing with Children

Entrance to the Villa Borghese Zoo

GENERAL TIPS

ROME DOES NOT have many museums with the sort of hands-on exhibits and activities that many other cities lay on for children. Instead, it has other things to entertain visitors. Bernini's marble elephant *(see p108)* and the fat *facchino*, or porter, *(p107)* appeal to children. The Capuchin cemetery at Santa Maria della Concezione *(p254)*, the catacombs *(pp264–7)* and the Mamertine Prison *(p91)* will grab more ghoulish, young imaginations.

Look for details like the dirty toenails on figures in Caravaggio's paintings, the Etruscan votives, which were offered to the gods, at the Villa Giulia *(pp262–3)*, and the illusory collapsing ceiling in the Chiesa Nuova as well as the fake dome of Sant' Ignazio di Loyola *(see p106)*.

Museums your children will enjoy include the Museo delle Arti e Tradizioni Popolari at EUR, with its antique toys, potty and crib scene *(p267)*, and the Museo delle Mura, which explores the length of the Aurelian Wall *(p196)*.

Among the churches, St Peter's, where they can climb to the top of the dome *(see p230)*, and San Clemente, where they can descend to the underground mithreum *(see pp186–7)*, are most fun.

At the Vatican most children will like the statues and mosaics of animals in the Animal Gallery and also the Sistine Ceiling *(p246)*, especially when they get to know that Michelangelo had to paint it hunched up on a scaffolding platform.

ANCIENT RUINS

THE ANCIENT RUINS best appreciated by children are the Colosseum *(see pp92–5)*, and Trajan's Markets *(see pp 88–9)*. You can still make out what both these buildings looked like from their remains. The scant ruins of the Forum and Palatine, on the other hand, may not appeal so strongly. Ostia Antica, where the remains include a theatre, shop and 20-seater public toilet, is much more likely to interest them *(see pp270–71)*.

Mosaic from the Vatican

MOSAICS

THERE ARE SCORES of vivid, sometimes quirky, mosaics in buildings all over Rome. Many of these are particularly appealing to children. Details in the mosaics range from brilliantly coloured flowers, leaves, animals and buildings (in the churches of San Clemente, Santa Prassede and Santa Maria in Trastevere, *see p186, p171 and pp212–13*) to the debris of a banquet (in the Vatican's Museo Gregorio Profano, *see pp234–5*).

Model trains in Villa Borghese

ENTERTAINMENT

Rome's cultural offerings for children are pretty sparse. To find out what's on, scour the cinema pages of the newspapers and the listings in *Trovaroma* and *Roma c'è (see p340)*. Most theatres and cinemas have reduced entry fees for children, but these are only useful if your children can speak Italian.

Language is not a barrier in cartoons and puppet shows. There are cartoons at Villa Borghese's Cinema dei Piccoli and traditional puppet shows every afternoon, except Wednesday, up on the Janiculum hill. If your hotel has a TV, you'll find plenty of cartoons there to keep your kids entertained.

Stall at the Christmas toy fair on Piazza Navona

**Resting
on the kerb side**

One of the most appealing times for children to be in Rome is over Christmas, when Piazza Navona hosts a Christmas toy fair, where stalls sell toys and sweets.

PARKS

Villa Borghese (see p258) has rowing boats to hire and ducks to feed; pony and pony-cart rides; bikes to rent; a mini cinema; a small fun fair; and a zoo. Villa Celimontana (see p193) has bike trails, and open-air theatre performances in the summer. The amusement park LUNEUR at EUR (see p267) is old-fashioned but can be good fun. The Bomarzo Monster Park, 95 km (60 miles) north of Rome, was built in the 16th century for a mad duke. Children can clamber over its giant stone monsters.

TOYS

A visit to a Roman toyshop can be a lot of fun. **Città del Sole** sells a range of delightful educational toys and games, while **Al Sogno** is a dream come true for children who love stuffed animals.

Città del Sole
Via della Scrofa 65.
Map 4 F3 & 12 D2.
06-687 54 04.

Al Sogno
Piazza Navona 53.
Map 4 E4 & 11 C3.
06-686 41 98.

CHILDREN'S CLOTHES

Italians adore dressing their children up, and on Sunday afternoons in particular, you are likely to encounter young children dressed as if they had walked straight out of a costume drama: girls in frills and flounces and boys in velvet breeches or knee-length shorts.

Many shops sell beautifully hand-crafted children's shoes and clothes – the downside is that they can often be expensive and impractical: dry-clean-only clothes are common and shoes are not made for mud.

Lavori Artigianali Femminili sells handmade silk and wool clothes for children up to eight. **Baby House** offers *haute couture* for children, including clothes by top designers, and **Benetton** sells smart casuals.

Baby House
Via Cola di Rienzo 117. **Map** 3 C2.
06-321 42 91.

Benetton
Via Condotti 19. **Map** 5 A2.
06-679 79 82.

Lavori Artigianali Femminili
Via Capo le Case 6. **Map** 5 A3 & 12 F1.
06-679 29 92.

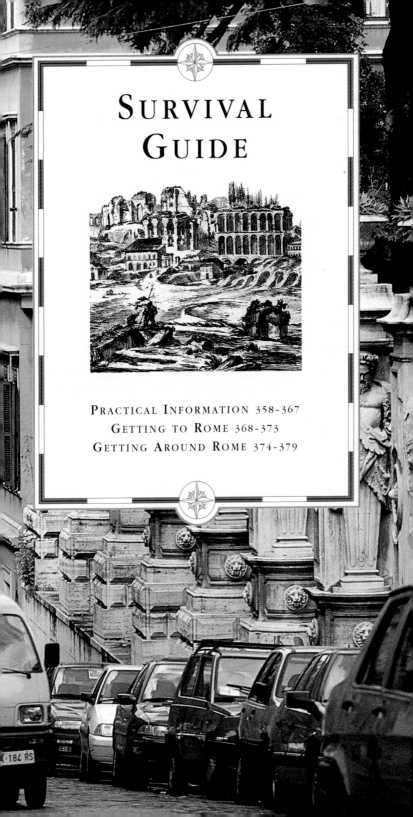

SURVIVAL
GUIDE

PRACTICAL INFORMATION

Romans often seem unconcerned by the priceless art treasures and ancient ruins which lie casually among the buildings and workings of their hectic 20th-century city. Visitors nearly always find these wonders very exciting, but it's not always easy to make the most of them. Relaxed local attitudes make for hundreds of variations on opening hours. Most places close for several hours over lunch and reopen in the late afternoon; some museums are open in the mornings only. Bank and shop hours can be just as difficult to pin down. On a more positive note, many of the main sights are within easy walking distance of one another. Start your day early and wear comfortable shoes for the Roman cobblestones. It can be a delightfully informal city to visit; but remember to observe dress rules to cover up in churches, as this is one area where the Italians are very strict.

MUSEUMS AND MONUMENTS

Many museums open only in the mornings and close all day on Mondays. If you are particularly keen to see a specific monument or museum, make sure it's open before you set out. Many museums don't allow visitors to enter in the last half an hour or so before they close.

EPT's guide to current exhibitions

There is usually an admission charge for museums and monuments, although some are free on Sundays. Many museums offer a reduced entrance fee for children under 18, students with the appropriate ID and senior citizens from the European Union. If you don't see any reductions advertised it is always worth asking. Entrance to all churches is free, and many contain works of art that are worthy of the world's greatest museums. Some of Rome's sights are accessible only on personal application or by written appointment. Examples include Nero's Aqueduct or the gardens at the Vatican.

The *Area by Area* section of this guide gives opening times for each sight and tells you whether there is an admission charge. The **EPT** publishes a useful leaflet called *Musei e Monumenti di Roma* which gives details of current exhibitions at Rome's main museums and galleries.

Typical traffic congestion in Via delle Quattro Fontane

TOURIST INFORMATION

The service at the main provincial tourist office (**EPT**) is better than at the station. You can pick up details of special tours here. EPT also help with accommodation *(see p289).* There are also several information kiosks in strategic positions, run by the Commune di Roma, with English-speaking staff providing free maps, leaflets and advice.

Besides the official tourist offices, good travel agents such as **CIT**, **Wagons Lits** or the **American Express** office can also be helpful to visitors. For information on Italian cities and areas outside Rome, contact **ENIT** (the National Tourist Board), who have offices in all the main cities.

A word of warning: prices and opening times change often, without notice, and sights can be closed for what seem to be unbelievably long periods of restoration *(chiuso per restauro)* or because of a strike *(sciopero).*

ENTE NAZIONALE ITALIANO PER IL TURISMO
ENIT logo

The 116 electric minibus: useful for the historic centre

ENTERTAINMENT INFORMATION

THE WEEKLY *Trovaroma*, in *La Repubblica*, and *Roma c'è*, both published on Thursdays, are the main guides to what's on. The bilingual fortnightly *Un Ospite a Roma* (A Guest in Rome) also has entertainment listings and is available free from newsagents. English listings are also in *Metropolitan* and *Wanted in Rome*. Full entertainment information is on page 340.

Trovaroma

GUIDED TOURS

SEVERAL COMPANIES offer tours with English-speaking guides; these include **CIT**, **American Express**, **Green Line Tours** and **Carrani Tours**. Full-day city tours including lunch cost around L95,000–110,000; half-day tours around L40,000– 50,000. Alternatively the No. 110 ATAC bus passes many of the main sights on a three-hour circuit. The journey costs around L6,000. Tour guides can be hired at many of the major sights, such as the Roman Forum *(see pp78–87)*. Employ only the official guides and make sure you establish the fee in advance; on average they charge around L100,000 for a half-day's tour.

ATAC, the Rome bus company

VISITING CHURCHES

MANY OF ITALY'S churches are very dark, but they usually have light meters to illuminate chapels and works of art. The meters are coin-operated (L100, L200 or L500 coins accepted). Recorded information in several languages is often available at coin-operated machines. Dress codes are firmly upheld in Roman churches; St Peter's *(see pp230–33)* is especially strict.

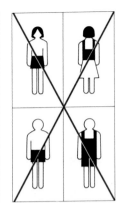

Unacceptable dress in church: both sexes should cover torsos and upper arms

ETIQUETTE

PEOPLE IN ROME are generally courteous and friendly to foreign visitors. Remember to show consideration for local residents and workers.

Italians are delighted at any effort to speak their language, so it's worth learning a few phrases *(see p431)*. Italians tend to drink only with meals and are unlikely to be seen drunk – obvious drunkenness is frowned upon. Smoking is common in bars, restaurants and on streets, but banned on public transport.

Roman style

TIPPING

FOREIGNERS ARE expected to tip, although Italians themselves don't always do so. Leave a few coins in bars or cafés; in restaurants where service is not included, leave around 10%. Keep L1,000 or L2,000 notes and coins handy for taxi drivers, sacristans, chambermaids, doormen, porters and usherettes.

ROME FOR THE DISABLED

ROME IS not particularly well organized to cater for the disabled. Its uneven cobbles and crowded pavements aren't suitable for those in wheelchairs and even the most agile must be alert when crossing the busy roads. Look before crossing at traffic lights and pedestrian crossings – not all vehicles stop when you expect. The seriously disabled will need to organize help getting around. Ramps, lifts and modified WCs exist in a few places, including Termini station and the Colosseum. If you have no escort, consider a specially-designed package tour, or contact an organization for disabled travellers before you set off. The Vatican Museums, Sistine Chapel and St Peter's are all accessible by wheelchair. The Vatican Museums recently received an EC award for improving accessibility for the disabled, and offer staff help if needed.

WCs

PUBLIC TOILETS are few and far between. There are clean ones by the Colosseum (with facilities for the disabled), at St Peter's and in the Rinascente store *(see p323)*. Most cafés let you use theirs if you ask. Take your own paper.

USEFUL ADDRESSES

American Express
Piazza di Spagna 38.
Map 5 A2.
06-676 41.

Carrani Tours
Via V. E. Orlando 95.
Map 5 C3.
06-488 05 10.

CIT
Piazza della Repubblica 65.
Map 5 C3.
06-474 65 55.

ENIT
Via Marghera 2.
Map 6 E3.
06-497 11.

EPT
Via Parigi 5.
Map 5 C2.
06-48 89 92 53.
Open 8.15am–7.15pm Mon–Fri, 8.15am–1.15pm Sat.

Green Line Tours
Via Farini 5A.
Map 6 D4.
06-481 57 64.

Personal Security and Health

O N THE WHOLE, Rome is a safe, unthreatening place for visitors, but petty street crime is a problem. Don't carry more money than you'll need for the day and leave other valuables or documents in a hotel safe. Cameras are less likely to be snatched if they're in a carrier bag rather than an obvious case. Take particular care in crowded places, such as stations, or on full buses, and steer clear of bands of innocent-looking children – they may be skilful professional pickpockets.

Pharmacy sign

ADVICE FOR VISITORS

T AKE OUT ADEQUATE property insurance before you travel (it is difficult to arrange once you are in Italy), and look after your belongings while you're in Rome. Some hotels now have personal safes in the bedrooms. You can programme these with your own memorable number. (Don't use your date of birth; it's on your passport and registration slip.) To be prepared for all eventualities, keep a separate photocopy of vital documents, such as your passport, to minimize the problem of replacing them, and take a spare photograph or two. Traveller's cheques are the safest way to carry large amounts of cash. Keep the receipts separate from the cheques for a refund in case they do go missing.

Be wary of bag-snatchers on mopeds who operate in quiet streets. You might want to take a discreet money belt or a securely-fastened, long-strapped shoulder bag, while

equipment like video cameras should be disguised. Pickpockets (sometimes children) adopt highly sophisticated distraction techniques with pieces of card or newspaper while they deftly sever you from your possessions in seconds. Take particular care of your valuables in market places or on public transport. Bus route No. 64, which runs between Termini station and the Vatican, is notorious for pickpockets. Thefts from cars

are also rife. Nothing portable like a jacket or bag should be left visible inside a car on Rome's streets, and don't carry luggage on a roof rack. The streets to the east and south of Termini station and around the Colosseum are well-known for prostitution and drug-peddling, and are unsavoury at night.

Women travelling alone (or even in small groups) may need to take extra care. Italian society is male-dominated, and women who are out without male escorts attract more attention than they do in much of the rest of Europe and Northern America.

Beware of unauthorized minicab drivers who are probably not insured and frequently overcharge. They operate in particular near the airport, waiting to profit from

Mounted police

Distinctive *carabinieri* motorcycle

Carabiniere – a member of the military police

Carabiniere in traffic police uniform

Municipal policeman directing traffic

new arrivals. Hotel touts and unofficial tour guides are also best avoided; instead stick to the official tourist agencies *(see p289 and pp358–9).*

Police car

POLICE

THE VIGILI URBANI, or municipal police, wear blue uniforms in winter and white in summer, and can most often be seen regulating traffic. The *carabinieri* are the military police, in red striped trousers. They deal with everything from fine art thefts to speeding offences. *La polizia* (the state police) wear blue uniforms with white belts and berets, and they specialize in serious crime. Any of these should be able to help you.

Green cross ambulance

Italian fire engine

MEDICAL MATTERS

NO INOCULATIONS are required for Rome, but take mosquito repellent and sun screen in the summer. The Tiber is polluted but the water from the taps and from many street fountains is piped straight from the hills, and is fresh and palatable. EU residents are officially entitled to reciprocal medical care, but the bureaucracy involved can be daunting. Before you travel, pick up form E111 from a post office. This covers you for emergencies – you'll need medical insurance for other needs. Form E111

Carabinieri **in dress uniform**

comes with a booklet of health advice and information on the procedure for claiming free medical treatment. It has to be stamped by a post office to be valid abroad.

Non-EU visitors should take out insurance to cover everything, including emergencies.

For urgent medical attention, contact the First Aid *(Pronto Soccorso)* department of a main hospital such as **Policlinico Umberto I** or check the Yellow Pages *(Pagine Gialle)* for a doctor *(medico)* or dentist *(dentista)*. English-speaking doctors can be found at the **Rome American Hospital** or by looking in the English Yellow Pages, available at some hotel receptions and international bookshops. Pharmacists post late-opening rosters on their doors (several stay open all night), and can usually supply the local equivalent of foreign medicines. The **Vatican Pharmacy** stocks some American and British pharmaceutical products.

Policlinico Umberto I
Viale del Policlinico 155. **Map** 6 F2.
[06-446 23 41.

Rome American Hospital
Via Emilio Longoni 69. [06-225 51.

Vatican Pharmacy
Via di Porta Angelica. **Map** 3 C2.
[06-686 41 46.

LOST PROPERTY

FOR ITEMS LOST on a bus or metro, contact the numbers below. Otherwise, ask at a police station. If you want to make an insurance claim on your lost property, you will need to report your loss to a police station and get a signed form. For lost passports, contact your embassy or consulate; for lost traveller's cheques, go to the issuing company's office *(see p362).*

Lost Property on Buses
[06-581 60 40. *Open* 7am–6pm.

Lost Property on the Metro
Line A [06-487 43 09. *Open* 9.30am–12.30pm Mon, Wed & Fri.
Line B [06-575 42 95. *Open* 9am–6pm daily.

Commissariato di Polizia – **a police station**

EMERGENCY TELEPHONE NUMBERS

Ambulance
[55 10 or 118.

Automobile Club d'Italia
[116.

Fire
[115.

General SOS
[113 (Free from any telephone).

Police
[112 (Carabinieri) or 06-468 61 (Polizia).

Samaritans
[06-70 45 44 44.
Line open 1pm–10pm daily.

Traffic Police
[06-888 76 20.

Banking and Local Currency

MONEY SERVICES are not always fast in Rome. Transactions can involve considerable paperwork and a lot of waiting around. On the whole, bank exchange rates are more favourable than those in travel agents and hotels – the deal just takes longer to complete. Small change is indispensable – especially the L100, L200 or L500 coins needed for telephones, tips and for illuminating works of art and chapels in churches *(see p359)*.

Eagle sculpture on the Ministry of Finance

CHANGING MONEY

IT'S BEST to have at least some local currency when you arrive, so you won't have to change money immediately. However, there are increasing numbers of convenient electronic exchange machines at arrival points. There are now several throughout the city too. Multilingual instructions are available. You simply feed in up to 14 notes of the same foreign currency, and should get some lire back. Exchange rates vary from place to place. The Banco di Santo Spirito office at Fiumicino airport offers reasonable rates.

For the best rates, change money at a bank (look for the sign *Cambio*). Hotels tend to give poor rates, even if they charge modest commissions. At the Vatican Museums *(see p235)*, you aren't charged any commission. The American Express office *(see p359)* offers good rates and is open on Saturday mornings. Cardholders may withdraw up to $1,000 (or £500) a week from the cash machine, but you have to pay a fee for this service and need to organize a PIN (personal identification number) linked to your account before you travel.

Automatic exchange machine

CREDIT CARDS

CREDIT CARDS, which used to be regarded with great suspicion in Italy, are now much more widely accepted in larger hotels, shops and restaurants in Rome. Some places, however, prefer Eurocheques, which can be cleared faster. All major credit and charge cards (American Express, Access/Mastercard, Visa, Diners Card) are well known. Banks and cash dispensers are more likely to accept Visa cards for cash advances, but Access (Mastercard) is accepted by more retail outlets in Italy. Take both if you have them. Paying for anything in foreign currency will almost always be expensive.

TRAVELLER'S CHEQUES

IF YOU OPT for traveller's cheques, choose a well-known name such as Thomas Cook or American Express, or take those issued through a major bank. Most issuers charge a 1% commission on traveller's cheques. Get some small denominations, so you won't be left with huge amounts of Italian currency at the end of your trip. But don't forget that the minimum commission charged for each transaction (and the amount of time involved) may make changing small amounts of money uneconomical. Always record the traveller's cheque numbers and refund addresses separately from the cheques themselves in case they are stolen. Some places will charge you for each cheque.

Check the exchange rates before you travel and decide whether lire, dollar or sterling cheques are more appropriate. Lire cheques are issued only by Italian banks, and may be more difficult to cash in Italy than dollar or sterling ones.

OPENING HOURS

BANKS ARE USUALLY open 8.30am–1.20pm and 3pm–4.30pm Mon–Fri, but opening times vary and banks are closed for public holidays and at weekends.

Bureaux de Change have more generous opening times, similar to shop hours. The exchange office at Termini station *(see p372)* is also open on Sunday mornings.

USING BANKS

QUEUES IN BANKS can be long and the form-filling involved in changing money can take up a lot of time. You usually have to queue first at the *cambio*, then at the *cassa* to obtain your cash. Take some form of identity with you, such as a passport. Metal objects may set off emergency detectors as you enter.

Exchange office at one of the Italian national banks

Credito Italiano
One of the major Italian banks

BANCA DI ROMA
The Bank of Rome, which has branches in other Italian cities

CURRENCY

ITALY'S CURRENCY unit is the *lira* (plural *lire*) and is usually abbreviated L or £. It became the national currency during the unification process in the mid-19th century.

Lira means pound and the English pound is referred to as *lira sterlina* to distinguish it.

Telephone tokens *(gettoni)* have been phased out so do not accept them if you recieve them in your change.

Shops and bars are usually not very keen on giving change for a high-value note, so ask for smaller denominations of bank notes when you change money. Coins are often in short supply.

The prospect of carrying around millions of units of currency may at first seem alarming. Plans to alter the basic unit have still not been realized, but you'll find in practice that the last three noughts are often ignored in spoken Italian: *sessanta* will usually mean L60,000 and not, as one may think, L60.

Bank Notes

Italian bank notes come in denominations of L100,000, L50,000, L10,000, L5,000, L2,000 and L1,000, which are easily identifiable by their colours and the historic people portrayed. Notes increase in size progressively according to their value. The lira is never divided into smaller units.

1,000 lire

2,000 lire

5,000 lire

10,000 lire

50,000 lire

100,000 lire

Coins

Coins exist in denominations of L500, L200, L100 and L50. Now there is also a L1,000 coin. Several versions of L100 and L50 coins in different sizes are in use (the larger, older ones shown here are still the most common).

50 lire

100 lire   200 lire   500 lire

THE EURO CURRENCY

On 1 Jan 1999, the Euro became the legal currency in 11 European Union countries: Austria, Belgium, Finland, France, Germany, Ireland, Italy, Luxembourg, the Netherlands, Portugal and Spain. Beginning 1 Jan 2002, national currencies will be replaced gradually by the Euro. There will be seven notes in the denominations of 500, 200, 100, 50, 20, 10 and 5 Euros. The eight coins (2 and 1 Euros, 50, 20, 10, 5, 2 and 1 Euro Cents) will have a common European design on one side and the Member States' own national designs on the reverse side.

Using Rome's Telephones

THE ROME TELEPHONE SYSTEM has recently undergone a major upheaval. Many numbers have been changed and new equipment has been installed alongside older machinery. At present, telephone numbers can have any number of digits from four to nine. Any telephone number dialled in Italy, even a local number, now needs to have the relevant local code in front of it.

Telephone company logo

CALL CHARGES

THE CHEAPEST times to phone within Italy are between 6.30pm and 8am Monday to Friday, after 1.30pm Saturday and all day Sunday. Check what time is best if you are making international calls: time variations throughout the world make a difference.

In general, it is cheaper to dial direct for international calls rather than going through the operator or making collect or credit card calls. Telephoning from hotel rooms is usually expensive and is sometimes marked up by several hundred per cent. Normally telephone calls cost more from Italy than they do from the UK or North America.

TELEPHONE OFFICES

TELEPHONE OFFICES (*Telefoni*) are run by Telecom Italia (previously called SIP) and ASST, and offer a convenient way of making long-distance or private calls. At the *Telefono* there will be several metered telephones, each in its own sound-proofed booth. An assistant will assign you a booth, and meter your call once you have been connected to the number you want. You do not need large amounts of change as you pay at the desk when you have finished. There is no extra charge for this service, but *Telefoni* opening hours rarely coincide with Italy's cheapest-rate calling times. The one at the **Palazzo delle Poste** on Piazza San Silvestro is an exception – it stays open 24 hours a day. Here you'll also find a 24-hour fax service, to the left of the main entrance. There are other *Telefoni* throughout Rome, including ones at Fiumicino airport, the main hall at Termini railway station, other major post offices and in the underground car park at Villa Borghese. To send an international telegram, either go to a main post office or dial 186 and dictate it over the telephone.

USING A TELECOM ITALIA COIN AND CARD TELEPHONE

1 Lift the receiver and wait for the dialling tone.

2 If you use coins insert them in the slot at the top. The slot for telephone cards is lower down.

3 The display shows how much credit is left.

4 Dial the number and wait to be connected.

5 If you still have credit and want to make a second call, press the "follow-on call" button.

6 If your telephone card is about to expire, place a new one in the telephone card slot. When the old card expires, it will feed through automatically.

7 After your call is finished, unused coins are returned from the left-hand slot. Cards are returned from the slot on the right.

Telephone cards have values of L5,000, L10,000 or L15,000.

To use a card, break off the marked corner and insert, arrow first.

L500

L200

L100

USING PUBLIC TELEPHONES

Newer payphones, called *interurbani*, are orange, and from these you can dial long-distance and most international calls direct. Payphones take L100, L200 and L500 coins. For long-distance direct-dial calls, have at least L2,000 of change ready. If you don't put enough coins in to start with, the telephone simply retains your money and disconnects you. After a successful call, any unused coins are usually returned.

Public telephone sign

The most up-to-date payphones (pictured opposite) take telephone cards (ask for a *scheda* or *carta telefonica*), costing L5,000, L10,000 or L15,000, as well as coins. Some payphones will now only accept cards. Cards are available from shops, bars and tobacconists displaying the black and white T sign. Break off the marked corner, insert the card arrow first, and the value of the unexpired units will show on a display window. After your call, the card can be retrieved and reused until its value expires.

For long-distance calls on older telephones it is best to find a metered phone (*telefono a scatti*). Ask if you can phone and the call will be metered. You pay afterwards.

REACHING THE RIGHT NUMBER

- The code for Rome is 06 (obligatory also within the city).
- International directory enquiries is on 176.
- International operator assistance is on 170. Reverse charge and credit card calls are also accepted.

- Italian directory enquiries is on 12.
- You can dial direct using the following codes. To reach the operator in your own country to place a collect or credit card call dial 172 then: 0044 for the UK; 1011 for AT&T, US; 1022 for MCI, US; 1877 for US Sprint; 1061 for Telstra, Australia; 1161 for Optus, Australia; and 1001 for Canada.

Stamps are available at tobacconists

- *See also* Emergency Numbers *p361*.

E-MAIL

The internet has made e-mail a viable alternative to the postal service. Two of the most popular places in Rome to access the web are:

Internet Café
Via dei Marrucini, 12. **Map** 6 F3.
📞 06-445 49 53. **Open** 9–2am Mon–Fri, 5pm–2am Sat, Sun.

The Netgate
Piazza Firenze 25. **Map** 12 D1.
📞 06-689 34 45. **Open** 10.30am–10.30pm Mon–Sat (summer).

Sending Letters

The Italian postal service is not especially efficient and it is said that letters travelled faster in the days of the old Roman Empire than they do today, in spite of modern technology. For leisurely postcards, the service is usually fine but expect anything sent abroad to take its

Rome letters   Other destinations

Post Office sign

time; the Italian postal service is particularly slow in August when it can take up to a month for a postcard to reach the UK. For anything urgent or important, it's better to use the more expensive express system, which knocks a day or two off the delivery time, or registered post. Otherwise, you can buy ordinary stamps (*francobolli*) at tobacconists with the black and white T sign as well as in post offices. Sub-post office hours are generally from around 8.30am

until 2pm (8.30am–noon on Saturdays and the last day of the month), but main offices stay open 24 hours a day or well into the evening for some services (such as registered post). Among the 24-hour ones are Piazza San Silvestro, at Termini and at the airport. Italian post boxes are red.

POSTE RESTANTE

Letters and parcels which are to be picked up at the post office are sent care of (*c/o*) Palazzo delle Poste, Roma, *Fermo Posta*. Print the surname clearly in block capitals and underline it to make sure the letters are filed correctly. To collect your post, you have to show your passport and pay a small charge. American Express *poste restante* is free to clients.

VATICAN POST

The Vatican postal service costs the same as the state post, but is faster. Buy cards and stamps at the post office near the Vatican Museums entrance, or in Piazza San Pietro. Letters bearing Vatican stamps can only be posted in blue Vatican post boxes.

Vatican post office sign

Vatican postage stamps

Postage stamps   Airmail sticker

Additional Information

Fiumicino airport, point of arrival for most visitors to Rome

CUSTOMS AND IMMIGRATION

EUROPEAN UNION nationals and citizens of the US, Canada, Australia and New Zealand do not need visas for stays of up to three months. All visitors are required to present a full passport on entry and, officially, need to declare their presence to the Italian police within eight days of arrival. If you are staying in a hotel or on a campsite, this will be done for you. Otherwise, contact the local **Questura** (police station).

Anyone wishing to stay for more than three months (eight days for citizens from countries other than those mentioned above) will have to work their way through complicated Italian bureaucracy to obtain a *permesso di soggiorno* (permit to stay). You can apply for a permit at any main police station, *Questura*. Depending on your motive for staying, you must apply for either a permit to work *(lavoro)* or a permit to study *(studio)*.

Duty-free allowances are as follows. Residents of the EU can bring duty-free goods into Italy for their own use: 800 cigarettes, 200 cigars, 400 cigarillos, 1 kg of smoking tobacco, 10 litres of spirits, 90 litres of wine and 100 litres of beer. Limits for non-EU citizens are stricter: 400 cigarettes, 100 cigars, 200 cigarillos or 500 grams of tobacco, 1 litre of spirits or 2 litres of wine and 50 grams of perfume. To find out what you can take back from Italy to a non-EU country, contact that country's customs department.

The refund system for Value Added Tax (IVA in Italy) for non-EU residents is very complex *(see p323)*.

Questura
(*06-46 86 1.*

CATHOLIC SERVICES

FOR MANY CATHOLICS, a visit to Rome means an audience with the pope. General audiences are usually held every Wednesday at 11am (10am in hot weather) in St Peter's square, the Audiences room, or at the summer residence at Castel Gandolfo. To attend an audience, apply to the **Prefettura della Casa Pontificia** before your visit. (Rome travel agencies may be able to arrange an audience as part of a coach tour during your stay.) There is no charge. Mass is held daily in the main churches of Rome (High Mass is on Sunday). Churches where confession is heard include St Peter's *(see pp230–33)*, San Giovanni in Laterano *(pp182–3)*, San Paolo fuori le Mura *(p267)*, Santa Maria Maggiore *(pp172–3)*, the Gesù *(pp114–15)*, Santa Sabina *(p204)* and Sant'Ignazio *(p106)*. English-speaking Catholic churches include San Silvestro (Piazza San Silvestro) and San Tommaso di Canterbury (Via di Monserrato 45).

Confession box, Gesù

Prefettura della Casa Pontificia
Città del Vaticano, 00120. **Map** 3 B3.
(*06-698 82 73.*

STUDENT INFORMATION

AN INTERNATIONAL Student Identity Card (ISIC) or a Youth International Educational Exchange Card (YIEE) are worth having for reductions on museum and other charges.

Students on the steps of Santa Maria Maggiore

Contact the **Centro Turistico Studentesco** for general student information. The **Associazione Italiana Alberghi per la Gioventù** (the Italian YHA) has four hostels in the city. **Transalpino** has information on rail discounts for students.

ISIC card

Associazione Italiana Alberghi per la Gioventù
Via Cavour 44, 00184.
Map 3 D3.
(FAX *06-488 04 92.*

Centro Turistico Studentesco
Via Genova 16. **Map** 5 C3.
(*06-467 91. Also branches at Via Appia Nuova 434 (06-7857 906) and Corso Vittorio Emanuele 297 (06-6872 672).*

Transalpino
Piazza Esquilino 10/Z. **Map** 6 D4.
(*06-487 08 70. (Branch at Stazione Termini, in main gallery).*

The pope on his balcony at St Peter's

Newspapers available in Rome

NEWSPAPERS, TV, RADIO

ROME'S MAIN newspapers are *La Repubblica* and *Il Messaggero*. British and American newspapers are readily available, and the *International Herald Tribune* is sold on the day of issue. The state TV channels are RAI Uno, Due and Tre; all of them are politically aligned. The advent of satellite and cable TV means there are European channels in many languages, plus sport and CNN news in English. The BBC World Service is broadcast on radio on 15.070MHz (short wave) in the mornings and 648KHz (medium wave) at night. Vatican Radio on 93.3MHz and 105MHz (FM) broadcasts news in English.

EMBASSIES AND CONSULATES

IF YOU LOSE your passport, or need other help, contact your national embassy or consulate as listed below.

Australia
Corso Trieste 25/C.
06-85 27 21.

Canada
Via Zara 30.
06-44 59 81.

New Zealand
Via Zara 28.
06-441 71 71.

United Kingdom
Via XX Settembre 80A. **Map** 6 D2.
06-482 54 41.

United States
Via Veneto 119A/121. **Map** 5 B2.
06-467 41.

ELECTRICAL ADAPTORS

ELECTRIC CURRENT in Italy is 220V AC, with two-pin round-pronged plugs. Adaptors can be purchased in most countries. In most hotels of three or more stars, there are hair dryers and shaving points in all the bedrooms.

Shaving point in hotel bedroom for 110V or 220V

Standard Italian plug

ROME TIME

ROME IS ONE HOUR ahead of Greenwich Mean Time (GMT). Examples of the time difference with Rome for other major cities are as follows: London: -1 hour; New York: -6 hours; Dallas: -7 hours; Los Angeles: -9 hours; Perth: +7 hours; Sydney: +9 hours; Auckland: +11 hours; Tokyo: +8 hours. These figures can vary slightly for brief periods with local changes in summer. For all official purposes, the Italians use the 24-hour clock.

CONVERSION TABLE

Imperial to Metric
1 inch	= 2.54 centimetres
1 foot	= 30 centimetres
1 mile	= 1.6 kilometres
1 ounce	= 28 grams
1 pound	= 454 grams
1 pint	= 0.57 litres
1 gallon	= 4.6 litres

Metric to Imperial
1 centimetre	= 0.4 inches
1 metre	= 3 feet 3 inches
1 kilometre	= 0.6 miles
1 gram	= 0.04 ounces
1 kilogram	= 2.2 pounds
1 litre	= 1.8 pints

SIGHTSEEING PERMITS

TO VISIT certain sights in Rome, you need to obtain a written permit and book the time of your visit in advance. This applies particularly to archaeological sites, which may sometimes be closed during excavations. Write to the address below, stating your name, the number of people in your party, the reason why you wish to visit the sight (for example study or tourism) and the days on which you are available to make the visit. Try and include a contact phone number in Rome. It is advisable to send the request by fax. Call a few days before to confirm your visit.

Ufficio Monumenti Antichi e Scavi
Via del Portico d'Ottavia 29.
Map 4 F5 & 12 E5.
06-67 10 34 31 or 06-67 10 37 34.
FAX 06-67 10 31 18.

OTHER RELIGIOUS SERVICES

Anglican
All Saints, Via del Babuino 153.
Map 4 F2. 06-36 00 18 81.

American Episcopal
St Paul's, Via Napoli 58. **Map** 5 C3.
06-488 33 39.

Jewish
Sinagoga, Lungotevere Cenci.
Map 4 F5 & 12 D5. 06-684 00 61.

Methodist
Via Firenze 38. **Map** 5 C3.
06-481 48 11.

Mosque
Viale della Moschea 85 (Parioli district).
Map 2 F1. 06-808 21 67.

Presbyterian
St Andrew's, Via XX Settembre 7.
Map 5 C3. 06-482 76 27.

The Mosque in Parioli

GETTING TO ROME

MANY NATIONAL AIRLINES, including Italy's Alitalia fly direct to Rome from most European cities and several in North America and Australia. There are no direct flights from New Zealand, but passengers can catch connections from either Frankfurt or London. Rome's Fiumicino airport has expanded considerably in the late 1990s

Alitalia aircraft

to accommodate the growing number of visitors. Rome also has train and coach links with the rest of Europe. These take a lot longer than flights (about 24 hours from London, compared with about 3 hours by air), but tend to cost about the same, so are only really worthwhile if you want to travel overland. The trains are often crowded in summer.

Part of the new extension to Fiumicino airport

BY AIR

IF YOU'RE FLYING from the United States, **TWA**, Delta and United Airlines operate regular direct scheduled flights to Rome, with services from about half a dozen cities (including New York, Boston, Washington, Los Angeles and Chicago). Flying time from New York is about eight and a half hours and it's about 13 hours from Los Angeles. **Canadian Airlines** flies from Montreal and Toronto; **Qantas** from Melbourne and Sydney. The Italian state

airline, **Alitalia**, also flies between Rome and New York, San Francisco, Philadelphia, Boston, Chicago, Detroit, Washington, Montreal, Toronto and Sydney. It may, however, be considerably cheaper for intercontinental travellers to take a budget flight to London, Paris, Frankfurt or Amsterdam and continue the journey to Rome from there. **British**

Alitalia flight tickets

Airways and Alitalia operate direct scheduled flights from London Heathrow to Rome, and you can fly from Manchester. Among the airlines using Rome as an intercontinental transit point are **Philippine Airlines**, Sudan Airways and Ethiopian Airlines: fares are cheaper, but flights tend to be less frequent and are sometimes subject to long delays.

APEX, PEX, or SuperPEX fares generally offer the best value in scheduled flights, but you must purchase them well in advance (for example, 7 or 14 days ahead in the UK; 21 days in the US). They are subject to penalty clauses if you cancel, so it's advisable to take out insurance as soon as you buy your ticket. If you're based in the UK, it's worth looking in the small ads of newspapers for cut-price charters (though even in low season these are

Check-in area at Fiumicino, Rome's main international airport

becoming increasingly rare). Regular charters run all year round. Most leave from Gatwick and Luton, but there are a couple of flights a week from Manchester and it's usually possible to fly from Glasgow and Birmingham. Fares vary greatly, peaking in summer, and in Holy Week for the Pope's Easter blessing.

If you want to book flights during your stay in Rome, travel agents, such as the **American Express** office, should be able to help.

Easy-to-follow signs at Ostiense

AIRLINE NUMBERS

Alitalia
[C] *1478-656 43 (information), 1478-656 42 (international flights), 1478-656 41 (domestic flights); all these are toll-free numbers that can only be used within Italy.*

American Express
[C] *06-676 41.*

British Airways
[C] *06-52 49 28 00.*

Canadian Airlines
[C] *06-655 71 17 or 1678-622 16 (toll free, within Italy only).*

Qantas
[C] *06-488 81 01 or 06-48 88 09 30.*

TWA
[C] *06-472 11 or 06-65 95 49 21.*

PACKAGE HOLIDAYS

PACKAGE HOLIDAYS to Rome can be much better value than travelling independently. For European visitors there are weekend packages and two- or three-centre holidays; Rome is frequently packaged with Florence and Venice. Those from further afield can visit the city during Europe-wide tours. Most package companies transport you free of charge from the airport to your hotel in Rome. Many, especially the more expensive ones, include a tour guide.

FIUMICINO AIRPORT

ROME HAS TWO international airports. Leonardo da Vinci – commonly known as Fiumicino – handles most scheduled flights, and is situated about 30 km (18 miles) southwest of the city. The airport is currently being expanded to accomodate the increasing number of flights, and will by year 2001 have 3 terminals (two of which were ready in 1999). Terminal A will service domestic flights, Terminal B is for domestic and international flights within the European Community, and Terminal C for international flights.

From Fiumicino there is a train to Fara Sabina station (6.15am– midnight; 30 min journey). It also stops at Trastevere, Ostiense, Tuscolana and Tiburtina stations. A faster, but more expensive, train runs non-stop to Termini every hour (7.50am–10.05pm, return trains departing hourly 7am– 9.15pm). If you are lucky the ticket office (which also sells Metro tickets) will be open; if not, you'll have to tackle the automatic ticket machine *(see p373)*.

Ostiense is linked with Piramide Metro (Line B) where you can catch an underground train to the city centre. This Metro line runs from 5.30am until 11.30pm every day. It can be difficult to find a taxi at Ostiense after 9pm, but there's a bus (the No. 95) to Piazza Venezia.

In addition, car hires are also available and have offices at the airport *(see p379)*.

Shuttle bus to car-hire lots at Fiumicino

The train linking Fiumicino airport to Stazione Termini

Efforts are made at Fiumicino to improve both the airport and the surrounding area at the beginning of the new Millennium. These developments include the institution of a People Mover rail transport system for travelling between various points within the airport, the expansion of Terminal A, and a four-star hotel located nearby the terminals.

CIAMPINO AIRPORT

THE OTHER AIRPORT that services Rome is Ciampino, about 15 km (9 miles) south-east and used by the majority of charter flights. Major car hire firms have a rental office at the airport, though you may find it less harrowing to get into the city centre on public transport or by taxi.

Although it is more difficult to travel to and from Ciampino via public transportation than Fiumicino, the swiftest way to get to the centre of Rome from Ciampino is by bus to Anagnina Metro station, then by underground train to Termini. Taxis from the airport are expensive; be careful and only use official cab. In addition, make sure that the fare meter is switched on and showing only the minimum charge before you leave the airport.

Ciampino, a more basic airport used by most charter flights

Arriving in Rome

THIS MAP shows the main bus, rail and Metro links used by travellers arriving in Rome. The connections between Rome's two airports and the city centre are shown, as well as links between Rome and the rest of Italy and the international rail routes from neighbouring European countries. Travel information, including details of journey times and service frequency, is listed separately in each box.

FS *National connections*
Links to Flaminio from Viterbo (2 hrs), Bracciano (90 mins).

M *Line A, northbound*
Stops after Ottaviano, due to open from year 2000, are: Mosca, Valle Aurelia, Baldo degli Ubaldi.

FS *Coastal route from Northern Italy*
Links with Termini station. Marseille (11 hrs), Nice (9 hrs), Turin (7 hrs 30 mins), Genova (6 hrs), Pisa (3 hrs 30 mins).

KEY

✈	Airport *see pp368–9*
FS	Railway *see pp372–3*
🚍	Coach & Bus Link *see p373*
M	Metro *see pp376–7*
——	Airport Link *see pp368–9*
——	State Rail Link *see pp374–5*
——	Metro Line A *see pp376–7*
——	Metro Line B *see pp376–7*
▪ ▪	Walkway
——	Tram 8

✈ **LEONARDO DA VINCI (FIUMICINO)**
Direct train links to Ostiense, Tiburtina and Termini. Linked with Piramide Metro station.
FS *Fiumicino–Fara Sabina (via Trastevere, Ostiense, Tiburtina) every 20 mins;*
Fiumicino–Termini every 60 mins.
🚍 *Fiumicino–Lepanto (via Fregene) every 30 mins.*
🚍 *Fiumicino–Ostiense (via Fiumicino village) every 45 mins.*

M *Line B, southbound*
Stops after Piramide are: Garbatella, Basilica San Paolo, Marconi, Magliana, EUR Palasport, EUR Fermi and Laurentina (end station).

Coach connections into Rome
International and national bus links at **Piazza dei Cinquecento** (in front of Termini). Buses for the Lazio region link at **Lepanto**. Connections to the city centre and other parts of Italy link at **Piazzale Ostiense**.

Coach arriving at Piazzale Ostiense

FS International and Northern Italy
Links with Termini. Trains arriving after midnight terminate at Tiburtina.
Paris (15 hrs), **Vienna** (14 hrs), **Geneva** (14 hrs), **Basle** (13 hrs), **Munich** (11 hrs), **Verona** (7 hrs), **Milan** (5 hrs), **Bologna** (3 hrs 30 mins), **Florence** (2 hrs).

M Line B, northbound
Stops after Tiburtina are: Monti Tiburtini, Pietralata, Santa Maria del Soccorso, Ponte Mammolo and Rebibbia (end station).

FS Eastern Italy
Links with Termini station.
Pescara (4 hrs), **L'Aquila** (3 hrs 30mins).

FS Southern Italy
Links with Termini station.
Palermo (12 hrs), **Reggio Calabria** (9 hrs 30 mins), **Bari** (6 hrs 30 mins), **Naples** (2 hrs).

Piazza Bologna

Policlinico

Tiburtina

Castro Pretorio

eneto

bblica

nal

Roma Termini

ur

Esquiline

Vittorio Emanuele

osseo

Manzoni

Lateran

San Giovanni

calla

Re di Roma

Tuscolana

Ponte Lungo

M Line A, southbound
Stops after Ponte Lungo are: Furio Camillo, Colli Albani, Arco di Travertino, Porta Furba, Numidio Quadrato, Lucio Sestio, Giulio Agricola, Subaugusta, Cinecittà and Anagnina (end station).

CIAMPINO
Bus link to Anagnina Metro station (on Line A).
Atac bus every 30 mins (10–20 mins). **ACOTRAL bus** every hour to Anagnina Metro station (10–20 mins). Metro line A links with Termini station.

Termini Metro station

Reaching Rome by Train, Coach or Car

ANY OVERLAND journey to Rome is fastest by train, though there are coach connections to most major European cities. Within Italy, journeys between large cities are usually also best done by train, but when travelling from towns which are not on the main Intercity rail routes, coaches can be quicker. For drivers, the Italian Automobile Club (see p361) provides free assistance and excellent maps to members of affiliated automobile clubs from all over the world.

The Eurostar – Italy's fastest train

The foyer of Stazione Termini

STAZIONE TERMINI

STAZIONE TERMINI, Rome's main train station, is also the hub of the urban transport system. Beneath it is the only interchange between the city's two Metro lines, and outside, on Piazza dei Cinquecento, is the central bus terminus. Though it is one of Rome's most stunning 20th-century buildings and was restored in 1999, it also has many unsavoury aspects, so it is unwise to linger longer than necessary.

FS logo

If you arrive late, aim to leave the neighbourhood as swiftly as you can. There are usually taxis (go to the official queue), even in the small hours, and most of the city's night buses start at Termini.

In summer the station gets very crowded, and you can expect long queues at ticket booths, bureaux de change and at both the transport and tourist information offices. There's a left luggage office, a police station where you should report anything lost or stolen on a train or in the station; and a small Citalia office where you can exchange money as well as

get travel information. In the foyer, there is an international telephone office (see p364), a bookshop, a post office and a tobacconist (where you can stock up on bus and Metro tickets). Other facilities at the station include a burger bar, a café, a ticket office for Transalpino and, downstairs in the gloomy Metro subway, a hairdresser, a pharmacy and an albergo diurno (day hotel), where, for a price, you can freshen up with a bath or shower.

Of Rome's other stations, four are most likely to be of interest to tourists. They are

BINARIO 17
Platform sign

← uscita
Exit sign

Ostiense and Trastevere, for trains to Fiumicino airport and Viterbo (see p271); Tiburtina, for some of the trains on the north-south line through Italy; and Roma Nord for trains to Prima Porta.

TRAVELLING BY TRAIN

ITALIAN STATE RAILWAYS (Ferrovie dello Stato or FS) have several levels of service, from Locale trains which stop at every station, to the Eurostar, a super-fast and extremely luxurious train, which offers first- and second-class service. The Eurostar runs between Rome and Milan, Turin, Genoa, Bari, Naples and Venice. You have to reserve and you're charged hefty supplements for the privileges of speed, hostess service and free newspapers. You also pay a supplement on Intercity trains. These trains are for fast long-distance journeys and have both first- and second-class carriages. They run from Rome to Venice, Milan, Florence, Naples and other cities. You should book in high season and at weekends. Booking is obligatory on

Termini, the heart of Italy's rail network and Rome's transport system

An international Eurocity train

some services, which are marked in the timetable by a black R on a white background. Tickets for immediate travel can be bought at the station, but allow plenty of time to queue. To book a ticket in advance or make a seat reservation it is usually much quicker to go to a travel agent displaying the FS symbol.

From Rome you can also take international or Eurocity (EC) trains to destinations all over Europe. It is worth reserving a seat on these services, especially during the summer when trains can become very crowded.

MACHINES FOR FS RAIL TICKETS

These self-service machines are easy to use, and most have instructions in four languages on a printed panel.

1 Select your destination.

3 Take your ticket and change.

2 The price is shown on the display. Insert coins, notes, or an American Express or Diners Club card.

Date

Length of journey

Price of ticket

Destination   Class

Number of adults and children travelling

COACH TRAVEL

Most regional and long-distance coaches are blue

LONG-DISTANCE coaches terminate at Tiburtina, which is the city's main coach station. Information and tickets for Euroline coaches to European cities are available from **Lazzi Express**. The **Appian Line** offers regular services within Italy. Its itineraries include Florence, Naples, Capri, Sorrento and Pompei, and, in summer, Venice and Assisi. Local buses, serving villages and towns within the Lazio region, are run by **COTRAL**. All bus stations used by COTRAL are linked

to Metro stations. Tickets for COTRAL services are bought on the spot and cannot be booked in advance. Some day trips from Rome by bus are described on pages 268–71.

Appian Line
Piazza dell Esquilino 6–7. **Map** 6 D4.
[C] 06-48 78 61.

COTRAL
[C] 167 43 17 84 (toll free).

Lazzi Express
Via Tagliamento 27. [C] 06-884 08 40.

TRAVELLING BY CAR

TO DRIVE YOUR own car in Italy you need an international Green Card (for insurance purposes) and the vehicle registration document. A translation of your driving licence, available at Italian tourist offices abroad, is also

Blue signs showing A roads and green signs showing motorways

useful. Wearing seatbelts is compulsory in Italy. You must also carry a warning triangle in case of breakdown. Main routes to Rome connect with the Grande Raccordo Anulare (GRA), Rome's ringroad.

Tolls are charged on all Italian motorways. You can buy magnetic motorway toll cards from motoring organizations before entering Italy.

Euroline coach running between Rome and the rest of Europe

GETTING AROUND ROME

ROME'S CENTRE is compact and, although walking absolutely everywhere would be over-ambitious, it is a city in which you can spend much of your time on foot. As the main streets in the centre are usually clogged with traffic, driving and cycling cannot be recommended, but courageous motorbike or scooter riders can have

A Roman family's solution to very heavy traffic

great fun buzzing around on a rented Vespa. Travelling by bus and tram can be very slow, so use overland public transport only when you have a long way to go. The Metro, designed to connect the suburbs with the centre, has no stops in the historic city centre near the Pantheon or Piazza Navona, though it is certainly the swiftest way of crossing the city.

WALKING

WANDERING through Rome's old centre is one of the most enjoyable aspects of being in the city. You can take in the architectural details, absorb the streetlife, make diversions at will, and peek into any church, shop or bar that catches your interest. And you can easily visit, or at least see, several of the main tourist sights in a few hours. The Colosseum, for example, is only about 2.5 km (1.5 miles) from the Spanish Steps. Your route could pass by the Forum, Piazza Venezia and several churches; other sights, such as the Trevi Fountain, the Galleria Doria Pamphilj and the Pantheon, are just a short detour away.

Explore the city area by area, using public transport when distances are too far.

Only very small patches of central Rome are pedestrianized, and a street which is closed to cars will still be used by cyclists and scooter riders. There have been many plans to create more traffic-free zones, and even to ban anything on wheels from some parts of the city – but imposing such measures on a population as insubordinate as Rome's is not easily done.

If you find the summer heat hard to bear, remember that the narrow cobbled streets get little sunlight and remain relatively cool, while walking into an open piazza can be like stepping into a furnace.

During the height of summer, you'll have a more enjoyable time if you follow the example of the Italians. Walk slowly on the shady side of the street; have a long lunch followed by a siesta in the hottest part of the day. You can continue exploring in the late afternoon, when churches and shops reopen and the streets are at their liveliest. Wandering at night is worthwhile, as the streets are cool and many facades floodlit.

■ **Directions for walkers**

Avanti: go! Pedestrians have right of way

Alt: stop! Traffic has right of way

Pedestrian crossing: only slightly safer than the open road

CROSSING ROADS

FIRST IMPRESSIONS suggest there can be only two sorts of pedestrian in Rome: the quick and the dead. Even if you cross roads by sets of traffic lights and pedestrian crossings strictly in your favour, there is sure to be some van or Vespa hurtling towards you with apparently homicidal intent. Fortunately, Roman drivers have quick reactions. The pious would attribute this to the protection of Santa Francesca Romana *(see p87),* cynics to the fact that according to Italian insurance law, drivers are responsible for any road accident. Whatever the inspiration, accidents are quite rare. The best tactic is to be as alert and confident

Pedestrian crossing   **Watch out for children**

as Romans. The roads are very busy. When crossing, try to leave as large a gap as possible between yourself and oncoming traffic. Step purposefully into the road, facing approaching motorists with a determined glare. The trick now is to keep going steadily: don't hesitate, or change your course, and don't run. As long as a driver can see you, he or she should stop, or at least swerve, albeit at the last moment.

Pedestrians and drivers must both take particular care at night, when the traffic lights are switched to a constantly flashing amber, turning the crossings into free-for-alls.

STREET SIGNS

THEORETICALLY, although it may not always seem to be the case, pedestrians have right of way at crossings when the green *avanti* sign is lit up. The red sign *alt* means you must wait. Underground crossings are indicated by a sign reading *sottopassaggio*.

It is easy to get lost in the maze of streets and piazzas that comprise the historic centre. Until you know your way around, you can follow the yellow signs marking routes between the sights and piazzas of particular interest to tourists. Routes leading to general landmarks are indicated by signs on a silver-grey background.

No stopping

continua
No parking

One-way street

strada senza uscita
No through road

DRIVING

DRIVING IN CENTRAL Rome can be an extremely intimidating experience for visitors. The flamboyant aggression of Italian drivers is notorious, pedestrians step out into the roads without warning, and the one-way system operating in much of the centre makes retaining a sense of direction impossible. You'll also find motorists overtaking on the

Directions to parking areas

wrong side, while scooters and Vespas zoom among the lanes of traffic and go the wrong way down one-way streets. One rule to remember is to give way to the right. Unless you are accustomed to driving in Italian cities, leave your car at home – or failing that, in a guarded car park.

Car thefts are rife in Rome, so never leave anything of value in your car, even out of sight: areas such as Campo de' Fiori are patrolled by gangs on the lookout for anyone leaving cameras, fur coats and other costly items in their boots. You should also remove your car radio – you won't be the only person carrying one into a bar, restaurant or disco.

Take extra care if driving late at night. Not only do traffic lights switch to flashing amber, but many Italians are astonishingly cavalier about driving under the influence of drink or drugs.

PARKING

THE MOST convenient car park is below the Villa Borghese. Much of the city centre is reserved for residents with permits but there are around 2,000 metered parking spaces (from 8am–8pm). If you do find a legal place to park, however, you may return and find you've been hemmed in by double parked cars. Locations of some of the most useful car parks are listed on page 379.

PETROL

PETROL IS very expensive. It can be bought from roadside petrol pumps throughout the city, as well as from regular garages, though the former don't always sell lead-free petrol *(senza piombo)*. In the afternoon and at night many pumps are self-service, operated by banknotes or credit cards. Late-night petrol stations are listed on page 379.

The state petrol company logo

ILLEGAL PARKING

Rome's traffic police are vigilant. If you've parked illegally, your car may be clamped or (if it's causing an obstruction) towed away, so phone 06-67 691 to check before reporting it stolen. No-parking zones should be clearly marked, but look carefully, in case the sign is hidden by a tree.

zona rimozione fermata consentita per salita e discesa con conducente a bordo
Signpost for a tow away area (*zona rimozione*)

A tow truck at work

Travelling by Bus, Tram and Metro

R OME'S PUBLIC TRANSPORT system is comparatively
cheap, comprehensive and as efficient as the busy
streets allow. Priests, nuns, tourists, pilgrims, businessmen and pickpockets all pile aboard, transforming the
buses and trams into mobile saunas during the summer.
Short distances are better covered on foot, because
heavy traffic often blocks the roads. Getting off at the
right stop can be difficult, but other passengers will
usually help if you ask for directions. Always keep a
tight hold on your valuables.

Weekly travelcard

BUSES AND TRAMS

R OME'S PUBLIC bus and tram
company is called **ATAC**
(Azienda Tramvie e Autobus
del Comune di Roma). Scores
of its orange buses and a
handful of rattling trams cover
most parts of the city. They
run from early morning until
about midnight. There are
also a few night buses.

Apart from a few electric
minibuses (115, 116, 117, 119),
no buses can run through the
narrow streets of the historic
centre. But there are plenty of
bus routes to take you within
a short walk of the main sights
(see map inside back cover).

Rome's new yellow bus
stops comprehensively list the
details of routes taken by all
the buses using that stop.
There are, however, still a
number of old-style bus stops
left. These list only a few of

the streets and piazzas that
the buses pass and are
mystifying until you know
Rome well.

USING BUSES AND TRAMS

T HE MAIN TERMINUS is on
Piazza dei Cinquecento
outside Termini station, but
there are other major route
hubs throughout the city, most
usefully those at Largo
Argentina, Piazza Venezia and
Piazza del Risorgimento.
Information on public transport
can be obtained from ATAC
kiosks. Tickets can be bought
from automatic machines
found at main bus stops and
also at Metro and train
stations or from newsagents
and tobacconists.

Most day buses have only a
driver; night buses usually
also have a conductor who
issues tickets. (You can't buy
tickets on day buses.)

In the day, if you have a
normal ticket, you should
board the bus at the back.
There will be an orange
machine there to time-stamp
your ticket. Timed tickets,
biglietto integrale a tempo
(BIT), are valid for 75
minutes or until the
end of the journey, if
you board before the
end of the 75 minutes.
BIT tickets can be
used on buses and
trams and for one-
way journeys on the
Metro or train.

INFORMATION

ATAC
Piazza dei Cinquecento.
Map 6 D3.
【 06-46 95 22 52.
Open 7.30am–8pm
daily.

**Ticket for one day's
unlimited travel**

**Ticket valid for
75 minutes**

TICKETS

T ICKETS FOR CITY buses, trams
and Metros have to be
bought before you travel. You
can buy them at bars, newsstands and tobacconists, as
well as at Metro stations and
bus termini. Look out for
places displaying ATAC (bus
and tram), COTRAL (Metro)
and FS (train) stickers. Most
of the outlets selling tickets
close by mid-evening but
there are automatic
ticket machines at
main bus stops and
train and Metro
stations which take
both coins and notes
and distribute change.

BIT tickets are
valid for 75 minutes,
during which time
you can hop on and
off as many buses, trams
and Metros as many times as
you like. If you are going to
make four or more
journeys in one day,
it is worth buying a
biglietto integrato

ATAC bus No. 64

Rome–Gubbio bus

FERMATA

**New-style bus stop
listing details of
routes served**

A Roman tram in the orange livery of ATAC

giornaliero (BIG) ticket. These give you a day's travel on the buses, trams and the Metros and one-way on urban train lines, except for Fiumicino airport. There are also available weekly tickets and monthly (calendar month) passes which are valid for the whole transport system, with discounts for students and people over 65. Fare-dodging is common, but incurs a hefty on-the-spot fine.

METROPOLITANA

ROME'S underground system, the Metropolitana, has two lines (A and B) which cross the city in a rough X-shape, converging at Termini station (*see inside back cover and pp370-71*). Line A (red) leads from Ottaviano near the Vatican to Anagnina in the southeast of the city,

Metro logo

where buses go to Ciampino airport. Line B (blue) runs from Rebibbia in the northeast, where you can catch a bus to Tivoli, down to EUR in the southwest, where buses leave for the coast. Stations are clearly marked by the Metro logo, a large white M on a red background.

The system was designed to ferry commuters in from the suburbs, so is not very useful within the centre, but the Metro is a relatively speedy way of crossing the city. Useful stations are Colosseo, Spagna, San Giovanni, Ottaviano and Piramide (for trains to Fiumicino). Metro Line C is due to be completed by 2005, linking St Peter's to the Colosseum. Both metro lines run from 5.30am until 11.30pm every day.

USEFUL BUS AND TRAM ROUTES

This map shows a selection of buses that go through interesting parts of the city with good views of major sights. The 64 is always full of tourists, since it is the one route from Termini to St Peter's. The other routes are likely to be less crowded. The 30b tram follows a long leisurely route around the southeast of the city, while 23 goes along the Tiber.

KEY

M	Metro station
FS	Railway station
—	Tram route 8
—	Tram route 30b
—	Bus route 23
—	Bus route 56
—	Bus route 64
—	Bus route 116
—	Bus route 117

BIKE AND MOPED HIRE

R OME'S NARROW streets and
heavy traffic, combined
with the seven steep hills on
which it was built, make it a
challenging place for even the
most serious of cyclists. However, there are a few areas,
such as the Villa Borghese,
the banks of the Tiber and
some pockets in the historic
centre (around the Pantheon
and Piazza Navona), where
cycling can be a relaxing way
to see the city. Make sure that
you have a loud bell though –
places that are good for
cyclists tend to be popular
with walkers and strollers too.

Mopeds *(motorini)* and
scooters, called Vespas or

Horse-drawn carriages outside the Pantheon

A Vespa scooter and helmet

wasps in Italy because of the
buzzing noise they make, are
an efficient way of getting
through the traffic. You may
want to stick to quiet streets
to begin with, though.

Although motorcyclists have
to wear helmets by law,
moped riders over 18 don't.
However, you can hire
helmets from most hire
shops in Rome.

Bikes and mopeds can be
hired from **Collalti**, **Roma
Rent**, **Scoot-a-Long**,
Happy Rent and **Scooters
for Rent**. **Biciroma** rents
from several spots around
the city and a **telephone
hire service** operates in the
summer and autumn.

You may have to leave a
credit card as deposit when
you pick up the bike.

HORSE-DRAWN CARRIAGES

T HESE ARE NOT as popular in
Rome as in Florence, but
you can hire horse-drawn
caleches *(carrozzelle)* for a
gentle tour of the historic
centre. Carriages carry up to
five people and can be hired
from many points: Piazza di
Spagna, the Colosseum, Trevi
Fountain, St Peter's, Via
Veneto, Villa Borghese, Piazza
Venezia and Piazza Navona.
Trips last half an hour, an
hour, half a day or a day.
They tend to be expensive,
but prices for longer rides are
negotiable; establish the price
before you set off and make
sure you understand whether
the rate is per person, or for
the whole carriage.

TAXIS

O FFICIAL TAXIS in Rome are
yellow or white and must
bear the "taxi" sign on the
roof. Only use these taxis, not
the ones offered by
touts at stations and
tourist spots; official
taxi drivers do not
tout for customers.
Official taxis can
be hailed either at
specially marked
stands or on the street (drivers
are not meant to stop in the
street but many of them do).
You can nearly always find
them at the main tourist sights,
at airports and stations
(including

**Taxi
stand
signpost**

Termini and Ostiense). Roman
taxi drivers are not renowned
for their friendliness and may
even refuse to take you too far
from the lucrative city centre.

Taxis aren't a particularly
cheap way of getting about,
so, unless you have heavy
luggage or screaming
toddlers, public transport is
usually a better option.
Taxi drivers always charge
supplements for: baggage,
night journeys (10pm–7am),
journeys on Sundays or
public holidays, and fares to
or from the airport. As with
taxis elsewhere, the meter
continues running while

Taxis lining up at Fiumicino

you're at a standstill so traffic
jams can become expensive.
Drivers may also take sus-
piciously circuitous routes to
your destination. While Native
Romans generally tip taxi
drivers small amounts or
nothing at all, visitors are
expected to give at least 10
per cent of the fare.

You can book in advance
from **Cosmos Radio Taxi**,
**Società Cooperativa
Autoradiotaxi Roma** or
**Società la Capitale Radio
Taxi**. There is a surcharge for
taxis booked in advance.

Official taxi with Commune di Roma sign

CAR HIRE

IN ITALY car hire is generally quite expensive, while petrol is among the highest-priced in Europe. Major international companies, including **Avis**, **Europcar**, **Hertz**, **Eurodollar** and **Thrifty** have rental offices at the airports and within the city centre. However, you may be able to get a better deal by booking a car before you arrive through a travel agent or tour operator. Local firms (such as **Maggiore**) are generally a lot cheaper, but check that breakdown service and collision damage waiver are included in the hire price.

Prospective renters should be aged 21 or over and have held a driving licence for at least one year. Theoretically you should also hold an international licence (available from your national automobile association) but most car rental firms do not usually insist on this.

If the expense does not discourage you, the aggressive style of driving might. Accident rates on Italian roads are very high, so make sure you are fully insured against all eventualities. It is also a good idea to join an internationally affiliated automobile association (such as the AA in Britain or the AAA in the US). If you are unfortunate enough to break down, it is best to phone the **ACI** (Italian Automobile Club) for assistance. Although they will tow away any car without charging, only members of affiliated associations are entitled to free repairs.

Details of current road and traffic conditions (in Italian) are available from a special **Road Conditions** number. You'll find more information about driving and parking in Rome on page 375.

Car rental offices at Fiumicino airport

DIRECTORY

BIKE AND MOPED HIRE ADDRESSES

Biciroma
Piazza del Popolo.
Map 4 F1.
Also: Piazza di Spagna.
Map 5 A2.
Also: Il Pincio in Villa Borghese.
Map 4 F1.

Collalti
Via del Pellegrino 82.
Map 4 E4 & 11 C4.
06-68 80 10 84
(bikes).

Happy Rent
Via Farini 3.
Map 6 D4.
06-481 81 85 (bikes, mopeds and scooters).

Scoot-a-Long
Via Cavour 302.
Map 5 B5.
06-678 02 06
(mopeds).

Scooters for Rent
Via della Purificazione 84.
06-488 54 85 (bikes and mopeds).

TAXI BOOKING NUMBERS

Cosmos Radio Taxi
06-881 77.

Società la Capitale Radio Taxi
06-49 94.

Società Cooperativa Autoradiotaxi Roma
06-35 70.

CAR HIRE ADDRESSES

Avis
06-41999 (centralized booking number).
Also: Ciampino airport.
06-79 34 01 95.
Also: Fiumicino airport.
06-65 01 15 79.
Also: Via Sardegna 38A.
Map 5 C1.
06-42 82 47 28.

Eurodollar
167 01 86 68
(toll free).

Europcar
Fiumicino airport.
06-65 01 08 79.
Also: Via Lombardia 7.
Map 5 B2.
06-487 12 74.

Hertz
Via Gregorio VII 207.
06-39 37 88 07.
Also: Stazione Termini.
Map 6 D3.
06-474 03 89
or 06-32 68 31.
Also: Fiumicino airport.
06-65 01 14 48.

Maggiore
147 867 07
(toll free).
Stazione Termini.
Map 6 D3.
06-488 00 49.
Also: Via Po 8A.
Map 5 C1.
06-854 86 98
or 06-884 01 37.

Thrifty
Via Ludovisi 60.
Map 5 B2.
06-482 09 66.
Also: Fiumicino airport.
06-652 91 34.
Also: Ciampino airport.
06-79 34 01 37.

CAR BREAKDOWN SERVICES

ACI Breakdown
116.
Autosoccorso CARA
Veientana Vetere 405.
06-332 01 19.
(24-hour rescue service).

Road Conditions
Via Magenta 5. **Map** 6 E3.
06-44 77.

MAIN CAR PARKS

Acqua Acetosa station.
Map 2 E1.
Also: Lepanto Metro station. **Map** 4 D1.
Also: Piazza del Popolo.
Map 4 F1.
Also: EUR Palasport Metro station.

USEFUL 24-HOUR PETROL STATIONS

Trastevere
Lungotevere Ripa.
Map 8 D1.

Portuense
Piazza della Radio.
Map 7 B5.

STREET FINDER

MAP REFERENCES given with sights, restaurants, hotels, shops and entertainment venues refer to the maps in this section *(see* How the Map References Work *opposite).* A complete index of the street names and places of interest marked on the maps follows on pages 382–91. The key map below shows the area of Rome covered by the *Street Finder.* This includes the sightseeing areas (which are colour-coded) as well as the whole of central Rome with all the districts important for restaurants, hotels and entertainment venues. Because the historic centre is so packed with sights, there is a large-scale map of this area on pages 11 and 12.

0 kilometres   2

0 miles   1

HOW THE MAP REFERENCES WORK

The first figure tells you which Street Finder map to turn to.

Trevi Fountain **7**

Fontana di Trevi. **Map** 5 A3 & 12 F2 🚌 52, 53, 56, 58, 58b, 60, 61, 62, 71, 95, 115, 116, 117, 492.

The letter and number are a grid reference. You will find the letters at the top and bottom of the map and the numbers at the sides.

The second reference refers to the large-scale maps of central Rome (11 & 12). It is read in exactly the same way as the first.

The map continues on map 8 of the Street Finder.

The key to the abbreviations used in the Street Finder is on page 382.

KEY TO STREET FINDER

▨	Major sight
▨	Places of interest
▨	Railway station
M	Metro station
🚌	Bus terminus
🚊	Tram terminus
P	Main car parks
i	Tourist information office
✚	Hospital with casualty unit
🚓	Police station
✝	Church
✡	Synagogue
⊠	Post office
=	Railway line
-	One-way street
▦	Steps
━	City wall

SCALE OF MAPS 1–10

0 metres	250
	1:13,000
0 yards	250

SCALE OF MAPS 11 & 12

0 metres	150
	1:8,000
0 yards	150

Street Finder Index

KEY TO ABBREVIATIONS USED IN THE STREET FINDER

B.go	Borgo	**M.te**	Monte	**Reg.**	Regina
d.	di, del, dell',	**P.**	Piazza	**S.**	San, Sant', Santa
	dello, della, dei,	**P.etta**	Piazzetta	**S. M.**	Santa Maria
	delle, degli	**P.le**	Piazzale	**SS.**	Santi, Santissima
Gall.	Galleria	**Princ.**	Principe	**V.**	Via
L.go	Largo	**P.ta**	Porta	**Vic.**	Vicolo
Lungot.	Lungotevere	**P.te**	Ponte	**V.le**	Viale

SEE PAGES 11, 12 FOR ENLARGEMENT OF THIS AREA

SEE PAGES 11, 12 FOR ENLARGEMENT OF THIS AREA

General Index

Acknowledgments

DORLING KINDERSLEY would like to thank the following people whose contributions and assistance have made the preparation of this book possible.

MAIN CONTRIBUTORS
Olivia Ercoli is an art historian and tour guide, who has lived all her life in Rome. Bilingual in English and Italian, she lectures on art history and writes on a range of subjects for English and Italian publications.

Travel writer Ros Belford conceived the idea of the Virago Woman's Guides, of which she is now series editor, and wrote the *Virago Woman's Guide to Rome*. She has travelled widely in Europe and as well as writing guide books contributes to a variety of publications including *The Guardian*.

Roberta Mitchell heads the editorial section of the UN's Publishing Division in Rome, where she has lived for many years. An experienced writer and editor with extensive knowledge of the city, she has contributed to a number of guides to Rome including the *American Express Guide to Rome*.

CONTRIBUTORS
Sam Cole, Mary Jane Cryan Pancani, Daphne Wilson Ercoli, Laura Ercoli, Lindsay Hunt, Adrian James, Christopher McDowall, Davina Palmer, Rodney Palmer, Debra Shipley.

DORLING KINDERSLEY wishes to thank the following editors and researchers at Websters International Publishers: Sandy Carr, Matthew Barrell, Siobhan Bremner, Serena Cross, Valeria Fabbri, Annie Galpin, Gemma Hancock, Celia Woolfrey.

ADDITIONAL PHOTOGRAPHY
Max Alexander, Andy Crawford, Philip Enticknap, Steve Gorton, John Heseltine, Neil Mersh, Poppy, David Sutherland, Martin Woodward.

ADDITIONAL ILLUSTRATIONS
Anne Bowes, Robin Carter, Gillie Newman, Chris D Orr.

ADDITIONAL PICTURE RESEARCH
Sharon Buckley.

CARTOGRAPHY
Advanced Illustration (Cheshire), Contour Publishing (Derby), Euromap Limited (Berkshire). Street Finder maps: ERA Maptec Ltd (Dublin) adapted with permission from original survey and mapping from Shobunsha (Japan).

CARTOGRAPHIC RESEARCH
James Anderson, Donna Rispoli, Joan Russell.

RESEARCH ASSISTANCE
Janet Abbott, Flaminia Allvin, Fabrizio Ardito, Licia Bronzin, Lupus Sabene.

DESIGN AND EDITORIAL ASSISTANCE
Kristin Dolina-Adamczyk, Hilary Bird, Vanessa Courtier, Claire Edwards, Jon Eldan, Simon Farbrother, Vanessa Hamilton, Marcus Hardy, Sasha Heseltine, Sally Ann Hibbard, Paul Hines, Stephanie Jackson, Steve Knowlden, Mary Lambert, Janette Leung, Jane Middleton, Fiona Morgan, Helen Partington, Naomi Peck, Carolyn Pyrah, Salim Qurashi, Jane Shaw, Clare Sullivan, Andrew Szudek, Daphne Trotter, Diana Vowles, Lynda Warrington.

SPECIAL ASSISTANCE
Dottore Riccardo Baldini, Signor Mario di Bartolomeo of the Soprintendenza dei Beni Artistici e Storici di Roma, Belloni, Dorling Kindersley picture department, David Gleave MW, Debbie Harris, Emma Hutton and Cooling Brown Partnership, Marina Tavolato, Dottoressa Todaro and Signora Camimiti at the Ministero dell'Interno, Trestini.

PHOTOGRAPHY PERMISSIONS
DORLING KINDERSLEY would like to thank the following for their kind permission to photograph at their establishments: Bathsheba Abse at the Keats-Shelley Memorial House, Accademia dei Lincei, Accanto, Aeroporti di Roma, Aldrovandi Palace, Alpheus, Banco di Santo Spirito at Palazzo del Monte di Pietà, Rory Bruck at Babington's, Caffè Giolitti, Caffè Latino, Comune di Roma (Ripartizione X), Comunità Ebraica di Roma, Guido Cornini at Monumenti Musei e Gallerie Ponteficie, Direzione Sanitaria Ospedale di Santo

Spirito, Dottoressa Laura Falsini at the
Soprintendenza Archeologica di Etruria
Meridionale, Hotel Gregoriana, Hotel Majestic,
Hotel Regina Baglioni, Marco Marchetti at Ente
EUR, Dottoressa Mercalli at the Museo
Nazionale di Castel Sant'Angelo, Ministero
dell'Interno, Plaza Minerva, Ristorante Alberto
Ciarla, Ristorante Filetti di Baccalà, Ristorante
Romolo, Signor Rulli and Signor Angeli at the
Soprintendenza Archeologica di Roma,
Soprintendenza Archeologica per il Lazio,
Soprintendenza per i Beni Ambientali e
Architettonici, Soprintendenza per i Beni
Artistici e Storici di Roma, Daniela Tabo at the
Musei Capitolini, Villa d'Este, Villa San Pio,
Mrs Marjorie Weeke at St Peter's.

PICTURE CREDITS

t = top; tl = top left; tc = top centre;
tr = top right; cla = centre left above;
ca = centre above; cra = centre right above;
cl = centre left; c = centre; cr = centre right;
clb = centre left below; cb = centre below;
crb = centre right below; bl = bottom left;
b = bottom; bc = bottom centre;
br = bottom right.

Every effort has been made to trace the copyright holders and we apologize for any
unintentional omissions. We would be pleased
to insert the appropriate acknowledgments in
any subsequent edition of this publication.

Works of art have been reproduced with the
permission of the following copyright holders:
© DACS: Città con Cattedrale Gotica, 1925 by
Paul Klee 241b.

The publishers are grateful to the following
individuals, companies and picture libraries
for permission to reproduce their photographs:

ACCADEMIA NAZIONALE DI SAN LUCA, Rome:
160b; AFE: 57b, 61cr; Sandro Battaglia 59c,
61clb, 61br, 324br; Louise Goldman 157t;
G La Malfa 251t; AEROPORTI DI ROMA: 368b;
AGENZIA SINTESI: Fabio Fiorani 360br, 361t,
361b; Antonella di Girolamo 361c; Marco
Marcotulli 360bc; R Venturi 360bl; ALITALIA:
368t, 369cl; ALLSPORT: David Cannon 39br;
ANCIENT ART AND ARCHITECTURE: 16bl, 20tl,
21tl, 25bc, 34crb, 35tc, 44cl; ARTOTHEK,
Stadelsches Kunstinstitut Frankfurt, Goethe in
the Roman Campagna by JHW Tischbein 136t.

BIBLIOTECA REALE, Torino: 28–29c; BRIDGEMAN
ART LIBRARY, LONDON/NEW YORK: 18br, 37tr;
Agnew & Sons, London 51tr; Antikenmuseum
Staatliches Museum, Berlin 19bl; Biblioteca
Publica Episcopal, Barcelona/Index 114bl;
Bibliothèque da la Sorbonne 28c, British
Museum, London 27ctr; Chateau de Versailles,
France/Giraudon 33tr, 54cl; Christie's, London
40, 55tr, 68b, 95t; The Fine Art Society, London
151tr, 279tl; Galleria degli Uffizi, Florence
31bl; Greek Museum, University of Newcastle-
upon-Tyne 16br; King Street Galleries, London
33br; Louvre, Paris/Lauros-Giraudon 56br;
Louvre, Paris/Giraudon 26br; Roy Miles Gallery,
29 Bruton St, London 228t; Musée des Beaux-
Arts, Nantes 53c; Museo e Gallerie Nazionali di
Capodimonte, Naples, Detail from the predella
of San Ludovico by Simone Martini 26tr;
Musée Condé, Chantilly f.71v Très Riches
Heures, 26tc; Museum of Fine Arts, Budapest
110bl; Museo Archeologico di Villa Giulia
48cl; Museo Poldi Pezzoli, Milan 54tr; Palazzo
Doria Pamphilj, Rome 107b; Piacenza Town
Hall, Italy/Index 27br; Private Collection 19br,
22bl, 24br, 27tr, 178b; Pushkin Museum,
Moscow 111t; Sotheby's, London 18bl;
Vatican Museums & Galleries 41ca, 237tr.

CEPHAS PICTURE LIBRARY: Mick Rock 306tr;
VANESSA COURTIER: 355t.

IL DAGHERROTIPO: Stefano Chieppa 152cl, 378b;
Giorgio Oddi 53cl; CM DIXON: 17bl, 24c, 268b,
269t, 269b.

ECOLE NATIONALE SUPERIEURE DES BEAUX-ARTS:
21cr, 22–23, 248t, 284–285b; ENTE NAZIONALE
ITALIANO PER IL TURISMO: 358cl, cr; ET ARCHIVE:
14, 17tr, 17clb, 18tr, 19tc, 23t, 27cl, 28tl, 31br,
32br, 37br, 48tl, 306tl; MARY EVANS PICTURE
LIBRARY: 9, 18cl, 23cl, 24cl, 29br, 30cb, 30b,
31t, 34tl, 34cr, 34bl, 54tl, 56tl, 67bl, 74t, 81b,
91t, 92b, 94bl, 127c, 135t, 213b.

CORALDO FALSINI: 38–39c, 340b, 341t, 341c;
WERNER FORMAN ARCHIVE: 17cr, 20bl, 22tl,
23cr, 23bl, 23br, 47tr, 155t, 163tr, 175c;
FOLKLORE MUSEUM, Rome: 210br.

GARDEN PICTURE LIBRARY: Bob Challinor 172cb;
GIRAUDON: 15b, 28br, 36br, 55tl; RONALD
GRANT: 52br, 340t.

SONIA HALLIDAY: 19c, 22br, 25cl; Laura
Lushington 24bl; ROBERT HARDING PICTURE
LIBRARY: 23cra, 32bl, 79cr, 177t, 268c, 353c;

Mario Carrieri 35tr; Caffè Greco, Rome by Ludwig Passini 309tr; John G Ross 38tl, 59cl, 341bl; Sheila Terry 39cl; G White 59br; MICHAEL HOLFORD: 70b; HULTON DEUTSCH: 36tl, 38bc, 57cr, 63, 175b, 287c, 357c.

MAGNUM: Erich Lessing 15t, 17tl, 89br; MANSELL COLLECTION: 19tr, 25bl, 26bc, 31cl, 54bc, 55tc, 56cl, 57cl, 75cl, 75cr, 78tc, 93b, 112c, 122t, 125tr, 126tl, 132br, 133cr, 136bl, 139bl, 139br, 162tr, 172bl, 172 br, 183br, 192bl, 196bl, 210c, 220bl, 227cr, 229cr; Alinari 80br, 141bl, 174t, 254b; Anderson 78cr, 138bl, 163tl, 228b; MORO ROMA: 36cl, 37cl, 38br, 39tr, 39bl.

NATIONAL PORTRAIT GALLERY, London: 55cr, 55b, 56tr, 57tr; © NIPPON TELEVISION NETWORK CORPORATION, Tokyo 1999: 244b and all pictures on 246-7.

LA REPUBBLICA TROVAROMA: 359tl; REX FEATURES: Sipa 366br; Today 39cr.

SCALA: 94t, 278cl, Casa di Augusto 97t, Chiesa del Gesù 115t, Galleria Borghese 32cla, 260tr, Galleria Colonna 157b, Galleria Doria Pamphilj 46br, 105cr, Galleria Spada 46cl, Galleria degli Uffizi 16–17, 27bl, Museo d'Arte Orientale 174t, 174br, Musei Capitolini 47bl, Museo della Civiltà Romana 48tr, 48b, Museo delle Terme 21tr, Museo Napoleonico 49cr, Museo Nazionale, Napoli 21cl, Museo Nazionale, Ravenna 22cl, Museo del Risorgimento, Milano 36clb, 36–37c, Museo del Risorgimento, Roma 37tl, Museo di San

Marco 54bl, Palazzo Barberini 253bl, Palazzo Ducale 8, 19tr, Palazzo della Farnesina 220ct, Palazzo Madama 20cl, Palazzo Venezia 47cr, 66bl, San Carlo alle Quattro Fontane 33cl, 33cr, Santa Cecilia in Trastevere 32tl, San Clemente 35bl, Santa Costanza 24–25c, Santa Maria Antiqua 24tl, Santa Maria dell'Anima 121t, Santa Maria Maggiore 43tr, Santa Maria del Popolo 139tr, 139c, Santa Prassede 26bl, 28bl, Santa Sabina 25tc, 29cl, Vatican Museums 19bc, 25t, 25cr, 25cra, 27cr, 29tl, 29cr, 30tl, 30ct, 31cr, 31bc, 32cr, 32clb, 41tr, 46tl, 48cr, 49bl, 224bl, 225cr, 235t, 238tl, 238br, 240t, 240b, 241t, 241c, 241b, 242tl, 242c, 242b, 243t, 243c, 243b, 245 (all 4); TONY STONE IMAGES: Richard Passmore 1c.

TOPHAM PICTURE SOURCE: 38cl.

ZEFA: 2, 39tl, 230cl, 231br, 356–7, 358t, 372t; Eric Carle 58t; Kohlhas 231t.

JACKET: All special photography except: BRIDGEMAN ART LIBRARY, LONDON/NEW YORK front cover cl; TONY STONE IMAGES: Richard Passmore spine c.

Thanks also to Dottoressa Giulia De Marchi of L'ACCADEMIA NAZIONALE DI SAN LUCA, Rome for 160b, Rettore Padre Libianchi of LA CHIESA DI SANT'IGNAZIO DI LOYOLA for 106t, ENTE NAZIONALE PER IL TURISMO, HASSLER HOTEL, Rome for 293tl, GRAND HOTEL, Rome for 293crb and to LA REPUBBLICA TROVAROMA.

Phrase Book

IN EMERGENCY

Help!	Aiuto!	eye-**yoo**-toh
Stop!	Fermate!	fair-**mah**-teb
Call a doctor	Chiama un medico	kee-**ah**-mah oon **meh**-dee-koh
Call an ambulance	Chiama un' ambulanza	kee-**ah**-mah oon am-boo-**lan**-tsa
Call the police	Chiama la polizia	kee-**ah**-mah lah pol-ee-**tsee**-ah
Call the fire brigade	Chiama i pompieri	kee-**ah**-mah ee pom-pee-**air**-ee
Where is the telephone?	Dov'è il telefono?	dov-**eb** eel teh-**leh**-foh-noh?
The nearest hospital?	L'ospedale più vicino?	loss-peh-**dah**-leh pee-oo vee-**chee**-noh?

COMMUNICATION ESSENTIALS

Yes/No	Sì/No	see/noh
Please	Per favore	pair fah-**vor**-eh
Thank you	Grazie	**grah**-tsee-eh
Excuse me	Mi scusi	mee **skoo**-zee
Hello	Buon giorno	bwon **jor**-noh
Good bye	Arrivederci	ah-ree-veh-**dair**-chee
Good evening	Buona sera	bwon-ah **sair**-ah
morning	la mattina	lah mah-**tee**-nah
afternoon	il pomeriggio	eel poh-meh-**ree**-joh
evening	la sera	lah **sair**-ah
yesterday	ieri	ee-**air**-ee
today	oggi	**oh**-jee
tomorrow	domani	doh-**mah**-nee
here	qui	**kwee**
there	la	**lah**
What?	Quale?	**kwah**-leh?
When?	Quando?	**kwan**-doh?
Why?	Perchè?	pair-**keh**?
Where?	Dove?	**doh**-veh

USEFUL PHRASES

How are you?	Come sta?	**koh**-meh stah?
Very well, thank you.	Molto bene, grazie.	**moll**-toh **beh**-neh **grah**-tsee-eh
Pleased to meet you.	Piacere di conoscerla.	pee-ah-**chair**-eh dee coh-**noh**-sbair-lah
See you soon.	A più tardi.	ah pee-oo **tar**-dee
That's fine.	Va bene.	va **beh**-neh
Where is/are ...?	Dov'è/Dove sono ...?	dov-**eb**/doveh **soh**-noh?
How long does it take to get to ...?	Quanto tempo ci vuole per andare a ...?	**kwan**-toh **tem**-poh chee voo-**oh**-leh pair an-**dar**-eh ah...?
How do I get to ...?	Come faccio per arrivare a ...?	**koh**-meh **fah**-choh pair arri-**var**-eh ah...?
Do you speak English?	Parla inglese?	**par**-lah een-**gleh**-zeh?
I don't understand.	Non capisco.	non ka-**pee**-skoh
Could you speak more slowly, please?	Può parlare più lentamente, per favore?	pwoh par-**lah**-reh pee-oo len-ta-**men**-teh pair fah-**vor**-eh?
I'm sorry.	Mi dispiace.	mee dee-spee-**ah**-cheh

USEFUL WORDS

big	grande	**gran**-deh
small	piccolo	**pee**-koh-loh
hot	caldo	**kal**-doh
cold	freddo	**fred**-doh
good	buono	**bwoh**-noh
bad	cattivo	kat-**tee**-voh
enough	basta	**bas**-tah
well	bene	**beh**-neh
open	aperto	ah-**pair**-toh
closed	chiuso	kee-**oo**-zoh
left	a sinistra	ah see-**nee**-strah
right	a destra	ah **dess**-trah
straight on	sempre dritto	**sem**-preh **dree**-toh
near	vicino	vee-**chee**-noh
far	lontano	lon-**tah**-noh
up	su	**soo**
down	giù	**joo**
early	presto	**press**-toh
late	tardi	**tar**-dee
entrance	entrata	en-**trah**-tah
exit	uscita	oo-**shee**-ta
toilet	il gabinetto	eel gab-bee-**net**-toh
free, unoccupied	libero	**lee**-bair-oh
free, no charge	gratuito	grah-**too**-ee-toh

MAKING A TELEPHONE CALL

I'd like to place a long-distance call.	Vorrei fare una interurbana.	vor-**ray far**-eh oona in-tair-oor-**bah**-nab
I'd like to make a reverse-charge call.	Vorrei fare una telefonata a carico del destinatario.	vor-**ray far**-eh oona teh-leh-fon-**ah**-tah ab **kar**-ee-koh dell dess-tee-nah-**tar**-ree-oh
I'll try again later.	Ritelefono più tardi.	ree-teh-**leh**-foh-noh pee-oo **tar**-dee
Can I leave a message?	Posso lasciare un messaggio?	**poss**-oh lasb-**ah**-reh oon mess-**sah**-joh?
Hold on	Un attimo, per favore	oon **ah**-tee-moh, pair fah-**vor**-eh
Could you speak up a little please?	Può parlare più forte, per favore?	pwoh par-**lah**-reh pee-oo **for**-teb, pair fah-**vor**-eh?
local call	la telefonata locale	lah teh-leh-fon-**ah**-ta loh-**kah**-leh

SHOPPING

How much does this cost?	Quant'è, per favore?	kwan-**teb** pair fah-**vor**-eh?
I would like ...	Vorrei ...	vor-**ray**
Do you have ...?	Avete ...?	ah-**veh**-teb..?
I'm just looking.	Sto soltanto guardando.	stoh sol-**tan**-toh gwar-**dan**-doh
Do you take credit cards?	Accettate carte di credito?	ah-chet-tah-teb **kar**-teb dee **creb**-dee-toh?
What time do you open/close?	A che ora apre/ chiude?	ah keh **or**-ah **ab**-preh/kee-**oo**-deb?
this one	questo	**kweb**-stoh
that one	quello	**kwell**-oh
expensive	caro	**kar**-oh
cheap	a buon prezzo	ah bwon **pret**-soh
size, clothes	la taglia	lah **tah**-lee-ah
size, shoes	il numero	eel **noo**-mair-oh
white	bianco	bee-**ang**-koh
black	nero	**neh**-roh
red	rosso	**ross**-oh
yellow	giallo	**jal**-loh
green	verde	**vair**-deb
blue	blu	bloo
brown	marrone	mar-**rob**-neb

TYPES OF SHOP

antique dealer	l'antiquario	lan-tee-**kwah**-ree-oh
bakery	la panetteria	lah pah-net-tair-**ree**-ah
bank	la banca	lah **bang**-kah
bookshop	la libreria	lah lee-breh-**ree**-ah
butcher's	la macelleria	lah mah-chell-eh-**ree**-ah
cake shop	la pasticceria	lah pass-tee-chair-ee-ah
chemist's	la farmacia	lah far-mah-**chee**-ah
department store	il grande magazzino	eel **gran**-deh mag-gad-**zee**-noh
delicatessen	la salumeria	lah sah-loo-meh-**ree**-ah
fishmonger's	la pescheria	lah pess-keh-**ree**-ah
florist	il fioraio	eel fee-or-**eye**-oh
greengrocer	il fruttivendolo	eel froo-tee-**ven**-doh-loh
grocery	alimentari	ah-lee-men-**tah**-ree
hairdresser	il parrucchiere	eel par-oo-kee-**air**-eh
ice cream parlour	la gelateria	lah jel-lah-tair-**ree**-ah
market	il mercato	eel mair-**kah**-toh
news-stand	l'edicola	leh-**dee**-koh-lah
post office	l'ufficio postale	loo-**fee**-choh pos-**tah**-leh
shoe shop	il negozio di scarpe	eel neh-**goh**-tsioh dee **skar**-peb
supermarket	il supermercato	su-pair-mair-**kah**-toh
tobacconist	il tabaccaio	eel tah-bak-**eye**-oh
travel agency	l'agenzia di viaggi	lah-jen-**tsee**-ah dee vee-**ad**-jee

SIGHTSEEING

art gallery	la pinacoteca	lah peena-koh-**teb**-kah
bus stop	la fermata dell'autobus	lah fair-**mah**-tah dell ow-toh-booss
church	la chiesa	lah kee-**eh**-zah
	la basilica	lah bah-**seel**-i-kab
garden	il giardino	eel jar-**dee**-no
library	la biblioteca	lah beeb-lee-oh-**teb**-kah
museum	il museo	eel moo-**zeb**-oh
railway station	la stazione	lah stab-tsee-**ob**-neb
tourist information	l'ufficio turistico	loo-**fee**-choh too-**ree**-stee-koh
closed for the public holiday	chiuso per la festa	kee-**oo**-zob pair lah **fess**-tah

STAYING IN A HOTEL

Do you have any vacant rooms?	Avete camere libere?	ah-veh-teh kab-mair-eh lee-bair-eh?
double room	una camera doppia	oona kab-mair-ah dob-pee-ah
with double bed	con letto matrimoniale	kon let-toh mab-tree-moh-nee-ab-leh
twin room	una camera con due letti	oona kab-mair-ah kon doo-eh let-tee
single room	una camera singola	oona kab-mair-ah sing-gob-lah
room with a bath, shower	una camera con bagno, con doccia	oona kab-mair-ah kon ban-yob, kon dot-chah
porter	il facchino	eel fab-kee-nob
key	la chiave	lah kee-ab-veh
I have a reservation.	Ho fatto una prenotazione.	ob fat-toh oona preb-nob-lab-tsee-ob-neh

EATING OUT

Have you got a table for ...?	Avete una tavola per ... ?	ah-veh-teh oona tab-vob-lah pair ...?
I'd like to reserve a table.	Vorrei riservare una tavola.	vor-ray ree-sair-vah-reb oona tab-vob-lah
breakfast	colazione	koh-lab-tsee-ob-neh
lunch	pranzo	pran-tsoh
dinner	cena	cheb-nah
The bill, please.	Il conto, per favore.	eel kon-toh pair fah-vor-eb
I am a vegetarian.	Sono vegetariano/a.	sob-nob veb-jeb-tar-ee-ab-nob/nab
waitress	cameriera	kab-mair-ee-air-ab
waiter	cameriere	kab-mair-ee-air-eh
fixed price menu	il menù a prezzo fisso	eel meb-noo ab pret-sob fee-sob
dish of the day	piatto del giorno	pee-ab-tob dell jor-no
starter	antipasto	an-tee-pass-tob
first course	il primo	eel pree-mob
main course	il secondo	eel seb-kon-dob
vegetables	il contorno	eel kon-tor-nob
dessert	il dolce	eel doll-cheb
cover charge	il coperto	eel kob-pair-tob
wine list	la lista dei vini	lah lee-stab day vee-nee
rare	al sangue	al sang-gweb
medium	al puntino	al poon-tee-nob
well done	ben cotto	ben kot-tob
glass	il bicchiere	eel bee-kee-air-eb
bottle	la bottiglia	lah bot-teel-yab
knife	il coltello	eel kol-tell-oh
fork	la forchetta	lah for-ket-tab
spoon	il cucchiaio	eel koo-kee-eye-ob

MENU DECODER

apple	la mela	lah meb-lah
artichoke	il carciofo	eel kar-choff-oh
aubergine	la melanzana	lah meb-lan-tsab-nab
baked	al forno	al for-nob
beans	i fagioli	ee fab-job-lee
beef	il manzo	eel man-tsob
beer	la birra	lah beer-rah
boiled	lesso	less-ob
bread	il pane	eel pab-neb
broth	il brodo	eel brob-dob
butter	il burro	eel boor-ob
cake	la torta	lah tor-tab
cheese	il formaggio	eel for-mad-job
chicken	il pollo	eel poll-ob
chips	patatine fritte	pab-tab-teen-eb free-teb
baby clams	le vongole	leb von-gob-leb
coffee	il caffè	eel kab-feb
courgettes	gli zucchini	lyee dzoo-kee-nee
dry	secco	sek-kob
duck	l'anatra	lab-nah-trab
egg	l'uovo	loo-ob-vob
fish	il pesce	eel pesb-eb
fresh fruit	frutta fresca	froo-tab fress-kab
garlic	l'aglio	labl-yob
grapes	l'uva	loo-vah
grilled	alla griglia	ab-lah greel-yah
ham	il prosciutto	eel pro-sboo-tob
cooked/cured	cotto/crudo	kot-toh/kroo-dob
ice cream	il gelato	eel jel-lab-tob
lamb	l'abbacchio	lah-back-kee-ob
lobster	l'aragosta	lab-rah-goss-tab
meat	la carne	la kar-neb

milk	il latte	eel labt-teb
mineral water	l'acqua minerale	lah-kwab mee-nair-ab-leh
fizzy/still	gasata/naturale	ab-leb gab-zab-tab/ nab-too-rab-leb
mushrooms	i funghi	ee foon-gee
oil	l'olio	loll-yob
olive	l'oliva	lob-lee-vab
onion	la cipolla	lah chee-poll-ab
orange	l'arancia	lab-ran-chab
orange/lemon juice	succo d'arancia/ di limone	soo-kob dab-ran-chab/ dee lee-mob-neb
peach	la pesca	lah pess-kab
pepper	il pepe	eel peb-peb
pork	carne di maiale	kar-neb dee mab-yab-leh
potatoes	le patate	leb pab-tab-teb
prawns	i gamberi	ee gam-bair-ee
rice	il riso	eel ree-zob
roast	arrosto	ar-ross-tob
roll	il panino	eel pab-nee-nob
salad	l'insalata	leen-sab-lab-tab
salt	il sale	eel sab-leb
sausage	la salsiccia	lah sal-see-chab
seafood	frutti di mare	froo-tee dee mab-reb
soup	la zuppa, la minestra	lah tsoo-pab, lah mee-ness-trab
steak	la bistecca	lah bee-stek-kab
strawberries	le fragole	leb frab-gob-leb
sugar	lo zucchero	lob zoo-kair-ob
tea	il tè	eel teb
herb tea	la tisana	lah tee-zab-nab
tomato	il pomodoro	eel pob-mob-dor-ob
tuna	il tonno	ton-nob
veal	il vitello	vee-tell-ob
vegetables	i legumi	ee leb-goo-mee
vinegar	l'aceto	lab-cheb-tob
water	l'acqua	lab-kwab
red wine	vino rosso	vee-nob ross-ob
white wine	vino bianco	vee-nob bee-ang-kob

NUMBERS

1	uno	oo-nob
2	due	doo-eb
3	tre	treb
4	quattro	kwat-rob
5	cinque	ching-kweb
6	sei	say-ee
7	sette	set-teb
8	otto	ot-tob
9	nove	nob-veb
10	dieci	dee-eb-chee
11	undici	oon-dee-chee
12	dodici	dob-dee-chee
13	tredici	tray-dee-chee
14	quattordici	kwat-tor-dee-chee
15	quindici	kwin-dee-chee
16	sedici	say-dee-chee
17	diciassette	dee-chab-set-teb
18	diciotto	dee-chot-tob
19	diciannove	dee-chab-nob-veb
20	venti	ven-tee
30	trenta	tren-tab
40	quaranta	kwah-ran-tab
50	cinquanta	ching-kwan-tab
60	sessanta	sess-an-tab
70	settanta	set-tan-tab
80	ottanta	ot-tan-tab
90	novanta	nob-van-tab
100	cento	chen-tob
1,000	mille	mee-leb
2,000	duemila	doo-eb mee-lah
5,000	cinquemila	ching-kweb mee-lab
1,000,000	un milione	oon meel-yob-neb

TIME

one minute	un minuto	oon mee-noo-tob
one hour	un'ora	oon or-ab
half an hour	mezz'ora	medz-or-ab
a day	un giorno	oon jor-nob
a week	una settimana	oona set-tee-mab-nah
Monday	lunedì	loo-neb-dee
Tuesday	martedì	mar-teb-dee
Wednesday	mercoledì	mair-kob-leb-dee
Thursday	giovedì	job-veb-dee
Friday	venerdì	ven-air-dee
Saturday	sabato	sab-bab-tob
Sunday	domenica	doh-meb-nee-kab